AMERICAN
MASS-MARKET
MAGAZINES

Recent Titles of
Historical Guides to the World's Periodicals and Newspapers

This series provides historically focused narrative and analytical profiles of periodicals and newspapers with accompanying bibliographical data.

American Indian and Alaska Native Newspapers and Periodicals, 1925–1970
Daniel F. Littlefield, Jr., and James W. Parins, editors

Magazines of the American South
Sam G. Riley

Religious Periodicals of the United States: Academic and Scholarly Journals
Charles H. Lippy, editor

British Literary Magazines: The Modern Age, 1914–1984
Alvin Sullivan, editor

American Indian and Alaska Native Newspapers and Periodicals, 1971–1985
Daniel F. Littlefield, Jr., and James W. Parins, editors

Index to Southern Periodicals
Sam G. Riley

American Literary Magazines: The Eighteenth and Nineteenth Centuries
Edward E. Chielens, editor

American Humor Magazines and Comic Periodicals
David E. E. Sloane, editor

Index to City and Regional Magazines of the United States
Sam G. Riley and Gary W. Selnow, compilers

International Music Journals
Linda M. Fidler and Richard S. James, editors

AMERICAN MASS-MARKET MAGAZINES

Edited by
Alan Nourie
and
Barbara Nourie

Historical Guides to the World's Periodicals and Newspapers

Greenwood Press
New York • Westport, Connecticut • London

Library of Congress Cataloging-in-Publication Data

American mass-market magazines / edited by Alan Nourie and Barbara
    Nourie.
        p.   cm.—(Historical guides to the world's periodicals and
    newspapers, ISSN 0742–5538)
    Includes bibliographical references.
    ISBN 0–313–25254–8 (lib. bdg. : alk. paper)
    1. American periodicals—History.   I. Nourie, Alan.   II. Nourie,
Barbara.   III. Series.
PN4877.A48   1990
051–dc20   89–17084

British Library Cataloguing in Publication Data is available.

Library of Congress Catalog Card Number: 89–17084
ISBN: 0–313–25254–8
ISSN: 0742–5538

First published in 1990

Greenwood Press, Inc.
88 Post Road West, Westport, Connecticut   06881

Printed in the United States of America

The paper used in this book complies with the
Permanent Paper Standard issued by the National
Information Standards Organization (Z39.48–1984).

10 9 8 7 6 5 4 3 2 1

Contents

Introduction

Mass-market, or general, periodicals are in the present age almost nonexistent. Except for a relative few, what one finds today are large numbers of magazines that have large circulations, but appeal to a specific audience or interest instead of being all things to large populations. In other words, in considering mass-market magazines, we find that the bulk of the titles appeals to fairly large populations within the much larger general population. Hence we have religious, children's, literary, men's, women's, sports, news, music, hobby, business, blacks', health, and fraternal magazines all capable of achieving circulations of more than 100,000 and many of more than a million. These magazines occupy a sort of middle ground between the true general magazines and the specialist magazines that require only a limited audience or circulation.

We have attempted to furnish periodical histories that in terms of length fall somewhere between those done by Frank Luther Mott in his seminal studies and the paragraph-length treatment in *Magazines for Libraries*, which is unfortunately often the only source of information available for many recent periodicals. In fact, to a large degree, the general publications from the late 1970s to the present are largely undocumented.

In some instances, general magazines of large circulations have not been included in this volume because while mass-market in terms of numbers, they are more accurately classed in another specific genre. *Southern Living*, for example, appears in a companion volume of the Historical Guides to the World's Periodicals and Newspapers series; *Ebony* is slated for another, as are *Sports Illustrated* and the majority of the "Women's Magazines." However, a generous selection of the more prominent examples of many mass-market titles has been included, if the focus was broad enough and the circulation high enough to warrant consideration. Others have been included if treatment in Mott was brief or incomplete, if other coverage was negligible, or if the title in question was somewhat unique in its focus.

Perhaps the most striking characteristic of the list of titles included in this volume is the tremendous variety of categories represented. Where other than in a treatment of mass-market magazines could one find *TV Guide*, *Playboy*, *Rolling Stone*, *National Enquirer*, *Collier's*, *Yankee*, and the *Atlantic* all cheek by jowl?

Theodore Peterson locates the beginnings of the "modern national magazine" or general, mass-market magazine as "sometime in the last decades of the nineteenth century . . . in no one year but in a period stretching across more than a decade" ranging from 1979 when Congress stimulated the growth of periodicals by providing low-cost mailing privileges to 1899 when George H. Lorimer assumed the editorship of the newly revitalized *Saturday Evening Post*.[1]

One hundred and six of the most significant mass-market or general U.S. periodicals have been included, for the most part originating in the late nineteenth and twentieth centuries. Although the emphasis of this volume is the modern mass-market periodical, thirty-three titles have been included that either existed in their entirety in the nineteenth century or had their roots there. In general, early American magazines were political, wanting to "disseminate political information and opinion."[2] A typical magazine might contain general essays, political opinion, poetry and fiction, criticism, economic and business news, and religious material—in other words, the coverage was very much like that of the more heavily circulated magazines that were to appear toward the end of the century. James Wood estimates that these early magazines typically had a brief life span, averaging fourteen months, due mainly to the paucity of advertising and restrictive postal regulations.[3] And while the number of subscribers was also quite small, seldom exceeding 1,600, Mott maintains that the influence they exerted far exceeded this. So, not unlike some more recent magazines, the readership exceeded the subscription list. The *American Magazine* is the earliest example provided in this volume, followed by the *North American Review*, *American Farmer*, and *Country Gentleman*. Midcentury titles include a southern magazine, *Debow's Review*, a precursor of the tabloids in the *National Police Gazette*, a pair of general, political organs—*American Whig Review* and *Democratic Review*, and the publishers' magazines, which with their eventual large circulations and use of advertising led to the modern mass-market publication: *Atlantic, Harper's, Lippincott's, Putnam's, Scribner's,* and *Frank Leslie's Popular Monthly*.

Frank Munsey, Frank Leslie, Cyrus Curtis, and S. S. McClure, owner-publishers at this time, were all major contributors to the formation of the twentieth-century popular magazine through their innovation in several areas: the low price of their magazines (five or ten cents), high circulation resulting from mass production and distribution, extensive use of advertising (to keep the price down), and popular, wide-ranging content.

As John Tebbel notes, a journal of opinion, the *Chicago Graphic*, observed in 1892: "The development of the magazine in the last quarter of a century in the United States has been marvelous. . . . Every field of human thought has been entered and as the field has broadened, new magazines have arisen to occupy the territory, and the magazine has become not only a school of literature, but of science, art and politics as well.''[4] With the increase in an educated population that was occurring at the time came an increased popularization of interest in what had heretofore been specialized areas: psychology, science, music, history, gardening, and so on.

The magazines originating in this period reflect this. *Scribner's*, for example, with a circulation in excess of 200,000 by 1911, applied the formula of furnishing coverage of ''popular topics in a literary way.'' The *Literary Digest* (1.5 million circulation by 1927) was a digest of political and sociological material, even from newspapers; two ten-cent ''muckrakers''—*McClure's* and *Cosmopolitan*— were soon achieving 300,000-plus circulations, mainly on the basis of their American social-political commentary. As Tebbel observes, ''The basis of the ten cent magazine's popular appeal was its liveliness and variety, its many and well-printed illustrations, its coverage of world events, and progress at home— and most of all, its head-on confrontation with contemporary social problems.''[5]

Generally, aside from a pretense at least to wide appeal, a circulation of 100,000 or more was the basic criterion for inclusion in this volume, and in fact, approximately 30 percent of the titles actually had circulations in excess of a million. But in a society of more than two hundred million, mostly literate people, no single magazine, not even *TV Guide, Modern Maturity*, or *Reader's Digest*, each with a sixteen million-plus circulation (and even higher readership, since they are usually subscribed to by families) can truly be considered a national, mass-market or popular magazine. What we have instead are a number of general, specialist titles: magazines such as *Modern Maturity*, for example (circulation 16,700,000), which technically appeals to a large audience, but in fact is fairly specific in its focus at the same time. The same case can be made for numerous million-plus circulation magazines: *Playboy, Sports Illustrated, Popular Science, Money, Popular Mechanics, Bon Appetit, Rolling Stone, Organic Gardening, Health, Prevention.*

And so, between the handful of magazines circulating to millions of subscribers and the true specialist, scholarly journals and reviews that academic libraries support, lies the area into which most of the titles included in this volume fall: *Horizon, GQ:Gentleman's Quarterly, Crawdaddy, Redbook*—periodicals with no commonality except for circulation figures.

A number of general periodicals that might also fall into the ''Women's Magazine'' category have been included as well. *Parents* is because of its title and the plurality spelled out there; clearly it is not limited to the female parent only. *Family Circle* and *Redbook* also are not gender specific, and one can safely assume that if they enter the household through a purchase by the female, the range and diversity of material offered will not deter cross-reading any more than in the case of, for example, *Reader's Digest*; they aspired to be magazines for the household. Two other titles, *McCall's* and *Vogue*, were included not only because of their high circulations, but also because of their early years, when they were among the more important general magazines of their day.

Presently in the United States daily newspapers number slightly over 1,600 and generate a total circulation of 63 million copies. This medium, together with the television news broadly and on a daily basis, serves the function of educating or at least informing the masses, which was originally the purview of the magazines of earlier times. However, the magazine supplements to the Sunday newspapers are in several instances true mass-oriented periodicals, and we have included several of them in this volume: *Parade, Family Weekly/USA Weekend*, and the *New York Times Magazine*. By the same token, examples of that disreputable genre, the tabloid, have also been included as well; hence the *National Enquirer* and *Grit*, with a combined circulation of nearly five million, find their way into these pages to be considered along with *Time* (4.6 million), *Newsweek* (3.2 million), and *U.S. News & World Report* (2.3 million).

If a title is followed by an asterisk, it is treated at length in this volume. "See references" have been provided in the case of title variations. (For example, for *Organic Gardening* see *Rodale's Organic Gardening*.)

Locations have been provided in cases that might prove problematic, but the existence of electronic national databases such as OCLC (Online Computer Library Center, Inc.) and others, various state and regional databases and union lists, plus the standard bibliographic control furnished via the *Union List of Serials* and *New Serial Titles* really make locations redundant in most cases. Since this is a "mass-market" or "general" volume, most titles are indeed "widely held": either in the original, in microform, or in reprinted hard copy. The *Guide to Microforms in Print* and the *Guide to Reprints* are both updated regularly, but for the majority of the titles under consideration here, the University Microfilms annually issued catalog of *Serials in Microform* will suffice—and will probably be more readily available in most libraries.

Alan Nourie

Notes

1. Theodore Peterson, *Magazines in the Twentieth Century*, p. 1.
2. James Playsted Wood, *Magazines in the United States*, p. 24.
3. Wood, p. 24.
4. John Tebbel, *The American Magazine: A Compact History*, pp. 119–20.
5. Tebbel, p. 166.

Bibliography

Peterson, Theodore. *Magazines in the Twentieth Century*. Urbana: University of Illinois Press, 1964.

Tebbel, John. *The American Magazine: A Compact History*. New York: Hawthorne Press, 1969.

Wood, James Playstead. *Magazines in the United States*. New York: Ronald Press, 1956.

AMERICAN MASS-MARKET MAGAZINES

A

THE AMERICAN FARMER

John Stuart Skinner, the founder of the *American Farmer,* was described in the memoirs of John Quincy Adams as "a man of mingled character of daring and pernicous principles, of restless and rash temper, and yet of useful and honorable enterprise. Ruffian, patriot, and philanthropist are so blended in him that I cannot appreciate him without a mingled sentiment of detestation and esteem."[1]

Skinner was born on a Maryland farm in 1788. He was admitted to the bar in 1809, and appointed to several government posts, finally settling in the postal service. During the War of 1812 he participated in two dramatic events. When he learned that the British had landed in Maryland and were marching on Washington, he rode ninety miles through the night to warn the city's defenders of the enemy approach. Later, during the siege of Baltimore, he stood next to Francis Scott Key on a British warship, watching the bombardment of Fort McHenry. When they were freed, Skinner accompanied Key to a Baltimore hotel where the latter wrote the words to "The Star-Spangled Banner." After the war Skinner continued his work in the postal service while also involved in privateering in the sea lanes around South America. By 1819 he was ready to begin a new enterprise.

In early nineteenth-century America, agricultural subjects were discussed in many scientific and popular periodicals. The first periodical devoted exclusively to agriculture was the *Agricultural Museum,* which began publishing in 1810 and lasted for less than two years. Seven years later Skinner bought a weekly newspaper and transformed it into the *American Farmer.*

First published on 2 April 1819, the *American Farmer* began as a weekly quarto of eight pages. The annual subscription rate was four dollars. It proclaimed its subject matter as "rural economy, internal improvements, new prices current.'' Skinner continued his full-time position in the postal service but devoted every spare minute to the new periodical. A large group of enlightened agriculturalists including Thomas Jefferson, James Madison, John C. Calhoun, and Henry Clay assisted him with contributions. Skinner himself wrote from his experiences traveling around the United States. He also reprinted chapters from books as well as articles from American and English journals. Another staple was articles in the form of letters from farmers around the country. These contributions tended to be from gentlemen farmers. Contributions from smaller farmers, while sought by the editor, were hard to obtain.

The makeup of the eight-page journal would, according to Skinner, have ''one half of four pages devoted to practical Agriculture: the remainder to Internal Improvements, Rural and Domestic Economy, selections for housekeepers and female readers, and Natural History and Rural Sports.''[2]

Practical agriculture covered all manner of subjects including plowing, sowing, crop rotation, the construction of water ponds for cattle, the care and feeding of various types of livestock, the care and diseases of fruit trees, new fertilizers, new inventions to aid the farmer, new crops, hedging, the art of building walls of dirt, agricultural chemistry, and the value of the ox. Results of cattle shows were regularly reported, as were meteorological observations beginning in 1824. Current prices of farm produce and items needed by farmers were obtained from Baltimore and later from New York markets.

A unique aspect of the *American Farmer* was the many articles printed on sports, recreation, and exercise. Skinner's rationale was that sports possessed ''the power to promote good health and prevent disease, produce sound and respectable morals, create a reputable character, and encourage pleasure and enjoyment.''[3]

While Skinner recognized the importance of the horse to the American farmer and printed all manner of information about the agricultural uses of the horse, he also included articles on horse racing and fox hunting. He continually urged farmers to work to improve the breeds of American horses used in all of these activities.

While the horsey sports dominated the sporting sections of the *American Farmer*, other sports were also covered. Fishing, shooting, archery, rowing, chess, sailing, and ice skating were among those discussed. Much of this material was reprinted from New York and English newspapers.

Medicine was also a common topic for the *American Farmer*. Hundreds of recipes were printed for the treatment of everything from colds to snakebite. Much of this material also came from other journals. Cures tended to be home remedies rather than conventional medicine. Garlic was prescribed for fevers; a salve of black pepper, ginger, rum, and hog lard for itching; olive oil for snakebite; a mixture of figs, water, yeast, and honey for sore throat.

Poems were scattered through the journal. These poems were usually uplifting, stressing moral values and the glories of farm life.

From the beginning, each issue had many illustrations. This was particularly true for articles on new machinery, but illustrations of livestock and plants were also included.

What was missing from the *American Farmer* was controversy. Two major disputes of this period that directly affected farmers were tariffs and slavery. One searches in vain for articles on these topics, although one article in 1827 did extoll the utility of slave labor in manufacturing.[4] This lack of controversy was the result of a deliberate editorial policy by Skinner that was followed by later editors. He expressly excluded party politics. An exception to this policy occurred on the advent of the Civil War. In the early 1860s the *American Farmer* was published by N. B. Worthington and T. B. Lewis. Both of these men had strong Southern sympathies. In the 1 May 1861 issue, along with the usual agricultural material, appeared a fire-breathing editorial calling upon Marylanders to stand with their Virginian brothers and stop the Northern invaders. Lewis was reported to be part of a group trying to stop Union troop trains from reaching Washington, D.C., through Baltimore. However, after hearing from their Northern readers, the June 1 editorial stated that the May editorial would be the last mention of the war in the *American Farmer*. This was not enough, however, and they were forced to suspend publication from January 1862 through June 1866.

Over the years the content of the *American Farmer* changed very little. Skinner gave up the editorship in 1830 and returned only briefly between 1839 and 1841. With time the journal went from weekly to biweekly to monthly. It expanded its pages and reduced its pages. It changed its title, its editors and publishers, and its place of publication, but through it all it remained true to the goals annunciated by Skinner. In the 1 January 1872 issue, the editors stated that the purpose of the *American Farmer* was

> to point out to the cultivator of the soil the improvements and aids to agriculture which are furnished by the discoveries of science and the inventions of art; to keep him fully advised of new processes and improved methods in culture affecting a savings either of time, labor, or money; and at the same time with exhortation to careful and thorough tillage of the earth, to persuade him to those tasteful but inexpensive decorations of the homestead which do so much towards making the home attractive and strengthening the affections which cluster around it.

This could have been written by Skinner.

As the nineteenth century progressed, the *American Farmer* was joined by many other agricultural journals but it "maintained its reputation as the only truly national magazine in both focus and circulation."[5] When it ceased in 1897, after seventy-eight years of publication, it had a circulation of 100,000 and was being read by farmers in every state in the Union.

Notes

1. Harold A. Bierck, Jr., "Spoils, Soils, and Skinner," *Maryland Historical Magazine,* March 1954, p. 26.
2. *American Farmer*, 16 February 1827, p. 387.
3. Jack W. Berryman, "John Stuart Skinner and the *American Farmer*, 1819–1829," *Associates NAL (National Agricultural Library) Today*, October 1976, p. 14.
4. *American Farmer*, October 19, 1827.
5. Berryman, p. 18.

Information Sources

BIBLIOGRAPHY
Berryman, Jack W. "John S. Skinner's American Farmer." *Maryland Historical Magazine,* June 1981, pp. 159–73.
————. "John Stuart Skinner and the *American Farmer*, 1819–1829." *Associates NAL (National Agricultural Library) Today*, October 1976, pp. 11–32.
Bierck, Harold A., Jr. "Spoils, Soils, and Skinner." *Maryland Historical Magazine*, March 1954, pp. 21–40.
Demaree, Albert Lowther. *The American Agricultural Press 1819–1860*. New York: Columbia University Press, 1941, pp. 23–38.
Herman, Bernard L. "Folk Medical Recipes in Nineteenth-Century American Farm Journals." *Pennsylvania Folklife*, Summer 1976, pp. 16–25.
Pinkett, Harold T. "The American Farmer." *Agricultural History*, July 1950, pp. 146–51.
————. "A Forgotten Patriot." *Social Studies*, December 1949, pp. 354–55.
INDEX SOURCES
Not indexed.
LOCATION SOURCES
Available in microform.

Publication History

MAGAZINE TITLE AND TITLE CHANGES
American Farmer, 1819–7 March 1834; *Farmer and Gardener and Live-Stock Breeder and Manager*, 9 May 1834–28 April 1835; *Farmer and Gardener*, 5 May 1835–23 April 1939; *American Farmer and Spirit of the Agricultural Journals of the Day*, 29 May 1839–June 1850; *American Farmer*, July 1850–December 1871; *American Farmer and Rural Register*, January 1872–December 1873; *American Farmer*, January 1874–February 1897.
VOLUME AND ISSUE DATA
Vols. 1–15, 2 April 1819–7 March 1834; series 2, vols. 1–6, 9 May 1834–22 May 1839; series 3, vols. 1–6, 29 May 1839–June 1845; series 4, vols. 1–14, July 1845–June 1859; series 5, vols. 1–3, July 1859–January 1862; series 6, vols. 1–4, July 1866–1869; series 7, vol. 1, 1870–1871; series 8, vols. 1–10, 1872–1881; series 9, vols. 1–9, 1882–1890; series 10, vol. 1, 1891; series 11, vol. 1, 1892; 74th–78th year, 1893–February 1897. Weekly, 2 April 1819–June 1845;

monthly, July 1845–1881; semimonthly, 1882–June 1894; monthly, July 1894–February 1897.

PUBLISHER AND PLACE OF PUBLICATION

John S. Skinner, 2 April 1819–27 August 1830, Baltimore; I. Irvine Hitchcock, 3 September 1830–28 April 1835, Baltimore; Sinclair and Moore and Robert Sinclair, Jr., 5 May 1835–21 November 1836, Baltimore; E. P. Roberts and Sands and Neilson, 29 November 1836–24 October 1837, Baltimore; E. P. Roberts and Samuel Sands, 31 October 1837–22 May 1839, Baltimore; Samuel Sands, 29 May 1839–June 1854, Baltimore; Samuel Sands and N. B. Worthington, July 1854–June 1858, Baltimore; N. B. Worthington, July 1858–1859, Baltimore; N. B. Worthington and Theos. B. Lewis, 1860–1869, Baltimore; Frank Lewis, 1870–1871, Baltimore; Samuel Sands and Son, 1872–July 1891, Baltimore; William H. Sands, August 1891–December 1891, Baltimore; Farmer's Publishing Company, 1 January 1892–February 1892, Middletown, Maryland; American Farmer Company, 15 February 1892–February 1897, Washington, D.C.

EDITORS

John S. Skinner, 2 April 1819–27 August 1830; Gideon Smith, 3 September 1830–25 October 1833; I. Irvine Hitchcock, 1 November 1833–28 April 1835; E. P. Roberts, 5 May 1835–23 April 1839; John S. Skinner, 29 May 1839–18 August 1841; no editor given, 25 August 1841–December 1871; Samuel Sands and William B. Sands, January 1872–15 July 1891; William B. Sands, 1 August 1891–15 December 1891; no editor given, 1 January 1892–February 1897.

CIRCULATION

100,000 (1896).

Willard Moonan

AMERICAN HERITAGE

Of the popular history magazines that have appeared since World War II, the most successful and influential has been *American Heritage*. For over thirty years it has presented the American past to a wide audience, and though its fortunes have declined since the fifties and sixties, it remains the standard of quality by which similar publications must be measured.

The creative force behind this success story was James Parton, who drew upon two popular history efforts already underway.[1]

One was *American Heritage* itself—the original version—a quarterly started in 1949 by Earle W. Newton, publisher of *Vermont Life*, for a mere $2,000.[2] Backed by the American Association for State and Local History (AASLH), this early *American Heritage* was patriotic and chauvinistic, grassroots and folksy. It published articles on such topics as the Franklin stove and colonial craftsmen. Special issues covered topics of regional interest, and the editors encouraged members of local historical societies to do research and present their findings. Newton and his contributors were unpaid, yet by 1952 the magazine found 17,000 subscribers. Despite this success, the small AASLH found it burdensome to edit and distribute the magazine, and in 1954 turned over control of it to Parton and two of his former Time-Life colleagues, Oliver Jensen and Joseph Thorndike, Jr.[3]

The other effort that Parton drew upon was that of Allan Nevins, a Columbia University history professor and former New York newspaperman. Dissatisfied with pedantic and dry-as-dust academic history writing, Nevins proposed the creation of a history magazine geared "to the multitude, not the learned few." This magazine, to be called *History*, was to be not only engagingly written but also thought-provoking, helping responsible citizens gain a historical perspective on current events. When the American Historical Association refused to endorse such a notion, Nevins, indignant, started a *new* historical association—the Society of American Historians. Uniting popular historians with converts from the ranks of academic historians, the society was to sponsor the projected magazine, but when it failed to come up with the needed funds, it joined the AASLH in backing the Parton enterprise.[4]

Using the existing subscription base of *American Heritage* and the format proposed by the Nevins group (hard covers and no ads), Parton and his associates started a new tradition. Officially beginning with volume 6, issue number 1, *American Heritage* became *American Heritage: The Magazine of History*, and switched from a quarterly to a bimonthly publication schedule. But although the new version took advantage of the two earlier efforts, it resembled neither in historical vision. A commercial venture rather than an organ of some historical society, the new *American Heritage* aimed neither at inspiring localistic sentiments nor at inspiring civic virtue. It aimed at achieving commercial success.[5]

The magazine's first editor, Bruce Catton—the Pulitzer Prize–winning Civil War historian—quickly set the tone. Far from promoting grassroots participation, Catton solicited vividly written articles from such established names as Carl Carmer, Paul Horgan, Philip Van Doren Stern, and Henry Steele Commager.[6] And although Catton said in the preface to the first issue that "Our beat . . . is anything that ever happened in America," the topics covered were less likely to shed light on the present than they were to provide escapes into the past.[7] Favorite topics included the Civil War and the presidents of the United States (especially George Washington).[8] Other typical articles were "A Drill Master from Valley Forge" and "The Mills of Early America." When such articles were placed between beautiful hard covers, printed on glossy paper, adorned with illustrations (many in color), and freed from footnotes and the clutter of advertising, the result was a publication both fun to read and fun to look at—a coffee-table book.[9]

The magazine was an instant hit. Within a year it had 100,000 subscribers, at $2.95 a copy and $12.50 a year.[10] Five years later, selling for $3.95 and needing 105,000 subscribers to break even, it had 310,000, and was more popular than *Harper's,** Atlantic,** and *Scientific American.*[11] Nor can *American Heritage's* success be measured by its subscription base alone. One must also consider its spin-offs. In 1958 Parton started an international version called *Horizon**; by

1960 the American Heritage Publishing Company had published three best-selling historical books; and by 1968 the company's book division had issued some 200 titles that brought in more than $33 million in sales. In addition, the company has conducted tours, sold catalog gifts, and produced television series.[12]

The magazine has been influential too. One need only examine its readership. Popular, yes, but not—probably owing to the high subscription price—democratic. A 1959 survey found that the magazine's readers were largely white collar and well educated, 80 percent of them in "executive-managerial-proprietor" positions and 60 percent holding at least a bachelor's degree. This occupational profile holds true today, and it is fair to conclude that the magazine has interpreted history to a powerful segment of American society.[13]

In the late 1960s the magazine's readership began to dwindle. One observer attributes this decline to changes that started creeping into the magazine's pages. Responding to the general social upheaval of the period, the magazine could no longer maintain the uniformly optimistic tone that its upper-middle-class readers had come to expect. Even the conservative editor Oliver Jensen (1960–1975) experimented in 1969 with a vigorous (but short-lived) section on conservation. Controversy increased under the liberal editorship of Alvin Josephy (1976–1978) and Geoffrey Ward (1978–1982), when along with the usual fare there appeared articles on such contemporary topics as birth control, illiteracy, and joblessness. Perhaps because of the presence of such articles, perhaps because of the magazine's doubleness of tone (escape and reality side by side), readers drifted away in droves. Between 1968 and 1980, subscriptions dropped from 320,000 to 120,000—a decline of over 60 percent. And as the older readers left they were not replaced with younger ones, the words "American" and "heritage" having become anathema to an entire generation.[14]

Instability set in. The struggling magazine was sold to McGraw-Hill in 1969, to Englehard Hanovia in 1976, to Samuel P. Reed in 1978, and to Forbes in 1986.[15] In 1980, to save money, the magazine dropped its hard covers, and in 1982 began to accept advertising.[16]

Nevertheless, there is hope. Articles are still well written, authoritative, and beautifully illustrated, so much so that in 1985 the magazine won a prize for general excellence.[17] And editor Byron Dobell (1982–present), sensing a renewal of interest in history and in the humanities in general, has been seeking ways to attract younger readers, even to the point of emphasizing the more recent past. Three quarters of the articles now published cover twentieth-century events—Watergate and Vietnam, for example, and the opening of Disney World.[18] In fact, since Dobell became editor, subscriptions have risen steadily (though modestly)—from 111,000 to 241,000.

One might argue that a coffee-table magazine is not a proper vehicle for communicating historical insights, that history is not something to be neatly packaged and treasured but rather something to be continually reexamined and revised.[19] But though one can question American Heritage's methods, one cannot question its success at bringing history to the multitude, not just the learned few.

Notes

1. Roy Rosenzweig, "Marketing the Past: *American Heritage* and Popular History in the United States," in *Presenting the Past: Essays on History and the Public*, ed. Susan Porter Benson, Stephen Brier, and Roy Rosenzweig (Philadelphia: Temple University Press, 1986), pp. 22–26.

2. Theodore Peterson, *Magazines in the Twentieth Century*, 2nd ed. (Urbana: University of Illinois Press, 1964), p. 398.

3. Rosenzweig, pp. 25–26.

4. Ibid., pp. 22–26.

5. Ibid., p. 26.

6. James Playsted Wood, *Magazines in the United States*, 2nd ed. (New York: Ronald Press, 1956), p. 341; Richard Tobin, "Is There a Renaissance for the History Magazines?" *Mankind*, 5, no. 12 (1977), p. 12.

7. Rosenzweig, p. 27.

8. Tobin, p. 12.

9. Ibid.; Rosenzweig, p. 27.

10. Tobin, p. 12.

11. "Merchant of History" [James Parton], *Time*, 21 March 1960, p. 60; Rosenzweig, p. 28.

12. Tobin, p. 12; Edwin McDowell, "A New Look Emerges for *American Heritage*," *New York Times*, 31 December, p. 11 (Late edition), 13 (National edition) 1984; "Merchant," p. 60; Rosenzweig, pp. 21–22.

13. Rosenzweig, p. 29.

14. Ibid., pp. 41–46.

15. McDowell, "New Look"; "Forbes Deal for *Heritage*," *New York Times*, 8 January 1986. Section D8 (Late edition), 28 (National edition).

16. Rosenzweig, p. 45; McDowell, "New Look."

17. "10 Magazines Win National Awards: Pair of Prizes Presented to both *American Heritage* and *The Washingtonian*" [American Society of Magazine Editors Awards]. *New York Times*, April 25, 1985. Section B11 (Late edition), 30 (National edition).

18. McDowell, "New Look."

19. Rosenzweig, p. 49.

Information Sources

BIBLIOGRAPHY

Dobell, Byron. "Keeping Shop" [magazine now accepts advertising]. *American Heritage*, August-September 1982, p. 3.

Dougherty, Philip H. "American Heritage to Accept Ads." *New York Times*, 11 June 1982. Section D17 (Late edition), 45 (National edition).

———. "Heritage Shifts Ad Plan Again." *New York Times*, 3 August 1983. Section D17 (Late edition), 39 (National edition).

"Forbes Deal for *Heritage*." *New York Times*, 8 January 1986. Section D8 (Late edition), 28 (National edition).

"Grumman Pioneers in Ad Campaign." *Sales and Marketing Management*, 25 April 1983, p. 46.

McDowell, Edwin. "A New Look Emerges for *American Heritage.*" *New York Times*, 31 December 1984, p. 11 (Late edition), 13 (National edition).

"Merchant of History" [James Parton]. *Time*, 21 March 1960, p. 60.

Peterson, Theodore. *Magazines in the Twentieth Century.* 2nd ed. Urbana: University of Illinois Press, 1964.

Radding, Alan. "American Heritage Rewrites History" [changes appearance; adds advertising]. *Advertising Age*, 3 October 1985, p. 32.

Rosenzweig, Roy. "Marketing the Past: *American Heritage* and Popular History in the United States." In *Presenting the Past: Essays on History and the Public.* Eds. Susan Porter Benson, Stephen Brier, and Roy Rosenzweig. Philadelphia: Temple University Press, 1986, pp. 21–49. An earlier version of this paper appeared in *Radical History Review* 32 (1985); 7–29.

"10 Magazines Win National Awards: Pair of Prizes Presented to Both *American Heritage* and *The Washingtonian*" [American Society of Magazine Editors Awards]. *New York Times*, 25 April 1985. Section B11 (Late edition), 30 (National edition).

Tobin, Richard L. "Is There a Renaissance for the History Magazines?" *Mankind*, 5, no. 12 (1977): 10–14.

"We're Really Turned on about Having *American Heritage*" [Forbes acquisition]. *Forbes*, 16 June 1986, p. 18.

Wood, James Playsted. *Magazines in the United States.* 2nd ed. New York: Ronald Press, 1956.

INDEX SOURCES

Abridged Readers' Guide to Periodical Literature; America: History & Life; Arts & Humanities Citation Index; Historical Abstracts; Magazine Index; Periodical Abstracts; Readers' Guide to Periodical Literature. In addition, cumulative indexes are available from the publisher.

LOCATION SOURCES

Library of Congress, many other libraries. Available in microform.

Publication History

MAGAZINE TITLE AND TITLE CHANGES

American Heritage, vols. 1–5; *American Heritage: The Magazine of History*, vol. 6, no. 1–present.

VOLUME AND ISSUE DATA

Vols. 1–5, September 1949–Summer 1954, quarterly; vols. 6–37, December 1954–November 1986, bimonthly (six issues a year); vols. 38–current December 1986-current (eight issues a year).

PUBLISHER AND PLACE OF PUBLICATION

American Heritage Publishing Company: James Parton, 1954–1966; Darby Perry, 1967–1969; Paul Gottlieb, 1970–1975; Marjorie C. Dyer, December 1975; Rhett Austell, 1976–1978; Tim Hill, 1978–1979; Beverly Hilowitz, 1979–1981; Paul E. Hale, 1981–1983; Byron S. Hollinshead, 1983–1984. American Heritage Press, Inc. 1985–1986 and American Heritage, Inc. 1986-current; Carol A. Smith, 1985–1986; Jeffrey M. Cunningham, 1986–present. New York, New York.

EDITORS

Earle W. Newton, 1949–1954; Bruce Catton, 1954–1959; Oliver Jensen, 1960–1975; Ernest M. Halliday, 1975–1976; Alvin M. Josephy, Jr., 1976–1978; Geoffrey C. Ward, 1978–1982; Byron Dobell, 1982–present.

CIRCULATION
   248,860 paid, 13,714 nonpaid.

David R. Kohut

AMERICAN MAGAZINE AND HISTORICAL CHRONICLE

In September 1743 a new magazine was printed in Boston under the auspices of Rogers and Fowle. Jeremiah Gridley, described by Frank Luther Mott as a "lawyer who had been editor of the *Weekly Rehearsal,* and was later to make a reputation as a patriot, was editor of the new magazine."[1]
   According to the editor, the magazine would endeavor to publish

A Variety of Subjects having a certain Quality of unbending and entertaining the Mind: And as we design a Collection of the best and most approved Pieces published in Great Britain and the Plantations, with summary Rehearsals and Quotations from the best Authors that treat of all the Parts of polite and useful Learning; . . . these Collections will amount to a Treasury of various Knowledge and Learning, of the Serious and pleasant, of the instructive and diverting, and help to furnish the Mind with store of choice well digested Apprehensions of Men and Things.[2]

Gridley also states that the opinions expressed, right or wrong, should not be blamed on the magazine's staff, for they were to be considered as "mere reporters of facts."
   Modeled after the *London Magazine,* the periodical covered several areas of interest. The first issue included an article by several pastors on the state of religion in North America, testifying against the "evil things of the present day" and promoting "pure and undefiled religion"; a "letter from a Jew" describing the effects of music on the psyche, as opposed to metaphysics; an article on preservatives, and extracts from Dr. Arbuthnot's essay on the diseases of infants with remedies; and some poetry, mostly anonymous. The "historical chronicle" section was devoted to the debates in Parliament, foreign affairs, the proceedings of colonial legislatures, the Indian treaty held in Philadelphia, European wars, and other current events. Reprints from *Gentleman's Magazine* and *London Magazine* abound. The magazine ceased publication in 1746.

Notes

   1. Frank Luther Mott, *A History of American Magazines 1741–1850* (Cambridge: Harvard University Press, 1938), p. 78.
   2. *American Magazine and Historical Chronicle,* "Introduction," September 1743, ii.

Information Sources

BIBLIOGRAPHY

Hoornstra, Jean. *American Periodicals, 1741–1900: An Index to the Microfilm Collections*. Ann Arbor: University Microfilms, 1979.

Mott, Frank Luther. *A History of American Magazines 1741–1850*. Cambridge: Harvard University Press, 1938, pp. 78–79.

Thomas, Isaiah. *History of Printing in America*. Worcester: From the press of Isaiah Thomas, 1810.

INDEX SOURCES

 By publisher.

LOCATION SOURCES

 Microfilm: *American Periodical Series: 18th Century*. vol. 1.

Publication History

MAGAZINE TITLE AND TITLE CHANGES

 The American Magazine and Historical Chronicle.

VOLUME AND ISSUE DATA

 Vol. 1–3; September 1743–December 1746. Monthly.

PUBLISHER AND PLACE OF PUBLICATION

 Rogers and Fowle, Boston.

EDITOR

 Jeremiah Gridley.

CIRCULATION

 n.a.

Heleni Pedersoli

AMERICAN MERCURY

"America in the 1920's was the decade of H. L. Mencken."[1] From 1924 until he stepped down as editor in 1933, the *American Mercury* was the primary vehicle of Mencken's influence. "The *American Mercury* was the voice of the skepticism and iconoclasm which in the twenties replaced the rebellious idealism and optimism of the days before the war."[2]

In 1914 H. L. Mencken and his friend and collaborator George Nathan began editing the *Smart Set*,* an avant-garde literary and satirical magazine. By 1923 they were ready to move on to something less literary and more satirical. A young publisher named Alfred A. Knopf offered to publish a new monthly magazine if Mencken would edit it. Mencken agreed if Nathan could be coeditor, and the *American Mercury* was born.

The first issue, with its bright green cover and fifty-cent cost, was published on 26 December 1923 and dated January 1924. Neither Mencken nor Knopf envisioned the *Mercury* as a mass-market magazine. However, the success of the first issue soon changed their minds. The original printing was a modest 10,000 copies. This was sold out in two days. There was a second and a third printing, bringing the total number of copies of the first issue to 15,500. By the end of 1924 they were printing 55,000 copies an issue.

It is obvious that this first issue struck a responsive chord that continued to resonate in the American magazine reading public for many years. The primary attraction is evident: a satirical approach to American life. As Mencken put it in his first editorial, "[The *Mercury*] would devote itself pleasantly to exposing the nonsensicality of political, social, and economic hallucinations and utopias." Mencken never felt obliged to offer solutions to the problems he uncovered. Over the years he insisted that many of mankind's problems are unsolvable. It was enough to point them out.

The first issue began with an article debunking parts of the Lincoln legend, namely Lincoln's lowly origins, his skills as a war leader, and his ability to judge the character of the men around him. Another article, titled "The Drool Method of History," ridiculed the tendency of history textbook publishers to rewrite history to make it more palatable to the general public and various pressure groups. A third article downplayed the then current communist scare, and a fourth, titled "A Second-Rate War," disparaged the poor training received by American troops in World War I.

One should not, however, get the idea that the content of the *Mercury* was uniformly negative. The first issue also included a laudatory article on Stephen Crane by Carl Van Doren, an analysis of the 1912 Treaty on the Limitations of Naval Armaments, supporting the treaty and other measures to limit the arms race, and a straightforward discussion of the philosopher George Santayana.

Six departments appeared in the first issue. The first, a monthly editorial, was written by Mencken as long as he was editor. A great favorite with readers was Americana. It was three to four pages of short news items reprinted from various sources around the country, arranged alphabetically by state, illustrating what the editors viewed as the sillier aspects of American life. Included in the first issue were items about a law forbidding golf and billiards on Sunday in Birmingham, Alabama, a Bible reading marathon in Connecticut, a new world's record for Bible study attendance in Missouri, and several examples of bad English grammar.

Clinical Notes, originally written by both editors but gradually taken over by Nathan, was a collection of short opinion pieces, in this first issue supporting humor, suggesting hedonism as a philosophy of life, debunking the argument for the existence of God based upon design, extolling the joys of marrying a homely woman, and ridiculing a Ku Klux Klan circular attacking the Catholic church.

A fourth department was Arts and Sciences, a collection of short factual pieces on the arts, sciences, business and economics, education, and social relationships by a variety of writers. Arts and sciences was followed by Theatre, reviews by Nathan of current plays. Although Nathan's position as editor ended in 1925, he continued to write Clinical Notes until 1930 and Theatre into the forties. The last department, Library, contained book reviews written by Mencken.

Interspersed among this material was a selection of creative work: four short stories, a play, and four poems. All items ranged from three to nine pages in length, giving a total of 128 pages for the first issue. This size, excluding later advertising, remained constant into the 1930s.

This mix of factual articles, exposés of the shams and pretensions of American life, and literature, remained the essence of the *Mercury* as long as Mencken was editor. Although there was less emphasis on the belles lettres in the *Mercury* than in the *Smart Set*, Mencken solicited material from new writers as well as established writers. Over the years he printed selections by Eugene O'Neill, Sinclair Lewis, Theodore Dreiser, William Saroyan, Erskine Caldwell, William Faulkner, F. Scott Fitzgerald, and a host of others.

However, it was in the nonfiction and satirical pieces that Mencken exerted his strongest editorial influence. These articles had to reflect Mencken's outlook. A list of his targets would include anything to do with Prohibition, including the temperance movement and the Anti-Saloon League, reformers of any sort, lodges such as the Rotarians and the Kiwanians, the Daughters of the American Revolution and the American Legion, morticians, beauticians, college professors, children, puritanism, chiropractors, the science of psychology, farmers, new religious movements and religion in general, pacifists, socialists, politicians, the American political system and democracy in general, noisy patriotism, soft drinks, and dining out.

Mencken did not engage in logical debate, but tried to destroy his opponents with wit and scorn. However, as Walter Lippmann put it, "He calls you a swine and an imbecile, and he increases your will to live."[3]

There were negative opinions of the *Mercury*. A *New Republic** editorial writer cited the inclination toward name calling, noting the frequency of such words as insane, ludicrous, idiots, dervishes, sorcerers, yokels, and ass. He felt that the role of the *Mercury* would be that of a mere flea in the American bed.[4]

Charles Angoff, who would become editor of the *Mercury* in 1934, recalled Mencken as "a man of few basic ideas, and perhaps half of them were absurd, cheap, and simply not true."[5] His literary tastes were limited and his political views were anti-democratic and anti-American.[6] Others found that articles and particularly items in Americana were not representative of American life but rather reflected Mencken's iconoclastic personality.[7] Or, as the Reverend Dr. Charles E. Jones put it in the *Gospel Call*, "If a buzzard had laid an egg in a dunghill and the sun had hatched a thing like Mencken, the buzzard would have been justly ashamed of its offspring."[8] But of course this was exactly what the readers of the *Mercury* were buying.

In the early 1930s there were signs that the popularity of the *Mercury* had peaked. Circulation dropped from 62,000 in 1930 to a little more than half that in 1933. The stock market crash of 1929 seemed to sound the death knell for Mencken's style of journalism. It was an age in desperate need of new, constructive ideas, and Mencken's sarcasm and debunking no longer found a wide audience. "Mencken was too conservative, too bourgeois, too pro-German, and too anti-Semite, [and] he failed to grasp the impact of the stock market crash."[9] Mencken resigned as editor at the end of 1933, giving as his main reason his desire for more time to write books. In truth, America was changing and Mencken's *Mercury* refused to change with it.

New editors did not reverse the sagging circulation and advertising revenues. In 1935 Knopf sold the *Mercury* to Paul Palmer and Lawrence Spivak. Palmer, who took over as editor, was convinced that major changes had to be made if the *Mercury* was to survive. He shortened the length of the articles, reduced the magazine's physical dimensions to *Reader's Digest** size, and lowered the cost to twenty-five cents. The *Mercury* took on a strongly conservative outlook, anti–New Deal and procapitalism.

The new format was an immediate success with the readers, and circulation climbed. However, advertising revenue continued to drop. In 1939 Spivak purchased full control and continued as publisher until 1950, serving as editor from 1944 to 1950. Spivak was a prominent anti-Soviet writer, and under his direction the *Mercury* became strongly anti-Stalinist and concerned with communist influence in the United States.

During the 1940s the *Mercury*'s content emphasized the war and the postwar political situation. The mainstay was factual articles and opinion pieces. Literary material had been reduced to an occasional short story. On politically sensitive issues, articles expressing opposing views would often be printed back-to-back. The magazine included articles opposing Jim Crow and discrimination against Japanese Americans. Three original *Mercury* departments continued, Americana, Library, and Theatre, the latter still written by Nathan. During the war years another column was added, variously titled Lunacy: Left and Right, and Lunacy Marches On. It was similar to Americana but reprinted items from extreme left- and right-wing publications. Political cartoons were also added during the war. Americana disappeared in the mid–1940s, but Life with the Experts was added. This monthly column reprinted bad predictions by so-called experts.

The *Mercury*'s circulation under Spivak never went below 50,000 and hit a peak of 84,000 in 1945. Yet the magazine still did not make money. Spivak supported it with profits from other publishing ventures.

In the fall of 1950 Spivak sold the *Mercury* to Clendenin J. Ryan, a millionaire investment banker. His editor was William Huie. The magazine continued to lose money, and in 1952 it was sold to J. Russell Maguire, with Huie remaining as editor. Maguire seemed determined to convert the *Mercury* into a reactionary publication. Within six months Huie walked out. Two years later most of the remaining editorial staff left in a body because of attempts to introduce anti-Semitic material into the magazine.[10]

In the 1950s and 1960s the *Mercury* continued its shift to the extreme right. Publishers during these years included the Defenders of the Christian Faith and the Legion for the Survival of Freedom. In the sixties, articles attacked com-

munism, the United Nations, labor unions, foreign aid, the mental health movement, the fluoridation of drinking water, the Peace Corps, Israel, and blacks.
In the seventies, more and more articles appeared lauding the white race and
supporting segregation.

When the *Mercury* ceased publication in 1980, the publisher was still listed
as the Legion for the Survival of Freedom, of Torrance, California.

Writing in 1959, Lawrence Spivak stated that if he had known what was going
to happen to the *Mercury*, he "would have buried it. . . . It is a shame that the
magazine that contributed so much and earned a great name in its day, should
come to such a state."[11] What was true in 1959 was even more true in 1980.

Notes

1. D. E. Shepardson, "In the Prime of His Time," *American History Illustrated,*
January 1975, p. 10.

2. Theodore Peterson, *Magazines in the Twentieth Century*, 2nd ed. (Urbana: University of Illinois Press, 1964), p. 429.

3. Shepardson, p. 14.

4. "The American Mercury," *New Republic*, 6 February 1924, p. 274.

5. Charles Angoff, "The Inside View of Mencken's *Mercury*," *New Republic*, 13
September 1954, p. 18.

6. Ibid., p. 19.

7. William Manchester, "Mencken and the *Mercury*," *Harper's Magazine*, August
1950, p. 71.

8. As quoted in Manchester, p. 73.

9. Jack Salzman, "Conroy, Mencken, and the *American Mercury*" *Journal of Popular Culture*, Winter 1973, p. 524.

10. "Blowup at the *Mercury*," *Time*, 3 October 1955, p. 72.

11. Frank Luther Mott, *A History of American Magazines, Vol. 5: Sketches of 21
Magazines, 1905–1930*, (Cambridge: Harvard University Press, 1968), p. 26.

Information Sources

BIBLIOGRAPHY

"American Mercury," *New Republic*, 6 February 1924, p. 274.

Anderson, Fenwick. "Inadequate to Prevent the Present." *Journalism Quarterly*, Summer
1974, pp. 297–302, 382.

Angoff, Charles. "The Inside View of Mencken's *Mercury*." *New Republic*, 13 September 1954, pp. 18–22.

"Blowup at the *Mercury*," *Time*, 3 October 1955, p. 72.

"50 Years of the *American Mercury*," *Patterns of Prejudice*, 8, no. 2 (1974): 27–29.

Manchester, William. "Mencken and the *Mercury*." *Harper's Magazine*, August 1950,
pp. 65–73.

Mott, Frank Luther. *A History of American Magazines, Vol. 5: Sketches of 21 Magazines,
1905–1930*. Cambridge: Harvard University Press, 1968, pp. 2–26.

Peterson, Theodore. *Magazines in the Twentieth Century.* 2nd ed. Urbana: University of Illinois Press, 1964, pp. 429–34.

Salzman, Jack. "Conroy, Mencken, and the *American Mercury.*" *Journal of Popular Culture*, Winter 1973, pp. 524–26.

Shepardson, D. E. "In the Prime of His Time." *American History Illustrated*, January 1975, pp. 10–19.

INDEX SOURCES
  Readers' Guide (1924–1961); by publisher.
LOCATION SOURCES
  Available in microform.

Publication History

MAGAZINE TITLE AND CHANGES
  American Mercury. (*New American Mercury,* December 1950–February 1951.)
VOLUME AND ISSUE DATA
  Vols. 1–116, 1924–1980. Monthly.
PUBLISHER AND PLACE OF PUBLICATION
  Alfred A. Knopf, 1924–1935, New York; Lawrence E. Spivak, 1935–1936, New York; Paul Palmer, 1936–1939, New York; Lawrence E. Spivak, 1939–1950, New York; Clendenin J. Ryan, 1950–1951, New York; J. Russell Maguire, 1952–1960, New York; Defenders of the Christian Faith, Inc., 1960–1962, Oklahoma City, Oklahoma; Legion for the Survival of Freedom, Inc., 1963–1965, McAllen, Texas; 1966, Houston, Texas; 1966–1980, Torrance, California.
EDITORS
  H. L. Mencken and George Nathan, 1924–1925; H. L. Mencken, 1925–1933; Henry Hazlitt, 1934; Charles Angoff, 1934–1935; Paul Palmer, 1935–1939; Eugene Lyons, 1939–1944; Lawrence Spivak, 1944–1950; William B. Huie, 1950–1953; John A. Clements, 1953–1955; J. R. Maguire, 1955–1957; William La Varre, 1957–1958; Maurine Halliburton, 1958–1960; Gerald S. Pope, 1960–1962; Marcia C. J. Matthews, 1963; Jason Matthews, 1963–1964; Edwin A. Walker, 1964–1965; La Vonne Doden Furr, 1966–1980.
CIRCULATION
  High 4,000 (1945); Low 8,000 (1979).

Willard Moonan

AMERICAN MONTHLY. See THE KNICKERBOCKER

AMERICAN REVIEW. See AMERICAN WHIG REVIEW

THE AMERICAN WHIG REVIEW

The American Review: A Whig Journal of Politics, Literature, Art and Science was founded in January 1845 to provide a forum of expression for the members of the rising Whig party and to compete with the opposition party's *Democratic*

*Review.** The candidacy of Henry Clay against the Democrat James Polk provided further impetus for the new magazine's establishment.

The Introductory essay of the first issue decried the false ideas of liberty and progress of the Democrats, warned of the dangers of a chief executive whose power was "most liable to be abused, and greater than is possessed by the crowned head of any constitutional monarchy in Christendom" (a reference to "King" Andrew Jackson), and at the same time called for more attention to the "great field of literature, philosophy and morals." The contents of the first number are fairly representative of this dual approach. After the "Introductory," readers found an essay on "The Position of Parties," a poem entitled "How Are We Living," "Steam Navigation," "The Infancy of American Manufactures," a critique of Elizabeth Barrett's poems, Clay on "The Texas Question," "Random Collections of Travels," and "Critical Notices" (book reviews).

Most of the articles in the *Whig Review* were anonymous, although the more prominent contributors were Daniel Webster, John P. Kennedy, Daniel Barnard, and George P. Marsh.[1] The initial circulation was approximately three thousand, and grew to approximately five thousand in its final year (1852).

George H. Colton, the author of *Tecumseh* (a long narrative poem in praise of General William Henry Harrison), was the first editor of the *Whig Review*. Under his leadership, the review printed "The Raven" by Edgar Allan Poe (signed "Quarles" in the February 1845 issue), an essay in praise of Nathaniel Hawthorne (September 1846), a two-part comparison of Longfellow's poetry with that being written in Europe (November-December 1846), and many other reviews favorable to American writers.

But politics was clearly the main focus of the *Whig Review*, and as elections approached and issues arose for debate, political subjects took precedence over literary and scientific entries. The January 1847 number condemned on the one hand President Polk's conduct of the Mexican War, and on the other hand published a laudatory biographical sketch of Rufus Choate, one of the stalwarts of the Whig party. The following issue (February 1847) sang the praises of General Winfield Scott, and the July 1848 number began with a glowing endorsement of General Zachary Taylor, the (successful) Whig candidate for president.

Regardless of the 1848 election victory of General Taylor, the Whigs were not able to deal effectively with the issue of slavery, which tore the country asunder, and the editors of the *Whig Review* antagonized readers from both North and South by printing articles by John C. Calhoun of South Carolina and John Davis of Massachusetts. The "Congressional Summary" of March 1850 quoted excerpts from Henry Clay's speech before the Senate in which he called for the admission of California to the United States but sidestepped the designation of it as a free or slave state. Also, an "Editorial Note" of June 1850 maintained the ambiguity: "The ground which they [the editors] have taken they esteem to be strictly Whig and constitutional, and therefore intermediate and conciliatory between the extreme positions of the North and South. The question of the extension of slavery is simply a controversy between a certain class of property holders and the rest of the nation, and tends to confound all other distinctions of party.'' This attempt at neutrality caused Southern Whigs to join the Democrats for fear of losing their slaveholding rights, and many Northern Whigs joined the antislavery Free Soil party. The rise of the Republican party completed the Whig's downfall.

But the American Whig party and its *Review* were also the victims of bad luck. President Taylor died shortly after taking office, and his successor, Millard Fillmore, was soundly defeated in the presidential canvass of 1852. Also in 1852, the deaths of both elder statesmen of the Whig party, Clay and Webster, added to the disarray, and the *Whig Review* survived only until the end of that year. The final issue contained, appropriately, a eulogy of Webster.

Notes

1. Frank Luther Mott, *A History of American Magazines 1741–1850* (New York: Appleton, 1930), pp. 751–53.

Information Sources

BIBLIOGRAPHY
Mott, Frank Luther. *A History of American Magazines, 1741–1850*. New York: Appleton, 1930, pp. 751–53.
INDEX SOURCES
Each volume indexed. *Poole's* (1845–1852).
LOCATION SOURCES
Reprint ed., AMS Press, Inc., 1965; widely held. Available in microform.

Publication History

MAGAZINE TITLE AND TITLE CHANGES
The American Review: A Whig Journal of Politics, Literature, Art and Science, 1846–1847; *A Whig Journal Devoted to Politics and Literature*, 1848–April 1850; *The American Whig Review*, May 1850–December 1852.
VOLUME AND ISSUE DATA
Vols. 1–16, January 1845–December 1852, monthly.
PUBLISHER AND PLACE OF PUBLICATION
Wiley and Putnam, January–June 1845; George H. Colton, 1845–1847; D. W. Holly, 1848–1852. New York.
EDITORS
George H. Colton, 1845–1847; James D. Whelpley, 1848–1849; George W. Peck, 1850–1852.

CIRCULATION
   5,000 (1852).

Lawrence W. Lynch

AMERICANA

Originally conceived in 1973 as a mere gratuity for readers of *American Heritage: The Magazine of History, Americana* soon took on a life, character, and readership of its own. Today its paid circulation of 350,000 far surpasses that of its former companion.

Americana was not at first intended to be a real magazine, not intended to stand by itself. It was intended to be a promotional throw-in, and was sent to *American Heritage* subscribers in the six months of the year that *American Heritage* did not publish.[1]

But by the end of the first year, American Heritage Publishing Company decided to promote *Americana* as an independent magazine.[2] A wise decision, it turned out, because as *American Heritage* was in the midst of a long, steady decline in subscriptions (dropping from over 300,000 in the mid–1960s to about 170,000 in the mid–1970s and continuing to drop till the early 1980s), *Americana* was taking off. It already had 134,000 subscribers by the beginning of 1977 and was approaching 200,000 by the end of the year. In addition, it was beginning to attract sophisticated advertising.[3] Facts like these prompted Rhett Austell, president of American Heritage Publishing Company, to remark, "*Americana* [not *American Heritage*] is the hot-ticket item."[4]

One might ask how companion publications could experience such a difference in fortune. Perhaps the answer lies in the whims of different readerships. "The *Americana Heritage* readers are the history buffs," said Michael Durham, editor of *Americana* from 1974 to 1986. "The *American* readers are interested in what they can do today that have their roots in the past—crafts, collecting, cooking, travel, etc. . . . [*Americana*] is not a magazine of history . . . It is a magazine that shows the readers how the uses of the past add to the enjoyment of the present."[5]

The typical *Americana* article is a careful blend of text and pictures—neither dominating the other.[6] Recent articles are as high in quality as earlier ones. The June 1987 issue, for example, anticipating the bicentennial of the signing of the U.S. Constitution, included a story about the constitutional exhibit at the New York Public Library. Neither a detailed history of the Constitution nor a photographic portfolio, the story contained just enough text to breathe life into the pictures of some of the exhibits. The same issue also included articles on hatpins, stencilers, the New English Song and Dance Companie, and flagstone paths— all in a format showing concern for total textual and visual effect.

Americana's consistent high quality can be attributed not only to editorial skill but also to editorial stability. After Peter Andrews guided the magazine through its first year, Michael Durham became editor and served for some twelve years, surviving four changes in publisher and the magazine's change in ownership (in 1979).[7] An eleven-year veteran of *Life** and a former free-lance writer, Durham enjoyed a reputation (one that he shared with his small staff) for being approachable. Writers' magazines remarked on his willingness to entertain story suggestions from photographers, writers, and writer-photographers—the free-lance talent on which *Americana* has always drawn.[8] The present editor is Sandra Wilmot, who not only joined the magazine (as researcher) the same year that Durham did, but who had earlier (in another job at American Heritage Publishing Company) helped Peter Andrews get the magazine started.[9]

Though *Americana* may be described as elementary in content, one must keep in mind that sophistication is not its goal. It does not pretend to be a history magazine and should not be considered an inferior version of *American Heritage*. Rather, it should be considered a superior popular magazine for collectors of America's past.

Notes

1. Howard Chapnick, "Markets & Careers: *Americana* Is a Free-lance Market for America's Past," *Popular Photography*, November 1976, p. 80; Richard Tobin, "Is There a Renaissance for the History Magazines?" *Mankind*, 5, no. 2 (1977): 12.

2. Chapnick, p. 80.

3. Tobin, p. 12.

4. Ibid.

5. Chapnick, pp. 80, 82.

6. Ibid., p. 82.

7. *Americana* was acquired from the American Heritage Publishing Company by New America. Philip H. Dougherty, "Jersey Group Acquires *Americana* Magazine," *New York Times*, 25 May 1979, D11 (Late edition); not in National edition.

8. Hayes B. Jacobs, "Variety, at *Americana*," *Writer's Digest*, March 1979, p. 20; Chapnick, p. 84.

9. Michael Durham, "Note from the Editor," *Americana*, March 1974.

Information Sources

BIBLIOGRAPHY

Chapnick, Howard. "Markets & Careers: *Americana* Is a Free-lance Market for America's Past." *Popular Photography*, November 1976.

Dougherty, Philip H. "Jersey Group Acquires *Americana* Magazine." *New York Times*, 25 May 1979, D11 (Late edition); not in National edition.

Durham, Michael. "Note from the Editor." *Americana*, March 1974.

Jacobs, Hayes B. "Variety, at *Americana*." *Writer's Digest*, March 1979, p. 20.

Tobin, Richard L. "Is There a Renaissance for the History Magazines?" *Mankind*, 5, no. 2 (1977): 10–14.

INDEX SOURCES

Magazine Index (1977–present); *Popular Magazine Review; Readers' Guide to Periodical Literature* (1978–present); *Periodical Abstracts*.

LOCATION SOURCES
Library of Congress, many other libraries (especially public). Available in microform.

Publication History

MAGAZINE TITLE AND TITLE CHANGES
Americana, 1973–present.
VOLUME AND ISSUE DATA
Vols. 1–15, March 1973–present. Bimonthly (six issues a year).
PUBLISHER AND PLACE OF PUBLICATION
American Heritage Society: Paul Gottlieb, 1973–1975; Marjorie C. Dyer, 1975–1976; Rhett Austell, 1976–1978; Tim Hill, 1979. Americana Magazine, Inc.: Jack Armstrong, 1979–present. New York, New York.
EDITORS
Peter Andrews, 1973–1974; Michael Durham, 1974–1986; Sandra J. Wilmot, 1986–present.
CIRCULATION
357,700 paid, 3,300 nonpaid.

David R. Kohut

APPAREL ARTS. See GQ: GENTLEMAN'S QUARTERLY

APPLETON'S JOURNAL

In the latter part of the nineteenth century, it was not uncommon for American book publishers to branch out into magazine publishing as a means of increasing their profits. One of the publishers who did this was D. Appleton and Company, who, in 1869, brought out a general-interest magazine entitled *Appleton's Journal of Literature, Science and Art.* Primarily a New York–oriented magazine, *Appleton's* enlightened the public on those subjects included in the title and advertised the publisher's latest books as well.

The magazine's mission was outlined by editor Edward Youmans in the first issue, dated 3 April 1869. *Appleton's* would focus on literature, science, art, and education. While it would impart "valuable information upon subjects of public importance,"[1] ordinary news was to be omitted from its pages.

During its twelve-year existence, *Appleton's* contained a wide variety of features. In any given issue, the reader might find poetry, essays, a chapter of a serialized novel, travel pieces, criticism of drama or art, brief articles on science, or a biographical sketch. Topics covered in articles were many and varied, including education, women, health concerns, current events, and manners. The tone of many of the pieces is similar to much popular writing of the time, genteel almost in the extreme. Dorothy Parker once commented of a book written in this style that it was "happily free from iconoclasm. There is not a sentence that you couldn't read to your most conservative relatives and still be reasonably sure of that legacy."[2]

Science was not an overly large part of *Appleton's,* and it was this fact that led to the resignation of Edward Youmans, the first editor, in 1870. Youmans, a friend and colleague of William Henry Appleton, had conceived of the magazine as a vehicle for reporting contemporary scientific ideas.[3] Unfortunately for Youmans, Appleton was of the opinion that too much science would bore the gentle reader, and the coverage of science was restricted to a few columns of very general interest.

Discouraged by Appleton's apathy toward the subject Youmans held so dear, the editor turned over his post to Robert Carter in 1870. Carter, an experienced editor and publisher who had been on the staff of Appleton's *Cyclopedia,* held the position for two years. It then passed to Oliver Bell Bunce, who remained as editor until *Appleton's* ceased publication in 1881. Trained as a publisher and popular writer, Bunce had the valuable combination of a talent for knowing popular taste and the necessary capacity for detail.[4] He wrote almost all of the "Table-Talk" columns, light essays that dealt with social concerns and manners. Colonel Charles H. Jones, a journalist, worked as Bunce's assistant.

Little information is available on circulation rates and advertising revenue. The first issue sold for a dime, and a yearly subscription cost $4.50. Although *Appleton's* had been expected to net a profit for the good of its parent company, the magazine did not do well for very long. By 1870, financial troubles had begun to crop up. To cut costs, the highly popular steel plates and folding cartoons, artwork that characterized *Appleton's* from others of its ilk, were discontinued. By July 1876, the magazine's financial status was such that it became necessary to publish it on a monthly basis rather than weekly. Three years later *Appleton's* had become merely an eclectic, comprised almost wholly of material taken from European periodicals; only the department of criticism was not European.[5]

Many women subscribed to *Appleton's Journal.* The tone of the magazine is conservatively feminist, with the emphasis (as one would expect) on the word *conservatively. Appleton's* approved of outdoor exercise for women but frowned upon public athletic competition among them.[6] The magazine's support of women was best stated in one of the first issues: "Having been idolized, sung and flattered through all the moods and tenses of poets' feeling, it seems at last women's destiny to be soberly considered."[7]

Appleton's readers were themselves conservative folk, educated and inclined to be interested in reading. They were the sort of people who patronized or would be given to patronizing establishments such as Lord and Taylor, Tiffany's, Mason and Hamlin, and—most importantly for the publisher—people who were given to buying books.

As *Appleton's Journal* wound down, it gave rise to other publications and ventures for the firm of D. Appleton and Company. *Picturesque America,* a two-volume publication that came out in 1872–1874, originated in the magazine as a series of pictures and sketches under that title; among the featured artists were Harry Fenn, A. R. Wand, and Winslow Homer. The year 1876 saw the birth of a new Appleton magazine entitled the *Art Journal*, containing the kinds of art that had been featured in *Appleton's Journal*. Upon deciding to end *Appleton's* in 1881, the publishers began to print the literary articles in their new *Appleton's Literary Bulletin*.

Appleton's Journal is worth the look of students of late nineteenth-century American history and literature. It would also most likely be of interest to persons studying women's history or doing research on late nineteenth-century New Yorkers.

Notes

1. "To the Public," *Appleton's Journal*, 3 April 1869, p. 22.
2. Dorothy Parker, "The Professor Goes In for Sweetness and Light," *The Common Reader* (New York: Viking Press, 1970), p. 20.
3. Frank Luther Mott, *A History of American Magazines*. Vol. 3: *1865–1885* (Cambridge: Harvard University Press, 1938), p. 417.
4. Ibid., p. 418.
5. Ibid., p. 421.
6. "Table-Talk," *Appleton's Journal*, 8 October 1870, p. 438.
7. "Table-Talk," *Appleton's Journal*, 17 April 1869, p. 89.

Information Sources

BIBLIOGRAPHY
Mott, Frank Luther. *A History of American Magazines*. Vol. 3: *1865–1885*. Cambridge: Harvard University Press, 1938.
Parker, Dorothy. "The Professor Goes In for Sweetness and Light." *The Common Reader*. New York: Viking Press, 1970. pp. 18–22.
"Table-Talk." *Appleton's Journal*, 17 April 1869, p. 89.
"Table-Talk." *Appleton's Journal*, 8 October 1870, p. 438.
"To the Public." *Appleton's Journal*, 3 April 1869, p. 22.
Wolfe, Gerard R. *The House of Appleton: The History of a Publishing House and Its Relationship to the Cultural, Social and Political Events That Helped Shape the Destiny of New York City*. Metuchen, N.J.: Scarecrow Press, 1981.
INDEX SOURCES
Poole's; Jones's; Subject-Contents Index.
LOCATION SOURCES
Library of Congress and many other libraries. The complete run of *Appleton's Journal* has been reproduced in the microfilm series *American Periodicals: 1850–1900, Civil War and Reconstruction* (Ann Arbor, Mich.: University Microfilms International. Reels 244–249.

Publication History

MAGAZINE TITLE AND TITLE CHANGES

> *Appleton's Journal of Literature, Science and Art,* 1869–June 1876; *Appleton's Journal: A Monthly Miscellany of Popular Literature,* July 1876–1878.

VOLUME AND ISSUE DATA

> Weekly, 1869–26 June 1876; monthly, July 1876–1881. Vol. 1, 3 April–14 August 1869; vol. 2, 21 August–25 December 1869; vols. 3–15, 1870–26 June 1876. New series: vols. 1–11 (16–26), July 1876–1881.

EDITORS

> Edward Livingston Youmans, 1869–1870; Robert Carter, 1870–1872; Oliver Bell Bunce and Charles Henry Jones, 1872–1881.

CIRCULATION

> n.a.

Sandra Wenner

ARCHITECTURAL DIGEST

Architectural Digest, today's number one magazine in the world of interior design, has been a family-run business since its establishment in 1920. Owned and operated by the Knapp Communications Corporation of Los Angeles, the publication is controlled by Cleon T. Knapp, the grandson of the magazine's founder, John C. Brasfield. *Architectural Digest's* evolution and growth from a small family-owned regional trade directory to the internationally acclaimed design periodical of today is primarily due to the foresight and perspicacity of its present owner.

When John Brasfield moved to southern California in the early 1900s, he found a community just beginning to grow. He was convinced that California's climate and casual way of life were going to draw many people to the state, and as a result he envisioned a publication that would record the growth and development of architectural style as well as feature the works of fledgling architects: "Land promoters, builders and retailers of course wanted this development publicized. Therein lay the nucleus for a publication."[1] The result was a pictorial digest for the professionals.

For forty years, the *Architectural Digest: A Pictorial Digest of Outstanding Architecture, Interior Decoration and Landscaping* featured the exteriors and interiors of homes and commercial buildings in black-and-white photography. No text accompanied these photos, but the names of the owners and architects appeared for identification. Issues of the magazine were published biannually and circulation was small. However, throughout this early period, the publication was recording changing styles and growing communities.

By the 1960s the *Architectural Digest,* as it was still then called, began to emphasize home interiors. Residences of such celebrities as Clark Gable, Eartha Kitt, and Laurence Harvey were featured together with those of important and affluent industrialists. In order to spotlight some truly outstanding examples of architectural design, two new issues were added, allowing subscribers access to the publication in the spring, summer, winter, and fall. One such extra addition highlighted the home of Mr. and Mrs. Cliff May. This home was singular both because of its design and its builder. Cliff May was considered "the foremost designer of the Western Ranch House which he has been building in California since 1932."[2]

When in 1960 *Architectural Digest* made the claim, "Always there has been the unvarying theme of quality in subject matter and presentation which has made *The Architectural Digest* the Aristocrat of all Periodicals on Intertior Design."[3] Their words were somewhat premature. However, in 1965 Cleon T. Knapp took over control of the magazine and the decisions he was to make did much to change the magazine from a limited pictorial digest to the elegant and artistic periodical it is today.

The first decisions the new publisher made were based on the conviction that there was a growing population of affluent homeowners who would be willing subscribers for an expanded, more elegant, more glamorous magazine. The price of the periodical was set high enough for it to cover the costs of the changes. These included an expanded use of color photography, a more international selection of homes, added features on fine art and antiques, and an increase in the number of annual issues from four to six. By 1971 the format of the magazine had changed to full-color photography, and the cover was redesigned "to create an improved cover layout consistent with *Architectural Digest's* history and future as well as portraying the quality of our editorial philosophy. . . . In this case we want the book to be known by its cover."[4] Despite these changes, three interrelated hurdles had to be surmounted for the publication to prosper in the 1970s.

The first hurdle was to gain the respect of the eastern design establishment. Second, the publication needed to increase its circulation widely to attract important designers. Third, the magazine had to gain the national advertising that would set the publication on its feet. What was more, all of these gains had to be made simultaneously.

To begin the process, Knapp made two vital decisions. The first was to hire a professional interior decorator as his new editor. The second was to abandon the old policy that dictated all decorators had to advertise to have their work published in the periodical. Through diligent and exhaustive public relations, the new editor, Paige Rense, was able to persuade several San Francisco designers to show in the magazine. Two other firsts for *Architectural Digest* included the much sought after photographic portrayal of the home of New York designer Angelo Donghia and the Paris apartment of the late fashion designer Coco Chanel. So it was that by the end of the 1970s, *Architectural Digest* had risen to the top of the "shelter," otherwise known as home-oriented, magazines. It became a bimonthly, averaging about 200 pages per issue, packed with national advertising selling expensive "quality" home furnishings and other high-priced items: luxury cars, jewelry, perfume, and imported alcoholic beverages. The magazine's circulation rose to over 300,000 by the end of the decade.

The 1980s have seen the consolidation of *Architectural Digest's* position. It now averages 300 pages an issue (there have been twelve issues per year since the beginning of the 1980s), and the photographic presentations continue to be of the highest artistic quality. Critics of the publication who in the past complained that the text was mediocre can applaud more sophisticated and accomplished writing. In recent issues well-known and celebrated authors such as John Updike and Brendan Gill have contributed special articles. Circulation continues to grow and is now over 500,000. The periodical has featured the homes and the work of most of the great designers around the world and, in doing so, has challenged the taste of its readers. Among the cognoscenti of the design profession, it is acknowledged that *Architectural Digest* portrays the very best that interior designers have to offer.

Similar to the state of California in which it was founded, *Architectural Digest* has experienced incredible growth in the last sixty-eight years.

Notes

1. "From the Publisher," *Architectural Digest,* November-December 1970, p. 8.
2. "Foreword," *Architectural Digest,* Summer 1960.
3. "Foreword," *Architectural Digest*, Spring 1960.
4. "Publisher's Prerogative," *Architectural Digest*, March-April 1971.

Information Sources

BIBLIOGRAPHY
Sansweet, Stephen J. "*Stylish Success.* 'Architectural Digest' Becomes a Big Power in the Design World." *Wall Street Journal,* 6 August 1976, p. 1.
Architectural Digest, 1960–1988.
INDEX SOURCES
    Readers' Guide to Periodical Literature.
LOCATION SOURCES
    St. Louis Public Library, other libraries, available in microfilm.

Publication History

MAGAZINE TITLE AND TITLE CHANGES
    The Architectural Digest: A Pictorial Digest of Outstanding Architecture, Interior Decoration and Landscaping, 1920–1966; Architectural Digest: The Quality Guide to Home Decorating Ideas, 1966–1971; Architectural Digest: The Connoisseur's Magazine of Fine Interiors, 1971–1976; Architectural Digest: The International Magazine of Fine Interior Design, 1976–present.
VOLUME AND ISSUE DATA
    Vols. 1–16, 1920–1959, periodicity unknown; vols. 17–27, 1960–1970, quarterly; vols. 28–33, 1970–1976, bimonthly; vols. 34–45, 1977–present, monthly.

PUBLISHER AND PLACE OF PUBLICATION
  John C. Brasfield, 1920–1965; Cleon T. Knapp, 1965–present, Los Angeles, California.
EDITORS
  John C. Brasfield, 1920–1960; Bradley Little, 1960–1965; Cleon T. Knapp, 1965–1974; Paige Rense, 1974–present.
CIRCULATION
  550,000.

Judith Bunker

ARGOSY

Frank Munsey, the future magazine publishing baron, arrived in New York City from Maine on 23 September 1882 with $40 in his pocket. Ten months later, using borrowed money, he started his first magazine, the *Golden Argosy: Freighted With Treasures for Boys and Girls*. Munsey described it as "an illustrated weekly paper for boys and girls [that] consisted of eight pages."[1] It was aimed at ten-to twenty-year-olds.

There were many children's magazines being published at that time including *Frank Leslie's Boys and Girls Weekly, St. Nicholas,* and Munsey's model for his magazine, *Golden Days*, published in Philadelphia. However, Munsey was convinced that "there [was] an abundance of room for another publication of high moral tone."[2]

The first issue, dated 9 December 1882, led off with a serial by Horatio Alger, Jr., entitled "Do and Dare, or a Brave Boy's Fight for a Fortune." It also contained another serial, "Nick and Nellie, or God Helps Them That Help Themselves," three short stories, and a puzzle department.

The publisher of the *Golden Argosy*, E. G. Rideout, went bankrupt five months later and Munsey took over the publishing duties. Malcolm Douglas became editor at $10 a week. His primary task was to peruse English juvenile weeklies looking for stories suitable for reprinting in the *Golden Argosy*. Whenever this source of material gave out, Munsey, who had little money to buy original material, would write his own stories.

During his first five years of publishing Munsey was often broke and usually in debt. He spent thousands of dollars advertising his magazine and used traveling salesmen and the U.S. mails to distribute sample copies throughout the country. He increased the number of pages, decreased the size, decreased and then increased the price, but was always on the brink of economic disaster. In the fall of 1887 Munsey stopped his advertising campaign, realizing that "the trouble was with juvenile papers."[3] He decided to begin publishing for adults. The content of the *Golden Argosy* became more adult. In 1886 the subtitle referring to boys and girls was dropped. Two years later the title was shortened to *Argosy*. However, the magazine continued to languish.

In 1889 Munsey began *Munsey's Weekly*, which later became the very successful *Munsey's Magazine*. He now had a beachhead in the adult market.

By 1890 the circulation of *Argosy* had dropped to a point where it was no longer profitable. It limped along as a monthly adult magazine, a "weak imitation of *Munsey's Magazine*."[4] Then, in October 1896, Munsey made two changes that turned the *Argosy* into one of the most popular magazines of the first half of the twentieth century and radically changed the magazine publishing industry.

First, Munsey changed to an all-fiction format. *Argosy* was the first to publish in this format for adults. Next, he began publishing on rough wood-pulp paper. Thus *Argosy* became the first pulp magazine. The content stressed adventure in exotic lands, mysteries, and much action and melodrama. The American magazine-reading public responded. Circulation shot up. It doubled in a matter of months, reached 300,000 on its twentieth birthday, and 500,000 on its twenty-fifth birthday.

This winning format remained virtually unchanged until World War II. *Argosy* switched back to weekly publication in 1917, and merged with several of Munsey's other magazines over the years. But it continued to publish "decent, red-blooded fiction for the millions."[5]

To illustrate the format and the continuity, the December 1909 issue contained 192 pages. There were two complete stories of 25 and 28 pages, six serial parts ranging from 10 to 16 pages, and sixteen short stories of 3 to 8 pages. The 15 December 1928 issue contained 144 pages. There was one complete story of 24 pages, four serial parts ranging from 15 to 25 pages, and four short stories of 3 to 11 pages.

The subject matter of these stories included adventures in the Caribbean, China, eleventh-century Constantinople, and Shakespeare's England. There was mystery and romance on Wall Street, on a cattle ranch, in the pre–Civil War South, and on board an ocean liner. There were stories about detectives and spies, and sports heroes. In the late 1920s science fiction stories began to appear.

Among the better known authors who contributed to *Argosy* were Frederick Van Rensselaer Dey, author of the Nick Carter detective series; Albert Payson Terhune, P. G. Wodehouse, Sidney Porter (O. Henry), Max Brand, Mary Roberts Rinehart, Erle Stanley Gardner, C. S. Forester, Luke Short, Van Wyck Mason, and Zane Grey.

Munsey died in 1925, his estate estimated at $20 million.[6] *Argosy* was purchased by William T. Dewart. In the 1920s circulation held around 400,000, but the depression hit the magazine industry hard. *Argosy* circulation dropped to 40,000 by 1940.

In 1942 its publisher, the Frank Munsey Company, decided to make radical changes. They changed the title to the *New Argosy*, dropped its all-fiction format, and devoted half of every issue to factual war stories and news articles. It changed its price twice and its size three times. Its contents became so lurid that in 1942 it was briefly banned from the U.S. mails. But nothing helped.

That same year the Frank Munsey Company sold *New Argosy*, along with six other magazines, to Popular Publications, a large pulp publisher. In 1943 the new publisher changed it from pulp to slick and returned to its all-fiction format. No improvement resulted from these changes.

In 1945 *Argosy*, whose full title was now *Argosy: The Complete Men's Magazine*, became a slick general magazine. Retaining some fiction, it also ran factual articles about adventures, sports, crime, and science. Nonfiction pages became double those of fiction. As Henry Steeger of Popular Publications put it, "The tendency today is toward more realism. After the second world war the 15 million veterans were no longer content to accept the whimsy and phoniness of fiction."[7]

A department that brought the *Argosy* much publicity was the Court of Last Resort, which investigated cases of persons *Argosy* believed to be unjustly imprisoned. The investigating team consisted of a private detective, a criminologist, a former prison warden, and Erle Stanley Gardner, the detective story writer. Several men serving prison sentences were freed as a result of these investigations.

The new formula worked. By 1953, riding a period of rapid growth for men's magazines following the war, *Argosy* had a guaranteed circulation of 1.25 million and was asking $5,250 for a full-page color ad. By 1962 advertising revenues approached $2 million.

In 1965 an *Argosy* editor described its typical reader as "factory-bound, desk-bound, work-bound, forced by economics and society to abandon his innate maleness and individuality to become a cog in the corporate machine. We try to give him a sense of identity as a man in a world which has almost destroyed identity."[8] Apparently they were successful. Circulation remained well over a million until the economics of the magazine publishing industry forced the termination of *Argosy* in 1979.

Notes

1. Frank A. Munsey, *The Founding of the Munsey Publishing House* (New York: De Vinne Press, 1907), p. 5.
2. George Britt, *Forty Years—Forty Millions* (New York: Farrar and Rinehart, 1935), p. 63.
3. Munsey, p. 30.
4. Ibid., p. 50.
5. Frank Luther Mott, *A History of American Magazines*. Vol. 4: *1885–1905*. (Cambridge: Harvard University Press, 1938), p. 422.
6. Ibid., p. 421.
7. "New Argosy Crew," *Newsweek*, 17 May 1954, p. 62.
8. Bruce Cassiday, "When Argosy Looks for Stories," *Writer*, August 1965, p. 25.

Information Sources

BIBLIOGRAPHY

Britt, George. *Forty Years—Forty Millions*. New York: Farrar and Rinehart, 1935.
Cassiday, Bruce. "When Argosy Looks for Stories." *Writer,* August 1965, p. 25.

"Last Resort." *Newsweek*, 27 March 1950, p. 60.

"A Man's World." *Time*, 6 February 1950, pp. 38–40.

Mott, Frank Luther. *A History of American Magazines*. Vol. 4: *1885–1905*. Cambridge: Harvard University Press, 1938, pp. 417–23.

Munsey, Frank A. *The Founding of the Munsey Publishing House*. New York: De Vinne Press, 1907.

"New Argosy Crew." *Newsweek*, 17 May 1954, p. 62.

Peterson, Theodore. *Magazines in the Twentieth Century*. Urbana: University of Illinois Press, 1956, pp. 289–91.

INDEX SOURCES

> *Access* (1975–1977).

LOCATION SOURCES

> Available in microform.

Publication History

MAGAZINE TITLE AND TITLE CHANGES

> *Golden Argosy,* 9 December 1882–24 November 1888; *Argosy,* 1 December 1888–17 July 1920; *Argosy Story Weekly,* 24 July 1920–28 September 1929; *Argosy,* 5 October 1929–February 1942; *New Argosy,* March–July 1942; *Argosy,* August 1942–October 1979.

VOLUME AND ISSUE DATA

> Vols. 1–388, 9 December 1882–October 1979. Weekly, 9 December 1882–March 1894; monthly, April 1894–September 1917; weekly, October 1917–October 1941; biweekly, November 1941–April 1942; monthly, May 1942–October 1979.

PUBLISHER AND PLACE OF PUBLICATION

> E. G. Rideout and Company, 1882–1883; Frank A. Munsey, 1883–1925; William T. Dewart, 1926–1941; Popular Publications, Inc., 1942–1979. New York.

EDITORS

> Frank A. Munsey, 1882; Malcolm Douglas, 1883–1887; Matthew White, Jr., 1887–1928; A. H. Bittner, 1928–1930; Don Moore, 1930–1931; Albert J. Gibney, 1931–1936; Chandler H. Whipple, 1937–1939; George W. Post, 1940–1942; Henry Steeger, 1942–1948; Jerry Mason, 1948–1953; Howard J. Lewis, 1953–1954; Ken W. Purdy, 1954–1955; Henry Steeger, 1955–1972; Milt Machlin, 1973–1974; Ernie Baxter, 1975–1976; Lou Sahadi, 1976–October 1979.

CIRCULATION

> 1,150,000 (1978).

Willard Moonan

ATKINSON'S CASKET. See GRAHAM'S MAGAZINE

ATLANTIC MONTHLY

Remarkable for its longevity, the *Atlantic* celebrated 130 years of continuous publication in 1987. Francis Underwood created it; Phillips, Sampson, and Company published it; and New England's finest minds during the 1850s formed it.

Phillips and Sampson's Moses Dresser Phillips is given credit for assembling, in April 1857, a small group of writers, including James Russell Lowell, Ralph Waldo Emerson, Oliver Wendell Holmes, and Henry Wadsworth Longfellow, to discuss Underwood's idea for a new literary and political magazine. They greeted the idea enthusiastically, for as Horace Elisha Scudder notes in his early biography of Lowell, "They had a great deal to say, which was ill-adapted to daily journalism and for which they could not wait till it should cool for book publication."[1] Lowell became the first editor, with Underwood his principal office assistant. Lowell accepted the editorship on the condition that Holmes would be a major contributor; in fact, all the assembled were regular contributors during the formative years of the *Atlantic*. Successive editors have remained faithful to the objective of the founders, "to concentrate the efforts of the best writers upon literature and politics, under the light of the highest morals."[2] Its founders believed as much in giving voice to their political concerns as they did to belles lettres, and the *Atlantic* has attempted to sustain equilibrium between the two.

The first issue, in November 1857, set the standard to which the *Atlantic* has conformed since its inception. Desiring to make its appearance as appealing as its content, Phillips and Sampson selected the finest printer in Boston. Mark A. D. Howe states, perhaps overenthusiastically, "The magazine inevitably scored an immediate success."[3] The premier issue was devoid of any illustration, and it was 128 pages of double-columned text. The contents were a varied mix of essays, short stories, poetry, and the inevitable section entitled Literary Notices. Twenty thousand copies were distributed in late October, and the annual subscription was $30. Today's *Atlantic* is not much different. Usually about 100 pages of lightly illustrated double-and triple-columned text, each issue is composed of several departments. These include Articles, Arts and Leisure, Reports and Comment, Humor, Fiction, and Poetry, Other Departments, and Books. In 1987 circulation was estimated at 457,000 and the annual subscription $14.95.

The first issue had a distinguished list of then anonymous contributors, including Emerson, Lowell, Charles Eliot Norton, Harriet Beecher Stowe, Parke Godwin, and John Greenleaf Whittier. Emerson justified the anonymity thus: "The names of contributors will be given out when the names are worth more than the articles."[4] Nevertheless, the identity of contributors, although generally a well-known secret, was not routinely revealed on the pages of the *Atlantic* until 1870. The magazine regularly published regional authors, as Frank Luther Mott points out: "Throughout the first fifteen years . . . about two-thirds of its contributors were from New England, and far more than two-thirds of its pages were filled with their writing."[5] Initially, the magazine paid its contributors significantly, if not extravagantly, for their work. A poet could expect to receive $50 for each poem selected for publication, and writers of prose received $6 per page ($10 if the author had name recognition, an interesting paradox since all the articles were anonymous).[6] Thoreau was one writer paid only the standard rate, receiving $198 for his thirty-three page "Chesuncook" in June and July

1858, the most he had ever been paid for a magazine contribution.[7] Incidentally, he became so enraged at what he considered excessive editorial meddling that subsequently his works were published only posthumously in the magazine.

The *Atlantic* has remained true to the intent of publishing equal amounts of *belles lettres* and political commentary, shifting slightly as public sentiment altered, and evolving from what was primarily a literary magazine to today's general-interest periodical. In both categories, however, writers have met the high standards imposed by the magazine. In contrast to some literary and general-interest magazines, particularly *Harper's*,* the *Atlantic* was unable to maintain extravagant rates for contributions. Despite the comparatively low pay, articles poured into the offices from the beginning. Lowell never had a problem securing enough material for publication, and his insistence on reviewing each contribution himself ensured consistency and quality. Ellery Sedgwick, editor from 1909 to 1938, boasted that "people of notoriety, then of eminence, began to show a disposition to write for the *Atlantic*."[8] In 1987 the magazine was receiving approximately 1,000 unsolicited fiction manuscripts each month.[9]

Unknown fiction writers would find themselves in good company should they have articles published in the *Atlantic*. Emerson, Thoreau, Lowell, Henry Wadsworth Longfellow, Henry James, Edith Wharton, Sarah Orne Jewett, William Dean Howells, Mark Twain, Dylan Thomas, Theodore Roethke, Gertrude Stein, Philip Roth, Joyce Carol Oates, Robert Graves, Albert Camus, Isaac Bashevis Singer, Bobbie Ann Mason, Paul Theroux, Ann Beattie—the list of accomplished writers seems endless. The *Atlantic* has not published these writers only after they have caught the eye or imagination of the public, but frequently before they have gained fame. Its editors have had a knack for finding new talent. According to Edward Weeks, editor from 1938 to 1966, the *Atlantic* "has been a discoverer and a champion of new authors; since our resources were limited, we had to find new people of promise."[10]

The *Atlantic* is not known only for the quality of its *belles lettres*, particularly during this century. As a general-interest political and social review, the *Atlantic* has few peers. Underwood and the founding fathers of the magazine shared a sympathy for the abolition movement; the *Atlantic* was recognized as an anti-slavery magazine at its inception, and throughout the Civil War. Julia Ward Howe's "Battle Hymn of the Republic" first appeared in its pages[11] she was paid the seemingly paltry sum of $4 for it. Essays have been lively and thought-provoking, covering topics from slavery to the arms race. Woodrow Wilson sent, unsolicited, "The Road away from Revolution."[12] Additional noteworthy contributions are "The English Governess at the Siamese Court,"[13] "Municipal Administration: The New York Police Force,"[14] "Newspaper Morals,"[15] "The World's Economic Outlook,"[16] "Neutrality and Common Sense,"[17] "The Negro Is Your Brother,"[18] and "The Education of David Stockman."[19]

The *Atlantic* contributors are a distinguished group, and so too are the *Atlantic* editors. Weeks believed that the longevity of the magazine may have been due, at least in part, to the relative frequency with which editorial responsibility changed hands: "We have changed editors more frequently than any other magazine in our field; whenever the circulation began to sag, a younger mind was brought in."[20] To expand Weeks's figures, six editors hailed from New England (Lowell, James T. Fields, Thomas Bailey Aldrich, Horace Scudder, Bliss Perry, and Ellery Sedgwick), and one each from Ohio (William Dean Howells), North Carolina (Walter Hines Page), New Jersey (Weeks), New York (Robert Manning), and Arkansas (William Whitworth).

Each editor of the *Atlantic* was to leave a mark on the magazine, while sustaining the reputation for quality it has gained over the years. Its first editor maintained his position as professor of literature at Harvard College throughout his four-year tenure at the *Atlantic*. Lowell was passionate about the magazine, and imbued it with a decidedly scholarly and literary tone. James T. Fields's publishing house, Ticknor and Fields, purchased the magazine in 1859, and Fields endured Lowell's editorship for just two years before he assumed the role himself. According to Ellery Sedgwick III, "If the Brahmin Lowell had often selected manuscripts from a sense of cultural responsibility to educate his audience, Fields's selection was more often circumscribed by a shrewd sense of what would appeal to readers."[21] During Fields's tenure, the *Atlantic* published a then infamous article, Harriet Beecher Stowe's "The True History of Lady Byron's Life."[22] The circulation that Fields had so conscientiously increased to 50,000 dropped to 35,000. Mott attributed the drop to the article, but it was only the beginning of a nearly thirty-year decline in circulation.[23] Fields edited the magazine for ten years, replaced by his former assistant and man of letters, William Dean Howells. At the time, one would have had to look long and hard to find an individual whose background seemed as far removed from Boston Brahminism as Howells's Ohio heritage. Like Fields, Howells edited the *Atlantic* for ten years. He believed himself responsible for broadening the scope of the magazine to the Midwest, the South, and the West, while at the same time retaining its New England roots. When Howells resigned in 1881, Thomas Bailey Aldrich replaced him. His tendency was to return to the *Atlantic* of the Lowell years. He was interested in New England and in literature, and not so interested in politics and social issues. Thus, the first four editors of the *Atlantic* had in common their interest in literature, and although the *Atlantic* was subtitled *A Magazine of Literature, Art and Politics*, it remained largely a magazine of literature. The first three decades of the *Atlantic* were characterized, furthermore, by contributions equal to the best of the literary magazines.

With circulation approaching its lowest point ever, the next editors were forced to employ different tactics. Horace Elisha Scudder was the first editor of this phase of the magazine's history. He maintained the long-standing tradition of relying on *belles lettres* as the foundation of the *Atlantic*, but also began the emphasis on political and social issues. John Adams Thayer proffered what seemed an extreme suggestion to the *Atlantic* men near the end of the century. He boasted that he could increase sales of the magazine to over 100,000 by making the content and cover more lively, and by adding illustrations. The publishers refused his generous offer.[24] Walter Hines Page, an assistant editor for two years, became the editor in 1898, and he, not Thayer, became the man to stir things up at the staid *Atlantic*.

He enjoyed political controversy and engaged in some mild muckraking. Page did begin to turn the fortunes of the *Atlantic* around but resigned after only one year. His successor was Bliss Perry, a Princeton English professor, who carefully balanced the political and literary in the magazine. It has been said of Perry that he was soon made "uncomfortably aware" that the New England literary tradition was, if not dead, at least in decline.[25] In 1909 he turned editorial responsibilities over to Ellery Sedgwick, who had organized the Atlantic Monthly Company and purchased the magazine one year earlier. The increased prestige and fortune of the *Atlantic* that Page had initiated, Sedgwick carried out with vigor and success. His management enacted still more changes in the magazine. It is fair to say that while Sedgwick was editor of the *Atlantic*, it became the general-interest magazine it is today. Peterson suggests that the change may be due to Sedgwick's belief that the literary magazines, such as *Harper's*, "were too remote from life; they avoided questions which really excited people."[26] The strategy of printing essays designed to excite worked; interest and readership increased, and sales surpassed 100,000 in 1921.[27]

The "new" *Atlantic*'s reputation and fortune continued to increase throughout Sedgwick's long (twenty-eight years) editorship, and also during that of the next editor, Edward Weeks, who held the title editor emeritus until his death in March 1989. In addition to maintaining the Sedgwick strategy, Weeks was responsible for making important visual changes in the magazine. As editor, he instituted the use of drawings and other illustration; the first colored pictorial cover was the November 1947 ninetieth anniversary issue. When he retired, and Robert Manning became editor, the *Atlantic*'s circulation was steady, its content was consistent with the vision of the founders, and it was 1966, the dawn of a new politically aware day. Initially Manning, a former *Time** editor, was able to capitalize on increased political activism, but when interest declined during the late 1970s, so too did the fortunes of the *Atlantic*. Then Mortimer Zuckerman, a Boston real estate developer, purchased the Atlantic Monthly Company in 1980. His choice for editor was William Whitworth, formerly of the *New Yorker*, and he assisted Whitworth with generous funding, which in part enabled him to get the magazine back on track. Sedgwick notes that Whitworth's *Atlantic* contains "both incisive political journalism and good fiction."[28]

Thus, over the last 130 years the *Atlantic* has suffered significant losses in circulation, but has regained its footing through prudent modifications of editorial policy, and recently through the infusion of capital. It has never, however, relinquished its standards for quality fiction and nonfiction, and what was said about the first 30 years of the *Atlantic* is applicable after 130: the *Atlantic* contributions are at least equal to and generally better than those found in other literary and general-interest magazines. The commitment to incisive, intelligent essays remains strong. If the *Atlantic* has become known primarily as a general-

interest magazine rather than a literary magazine, it is to its credit. Never overly scholarly in its pursuit of literary and political issues, it was, and remains, an attractive and informative magazine whose name and long history assure the reader of intelligent fiction, poetry, and essays.

Notes

1. Horace Elisha Scudder, *James Russell Lowell: A Biography,* vol. 1 (Boston: Houghton Mifflin, 1901), p. 420.

2. *Atlantic Monthly,* November 1957, p. 37.

3. Mark A. D. Howe, *The Atlantic Monthly and Its Makers* (Boston: Atlantic Monthly Press, 1919), p. 26.

4. Ibid., p. 25.

5. Frank Luther Mott, "The Atlantic Monthly," in *A History of American Magazines,* vol. 2: 1850–1865 (Cambridge: Harvard University Press, 1938), p. 495.

6. Scudder, p. 421.

7. James Playsted Wood, *Magazines in the United States,* 2nd ed. (New York: Ronald Press, 1956), p. 66.

8. Ellery Sedgwick, *The Happy Profession* (Boston: Atlantic Monthly Press, 1946), p. 55.

9. Laurie Henry, ed., *Fiction Writer's Market* (Cincinnati: Writer's Digest Books, 1987), p. 292.

10. *Atlantic Monthly,* November 1957, p. 37.

11. *Atlantic Monthly,* February 1862, p. 1.

12. *Atlantic Monthly,* August 1923, pp. 145–46.

13. Anna Leonowens, *Atlantic Monthly,* April, May, and June 1879, pp. 396–410, 554–65, and 730–43. Anna Leonowens's memoirs were popularized first in Margaret Landon's *Anna and the King of Siam,* and later in the musical *The King and I.*

14. Theodore Roosevelt, *Atlantic Monthly,* September 1897, pp. 289–300.

15. H. L. Mencken, *Atlantic Monthly,* March 1914, pp. 289–97.

16. John Maynard Keynes, *Atlantic Monthly,* May 1932, pp. 521–26.

17. Bernard Baruch, *Atlantic Monthly,* March 1937, pp. 368–72.

18. Martin Luther King, Jr., *Atlantic Monthly,* August 1963, pp. 78–88.

19. William Greider, *Atlantic Monthly,* December 1981, pp. 27–54.

20. *Atlantic Monthly,* November 1957, p. 37.

21. Ellery Sedgwick III, "The Atlantic Monthly," in *American Literary Magazines: The Eighteenth and Nineteenth Centuries,* ed. Edward E. Chielens (New York: Greenwood Press, 1986), p. 52. Sedgwick's editorial history of the magazine is very informative.

22. *Atlantic Monthly,* September 1869, pp. 295–313.

23. Mott, p. 505. According to Theodore Peterson in *Magazines in the Twentieth Century* (Urbana: University of Illinois Press, 1964), circulation continued to decline, however, reaching a low of 7,000 by 1887 (p. 406).

24. Peterson, p. 406.

25. Sedgwick, "The Atlantic Monthly," p. 54.

26. Peterson, p. 407.

27. Ibid.

28. Sedgwick, "The Atlantic Monthly," p. 55.

Information Sources

BIBLIOGRAPHY

Austin, James C. *Fields of the Atlantic Monthly: Letters to an Editor, 1861–1870*. San
    Marino, Calif.: Huntington Library, 1953.
Howe, Mark A. D. *The Atlantic Monthly and Its Makers*. Boston: Atlantic Monthly Press,
    1919.
Mott, Frank Luther. *A History of American Magazines*. vol. 2: 1850–1865. Cambridge:
    Harvard University Press, 1938, pp. 493–515.
Perry, Bliss. *And Gladly Teach*. Boston: Houghton Mifflin, 1935, pp. 160–98.
———. *Park Street Papers*. Boston: Houghton Mifflin, 1908.
Scudder, Horace Elisha. *James Russell Lowell: A Biography*. 2 vols. Boston: Houghton
    Mifflin, 1901.
Sedgwick, Ellery III. "The Atlantic Monthly." *American Literary Magazines: The Eigh-
    teenth and Nineteenth Centuries*. Ed. Edward E. Chielens. New York: Greenwood
    Press, 1986, pp. 50–57.
Weeks, Edward. *Writers and Friends*. Boston: Atlantic Monthly Press, 1981.

INDEX SOURCES

    Semiannual. Cumulative Atlantic Indexes, vols. 1–38, 1877; vols. 39–62, 1889;
    vols. 63–88, 1903. Also: *Abstrax; America: History and Life; American Bibli-
    ography of Slavic and East European Studies; Annual Library Index; Engineering
    Index; Film Literature Index; Future Survey; Historical Abstracts; Index to Book
    Reviews in the Humanities; Magazine Index; Peace Research Abstracts Journal;
    Poole's; Poole's Abridged; PROMT; Reader's Guide; Review of Reviews.*

LOCATION SOURCES

    Widely available. Reprint sources: Bell and Howell, Microforms International
    Marketing, University Microfilms International.

Publication History

MAGAZINE TITLE AND TITLE CHANGES

    The Atlantic Monthly: A Magazine of Literature, Art and Politics, November
    1857–September 1865; *The Atlantic Monthly: A Magazine of Literature, Science,
    Art and Politics*, October 1865–June 1952; *The Atlantic*, July 1952–present.

VOLUME AND ISSUE DATA

    Semiannual volumes; November 1857–present. Monthly.

PUBLISHERS AND PLACE OF PUBLICATION

    Phillips, Sampson and Company, November 1857–October 1859; Ticknor and
    Fields, November 1859–June 1868; Fields, Osgood and Company, July 1868–
    1870; James Osgood and Company, 1871–1873; H. O. Houghton and Company,
    1874–1877; Houghton, Osgood and Company, 1878–1879; Houghton Mifflin and
    Company, 1880–July 1908; Atlantic Monthly, August 1908–present. Boston.

EDITORS

    James Russell Lowell, November 1857–June 1861; James T. Fields, July 1861–
    July 1871; William Dean Howells, August 1871–January 1881; Thomas Bailey
    Aldrich, February 1881–March 1890; Horace Elisha Scudder, April 1890–July

1898; Walter Hines Page, August 1898–July 1899; Bliss Perry, August 1899–July 1909; Ellery Sedgwick, August 1909–June 1938; Edward A. Weeks, Jr., July 1938–January 1966; Robert Manning, February 1966–December 1980; William Whitworth, April 1981–present.

CIRCULATION
457,000.

Jean M. Parker

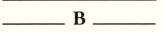

B

BON APPÉTIT

"Publishers have always been quick in sensing new interests within the public and then establishing new publications to cater to them."[1] Cleon T. (Bud) Knapp was quick in sensing America's food revolution of the 1970s. Bud Knapp, owner and chairman of Knapp Communications Corporation (publisher of *Architectural Digest**), purchased a small food and beverage magazine called *Bon Appétit* from the Pillsbury Company in the mid–1970s[2] and, with the aid of a new editor Paige Rense, transformed this liquor store giveaway into one of America's most successful gourmet food magazines.[3]

America's food revolution of the 1970s was due to many factors. A health and fitness craze was sweeping the country. The hippies of the 1960s were growing up and making money, yet they still wanted healthful and natural foods. Due to smaller families and two-income households, Americans had more money to spend.[4] The young urban professionals (yuppies) were discovering cooking as a way to spend their newly earned leisure dollars. Greater numbers of men, as well as the affluent, were discovering cooking for fun and entertainment. Other people were cooking as a way of rebelling against the country's fast-food restaurants. New products, such as food processors and microwave ovens, were saving people time and effort.[5] Even the recession of the 1970s helped popularize fine food and cooking: "Unable to make a down payment for a house, a couple happily pays $8 for a jar of gourmet mustard."[6]

Bon Appétit began in 1956 as a free promotional magazine edited by James A. Shanahan and published by American Colortype Company of Chicago, Illinois. After years as a liquor store giveaway, and under various editors and publishers,[7] *Bon Appétit* was acquired by the Pillsbury Company in 1970. Pillsbury published *Bon Appétit* bimonthly, and over the next five years increased the magazine's paid circulation to 250,000, with 50,000 newsstand sales and

200,000 distributed free by liquor stores making bulk purchases.[8] In 1975 Bud Knapp bought *Bon Appétit* for $80,000.[9] He moved the magazine to Los Angeles, and by the end of that year turned it into a monthly periodical. Within the next three years *Bon Appétit*'s paid circulation doubled twice.[10] By the mid–1980s circulation reached 1,300,834, with newsstand sales of 152,861 and subscriptions of 1,147,973.[11] The cover price increased to the present $2.50, and the annual subscription rate to $18.00.

Since a fine food magazine aimed at very wealthy gourmets already existed (*Gourmet*), Bud Knapp aimed *Bon Appétit* at a slightly more medium-income group.[12] Knapp stated, "Our editorial will be less esoteric than *Gourmet* and a little more creative than the tuna-fish-casserole type."[13] *Bon Appétit* was for readers "in the kitchen with their sleeves rolled up trying recipes in the latest issue . . . the magazine will spend many hours in the kitchen and emerge spattered and stained, evidence that it is being used."[14] This was a magazine "for the kitchen counter, not the coffee table."[15]

Therefore, *Bon Appétit* contained about 80–100 recipes per issue, with step-by-step instructions on preparing food, and choosing and serving wine and other beverages.[16] Every recipe was tasted and tasted by *Bon Appétit*'s staff, and every recipe was to contain ingredients found on the shelves of any supermarket.[17] Also, *Bon Appétit* featured entertainment and travel articles, book reviews,[18] and columns such as "Too Busy to Cook?" and "Cooking for Two."[19] Extremely attractive photographs colored the pages throughout each issue.

The readers of *Bon Appétit* often were called "upscale." A 1981 study showed the magazine's readers having a median income of $26,752, with 75.2 percent of them being female, 24.8 percent male, and a median age of 41.5.[20] A 1987 study listed *Bon Appétit*'s readers as having incomes of $46,000 + per year, with 70 percent of them employed, and throwing 61 million parties a year.[21]

In 1980 *Bon Appétit* began a three-year survey of its "upscale readers," and published its results in a study called "Tracking the Food Enthusiasts." Out of 3,000 subscribers polled, 2,376 replied. Of those responding, 86 percent said they cooked for fun; only 4 percent thought cooking was a chore. Eighty-four percent said they considered themselves creative cooks, and 95 percent considered cooking a form of self-expression.[22]

Advertisers were very eager to appeal to *Bon Appétit*'s upscale readers. They saw the food enthusiast as "a potential customer for a wide variety of products. . . . An interest in good food usually includes a desire to travel to a multitude of gourmet spots around the world. In addition, the food connoisseur often appreciates the best in everything—automobiles, liquor, jewelry, furniture and *objets d'art*."[23] Needless to say, *Bon Appétit* attracted advertisers of many kinds of upscale products. In 1981 *Bon Appétit* earned $17.25 million from 1,119 pages of advertising.[24] A 1987 study listed a four-color advertising page as costing $28,340.[25] The advertising revenues, and the circulation figures exceeding 1,300,000, make *Bon Appétit* an extremely successful magazine.

One of the persons mainly responsible for *Bon Appétit's* success under Knapp was its founding editor Paige Rense. To describe Paige Rense's talent, Bud Knapp said, "It's taste and it's guts and it's a matching of her vision with that of readers. . . . Paige has an ability to work with people in an extraordinarily successful way. I think all good editors have that same quality. It's a degree of integrity that she has that I've supported and tried to enhance. . . . I haven't seen anyone better at getting the best out of a creative group."[26]

Yet some people criticized *Bon Appétit's* editorial content: "The vast majority of *Bon Appétit* recipes have failed me. . . . I followed *BA's* instructions. . . . Why then, have most of my *Bon Appétit* cooking sprees ended in disaster?"[27] Paige Rense has said that her "aim is that anybody should be able to make these recipes."[28] Paige Rense also has said, "I think that food is love and I think we should make love, easy."[29] One critic disliked *Bon Appétit's* "lack of humor,"[30] and called the magazine "too bustling, too socially aggressive, too Yuppie to really have class."[31] However, that same critic admitted, "But when it comes to recipes, and for many readers it does come down to recipes, *Bon Appétit* seems to me the winner. . . . [Its recipes] seem more appealing than those in *Gourmet*; less exotic, a bit more conventional, perhaps, but more sumptuous, the ones you'd like to eat."[32]

Indeed, so many people liked to eat "*bon appétit*," that the magazine branched into several different directions. *Bon Appétit* cookbooks were published by Knapp Press, a book division of Knapp Communications Corporate.[33] *Bon Appétit* merchandise such as cookware, cutlery, paper goods, and dinnerware were developed by Wilshire Marketing Company, a marketing division of Knapp.[34] *Bon Appétit* food stores opened as a joint venture between Knapp and Safeway Stores Company, America's largest grocery chain.[35] *Bon Appétit* days were held in department stores such as J. W. Robinson Company, and featured the magazine's staff demonstrating equipment and craftsmanship.[36] By the mid–1980s *Bon Appétit* indeed had grown into the largest and most successful epicurean magazine of its time.

Notes

1. Benjamin M. Compaine, "The Magazine Industry: Developing the Special Interest Audience," *Journal of Communications*, Spring 1980, p. 101.

2. Philip H. Daugherty, "Architecture and Bon Appétit," *New York Times*, 4 April 1975, p. 51.

3. Robert V. Hudson. *Mass Media: A Chronological Encyclopedia of Television, Radio, Motion Pictures, Magazines, Newspapers, and Books in the United States* (New York: Garland Publishing, 1987), p. 278.

4. Jaye Scholl, "Hot Cuisine: Americans Develop a Taste for Gourmet Foods," *Barron's*, 27 September 1982, p. 34.

5. Dan Zenka, "Cashing in on Creative Cookery," *Marketing Communications*, May 1983, p. 34.

6. Scholl, "Hot Cuisine," p. 34.

7. Mark McHugh, Library Aide, Minneapolis Public Library, in telephone conversations 3–4, November, 1988.

8. Daugherty, "Architecture," p. 51.

9. N. R. Kleinfield, "Knapp Publishes the Good Life," *New York Times*, 9 February, 1979, p. D16.

10. Rosalie Bruno, "Knapp Communications: A Publishing Success Story," *Direct Marketing*, May 1983, p. 24.

11. *The National Directory of Magazines* (New York: Oxbridge Communications, 1988), p. 291.

12. Kleinfield, "Knapp Publishes," p. D16.

13. Daugherty, "Architecture," p. 51.

14. Charlene Canape, "Five Upscale Magazines Battle for the Epicurean Market," *Advertising Age*, 12 September, 1983, p. M4.

15. Mark Bittman, "Publishers Have Taste for More Than Food," *Advertising Age*, 3 October 1985, p. 54.

16. *National Directory*, p. 291.

17. Kleinfield, "Knapp Publishes," p. D16.

18. *National Directory*, p. 291.

19. Judith Sims, "Cooking by the Book . . . er, Magazine," *Los Angeles*, 1 December 1980, p. 376.

20. Renee Blakkan, "Pinch of Snob Appeal Leads to Healthy Circulation," *Advertising Age*, 25 October 1982, p. M58.

21. "Magazine Scene: Bon Appétit," *HFD–Retailing Home Furnishings*, 1 June 1987, p. 12.

22. Canape, "Five Upscale Magazines," p. M38.

23. Ibid., p. M4.

24. Blakkan, "Pinch of Snob Appeal," p. M58.

25. "Magazine Scene," p. 12.

26. Joanna Powell, "Paige Rense: Editor-in-Chief of *Architectural Digest, Bon Appétit*, and *GEO*," *Washington Journalism Review*, 5 May 1983, p. 41.

27. Sims, "Cooking by the Book," p. 376.

28. Kleinfield, "Knapp Publishes," p. D16.

29. N. R. Kleinfield, "A Growing Appetite for Food Magazines," *New York Times*, 1 July 1980, p. B10.

30. Gail Pool, "Magazines," *Wilson Library Bulletin*, December 1984, p. 282.

31. Ibid., p. 283.

32. Ibid.

33. Kleinfield, "Knapp Publishes," p. D16.

34. Steven Beitler, "Bon Jour, Bon Appétit," *Advertising Age*, 15 March 1982, p. M44.

35. "Safeway Says, Bon Appétit!," *Sales and Marketing Management*, 15 March 1982, p. 15.

36. Beitler, "Bon Jour," p. M44.

Information Sources

BIBLIOGRAPHY

Beitler, Steven. "Bon Jour, Bon Appétit." *Advertising Age,* 15 March 1982, p. M44.
Bittman, Mark. "Publishers Have Taste for More Than Food." *Advertising Age*, 3 October 1985, pp. 54–55.

Blakkan, Renee. "Pinch of Snob Appeal Leads to Healthy Circulation." *Advertising Age*, 25 October 1982, pp. M58–M59.

Bruno, Rosalie. "Knapp Communications: A Publishing Success Story." *Direct Marketing*, May 1983, pp. 24, 26.

Canape, Charlene. "Five Upscale Magazines Battle for the Epicurean Market." *Advertising Age*, 12 September 1983, pp. M4–M5, M38.

Compaine, Benjamin M. "The Magazine Industry: Developing the Special Interest Audience." *Journal of Communication*, Spring 1980, pp. 98–103.

Daugherty, Philip H. "Architecture and Bon Appétit." *New York Times*, 4 April 1975, p. 51.

———. "Food Magazine Establishes Survey." *New York Times*, 11 March 1980, p. D17.

Hudson, Robert V. *Mass Media: A Chronological Encyclopedia of Television, Radio, Motion Pictures, Magazines, Newspapers, and Books in the United States*. New York: Garland Publishing, 1987.

Kleinfield, N. R. "A Growing Appetite for Food Magazines." *New York Times*, 1 July 1980, p. B10.

———. "Knapp Publishes the Good Life." *New York Times*, 9 February 1979, pp. D1, D16.

"Magazine Scene: Bon Appétit." *HFD–Retailing Home Furnishings*, 1 June 1987, p. 12.

Pool, Gail. "Magazines." *Wilson Library Bulletin*, December 1984, pp. 282–83.

Powell, Joanna. "Paige Rense: Editor-in-Chief of *Architectural Digest*, *Bon Appétit* and *GEO*." *Washington Journalism Review*, 5 May 1983, pp. 36–41.

"Safeway Says, Bon Appétit!" *Sales and Marketing Management*, 15 March 1982, pp. 15, 17.

"Safeway Stores Forms Joint Venture." *Wall Street Journal*, 19 January 1982, p. 45.

Scholl, Jaye. "Hot Cuisine: Americans Develop a Taste for Gourmet Foods." *Barron's*, 27 September 1982, pp. 34–37.

Sims, Judith. "Cooking by the Book . . . er, Magazine." *Los Angeles*, 1 December 1980, p. 376.

Zenka, Dan. "Cashing In On Creative Cooking." *Marketing Communications*, May 1983, pp. 33–36.

INDEX SOURCES
    Popular Magazine Review; Consumers Index to Evaluations and Information Sources; Recipe Periodical Index; Access: The Supplementary Index to Periodicals.

LOCATION SOURCES
    Library of Congress, New York Public Library, and many other libraries.

Publication History

TITLE AND TITLE CHANGES
    Bon Appétit: A Magazine of Good Taste, 1956–1976; *Bon Appétit*, 1976–1980; *Bon Appétit: America's Food and Entertaining Magazine*, 1980–present.

VOLUME AND ISSUE DATA
    Vols. 1–20, no. 4, November/December 1956–September 1975, bimonthly; Vol. 20, no. 5–33, November 1975–present, monthly.

PUBLISHERS AND PLACES OF PUBLICATION
American Colortype Company, Chicago, Illinois: James A. Shanahan, 1956–1959. Home Publications, Inc., San Francisco, California: James A. Shanahan, 1959–1961; Duncan Scott, 1961–1962. Beverage News, Inc., Wichita, Kansas: Betty Paige, 1962–1964. Billett Publishing Company, Wichita, Kansas: W. C. Carreras, 1964. Financial Publications, Kansas City, Missouri: Henry Bodendiek, 1964–1965; M. Frank Jones, 1965–1970. Bon Appétit Division of Pillsbury Company, Kansas City, Missouri: M. Frank Jones, 1970–1975. Bon Appétit Publishing Corporation (Subsidiary of Knapp Communications Corporation), Los Angeles, California: Cleon T. Knapp, 1975–1978; John L. Decker, 1978–1981; Ernest M. Walker, 1981–1982; Leda Sanford Gordon, 1982–1983; Robert B. Phelps, 1983–1988, George B. Dippy, 1988–present.

EDITORS
James A. Shanahan, 1956–1961; Alan Shearer, 1961–1962; Charles Walters, 1962–1963; Betty Paige, 1963–1964; W. C. Carreras, 1964; Floyd Sageser, 1964–1965; M. Frank Jones, 1965–1976; Paige Rense, 1976–1983; Marilou Vaughan, 1983–1985; William J. Garry, 1985–present.

CIRCULATION
1,300,834.

Irene Hansen

C

THE CASKET. See GRAHAM'S MAGAZINE

CENTURY. See SCRIBNER'S

CHANGING TIMES: THE KIPLINGER MAGAZINE

Changing Times, one of the first post–World War II monthly magazines, is published by Kiplinger Washington Editors. It was not designed to replace newspapers or news magazines, but rather it was to be devoted to providing small businesses and their families with information on the practical economics of personal finance and planning for the futures.[1] Today, the median age of the readership is about forty-five. However, above one-third are in their thirties or younger and the age of management's targeted audience is now twenty-eight to forty-four.[2]

The magazine was first titled *The Kiplinger Magazine: Changing Times* by the founder, Willard M. Kiplinger, who had successfully pioneered the business-forecasting newsletter, *The Kiplinger Washington Letter* (1923). The change of name to the present title occurred May 1949 by switching the word order to *Changing Times: The Kiplinger Magazine*. The magazine became available at the newsstands with the same issue.

The articles were mainly brief nontechnical reports on economic topics of interest to the small businessman and his family. Kiplinger's aim was to present the "changing times with an emphasis on the times ahead."[3] Kiplinger wanted his readers to have a better understanding of current business planning; he would help them to "look, think, and plan ahead."[4]

The timing for the magazine was nearly perfect. The impact of the baby boom during the late 1940s and 1950s, economic adjustments following World War II, the Korean War, and the politically and economically turbulent sixties and seventies have all contributed to the continued need for a consumer finance magazine.

In June 1946 Kiplinger announced to the *Newsletter* subscribers his plan for a consumer-type magazine to be sold by subscription only. Kiplinger was so well respected as a business forecaster-economist that his announcement resulted in 30,000 charter subscriptions for the forty-eight page magazine, which was printed on paper stock. The magazine was made up of down-to-earth articles about labor relations, small business concerns, and major companies. Initially, no advertising was accepted because Kiplinger wished to be free of any possible influence of advertisers.

The first managing editor was Charles M. Stevenson, who was followed shortly by John Denson. Early on, Austin Kiplinger, the founder's son, became the executive editor, and he continues today as the editorial chairman, while Knight A. Kiplinger, the founder's grandson, is the editor-in-chief.[5] Other editors of long service were Herb Brown, Margaret White, and Theodore Miller.

With an emphasis on financial planning, Kiplinger designed a readable consumer's magazine containing articles that discussed in depth topics related to business and family financial health. Recently articles on health and fitness have begun appearing. The articles are usually researched and written by the magazine staff, with as few as 10 percent of the thoroughly documented articles coming from free-lance writers. Until the 1980s there were few signed articles because the editors usually collaborated on the articles as a team.[6] However, regular feature columns that remain today are "The Months Ahead" and "Letters" or "Readers Talk Back."

The magazine articles emphasize future need, since Kiplinger believed that a technical, easy-to-read economic service for the small businessman would help his use of the tools of freedom—opportunity and information—in a practical manner in order to plan for the future needs of his business and family.[7] During the 1950s the editors often chose articles that extolled the virtues of education and pushed for public education because they felt that education was the backbone of a free society and that education was a useful tool for day-to-day living.[8]

For thirty-three years the publisher resisted accepting advertising and had editorially asserted that they were "a no-strings attached operation" free of any pressure from advertisers. Then the policy changed. It was the increasing costs of paper, printing, and postage that forced the change in 1980. The magazine decided that it either had to increase the subscription rates or accept advertising. After surveying a cross section of subscribers, the editors announced they would begin accepting advertising with the March 1980 issue. This issue carried 38.6 pages of advertising that provided revenue of $485,000. Later in 1983 the magazine had a total of 511 pages of advertising that provided $11.6 million in revenues.[9] With the addition of advertising they also changed from paper stock to slick paper, and added more color photographs in place of line drawings. They believed that they would have more editorial space in which to continue their objective reporting. Early advertisers came from the automobile and tobacco industries, publishing, investment houses, and insurance companies. Today, in addition to the advertisers listed above, the advertisers include high-tech and health and fitness ads.

Long-time editor Herb Brown summed up the objectives of the magazine by stating that Americans may not like economics but "we eat, breathe, and dream by economics."[10] That philosophy and a responsive readership have kept *Changing Times* at the forefront in providing important consumer information and financial advice to its readership.

Notes

1. Knight A. Kiplinger, "The Shape of Things to Come, Special Report: 1987 & Beyond," *Changing Times,* January 1987, p. 28.

2. Beth Bogart, "Kiplinger Changes with the Times," *Advertising Age,* 18 October 1984, p. 26.

3. Willard M. Kiplinger, "Tell Your Friends This . . . ," *Changing Times*, April 1948, back cover.

4. Ibid.

5. "Kiplinger's Business Baby," *Newsweek*, 6 January 1947, p. 50.

6. Editors, "What—No By-lines?" *Changing Times*, July 1950, p. 2.

7. Herb Brown, "Chat with the Editor," *Changing Times*, August 1956, [p. 1.]

8. Editorial, *Changing Times*, September 1958, p. 1.

9. Charlene Canape, "Persistence Pays Dividends," *Advertising Age*, 6 February 1984, p. M4.

10. Brown, p. 1.

Information Sources

BIBLIOGRAPHY

Bogart, Beth. "Kiplinger Changes with the Times." *Advertising Age,* 18 October 1984, p. 26.

Brown, Herb. "Chat with the Editor." *Changing Times*, August 1956, p. 1.

Canape, Charlene. "Persistence Pays Dividends." *Advertising Age,* 6 February 1984, p. M4.

"Changing Times Happy with Ad Move." *Advertising Age*, 14 June 1987, p. 37.

Editorial. *Changing Times*, September 1958, [p. 1.].

Editors. "What—No By-lines?" *Changing Times*, July 1950, p. 2.

"Kiplinger's Business Baby." *Newsweek*, 6 January 1947, p. 50.

Kiplinger, Knight A. "The Shape of Things to Come, Special Report: 1987 & Beyond." *Changing Times*, January 1987, pp. 28–48.

Kiplinger, Willard M. "Tell Your Friends This . . . " *Changing Times*, April 1948, back cover.

INDEX SOURCES
  Readers' Guide to Periodical Literature (1953–present);
  Magazine Index Plus; Business Periodical Index; Periodical Abstracts.
LOCATION SOURCES
  Milner Library, Illinois State University, many other libraries. Available in microform.

Publication History

MAGAZINE TITLE AND TITLE CHANGES
  The Kiplinger Magazine: Changing Times, 1947–April 1949; *Changing Times: The Kiplinger Magazine,* 1949–present.
VOLUME AND ISSUE DATA
  Vols. 1– , 1947–present.
PUBLISHER AND PLACE OF PUBLICATION
  Kiplinger Washington Editors, 1729 H Street N.W., Washington, D.C.
EDITORS
  Willard M. Kiplinger, 1947–1967; Austin A. Kiplinger, 1968–1985; Knight A. Kiplinger, 1985–present.
CIRCULATION PAID
  1,377,567. Newsstands, 37,143.

Katherine Shaw

CHAUTAUQUAN

The *Chautauquan* grew out of the Chautauqua movement, a combination of popular education combined with entertainment from concerts, dramatic performances, and lectures that flourished in the late nineteenth and early twentieth centuries. The first institution of this kind was located in Chautauqua, New York, which lent its name to the movement and, later, the magazine itself. Those attending the fall assemblies at Chautauqua often wrote back to ask what books they should read during the winter. Systematic answers to these questions were soon provided by a four-year home study program, the Chautauqua Literary and Scientific Circle.[1] Reconvening annually for the assembly, Chautauqua students read the *Chautauqua Assembly Daily Herald,* which was published for the three weeks of August when the assembly was held. This newspaper, published by the Reverend Theodore L. Flood, contained the texts of addresses given by notable speakers who appeared at the assembly. After four years of offering this newspaper, first as a daily, then as a monthly with a daily edition, Flood decided to tie his publication to the reading courses of the Chautauqua Literary and Scientific Circle, had his plan approved by the Chautauqua management, and in the fall of 1880, published the first number of his new monthly, the *Chautauquan.*[2]

Since colleges and universities of the time emphasized Greek and Latin classics and closed their doors to the less scholarly, women and businessmen found a substitute education in the Chautauqua-style home study courses; the literary and scientific circles soon claimed an "alumni group" of 80,000.[3] From an initial printing of 15,000 in 1880, the *Chautauquan* reached a circulation of 50,000 just five years later.[4] The first *Chautauquan* opened with "Required Reading: History of the World," a history beginning with the creation of man on the sixth day. Readings in other courses—among them science, theology, and literature—as well as lectures delivered at Chautauqua, a section about current events, and Sunday school aids supplemented the required reading. The sensibility of Flood, a former Methodist minister, is seldom disguised in the early numbers: apologies for Homer's polytheism, support for Prohibition, and other writings of clergymen and reformers are prominent. By the late 1880s, Flood's link with the successful self-culture organization was attracting contributions to the *Chautauquan* by leading intellectuals of the time—articles by J. P. Mahaffy, H. H. Boyesen, H. B. Adams, and John Burroughs were accompanied by serial courses by E. E. Hale, Arthur Gilman, and W. T. Harris.

While the *Chautauquan*'s connection with adult education programs brought a large readership and distinguished contributors, the resulting emphasis on required readings, courses, study aids, and annotations of texts threatened to condemn the magazine to a dreary pace and dry tone. Flood tried to combat this threat by giving increasing variety to the contents, using less space for the required readings, and including general articles about historical and current topics, news from local reading circles, questions from readers, and articles by figures like Theodore Roosevelt, Woodrow Wilson, Artemus Ward, George Rawlinson, and James B. McMaster. Flood also enlisted the editorial assistance of Ida Tarbell, who provided answers to readers who needed to know how to pronounce a word or translate a foreign phrase.[5] The use of a size and format similar to that of the *Harper's** and *Century** of the time, and of ads for patent medicines and corsets, are reminders that the *Chautauquan*, under Flood, was run for profit.

Flood's efforts to establish the *Chautauquan* as a well-rounded, comprehensive magazine with a liberal outlook were punctuated by his change of the subtitle to *A Monthly Magazine* in 1889. This change was accompanied by enlarged pages (and price—a subscription rose from $1.50 to $2.00 per year[6]), more articles about literary criticism, politics, travel, science, art, biography, and history. Fiction appeared occasionally. A department of Current History and Opinion gave excerpts from the editorials of leading newspapers, and the Woman's Council Table included pieces about women's activities, often written by famous women. Despite these changes, the *Chautauquan* remained the official organ of the Literary and Scientific Circle, and required readings were still directed at readers who were dead earnest in their desire for education. These readings varied considerably in content and tone: "Masterpieces of French Painting," "Social Life in Ancient Greece," "The Geographical Position of France," "A Century of French Costume," and "Insect Communities" were some of the required readings. While an occasional article showed style or grace, most of the writing remained somber and didactic; questions from the syllabus of readings asked readers to describe and give reasons for the English climate or to describe the composition of the German government.

By the turn of the century, decreasing circulation led Flood to relinquish both ownership and editorship of the *Chautauquan*. The Chautauqua Association became the owner, and the Chautauqua Press became the publisher. The new editor was Frank Chapin Bray, a career journalist with long-time connections with Chautauqua-style education. Bray was not committed to producing a general magazine, and the *Chautauquan* under his editorship more completely reflected its function as an organ of the Chautauqua assemblies. He added more illustrations (in 1903, he changed the subtitle to indicate this), more travel articles, especially about the East, and more material about social and civic reform. In 1906, Bray changed the size of the magazine to duodecimo[7] and limited the contents to local announcements and news. As the national enrollment in the Literary and Scientific Circles declined, the magazine was changed to "a weekly newsmagazine" (in 1913), and absorbed by the *Independent* in 1914.

Certainly the foremost of the organs of the organized adult education programs so important at the time, the *Chautauquan* fulfilled its unique function well— at times with surprising style and variety. Old *Chautauquans* are now likely to be found in attics,[8] reminders of an effort to carry the Chautauqua inspiration and culture to every fireside.

Notes

1. Victoria Case and Robert Ormond Case, *We Called It Culture* (New York: Doubleday, 1948), p. 15.

2. Frank Luther Mott, *A History of American Magazines*. Vol. 3: *1865–1885* (Cambridge: Harvard University Press, 1938), p. 545.

3. Case and Case, p. 16.

4. Theodore Morrison, *Chautauqua* (Chicago: University of Chicago Press, 1974), p. 62.

5. Ibid., p. 63.

6. Mott, p. 545.

7. Ibid., p. 547.

8. Case and Case, p. 15.

Information Sources

BIBLIOGRAPHY

Case, Victoria, and Robert Ormond Case. *We Called It Culture*. New York: Doubleday, 1948.

Hurlbert, Jesse L. *The Story of Chautauqua*. New York: Putnam's, 1921.

Morrison, Theodore. *Chautauqua*. Chicago: University of Chicago Press, 1974.

Mott, Frank Luther. *A History of American Magazines*. Vol. 3: 1865–1885. Cambridge: Harvard University Press, 1938.

INDEX SOURCES
   Poole's; Poole's Abridged; Readers' Guide; Annual Library Index; Review of Reviews Index; Engineering Index; Dramatic Index.
LOCATION SOURCES
   Library of Congress, Grand Rapids Public Library (Michigan).

Publication History

MAGAZINE TITLE AND TITLE CHANGES
   The Chautauquan. Subtitles: (1) *A Monthly Magazine Devoted to the Promotion of True Culture, Organ of the Chautauquan Literary and Scientific Circle,* 1880–1889; (2) *A Monthly Magazine,* 1889–1899; (3) *A Monthly Magazine for Self-Education,* 1900–1902; (4) *Issued Monthly with Illustrations,* 1903–1913; (5) *A Weekly Newsmagazine,* 1913–1914.
VOLUME AND ISSUE DATA
   Vols. 1–72, 1880–1914. A preliminary number appeared in September 1880. The first number was October 1880; the last issue was 23 May 1914. Monthly except August and September, 1880–1889; monthly, 1890–May 1913; weekly, June 1913–23 May 1914.
PUBLISHERS AND PLACE OF PUBLICATION
   Theodore L. Flood, Meadville, Pennsylvania, 1880–1899; Chautauqua Press, 1899–1914. At Cleveland, 1899–1902; Springfield, Ohio, 1902–1904; Chautauqua, New York, 1904–1914.
EDITORS
   Theodore L. Flood, 1880–1899; Frank Chapin Bray, 1899–1914.
CIRCULATION
   50,000 (1885).

Glenn Anderson

CHILDREN: THE MAGAZINE FOR PARENTS. See PARENTS

COLLIER'S

Collier's was founded as *Collier's Once a Week* by a successful Irish immigrant, Peter Fenlon Collier, on 28 April 1888, as a premium for books he sold on the installment plan.[1] Collier was successful in accomplishing his early mission of providing "fiction, fact, sensation, wit, humor and news," which the new magazine so boldly proclaimed on its cover. The magazine became known as *Collier's Weekly: An Illustrated Journal* in 1895, and three years later Collier's son Robert became its publisher. Adopting the subtitle *The National Weekly,* he was largely responsible for furthering *Collier's* popularity. To compete with other mass magazines at the time, he hired well-known writers and artists to establish the reputation of *Collier's.* Rudyard Kipling, Robert Chambers, and Frank Norris wrote for him. James Whitcomb Riley's poetry helped to further

Collier's literary reputation, and Henry James's *The Turn of the Screw* appeared as one of the first serials he published. Even though Robert was quite an innovator, he borrowed heavily to further his enterprise.[2] His leadership in the early 1900s brought *Collier's* to the forefront of magazine color illustration.[3] Frederick Remington produced his famous Southwestern scenes. Maxfield Parrish contributed his colorful fantasies including an *Arabian Nights* series, and Charles Dana Gibson delighted readers with his Gibson girls.

Under Norman Hapgood's ten-year editorship beginning in 1902, *Collier's* "achieved a certain editorial distinction."[4] His editorials, or essays as some preferred to call them, became known as influencers of public opinion.[5] It was during Hapgood's regime that *Collier's* came to be known as one of the most influential magazines in the country. Following the successful Hapgood years, *Collier's* fell on bad times when changes of editors, the 1920s depression, and a loss of advertisers combined to take their toll on this venerable magazine.[6]

Collier's was rejuvenated in 1925 when William Ludlow Chenery became the editor and provided the transfusion that spurred *Collier's* on to a solid period of growth and editorial leadership. Chenery served as editor until 1943 and provided *Collier's* with one of its finest eras. It was under Chenery's leadership that brevity became a distinctive characteristic of *Collier's* publishing.[7] Chenery was interested in exposing the public to new ideas and facts and was successful by providing a variety of quality reading matter. In a speech at the University of Virginia in 1936, Chenery observed that "the national magazine of mass circulation can treat only those national problems about which millions of people are willing to read. . . . If it does not interest its readers it cannot endure."[8]

After World War II American attitudes and tastes changed, and *Collier's*, finding it difficult to keep pace with the times, took another nosedive. Editor Louis Ruppel attempted to bring new life to the magazine through sensationalism. A famous example occurred when *Collier's* accomplished a journalistic coup by devoting its whole 27 October 1951 issue to a fictional account of World War III entitled "Preview of the War We Do Not Want." The detailed description of an imagined third world war was the work of many famous contributors, among them Edward R. Murrow, Lowell Thomas, and Robert E. Sherwood.[9] Circulation was given a temporary boost by this bit of sensational journalism, but it created adverse criticism around the world.[10] Ruppel's further attempt to give *Collier's* new life with an "exposé a week" was not entirely successful, and *Collier's* never fully recovered.[11]

Covering a period of sixty-eight years—from the late 1800s to the mid–twentieth century—*Collier's* spanned an era of change and development. The evolution of a "typical" issue reflected cultural and technological changes, tastes, and literary expectations.

In the early years as *Collier's: An Illustrated Journal*, the publication included fiction and humor with an emphasis on news and illustration. As *Collier's* grew, there was a decided improvement in all aspects of its makeup. *Collier's* soon became known for its color illustration and memorable writing, and even poetry was included in its pages. James H. Hare, a great pioneer news photographer, contributed to *Collier's* success in this early period. Stories by Conan Doyle, O. Henry, and Frank Norris and poetry by Frank R. Stanton added prestige to a typical issue.

A pattern that developed under editor William Chenery in the mid-twenties and continued into the thirties gave *Collier's* a certain sameness about it. One could expect to find an article about sports, an entertainment personality, politics, or economics; a topic of interest to women; two or three short short stories; two serials—usually a love story and a mystery; a general column; an editorial; and a few cartoons.[12]

The magazine took on a new appearance in the late thirties. Color illustrations appeared more frequently and the covers, illustrated by Ben Jorj Harris, Robert O. Reid, and others, reflected a new style.[13] The weekly lead article became the main feature of each issue, and more often than not it was this topic that was featured on the cover. In the mid and late forties, *Collier's* contained less fiction and emphasized feature articles about war. Each issue now had only one serial and only a few short stories. In the early to mid-forties sports continued to be an important feature, and Francis Wallace's football previews were a popular staple.

Crowell-Collier's profits declined in the late forties, and their problems continued into the early part of the 1950s when advertising revenue was insufficient.[14] In a bid for wider circulation *Collier's* became more sensational under editors Louis Ruppel and Roger Dakin.[15] However, the rising popularity of television too had a large measure of effect on the magazine's future as did competition from the extremely popular *Saturday Evening Post*.* Facing this dilemma, the management decided to change *Collier's*, after sixty-five years as a weekly, to a biweekly with the 7 August 1953 issue. With no price increase, *Collier's* was expanded to almost twice its previous size. In its first editorial as a biweekly, *Collier's* reiterated its philosophy, that *"Collier's* is a popular magazine, first and last, and it means to remain one."[16] With a renewed emphasis on fiction, the expanded magazine now included seven articles, two special features, five short stories, one serial, and a host of popular cartoons. A substantial number of pages of advertising often consisted of full-page ads including categories of automobiles, liquor, wine, beer, tobacco, toiletries, food, and public utilities. Along with contributions by Fulton Oursler and Pearl Buck, there were many color illustrations and the standard features such as Collier's Credits and Walter Davenport's "48 States of Mind." Having established a solid pattern as a biweekly, *Collier's*, with its format and editorial policy firmly in place, remained basically the same throughout its existence.

The audience that *Collier's* appealed to was the middle-class American—the broad cross section of men and women who came from widely different economic and educational backgrounds. It was this average American who wanted "stories," not "literature."[17] William Chenery's philosophy was that "successful magazine fiction is, of course, not necessarily identical with great literature."[18]

In its maturity, the flamboyant tone of *Collier's* appealed to the man in the street. The editors of *Collier's* liked action and adventure, and their prime concern was entertainment.[19] During *Collier's* lifetime, fiction was contributed by almost every writer of consequence. Typical names include Henry James, H. G. Wells, Bret Harte, Jack London, John Steinbeck, and Kathleen Norris to name a few.

Though *Collier's* relied to a great extent on fiction, its nonfiction coverage was plentiful indeed. Nonfiction articles covered a broad range of interest and included politics, foreign and national affairs, sports, theater, movies, profiles of personalities, and any type of human interest story. *Collier's* neither neglected important social and economic issues nor gave comments on public affairs short shrift. In the early 1900s *Collier's* battled the Beef Trust, the Oil Trust, William Randolph Hearst, liquor, child labor, and food labeling. The latter resulted in the adoption of the first food and drug laws.[20]

Collier's was known for its brevity. Articles were generally between 2,500 and 3,500 words with rare exceptions. Even such dignitaries as Winston Churchill and Franklin Delano Roosevelt were known to bow to *Collier's* policy on conciseness. *Collier's* was also a pioneer in the development of the short short story.[21] This journalistic art form was usually 750–1,200 words in length and generally was limited to one page with an illustration. The short short story was a prominent feature for the entire run of the magazine.

For the better part of its lifetime, *Collier's* had been a popular and successful magazine. It flourished and gained a deserved reputation early on as a serious magazine of fiction and opinion and contributed greatly to the history of American journalism. In spite of editor Kenneth McArdle's futile attempt to rebuild the magazine in the mid-fifties by giving it a new and modern look, *Collier's* gave up the fight to stay in the magazine business and published its last issue on 4 January 1957. The good intentions of a dedicated staff could not overbalance the heavy financial losses.

Collier's circulation rose from 2.7 million in 1939[22] to an estimated 3.8 million in 1953[23] and finally to 4,165,000 at the end of 1956.[24] However, advertisers lost confidence in a magazine they considered to be not contemporary enough and paid for only 1,008 ad pages in 1956 as compared to 1,718 in 1951.[25] Skyrocketing costs and formidable competition with other popular magazines simply took their toll.

Notes

1. Frank Luther Mott, *A History of American Magazines Vol. 4: 1885–1905* (Cambridge: Harvard University Press, 1957), p. 453.

2. Ibid., p. 456.

3. Ibid.

4. Theodore Peterson, *Magazines in the Twentieth Century*, 2nd ed. (Urbana: University of Illinois Press, 1964), p. 134.

5. Hickman Powell, "Collier's," *Scribner's Magazine*, May 1939, p. 20.

6. Ibid.

7. John E. Drewry, *Contemporary American Magazines*, 2nd ed. (Athens: University of Georgia Press, 1939), p. 17.

8. William Ludlow Chenery, "The Magazine and Public Opinion," *Vital Speeches of the Day*, 15 August 1936, p. 720.

9. For a discussion of this issue, see D. F. Fleming, "Collier's Wins World War III," *Nation*, 10 November 1951, pp. 392–95, and "Postscript to Collier's World War III," *Nation*, 1 December 1951, pp. 498–99.

10. James Playsted Wood, *Magazines in the United States*, 3rd ed. (New York: Ronald Press, 1971), p. 412.

11. Peterson, p. 138.

12. A typical issue under Chenery is very well described in Powell. p. 21.

13. Mott, pp. 474–75.

14. "Change at Collier's," *Newsweek*, 18 May 1953, p. 98.

15. Mott, pp. 478–79.

16. "A Restatement of What Collier's Stands For," *Collier's*, 7 August 1953, p. 110.

17. Powell, p. 19.

18. William Ludlow Chenery, *So It Seemed* (New York: Harcourt Brace and Company, 1952), p. 197.

19. Denver Lindley and Allen Marple, "What Is a Collier's Story?," *Writer*, July 1943, p. 208.

20. Mott, p. 460.

21. Ibid., p. 472.

22. Powell, p. 19.

23. A. J. Van Zuilen, *The Life Cycle of Magazines* (Uithoorn, The Netherlands: Graduate Press, 1977), p. 199.

24. "Crowell-Collier's Christmas," *Time*, 24 December 1956, p. 44.

25. Ibid.

Information Sources

BIBLIOGRAPHY

Burger, Knox. "Collier's Best." *Writer,* July 1951, pp. 217–18.

"Change at Collier's." *Newsweek*, 18 May 1953, pp. 98–99.

Chenery, William Ludlow. "The Magazine and Public Opinion." *Vital Speeches of the Day*, 15 August 1936, pp. 717–20.

———. *So It Seemed*. New York: Harcourt Brace and Company, 1952.

"Crowell-Collier's Christmas." *Time*, 24 December 1956, pp. 44–45.

Drewry, John E. *Contemporary American Magazines*. 2nd ed. Athens: University of Georgia Press, 1939.

Fleming, D. F. "Collier's Wins World War III." *Nation*, 10 November 1951, pp. 392–95.

Lindley, Denver, and Allen Marple. "What Is a Collier's Story?" *Writer*, July 1943, pp. 208–9.

Mott, Frank Luther. *A History of American Magazines 1885–1905 Vol. 4.: 1885–1905* Cambridge: Harvard University Press, 1957.

Peterson, Theodore B. *Magazines in the Twentieth Century*. 2nd ed. Urbana: University of Illinois Press, 1964.

"Postscript to Collier's World War III." *Nation*, 1 December 1951, pp. 498–99.

Powell, Hickman. "Collier's." *Scribner's Magazines*, May 1939, pp. 19–23.

"A Restatement of What Collier's Stands For." *Collier's*, 7 August 1983, p. 110.

Wood, James Playsted. *Magazines in the United States*. 3rd ed. New York: Ronald Press, 1971.

van Zuilen, A. J. *The Life Cycle of Magazines*. Uithoorn, The Netherlands: Graduate Press, 1977.

INDEX SOURCES

> *Readers' Guide to Periodical Literature*, 1909–January 1957; *Cumulated Dramatic Index*, 1909–1949; *Bulletin of Bibliography Dramatic Index*, 1912–1953.

LOCATION SOURCES

> Library of Congress, Chicago Public Library, Indiana University Library, New York State Library, various other libraries. Available in microform (1891–1915).

Publication History

MAGAZINE TITLE AND TITLE CHANGES

> *Collier's Once a Week*, 1888–1889; *Once a Week, An Illustrated Weekly Newspaper*, 1889–1895; *Collier's Weekly, An Illustrated Journal*, 1895–1904; *Collier's, The National Weekly*, 1905–1957. (The title on the cover, title page, and page captions after 1949 was *Collier's*.)

VOLUME AND ISSUE DATA

> First issue: 28 April 1888. Last issue: 4 January 1957. Weekly, 1888–1953; biweekly, 7 August 1953–1957. Vols. 1–61, semiannual volumes ending in September and March, 1888–1918; vol. 62, 14 September–21 December 1918; vol. 63, January-June 1919; vol. 64, July-December 1919 (including only 21 numbers); vols. 65–140, no. 1, regular semiannual volumes, 1920–4 January 1957.

PUBLISHER AND PLACE OF PUBLICATION

> P. F. Collier, New York, 1888–1900; P. F. Collier and Son, New York, 1900–1934; Crowell Publishing Company, New York, 1934–1939; Crowell-Collier Publishing Company, New York, 1939–1957.

EDITORS

> Nugent Robinson, 1888–1890; Mayo Williamson Hazeltine, 1891; Julius Chambers, 1892–1893; T. B. Connery, 1893–1896; Daniel Lyons, 1896–1898; Robert Joseph Collier, 1898–1902, 1912–1913; Norman Hapgood, 1902–1912; Mark Sullivan, 1914–1917; Finley Peter Dunne, 1917–1919; Harford Powel, Jr., 1919–1922; Richard John Walsh, 1922–1924; Loren Palmer, 1924–1925; William Ludlow Chenery, 1925–1943; Charles Henry Colebaugh, 1943–1944; Henry La Cossitt, 1944–1946; Walter Davenport, 1946–1949; Louis Ruppel, 1949–1952; Roger Dakin, 1952–1955; Kenneth McArdle, 1953–1957.

CIRCULATION

> 3,776,538 (1957).

Norman Vogt

THE COLUMBIAN LADY'S AND GENTLEMAN'S MAGAZINE

John Inman, brother of celebrated portrait painter Henry Inman and the first editor of the *Columbian Magazine*, was associated with it throughout its publication: as editor, as coeditor, as senior editor, and as contributor. Before that professional association, however, in 1823 he became principal or headmaster of a school in North Carolina; two years later he spent twelve months touring Europe. Upon returning to the United States he practiced law for some time; then in 1928 he began his journalism career as editor of the *Standard*, a New York newspaper; in 1830 he joined the staff of the *Mirror*, and in 1833 he became assistant to William L. Stone, editor of the *Commercial Advertiser*. With Stone's death in 1844, Inman became editor of the *Commercial Advertiser*, and that same year he began as editor of the *Columbian Magazine*. In addition, throughout this period he was a frequent contributor to the *New York Review* and the *Spirit of the Times* with occasional poems, sketches, and tales.[1]

Inman assessed the importance of magazines in the first article of the first issue of the *Columbian Magazine*: "Decidedly this is the age of the magazine, as well as of railroads, Ericson propellers, miracle-working pills, and medicated candy. All literature approximates to the magazine, either in form or character." He cited many examples of how newspapers of the era had tried to be magazines and failed in the attempt; then he noted the intent of his new magazine: "the magazine is the true channel into which talent should direct itself for the acquisition of literary fame. The newspaper is too ephemeral—the book is not of sufficiently rapid and frequent production." Inman recalled Joseph Addison, Sir Richard Steele, Jonathan Swift, and Benjamin Franklin to illustrate this point and observed that many novels appear serially through magazines. Finally, he expressed the hope that "the first compensation given by the publisher of a magazine to a new contributor may afford that stimulus which alone was wanting to bring out talents of the highest order."[2]

The first issue was forty-nine pages, including essays, poetry, steel engravings (line and mezzotint), and sheet music. With the second issue there began a series of reviews of contemporary books, and with the third issue in March, the editor complained about some of the manuscripts he had received. In a note to correspondents, Inman remarked that some of the handwriting was "crabbed" and difficult to read, all of which led to his refusal to print that particular material. Several manuscripts were too long; one such, forty-eight foolscap pages, Inman described as "three times too long for a magazine article." Another of twenty-seven foolscap pages, relatively too long, he might have used but it was "only a pleasant sketch tale of which the chief merit [was] the lively, agreeable style," and Inman was reluctant to give that much space to such a light piece.[3] Inman then described the kinds of pieces he would and would not use: "There is no kind of article less agreeable to the editor than stories, the only aim of which is to excite and satisfy curiosity by the mere detail of incidents. . . . The editor will always prefer . . . such as develope [*sic*] some profitable thought, enforce some moral, or illustrate some passage in history."[4] Later he noted that "15 foolscap pages of moderate handwriting are enough," for he did not wish to continue pieces from one issue to the next.[5]

Several noteworthy writers published works in the *Columbian*. In the first issue, William Cullen Bryant's "The White-Footed Deer" appeared. That same year his volume of poetry entitled *The White-Footed Deer and Other Poems* was published. In the first volume of the *Columbian Magazine* two articles by Walter Whitman were published: "Dumb Kate: An Early Death" and "Eris, a Spirit Record." (Whitman referred to himself as Walt after 1855 to distinguish his name from that of his father Walter.)[6] From 1841 to 1848 Whitman spent brief periods of time working for at least ten New York papers and magazines, writing editorials and stories rather than poems.[7] "The Little Sleighers" and "The Child and the Profligate" by Walter Whitman appeared in the second volume of the *Columbian Magazine*; of these four pieces all but "The Child and the Profligate" were first published by Inman.[8] Also in the second volume were two poems, "Mesmeric Revelation" and "The Angel of the Odd—An Extravaganza," and an essay, "Byron and Chaworth," by Edgar Allan Poe. In 1844 Poe, too, was working in New York, first for the *Evening Mirror* and then for the *Broadway Journal*, of which he eventually became owner. Because there were no international copyright laws and because authors were paid as little as $4 per article or $15 per story, writers even of Poe's caliber often suffered financially.[9] In March 1847, Poe's "The Domain of Arnheim" was published in the *Columbian Magazine*; volume 9 of Inman's magazine held the last of Poe's contributions: "To———" ("Not long ago, the writer of these lines, / In the mad pride of intellectuality").

Poe once remarked in his *Broadway Journal* that *Godey's, Graham's** and the *Columbian* "are so nearly alike that if the covers changed it would not be easy to distinguish one from the other. They nearly all have the same contributors and the same embellishers."[10] Among those same contributors was H. T. Tuckerman ("Thoughts on the Poets," "Clevenger," "Impromptu Sonnet," "Chansonette," "When Silent Grows the Plaintive Lady," "Leaves from the Diary of a Dreamer," "Much Ado About Nothing," and "Sonnet"), author of poems, travels, biographies, essays, and criticism, each of which represented some phase of experience or study as viewed by a scholar. Another was James Kirke Paulding ("The Fountain of Youth," "Sketch of the Great Western Lakes," "The Quiet Home," "The Happiness of Wealth," "A Panegyric on Witchcraft, Mesmerism and Cheap Literature," "Peter Pettifog, The Great Traveler," "The Creole's Daughter," and "The All-Seeing Eye"), whose sister married Washington Irving's elder brother and who worked jointly with Irving on the *Salmagundi*.[11] His favorite mode was to exemplify some moral in a story or allegory; he made many free and anonymous contributions to a number of different magazines during this era. T. S. Arthur ("The Bargain Buyer," "Brother's Temptation," "The Set of China," "The Moustache and the Imperial," "The Wise Forethought," "The True Friend," "The Perfect Wife," "Debtor and Creditor," "The Mother and Son," "A Leaf from the Book of Human Life," "The Lottery Ticket," "Charity Begins at Home," "Making Haste to be Rich," "Visiting as Neighbors," "Forgive and Forget," "Going to the Dogs," and "The Over-Paid Check"), editor and owner of *Arthur's Home Magazine*, also contributed works of fiction of a "moral character."[12] Thomas Buchanan Read ("Liberty") devoted himself to art and often contributed poetry. Charles Fenno Hoffman

("Rio Bravo!") was a lawyer for Charles King, who was editor of the *New York American*. Hoffman then became a journalist and in 1833 edited the *Knicker-bocker**; in the next decade he also contributed to the *Columbian*.[13] Alfred B. Street ("A Day or Two's Fishing in Pike Pond"), also a lawyer, wrote poetry and descriptive pieces, focusing on varied aspects of American scenery.

Among the leading female writers of the period, Elizabeth Fries Ellet ("Artist's Lesson," "The Kabotermann," "An Artist's Fortunes," "A Country Recollection; or, the Reformed Inebriate," "The Fanfare of Death," "Mozart's First Visit to Paris," "The Witch Caprushe," "The Maiden's Leap," "A Passage in Russian History," "The Shade of Wands," "The Castilian Princess," "The Haunted House in Georgia," "Zellie," "Olden Traditions," "The Picture Frame," "Eugene Le May," "Marry in Your Own Sphere," "Another Story of the Kyffhauser," "Illustrations of Popular Phrases," and "Handel—A Tale of Art") was a frequent contributor to Inman's *Columbian*. She generally wrote poems for magazines and researched memoirs for biographies of famous American women. Lydia Maria Child ("Thot and Freia," "The Children of Mount Ida," "Elizabeth Wilson—The Youthful Immigrant," "An Hour in the Nursery," "Hilda Silverling," "The Irish Heart," "The Beloved Time," "Fragments of Life in Small Pictures," "The Beauty of Peace," "Reflections of Ole Bull," "The Self-Conscious and the Unconscious," "The Neighbor-in-law," "A Poet's Dream of the Soul," "Rosenglory," "The Northmen," "The Rival Mechanicians," "My Fairy Friend," and "The Man That Killed His Neighbors"), who alone edited several monthly magazines for female readers and with her husband edited the *National Anti-Slavery Standard* in 1841, also contributed to the *Columbian*.[14] Elizabeth Oakes Smith ("Love Quarrel," "To Charlotte and Grace," "Childhood," "Retribution, or the Three Chimnies," and "Borrowing Neighbor") sent her earliest poems anonymously to various magazines, but eventually when her family's financial affairs were in jeopardy, she published openly.[15] Frances Sargent Osgood ("The Lady's Shadow," "The Hour Before the Duel," "Bois Ton Sang Beaumanoir," "To———," "To My Mother," "To The Spirit of Poetry," "To Amelia Welby," "Golden Rules in Rhyme," "Mabel, A German Legend," "A Flight of Fancy," "The Sunbeam's Love," "Lady Jane, a Song," "To Sybil," "A Mother's Prayer in Illness," "A Remembrance," "A Lover's Lay," "Ida's Farewell," "The Good Angel," "A Dream," "The Lost Lily," "Reflections," "To My Pen," "Sorrow's Holiday," "To———," "Kate Carol to Mary S." "An Exhortation, to one who will hardly understand it," "No!," "The Magic Prism," "The Poet to a Coquette," "The Poet to One who Loves Him," "The Poet's Reply to Undeserved Praise," "Sorrow and Joy," and "Stanzas for Music"), wife of S. S. Osgood the painter, wrote for the *Columbian*, as did Caroline M. Kirkland, most famous for her letters from the West. Kirkland ("Sinecures, or Parson Thatcher's Day," "The Voige and Travels of Sir John Maundeville," "What Must Be, Must," and "The Prince of Tezcuco") edited *Union Magazine* in 1847; all her pieces were noted for their "clear common sense, purity of style, and animated thought.''[16] Lydia H. Sigourney ("Intercession of the Indian for the Charter Oak of Connecticut," "The Lot of the Earth," "Micah and the Levite," "Montauk Point," "Passage up the Connecticut, from Hartford to Springfield," "Columbia's Ship's," "Father," "Farewell to Flowers," "Running Away," "The Victim of the Deep," "Friendship with Nature," "The Boy and the Wreck," "The Passing Bell," "The Sister's Intervention," "The Cyclamen Persicum," "The Feline Friend," "The Rock and the Flowers," "The Lost Friend," "Advertisement of a Lost Day," "Louisa Wilson," "The Royal Clock," "Lines on the Death of Mrs James Harper," "Epitaph on a Young Lady," "Reef Sails," "The Ivy," "Aurora," "Aurora, from Herder," "The Emigrant Mother," and "Mohawk Warrior"), who began a select school in 1814, toured Europe in 1840 and wrote many pieces describing her tour for several magazines, including the *Columbian*.[17] Other prominent female writers of the period who contributed frequently to this magazine were Fanny Forester, whose long fiction works were often a major portion of the issue; Caroline H. Butler; Emily E. Chubbuck; C. M. Sedgwick; and D. Ellen Goodman.

Of the popular writers, Paulding drew some critical notice of his contributions specifically to the *Columbian*. Mentor L. Williams notes that a survey of these articles "does not reveal any genius." In a concluding statement he notes that "Paulding's work in the *The Columbian* is sentimental junk unrelieved by imagination or real human emotion; canned, stereotyped nonsense." At the time, Paulding's style was being "challenged by a new type of fiction, the sensational. From the vantage point of a hundred years, however, the form may have changed but the substance never."[18]

With volume 3, Inman was joined by Robert A. West as coeditor. Both men contributed editorial pieces, stories, and poetry. According to Evert A. Duyckinck and George L. Duyckinck, however, Inman, once wrote an entire number of the *Columbian* alone.[19] Beginning with volume 9 a different typeface is used, thinner and smaller than before. Although Stephen M. Chester is listed as editor at the beginning of the volume, an article by the senior editor (J.I.) appeared in an early number, and Inman wrote his "Farewell Editorial" in the May issue. In this farewell, Inman began with an illustrative story about a horse, badly treated and unhappy with his lot in life, who plotted and finally achieved an escape from his farm. Soon, hungry and cold, he decided to return home. Although Inman emphasized that his own lot was far from miserable, he stated that he, too, would miss the "habit" of work. He noted that he had never intended to stay with the magazine for more than one year, chiefly because of his failing health. For that reason, a second editor was added in 1845, but both Inman and the coeditor West were in poor health. Then a publisher change occurred, again necessitating that Inman as well as West remain with the *Columbian*. Inman concluded: "Now the writer has the comforting assurance that he leaves (it) in good hands; that its interests, and the gratification of its readers, will be better cared for than they have been or could be, under the last two years of his administration."[20]

The first eight volumes were each six months; volume 9, however, was a full year with twelve issues, despite the change in editors and publishers. In the January issue of volume 9 one of the editors noted that, rather than the usual book reviews, this issue contained books for the "holydays" [sic] for the publishers "scarcely enable or permit us to speak of any but gift books."[21] This seems to indicate that the January issue must have been available for sale before the December holidays. This same volume also contained a "to be continued" article, a practice that Inman had never allowed.

Although both Inman and West wrote articles for the final issues in volume 10, the Reverend Darius Mead assumed the editor's role as well as that of publisher. Mead used a new cover, title page, and typeface. He listed the "potage" (postage) as 4.5 cents to any part of the United States on these terms: $3 per annum in advance, two copies for $5. Mead assured his readers: "It is our aim to blend valuable information and sound morality with the gratification of a literary and imaginative taste."[22] At the end of the first number he issued, Mead apologized for the short time he had had to prepare this first publication because of the recent change in editorship. Another note, in headlines, proclaimed: "Contents—Entirely Original." Although the February issue was the last, there was no comment to that effect, no farewell remarks.

Frank Luther Mott compared the *Columbian Lady's and Gentleman's Magazine to Peterson's and Lady's Book*—similar but shorter lived. He noted that several important engravers of the age appeared in the *Columbian*—Thomas Coney, S. H. Gimber, and A. L. Dick. The *Columbian* "published two mezzotints and a colored fashion plate in each number for the first two years, but in 1846 it renounced the fashions."[23] The music published included lyrics and score.

The early ambitions of the magazine, as expressed by Inman, were realized to a degree, for at least three authors of continuing literary significance were recognized: Bryant, Whitman, and Poe. In addition, those authors popular at the time in this and other magazines of the same caliber were also published. Perhaps, if Inman's health had been better, this magazine could have flourished and found a lasting place in the history of American magazines. As it is, the magazine is still significant despite its short-lived duration.

Notes

1. Evert A. Duyckinck and George L. Duyckinck, *Cyclopaedia of American Literature (2 vols.), Embracing Personal and Critical Notices of Authors, and Selections from the Earliest Period to the Present Day, with Portraits, Autographs, and Other Illustrations,* edited to date by M. Laird Simons (Philadelphia: Baxter Publishing, 1881), 2:244.

2. John Inman, "Magazine Literature," *Columbian Magazine,* January 1844, pp. 1–5.

3. John Inman, "Notice to Correspondents," *Columbian Magazine,* March 1844, p. 142.

4. Ibid.

5. John Inman, "Notice to Correspondents," *Columbian Magazine*, May 1844, p. 238.

6. "Walt Whitman 1819–1892," *American Authors 1600–1900: A Biographical Dictionary of American Literature*, ed. Stanley J. Kunitz and Howard Haycraft (New York: H. W. Wilson, 1938), p. 807.

7. Ibid., p. 808.

8. Richard Maurice Burke, Thomas B. Harned, and Horace L. Traubel, eds., *The Complete Writings of Walt Whitman*, 10 vols. (New York: Knickerbocker Press, 1902, Volume VI republished by Scholarly Press), 3:68, 6:60, 85.

9. "Edgar Allan Poe 1809–1849," *American Authors 1800–1900*, p. 624.

10. Frank Luther Mott, *A History of American Magazines, 5 vols. Vol 1: 1741–1850*, (New York: D. Appleton and Company, 1930), p. 352n.(From *Broadway Journal*, 25 January 1845, p. 60.)

11. Duyckinck and Duyckinck, *Cyclopaedia* 2:1.

12. Ibid. 2:516.

13. Ibid. 2:319.

14. Ibid. 2:210.

15. Ibid. 2:459.

16. Ibid. 2:456.

17. Ibid. 1:838.

18. Mentor L. Williams, "Notes and Queries," *American Literature* 21 (1949); 227.

19. Duyckinck and Duyckinck, *Cyclopaedia* 2:244.

20. John Inman, "Farewell Editorial," *Columbian Magazine*, May 1848, p. 236.

21. "Books for the Holydays," *Columbian Magazine*, January 1848, p. 48.

22. Darius Mead, *Columbian Magazine*, January 1849, inside cover.

23. Mott, I, pp. 743–44.

Information Sources

BIBLIOGRAPHY

Burke, Richard Maurice, Thomas B. Harned, and Horace L. Traubel, eds. *The Complete Prose Works of Walt Whitman*. 10 vols. New York: Knickerbocker Press, 1902.

Duyckinck, Evert A., And George L. Duyckinck. *Cyclopaedia of American Literature*. vols. 1 and 2. Philadelphia: Baxter Publishing, 1881.

Inman, John, ed. *Columbian Lady's and Gentleman's Magazine*, vols. 1–9, January 1844–May 1848.

Kunitz, Stanley J., and Howard Haycraft, eds. *American Authors 1800–1900: A Biographical Dictionary of American Literature*. New York: H. W. Wilson, 1938.

Mead, Darius, ed. *Columbian Lady's and Gentleman's Magazine*, vol. 10, January and February 1829.

Mott, Frank Luther. *A History of American Magazines, 5 vols. Vol. 1: 1741–1850*. New York: D. Appleton and Company, 1930.

Williams, Mentor L. "Notes and Queries." *American Literature*, 21 (1949); 222–27.

INDEX SOURCES:

n.a.

LOCATION SOURCES

Library of Congress; in many libraries in microform.

Publication History

MAGAZINE TITLE AND TITLE CHANGES:
> *The Columbian Lady's and Gentleman's Magazine, Embracing Literature in Every Department: Embellished with the Finest Steel and Mezzotint Engravings, Music and Colored Fashions.* (Half title and running head: *The Columbian Magazine.*)

VOLUME AND ISSUE DATA
> January 1844–February 1849. Monthly. vols. 1–8, regular semiannual volumes; vol. 9, 1848, 12 numbers; vol. 10, January and February 1849, incomplete in two numbers.

PUBLISHERS AND PLACE OF PUBLICATION
> Israel Post, New York, 1844–1846; Ormsby and Jackett, New York, 1847; John S. Taylor, New York, 1848; Darius Mead, New York, 1849.

EDITORS
> John Inman, 1844; John Inman and Robert A. West, 1845–April 1848; Stephen M. Chester, May-December 1848; Darius Mead, 1849.

CIRCULATION
> n.a.

Barbara Nourie

COMMERCIAL REVIEW. See DEBOW'S REVIEW

CONSUMER REPORTS

While the movement to establish protection for consumers is thought to be a phenomenon of the twentieth century, consumers, producers, and government authorities have attempted to protect buyers from deception and fraud for thousands of years. Roman emperors, for example, tried to govern trade practices in their grain markets; medieval guilds established standards for quality; Napoleonic health councils devised tests to measure the purity of wine and medicine and the nutritional value of bread.[1] In the United States, nineteenth-century authors including Catherine Beecher and Harriet Beecher Stowe wrote about the need for consumers to gain greater control over their increasing purchases of store-bought goods. As large companies began to recognize their need to evaluate the quality of raw materials supplied to them, many established laboratories to increase their oversight in this area.[2] These private initiatives paralleled the federal government's establishment of the National Bureau of Standards early in this century to test the quality of government-bought goods. This oversight by government and industry had little impact on private citizens: most consumers trusted brand names or endorsements like the *Good Housekeeping* Seal of Approval (begun in 1912).[3] This confidence in brand names was shaken by the work of Upton Sinclair, Lincoln Steffens, and other muckrakers; Sinclair deplored the conditions of the meat and dairy industries and the others also pointed out vivid examples of deception and adulteration. (The first Pure Food and Drug Act in 1906 was the result of public outrage over a wide range of deceptive practices.)[4]

Another ingredient in the assortment of conditions that led to increased consumer protection was the description of America by Thorstein Veblen as irrational and wasteful because of its emulation of the leisure class. Veblen thought that only when the natural values of utility and thrift gained ascendancy would the "conspicuous consumption" that characterized Americans be slowed. His ideal of an engineer's standards to counter the weight of advertising and subjective judgment was to form a major theme in the consumer movement. The specifications and standards adopted in the United States after World War I to attack inefficiency and waste and to promote a scientific approach to manufacturing and consumption became a characteristically American theme—Herbert Hoover was a leader in this movement toward adopting standards.[5] Each of these strands of consumer protection helped to even the balance of power between producers and consumers.

In 1927, Frederick Schlink and Stuart Chase combined several strands of consumer protest in *Your Money's Worth*, a Book-of-the-Month best-seller that urged consumers to purchase goods based on specifications, standards, and tests. Buoyed by the success of this book, Schlink and Chase established Consumers' Research and began publishing *Consumers' Research Bulletin*, a magazine that tested products and reported to readers about commodities they might purchase. A labor strike by the magazine's staff in 1935 eventually led to the formation of Consumers Union, a nonprofit corporation that began publishing *Consumer Reports* (then called *Consumers Union Reports*) in May 1936. While the *Consumers' Research Bulletin* had given priority to testing products, the newer *Consumer Union Reports* tried to unite political activism, educational activities, and boycotts with product testing. The early Consumers Union membership consisted of an alliance of radical trade unionists, journalists, and academicians.[6] For the first year, the organization was run as a cooperative socialist experiment: decisions were determined by the will of the member-subscribers, and everyone from secretary to editor received the same salary. By March of 1937, director Arthur Kallet and the magazine's board had realized that to retain the strongest staff, varying salaries would be required.[7]

For today's reader of *Consumer Reports*, the history of the magazine's origin may appear to be an accumulation of unnecessary baggage—what could be less revolutionary than an established popular magazine that guides its affluent readers' choices of stereo equipment, automobiles, and videocassette recorders (VCRs)? Such a vision of *Consumer Reports*, however, ignores the ongoing efforts of Consumers Union to balance product testing and consumer advocacy. The rising circulation of *Consumer Reports* (one of the few popular magazines that accept no advertising) funds the testing reported in the magazine as well as consumer advocacy offices, a magazine (*Penny Power*) that offers advice to children about products and money management, and a variety of consumer education projects and publications. This effort to retain activist ties along with product-testing credibility has characterized *Consumer Reports* during its first fifty years of publication. The early numbers included articles about the conditions of labor where a tested product was manufactured, transportation costs, utility bills, legislative proposals, and cooperative buying plans. Product testing, although less emphasized than it is today, was an important area of activity. Dewey Palmer, the first technical supervisor, acquired data about testing techniques, arranged for testing work to be done, and exchanged information with testing laboratories, the Bureau of Standards, the Department of Agriculture, and private chemists.[8] There was an emphasis on economy: articles indicated which cereal provided the most bulk for the money or whether Grade B milk was as safe as costlier Grade A milk. Something of this earnest concern for consumers can be found in an evaluation of bath soap: "Good soap, like good wine, improves with age. It will be found decidedly more economical to buy toilet bars in lots of a dozen or more cakes . . . and to let the soap dry out on a shelf before use. When dried out, the soap dissolves away at a much slower rate" (May 1936, p. 16). The high priority given to advocacy and activism and the lower priority given to technical work (in 1939, only seven of the fifty staff members were technicians, and only one was a scientist[9]) resulted in a lack of quality on the testing side. This deficiency became apparent to the staff when in May 1938 *Consumer Reports* accused the Libby Company of permitting poisonous belladonna in its canned peas—in fact, the debris identified as belladonna was later found to be harmless.

The less than rigorous testing approach, sometimes based on opinion rather than scientific testing, and *Consumer Reports'* surprising circulation (85,000 in 1939) combined to moderate the magazine's political stance. Like the consumer movement as a whole, Consumers Union found that its members were mostly middle-class—the targeted lower-income groups seemed barely to have heard of the magazine (*Consumer Reports*, June 1937, p. 32; October 1939, pp. 8–9). (As late as the mid-sixties, Walker Sandbach noticed that everyone who sat next to him on plane flights read and thought highly of *Consumer Reports*, but not one of his father's acquaintances in Mount Vernon, Iowa, had heard of the magazine. Ads in *TV Guide** and other promotions addressed this lack of recognition.[10]) Several early initiatives emphasized the importance of scientific testing and de-emphasized political activism on the part of Consumers Union. Arthur Kallet, director of Consumers Union from 1936 to 1957, redirected resources to stress technical tests and established a new laboratory in 1939. While the early members of the board of directors (especially Kallet, Colston Warne, and Bernard Reis) were open exponents of radical political and consumer philosophies, the organization carefully assumed a nonpartisan stance. World War II temporarily slowed the growth in *Consumer Reports'* circulation (although a weekly newsletter published by Consumers Union, *Bread and Butter*, had a circulation of over 50,000), but in the period between 1945 and 1950 circulation rose from 90,000 to over 400,000. Added income from subscriptions permitted

Consumers Union to expand both staff and testing programs—during 1949, 1,793 brands were evaluated.[11] A new technical director, Morris Kaplan, helped split the technical work into electronics, textiles, appliances, chemistry, food, and special projects. In addition, a staff member was permitted to work under Department of Agriculture supervision on the grading of canned food. Since both *Consumer Reports'* readers and staff were less interested in the radical context from which the magazine had emerged, Kallet tried to guide the magazine away from too close a connection with its origin. A more conservative board of directors, a distinction between "members" and "subscribers" (so that if the smaller number of members could be accused of radicalism, the larger group of subscribers could not), an end to coverage of labor conditions—each of these contributed to a more middle-class image.[12] The emphasis in testing changed from the earlier themes of economy and function to safety and convenience. By 1959, just five years after Consumers Union had cleared its name from the House Un-American Activities Committee's list of subversive organizations, *Consumer Reports* had achieved the status of a fixture in consumer affairs. As a business reporter for the *New York Times* wrote: "What Dr. Spock is to freshman parents, the Consumers Union is to bewildered housewives" (November 30, 1959). At the time of this comment, *Consumer Reports'* annual circulation was just under one million and its annual expenses were about $14 million; by 1980, circulation was over two million and annual expenses about $30 million.[13] A consumer institution founded in protest had found a place for itself within the establishment.

Despite this status as an established magazine with a solidly middle-class readership (the median income of *Consumer Reports'* readers is over $30,000[14]), *Consumer Reports* has never wholly disowned the activism characteristic at the time of its founding. In the 1950s, for example, an editorial director (Mildred Brady) spent much of her time "dredging up the sludge of sociological abuse"[15]—one of her best-known articles was about the watering of ham to increase its weight. Later, when Rhoda Karpatkin became executive director in 1975, consumer advocacy offices were opened in San Francisco, Washington, D.C., and Austin, Texas; *Penny Power* first appeared in 1980 as a children's alternative to corporate advertising; and higher pay scales were initiated ($16,400 for a file clerk, $20,600 for a secretary[16]) to emphasize the organization's commitment to labor. The response of the Consumers Union staff to Karpatkin's reemphasis of consumer activism was to call for her resignation—the staff was especially distressed about austerity measures that were taken in the early 1980s after a deficit of $5.7 million had accumulated.[17] Despite this periodic discontent, money from *Consumer Reports'* circulation seems able to finance both advocacy activities and product testing with subscription income. (The magazine's anticipated move into the new *Consumer Reports* National Testing and Research Center should accommodate large-scale testing on a regular basis—recent tests, in January and March 1987, have compared 186 videocassette recorders and 169 televisions.)

The testing projects with which *Consumer Reports'* activism is most closely associated include a long-time examination of cigarette smoking (culminating in the publication of a separate book—the *CU Report on Smoking* in 1963—which was a key document for the Surgeon General's Committee that warned against smoking in 1964), an ongoing rating of the comparative performance and safety of automobiles (Ralph Nader's presence on the board of directors of Consumers Union has encouraged a perception of cooperation between the two that is not always accurate), and warnings about a variety of radioactive hazards (from well-publicized warnings in 1959 about fallout in milk—which some regard as an important stimulus to the later treaty banning nuclear testing—to tests of X-rays, color televisions, and microwave ovens).[18] The often-politicized use made of *Consumer Reports'* studies by others tends to diminish the public's recognition of the range, quality, and impartiality of the magazine's testing. Despite frequent suits against it, Consumers Union never lost a court case or received any unfavorable settlement out of court during its first forty-six years. (Its first unfavorable ruling came in 1982, when a court ruled in favor of Bose Corporation and found Consumers Union guilty of knowingly publishing "a false statement of material fact."[19]) *Consumer Reports* has never accepted advertising and has never authorized the use of its testing results by other advertisers—the magazine actively encourages its readers to notify Consumers Union if its testing results are used in ads. While budgetary considerations have sometimes forced alterations in testing and format (for example, *Consumer Reports* reduced its average issue size from sixty to fifty-two pages in response to the deficits in the early 1980s), the format has remained stable—reviews of six major types of products and a report on an automobile test in each issue.

A comparison of the first issue of *Consumer Reports* and a recent issue illustrates both the continuity of the testing reports and the magazine's accommodation to more affluent readers. The May 1936 issue gave test results on breakfast cereal, antacid, toilet soaps, stockings, milk, and toothbrushes; an informative article cautioning readers about the presence of lead in toys also appeared. The May 1987 issue gave test results on electric ranges, travel irons and steamers, compact disc players, automobiles, rechargeable lights, computer printers, and blood pressure monitors; informative articles cautioning readers about telephone fraud and bargain travel fares also appeared. Although written over fifty years from one another, both sets of articles provide technical information about a variety of brands and make recommendations based on the technical testing data—the sophistication of the tests has increased to allow tests of increasingly complex products. As has been the case throughout *Consumer Reports'* history, each of these articles would be of use to readers interested in comparing different brands of a given item. (The influence the magazine has on its readers and their buying habits has been studied often—many of these studies have taken the form of doctoral dissertations. Critics of *Consumer Reports* question the validity of ratings that fail to take style, fashion, and status into account; balk at the implication that one purchases something only for replacement or utility purposes;[20]

or reject an approach that assumes the importance of consuming and questions only which brand to buy.[21] Still others have suggested that rather than introduce a rational element into consumer choice, *Consumer Reports* merely makes consumers feel more rational about and satisfied with their purchases.[22])

While each of these criticisms retains an isolated validity, each limits itself by taking the role of *Consumer Reports* as seriously as the magazine takes itself. The Veblen-intoned ideals of utility and thrift seem as far from the ascendancy as they were sixty years ago; many observers might regard the intervening years as the triumph of conspicuous consumption rather than its defeat. The often-remarked power of American society to absorb its dissenters without wholly accepting or rejecting their position is well illustrated by the status of *Consumer Reports*, which has become a fixture despite the triumph of conspicuous consumption. *Consumer Reports*, like Veblen's voice, has been a tiny dam against the surge of leisurely consumption. Unable to remake the world along the restrained utilitarian lines Veblen valued, *Consumer Reports* has nonetheless carved out a valued place for itself within the free arena of American consumer affairs.

Notes

1. Robert Lynd, "The Problem of the Consumer," *Annals of the American Academy of Arts and Sciences*, May 1936, pp. 1–7.

2. Daniel Boorstin, *The Americans* (New York: Random House, 1973), pp. 193–99.

3. Otis Pease, *The Responsibilities of American Advertising: Private Control and Public Influence* (New Haven: Yale University Press, 1958), chapters 1–4.

4. Oscar E. Anderson, *The Health of a Nation* (Chicago: University of Chicago Press, 1958), pp. 172–96.

5. W. Whitney, "The Place of Standardization in Modern Life," *Annals of the American Academy of Arts and Sciences*, May 1928, pp. 32–39.

6. Norman I. Silber, *Test and Protest: The Influence of Consumers Union* (New York: Holmes and Meier, 1983), pp. 22–23.

7. Ibid.

8. Ibid., p. 27.

9. Ibid.

10. Elin Schoen, "*Consumer Reports*' Knows What's Best for Us All," *Esquire*, February 1974, p. 111.

11. Silber, p. 29.

12. Ibid., p. 33.

13. Ibid., p. 130.

14. G. Kinkead, "Soulful Trouble at *Consumers Union*," *Fortune*, 22 February 1982, p. 124.

15. Schoen, p. 146.

16. Kinkead, p. 124.

17. Ibid.

18. For a detailed study of the smoking, automobile, and milk testing, the reader should refer to Silber's *Test and Protest*, which includes a general history of Consumers Union.

19. Kinkead, p. 120.
20. Silber, p. 33.
21. Schoen, p. 146.
22. Silber, p. 27.

Information Sources

BIBLIOGRAPHY

Engledow, Jack. *The Impact of "Consumer Reports" Ratings on Purchase Behavior and Post-Purchase Product Satisfaction.* Ph.D. diss., Indiana University, 1971.

English, Deirdre. *For Her Own Good: 150 Years of Experts' Advice to Women.* New York: Anchor, 1978.

Florman, Monte, ed. *Testing: Behind the Scenes at Consumer Reports, 1936–1986.* Mt. Vernon, N.Y.: Consumers Union, 1986.

Katz, Norman. *Consumers Union, The Movement and the Magazine, 1936–1957.* Ph.D. diss., Rutgers University, 1977.

Kinkead, G. "Soulful Trouble at Consumers Union." *Fortune,* 22 February 1982, pp. 119–20.

Schoen, Elin. " 'Consumer Reports' Knows What's Best for Us All." *Esquire,* February 1974, pp. 108–11.

Sorenson, Helen. *The Consumer Movement.* New York: Harper, 1941.

INDEX SOURCES

    Readers' Guide (1949–present); *Consumers Index; Magazine Index (1977–present); P.A.I.S.; Key to Economic Science (Consumer Reports* provides an annual index).

LOCATION SOURCES

    Library of Congress, many other libraries. Available in microform.

Publication History

MAGAZINE TITLE AND TITLE CHANGES

    Consumers Union Reports, May 1936–May 1942; *Consumer Report,* June 1942–April 1947; *CU Consumer Reports,* May 1947–October 1948; *Consumer Reports,* November 1948–present.

VOLUME AND ISSUE DATA

    Vols. 1–52, May 1936–present, monthly. (Since 1940 the December issue has been the annual buyers guide.)

PUBLISHER AND PLACE OF PUBLICATION

    Consumers Union, Directors Arthur Kallet, 1936–1957; Colston E. Warne, 1958; Dexter Masters, 1959–1963; Wray Smith, 1964–1965; Walker Sandbach, 1966–1974; Rhoda Karpatkin, 1975–present. Mt. Vernon, New York.

EDITORS

    (Note: The staff of *Consumer Reports* was initially organized as a cooperative experiment. Various designations were assigned to staff members; no separate "editor" was recognized for much of the magazine's history.) Dexter Masters, February 1938; Rachel Lynn Palmer, July–October 1938; Dexter Masters, June–

November 1942; Madeline Ross, June 1943–June 1947; Dexter Masters, June 1948–October 1950; Sidney Hertzberg, 1965; Helen Jacobs, 1966; Patricia Jenkins, 1967–1968; Donal Dinwiddie, 1969–1974; Irwin Landau, 1975–present.
CIRCULATION
    3,000,000.

Glenn Anderson

CONSUMERS UNION REPORTS. See CONSUMER REPORTS

CORONET

Jeane Honoré Fragonard's glorious *Jeune Fille aux Chiens* was the last classical art reproduction to appear on the cover of *Coronet*: the date was August 1939. The first art reproduction had appeared on the cover of the first issue of *Coronet*— November 1936. The September 1939 cover featured a color photograph of a cover girl (on her back, arms behind her head). Harbingering future content, the price of an issue of *Coronet* also changed: from thirty-five cents in August 1939 to twenty-five cents in September 1939.

That dramatic switch in gears occurred in part because the publication had achieved "only mediocre success in sowing culture."[1] If one's purpose was basically to be a "class magazine for arty intellectuals,"[2] there was a built-in limit as to how many issues could be sold.

Some of Fragonard's predecessors on the cover of *Coronet* included Pierre Bonnard, Frans Hals, Hans Holbein, Peter Paul Rubens, and Paolo Uccello. Artists of that caliber were also featured in the magazine itself. When the art reproductions stopped appearing on the cover, "Infinite Riches in a Little Room" also stopped appearing under the title.

Because of the profusion of pages dedicated in the first few years of *Coronet* to art and photography (Brassaï, Alfred Blumenfeld, and Erwin Eisenstaedt are all there), the early *Coronet* was different from the later *Coronet*. The former was not *Reader's Digest**–like; the latter was. *Coronet* always maintained its *Reader's Digest*–like size; it was "pocket size" at the beginning and at the end.

Begun by the Smart brothers (David and Alfred), publishers of *Esquire*,* *Coronet* was initially looked upon as a "four-color and metallic ink luxury little brother to *Esquire*."[3]

While it was struggling to establish itself as an arty magazine, *Coronet* was above merely having a table of contents or list of articles and sections. Instead, it had Textual Features and Pictorial Features. Under the textual, usually, were the categories of factual, conversational, fictional, personal, satirical, historical, cultural, regional, and biographical. "A Portfolio from the Louvre," with the particular Renoirs and Manets listed, was a typical entry under Pictorial Features.

Graphically, the features pages were very attractive. When *Coronet* decided to take the "mass appeal" route,[4] Textual Features and Pictorial Features were replaced by In This Issue and Contents—a change both literal and figurative.

For a brief time in its early existence *Coronet* offered its readers "salon-size contact prints, handsomely matted, of any of the photographs appearing"[5] in the magazine (later suspended only because of copyright problems). Also early in its existence *Coronet* offered (for a small fee) to bind, for its subscribers and anyone else, back issues of the magazine. Certainly, according to management, the magazine was of bookshelf-quality, keepable-quality.

And the first eleven issues of *Coronet* were booklike: they contained no advertisements whatsoever. Advertisements appeared for the first time in *Coronet* with the October 1937 issue, extolling the virtues of cruise ships, foundations/ girdles, book clubs, tomato juice, and a peace agency. A cry went up, out, and forth: *Coronet*'s management said that it was "barraged [by subscribers] with pleas to reconsider."[6] One plea included the assertion that "advertisements are as out of place in . . . *Coronet* . . . as they would be in . . . our set of Shakespeare."[7] There were no more advertisements in *Coronet* for over ten years. They reappeared, however, with the March 1948 issue. Revenue was the name of the game—and subscriptions alone did not generate enough revenue. *Coronet* management said its costs were rising, but it did not want to increase the price of an issue beyond twenty-five cents.[8]

Coronet had no more faithful advertiser than Kraft, the food manufacturer and producer. Certainly many Americans were first introduced to Cheez Whiz and Miracle Sandwich Spread in the pages of *Coronet*.

Coronet can lay claim to an advertising piece of fame. The twenty-eight–page, lift-out cookbook of Bisquick recipes from General Mills that was part of the January 1957 issue was, according to *Coronet*'s editor, "the largest single insertion any general magazine ha[d] ever carried."[9] At that time, *Coronet*'s circulation was nearly three million.

Possibly obsessed with letting the world know what it was all about, *Coronet* in October 1937 sponsored a contest for its readers: they were to answer the question, "What *Is* Coronet?" In a three-page essay, the winner suggested that "perusal of *Coronet* is like a steady streak of luck in shopping—one is continually coming across something *unusual* one wanted to know but was never conscious of looking for, as well as discovering something one should have known but somehow didn't about the *standard* topics of significant conversation."[10]

The articles—there had always been articles in *Coronet*—were praised by the essay winner for being "as perfectly developed as the intricate entrails of small watches."[11] The winner was the winner probably because he paid attention to both the words and the pictures in the magazine: *Coronet* "trains the eyes by painless instruction and pleasant practice, to read pictures as well as print."[12] Another respondent felt that *Coronet* was "a liberal education for those who cannot spend much time in the great art galleries of the world."[13] Should the winner have been the writer of the following sentiments? "*Coronet* is a magazine like great people. By my association with its 'infinite riches,' I, a commoner, am able to reap the benefits it willingly offers without my first falsely assuming the air of sophistication demanded by other and lesser periodicals. *Coronet* is the aristocrat most democratic.''[14]

The gatefolds, or folded inserts, in the center of *Coronet* for several years were an appealing feature of the magazine: one month it was a Thomas Hart Benton painting; another month it was Disney's Dumbo of the Circus. Subscribers could obtain unfolded reprints of the gatefolds.

Since that which is artistic is not without controversy, it is not surprising that a less-than-one-year-old *Coronet* announced that some of its subscribers were saying "that they feel that . . . nude photographs are out of place [in the magazine]."[15] Attempting to assuage the offended on all sides, *Coronet* management said that none of the letter writers "objected to nudity in art [and that many had] gone to great length to differentiate between nudes in paintings and sculpture and nudes in photographs."[16] Rest assured, continued management, this was not a battle of "Aesthetes and Philistines."[17] More readers contacted *Coronet*, and almost all of them wanted to retain, maintain, and sustain the photographic nudes—and so they were, although as time went by fewer nudes actually appeared in *Coronet*. They came not to be emphasized very much.

In its early, pre-television days *Coronet* established an intimacy with its readers through such features as the Coronet Workshop. Readers could vote each month on what a particular editorial policy should be. Those voters helped determine, among other issues, whether there would be cartoons in *Coronet*, whether the Gallup Report would appear, and how much fiction there would be. Results of the balloting were always reported in later issues.

The Coronet Round Table was another special feature. A famous person took a pro or con position on a controversial topic. W. Somerset Maugham, for example, addressed the issue of whether children should be conceived and brought into a warring world. A pre–1960 topic was "Should Teenagers Be Allowed to Vote?" A 1944 topic was "Is Jive a Cause of Delinquency?"

For much of the 1940s (with a start in the late 1930s) the Game Book appeared regularly in *Coronet*. A variety of quizzes, puzzles, rhyming games, anagrams, "checkers brainteasers," and "whodunits" were presented for the entertainment of readers.

The pictorials, or photographic essays, and picture stories remained until *Coronet*'s demise—and proved to be one of its most enduring and distinctive features. The pictorials took the readers-viewers practically everywhere—and it was not all pleasant. Sometimes there was misery, suffering, and sadness in the faces of the people in the pictures. June 1949 was a highwater mark for the pictorial: eighteen of them appeared in that issue. The pictorials ranged from "The Splendor of the Southwest" to "The Royal Danish Ballet," from "The Lonely Women of Las Vegas" to "Moslem Wedding," and from "Teen-Ager's Hangout" to "The Strange Vision of Ingmar Bergman."

Among *Coronet*'s nonarticle, nonpicture features were the following: Grin and Share It, Human Comedy, Political Palaver, Roamin' Numerals, and Sharpen Your Word Sense. Such sections and departments added to the variety of the magazine.

Articles on a vast array of topics appeared in *Coronet* over its twenty-five–year history, ranging from the silly to the serious, from the sappy and sickening to the stirring and substantial. For every "Go Ahead and Flirt!," "There's Something about a Moustache," "Lemon Peel Helps to Combat Cancer," and "Hubert the Hypoed Hypo" –type article, there was a "The Massacre of Wounded Knee," "Are We Executing Sick People?," "The Story of the NAACP," and "The Tragedy of *The Beloved Country*" –type article.

Pop psychology–type articles were always in abundance in *Coronet*. Representative examples include "How to Live with Others and Like It," "How to Test Your Emotional Maturity," "How to Cure an Inferiority Complex," as well as "There's No Need to Be Lonely," "The Deadly Sin of Jealousy," and "I Am a Psycho-Neurotic."

While it was never the *New Left Review*, *Coronet* did more than only take the middle ground: it ran some courageous, forward-looking, progressive articles. It never ran racist or anti-Semitic articles. It tried, sometimes, to present more than one way of thinking. "The Kids Who Speak for Brotherhood" could only have done good, likewise "Democracy in Our Church" ("an experiment in human brotherhood"),[18] "My Battle against the Klan" (by Georgia's governor in 1946), and "Prejudice Won't Make Us Sell *Our* House!"

The comments by a *Coronet* associate editor in 1948 that "*Coronet* is primarily a magazine of entertainment, so controversial, political and foreign affairs articles are seldom published"[19] would have been different had he been offering them a decade later.

In 1946 and 1948, respectively, *Coronet* included articles about Senator Robert Wagner of New York and Representative Henry Gonzalez of Texas. Unopprobriously, Wagner was referred to as a "liberal lawmaker."[20] The Gonzalez article also unopprobriously referred to his "battle in behalf of minorities."[21]

Another 1946 article, "How Open Is Your Mind?," exposed the evils of prejudice and "tabloid thinking."[22] A 1945 piece by Eleanor Roosevelt cried out for liking and loving among all people and peoples. "The Right to Be an Atheist" and "A Parent's Prayer" appeared in the same issue.

While *Coronet* was sometimes ahead of the times, most often it reflected the times. In 1950, homosexuality was the "New Moral Menace to Our Youth," and reactionaries, according to Herbert Hoover in "What Is a Reactionary?," were to be commended for "[holding] to basic freedoms of mind and spirit."[23]

As the 1950s progressed, *Coronet* included articles such as "When Communism Failed in Iowa," "Malenkov's Plan for World Conquest," and "Communism's Most Dangerous Enemy."

Coronet never lacked for articles about dating, marriage, love, and sex. Sometimes an issue (September 1958, for example) contained two articles on those topics: "20 Questions Most Often Asked about Sex" and "Myths That Imperil Married Love." A 1950 *Coronet* admonishment was "More Love, Less Sex"; a 1952 *Coronet* warning was "You Can't Get Away with Marriage Infidelity." An important question in 1954 in *Coronet* was "Does Chastity Make Sense?" A 1955 *Coronet* reassurance was that "Promiscuous Women Can Be Cured."

"A Case for Spinsterhood" was presented in the mid–1940s. Earlier in the decade, "Wanted: A Woman's Bill of Rights" appeared.

Probably no more earth-shattering article than " 'Nice Girls' Are Dangerous" ever appeared in *Coronet*. That 1954 piece asserted that women "ha[d] been taught . . . to live according to a . . . social pattern of human relations which was laid down in Victorian days."[24] A 1959 article similarly asserted that "women . . . ha[d] been hampered . . . by outworn mores."[25]

A female medical doctor, a contributor to *Coronet* in the late 1940s, wrote pieces such as "The Tragic Failure of America's Women" (they were "trying to compete with men or serving as men's lackeys")[26] and "Who Wears the Pants in Your Family?" ("the happiest homes are the ones in which firm, self-reliant husbands have the final say").[27]

Articles and pictorials about movie stars, performers, and celebrities could almost always be found in *Coronet*: Ingrid Bergman, Sammy Davis, Jr., Zsa Zsa Gabor, Bob Hope, and John Wayne are all there. An article by Liberace, "Mature Women Are Best," appeared in 1954.

"Bookettes," or book condensations, appeared with some frequency in *Coronet* throughout much of its existence. Those excerpts, or chapters from full-length books, averaged from ten to twenty pages. As with the articles, a great variety of kinds and types of subjects—and authors—were covered and represented. Richard Wright's *Black Boy* was a bookette, as was John Steinbeck's *Cannery Row*. Washington Irving's *Rip Van Winkle* found new life in *Coronet*. Mrs. Dale Carnegie's *How to Help Your Husband Get Ahead* was featured, as well as Norman Vincent Peale's *The Power of Positive Thinking*. Many "lighter," pure-pleasure books were included. Self-help books and books on marriage were not uncommon. John Hersey, Betty Smith, and Irving Stone were also among the condensed authors.

The short stories in *Coronet* were written by known as well as unknown authors. Some of the authors, of course, were in the process of gaining their fame.

Summer 1961 found *Coronet* subscribers still able to obtain, as they had for almost twenty-three years, two years' worth of the magazine (twenty-four issues) for five dollars. More than three million individuals had taken *Coronet* up on its offer. But there would be no two more years' worth of *Coronet*: the October 1961 issue was the last issue ever published. A poignant "Special Message" from publisher Arthur Stein and editor Lewis W. Gillenson appeared in that final issue. After pointing out that "the reasons for the demise of the magazine are etched in the red ink of the business ledger,"[28] the gentlemen delivered a eulogy for their beloved *Coronet*: "a magazine is . . . a living contact. . . . [W]hen it must depart, it does so not unlike a human—bereft of material body but ever available in spirit."[29] They heaped praise on *Coronet*'s writers, artists, and photographers for "always tread[ing] the rim of the event to fashion that special reaction which separates the banal from the artistic."[30] While there was much that was artistic in *Coronet*, the banal now and then made its appearance. In many senses, *Coronet* was a piece of Americana: for most of its existence it captured, reflected, and conveyed the common culture.

Notes

1. "Ads in *Coronet*," *Business Week*, 1 March 1947, p. 22.
2. Ibid.
3. " 'Coronet': Culture in Capsule Form," *Literary Digest*, 31 October 1936, p. 43.
4. Ibid.
5. "Salon-Size Prints of *Coronet* Photographs," *Coronet*, May 1937, p. 190.
6. "[Editor's Page]," *Coronet*, November 1937, p. 194.
7. Ibid.
8. "Ads in *Coronet*," p. 21.
9. William M. Freeman, "Betty Crocker, General Mills, *Coronet* Join Forces in New Idea," *New York Times*, 2 December 1956, sec. 3, p. 10F.
10. Ernest R. Buckler, "What Is *Coronet*?," *Coronet*, January 1938, p. 192.
11. Ibid.
12. Ibid.
13. Jean Flickinger, "What Is *Coronet*?," *Coronet*, February 1938, p. 194.
14. John Binnes, "Like Great People," *Coronet*, April 1939, p. [177].
15. "[Editor's Page]," *Coronet*, July 1937, p. 4.
16. Ibid.
17. Ibid.
18. John H. Holmes, "Democracy in Our Church," *Coronet*, November 1943, p. 3.
19. Ralph H. Major, Jr., "Read Before You Write," *Writer*, December 1948, p. 402.
20. Jack H. Pollack, "Bob Wagner: Liberal Lawmaker," *Coronet*, April 1946, p. 36.
21. Hart Stilwell, "Texas Rebel with a Cause," *Coronet*, August 1958, p. 43.
22. Roger W. Riis, "How Open Is Your Mind?," *Coronet*, December 1946, p. 7.
23. Herbert Hoover, "What Is a Reactionary?," *Coronet*, February 1950, p. 51.
24. Anne Fromer, " 'Nice Girls' Are Dangerous," *Coronet*, September 1954, p. 79.
25. Jerome Rainer and Julia Rainer, "The Responsive Wife in Modern Marriage," *Coronet*, August 1959, p. 60.
26. Marynia F. Farnham, "The Tragic Failure of America's Women," *Coronet*, September 1947, p. 5.
27. Marynia F. Farnham, "Who Wears the Pants in Your Family?," *Coronet*, March 1948, p. 14.
28. Arthur Stein and Lewis W. Gillenson, "A Special Message," *Coronet*, October 1961, p. [25].
29. Ibid.
30. Ibid.

Information Sources

BIBLIOGRAPHY

"Ads in *Coronet*." *Business Week,* 1 March 1947, pp. 21–22.

"*Coronet*: Book-Sized Materials Issued for Non-*Esquire* Minds." *News-Week*, 31 October 1936, 3.

" 'Coronet': Culture in Capsule Form." *Literary Digest*, 31 October 1936, p. 43.

"Cut-Price Circulation Economics Led to Demise of *Coronet*, Stein Declares." *Advertising Age*, 7 July 1961, pp. 6, 52.

"*Esquire* in Talks to Sell *Coronet*: Company Denies Macfadden Has Part in Negotiations." *New York Times*, 21 June 1961, p. 47.

"Final Touches." *Newsweek*, 24 July 1961, p. 45.

Freeman, William M. "Betty Crocker, General Mills, *Coronet* Join Forces in New Idea." *New York Times*, 2 December 1956, sec. 2, p. 10F.

Major, Ralph H., Jr. "Read Before You Write." *Writer*, December 1948; pp. 401–403.

"New Man at *Coronet*." *Newsweek*, 14 November 1955, p. 98.

O'Gara, James. "End of a Magazine." *Commonweal*, 29 September 1961, p. 32.

"Out Looking." *Newsweek*, 3 July 1961, p. 71.

INDEX SOURCES

Readers' Guide to Periodical Literature. (1948–1961).

LOCATION SOURCES

Library of Congress, many other libraries. Available in microform.

Publication History

MAGAZINE TITLE AND TITLE CHANGES

Coronet, 1936–1961.

VOLUME AND ISSUE DATA

Vol. 1–vol. 50, no. 6, November 1936–October 1961.

PUBLISHERS AND PLACE OF PUBLICATION

Coronet, Inc. (part of Esquire, Inc.) and Esquire, Inc. Chicago. David A. Smart, 1936–1952; Gordon Carroll, 1953–1955; no publisher, January 1956; Arthur Stein, February 1956–October 1961.

EDITORS

Arnold Gingrich, November 1936–August 1938; Arnold Gingrich and Bernard Geis, September 1938–February 1942; Oscar Dystel and Bernard Geis, March–December 1942; Bernard Geis and Harris Shevelson, 1943–March 1945; Oscar Dystel, editor-in-chief, April 1945–June 1948; Gordon Carroll, executive editor, 1946–July 1948; Gordon Carroll, August 1948–1952; Fritz Bamberger, 1953–February 1956; Lewis W. Gillenson, March 1956–October 1961.

CIRCULATION

Spring 1961: 3,100,000; October 1961: 2,000,000 (estimate).

Katherine Dahl

COSMOPOLITAN

First published in 1886, *Cosmopolitan (Cosmo)* has metamorphosed radically in its hundred-year history of publication. Current readers of the new *Cosmo* wouldn't recognize the older version of the title, and the Victorians would have even greater difficulty dealing with the modern emphasis on sex and the single girl.

The *Cosmopolitan* was begun by Paul Schlicht as a family periodical with a heavily literary emphasis. Current events and biography, as well as sections called "The Household" and "The Little Ones," broadened the publication's appeal to a mass audience. Despite the success that seemed assured for the new magazine, the publisher's ambition almost immediately outran sales. In 1888 it changed hands twice before being purchased by real estate and newspaper magnate John Brisben Walker.

During Walker's seventeen-year ownership the *Cosmopolitan* became a true general-interest magazine, known for both its current events coverage and its fiction. It was highly successful, rising from 20,000 to over 300,000 circulation in 1898. Walker, though drawing on many of the top-notch editorial and creative personnel of the period (William Dean Howells, Edward Everett Hale, and Jack London, for example), imbued the *Cosmopolitan* with much of his own forceful personality and multiple interests. He was an early champion of the automobile, the airplane, and modern technology in general. A proponent of educational reform, in 1897 he established the Cosmopolitan University for free correspondence studies—a project so popular it was swamped with applicants and died from its own success. Eventually, however, the *Cosmopolitan* suffered from the competing claims of Walker's other enthusiasms, and in 1905 it was sold to William Randolph Hearst.

Hearst continued the mix of fiction and nonfiction characteristic of the Walker years but under a succession of editors made the magazine immediately known for a newspaper-like sensationalism. The magazine attacked political corruption in the Senate, wealthy industrialists, and the Mormon church in a last gasp of muckraking fever. Fiction replaced exposé in 1912, an editorial decision that assured the financial and critical success of the *Cosmopolitan* for the next thirty-five years. World War I came and went with little *Cosmopolitan* attention to it, whereas romantic fiction by Robert W. Chambers and pictures of attractive stage stars like the Dolly Sisters were featured prominently. Along with fiction came an emphasis on illustration, and for several decades the illustrators of each story (Charles Dana Gibson, James Montgomery Flagg, and others) were mentioned in the contents. On this basis, the *Cosmopolitan* sold well, reaching a million circulation in 1914.

By 1918, *Cosmopolitan's* reputation for fiction was well established, but the formula was polished to perfection during Ray Long's tenure as editor (1918–1931). Under Long's savvy direction, the magazine was packed with more stories, more serials, and more illustrations, and the contents read like a Who's Who of bankable authors. The December 1922 issue, for example, had (for twenty-five cents) a poem by Edgar Guest, short stories by Fannie Hurst, Ring Lardner, Gouverneur Morris, Adela Rogers St. Johns, Kathleen Norris, and P. G. Wodehouse. The magazine continued to be profitable, especially after the *Cosmopolitan* was combined with another similar Hearst publication in 1925. While the new offering was officially called *Hearst's International Combined with Cosmopolitan*, *Cosmopolitan* retained much of its old identity.

Hearst successfully continued the Long formula under H. P. Burton (1931–1942) and Frances Whiting (1942–1945) during the 1930s and 1940s. April 1939, for example, included a book-length novel, a novelette, eight short stories by authors of some renown, including W. Somerset Maugham, Paul Gallico, and A. J. Cronin, two serials, and twelve articles. The magazine, at 140 small-type pages, was a good value, providing a great deal of popular reading material for the middle class. By 1942 it was billing itself as "the four book magazine." Readers of the 1940s could count on regular contributions from stalwarts Faith Baldwin, Louis Bromfield, and Vina Delmar, with occasional stories from Edna Ferber, Mary Roberts Rinehart, and Agatha Christie.

Despite the long-term success of *Cosmopolitan*, after World War II fiction was abandoned in favor of nonfiction for the young housewife in an attempt to combat rising production costs. Quizzes and cartoons in the back pages of articles titled "What Not to Tell Your Husband" and "I Was Sure I Was Sterile," and photo essays about Ralph Edwards, Jane Russell, and Jack Webb, began to appear. There was at least one novel included, usually a mystery, but more pages were devoted to light nonfiction and entertainment personalities. Photographs of popular stars finally replaced the painted "Cosmopolitan girl" covers made famous by Harrison Fisher and Bradshaw Crandell. Under John J. O'Connell (1951–1959) and Richard Atherton (1959–1965), "Special Sections" became the norm, each composed of several articles on the same subject. "The American Wife" (January 1958), "The Fascination of the Unknown" (January 1960), and "Psychiatry and Emotions" (April 1962) were topics designed to attract increasingly critical newsstand sales. Despite these measures, *Cosmopolitan*'s circulation dropped drastically in the early 1960s and its future seemed short.

Just as *Cosmopolitan*'s demise seemed imminent, salvation came from an unlikely source. A change in policy at the hands of a new editor, Helen Gurley Brown, determined that the magazine should address the needs and interests of a totally new audience whom Brown called "mouseburgers," young women whose main interest lay in catching a man. This was radical thinking in 1965 but predictable stuff from the author of best-seller *Sex and the Single Girl* (1962). Under Brown, the "Cosmopolitan Girl" resurfaced with a dangerously low décolletage and the cover noted articles like "How to Make Good at the Beach."

The success of the new *Cosmo* was phenomenal. Within months of the change-over, *Cosmopolitan* readership was up 15 percent and the advertising revenues has risen 50 percent.[1] Well-publicized hostility from the feminist press and the clever promotion of male centerfolds like actor Burt Reynolds continued to keep the magazine alive and thriving through the 1970s. By the early 1980s, *Cosmopolitan* could be relied upon for over twenty short articles and features relating to sex or dating per 330-page issue. Attention was also given to celebrities, beauty, food, and decorating as well as regular departments on books, movies, health, and money. This formula made *Cosmopolitan* the nineteenth largest-selling magazine in 1980 with a circulation of 2,837,000.[2]

Helen Gurley Brown's *Cosmopolitan* could be called a ''junk food'' magazine, but if so, the public has maintained an enormous appetite for it. Whether it will still be as palatable after Brown's retirement is anyone's guess, but at the moment, its popularity seems as predictable as McDonald's.

Notes

1. Chris Welles, ''Helen Gurley Brown Turns Editor: Soaring Success of the Iron Butterfly,'' *Life,* 19 November 1965, p. 65.
2. Benjamin Compaine, *The Business of Consumer Magazines* (White Plains, N.Y.: Knowledge Publications, 1982), p. 50.

Information Sources

BIBLIOGRAPHY
Buckley, William F. ''You Are the More Cupcakeable for Being a Cosmopolitan Girl.'' *National Review,* 22 September 1970, pp. 999–1000.
Carlson, Oliver, and Ernest Sutherland Bates. *Hearst, Lord of San Simeon.* New York: Viking, 1936.
Chaney, Lindsay, and Michael Cieply. *The Hearsts.* New York: Simon and Schuster, 1981.
Compaine, Benjamin. *The Business of Consumer Magazines.* White Plains, N.Y.: Knowledge Publications, 1982.
''The *Cosmopolitan* of Ray Long.'' *Fortune,* March 1931, pp. 51–55.
''Down with Pippypoo.'' *Newsweek,* 18 July 1966, p. 60.
Ephron, Nora. ''Helen Gurley Brown Only Wants to Help.'' *Esquire,* February 1970, pp. 74, 117–118.
Greene, Bob. ''American Beat: Bachelor of the Month.'' *Esquire,* August 1981, pp. 19, 22.
Katz, Bill, and Linda Sternberg Katz. *Magazines for Libraries.* 5th ed. New York and London: R. R. Bowker, 1986.
Mott, Frank Luther. *A History of American Magazines 1885–1905.* Cambridge: Belknap Press of Harvard University Press, 1957.
Peterson, Theodore. *Magazines in the Twentieth Century.* Urbana: University of Illinois Press, 1964.
Reisig, Robin. ''The Feminine Plastique.'' *Ramparts,* March 1973, pp. 25–29, 55–59.
Rosenblatt, Roger. ''The Back of the Book: That Girl.'' *New Republic,* 6 December 1975, pp. 30–31.
''Sex and the Editor.'' *Time,* 26 March 1965, p. 40.
Sobran, M. J., Jr. ''The Printed Word: Diets and Diaphragms.'' *National Review,* 2 April 1976, p. 335.
Welles, Chris. ''Helen Gurley Brown Turns Editor: Soaring Success of the Iron Butterfly.'' *Life,* 19 November 1965, pp. 65–72.
Wood, James Playsted. *Magazines in the United States.* 3rd ed. New York: Ronald Press, 1971.

INDEX SOURCES
>   *Abstrax; Access* (1975–present); *Biography Index; Readers' Guide* (1900–1913, 1953–1961); *Magazine Index* (1977–present); *Poole's Index* (1886–1906); *Engineering Index; Dramatic Index.*

LOCATION SOURCES
>   Widely available. Available in microform.

Publication History

MAGAZINE TITLE AND TITLE CHANGES
>   *Cosmopolitan Magazine,* 1886–1925; *Hearst's International Combined with Cosmopolitan,* 1925–1952; *Cosmopolitan,* 1952–present.

VOLUME AND ISSUE DATA
>   March 1886–present; monthly.

PUBLISHER AND PLACE OF PUBLICATION
>   Schlicht and Field, Rochester, New York, 1886–1887; Schlicht and Field Company, New York, 1887–1888; Joseph N. Hallock, 1888, New York; John Brisben Walker, in New York, 1889–1894, and in Irvington-on-the-Hudson, 1895–1905; International Magazine Company, 1905–1936; Hearst Magazines, 1936–1952; Hearst Corporation, 1952–present, New York.

EDITORS
>   Frank P. Smith, 1886–1888; E. D. Walker, 1888; John Brisben Walker, 1889–1905, with William Dean Howells (1890) and with Arthur S. Hardy (1893–1895); Bailey Milliard, 1905–1907; S. S. Chamberlain, 1907–1908; C. P. Narcross, 1908–1913; Sewell Haggard, 1914; Edgar G. Sisson, 1914–1917; Douglas Z. Doty, 1917–1918; Ray Long, 1918–1931; H. P. Burton, 1931–1942; Frances Whiting, 1942–1945; Arthur Gordon, 1946–1948; Herbert R. Mayes, 1948–1951; John J. O'Connell, 1951–1959; Richard Atherton, 1959–1965; Helen Gurley Brown, 1965–present.

CIRCULATION
>   2,350,000 (1985).

Stephanie Childs Sigala

COUNTRY GENTLEMAN

Few magazines have enjoyed either the longevity or readership of *Country Gentleman,* which for nearly a century was the most popular farm journal in America. However, the story of *Country Gentleman* falls into three separate and very distinctive periods, and only the continuity of the title links the three generations of the magazine.

In 1853 the full title of the first volume of *Country Gentleman* explained its purpose: "The Country Gentleman, A journal for the farm, the garden and the fireside; devoted to improvement in agriculture, horticulture, and rural taste; to elevation in mental, moral and social character, and the spread of useful knowledge and current news." Luther Tucker created the vision that guided *Country*

Gentleman from 1853 to 1911 under his editorship and that of his sons, Luther H. and Gilbert M. Tucker. His magazine was rooted in the nineteenth-century concept of the gentleman:

> In its best and proper signification, the word is defined to mean a man of cultivated mind, of refined manners, of genuine kindness of heart, and consequently purity of life. . . . Wherever the honest, earnest feeling of the heart finds utterance—wherever the deed of generous sympathy is performed—wherever the life is ruled by the principles of honor and religion, do we find the gentleman.[1]

Tucker dedicated his magazine to the interests and pursuits of farmers as gentlemen.

Luther Tucker was born on 7 May 1802 in Brandon, Vermont. He became apprenticed to a printer and worked as a journeyman. In 1826 he became editor and publisher of the *Rochester Daily Advertiser* in Rochester, New York. In 1831 he established a weekly farm paper, the *Genesee Farmer*, which may be claimed as the genesis for if not the immediate predecessor of the *Country Gentleman*. In 1839 Tucker sold the *Advertiser* to purchase a farm and devote his full attention to the *Genesee Farmer*. However, before the end of the year, Jesse Buel, editor of another major farm journal, the *Cultivator*, died, and Tucker sold his farm, purchased the *Cultivator*, and moved to Albany, where he consolidated the two agricultural papers into a monthly under the *Cultivator* title. The *Country Gentleman*, begun in 1853, was in essence a weekly edition of the *Cultivator*. Over the next decade interest in his weekly rose while the *Cultivator*'s readership diminished, and in 1865 Tucker consolidated them as the *Cultivator & Country Gentleman*.

Luther Tucker's clear goal in publishing the *Genesee Farmer*, the *Cultivator*, and the *Country Gentleman* was rural improvement. He desired to promote "high culture," defined as "a taste for literature, for home embellishment, and true refinement."[2] A focus for these efforts throughout the Tucker family's editorship of the magazine was a column entitled "The Fireside." Here one found literary notices, short stories, poems, and other materials to "cultivate the mind." Tucker called these the "higher and purer enjoyments" and concluded that the delight of reading fails "if the idea of improvement does not mingle in all its pleasures."[3] "The Fireside" also contained practical advice on interior decorating and other home improvements.

Nevertheless, the Tuckers' *Country Gentleman* was first and foremost a journal for farmers. The early feature columns included "The Grazier," "The Horticultural Department," and "Farm Product Markets," and these soon became more specific: "The Stock Breeder and Wool Grower," "The Dairyman," "The Poultry Keeper," "The Apiarist," and even "Entomology." A column on housekeeping expanded earlier tips for the housewife on canning, gardening, and other labor-saving recommendations. A short section summarized nonagricultural news. While the *Country Gentleman* was not a technical or scientific agricultural journal, it also was clearly not a coffee-table magazine. The market reports and extensive advertisements for farm products emphasized its practical aim.

Yet the *Country Gentleman* of the Tuckers was not drab and unattractive. Every issue was filled with illustrations of farm produce and animals, machinery, and even sketches of barns, farmhouses, and gazebos or of garden arrangements. The publication was a large quarto, 9.5″ x 12.75″, printed in three columns, and sixteen pages per issue. The paper was of good quality throughout the nineteenth century, with clear typography—especially the consistent use of headings for each regular department or feature column. The price was $2.00 (if paid in advance) or $2.50 until 1866 when a $.50 increase occurred and the number of pages per issue doubled to thirty-two.[4] In 1870 the size increased to 11″ x 14.75″ and the number of columns to four, while the length dropped to sixteen or twenty pages per issue.[5] The circulation generally remained between twenty and thirty thousand until after the Tucker family sold the magazine in 1911.

It is remarkable that for a period of nearly sixty years the format and content of *Country Gentleman* remained essentially unchanged. Luther Tucker had died in 1873, but his sons, Luther H. and Gilbert M., continued the magazine without interruption, philosophic or otherwise. The amount of advertising increased from an average of two pages during the first thirty years to five to six pages at the turn of the century, but the advertisements remained simple, mostly without illustration or special graphics, and always directly related to agricultural products. In 1898 the title reverted to *Country Gentleman*, and the editors explained that the double title including the *Cultivator* was cumbersome and anachronistic. They proclaimed "a paper of today and of tomorrow rather than of yesterday, fonder of looking forward into the twentieth century than back to the nineteenth." (January 6, 1898) The announcement presaged the modernization to come a decade later following the change in publishers, but *Country Gentleman* entered the twentieth century with few perceptible differences from a half-century earlier. In the late 1890s half-tones began to replace the etchings. While the writers in each department were nationally recognized specialists, the scope and purpose of their columns had changed little.

In 1911 Cyrus H. K. Curtis and his Curtis Publishing Company, publishers of *Ladies' Home Journal* and the *Saturday Evening Post** moved into a modern building on Independence Square in Philadelphia. Curtis almost immediately purchased *Country Gentleman*, as a means to acquire a third periodical without greatly increasing his overhead. Curtis was soon surprised to discover that only about 2,000 of a claimed 24,000 subscribers were not in arrears on their payments. The history of *Country Gentleman* soon entered a new generation. After about five years and an investment of $2 million, circulation began to boom and did not stop until it passed two and a half million in the mid-1940s. A revolution in agriculture had begun in the early twentieth century, and Curtis successfully predicted the trend and molded *Country Gentleman* to fit the new rural society.

While its subtitle proclaimed it as the oldest agricultural journal in the world, *Country Gentleman* soon left the dozens of other specialized farm magazines far behind in circulation. Technical publications and county agents existed for poultry, dairy, or other specialized interests. In essence, Curtis advocated for the modern farmer exactly what Tucker had promoted for the nineteenth-century farmer. *Country Gentleman* remained a general-interest or mass-market periodical. *Country Gentleman* promised improvement (and entertainment/culture) for a modernizing rural society that was deeply influenced by urbanization. Farming had become a business, and the new *Country Gentleman* examined marketing and product trends. How could production be increased? Luther Tucker had often raised the same question, but the context had changed.

The changes in *Country Gentleman* were highly visible. Curtis improved the paper on which *Country Gentleman* was printed to a coated white stock, and the cover boasted a full-page four-color illustration rather than a newspaper-style masthead. The layout and headlines for feature articles reflected a more modern and popular style. The space devoted to fiction increased, and well-known authors such as Zane Grey produced feature stories. The nature of the advertising in *Country Gentleman* also changed dramatically, with Kodak, Wrigley's, and dozens of other general products assuming a position beside implement promotions. Gone were most small ads for farm animals and products. In 1925 *Country Gentleman* became a monthly instead of a weekly. After over a half-century under the direction of the three Tuckers, the editorial turnover increased, with eight editors between 1911 and 1942.

Country Gentleman suffered greatly during the depression. The price fell from $1.50 per year to three years for $1.00. In the late 1920s some of the monthly issues had approached two hundred pages, but the length dropped to around fifty pages per issue in the 1930s.[6] The 1940s *Country Gentleman* expanded some of the features that had been popular fifty years earlier under the Tuckers such as recipes and patterns for women and floor plans for houses and barns. In 1953 Curtis reduced the size of *Country Gentleman* to 8″ x 10.5″, about half the 11″ x 14″ size since 1914. While the race for new subscribers was successful and readership grew from two to two and a half million, the magazine failed to increase its advertising revenues. The readership had become too urban, and the major advertisers demanded more rural subscribers. Curtis worked to promote *Country Gentleman* to farmers and even changed the title in a final desperate move to save the venerable magazine. The subtitle of the magazine had changed several times over the previous century, and ''The Magazine for Better Farming'' was added to the cover in August 1954. In January 1955, *Better Farming* became the title with ''Country Gentleman the magazine for'' in small type. Advertising in 1954 rose briefly to a record gross of $1 million and 508 advertisers, but a drastic decline in early 1955 coupled with increased production costs spelled the end of *Country Gentleman*. The August 1955 issue (vol. 125, no. 8) was the last published by Curtis.

In 1955 *Country Gentleman* was sold to its chief competitor, *Farm Journal*, for about $5 million. *Farm Journal* added some of the regular features of *Country Gentleman* and changed its title to *Farm Journal and Country Gentleman* in September 1955. Following the November 1956 issue, *Farm Journal* dropped *Country Gentleman* from its title. Nevertheless, the disappearance of *Country Gentleman* was not permanent, and a third and final generation of *Country Gentleman* appeared nearly two decades later. In 1975 Country Gentleman Publishing Company, a subsidiary of Curtis Publishing Company, chaired by Beurt SerVaas, revived *Country Gentleman* in Indianapolis. The first issue even used the old subtitle, "The oldest agricultural journal in the world," and carried forward the original volume numbering.[7] The new journal was quarterly and sold for $1.25 on the newsstands or $6.00 per year. Frederick A. Birmingham was the first of six editors during the revival, which was to last only seven years.

The editorial philosophy of the revival would have disturbed the Tuckers and even many of their successors at Curtis:

> Farming has become an industry. Yet there is still the "gentleman farmer" with only a couple acres, still the exurbanite and the suburbanite, not to overlook the man in a city apartment with dreams of open spaces in his heart—to all of whom this magazine is addressed.[8]

Country Gentleman now carried information for the enjoyment of country living, and the subtitle was soon changed to *The Magazine of Country Living*. The *Country Gentleman* of the Tuckers had been written for and read by farmers, and the loss of this audience by the *Country Gentleman* of Curtis Publishing Company had eventually doomed the magazine. The new *Country Gentleman* of the 1970s tried to take advantage of the urban and suburban popularity of *Country Gentleman* in the 1930s and 1940s, but the revival fared poorly and ceased in 1982. While an interest in the rural life style had once attracted millions of readers, by the 1970s the rural roots of American society had become too distant for a mass-market periodical for gentleman farmers to succeed.

Notes

1. *Country Gentleman*, 6 January 1853, p. 1.
2. Ibid.
3. Ibid., p. 8.
4. The price dropped to $2 in 1897, when *Country Gentleman* began to offer discounts on other publications such as *Life* and *Ladies' Home Journal* if subscribers paid their *Country Gentleman* subscription in advance. From the beginning the Tuckers had offered discounts for club or group purchases of *Country Gentleman*, and the lower price boosted circulation to a high under the Tuckers of about 50,000 in 1898.
5. The number of pages per year varied from 828 to 1,028 in the late nineteenth century.
6. In the 1940s and early 1950s the length was back up to around 200 pages per issue.

7. The winter 1975–1976 issue of the revived *Country Gentleman* mistakenly used the same number, vol. 125, no. 8, as the August 1954 issue.

8. *Country Gentleman*, Winter 1975–1976, p. 50.

Information Sources

BIBLIOGRAPHY

Bok, Edward W. *A Man from Maine*. New York: Charles Scribner's Sons, 1923.
Ogilvie, William Edward. *Pioneer Agricultural Journalists*. Chicago: Arthur G. Leonard, 1927, pp. 19–27.
"Luther Tucker." *Dictionary of American Biography*. 19:35–36.
Wood, James Playsted. *The Curtis Magazines*. New York: Ronald Press, 1971.
INDEX SOURCES
   Biological and Agricultural Index (1916–1955); *Access* (1975–1982).
LOCATION SOURCES
   Available in microform (1949–present).

Publication History

MAGAZINE TITLE AND TITLE CHANGES
   The Cultivator, 1834–1839; *The Genesee Farmer*, 1831–1839; *The Cultivator: A Consolidation of Buel's Cultivator and The Genesee Farmer*, 1840–1852; *The Country Gentleman*, 1853–1865; *The Cultivator & Country Gentleman*, 1865–1897; *The Country Gentleman*, 1898–1954; [*Better Farming*, 1955]; *Farm Journal and Country Gentleman*, 1955–1956; *Country Gentleman*, 1975–1982.
VOLUME AND ISSUE DATA
   Vols. 1–34, 1853–1869, weekly with semiannual volumes; vols. 35–90, 1870–1925, weekly with annual volumes; vols. 91–125, 1925–1955, monthly with annual volumes (skips from vol. 95 to vol. 101); vols. 125–132, 1975–1982, quarterly with annual volumes.
PUBLISHER AND PLACE OF PUBLICATION
   Luther Tucker & Sons, Albany, New York, 1853–1911; Cyrus H. K. Curtis, Curtis Publishing Company, Philadelphia, Pennsylvania, 1911–1955; Graham Patterson, Farm Journal, Inc., Philadelphia, 1955–1956; and Beurt SerVaas, Country Gentleman Publishing Company, a subsidiary of Curtis, Indianapolis, Indiana, 1975–1982.
EDITORS
   Luther Tucker, 1853–1873; Luther H. Tucker, 1873–1897; Gilbert M. Tucker, 1897–1911; J. Clyde Marquis, 1911–1912; Harry A. Thompson, 1912–1917; Barton W. Currie, 1917–1920; John E. Pickett, 1920–1924; Loring A. Schuler, 1924–1928; Philip S. Rose, 1928–1940; Ben Hibbs, 1940–1942; Robert H. Reed, 1942–1955; Frederick A. Birmingham, 1975–1977; Starkey Flythe, Jr., 1977–1979; Kurt Owen, 1979; Bruce Kinnaird, 1979–1982; Melinda A. Dunlevy, 1982; Robert A Scott, 1982.

CIRCULATION
    10,000–50,000 (1853–1911); 2,000,000–2,500,000 (1920s–1955).

David Haury

CRAWDADDY

At its inception, *Crawdaddy* was hailed as the first magazine to treat rock music seriously. Previously rock had been covered only by trade magazines such as *Billboard* that were primarily concerned with a record's future on the charts or by teen fan magazines that gushed over rather than analyzed a musician and his work. *Crawdaddy* met a need, and throughout its erratic publishing history, it continued to be applauded for its intelligent analyses of the contemporary music scene.

Named after England's Crawdaddy Club, early home to the Rolling Stones and the Yardbirds, the first issue of *Crawdaddy* appeared on 7 February 1966– 500 copies of ten mimeographed pages of staple-bound yellow paper.[1] Its founder and sole contributor, Paul Williams, was a seventeen-year-old Swarthmore College freshman who believed that there was an audience for "intelligent writing about pop music" and that "someone in the United States might be interested in what others have to say about the music they like."[2] In writing about rock music, he wanted "not to judge the records (like a critic) or report on the scene (like a journalist) but to explore (as an essayist) the experience of listening to certain records and feeling the whole world through them."[3] *Crawdaddy* was to serve the music industry only in that it would promote music that might otherwise be overlooked, provide buyers with a critical evaluation of new works to help them make more informed choices, and offer artists a critical response to their work.[4]

The first issue included reviews of single records and one album, Simon and Garfunkel's *Sounds of Silence*. A later writer for *Crawdaddy* notes that the "style was crude and Paul's taste tended to make it sound too much like a folk magazine."[5] Still, *Crawdaddy* endured although the announced intention to publish weekly was abandoned when it took Williams over a month to produce the second issue (number 3) and five months to put out number 4.

With number 5 *Crawdaddy*'s editorial direction was becoming clear: feature articles on artists and the music industry, reviews of albums and singles, and Williams's news column, "What Goes On," gave the magazine "the definite impression of chronicling a fast-developing scene."[6] By this time Williams had been joined by Jon Landau, who contributed reviews of albums by the Fifth Dimension, the Byrds, and the Young Rascals as well as a feature article on a local New York group called the Remains.

With number 8, the original staple-bound format was replaced by a more traditional magazine one. Williams had also begun to attract other talented writers equally devoted to the idea that rock music was an art form, most notably Sandy

Pearlman and Richard Meltzer. Where Landau was noted for a critical style that combined close attention to musical detail with *auteur* criticism (the search for the artist in a piece of music), Pearlman and Meltzer were primarily interested in the music itself, not the personality that created the music. In addition, they approached their criticism with an offbeat sense of humor sometimes at odds with the serious criticism of Landau and others; pieces such as Meltzer's "A Goddam Great Second Cream Album" were not always well-received.[7] Ironically, Meltzer, the most irreverent of the early *Crawdaddy* writers, was also the most scholarly, one writer noting that his analyses "carry the erudition of a thesis on Nietzsche."[8] Meltzer's first piece for *Crawdaddy*, "The Aesthetics of Rock," consisted of selections from a book turned down by Grove Press because "they didn't understand it."[9] In it he writes, "Rock is the only possible future for philosophy and art."[10]

For ten more issues, until number 19, *Crawdaddy* continued to publish reviews and articles about the world of popular music—Pearlman on the Jefferson Airplane, Byrds, Doors, and Kinks; Williams on the Beach Boys, Stones, Beatles, and Smoky Robinson; Meltzer on whatever took his fancy; and Landau on Motown, Otis Redding, and Wilson Pickett. In a late 1967 interview Williams stated, "Rock 'n' roll has given us a whole new playground . . . we're creating a whole new esthetic."[11]

Enthusiasm, however, was not enough to sustain *Crawdaddy*, and with number 19, Williams turned over financial and editorial responsibility to Chester Anderson. *Crawdaddy* was no longer unique; *Rolling Stone** had appeared in late 1967 and serious rock criticism was also being published in newspapers and general-interest magazines. Anderson kept *Crawdaddy* alive for four more issues, until June 1969 (number 23), at which time it ceased publication. Landau began writing for *Rolling Stone* and the *Real Paper* and Pearlman and Meltzer for a new counterculture magazine titled *Fusion*.[12]

Crawdaddy appeared again in 1970 under the direction of Peter Stafford, printed on newsprint paper stock and in a tabloid format closely resembling *Rolling Stone*'s. The magazine consisted of two sections: the first composed of columns and reviews and the second of feature articles and interviews. Stafford's *Crawdaddy* lasted for fourteen monthly issues before once again folding.

Six months later *Crawdaddy* was resurrected for the last time, appearing biweekly under the editorship of Raeanne Rubenstein from 5 December 1971 (number 1), to 11 June 1972 (number 13). Then, for two monthly issues, Rubenstein served as coeditor with Peter Knobler, son of *Crawdaddy*'s publisher, Alfred Knobler. Knobler assumed sole editorship with the September 1972 issue (number 16), a position he would hold until *Crawdaddy*'s final demise in April 1979. Knobler had begun writing for *Crawdaddy* in 1968 while Williams was still editor and, following its failure in 1969, helped found and edit the short-lived tabloid *Zygote*.

The tabloid, two-section format begun by Stafford continued through September 1972 with section 1 consisting of columns and reviews and section 2 devoted to feature articles and interviews. In addition, *Crawdaddy* continued to broaden its coverage to include topics that touched on social, political, and cultural aspects of the 1970s counterculture other than music—film, art, politics, and alternative life styles.

Columns devoted primarily to music-oriented topics included "Whisperings," news of live performances; "Half Notes," newsy and gossipy items about musicians and other pop-culture personalities; and "AudiOhm," surveys of the latest audio equipment. Notable nonmusic columns included Paul Krassner's "The Naked Emperor," musings by the controversial editor of the *Realist* on whatever was on his mind at the moment—Lenny Bruce, Kennedy's assassination, or television; "Thrilling Wonder Stories," a column about science fiction; "Fanzines," a unique survey of fan magazines; and "Pot Shots," a collection of "buried" news items intended to reveal the absurdity of life in the United States and the nefariousness of our public officials.

Crawdaddy continued to publish insightful, intelligent reviews of popular music, primarily rock and occasionally jazz and blues. Country and folk artists were rarely reviewed unless, as in the case of Kris Kristofferson or Country Joe and the Fish, they appealed to a broad audience. In addition to records, *Crawdaddy* regularly reviewed films, stage productions, and books.

Music dominated *Crawdaddy*'s feature articles during this period, with at least two-thirds of an issue devoted to interviews with musicians and analyses of the current music scene. Notable features include a rare interview with Chuck Berry (16 April 1972) and a special issue on the music industry, "Inside the Music Business" (August 1972). At the same time *Crawdaddy* was exploring nonmusical topics of interest to the politically and socially conscious younger generation of the 1970s: interviews with John Cassavetes (5 March 1972) and Ralph Nader (11 June 1972), an article on the war in Bangladesh (2 April 1972), and a special issue on the beat generation, "Roots: Bohemia and the Ancestry of Hip," which asserts that the counterculture of the late 1960s and 1970s had its roots in the beat generation that preceded it (2 February 1972).

Beginning with the October 1972 issue (number 17), Knobler reinstated a traditional magazine format complete with glossy cover. The two-section distinction between feature articles and columns was eliminated. Calling the "new" *Crawdaddy* between feature articles and columns was eliminated. Calling the "new" *Crawdaddy* "professional, but not slick. Broad but not dull," Knobler announced that it would continue to expand its content to include those areas to which "rock and roll awareness leads: culture, politics, film, arts and leisure."[13] And indeed it did. Although *Crawdaddy* continued to publish lengthy reviews of current music and interviews with performers, music-oriented topics were featured less and less.

Still, *Crawdaddy* published many noteworthy columns and features. More or less regular contributors included the novelist William S. Burroughs; William Kunstler, the lawyer for the Chicago 7 and other antiestablishment figures;

Paul Williams, *Crawdaddy*'s founder and original editor; and Abbie Hoffman, then living underground and serving as "travel editor." Feature articles included interviews with John Lennon and Ken Kesey; a one-act play by Joseph Heller; Martin Mull interviewing Woody Allen; coverage of Watergate and the elections of 1972 and 1976; and several articles on the Jefferson Airplane that led Paul Williams to accuse *Crawdaddy* of being "stuck in the 1960's"[14]

Until December 1978, *Crawdaddy* continued to maintain a "precarious balance" between its musical and social-political coverage.[15] During this time Knobler indulged in frequent soul-searching and exhortations to his readers to help him determine what direction the magazine should take—"More rock'n roll? More fiction and satire? Fuller political coverage? All glossy color photos? What?"[16] Then, in the December 1978 issue (number 91), Knobler announced that *Crawdaddy*'s name would change to *Feature* beginning with the January 1979 issue.

In his first *Feature* editorial, Knobler wrote that the premier issue was "starting a new year with a new name and an original outlook." In truth, other than the name, little was new; contributors, columns, content, even the typeface went virtually unchanged. Indeed, "Crawdaddy" even appeared in small print above "Feature" on the cover. *Feature* lasted for only five monthly issues, until May 1979. With that issue, number 96, *Crawdaddy/Feature* ceased altogether.

There are any number of reasons for *Crawdaddy*'s failure to survive into the 1980s. Certainly when Paul Williams created it, it filled a void in the coverage of popular music. However, it fell victim to an erratic publishing history, stiff competition from the better-managed and more editorially consistent *Rolling Stone*, and, especially in its later years, a lack of editorial focus. And, finally, perhaps there was simply no more place for it, as Knobler intimated in his final *Crawdaddy* editorial. The underground had entered the mainstream; the counterculture that *Crawdaddy* wrote about and wrote for had become *the* culture.[17]

Notes

1. John Swenson, "Rock Dreams/Schemes: The History of *Crawdaddy!*," *Crawdaddy*, March 1976, p. 68. Early issues of *Crawdaddy* (1966–November 1971) were unavailable for examination. Information regarding these years was obtained from this and other secondary sources.

2. Paul Williams, "Got Off of My Cloud!" *Crawdaddy*, 7 February 1966, n.p.

3. "Williams, Paul (Steven)," *Contemporary Authors*, vol. 81–84 (1979).

4. Williams, "Got Off of My Cloud!" n.p.

5. Swenson. p. 67.

6. Ibid.

7. Ibid., pp. 68–69.

8. "Crawdaddy!" *Newsweek*, 11 December 1967, p. 114.

9. Swenson, p. 68.

10. R[ichard] Meltzer, *The Aesthetics of Rock* (New York: Something Else Press, 1970), p. 7.

11. "Crawdaddy!" *Newsweek*, p. 114.

12. Swenson, p. 69.

13. Peter Knobler, Editorial, *Crawdaddy*, October 1979, p. 4.

14. Paul Williams, "The Sources of the Nile," *Crawdaddy*, February 1973, p. 8.

15. Peter Knobler, Editorial, *Crawdaddy*, March 1975, p. 4.

16. Peter Knobler, Editorial, *Crawdaddy*, December 1974, p. 4.

17. Peter Knobler, Editorial, *Crawdaddy*, December 1978, n.p.

Information Sources

BIBLIOGRAPHY

"Crawdaddy!" *Newsweek*, 11 December 1967, p. 114.

Ginsburg, David D. "Rock Is a Way of Life: The World of Rock 'n' Roll Fanzines and Fandom." *Serials Review*, January/March 1979, pp. 29–46.

Meltzer, R[ichard]. *The Aesthetics of Rock*. New York: Something Else Press, 1970.

Rockwell, John. "Crawdaddy Party Mirrors Magazine." *New York Times*, 9 June 1976, p. 34.

Swenson, John. "Rock Dreams/Schemes: The History of *Crawdaddy!*" *Crawdaddy*, March 1976, pp. 67–69.

Williams, Paul. "Sources of the Nile." *Crawdaddy*, February 1973, p. 8.

"Williams, Paul (Steven)." *Contemporary Authors*, vol. 81–84, 1979.

INDEX SOURCES

Access (1975–1978); *Music Index* (1972–1978); *Popular Periodicals Index* (1973–1978).

LOCATION SOURCES

1970–1979: Library of Congress and many other libraries. 1966–1969: incomplete runs at Library of Congress and other libraries; a nearly full run in the Folklore Collection, Indiana University Library, Bloomington, Indiana. Available in microform.

Publication History

MAGAZINE TITLE AND TITLE CHANGES

Crawdaddy, 1966–1978; *Feature*, 1979.

VOLUME AND ISSUE DATA

Various inconsistent numbering systems and publishing dates. *Crawdaddy*: nos. 1–23, 1966–1969; vol. 4, 1970–1971(?); nos. 1–91, 1971–1978. *Feature*: nos. 92–96, 1979. Monthly.

PUBLISHER AND PLACE OF PUBLICATION

Crawdaddy Magazine, Inc.: Paul Williams, 1966–1970; Crawdaddy Publishing Company: Alfred Knobler, 1971–1978; Feature Publishing Company: Alfred Knobler, 1979.

EDITORS

Paul Williams, 1966–1969; Chester Anderson, 1969; Peter Stafford, 1970–1971; Raeanne Rubenstein, 1971–1972; Raeanne Rubenstein and Peter Knobler, 1972; Peter Knobler, 1972–1978.

CIRCULATION

Highest posted figures: *Crawdaddy*, 125,000 (1975–1978); *Feature*, 200,000 (1979).

Loretta Rielly

CULTIVATOR. See COUNTRY GENTLEMAN

D

DEBOW'S REVIEW

One of the leading magazines of the Old South, *DeBow's Review* promoted and defended Southern institutions and aspirations—economic, social, political, intellectual.[1] Although it ceased publication in 1880, its importance is still being felt: it is the premier source of information on antebellum Southern life and attitudes and the changes effected by the war.[2]

The inspiration for *DeBow's* was the Commercial Convention of the Southern and Western States that was held in Memphis in 1845 and presided over by John C. Calhoun. The central message of the convention was that the South, far behind the North in prosperity, could best close the gap not by engaging in politics but by exploiting its resources. At the convention was a young secretary named James Dunwoody Brownson DeBow, who was so impressed by this idea that he decided to found a magazine that would promote it.[3]

Although DeBow was young—he had been born in Charleston, South Carolina, in 1820—he was by no means callow. Left an orphan and in poverty at sixteen, he managed largely by his own efforts to continue his education beyond the public school, first at Cokesbury College, a small labor school, then at the College of Charleston, where he finished his studies in three years and graduated in 1843 at the head of his class. He was so diligent in his studies that his fellow students called him "Old DeBow."[4] After considering careers in religion, politics, and the law, he turned to journalism, publishing a series of articles in the *Southern Quarterly Review* and becoming its associate editor. The most notable of these articles was "The Northern Pacific; California, Oregon, and the Oregon Question," which, in addition to being widely discussed in the United States, found its way into Europe, where it was discussed by statesmen in Great Britain and France.[5] DeBow now had some critical respect and was ready to move on. In January of 1846, inspired by the commercial convention, he established his magazine, the *Commercial Review of the South and West*, otherwise known as *DeBow's Review*. Having noticed that many magazines had perished in his native Charleston, he selected a more promising location—New Orleans.[6]

Whereas the other leading Southern magazines of the time were literary, *DeBow's* was practical, even prosaic. DeBow recognized that biological needs precede intellectual ones, and that the undeveloped South and West necessarily placed "ploughshares before philosophy."[7] He selected as the motto for his magazine Thomas Carlyle's pronouncement "Commerce is King," believing in the basic importance of commerce for economic and social betterment, but his scope was actually much broader, as *DeBow's* first subtitle indicates: *A Monthly Journal of Trade, Commerce, Commercial Polity, Agriculture, Manufactures, Internal Improvements, and General Literature.*[8] Volume 1 contained such articles as "The Mississippi and Atlantic Railroad," "Morse's Magnetic Telegraph," "Agricultural Associations," "The Cotton Plant," "The Rice Plant," and "Louisiana Sugar." Some were written by DeBow, some were contributed by competent (though not necessarily prominent) men, and some were extracted from articles previously published.[9] But whatever their source, they addressed the need for the South to exploit its resources, develop its industry, strengthen its institutions, and forge an alliance with the West in economic competition with the North.[10]

By devoting his magazine to practical matters, DeBow thought he could avoid the problems faced by literary magazines like the *Southern Quarterly Review*, which had to struggle to survive. His magazine would not only survive, he thought, but prosper.[11]

Yet owing largely to readers who were poor and dispersed in comparison with Northern ones and to a $5-a-year subscription price, *DeBow's* struggled at the outset as much as its literary competitors. In 1848 it had fewer than one thousand subscribers, and two-thirds of these were behind in their payments.[12] *DeBow's* at this stage depended for its survival on subscriptions—advertising did not come much into play till later—and would have perished in 1848 if it had not been rescued financially by Maunsel White, a wealthy New Orleans merchant and sugar planter.[13]

The crisis over, *DeBow's* prospects brightened. Although DeBow never realized his dream of a lengthy subscription list, yet by 1855, through word of mouth and the services of roving subscription agents, he had amassed as many as 4,500 subscribers.[14] That number compared favorably, or at least kept pace, with the number of subscribers estimated for other $5-a-year magazines such as the *Southern Quarterly Review* and the *Southern Literary Messenger*.[15] Even the Northern *Hunt's Merchants' Magazine*, which DeBow took as his model, probably never attracted more subscribers than did *DeBow's Review*.[16] With an increased subscription list came some attention to advertising, and by 1856 DeBow was reaping large profits from this source.[17] And as the magazine grew in subscriptions and financial success, so did its influence. Praised from the beginning by various chambers of commerce and by such prominent men as

John C. Calhoun and Henry Clay, it had by 1855 become the voice of the South.[18]

DeBow shifted *DeBow's* focus according to conditions. When in the early 1850s he feared that abolitionists were threatening the existence of slavery, he published so many defenses of slavery that even he grew weary of the topic.[19] When in the middle of the 1850s the growing sectional controversy began to threaten the Union, he turned from economic defenses of the South to political ones.[20] When secession had been accomplished, he aimed at strengthening the economy of the Confederacy.[21] During the war, he managed to put out fourteen issues defending the Davis administration and boosting morale.[22] After the war, accepting the altered conditions, he devoted his magazine to the reestablishment of Southern prosperity.[23]

DeBow was thwarted in this last goal too. Learning that his brother, Frank, was seriously ill in New Jersey, he rushed to his bedside. There he was stricken himself, with peritonitis, and died a week later, in February 1867. Frank, who had been the business manager for *DeBow's*, died the following month.[24]

After DeBow's death, *DeBow's* declined rapidly. R. G. Barnwell, an agent, and Edwin Q. Bell, a staff member, continued *DeBow's* till 1868, when William MacCreary Burwell, a writer on economics, acquired the property and became editor. The magazine was suspended in 1870. Then in October 1879 L. Graham and Company took over, putting out four issues edited by Burwell, the last in June 1880. In 1884 the struggling *Agricultural Review* of New York acquired the magazine, but folded within the year.[25]

The name James D. B. DeBow has since fallen into oblivion, no doubt because of DeBow's association with "dull," practical subjects and with actions in lost causes—slavery, secession, the Confederacy.[26] But for those seeking information on the Old South and its transformation by the war, *DeBow's Review* remains an indispensable source.

Notes

1. Rollin Gustav Osterweis, *Romanticism and Nationalism in the Old South* (Gloucester, Mass.: P. Smith, 1964), p. 26; Herman Clarence Nixon, "DeBow's Review," *Sewanee Review*, January–March 1931, p. 54; Ottis Clark Skipper, *J. D. B. DeBow: Magazinist of the Old South* (Athens: University of Georgia Press, 1958), p. 215. Originally published in 1949, reprinted in 1964.

2. Nixon, p. 54, 61.

3. Frank Luther Mott, *A History of American Magazines* (Cambridge, vol. 2:1850–1865.: Harvard University Press, 1938), pp. 338–39; Skipper, p. 16.

4. Edward Reinhold Rogers, "Four Southern Magazines" (Ph.D. diss., University of Virginia, 1902), pp. 20–21; Skipper, pp. 2–11.

5. Skipper, pp. 12–15; W. D. Weatherford, *James Dunwoody Brownson DeBow*, Southern Sketches no. 3, (Charlottesville, Virginia: Historical Publishing, 1935), pp. 9–10.

6. Mott, 2:339.

7. Nixon, p. 56; Skipper, p. 21.
8. Osterweis, p. 159; Nixon, p. 55.
9. Skipper, pp. 22, 218.
10. Ibid., p. 218.
11. Ibid., p. 21.
12. Ibid., p. 24.
13. Ibid., p. 25; Nixon, p. 57.
14. Skipper, p. 88.
15. The circulation for the *Southern Literary Messenger*, in 1842, was probably about 4,000; the circulation for the *Southern Quarterly Review*, in 1846, was probably about 2,000. These estimates were taken from Frank Luther Mott, *A History of American Magazines*. (Cambridge: Harvard University Press, 1939), 1:645, 724.
16. Skipper, p. 218.
17. Ibid., p. 129.
18. Ibid., p. 26, 218.
19. Ibid., pp. 61, 93.
20. Ibid., p. 113.
21. Ibid., p. 131.
22. Ibid., p. 150.
23. Nixon, p. 58.
24. Mott, 2:348; Skipper, p. 223.
25. Mott, 2:348; Skipper, p. 215.
26. Skipper, pp. ix, 224.

Information Sources

BIBLIOGRAPHY

Francis, David W. "Antebellum Agricultural Reform in *DeBow's Review*." *Louisiana History*, 14, no. 2 (1973): 165–77.
Mott, Frank Luther. *A History of American Magazines*. 5 vols. Cambridge, Mass.: Harvard University Press, 1938. (Sketch of *DeBow's Review*, 2: 338–48.)
Nixon, Herman Clarence. "DeBow's Review." *Sewanee Review*, January-March 1931, p. 54–61.
Osterweis, Rollin Gustav. *Romanticism and Nationalism in the Old South*. Gloucester, Mass.: P. Smith, 1964, 1949. Originally published in 1949, reprinted in 1964.
Rogers, Edward Reinhold. "Four Southern Magazines." Ph.D. diss., University of Virginia, 1902.
Skipper, Ottis Clark. *J.D.B. DeBow: Magazinist of the Old South*. Athens: University of Georgia Press, 1958.
Tebbel, John. *The American Magazine: A Compact History*. New York: Hawthorne Books, 1969.
Weatherford, W. D. *James Dunwoody Brownson DeBow*. Southern Sketches no. 3. Charlottesville, Va.: Historical Publishing, 1935.
INDEX SOURCES
Poole's Index to Periodical Literature (1846–1870).
LOCATION SOURCES
Library of Congress and well over a hundred other libraries. Holdings tend to be incomplete. Available in microform.

Publication History

MAGAZINE TITLE AND TITLE CHANGES

The Commercial Review of the South and West: A Monthly Journal of Trade, Commerce, Commercial Polity, Agriculture, Manufactures, Internal Improvements, and General Literature, January 1846–June 1850 [cover title: *DeBow's Commercial Review of the South and West*, 1847–1850]; *DeBow's Review of the Southern and Western States: Devoted to Commerce, Agriculture, Manufactures*, July 1850–December 1852; *DeBow's Review and Industrial Resources, Statistics, etc.: Devoted to Commerce, Agriculture, Manufactures*, January 1853–July/August 1864; *DeBow's Review: Devoted to the Restoration of the Southern States*, January 1866–December 1867; *DeBow's Review: Agricultural, Commercial, Industrial Progress and Resources*, 1868–1880 [cover title: *DeBow's New Orleans Monthly Review*, April 1869–October 1870].

VOLUME AND ISSUE DATA

Vols. 1–34, January 1846–August 1864; After the War Series, vols. 1–8, January 1866–October 1870; New Series, vol. 1, nos. 1–4, October 1879–June 1880. Monthly.

PUBLISHER AND PLACE OF PUBLICATION

James Dunwoody Brownson DeBow, 1846–1867; Mrs. J. D. B. DeBow, 1867–1868; William MacCreary Burwell, 1868–1870; L. Graham & Company, 1879–1880. New Orleans, 1846–1852; Washington, 1853–1860; New Orleans, 1859–1861, Charleston, South Carolina, 1861–1862; Columbia, South Carolina, 1864; Nashville, Tennessee, 1866–1868; New Orleans, 1868–1870, 1879–1880.

EDITORS

James Dunwoody Brownson DeBow, 1846–1867; R. G. Barnwell and Edwin Q. Bell, 1867–1868; William MacCreary Burwell, 1868–1870, 1880.

CIRCULATION

Largely unknown, but it is estimated to have been 4,500 in 1855.

David R. Kohut

THE DEMOCRATIC REVIEW

Politics and literature, on the face of things, seem an odd combination from which to make a magazine. All the more remarkable, then, that the *Democratic Review*, under spirited editorial leadership, became one of nineteenth-century America's outstanding periodicals.

First issued in late 1837, the *United States Magazine and Democratic Review* proclaimed its intent to provide the nation with the finest literature on a scale not seen before. And the first issues were certainly auspicious, replete with original poetry and prose, literary criticism, and translations from Latin, Greek, and European authors. Preeminent among the writers for the *Review* was Nathaniel Hawthorne, whose stories were frequent features of the journal for many years, and who symbolized the literary excellence of the *Review*.

Hawthorne alone, however, by no means carried the monthly, for his works were very quickly joined by those of other leading or rising authors. Contributions by John Greenleaf Whittier, William Cullen Bryant, Francis Scott Key, William Gilmore Simms, and James Russell Lowell gave the *Review* a well-deserved reputation for quality. That reputation was enhanced later by the early poems of a young man calling himself Walter Whitman. And of similar caliber was the literary criticism, including book reviews, bibliographic essays, and "Marginalia" by Edgar Allan Poe.

The driving force that assembled this collection of America's best writing was the *Review*'s equally amazing founder and long-time editor, John O'Sullivan. An adventurer who dreamed grandiose schemes, and a fierce political partisan, O'Sullivan possessed the perfect combination of vision and efficiency to make the *Review* a success.[1] Generally charming, O'Sullivan could also be abrasive and annoying, and was characterised by Poe as "that ass O'Sullivan."[2] But whether he cajoled or carped, O'Sullivan did what was necessary in order to get excellent writers to write, and the success of the *Review* is directly attributable to the presence and efforts of O'Sullivan.

Excellent as was the *Review*'s literature, O'Sullivan himself was nothing if not political, and his journal was, as the title indicates, a political one. Mixed in among the literature were lengthy political opinions, essays on current affairs, and transcripts of speeches from Washington. The *Review* was established primarily as a voice for the Democratic party, but to label it according to today's parties, or by the labels "conservative" or "liberal," would be futile.

O'Sullivan, in fact, was rather independent in his thinking, so independent that the political nature of the *Review*, while its raison d'être, also became its nemesis. As the nation and the Democratic party became divided by region, O'Sullivan stayed above the fracas, criticizing Northern Democrats for abolitionist leanings, and blasting Southern Democrats for intransigence. His original independence was biting and bold. Probably as a result of his failure to be obsequious, O'Sullivan lost his bid for the government's printing contract, one of the plums for which he had been originally angling when founding the *Review*![3]

In spite of this rebuff, the *Review* strengthened its activity as a leading political voice, attracting essayists as eminent as were the literati: George Bancroft, Henry David Thoreau, Lewis Cass, and Samuel J. Tilden provided thoughtful and provocative points of view. Overwhelmingly, the theme of the *Review* was its enthusiastic nationalism, especially in the era of the Mexican War. It was, in fact, the *Review* that coined the phrase "Manifest Destiny," which would echo down through the years.[4]

Although its original composition of literature and politics remained basic to the *Review*, other features were tried with various results. An early attempt to report news was quickly scuttled, and other unsuccessful experiments were a section of New York gossip, double-columned pages, and even publication in a newspaper format. Ideas that worked included book reviews, literary news, and a regular section on business and economic information. Perhaps the feature that most distinguished the *Review* was its very fine series of political portraits, in which essays describing great (i.e., Democratic) men were accompanied by engravings of the subjects. The engravings have become justly famous, both for their quality of work and for their imaginative designs.

Ultimately, politics proved the albatross around the neck of the *Review*, committed as the magazine was to the fortunes of an increasingly divided and troubled Democratic party. Reflecting the position of Northern Democrats, the *Review* tried to defend the ideas of Southerners as well. Siding with the moderation of President James Buchanan, villifying abolitionists as troublemaking Whig or Republican agitators—such views became more and more difficult in perilous times.

The fortunes of the *Review* were finally tied to the presence of O'Sullivan, who was openly or covertly editor-in-chief of the journal until 1849. Those were the years of greatness and prosperity. After 1849, O'Sullivan left the *Review*, and the fortunes of the magazine declined.[5] Compared to the volumes of the first decade, the *Review* of the 1850s is obviously lacking the fine writers and the spark of before. Eventually, the lack of O'Sullivan and the increasingly impossible Democratic politics doomed the *Review*. Attempts at merger, cries for payment of subscriptions, and complaints of no worthy material, all mark the last issues of the *Review*, which sputtered to its end in 1859, shortly before the war that would decide with blood what ink could not.

As an example of intelligent political comment, combined with outstanding original literature, the *Democratic Review* carved for itself a remarkable niche in American history.

Notes

1. Julius W. Pratt, "John Louis O'Sullivan," *Dictionary of American Biography*, ed. Allen Johnson and Dumas Malone, 20 vols. (New York: Charles Scribner's Sons, 1934), 14:89.

2. Edgar Allan Poe, letter of 12 September 1842 in *The Complete Works*, ed. James A. Harrison, 17 vols. (New York: Thomas Crowell, 1902), 17:117–18.

3. Frank Luther Mott, *A History of American Magazines*, vol. 1, 1741–1850 (Cambridge: Harvard University Press, 1957), p. 679.

4. Julius W. Pratt, "The Origin of 'Manifest Destiny,' " *American Historical Review*, July 1927, p. 795–99.

5. Ibid., p. 796.

Information Sources

BIBLIOGRAPHY

Mott, Frank Luther. *A History of American Magazines*, vol. 1, 1741–1850. Cambridge: Harvard University Press, 1957. pp. 677–684.

Poe, Edgar Allan. *The Complete Works*. Ed. James A Harrison. 17 vols. New York: Thomas Crowell, 1902.

Pratt, Julius W. "The Origin of 'Manifest Destiny,' " *American Historical Review*, July 1927, pp. 795–99.
———. "John Louis O'Sullivan." *Dictionary of American Biography*. Ed. Allen Johnson and Dumas Malone. 20 vols. New York: Charles Scribner's Sons, 1928. 14:89.
INDEX SOURCES
  Poole's Index to Periodical Literature, vol. 1 (1838–1859).
LOCATION SOURCES
  Library of Congress; many other libraries listed in the *Union List of Serials* 5:4320. Available in microform.

Publication History

MAGAZINE TITLE AND TITLE CHANGES
  The United States Magazine and Democratic Review, 1837–1851; *Democratic Review*, 1852; *The United States Review and State Rights Register*, August 1853–November 1854; *The United States Review*, 1853–1855; *The United States Democratic Review*, 1856–1859.
VOLUME AND ISSUE DATA
  Vols. 1–38, October 1837–December 1856, monthly. Vol. 39, January-June 1857, weekly. Vols. 40–42, July 1857–December 1858, monthly. Vol. 43, April-October 1859, quarterly. Vols. 30–31 also called New Series, vols. 1–2. Vols. 32–38 also called New Series, vols. 1–7. Vols. 9–29, 40–41 also called New Series. Suspended November-December 1837, August 1838, January-June 1841, October 1853–May 1854, January and June 1859.
PUBLISHER AND PLACE OF PUBLICATION
  Langtree & O'Sullivan, 1837–1839; S. D. Langtree, 1840; Washington, D.C. J. & H. G. Langley, 1841–1843; Henry G. Langley, 1844–1845; J. L. O'Sullivan & O. C. Gardiner, 1846; H. Wickoff, 1846–1849; Kettell & Moore, 1849–1851; D. W. Holly, 1852; Theodore A. Foster, 1853; Lloyd & Brainard, 1854; Lloyd & Campbell, 1855; Wright, Cone, & Co., 1856; Lloyd & Co., 1856; Conrad Swackhamer, 1857–1859; New York.
EDITORS
  J. L. O'Sullivan and S. D. Langtree, 1837–1839; S. D. Langtree, 1839–1840; J. L. O'Sullivan, 1841–1846; Thomas Prentice Kettell, 1846–1851; George N. Sanders, 1852; Theodore A. Foster et al., 1853; D. W. Holly, 1854–1855; Spencer W. Cone, 1856; Conrad Swackhamer, 1857–1858; Conrad Swackhamer and Isaac Lawrence, 1859.
CIRCULATION
  n.a.

Daniel Boice

THE DIGEST: REVIEW OF REVIEWS. See LITERARY DIGEST

DOMAIN. See TEXAS MONTHLY

DRESS AND VANITY FAIR. See VANITY FAIR

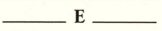

E

EARLY AMERICAN LIFE

From an inauspicious start as a magazine intended to serve a limited clientele, *Early American Life* has gone on to prove its mass audience appeal and durability. Beginning with a first issue printing estimate of a mere 5,000 copies,[1] the magazine's circulation has exceeded 300,000 since its tenth year. During the nearly two decades since its creation in 1970, it has changed addresses more frequently than publishers or editors; and that, seldom. Three editors and three publishers have shaped its pages. Four addresses in three states have been home to the publication, two of its three moves occurring during the first couple of years.

Founding editor James E. Betts initially planned only to determine and meet the interests and needs of the select membership of the newly formed Early American Society, and to promote attendance at museums and historic sites. In keeping with the publication's emphasis on decorating, Betts chose the serial's title as indicative of "furnishing that is traditional, comfortable, warm and secure."[2] He set out to span several centuries of early American arts and crafts "from hand-carved wooden spoons to canning—log huts to plastic replicas."[3] The magazine's current range of years is from approximately 1600 to 1900.

The Early American Society was to be a small organization catering to an elite group of early American buffs.[4] Membership in the organization was to include a subscription to *Early American Life*. However, it became apparent early on that demand was heavier than anticipated. The initial print run was upped to 8,000 copies, and was still insufficient. In one year's time, the Early American Society claimed a membership (and *Early American Life*, a readership) of 30,000. At first, Betts intended to expand the bimonthly magazine to a monthly one by the third issue. That plan, although revived in late 1972, was never realized. Instead, the staff opted for the larger, bimonthly issues that would hold subscription rates down.

By the middle of the second year, a statement appearing on the magazine's masthead summarized its broader purpose, as then perceived:

> *Early American Life* is the official magazine of the Early American Society, Inc., the national organization of persons interested in advancing their understanding of American social history and in modern interpretations of early arts, crafts, furnishings, and architecture. The magazine is owned by the Society and published under the direction and control of its board of directors.[5]

During the third year of publication, gardening was added to the list of covered topics. By that time, the magazine had a narrowed focus reflecting then-editor Robert G. Miner's (and, presumably, readers') interests in "shut[ting] out the world and its problems."[6] The staff perceived its role to be, in part, providing a respite from the overly introspective times. The magazine was, and is, decidedly apolitical. Early perspectives are still apparent. Present-day issues maintain the commitment to the history of the daily lives of common people and attempt to both entertain and inform readers.

The dual emphasis on entertaining and informing is perhaps pivotal to the magazine's success. From the first issue, editors' columns have included requests for reader input in the form of questions, suggestions, observations, picture postcards, and clippings. The magazine is characterized, not by sophisticated statistical data, but rather by an editorial staff that pays attention. The steady, quietly-going-about-their-business approach works.

From the beginning, an effort was made not only to listen to readers already acquired but to attract a certain type of readership. Early issues were offered free of charge to clubs and organizations. When Historical Times assumed control, group discounts were offered to historical societies and folk groups at all levels from local to regional to national.

A genuine concern for responsiveness to needs coupled with low subscription rates has encouraged the active participation of many more people than Betts envisioned serving. The magazine was first offered at a rate of $6 per year ($1 per issue). Its current rate of $15 per year ($3 per issue) maintains it as a relatively inexpensive publication.

The content has been so true and consistent that a first-year reader who returned to it today, not having read the publication in the intervening eighteen-years, would still recognize and identify with it. Major articles have involved social history, travel, cooking, gardening, furniture, crafts, and home plans. Special features have included instructions in setting up and conducting a festival, how-to articles on home restoration with bargaining hints on purchasing a house to restore, origins of sayings and expressions, tombstoning as a hobby, America's first woman realtor, Christmas in a variety of historical settings, apartment decorating in early American style, and Thomas Jefferson's garden.

The variety and currency of topics keep the magazine lively. Travel articles, by nature of the time period covered emphasizing the original colonies, have included information on historical sites in many states. Among many that stand out were articles about Eric Sloane's museum of early tools, the top historic sites and landmarks in the United States, Mackinac Island, and historical farms. Dishes discussed have ranged from portable soup, to summer drinks, to waffles and wafers (along with photographs and descriptions of antique waffle irons), to prize dishes from inns.

Reader preference for how-to information is evident in regular columns over the years, as well as features. Among these are crafts articles on such topics as collecting pressed glass, designing sconces, pewter-casting, constructing a Lexington cradle, sewing curtains, and making corn husk dolls. A continuing series on simple furniture that amateur carpenters can build has included a trestle table, quilt racks, bookcases, a chest, colonial farm lanterns, and information about easy-assembly kits. Regular question-and-answer columns deal with restoring, constructing, collecting, and investing. A Merit Award Program of several years' duration included reader-submitted photographs of completed craft and furniture projects.

Related series, beginning with the first year of publication with plans developed by William Thompson, include house plans and designs by on-staff architects. These have ranged from preexisting plans to designs commissioned for the Early American Society. The plans have kept abreast of the times, as evidenced by a passive solar post and beam house once featured.

In addition to the articles, the magazine has been noted for special projects sponsored by the Early American Society or by the National Historical Society. These have included charter bus tours, motor tour maps, a Mississippi River cruise on the *Delta Queen*, and discount coupons to historic sites. Over the years, the Early American Society has marketed special items to members, including traditional quilts, needlepoint kits, a reproduction of a nineteenth-century schoolmaster's desk, and one of an eighteenth-century gaming table. One of the most distinctive products offered was Early American Sites notepaper, which featured a color print of historic buildings and ships. The artwork on the stationery, from an original painting by Jack Woodson, adorned the cover of *Early American Life* for several years.

The original edition of *Early American Life* was the work of one man: founder and first editor James E. Betts. What began as a hobby of early Americana became an obsession: so certain was he of interest and demand, Betts put everything into the infant publication. His early editorial columns were often apologetic in tone, because his involvement in related projects (such as bicentennial plans), and the rapid and unexpected growth of membership, meant delays in publication. Nonetheless, by the end of the first year, he had recouped an initial investment of $25,000 and developed a loyal, devoted readership.[7] Betts oversaw a move of the Early American Society from its first home in Richmond, Virginia, to one in Annapolis, Maryland, during the nearly two years that he ran the society and its publication; first, by himself; later, with a small staff of mostly part-time devotees.

Robert Gordon Miner's ten-year reign as editor began in mid–1971, when the Early American Society became a subsidiary of Historical Times. As a twenty-year publishing veteran and former publisher of *Home Garden* magazine, he was hired to run *Early American Life* by the organization. The changeover was apparently amicable. Betts stayed on as consulting editor while Miner praised his work and noted the personal interest evident among the magazine's growing readership.

The magazine's editorial column, previously known as the "President's Report," became "The Weathervane." It was through the column that Miner set the tenor for the magazine. He further refined the original concept, enhanced *Early American Life's* homespun, informal qualities, and emphasized the publication's function as a haven from a troubled world. The editor's column became a series of friendly chats with readers, not unlike some of the regular columns in the magazine. By turns, the column was filled with practical advice and reassurances on restoring and collecting, reminiscences, descriptions of travel, and the saga of Bob and Betty Miner's restoration of the oldest house in Mechanicsburg, Pennsylvania.

Miner's editorship and the relationship with Historical Times provided a favorable climate for the Early American Society. Circulation grew from 25,000 to over 300,000. What had now become a complete full-time staff was housed in Gettysburg, Pennsylvania. *Early American Life* meshed well with the other publications of its parent organization and with the intent and purpose of the National Historical Society, devoted not to scholarly interests, but to amateur interests in everyday history.

The December 1982 issue marked Miner's announced retirement and the last mention of the Early American Society. After assuming the helm, the present editor, Frances Carnahan, reminisced about her interview with Miner during his first year as editor. She noted it was more a friendly visit than a formal job interview, and that she was hired on the basis of "mutual enthusiasm for old houses, for fine craftsmanship, for travel, for reading, for good food—the very stuff of *Early American Life*."[8] As his predecessor had done, Miner continued to contribute to the magazine after his departure. Carnahan's editorial column, called "The Keeping Room," bears the same personable sense of warmth and sharing that has typified the editorials through the years. Her regard for her former boss is evident in the continuance of tradition.

In 1982, *Early American Life* was acquired by Cowles Magazines of Harrisburg, Pennsylvania. Major differences since its acquisition have been in the cover layout, the number and frequency of color photographs, and the slick paper (once a heavy ivory). Content remains consistent with that of earlier years, and the continued rise in circulation attests to its popularity.

In summary, *Early American Life* has maintained content while undergoing a number of minor shifts. The publication has shifted from a vehicle for collectors and buffs to a resource for amateurs, from vendor-oriented to member-oriented, from near-scholarly to practical, from esoteric to commercial, and from 100 percent staff-contributed to 70 percent free-lance written.[9] Those shifts, although following a path different from that originally intended, have increased readership by responding to readers' initiatives.

Notes

1. James E. Betts, "President's Report," *Early American Life*, January-February 1970, p. 4.
2. Ibid., p. 47.
3. Ibid.
4. James E. Betts, "President's Report," *Early American Life*, September-October 1970, p. 7.
5. *Early American Life*, July-December 1971, p. 3.
6. Robert G. Miner, "The Weathervane," *Early American Life*, March-April 1972, p. 62.
7. James E. Betts, "President's Report," *Early American Life*, January-February 1971, p. 5.
8. Frances Carnahan, "The Weathervane," *Early American Life*, April 1982, p. 1.
9. Becky Hall Williams, ed., "Early American Life," *Writer's Market* (Cincinnati: Writer's Digest Books, 1987), p. 328.

Information Sources

BIBLIOGRAPHY
Early American Life back issues, 1970–present, especially editorial columns by James E. Betts, Robert G. Miner, and Frances Carnahan.
Gill, Kay, and Donald P. Boyden, eds. *Gale Directory of Publications*. 120th ed. vol. 1. Detroit: Gale Research, 1988.
Katz, Bill, and Linda Sternberg Katz. *Magazines for Libraries*. 5th ed. New York: R. R. Bowker, 1986.
Taft, William H. *American Magazines for the 1980s*. New York: Hastings House, 1982.
Ulrich's International Periodicals Directory, 1987–88. 26th ed. vol. 1. New York: R. R. Bowker, 1987.
Williams, Becky Hall, ed. *Writer's Market*. Cincinnati: Writer's Digest Books, 1987.
INDEX SOURCES
Access: The Supplementary Index to Periodicals (1976–present) *America: History and Life; Historical Abstracts; Index to How to Do It Information; Magazine Index* (1977–present).
LOCATION SOURCES
Library of Congress and many other libraries. Available in microform.

Publication History

MAGAZINE TITLE AND TITLE CHANGES
Early American Life, 1970–present.

VOLUME AND ISSUE DATA
     Vols. 1–19, January-February 1970–present, bimonthly.
PUBLISHER AND PLACE OF PUBLICATION
     Early American Society, Inc., 1970–1971; Early American Society as subsidiary
     of Historical Times, Inc., 1971–1982; Cowles Magazines, Inc., 1982–present.
     Harrisburg, Pennsylvania.
EDITORS
     James E. Betts, 1970–1971; Robert G. Miner, 1971–1981; Frances Carnahan,
     1981–present.
CIRCULATION
     366, 349.

                                                          Patricia A. Cannon

ESQUIRE

Beginning in 1933, during the middle of the depression, at what was considered the outrageous price of fifty cents per issue, *Esquire* surprised everyone by becoming one of the most successful magazines in the history of American publishing. Credit for its success lies with its founding editor, Arnold Gingrich, who combined publishing the leading writers of America with humor and a slick style. Although changes in look and content have occurred over the years, the style remains, making it as successful today as it was over fifty years ago.

Esquire's byline, "Man at his best," defines its audience and its emphasis. The first issue specified its aim "to become the common denominator of masculine interests—to be all things to all men."[1] This goal was reasserted in 1987 when the current editor-in-chief, Lee Eisenberg, stated that the magazine was for "men who are men." It is " ... a kind of sanctuary, where we can share the male experience with like-minded friends, there to stimulate the mind and senses."[2]

Not surprisingly, men make up the majority of readers. However, the 35 percent female audience suggests that the magazine does carry a nongender appeal. While it covers subjects such as business, sports, and fashion angled toward a male perspective, it also publishes features ranging from national and international politics to fiction.

As the title *Esquire* denotes, the target group reading this publication are men of a certain social rank. While the audience has varied over the years, their main readership rests in the middle-to upper-income bracket: college-educated, often professional men, aged twenty-five to forty-five.[3] Until 1933, the males in this audience had no magazine geared toward them, which could partially explain why it became so instantly popular. However, the creators of *Esquire* were not quite sure just what type of publication they were creating in the beginning.

David Smart and his brother, Alfred Smart, began in advertising in 1921 in Chicago; they were joined in 1927 by William H. Weintraub. One of their main interests was menswear, and they ventured into advertising booklets as a way to inform buyers in local retail shops about the latest products. Encouraged by the moderate success of three ad booklets, the *Observer, Club and Campus*, and *Gentleman's Quarterly*,* they decided to enter the menswear field in full force.

Apparel Arts, a very colorful and successful trade publication, was the result. As David Smart explained, "The idea was to give the customer something to consult so that he would not have to depend on the taste of the clerk or tailor."[4] Even at the $1.50 price, the publication sold well. The Smarts and Gingrich adapted this idea to two other trade journals, *Homefurnishing Arts* and *Fabrics and Fashions*.[5]

While retailers were very happy with *Apparel Arts*, they missed the ad booklets. They suggested the firm could publish a fashion booklet to sell to their customers for ten cents. That was the seed of the idea for *Esquire*: to sell a magazine to men geared toward their interests, through clothing stores.

With Roosevelt's New Deal came a new optimism. The time was ripe for *Esquire* to attract a new man of leisure: the one who worked a five-day week and had time to read, relax, and think about the finer things in life. The high style that had made the Smarts' and Gingrich's trade booklets a success would provide the format.

Original plans were to publish 100,000 copies for the clothing stores, and 5,000 for the newsstands on a quarterly basis, beginning with the autumn 1933 issue. That was considered a large number in 1933. However, they hoped to commit clothing stores to the idea before going to press. They did not expect to sell even half of the 5,000 going to the newsstands. But the day it went on sale, the newsstand copies were sold out in five hours, and they pulled 95,000 copies back before shipping them off to clothing stores.[6] The newsstand response was so great that they immediately started plans to publish monthly beginning in January 1934.

Arnold Gingrich (1903–1976), one of their young employees, served as editor for both *Apparel Arts* and *Esquire*. Raised in Grand Rapids and a graduate of the University of Michigan, Gingrich wanted to be a writer. Before graduating, he was secretly married, knowing that his wife's mother would not approve. When the young couple did tell her, she agreed to give her blessing only if Gingrich held a job paying fifty dollars per week. With this motivation, he talked and worked his way into copywriting for a small advertising firm.[7] He joined forces with the Smarts and Weintraub as a copywriter late in 1928, writing radio scripts and novels on the side. With the *Esquire* assignment, he was destined to become one of the notable editors of American publishing.

Gingrich met Ernest Hemingway through a mutual friend, the owner of a bookstore in New York. Hemingway was already well known and could demand top dollar for his work. *Esquire* did not have unlimited funds, but Gingrich suggested that Hemingway write a column as he traveled about, at twice the pay other writers were receiving. It was agreed.

On the success of *Esquire*, Gingrich said, "Hell, I just went around New York with a checkbook signing up people I like and then naturally they wrote

things I liked and I printed them. After that, the mailman was our best friend.''[8]
The Hemingway name helped attract other top writers, resulting in an impressive
list of writers for the new magazine. Appearing in the first issue were Ernest
Hemingway, John Dos Passos, George Ade, Erskine Caldwell, Dashiell Ham-
mett, and Ring Lardner among others. Bobby Jones, the famous golfer, contributed an article on putting, and James T. Farrell reviewed books.

The whole tone of this publication was quality: quality clothes, writing, art,
photography, and features. Throughout *Esquire*'s history the drive for quality
has often yielded impressive results. Most notable was the first publication of
Hemingway's "The Snows of Kilimanjaro" in August 1936.

Gingrich also became a friend of F. Scott Fitzgerald. He told the story of how
the auditor at *Esquire* was tired of paying out money to authors who were not
submitting work. Fitzgerald complained of writer's block because he could no
longer write stories about young love for the *Saturday Evening Post.** Gingrich
suggested that he should write about that block. The result was the three stories
of ''The Crack Up.''[9]

There are too many authors who have published in *Esquire* to list them all
here.[10] Notables include Theodore Dreiser, H. L. Mencken, John Steinbeck,
Ezra Pound, Irwin Shaw, James Jones, Arthur Miller, Philip Roth, Stanley Elkin,
Bernard Malamud, Flannery O'Connor, Raymond Carver, William Kotzwinkle,
Ivan Bashevis Singer, John Cheever, James Baldwin, William Styron, Tim
O'Brien, John Updike, Jim Harrison, John Gardner, William Faulkner, Joseph
Heller, Saul Bellow, Kurt Vonnegut, Dorothy Parker, Robert Penn Warren,
Tennessee Williams, Joyce Carol Oates, John Gregory Dunne, and Joan Didion.
The list just touches the surface, and omits many well-known writers who have
contributed to the reputation of the magazine.

Esquire also searched for new and fresh voices to publish in its pages. During
the Gingrich years, it sponsored College Film Festivals aimed at talented young
filmmakers, Business in the Arts Awards, Corporate Social Responsibility
Awards, and writing seminars at campuses across the country. These activities
were reported in the magazine as a part of its effort to keep readers aware of
creative trends in the country, and to support new talent.

The cartoons appearing in the first issue were a full page, many in color, and
were featured throughout the issue. Full-page cartoons had appeared before in
the *New Yorker*, but this was the first time they were published in color. Gingrich
gives the cartoons much credit for the initial success of the magazine. ''Without
a doubt, it was the full-page cartoons in color, an ingredient that we hadn't even
thought of in the first place, that catapulted the magazine's circulation from the
start. They were such a novelty as almost to seem to lend the magazine another
dimension.''[11]

The cartoons often centered on the leering man and the barely dressed, beautiful
woman. Esky, a bug-eyed man with a moustache, typically dressed in tails, was
adopted as the magazine's trademark. Created by cartoonist E. Simms Campbell,
Esky first appeared on the cover of the January 1934 issue. He was to remain

on the cover, in one form or another, until 1978. His last appearance was as a formalized dot on the "i" in the magazine's title.

Esquire has never retreated from controversy. An early piece called "Latins Are Lousy Lovers," written anonymously in 1936 by Helen Lawrenson, caused such an uproar in Cuba that the magazine was banned and issues confiscated there. The magazine was confiscated again a month later when it published a reply to the incident with an editorial entitled "The Latin Lack of a Sense of Humor."

Humor is an *Esquire* forte, along with its hard-hitting, controversial subject matter. In 1970, it published a series of interviews with Lt. William Calley about Vietnam and the My Lai incident. The brutally truthful descriptions are said to have cost the publication advertisers. This represents the magazine's approach: to go after the unique, new, and challenging story, filling it with features that were more substantial than last week's news. *Esquire* published stories that stood by themselves, on subjects present on everyone's mind. Its early issues still read as absorbing accounts today.

Not only did *Esquire* publish controversial stories, but it also used controversial methods. The February 1976 issue printed an article titled "Travel Through America" by Harrison E. Salisbury, sponsored by and paid for by Xerox Corporation. Xerox could pay the author a much higher fee than *Esquire*, and also guaranteed the magazine $115,000 worth of additional advertising. *Esquire* kept editing rights and full ownership of the article.[12] As far as *Esquire* was concerned, this was patronage, similar to Xerox's sponsoring a television show. However, the media response proved intense. The joint effort was thought to be crossing sacred lines between business and free expression.

In recent years the June and December issues often center around a theme. For the fiftieth anniversary issue, they explored "How We Lived" from 1933 to 1983. Other issues have been titled "The American Man" and "Man Power." In 1984 *Esquire* introduced "The Best of a New Generation," a register of people who are leaders or innovators in their fields. This register is updated yearly. In addition, every January, *Esquire* publishes its "Dubious Achievements" for the year, a humorous look at the not so great moments of the previous year.

Esquire always welcomed criticism, and the beautiful women featured in cartoons, drawings, or photographs often caused much comment through the early years. Artist George Petty became famous for his drawings of women, as did Alberto Vargas later. In the 1940s *Esquire* featured the Petty and "Vargas" girls in foldouts. The presence of these beautiful women made the postmaster general, Frank C. Walker, nervous enough in 1943 to request a hearing to cancel *Esquire's* right to use second-class postage. A three-year battle with the U.S. Post Office ensued. Second-class postage is reserved for magazines being "originated and published for the dissemination of information of a public character or devoted to literature, the sciences, arts, or some special industry." The Post Office found *Esquire* to be obscene, lewd, and lascivious.[13] *Esquire* recruited famous authors in its defense, including H. L. Mencken, and enlisted psychologists to defend the "Vargas" girls.

Esquire won its case by a unanimous decision of the Supreme Court in early 1946. Justice William O. Douglas's opinion stated that supporting the postmaster general would give the Post Office "a power of censorship abhorrent to our traditions." It asserted that "a requirement that literature or art conforms to some norm prescribed by an official smacks of an ideology foreign to our system."[14]

The foldout lasted until 1957. By that time the more revealing foldouts of *Playboy** were being published.[15] *Esquire* does, however, maintain an interest in women. In fact, the August 1988 cover story is titled "The Women We Love." The women listed were chosen for "the qualities we crave: wit and power and guts and glamour and mystery and depth."[16]

Arnold Gingrich left to live in Europe in 1946, and David Smart took over as editor. The magazine began publishing light fiction, more mysteries and Westerns rather than the frequent highbrow fiction of the thirties. In 1952, the year Smart died, Gingrich returned to reestablish *Esquire's* original direction and standards.

Gingrich felt that for *Esquire* to continue to appeal to its targeted audience, men aged twenty-five to forty-five, it had to have men that age shaping the magazine. Gingrich had just turned thirty when he first started editing the magazine. To this end, in the late 1950s, Gingrich brought in a team of editors he called the "Young Turks" : Harold Hayes, Clay Felker, Ralph Ginzburg, and Rust Hills. They brought to *Esquire* what was called the "new journalism," represented by Tom Wolfe, Gay Talese, Norman Mailer, and Truman Capote. Harold Hayes emerged the leader of the group and took over as editor from 1963 to 1973.

It was during the Hayes period that advertising man George Lois was brought in to design the now famous covers. Like the articles inside, these covers could be entertaining or disturbing. A head shot of Sonny Liston dressed as Santa Claus, for example, at once makes fun of the traditional image of Santa, while also expressing a sense of racial rage. A cover concerning pop art pictures Andy Warhol, with arms outstretched, sinking into a huge open can of Campbell's Soup. The covers in themselves brought *Esquire* praise and criticism.

Gingrich died in 1976, and *Esquire* began a series of new ownerships. A company had grown up around the magazine, of which publishing was only a small part. Because the magazine was losing money it was sold to a British company, Associated Newspapers Group, and Clay Felker in 1977. Felker had been on *Esquire's* editorial staff in the late 1950s, but had gone on to establish *New York** magazine. He converted his new acquisition into *Esquire Fortnightly*, but circulation, already in trouble, continued to drop.

In 1979, the magazine was again sold, this time to a small publishing concern called 13–30 Corporation of Knoxville, Tennessee. The young blood of this energetic company brought *Esquire* back to life. H. Christopher Whittle, thirty-one, became the publisher, and Phillip Moffitt, thirty-two, the editor. *Esquire* was reestablished as a monthly, and many of the long-time editors were retained to help restore the successful formula of the magazine. These included Rust Hills, Byron Dobel, Don Erickson, and Lee Eisenberg.

By the time *Esquire* reached the age of fifty, it was again a profitable venture. The two young outsiders turned the magazine around and raised circulation back up to the 700,000 mark, where it has remained. In 1987 Whittle and Moffitt sold the magazine to Hearst Corporation, but left Lee Eisenberg as editor-in-chief.

Established in 1933, *Esquire* has had the ability to adapt with the times. Sometimes bold, sometimes brash, it rings of American style and humor. Arnold Gingrich's edict—"He edits best who edits least"—allowed for a free range of literary styles, often new and challenging. In the Fiftieth Anniversary Collector's Issue, Gay Talese said:

> More saucy than sophisticated, incessantly skeptical but never reactionary, *Esquire* depicted through its fiction and reportage the vast range of America's conscience and conflict; and though the level of *Esquire's* prose was often uneven, like the configuration of the country it covered, the magazine maintained throughout Gingrich's lifetime, and beyond it . . . what he once called an editor's most essential talent: "a continuing sense of wonder."[17]

Notes

1. *Esquire*, Autumn 1933, p. 3.

2. *Esquire*, April 1987, p. 1.

3. The median age is thirty-four and the median income is $34,119 according to the "Esquire Readership Profile," spring 1987 Mediamark Research, Incorporated figures. Very similar figures are found in the *Esquire Subscribers Survey*, prepared for Esquire by Universal Marketing Research, March 1965.

4. Henry F. Pringle, "Sex, Esq.," *Scribner's Magazine*, March 1938, p. 36.

5. In 1957, *Apparel Arts* and *Fabrics and Fashions* would be combined into the consumer publication *Gentleman's Quarterly*.

6. Arnold Gingrich, *Nothing But People* (New York: Crown Publishers, 1971), p. 106.

7. The complete story is in the chapter titled "What Makes the Wheels Go Round," in *Toys of a Lifetime* by Arnold Gingrich (New York: Alfred A. Knopf, 1966), p. 259.

8. "Some Words and Pictures about Arnold Gingrich, Founding Editor of Esquire, 1903–1976," *Esquire*, October 1976, p. 66.

9. Arnold Gingrich, *Nothing But People*, pp. 241–43. Also, this story told in "Arnold Gingrich, Esquire" by Harold T. P. Hayes, *New Republic*, 4 September 1976, p. 35.

10. A good source is Herman Baron, *Author Index to Esquire 1933–1973* (Metuchen, N.J.: Scarecrow Press, 1976).

11. Gingrich, *Nothing But People*, p. 97.

12. David Gelman. "Words From the Sponsor." *Newsweek*, 29 December 1975, p. 40.

13. Associated Press. "Mail Rights Denied to Esquire; Magazine to Fight Court Order." *New York Times*, 31 December 1943, p. 1 col. 6.

14. Lewis Wood. "High Court Lifts Esquire Mail Curb." 5 February 1946, p. 25 col. 1.

15. Hugh Hefner, editor of *Playboy*, had worked as a copy editor for *Esquire* early in his career. He quit when refused a $5 weekly raise. See Gingrich, *Nothing But People*, p. 193.

16. "Women We Love . . . Women We Don't," *Esquire*, August 1988, p. 99.

17. Gay Talese, *Esquire*, June 1983, p. 18.

Information Sources

BIBLIOGRAPHY

Baron, Herman. *Author Index to Esquire 1933–1973*. Metuchen, N.J.: Scarecrow Press, 1976.

Eisenberg, Lee. "Welcome to the Magazine of the 1990s." *Esquire,* April 1987, p. 1.

Erickson, Don, et al. "Some Words and Pictures about Arnold Gingrich, Founding Editor of Esquire, 1903–1976." *Esquire*, October 1976, pp. 65–70.

Gingrich, Arnold. *Nothing But People*. New York: Crown Publishers, 1971.

———. *Toys of a Lifetime*. New York: Alfred A. Knopf, 1966.

Hayes, Harold T. P. "Arnold Gingrich, Esquire." *New Republic*, 4 September 1976, pp. 33–37.

Moffitt, Phillip. "Esquire from the Beginning." *Esquire*, June 1963, pp. 13–14.

Pringle, Henry F. "Sex, Esq." *Scribner's Magazine*, March 1983, pp. 33–39.

Talese, Gay. "Arnold Gingrich." *Esquire*, June 1983, p. 18.

INDEX SOURCES

Readers' Guide (1961–present); *Magazine Index* (1977–present).

LOCATION SOURCES

Available in microform.

Publication History

MAGAZINE TITLE AND TITLE CHANGES

Esquire, Autumn 1933–February 1978; *Esquire Fortnightly*, March 1978–July 1979; *Esquire*, August 1979–present.

VOLUME AND ISSUE DATA

Volume ends June and December. Vol. 1, no. 1, Autumn 1933, quarterly; vol. 1, no. 2–vol. 89, no. 1, January 1934–February 1978, monthly; vol. 89, no. 2–vol. 92, no. 1, 1 March 1978–3–19 July 1979, fortnightly; vol. 92, no. 2–vol. 110, August 1979–present, monthly.

PUBLISHER AND PLACE OF PUBLICATION

Published by Esquire, New York, New York, 1933–present. *Esquire* originally was owned by Esquire, Inc., but was sold in 1977 to associated Newspapers Group (Great Britain) and Clay Felker. In 1979 *Esquire* was sold to 13–30 Corporation, Knoxville. In 1987 it was sold to the Hearst Corporation, New York. David A. Smart and William H. Weintraub, Autumn 1933–January 1941; David A. Smart, February 1941–December 1946. Alfred Smart added as co-publisher, January

1947; G. T. Sweetser, August 1948–December 1952; Arnold Gingrich, January 1953–June 1974; Samuel Ferber, July 1974–August 1976; David M. O'Brasky, September 1976–February 1979; Clay Felker, March 1979–May 1979; Christopher Whittle, June 1979–May 1982; Alan Greenberg, June 1982–December 1986; W. Randall Jones, January 1987–present.

EDITORS

Arnold Gingrich, Autumn 1933–October 1945; David Smart, November 1945–July 1948; Frederic A. Birmingham, August 1948–January 1953; Arnold Gingrich, January 1953–December 1962; Harold T. P. Hayes, January 1963–July 1973; Don Erickson, August 1973–June 1974; Arnold Gingrich, July 1974–May 1976; Don Erickson, June 1976–April 1977; Byron Dobell, May 1977–December 1977; Clay Felker, January 1978–May 1979; Phillip Moffitt, June 1979–May 1984; Lee Eisenberg, June 1984–present.

CIRCULATION

700,000 paid; 38,385 nonpaid.

Dean Howd

EVERYBODY'S MAGAZINE

"If it's in *Everybody's* it's a good story!" proclaimed the masthead of this magazine in the late 1920s—when it was no longer popular, and when the stories were not as good as they once were. For rollicking good stories had indeed been the backbone of *Everybody's Magazine* for decades, good stories and a fair sense of what folks wanted to read.

First published in 1899, *Everybody's Magazine* was a scion of John Wanamaker's New York department store, and sold for ten cents per copy, or a dollar for a year's subscription. The mighty Wanamaker himself is not apparent in the issues, and seems to have left the business entirely to the editors. The magazine struggled at first to find its own image, one that would sell. The obvious tack of popular fiction was an easy choice, and a notice stated that "the editors of *Everybody's Magazine* wish good short stories dealing in a vital way with American life and affairs."[1]

The "good short stories," at least for a while, were purchased from English publishers, but, in time, original American stories appeared. Theodore Dreiser was an early contributor of potboiling fiction, as was O. Henry, whose stories would pepper *Everybody's* issues for many years. In fact, one 1903 issue carried a short story by O. Henry and another by Sydney Porter![2] Most of *Everybody's* fiction was aimed at a broad readership, and was therefore mediocre, but sometimes it excelled, as bylines of Willa Cather, Jack London, Zane Grey, and Sinclair Lewis show. George Bernard Shaw contributed both *Androcles and the Lion* and *Pygmalion*, and the occasional bits of verse once included the poetry of Alfred Noyes. Even A. A. Milne once contributed a six-part detective story!

Current events and items of general interest also provided much of *Everybody's* material. Early essays for women, for example, suggested ideas for more efficient housework and for making spending money. The improving technology of photography illustrated news and stories with well-printed pictures. Besides photographs, illustrations for fiction included a vast number of drawings and paintings, many of which were colorful, and a few of which, by such artists as N. C. Wyeth, were superb. Often, the editors provided discussions or debates on quite controversial topics such as socialism or war, as in 1908 when trouble in the Philippines was analyzed by presidential candidates William Jennings Bryan and William Howard Taft. Booker T. Washington contributed a remarkable series, "Work with the Hands," in 1903. Royal families, baseball, explorations, and the like made for articles of interesting format. Letters to and responses from the editor provided a chatty, friendly forum, and a popular column of anecdotes, "Under the Spreading Chestnut Tree," also lent a homely touch to the magazine.

Still, *Everybody's* did not immediately find the distinguishing feature that would set it apart from other general-interest magazines and that would, not coincidentally, boost circulation. In 1903, *Everybody's* had a circulation of 150,000 when it was sold by Wanamaker to E. J. Ridgway, whose intrepid entrepreneurship soon found *Everybody's* ticket to the big time. Thomas Lawson, a former stock-market speculator, produced for the magazine a twenty-month series of exposés on big business. The series, called "Frenzied Finance," became one of the best known of all muckraking literature. Ballyhooed by a huge advertising campaign, the essays by Lawson claimed to lay open the sinister secrets of the corrupt moguls of high finance. Lawson's rough-and-tumble attacks and his slashing prose stung many important targets, some of whom retaliated by suing, although none were successful. The much-publicized series attracted immediate attention, and circulation soared, so that by 1905 there were nearly 750,000 subscribers, and *Everybody's* prospered. Advertising and subscriptions remained healthy through the rest of the magazine's first decade.[3]

This was *Everybody's* period of glory and fortune, achieved by the criticism of how others obtained their gold. Unfortunately for the magazine, the novelty— and the profit—of muckraking did not long endure. While lesser guns continued to grumble, Lawson himself was silent from 1907 to 1912, and his long-awaited return caused no excitement among the public. *Everybody's* gradually eliminated their erstwhile popular investigative journalism, although a late (1912) series neatly connected America's judicial system to the unholy dollar thus:

> This is the people bound and sold
> by the crafty Boss, all brazen and bold,
> That joins with Business, out for gold,
> To send the Lawyer in to mold
> The mind of the Judge, all proud and cold.[4]

As the interest in muckraking waned, the growing tensions in Europe and the advent of a world war sparked a vigorous and colorful response from *Everybody's*. The problems across the Atlantic were argued in many essays and debates. Theodore Roosevelt sounded a reveille with his "America: On Guard!" and such luminaries as H. G. Wells, G. B. Shaw, and G. K. Chesterton discussed American neutrality in the 1916 issues. When the United States finally entered the fracas, *Everybody's* enlarged its dimensions, and reported the war with good photographs, maps, and style.

In spite of these good efforts, success was slowly ebbing from *Everybody's* shore. Since the glorious days of 1905–1910, the fortunes of the magazine had been in a gradual decline, which even World War I could not stop. *Everybody's*, from 1910 to 1920, was still a pretty good magazine, with decent material and balanced formats, but subscriptions sank, and those of competitors rose. Eventually, desperate remedies were tried. In an effort to specialize, *Everybody's* became entirely fiction, scuttling all other departments, and including increasingly bad stories.

Eventually, as the quality of the fiction declined, so did the quality of the printed paper itself, and, in turn, circulation. Finally, in 1929, *Everybody's* was merged into a horrible confession magazine, and soon died an ignominious death.

Everybody's had found muckraking, whether sincere or not, an early key to success, but when the public's ardor for reform cooled, *Everybody's* could find nothing else upon which to stand. For three decades, *Everybody's* was not great, but it occasionally was good enough to merit public acceptance and, now, some critical acclaim. *Everybody's* failure was its inability to excel, and it doomed itself.

Notes

1. *Everybody's,* December 1900, contents page.

2. Ibid., July 1903. "The Atavism of John Tom Little Bear," by O. Henry on pp. 57–64 and Sydney Porter's "A Call Loan" on pp. 133–35.

3. Alvin F. Harlow, "Thomas William Lawson," in *Dictionary of American Biography*, eds. Allen Johnson, Dumas Malone, vol. 6 (New York: Charles Scribner's Sons, 1928–1936), pp. 59–60.

4. C. P. Connolly, "Bit Business and the Bench, Part 6," *Everybody's*, July 1912, p. 119.

Information Sources

BIBLIOGRAPHY
Harlow, Alvin F. "Thomas William Lawson." *Dictionary of American Biography*. Eds. Allen Johnson and Dumas Malone. vol. 6. New York: Charles Scribner's Sons, 1928–1936, pp. 59–60.
Mott, Frank Luther. *A History of American Magazines*. Vol. 5: Sketches of 21 Magazines, 1905–1930. Cambridge, MA: Harvard University Press, 1968, pp. 72–87.
INDEX SOURCES
Poole's *Index to Periodicals* (1902–1906 covered); *Readers' Guide to Periodical Literature* (covers only 1905–1921).

LOCATION SOURCES
> Library of Congress; many other libraries listed in *Union List of Serials*. Available in microform.

Publication History

MAGAZINE TITLE AND TITLE CHANGES
> *Everybody's Magazine,* 1899–1923; *Everybody's,* 1923–1929.

VOLUME AND ISSUE DATA
> Vol. 1, September–December 1899; vol. 2–59, 1899–1928; vol. 60, January–March 1929. Monthly. Semiannual volumes.

PUBLISHER AND DATE OF PUBLICATION
> John Wanamaker, 1899–1903; Ridgway-Thayer Company, 1903–1906; Ridgway Company, 1906–1929. New York.

EDITORS
> Chauncey Montgomery M'Govern, 1899–1900; John O'Hara Cosgrave, 1900–1903, 1906–1911; E. J. Ridgway, 1903–1906; Trumbull White, 1911–1914; William Hard, 1915; Howard Wheeler, 1916–1918; S. V. Roderick, 1919–1921; Sewell Haggard, 1921–1925; Frank Quinn, 1925–1926; Oscar Graeve, 1927; William Corcoran, 1928–1929.

CIRCULATION
> n.a.

Daniel Boice

EVERYWOMAN'S FAMILY CIRCLE. See FAMILY CIRCLE

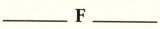

F

FAMILY CIRCLE

Family Circle is one of the leading women's magazines in the United States. Its average paid circulation per issue for July-December 1987 was 5,773,484 (there are seventeen issues a year), and the number of advertising pages it carried in 1987 was 1,650. With advertising revenues that totaled $123,975,448 in 1987, it ranks tenth in this area among all Publishers' Information Bureau (PIB) publications.[1]

But *Family Circle* is not only a local enterprise. In addition to the American version (which is also distributed in Canada), there are British, Australian, and Japanese versions. The British *Family Circle*, which began in 1964, is published under a licensing agreement, and is also distributed in Ireland. It is now a bimonthly, with a circulation of more than 800,000. The Australian *Family Circle* (founded in 1973) has become one of the most popular women's magazines in that country, with a circulation of about 400,000; it is published seventeen times a year, and is distributed in New Zealand as well. The Japanese version of *Family Circle* came out in 1978, under license of the Blue Chip Stamp Company of Japan. *Family Circle* and its international versions are now part of the New York Times Magazine Group, a large communications conglomerate that has diverse interests in magazines, newspapers, and television and radio stations.

Family Circle was first published on 9 September 1932. It was conceived by Harry Evans, a former film critic and managing editor of the old *Life** magazine, and financed by Charles Merrill, of Merrill Lynch and Company. *Family Circle* began as a weekly tabloid; Evans's idea was to bring out a publication whose purpose would be to help boost retailers' sales, especially in the expanding supermarket business. The tabloid was sold to retailers, who then distributed it for free to all customers.[2]

Family Circle contained a lot of food ideas and cooking tips as well as articles about movies, radio, fashion, and beauty, all of which indeed helped move products off supermarket shelves at a fast rate. Soon *Family Circle* became an efficient, highly targeted marketing medium, among the very first to be mass-marketed in grocery chain stores. After World War II, in September 1946, *Family Circle* became a monthly, and assumed a five-cent cover price.

The magazine remained under the financial control of Charles Merrill until December 1954, when it was acquired by its principal officers, Palmer K. Leberman (its publisher), Carl J. Schaefer, and Harry Evans. It is during this period (in 1958) that the magazine changed its name to *Everywoman's Family Circle*, although the word "everywoman's" was printed in very small print. The reason for the title change was the acquisition of *Everywoman's*, a competing magazine, by *Family Circle*. Theodore Peterson reports that "when it was merged with *Family Circle* in 1958, the combined *Everywoman's Family Circle* emerged with a circulation of 5,000,000 and access to 12,657 grocery stores in the United States and Canada—1,000,000 circulation and 5,367 stores from *Everywoman's*, 4,000,000 and 7,290 stores from *Family Circle*."[3]

In December 1961 *Family Circle* published its first annual special publication, *Christmas Helps*. Later in the sixties other special issues were published, such as *Great Ground Beef* and *Diet and Exercise*.

In December 1962 *Family Circle* was sold to Cowles Magazines and Broadcasting, publishers of (among other things) *Look** magazine. *Look*, just like *Family Circle*, was a mass-market magazine, but unlike *Family Circle*, whose main advertising category was food, *Look's* was automotive, with food being a minor category. In acquiring *Family Circle*, Gardner Cowles (president of Cowles) hoped not only to profit from an increase in revenues from advertisements, but also to learn about *Family Circle's* ingenious distribution channels. For *Family Circle*, unlike *Look* and other similar magazines, was not sold by subscription; it was shipped to the warehouses of giant food chains, where it was treated just like any other product on the supermarket shelves.

The supermarket method of distribution intrigued Cowles because "the cost of increasing and keeping subscriptions is the most frightening problem in the mass magazine market."[4] Cowles thought he could use *Family Circle's* proven channels to increase *Look's* distribution as well. In 1963, after the Cowles purchase, the word "everywoman's" was dropped from the title, and *Family Circle* assumed its former name, *Family Circle*. However, despite the title changes, the magazine has always been targeted to and bought by women (mostly women with families), and the topics of the articles and advertisements appearing in its pages have changed very little since the magazine's beginnings.

Advertising Age of 1962 reports that Gardner Cowles made a good decision in acquiring *Family Circle*, because "*Family Circle's* net profit for the fiscal year ended last June 30 was $750,000, compared with $350,000 the year before."[5]

In 1971, when *Look* folded, Cowles sold *Family Circle* along with other publications to the *New York Times*. Since then it has continued to thrive, increasing its frequency from twelve issues a year to thirteen in 1977, to fourteen in 1978, and since 1979 it has been put out seventeen times a year—every three weeks. The price of a 1988 issue is 99¢, and a subscription costs $16.15 a year. *Family Circle* is published in twenty-six regional and fifty-four subregional editions. Page numbers vary, with an average of 150 pages an issue. More than 60 percent is devoted to advertisements. Since *Family Circle* carries approximately 1,700 pages of advertisements a year, and is published seventeen times a year, on average each issue contains about 100 pages of advertisements.

Although subscriptions to the magazine were previously made available, they were not actively promoted until 1986. And, in fact, the subscriptions figure for July-December 1987 was 1,146,591, a 100 percent increase over the same period the previous year.[6]

In 1975, the special issues that had been published irregularly since 1961 were formalized as the Great Ideas Program. *Family Circle* now publishes nine Great Ideas specials a year that focus on popular subjects such as cooking, health, and nutrition.

Beginning in 1973 *Family Circle's* name became associated with tennis, because 1973 was the first year that *Family Circle* sponsored the National Women's Tennis Cup, which has become an important annual sports event. Quite understandably, this event has been thoroughly covered and publicized by the *New York Times*. Other *Family Circle* activities include the establishment of the Gold Leaf Awards that recognize excellence in nutrition education (1973), and the cosponsoring of the first Conference on Nutrition and the American Food System (1977).

What can one find in a regular issue of *Family Circle* today? There is a beauty and fashions section, with tips on clothes and makeup, which is quite conservative in approach. There is also a food section that contains recipes that aim at simplicity rather than at rarefied gastronomic tastes, and a crafts section, with detailed instructions on how to sew, knit, redecorate, or remodel. Many issues have a "free bonus" section or two, such as "8 exercise cards" to pull out and save (7 June 1988), or a "free calendar" to clip and save (28 June 1977). There is a regular Articles section, with practical types of information (i.e., "vacations your family will never forget"), health-related matters ("Can Carrots Prevent Cancer?"), or nonfiction stories ("Jennifer O'Neill: A New Beginning. After failed marriages, miscarriages and professional setbacks, she's back on top with a new family and a new career"). Other regular features include Voilá!, which lists practical advice;[7] Inside FC, which is the editorial page; Here's News in Medicine; Buyer's Guide (another advertising section); Recipe Index, which indexes all recipes presented in the issue; and Sneak Preview—a preview of subjects to be found in the next issue.

Gay Bryant, a former *Family Circle* editor, described exactly the kind of material *Family Circle* will accept for publication:

We want to give our reader ways to make her life (and her family's) better. This means giving her the information she needs to help her make the best decisions about everything from saving money to buying a car. Such pieces are full of nitty-gritty information: How to protect your home against crime; how to buy a refrigerator; the safest new cars; how to bank your money, etc.[8]

To retain the "service" image of the magazine, the space devoted to fiction is minimal, and most stories published are nonfiction, in which the reader is told how a person coped with a problem, and overcame it, or gained some deep insight from it. When the magazine does publish fiction, the editors make their stand very clear: "We want realistic fiction, fiction that depicts believable characters, particularly women, who are dealing with problems that strike a chord with our readers."[9]

Cynthia White points to another possible reason (besides the service approach) for *Family Circle's* policy of minimizing fiction: "In order to maximise the impact of any publication, and in particular its advertising content, it is necessary to secure the highest possible number of primary readers."[10] Primary readers are readers who buy and retain the magazine, as opposed to those who have it passed on to them. Presumably, fiction is more likely to be passed on than recipes and do-it-yourself instructions. By almost excluding pure fiction, *Family Circle* apparently seeks to eliminate casual readers, and restrict the amount of "passing on"; this, in turn, might prove to potential advertisers that their investments will be worthwhile.

Who are the people who read *Family Circle*? They are primarily women, although some men read it as well. In her dissertation of 1979,[11] Alice Miller quotes the 1978–1979 Simmons Report: the total adult female audience for that period was 17,701,000; and the total adult male audience was 2,801,000. Miller further breaks down the female audience of *Family Circle* by ages, income, and other variables. For example, the total women audience's median age was 38.5, with 2,870,000 women readers between the ages of 18 and 24; 4,756,000 between 25 and 34; 4,648,000 between 35 and 49; and 5,844,000 aged 50 and above. The relatively high median age of *Family Circle* readers is what probably prompted Gay Bryant to say in 1985, "Right now we are trying to attract the 'younger' reader (the 28-to 34-year-olds just starting a family), so we are running more pieces relating to children."[12]

The median income of the total female audience of *Family Circle* was $16,714; and out of the *Family Circle* female audience only 2,409,000 graduated from college. Most of the women (12,684,000) were married, but of the married women, only about half were also working (6,288,000). The fact that a majority of women readers (9,356,000) had children under eighteen in their households is probably an explanation for the motto picked by *Family Circle*: "for the women of today raising the generation of tomorrow."[13]

Gardner Cowles, the former owner of *Family Circle*, is quoted as having said, "I can't get it out of my head that 7-million women every month voluntarily

pick this *Family Circle* up and buy it.''[14] And his bewilderment is easily understood. For one thing, the accuracy of the information provided on nutrition (a
topic that receives high coverage in *Family Circle*) is questionable.[15] For another,
Family Circle has never hidden its marketing-oriented approach. A major portion
of every issue contains pure advertisements (that is, advertisements that are easy
to discern), and much of the rest of the magazine is full of implied advertisements.
For example, in the June 7, 1988, issue, under the rubric ''Here's News in
Medicine'' (p. 150), there is a piece entitled ''Detecting Radon in Your Home.''
Besides discussing the radon problem and listing an Environmental Protection
Agency (EPA) pamphlet as a source of information about radon and available
radon-detection equipment, *Family Circle* goes one step further: ''one such EPA-
approved kit . . . [is] produced by the Radon Testing Corporation of America . . .
For more information call RTCA at 800–457–2366.'' Even in a demonstration
for making yeast bread (same issue), it is possible to see the label of the brand
of dry yeast being used. In fact, because *Family Circle* is so intent on selling,
many times it is difficult to tell where an article ends and where the advertising
begins. The high-pitched selling intent of the magazine is particularly strident
in the case of cigarette advertisements: on the one hand *Family Circle* publishes
numerous articles on health, and on the other, it carries full-page ads for Virginia
Slims cigarettes, with the slogan ''you've come a long way baby.'' In the 7
June 1988 issue there is even a pop-up cigarette ad for Now cigarettes.

What is it, then, in this magazine that attracts so many women? One of the
most important factors may be its approach to recipes: practically every single
recipe is thoroughly tested by *Family Circle* in its own large kitchen to ensure
good quality and simplicity of instruction. In an article in *National Review*,*
Nika Hazelton substantiates this testing.[16] The recipes (and other how-to
instructions) actually work, and work very well the first time around. When
something taught by *Family Circle* does not work well, it is an exception, and
Family Circle takes pains to apologize and make sure that such incidents do not
happen again.[17]

Although James Playsted Wood notes that in *Family Circle* ''there is little
that will strain the intellect or titivate the sensibilities,''[18] *Family Circle* magazine
seems to have hit on a formula that appeals to millions of women worldwide.

Notes

1. I thank the Magazine Publishers' Association (MPA), the Publishers' Information
Bureau (PIB), and the Audit Bureau of Circulations (ABC) for these figures. I also thank
the staff of *Family Circle* for the information they have provided.

2. Evans explains the benefits of giveaway items in an article (''Graduates of Life'')
in *Time*, 3 October 1932, p. 19.

3. Theodore Peterson, *Magazines in the Twentieth Century* (Urbana: University of
Illinois Press, 1964), p. 283.

4. ''Cowles Finds Running Mate for *Look*,'' *Business Week*, 15 September 1962,
p. 33.

5. "Cowles Reveals Stock Deal for 'Family Circle,' " *Advertising Age*, 8 October 1962, p. 2.

6. MPA report. Magazine Publishers of America. 575 Lexington Avenue, New York, NY 10022.

7. One such piece of information reads, "If one of your feet is larger than the other, the . . . National Odd Shoe Exchange may offer a solution . . . For an initial membership fee of $22.50 and $7.50 yearly thereafter, you'll receive the names of other members who match your left or right odd-shoe size . . . you can then exchange extra shoes, splitting the cost" (28 June 1988, p. 7).

8. Gay Bryant, "Writing for *Family Circle,*" *Writer*, August 1985, p. 22.

9. Ibid., p. 23.

10. Cynthia L. White, *Women's Magazines 1693–1968* (London: Michael Joseph, 1970) p. 191.

11. Alice E. Miller, "A Descriptive Analysis of Health-Related Articles in the Six Leading Women's Magazines: Content Coverage and Readership profile," Ph.D. diss., Southern Illinois University at Carbondale, 1979.

12. Bryant, "Writing for *Family Circle,*" p. 22.

13. This is the motto on the promotional material of *Family Circle*.

14. "Cowles Finds Running Mate," p. 33.

15. See Denise Hatfield, "New ACSH Survey Rates Magazine Nutrition Accuracy," *ACSH News & Views*, May-June 1984, pp. 8–9.

16. Nika Hazelton, "In the Bosom of the Family," *National Review*, 10 July 1981, p. 794.

17. In the 19 July 1988 issue (p. 17), a reader complains about having been misinformed about floor paint by *Family Circle*. *Family Circle* apologizes, and provides the toll-free phone number of the National Wood Flooring Association.

18. James Playsted Wood, *Magazines in the United States* (New York: Ronald Press, 1956), p. 265.

Information Sources

BIBLIOGRAPHY

Ashby, Babette. "*Family Circle* Is Looking for New Talent, But. . . . " *Writer*, November 1978, pp. 20–22.

Bryant, Gay. "Writing for *Family Circle*." *Writer*, August 1985, pp. 22–23.

"Cowles Finds Running Mate for *Look*." *Business Week*, 15 September 1962, pp. 33–34.

"Cowles Reveals Stock Deal for 'Family Circle.' " *Advertising Age*, 8 October 1962, p. 2.

Ferguson, M. *Forever Feminine: Women's Magazines and the Cult of Femininity*. London: Heinemann, 1983.

Hatfield, Denise. "New ACSH Survey Rates Magazine Nutrition Accuracy." *ACSH News & Views*, May-June 1984, pp. 7–10.

Hazelton, Nika. "In the Bosom of the Family." *National Review*, 10 July 1981, p. 794.

Henry, Susan. "Juggling the Frying Pan and the Fire: The Portrayal of Employment and Family Life in Seven Women's Magazines, 1975–1982." *Social Science Journal*, October 1984, pp. 87–107.

Miller, Alice E. "A Descriptive Analysis of Health-Related Articles in the Six Leading Women's Magazines: Content Coverage and Readership Profile." Ph.D. diss., Southern Illinois University at Carbondale, 1979.

Millum, Trevor. *Images of Woman: Advertising in Women's Magazines*. Totowa, N.J: Rowman and Littlefield, 1975.

Parham, Ellen S. "Weight Control Content of Women's Magazines: Bias and Accuracy." *International Journal of Obesity*, pp. 10 (1986): 19–27.

Peterson, Theodore. *Magazines in the Twentieth Century*. Urbana: University of Illinois Press, 1964.

White, Cynthia L. *Women's Magazines 1693–1968*. London: Michael Joseph, 1970.

Winship, Janice. *Inside Women's Magazines*. New York: Pandora, 1987.

Wolseley, Roland E. *Understanding Magazines*. Ames: Iowa State University Press, 1965.

Wood, James Playsted. *Magazines in the United States*. New York: Ronald Press, 1956.

INDEX SOURCES

Access: The Supplementary Index to Periodicals (1975–present); *Consumer's Index; Current Literature in Family Planning; Index to How to Do It Information; Recipe Periodical Index.*

LOCATION SOURCES

Library of Congress (vol. 7, 1935–); scattered volumes in other libraries. Available in microform (1974–present).

Publication History

MAGAZINE TITLE AND TITLE CHANGES

The Family Circle, 1932–May 1958; *Everywoman's Family Circle*, June 1958–December 1962; *Family Circle*, January 1963–present.

VOLUME AND ISSUE DATA

Vols. 1–29, 9 September 1932–16 August 1946, weekly; vols. 29–89, September 1946–1976, monthly; vol. 90, 1977, 13 times a year; vol. 91, 1978, 14 times a year; vols. 92–present, 1979–present, 17 times a year. One volume a year in 1932. Two volumes a year 1933–1976. One volume a year 1977–present.

PUBLISHER AND PLACE OF PUBLICATION

Evans Publishing Company, New York, New York, 1932–May 1958; Family Circle, Inc. Mount Morris, Illinois June 1958–June 1969; Family Circle, Inc. Mattoon, Illinois July 1969–1988.

EDITORS

Harry Evans, 1932–1936; Robert Endicott, 1936–1954; Robert Jones, 1955–1965; Arthur Hettich, 1965–June 1985; Gay Bryant, July 1985–August 1986; Arthur Hettich, September 1986–June 7, 1988; Jacqueline Leo, June 28, 1988–present.

CIRCULATION
    5,773,484 (average paid circulation per issue in July–December 1987; an ABC
    statement).

Sharon Tabachnick

FAMILY HEALTH. See HEALTH

FAMILY WEEKLY. See USA WEEKEND

FARM JOURNAL AND COUNTRY GENTLEMAN. See COUNTRY
GENTLEMAN

**FARMER AND GARDENER AND LIVE-STOCK BREEDER AND MAN-
AGER.** See AMERICAN FARMER

FEATURE. See CRAWDADDY

FEDERAL AMERICAN MONTHLY. See THE KNICKERBOCKER

FORUM

The *Forum,* a magazine of political and social commentary, was founded in
1886 by a group of New York businessmen led by Isaac Leopold Rice. The first
editor was Lorettus Sutton Metcalf, a former editor of the *North American
Review*, who left that periodical in order to attain greater editorial freedom. Both
Rice and Metcalf felt that popular government required a source of enlightened
information about important issues. The *Forum* was officially launched in March
of 1886 with an initial investment of approximately $100,000.[1]
    The first issue of the *Forum* contained articles dealing with Prohibition, Chris-
tianity, college sports, Roman Catholicism, women's pay, and Florida. The
periodical was designed to be "a public magazine for the discussion sanely and
seriously of all vital questions."[2] Metcalf was somewhat disappointed that he
had to include a few articles of a light nature in order to keep up circulation.
Nonetheless, for years the *Forum* stumbled along with 2,000 subscribers.[3]
    In 1887 Walter Hines Page, a transplanted North Carolina newspaperman,
was hired as business manager of the *Forum*. He struggled unsuccessfully to
increase circulation under Metcalf. The situation changed dramatically in 1891

when Page assumed the editorship. By 1894 the journal had 30,000 subscribers. Page proved to be an innovative editor. He outlined and gave direction to each issue of the magazine, soliciting the work of authorities such as Theodore Roosevelt, Woodrow Wilson, and William Graham Sumner. The *Forum* became one of the most influential periodicals of opinion in the country. In 1895, after a dispute over control of the publication, Page relinquished the editorial chair.[4] He later became editor of the *Atlantic Monthly*.

After Page's departure, the fortunes of *Forum* fluctuated. The immediate result of Page's resignation as editor was a decline in circulation. However, the *Forum's* stature was clearly established, as was evidenced by its inclusion in *Readers' Guide to Periodical Literature*. In 1902 the *Forum*, under the direction of Joseph M. Rice, went from a monthly written by experts to a quarterly largely written by the editorial staff. This policy was very unsuccessful and was altered in 1907 when Frederic T. Cooper, a professor of Sanskrit and Latin, became editor. Cooper once again opened the periodical to outsiders, returned to monthly, and started the publication of fiction and poetry. These changes led to a resurgence of the *Forum* and were continued by later editors such as Benjamin R. Herts and Mitchell Kennerley.[5]

During and immediately after World War I the *Forum* suffered some financial setbacks. By 1923 the circulation had again declined to 2,000. But with the appointment that same year of Henry Goddard Leach as editor, the situation started to improve. By 1926 *Forum* boasted a circulation of over 63,000. Leach changed the editorial policy so that the *Forum* was "no longer a magazine of discussion merely, but a magazine of controversy."[6] Leach delighted in pointing to a letter from an ailing reader whom doctors said needed "peace of mind," and who wrote: "To give me that you will have to do something about the Forum. It is too damn exciting."[7] Accompanying the editorial changes, Leach also moved to improve the design of the *Forum*. He instituted a "mandarin red" cover with a border design from symbols found on Mayan temple walls.[8]

Leon Whipple of New York University, writing in *Survey-Graphic*, noted that the *Forum* always attempted to give opposing viewpoints on important questions. It printed an attack on the Klan and then got the head wizard himself to respond. "It is more civilized than The Mercury," concluded Whipple, "for when did Mr. [H. L.] Mencken print the side of George Babbitt or Judge Gary or Wayne B. Wheeler?" The *Forum* took on the hard issues of the 1920s such as separation of church and state and fundamentalism versus evolution.[9]

In 1930 the *Forum* absorbed the *Century*, a magazine founded in 1870 that had fallen on hard times. For a while the combined periodical was entitled the *Forum and Century*. It was, according to John E. Drewry of the University of Georgia School of Journalism, "dedicated to open-mindedness." The new magazine attracted such notable authors as John Maynard Keynes, Charles A. Beard, G. K. Chesterton, and James Truslow Adams. Unfortunately, by 1935 circulation had declined to 33,000 and times were hard.[10]

In 1940 the *Forum* was sold to *Current History*, and the two periodicals were combined. The *Forum* volume count ended with 103. In 1945 Events Publishing Company bought *Current History and Forum* and combined the *Forum* with the *Column Review*, published in Philadelphia. The new periodical started with volume 104. The title was soon simplified to *Forum*. The periodical finally ceased publication in 1950, never having achieved in its last years its former stature. "It seems a pity that the *Forum* could not have died in 1940," concluded Frank Luther Mott. "The admirer of a magazine that has once enjoyed something of greatness hates to see it kicked around as the football of foredoomed failures."[11]

Notes

1. Norman LaCour Olsen, Jr., "The *Forum* as a Magazine of Literary Comment: 1886–1907" (Ph.D. diss., Duke University, 1963), pp. 2–5.

2. Leon Whipple, "The Revolution on Quality Street," *Survey-Graphic*, November-January 1926–1927, p. 121; Olsen, "The *Forum* as a Magazine of Literary Comment," p. 3.

3. Burton J. Hendrick, *The Training of an American: The Earlier Life and Letters of Walter H. Page, 1855–1913* (Boston: Houghton Mifflin Company, 1928), p. 203.

4. Ross Gregory, *Walter Hines Page: Ambassador to the Court of St. James's* (Lexington: University of Kentucky Press, 1970), p. 9; Theodore Peterson, *Magazines in the Twentieth Century* (Urbana: University of Illinois Press, 1964), pp. 151–152.

5. Olsen, "The *Forum* as a Magazine of Literary Comment," pp. 10–13; Frank Luther Mott, *A History of American Magazines*, vol. 4: *1885–1905* (Cambridge: Harvard University Press, 1957), p. 517.

6. Henry Goddard Leach, "The Next Forty Years," *Forum*, March 1926, p. 414; Mott, *A History of American Magazines*, 4: 518–21.

7. Quoted in Whipple, "The Revolution on Quality Street," p. 469.

8. Ibid., p. 430.

9. Ibid., p. 470.

10. John E. Drewry, "The Forum-Century: Dedicated to Open-Mindedness," *Writer*, January 1936, p. 20; Mott, *A History of American Magazines* 4: 521–22.

11. Mott, *A History of American Magazines* 4: 523.

Information Sources

BIBLIOGRAPHY

Drewry, John E. "The Forum-Century: Dedicated to Open-Mindedness." *Writer,* January 1936, pp. 20–21, 25–26.

Eaton, Charles H. "A Decade of Magazine Literature—1888–1897." *Forum,* 26, 1898, pp. 211–216.

"The *Forum* and Its Editor." *Review of Reviews*, April 1891, pp. 287–88.

Gregory, Ross. *Walter Hines Page: Ambassador to the Court of St. James's.* Lexington: University of Kentucky Press, 1970.

Hendrick, Burton J. *The Training of an American: The Earlier Life and Letters of Walter H. Page, 1855–1913*. Boston: Houghton Mifflin Company, 1928.

Leach, Henry Goddard. "The Next Forty Years." *Forum*, March 1926, pp. 414–19.

Mott, Frank Luther. *A History of American Magazines*, vol. 4: *1885–1905*. Cambridge: Harvard University Press, 1957.

Olsen, Norman LaCour, Jr. "The *Forum* as a Magazine of Literary Comment: 1886–1907." Ph.D. diss., Duke University, 1963.

Peterson, Theodore. *Magazines in the Twentieth Century*. Urbana: University of Illinois Press, 1964.

Whipple, Leon. "The Revolution on Quality Street." *Survey-Graphic*, November-January 1926–1927, pp. 19–24, 177–179, 427–432, 469–472.

INDEX SOURCES
> *Nineteenth Century Readers' Guide; Readers' Guide to Periodical Literature* (1890–1940); Poole's (1886–1906).

LOCATION SOURCES
> Library of Congress, many other libraries. Available in microform.

Publication History

MAGAZINE TITLE AND TITLE CHANGES
> *Forum*, 1886–1930; *Forum and Century*, 1930–1940; *Forum and Column Review*, 1945; *Forum*, 1945–1950.

VOLUMES AND ISSUE DATA
> Vols. 1–103, 1886–1940; vols. 104–113, 1945–1950; monthly and quarterly.

PUBLISHER AND PLACE OF PUBLICATION
> Forum Publishing Company, New York, New York, 1886–1940; Events Publishing Company, Philadelphia, Pennsylvania, 1945–1950.

EDITORS
> Lorettus Metcalf, 1886–1891; Walter Hines Page, 1891–1895; Alfred E. Keet, 1895–1897; Joseph M. Rice, 1897–1907; Frederic T. Cooper, 1907–1909; Benjamin Russell Herts, 1909–1910; Mitchell Kennerley, 1910–1916; H. Thompson Rich, 1916–1918; Edwin Wildman, 1918–1920; George Harvey Payne, 1920–1923; Henry Goddard Leach, 1923–1940; D. G. Redmond, 1945–1950.

CIRCULATION
> Fluctuated between 2,000 and 63,000.

Ronnie W. Faulkner

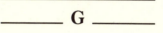

G

GEO

The publication of *Geo* in the United States was an extraordinary experiment that provided an elegant magazine with a wide range of high-quality articles and photographs over many different subjects. Unfortunately, *Geo* never developed a large enough audience to sustain its publication and became a very short-lived and very expensive failure.

The German firm Gruner and Jahr began publishing *Geo* in Germany in 1977. Gruner and Jahr is the parent company of *Stern* and other successful German magazines and with *Geo* expanded its base with a high-quality general-interest magazine. *Geo* filled an empty niche among German magazine readers and became an instant success. German antitrust laws prevented Gruner and Jahr from expanding any further in Germany and the company decided to expand by publishing *Geo* internationally. The next edition of *Geo* was published in France and also resulted in a great success. Both of these editions are still being published, with circulation of the German edition at 520,000 and the French edition at 500,000.[1] Gruner and Jahr decided to develop a U.S. edition and intended to publish editions in Japan, Great Britain, and Italy.

Gruner and Jahr entered the American market expecting the same type of instant success as they had had with the German and French editions. *Geo* was introduced in the United States with a large amount of fanfare and no expense was spared in attempts to lure potential subscribers. Some of the advertising for this new magazine consisted of a six-page four-color bleed spread with reply cards that was placed in *Time,* * *Business Week*, and *Newsweek** and had an estimated cost of approximately one million dollars. Direct marketing included two gigantic mailings of 3.2 million pieces and 1.6 million pieces with names of potential subscribers selected from many different mailing lists.[2]

As a magazine, *Geo* was first-class in every aspect. In the charter issue (April 1979), the managing editor, H. J. Kaplan, defined the focus as "broadly anthropological," saying "our ambition, then, is to produce a magazine of compelling style and beauty which at the same time boldly and thoughtfully addresses the realities of our time, raises the fateful questions, opens windows on a more various and meaningful world." Excellent, well-known writers, such as Edward Abbey, Isaac Asimov, Roger Caras, and René Dubois contributed articles in the first issues. The photographs corresponding to the articles in *Geo* were exquisite. Within the first year of its publication, *Geo* was awarded the Best Use of Photos Award and the Magazine Picture Editors Award in the Annual Pictures of the Year Competition sponsored by the University of Missouri School of Photojournalism, the National Press Photographers Association, and Nikon.[3]

Gruner and Jahr attempted to use a very different philosophy of advertising within *Geo*. Their strategy was to produce the majority of the magazine's revenue from the subscribers and not from the advertisers. The ad ratio was set at 80–20, which is 80 percent editorial and 20 percent advertising. *Geo* limited the advertising to twenty-nine pages, and only full-page color ads were permitted. Within these restrictions, *Geo* had to command a high price from its subscribers. The annual subscription rate was $36 and a single issue cost $4, which made *Geo* one of the most expensive general-interest magazines on the market.

But even with the massive advertising campaign and high standards of quality, *Geo* did not have a successful beginning in the United States. Gruner and Jahr had intended to use translations of articles from the German edition, but found that many were not suitable for the American audience. Significant differences of opinion occurred between the German and American editors and managers. The first president and publisher, Charles C. (Jim) Randolph, left before the first issue was ever published. The enormous and expensive advertising campaign failed to attract the expected number of subscribers needed to make *Geo* profitable. Advertisers were confused by the magazine's lack of focus and lack of a targeted audience.

Gruner and Jahr also had not anticipated the seriousness of *Geo*'s competitors in the American market. This niche was not as empty as in the German and French markets. The market already had several well-established publications such as *National Geographic,* * *Natural History, Audubon*, and *Smithsonian,* * whose subscription rates were much lower than those of *Geo*.

Geo subscribers never quite knew what to expect of the six lengthy articles in each issue. *Geo*'s subtitle, *A New View of the World*, hinted that the subject matter would be unusual. Articles and photographs ranged from the beautiful and exquisite to the shocking and controversial. In the first issues, articles on California ghost towns (May 1979), roller coasters (June 1979), triggerfish and sea urchins (June 1979), the space shuttle (July 1979), and art in machinery (November 1979) provided the reader with enjoyable text and unusual, appealing pictures. But these quietly beautiful articles were overshadowed by other articles that contained descriptions and photographs of the unpleasant aspects of life.

Examples of these types of articles include rattlesnakes (May 1979), racism in Kenya (June 1979), Haiti's squalor (September 1979), Mexican-American border and illegal immigrants (November 1979), poverty in Naples (January 1980), and orphaned street children of Brazil (February 1980).

An article on illegal dogfighting in the United States (November 1979) especially disturbed readers and reviewers. The author of this article had infiltrated groups that organized illegal dogfighting. The article contained graphic descriptions of the fights and the people associated with illegal dogfighting. The photographs showed bloodied dogs locked in combat while spectators cheered. The article was difficult to ignore, and in almost every review or article written about *Geo*, the dogfighting article is mentioned.

All these factors gave *Geo* a rather unstable beginning, and within eighteen months, Gruner and Jahr began to initiate changes. In June 1980, the staff was reduced from thirty-six to twenty-two, and managing editor Robert Christoper left to develop the Japanese edition of *Geo*. Several months later, Peter Diamandis became publisher and was given the task of relaunching *Geo*. One of his first moves was to change the subtitle on the masthead to *The Earth Diary*. Articles were categorized into fields such as Geo Wildlife, Geo Knowledge, and Geo Explorations. Two new features were added: Geosphere was added at the end of the magazine and contained very short articles, and Geo Data Bank Box occurred within stories and complemented them with additional factual information. The tone of the articles was softened, and more entertaining articles were included. Richard Burton was enticed at a price of $200,000 into his first advertising campaign and did radio and television ads promoting *Geo*. The restrictions on advertisements were reviewed and changed, and *Geo* began accepting all types of ads. The ad ratio was changed from 80–20 to 65–35. The limit of twenty-nine pages of advertising was dropped, and black-and-white ads and partial pages were welcome. The expensive subscription price was lowered to $29.95 per year.[4]

But these changes did not significantly increase the number of subscribers, which ranged between 200,000 and 250,000 throughout *Geo*'s history. Within the year, Gruner and Jahr began discussing the sale of *Geo* in the United States. Estimates were that the magazine had lost over $35 million.[5]

In September 1981, *Geo* was sold to the Los Angeles–based Knapp Communications. Knapp Communications had success in developing high-quality publications such as *Architectural Digest** and *Bon Appétit.** These magazines were designed to attract the affluent subscriber and the daydreamers. New editor-in-chief Paige Rense and publisher T. Swift Lockard were given the charge to revitalize *Geo* and make it attractive to wealthy subscribers.

Rense began by initiating more changes in *Geo*. The magazine's trademark lime green border on the cover and its logo and subtitle were abandoned for dramatic full-color covers. The tone of the magazine was to be completely turned around to reflect a more optimistic view of life. According to Rense, "The magazine will have no more news, no more ecology, no more people lying in gutters with open sores. It will be timeless and a pleasure to read.''[6] The magazine would now concentrate on people and would include more stories from the world of culture and entertainment. In each issue, the number of articles was increased to eight or nine, and the length of these articles was shortened. The high-class quality of the photographs and stories was to be maintained. Another new section, Geo Conversation, featured interviews with prominent and interesting people such as Roger Tory Peterson, world's most famous birdwatcher (April 1982); Daniel J. Boorstin, author and former librarian of Congress (May 1982); Clare Booth Luce, journalist and politician (September 1982); Dian Fossey, research scientist who studied gorillas in Rwanda (November 1982); Jim Henson, creator of the Muppets (January 1983); and Rudolf Nureyev, ballet dancer (August 1983).

Even with these changes, the high contrast between the story's subjects continued to confuse readers and advertisers. For example, the August 1982 issue contained an interview with William Conway as the director of the New York City Zoo, articles on ultralight flying, truckers' life styles, elephant seals, British butlers, Henry Aaron, growing up Amish, and letters from a Civil War soldier. There was something for everyone in each issue, but not enough of any one thing to capture the subscriber's attention and dollars.

When Cleon Knapp acquired Geo, he predicted that ''the monthly would be profitable within three years.''[7] In September 1984, which was the end of these three years, Geo was still not getting close to making a profit. The magazine was given one more chance and one more transformation. In its final phase, Geo shifted to an all-travel magazine, and the masthead was given a new subtitle, Travel and Discover the World. Advertising in Geo increased slightly with this new format, but it was too little too late. Knapp decided to cease publication, and Geo's final issue was February 1985.

Geo had a turbulent six-year history. It had a constantly changing framework with two owners, six publishers, four editors-in-chief, and numerous other personnel changes. The magazine won at least twenty-six awards for excellence and lost an estimated $70 million for its two owners.[8] Geo's major failure was not developing a clearly defined identity for subscribers and advertisers. Geo will be remembered as an elegant, beautiful magazine whose stories and pictures highlighted a diverse group of untraditional subjects.

Notes

1. *Ulrich's International Periodicals Directory*, 1988–1989.

2. Philip H. Dougherty, ''*Geo* Goes Nationwide in 4 Colors,'' *New York Times*, 2 January 1979.

3. *Geo*, May 1980, p. 4.

4. N. R. Kleinfield, ''*Geo*: Lime Green Edsel of a Magazine Searches for an Image That Works: It's Had Three Publishers and Three Editors in Just Two Years. And It's Still Leaking Red Ink,'' *New York Times*, 10 May 1981.

5. N. R. Kleinfield, "U.S. *Geo* Is Sold to Knapp: Woes Stymied Gruner & Jahr," *New York Times*, 18 September 1981.

6. Janice Castro, "*Geo* Goes Upbeat—and Uptown," *Time*, 9 November 1981, p. 104.

7. Kleinfield, "U.S. *Geo* Is Sold to Knapp," p. D3.

8. William F. Gloede, " 'Geo' Goes Off Without a Niche." *Advertising Age*, 21 January 1985, p. 2.

Information Sources

BIBLIOGRAPHY

Bruno, Rosalie. "Knapp Communications: A Publishing Success Story." *Direct Marketing,* May 1983, p. 24–26.

Castro, Janice. "*Geo* Goes Upbeat—and Uptown." *Time*, 9 November 1981, p. 104.

Dougherty, Philip H. "*Geo* Goes Nationwide in 4 Colors." *New York Times*, 2 January 1979.

———. "New Look for *Geo* Magazine." *New York Times*, 29 October 1980.

Gloede, William F. " 'Geo' Goes Off Without a Niche." *Advertising Age*, 21 January 1985, p. 2.

Hammonds, Keith. "A New Publisher Gives *Geo* Magazine a Facelift." *New York Times*, 22 August 1982.

Jones, Alex S. "*Geo* Magazine to Stop Publication." *New York Times*, 16 January 1985.

Katz, William. "*Geo*." *Library Journal*, 1 April 1980, p. 792.

Kleinfield, N. R. "*Geo*: Lime Green Edsel of a Magazine Searches for an Image That Works: It's Had Three Publishers and Three Editors in Just Two Years. And It's Still Leaking Red Ink." *New York Times*, 10 May 1981.

———. "U.S. *Geo* Is Sold to Knapp: Woes Stymied Gruner & Jahr." *New York Times*, 18 September 1981.

Lachlan, E. C. "*Geo* Magazines Proliferate Around the World." *Advertising World*, December 1983, pp. 13–14.

Machalaba, Daniel. "Carving Out Identity Is the Crucial Task for a New Magazine: 'New View of the World's Is Promise of *Geo*, Monthly That Stresses the Offbeat.' " *Wall Street Journal*, 24 March 1980.

Millman, Nancy. "*Geo* Puts on a New Face." *Advertising Age*, 5 April 1982, pp. M2–M6.

Schardt, Arlie, and George Hackett. "Chapter Two Begins at *Geo*." *Newsweek*, 7 July 1980.

Wallach, Van. "*Geo*, Science 86: Some Success Stories Don't Work." *Advertising Age*, 10 November 1986, pp. 510–514.

INDEX SOURCES

Online databases of *Magazine Index, National Newspaper Index,* and *Trade and Industry Index.*

LOCATION SOURCES

R. M. Cooper Library at Clemson University, many other libraries.

Publication History

MAGAZINE TITLE AND TITLE CHANGES

Geo, 1979–1985.

VOLUME AND ISSUE DATA
 Vols. 1–7, April 1979–February 1985, monthly.
PUBLISHER AND PLACE OF PUBLICATION
 Gruner and Jahr: Igor Gordevitch, 1980–1981; Peter Diamandis, 1981; New York,
 New York. Knapp Corporation: T. Swift Lockard, 1981–1982; Harry Myers,
 1982–1983; John F. Grant, 1983–1985; Los Angeles, California.
EDITORS
 H. J. Kaplan, 1979–1981; Paige Rense, 1981–1983; David Maxey, 1984; Kevin
 Buckley, 1984–1985.
CIRCULATION
 200,000—250,000

Kathy Wood

GENTLEMAN'S QUARTERLY. See GQ: GENTLEMAN'S QUARTERLY

GOLDEN ARGOSY. See ARGOSY

GQ: GENTLEMAN'S QUARTERLY

The first *Gentleman's Quarterly* appeared for the Christmas season of 1926.
It was produced by two "natural salesmen" David A. Smart, later the publisher
of *Esquire*,* and William H. Weintraub, a part-publisher of a monthly booklet
of menswear called *The Man of Today*. The two formed the Men's Wear Service
Corporation to publish a quarterly booklet of men's fashions sold to stores as
ersatz catalogs.

 Gentleman's Quarterly was innovative in two significant ways. It was one of
the first catalogs issued in the guise of a magazine at regular intervals. It was
the store, not the customer, that paid twenty cents for each issue to give away.
Then, rather than cater to the routine needs of the stores' customers, *Gentleman's
Quarterly* forced stores into the new role of stimulating customers' unsuspected
wants with items of new fashion featured each quarter. A subscribing store
received a sample shipment of all the menswear in each issue with price and
delivery information.

 The partners' slick trade paper, *Apparel Arts*, replaced *Gentleman's Quarterly*
in the depression year of 1932. Stores could not afford the booklets, but they
could use a trade paper to show the customers affordable clothing. Another trade
paper, *Fabrics and Fashions*, which actually had cloth swatches inserted, was
issued concurrently in place of sample shipments. When the consumer's publication that we know as *GQ*, was reborn in 1957, the partners simply transformed
the two old trade papers using their oldest title.[1]

 The editor for *Apparel Arts*, Arnold Gingrich, freely admitted he and publisher
David Smart had modeled the magazine after the new "classy" *Fortune*. He
began in 1933 editing the men's magazine that was to define the genre for the
next half-century. *Esquire* was a fashion-oriented men's magazine that combined

quality writing with current trends in apparel. Gingrich was the vice-president of *Esquire* in 1957 when *Gentleman's Quarterly* was reborn. (David Smart had died in 1952, and John Smart had succeeded his brother as president.)

The first issue of the modern *GQ* was published as volume 27, number 6 of *Apparel Arts* for June 1957. The cover and title page actually read ''Apparel Arts'' with ''Gentleman's Quarterly'' in smaller print underneath. Bernard J. Miller was the publisher and Everett Mattlin the editor and columnist. It had a hefty 248 oversize pages with eight fashion articles and eight features of the type that graced *Esquire*, but no fiction. The list of advertisers ran to nearly 200. Each issue was $1.

The next issue was volume 28, number 2, for spring 1958. Everett Mattlin continued as editor for twelve years, and the initial pattern changed very little. The mix of fashion and feature articles varied, usually on the side of more fashion, and a number of different departments were started and stopped. Fiction was not uncommon, but the emphasis was on Fashion, while its ''brother'' magazine, *Esquire*, emphasized the new fiction for which it had become justly famous.

GQ had, in fact, begun as a vehicle for the overflow of fashion advertising to *Esquire* as upwardly mobile males' interest in fashion began to increase. This was the era of *Playboy** with its total emphasis on the male life style. *GQ* soon became the reading material of the young man attempting to get to the *Playboy* and *Esquire* image of the successful man.

In October 1969, Jack Haber became editor of *GQ*. Within the year, the magazine had changed its size to the smaller, more standard size from the big folios. Haber started many new departments, including ''Inside,'' which discussed what the ''new'' *GQ* was attempting to do. Little changed in the feature/fashion mix, however, and the magazine started 1970 with a slim 134 pages. In 1972, Haber revamped the magazine again into more of a consumer publication with broader editorial recognition of life-style features.

During the next six years, *GQ* had increasing success. By 1978, however, the traditional leadership of both *Esquire* and *GQ* had changed considerably. Founding editor Arnold Gingrich had died in 1976, and Jack Haber had become editor-in-chief. The readership also had aged, and circulation had declined.

In 1979, *GQ* was bought by Condé Nast Magazines, owned by the newspaper-based Newhouse family along with *Vogue,** *Gourmet, Vanity Fair,** *HQ,* and *Parade** (the Sunday Magazine). *Esquire* was sold to a different publishing group. The new publishers felt that *GQ* was perceived in two negative ways. Its attempt to be on the cutting edge of style was too avant-garde, resulting in readers going over to the life-style magazines that packaged a ''complete'' male look. *GQ* had also frequently been characterized as a magazine for homosexuals because of its young models and narcissistic fashion layouts.[2]

By 1984, *GQ* was the fastest growing magazine in the marketplace, closely followed by *Esquire*. It had become a complete life-style magazine. Editor-in-chief Arthur Cooper brought a new look to *GQ*. He introduced older, more natural models to mirror the magazine's readers. Also, *GQ* went head-to-head with *Esquire* for feature articles by well-known writers to improve the written content.[3] Writers Joseph Heller, Garry Wills, and Roy Blount, Jr., were featured. Richard Avedon was hired to photograph all covers in 1984 to give them a distinctive look reflecting the new approach in content.

Publisher Steve Florio positioned *GQ* completely in the life-style market. An alumnus of *Esquire* under Gingrich, he aimed *GQ* squarely at his former employer's readers. Florio added numerous articles about men's services such as grooming, health, food, and travel. The number of departments soared to over twenty, with music, cars, theater, and movies added to the mix.

Still, differences between *Esquire* and *GQ* remained. Robert Farley, senior vice-president of the Magazine Publisher's Association, divided up the market in 1984 demographically by theme. For *M*,* Fairchild Publications' entry in the field, the theme is "Having It Made." *Esquire's* theme is "Man at His Best," which appears as the motto on the cover, and *GQ*'s theme is "Making It."[4]

By the end of 1984, *GQ* had an audited circulation of 607,177, an increase of 8.3 percent over the previous year. Its ad pages were up 43.5 percent with a ratio of ads to editorial copy of 55–45. The September 1984 issue had 470 pages, "so fat with ads that specially reinforced coffee tables may be required to hold it."[5] Certainly, the economics of *GQ* have matured along with its readers. Gail Pool, a magazine reviewer, wrote:

> It might be argued that the current trend in men's magazines is a response to the women's movement—that men are more vulnerable, more concerned about looking good and pleasing women, more open to advice. A more likely explanation, however, is that service magazines, with their advertising links, are economically safer than other types. Thus Mr. Reader is now addressed as Miss and Mrs. Reader have long been addressed: as M. Consumer.
>
> I suspect that men's life style magazines will continue in this direction, attempting, as literally as possible, to find answers to the question: What do men want . . . to buy?[6]

In September 1988, *GQ* was a clear leader among men's life-style magazines, and Pool's predictions were holding true. Over 139 advertisers were represented in 492 pages. The mix of fashion and features established in 1957 is intact, as are the departments added in the early eighties. *GQ* is positioned in the middle of the "baby boom" generation of American men. If *GQ* does not know what most men want, it is nevertheless a success at giving upper middle-class men suggestions about what to buy.

Notes

1. Arnold Gingrich, *Nothing But People* (New York: Crown Publishers, 1971), pp. 24–33, 67.

2. Charlene Canape, "Refashioning the Male Marketplace," *Marketing & Media Decisions*, March 1985, p. 88.

3. Ibid.

4. Bill Thomas, "What Does a Man Want?," *Washington Journalism Review*, December 1984, p. 23.

5. Ibid., p. 24.

6. Gail Pool, "Magazines," *Wilson Library Bulletin*, April 1983, p. 701.

Information Sources

BIBLIOGRAPHY

Barol, Bill. "20 Things a 30-Year-Old Regular Guy Should Know." *Newsweek*, 22 June 1987, p. 82.

Canape, Charlene. "Refashioning the Male Marketplace." *Marketing & Media Decisions*, March 1985, pp. 84–90.

Gingrich, Arnold. *Nothing But People.* New York: Crown Publishers, 1971. Joyce, Walter. "Muscular Merchandising." *Folio*, June 1986, p. 124.

Kanner, Bernice. "Peacock Alley." *New York*, 26 September 1983, pp. 24–26.

Langway, Lynn, and Tenley-Ann Jackson. "Courting the Clothes Hound." *Newsweek*, 3 October 1983, p. 92.

Peterson, Theodore. *Magazines in the Twentieth Century.* 2nd ed. Urbana: University of Illinois Press, 1964.

Pool, Gail. "Magazines." *Wilson Library Bulletin*, April 1983, pp. 700–701.

Taft, William H. *American Magazines for the 1980s.* New York: Hastings House, 1982.

Thomas, Bill. "What Does A Man Want?" *Washington Journalism Review*, December 1984, pp. 21–23.

INDEX SOURCES

Access (1986–present); *Readers' Guide* (1988–present).

LOCATION SOURCES

Available in microform.

Publication History

MAGAZINE TITLE AND TITLE CHANGES

Gentleman's Quarterly, Winter 1926–Spring 1932; *Apparel Arts/Gentleman's Quarterly,* June 1957; *GQ/Gentleman's Quarterly,* Spring 1958–present.

VOLUME AND ISSUE DATA

Volume ends December. Vol. 1, no. 1, Fall 1930, as *Apparel Arts.* Quarterly. Vol. 27, no. 6, June 1957, as *Apparel Arts/Gentleman's Quarterly.* Vol. 28, no. 2–vol. 47, no. 8, Spring 1958–Winter 1977, as *GQ/Gentleman's Quarterly.* Eight times a year: March, April, May, Summer, September, October, November, Winter. Vol. 48, no. 1–present, February 1978–present. Ten times a year, monthly except January and July.

PUBLISHER AND PLACE OF PUBLICATION

Published by Esquire, Inc., Chicago, Illinois, 1957–May 1977; by GQ, Inc., Chicago, Illinois, June 1977–1979; by Conde Nast Magazines, Inc., New York, New York, 1979–present. Publishers: Bernard J. Miller, June 1957–Summer 1974;

David M. O'Brasky, September 1974–November 1975; Sal M. Schiliro, Winter 1975–1976–1979; Steven Florio, 1979–June 1985; Jack Kliger, Summer 1985– November 1988; Michael Clinton, December 1988–present.

EDITORS

Everett Mattlin, June 1957–September 1969; Jack Haber, October 1969–1979; Arthur Cooper, 1979–present.

CIRCULATION

662,801 paid.

Carroll Varner

GRAHAM'S MAGAZINE

Energetic editor and publisher George R. Graham formed *Graham's Magazine* by merging *Burton's Gentleman's Magazine* with the *Casket* in 1840. At the time, he had little experience with magazines. Previously he apprenticed as a cabinetmaker, and he was admitted to the bar just two months before becoming an editor at a different periodical, the *Saturday Evening Post*.* Despite his lack of experience, he had a grand idea for his new magazine, and both he and the magazine achieved their greatest success during the 1840s. From 1841 to 1845, according to Frank Luther Mott, *Graham's* "displayed a brilliance which has seldom been matched in American magazine history."[1]

The two magazines that, once united, would later become so popular, were mixtures of articles, letters, sentimental essays and poetry, and literary reviews. Samuel C. Atkinson and Charles Alexander founded the *Casket* in 1826. Aimed chiefly at women readers, it was composed of stories and articles, poetry, fashion, and music. Typical of its articles were a biographical sketch and engraving of Simon Bolivar (January 1830), a "map of Europe and statistical tables" (1832), and an excerpt from "Elizabeth Bennet, or Pride and Prejudice" (October 1832). In addition to the *Casket*, Atkinson and Alexander also published the *Saturday Evening Post*. Mott notes that the *Casket* was often simply a place where items from the *Saturday Evening Post* were reprinted.[2] Graham purchased the *Casket* in 1839, and according to John Tebbel, transformed it from a "cheap-looking miscellany to a well-printed entertaining magazine."[3] While the *Casket* had a fairly long history, and was quite popular,[4] *Burton's* originated only three and a half years before Graham purchased it, existing from July 1837 to December 1840. William E. Burton edited it, and the same Charles Alexander published it. The magazine achieved some success, printing poetry and stories (including Edgar Allan Poe's "The Fall of the House of Usher"), book reviews, and tales of adventure. Desiring to return to his first love, the stage, Burton offered the periodical to Graham, who purchased the magazine, and its subscription list, for $3,500.[5] The new periodical became one of the country's most popular magazines and was a major literary title. Despite the title change and a change in format (to that of *Burton's*), *Graham's* retained the numbering of the *Casket*.

At the height of its success, each issue of *Graham's* generally contained an essay, several short stories, a significant amount of poetry, a travel piece, and a section of unsigned literary reviews. Graham remains well known for his expansive attitude regarding contributors, having paid handsomely for the articles and poetry in the magazine. Rather than paying a standard rate, Graham was more generous with famous contributors. William Cullen Bryant and Henry Wadsworth Longfellow received $50 for each poem printed in *Graham's* for example, and James Fenimore Cooper was paid $10 per page.[6] In addition to Bryant, Longfellow, and Cooper, frequent contributors were James Russell Lowell and Edgar Allan Poe (who also served as literary editor for fifteen months in 1841 and 1842). Poe's "Murders in the Rue Morgue" first appeared in *Graham's*, in the April 1841 issue. Unfortunately, he did not enjoy Graham's generosity, and was generally paid only $4 to $5 for each page.[7] In addition, unlike most other periodicals, whose articles remained anonymous, *Graham's* listed contributors' names on the cover, thus advertising the contents of each issue.

A predominant feature in the magazine was the presence of colored plates—both fashion and art. At the time, they were an unusual feature in the monthlies, according to John Sartain, who designed many of those used by Graham.[8] The fashion plates and illustrations in the magazine were appealing to its women readers, and it has been said that "[Graham] made pictorial illustration a distinctive feature of American magazines."[9] Previously if plates were used at all, they were generally old, often worn, and purchased for as little as possible. George Graham's philosophy of paying well for written contributions to his magazine extended to the engravings: they would be an outstanding feature of the magazine, and he would pay well for them. He is reported to have paid at least $405 for an engraving of Longfellow that appeared in the May 1843 issue.[10] Sartain boasted that the plates he engraved specifically for each issue were instrumental in the magazine's success.

Whatever the reason for *Graham's* popularity, the circulation reportedly increased from 5,500 in 1841 to 40,000 by the end of 1842.[11] The status of *Graham's* demonstrated that by expending money for quality writing and artwork, a magazine could retain good writers and artists, and increase its circulation.[12] The success of the periodical, however, was partly responsible for George Graham's eventual financial difficulty. He speculated heavily with his newfound wealth, and in 1848 was forced to sell the magazine to Samuel C. Patterson. He regained control in 1850, but the days of *Graham's* supremacy among the literary magazines were over. *Harper's** provided competition that was too strong, and despite many attempts to revive it, *Graham's* circulation declined rapidly. Graham was forced to sell the magazine again for financial reasons in 1853. It is unclear whether he retained any editorial position, although Arthur Wrobel states he was editor through 1857.[13] By 1857 Charles Godfrey Leland was sole editor.

During the decade of *Graham's* decline, it had a different look. Sentimental poetry and short stories were still dominant features, but there were new features such as the Monthly Summary, which apprised readers of the news of the country and the world. Other features were Recipes for the House and Toilet, Medical Suggestions, Fashion Gossip, the Ladies Work Table, and Editor's Easy Talk. Finally, in the December 1858 issue, this announcement appeared, signed by the publishers, Watson and Company:

> Owing to arrangements which have been for some time in preparation, it becomes our duty to inform our readers that after the first of January next, *Graham's Magazine* will be incorporated with a new publication to be entitled the *American Monthly*.

It is not clear, however, what exactly did happen to *Graham's* magazine. According to Mott, it appears to have become the *Ladies Illustrated Magazine*, which was swallowed into "blind oblivion."[14]

Graham's Magazine was a significant magazine in its time and remains so for a number of reasons. It was one of the first literary magazines to pay well for contributions, and it published some fine essays and stories by the best-known writers of the day along with its popular sentimental pieces. Its list of contributors is impressive, and the use of colored plates set a new standard for the monthlies. In addition, *Graham's* is said to have begun "magazinish writing in contradistinction from the dull and heavy review style all too prominent at that time."[15] A magazine that at one time claimed a circulation of 40,000 must be recognized as a major publication in the mid–nineteenth century; one with the contributors of *Graham's* must be recognized as not just popular but significant.

Notes

1. Frank Luther Mott, *A History of American Magazines*, vol. 1: *1741–1850* (Cambridge: Harvard University Press, 1938), p. 544.

2. Ibid, p. 545.

3. John Tebbel, *The American Magazine: A Compact History* (New York: Hawthorn Books, 1969), p. 49.

4. It was said by Lambert A. Wellmer to be "the most widely circulated monthly" in the country (Mott, p. 544).

5. Mott, p. 676.

6. Joy Bayless, *Rufus Wilmot Griswold: Poe's Literary Executor* (Nashville: Valderbilt University Press, 1943), pp. 55, 59; and Tebbel, p. 71. According to Tebbel, Graham paid anywhere from four to twelve dollars a page for prose, and ten to fifty dollars for a poem. . . . This rate scale had an inflationary effect on all magazines able to afford it, and the result was highly beneficial for writers" (p. 71).

7. Tebbel, p. 71.

8. John Sartain, *The Reminiscences of a Very Old Man, 1808–1897* (1899; repr. New York: Benjamin Blom, 1969), p. 197.

9. James Playsted Wood, *Magazines in the United States*, 2nd ed. (New York: Ronald Press, 1956), p. 50.

10. Bayless, pp. 57–58.

11. Sartain, p. 198.

12. Tebbel, p. 84. Furthermore, "Writers were loyal to him. He shared his success with them, as well as enjoying it himself." (p. 84).

13. Arthur Wrobel, "Graham's Lady's and Gentleman's Magazine," in *American Literary Magazines: The Eighteenth and Nineteenth Centuries*, ed. Edward E. Chielens (New York: Greenwood Press, 1986), p. 164.

14. Mott, p. 555.

15. Ibid.

Information Sources

BIBLIOGRAPHY

Bayless, Joy. *Rufus Wilmot Griswold: Poe's Literary Executor*. Nashville: Vanderbilt University Press, 1943.

Mott, Frank Luther. *A History of American Magazines*, vol. 1: *1741–1850*. Cambridge: Harvard University Press, 1938, pp. 544–555.

Sartain, John. *The Reminiscences of a Very Old Man, 1808–1897*. 1899; repr. New York: Benjamin Blom, 1969.

Tebbel, John. *The American Magazine: A Compact History*. New York: Hawthorn Books, 1969.

Wood, James Playsted. *Magazines in the United States*. 2nd ed. New York: Ronald Press, 1956.

Wrobel, Arthur. "Graham's Lady's and Gentleman's Magazine." In *American Literary Magazines: The Eighteenth and Nineteenth Centuries*. Ed. Edward E. Chielens. Westport, CT: Greenwood Press, 1986, pp. 156–161.

INDEX SOURCES
Annual, 1827–1837; semiannual, 1840–1858. Not indexed elsewhere.

LOCATION SOURCES
Widely available (American Periodical Series). *Graham's Magazine,* vol. 1–53, 1826–1858, from AMS (New York) reprints. Available in Microform.

Publication History

MAGAZINE TITLE AND TITLE CHANGES
Graham's Magazine. The Casket: Flowers of Literature, Wit and Sentiment (also, *Atkinson's Casket, or Gems of Literature, Wit and Sentiment*), vol. 1–13; *The Casket, and Philadelphia Monthly Magazine*, vol. 14–16; *Graham's Lady's and Gentleman's Magazine*, vols. 17–21 and vol. 23; *Graham's Magazine of Literature and Art*, vol. 22; *Graham's American Monthly Magazine of Literature and Art*, vol. 24–46; *Graham's American Monthly of Literature, Art and Fashion*, vol. 47–48; *Graham's Illustrated Magazine of Literature, Romance, Art and Fashion*, vols. 49–53. From volume 18 (1841) through volume 53 (1858), the title page consistently reads *Graham's Magazine*.

VOLUME AND ISSUE DATA

> Vol. 1–13, 1826–1838, called *The Casket,* 12 numbers each; vols. 14–53, 1839–1858, *Graham's Magazine*, 6 numbers each. Volume numbers for October 1843 through November 1845 are misnumbered vol. 24, no. 4 through vol. 28, no. 5; volume numbering is corrected with December 1845, vol. 27, no. 6. January 1846 is vol. 28, no. 1. Monthly.

PUBLISHERS AND PLACE OF PUBLICATION

> Atkinson and Alexander, 1826–1827; Samuel C. Atkinson, 1828–April 1839; George R. Graham, May 1839–July 1848; Samuel D. Patterson and Company, 1848–March 1850; George R. Graham, April 1850–December 1853; Samuel D. Patterson and Company, 1854–June 1856; R. H. See and Company, 1854–June 1856; Watson and Company, July 1856–1858. New York(?).

EDITORS

> Samuel C. Atkinson, 1826–1839; George R. Graham and Charles J. Peterson, 1839–1840; George R. Graham, Charles J. Peterson, Edgar Allan Poe (literary editor), 1841; George R. Graham, Charles J. Peterson, Edgar Allan Poe (until May), Emma C. Embury, Amy S. Stephens, Rufus Griswold, 1842; George R. Graham and Rufus Griswold, 1843; George R. Graham, 1844–1847; George R. Graham, Robert T. Conrad, J. R. Chandler, J. B. Taylor, 1848; George R. Graham, J. R. Chandler, and J. B. Taylor, 1849; George R. Graham, 1850–1852; Charles Godfrey Leland, 1857(?)–1858.

CIRCULATION

> 40,000 (1842—peak circulation).

Jean M. Parker

GRIT

Grit, considered one of the leading local and national periodicals of a general type, began as a weekend newspaper on 10 December 1882 in Williamsport, Pennsylvania, and is still in existence.[1] The periodical offers a forum to ordinary people with special stories to tell who live in small towns or the country; however, big-city folks who find the simple life attractive also contribute to and read *Grit.*

Planning of *Grit* was far from being ideal. Even though America and especially Williamsport could have supported another small-town folksy paper in 1882, it was not ready for another periodical that was uninteresting and "colorless." During its first fifteen months of existence, *Grit* would have perished if Dietrich Lamade (and partners) had not purchased it by borrowing $100 here and $100 there to acquire the fledgling paper. With his creative instincts, Lamade turned the paper into a bright, newsy, entertaining family paper. Part of his plot involved developing, in 1885, a lottery to attract readers. Giveaway prizes initially included a piano, a marble-topped bedroom suite, and a silk dress. The scheme worked, and within a few months, circulation tripled, reaching 50,000 by 1890. Trumpeting "Americanism" and rejecting "statism," the magazine began including plenty of pictures, fast-moving fiction (mostly Westerns) and the news, patterned to suit small towns.

Emphasizing traditional American values and individual integrity, the ''chatty, shirt-sleeved homebody of a newspaper''[2] continues to attract contributors with original stories to tell from the heartland of America, suggestions for successful living, and inspirational messages. Also included are romantic and adventuresome novelettes. Over a hundred years later, *Grit* continues to include articles and stories that appeal to the entire family—a woman from Sherman, Texas, has a collection of nearly 10,000 pens and pencils; a Mantua Township, New Jersey man built a model of the Eiffel Tower from 3,200 toothpicks.[3] Recent issues feature weekly columns by *Grit*'s editor Mike Rafferty and ''Viewpoints,'' written by the noted Paul Harvey. Additionally, each issue displays a colorful cover and a centerfold featuring food recipes. Classifieds abound; entertainment features people such as ''Tom Selleck's Set for Comedy Role'' and ''Dick Van Patten Presents 1½ Ton Birthday Cake.''[4] And an interesting section titled ''Etcetera'' gives pet peeves and thrift tips. The tone of *Grit* is cheery rather than sordid and sin and sensation are taboo. Divorcées rarely appear in its fiction. Obviously, the paper's story-section heroines do not smoke or drink.

With *Grit*'s inspirational nature, it might be reasoned that the focus of the magazine might deter purchase of it, thereby eventually reducing circulation. However, *Grit*'s circulation and profitability grew steadily as the periodical assumed national readership.

From 1882 to 1890 as the *Williamsport Grit*, to it attained a circulation of 50,000. By 1887 it became known as the *Pennsylvania Grit*; due to its national exposure, in 1907 the name was changed to *Grit, the National Small-town Weekly*. Circulation increased to 665,000 in 1949, with two-thirds of the readers from families living in villages of less than 1,000.

During the 1960s, circulation reached 1.5 million, and in 1969, circulation actually accounted for 75 percent of *Grit*'s $12 million gross revenues generated that year, with advertising accounting for 25 percent.[5] Shareholders enjoyed healthy dividends. However, by 1979, circulation declined to 900,000,[6] and in 1982, it was reported in *Newsweek* that the magazine was fighting to survive with a circulation of only 650,000.[7]

It is speculated that the decline in circulation after 1962 could be partially attributed to a decrease in the numbers of anxious kids recruited to peddle the periodical from house to house. To distribute *Grit*, Lamade's idea of creating an army of 30,000 boys to peddle it in towns with populations of less than 2,500 began in 1890, and in 1949, this was still the primary way by which the weekly was disseminated. Prizes and pay were incentive enough to keep such a formidable army of youngsters viable until the 1960s. The prospering fast-food industry and inflated allowances from parents provided teenagers with other avenues of acquiring money. By the 1980s the army of youngsters willing to distribute the weekly dropped by nearly two-thirds.

Additionally, small-town folks began to move to cities in increasing numbers; postal rates increased, making distribution more expensive; and it became more costly to find new subscribers. Advertisers who supported most publications began to lose interest in *Grit* because of its image as a periodical read by aging working-class people. According to Bob Cunnion, advertising director in 1983, "They (working-class folks) may have been God-fearing people, but they didn't have money to buy anything."[8]

Changing times have also brought about alterations in the appearance and cost of *Grit*. Two chubby cherubs tug-of-warring with a banner emblazoned "*Grit*" on the front cover of early issues have given way to a tabloid displaying brightly colored pictures of featured persons. Today, the emblazoned title remains void of its once accompanying banner, yet the magazine's overall appearance is appealing and the newsprint is easy to read.

Grit continues to be successful with advertising, devoting about a fourth of the periodical to it. Current issues of *Grit* cost seventy-five cents; however, the cost of five-cents per copy was not raised to seven cents until 1944 when the periodical adopted a tabloid format. By 1949, the cost per copy became ten cents.

The magazine's features have been criticized for their folksy content and its focus on only cheery aspects of life. Some issues feature sermons, and some of its editorial pages have been written by retired or former ministers hired as columnists. *Grit*'s sanctimonious tone has been seen as a bit too much for the sophisticated reader. Additionally, *Grit*'s publisher and editor allege the magazine is for the entire family, but many of its items are traditionally thought of as for women: food, fashions, beauty hints, and the home. Despite these criticisms, current issues of *Grit* tend to follow the traditional format.

As *Grit* continues to survive, the tabloid, newspaper-printed format gives it a very "homey" informal appearance. Photography is of a fairly high quality, yet the layout of the magazine tends toward crowdedness. Very helpful is the table of contents, which includes all of its standard features and columns.

The person most responsible for *Grit*'s success was Dietrich Lamade, a canny young German immigrant who was adept at cutting costs to produce the magazine, thereby assuring its success. Lamade believed in traditional American values. In creating a closely held company with a tradition in community paternalism, he practiced what was preached in *Grit*. Employees were treated with a great deal of respect, yet they were not allowed to smoke in the newsroom. "Once-hired, never-fired" was the Lamade policy, which remained part of the ninety-year-old institution until 1983, when it became counterproductive to maintain some of these traditional ideas. "Let us do nothing that will encourage fear, worry, temptation, or other forms of weakness. Let us make every issue of *Grit* ring the joybells of life."[9] Such was Lamade's admonition, which was framed on one of the walls of a newsroom.

Succeeding Deitrich after his death in 1938 were his sons Howard and George, who continued the tradition of their father. However, the *Grit* institution experienced a major change in 1983 when Dietrich Lamade's grandsons Jim, Bob, and Pete discovered that to remain viable layoffs might be necessary, and innovative new products would be needed while unproductive assets would have to be sold.

The catalyst for this transformation was Andy Stabler, a quiet and self-effacing man, hired in 1983 as chief executive officer of *Grit* Publishing Company. Stabler hired two consultants shortly after taking this position to help bring about the necessary changes. With their advice, the periodical was transformed into a diversified communications holding company. No longer was Grit a single-product company; it acquired television and radio stations plus cable television. Lamco Communications was created to oversee the management of this communications system in 1983. The Lamade grandsons accepted their diversified communications company; however, as they begin thinking of retirement, no fourth generation Lamade has yet shown interest in *Grit*.

Notes

1. Research sources provided no information indicating the owner-publisher of *Grit* when the paper originated. Sources begin with Dietrich Lamade, who bought the paper fifteen months after its beginning.

2. "Joybells Every Week," *Newsweek*, 7 November 1949, p. 59.

3. *Grit* is voluminous with examples like these of individuals who have done things that might appear to be trivial, but seemingly appeal to certain types of families.

4. Taken from issues 24–30 July 1988.

5. The year 1962 was recorded in *Newsweek*, 2 September 1982, as the period of *Grit*'s peak circulation of 1.5 million. *Inc., Magazine*, August 1983, recorded the exact year of 1969 as the year of peak circulation.

6. James Crossley, the company's new president in 1982, refuted this accusation and blamed the decline on distribution problems. He further indicated that mail subscriptions, which accounted for more than half of the sales, would reverse the circulation decline. According to the *Gale Directory of Publications* for 1987, *Grit*'s circulation was 575, 124.

7. "Here's Good News: *Grit* Battles On," *Newsweek*, 27 September 1982, p. 12.

8. *Inc., Magazine*, "What Business Are You Really In?" August 1983, p. 82.

9. "Joybells Every Week," 7 November 1949, p. 59.

Information Sources

BIBLIOGRAPHY

Gale Directory of Publications. Detroit: Gale Research Company, 1987.

Grit, America's Family Magazine. Selected issues.

"Here's Good News: *Grit* Battles On." *Newsweek*, 27 September 1982, p. 12.

"Joybells Every Week." *Newsweek*, 7 November 1949, p. 59.

Katz, Bill, and Linda Sternberg Katz. *Magazines for Libraries*. 5th ed. New York: R. R. Bowker, 1986, p. 481.

Mott, Frank Luther. *A History of American Magazines 1885–1905*. vol. 4. Cambridge: Harvard University Press, 1957, pp. 68–69.

"What Business Are You Really In?" *Inc.*, August 1983, pp. 80–84.

INDEX SOURCES
    n. a.
LOCATION SOURCES
    n.a.

Publication History

MAGAZINE TITLE AND TITLE CHANGES
    Williamsport Grit, 1882–1890; *Pennsylvania Grit; GRIT, the National Small-Town Weekly,* 1907—; *GRIT, America's Family Magazine,* —1989.
VOLUME AND ISSUE DATA
    Volume 1, December 10, 1882, to current issues, Volume 47, October 30–November 5. Printed in five editions. Weekly current [1988] cost, 75 cents per issue.
PUBLISHER AND PLACE OF PUBLICATION
    Grit Publishing Company, Subsidiary of Stauffer Communications Company, 208 West Third Street, Williamsport, Pennsylvania. Evan Anderson, publisher.
EDITORS
    Howard Rothrock Davis, 1905; Kenneth Dean Rhone, 1949; Rhone was *Grit's* seventh editor. Information about other editors not found. Michael R. Rafferty, 1988.
CIRCULATION
    Peak circulation of 1.5 million in either 1962 or 1969; 1987 circulation, 575,124.

Frances Moore-Bond

H

HARPER'S MAGAZINE

In its 138-year history, *Harper's* has undergone a number of changes, each calculated to perpetuate or recapture its past popularity. Harper and Brothers began publishing it because they had extra time to fill on their printing presses.[1] In the beginning it was a collection of miscellaneous material reprinted from British periodicals. It was 144 pages of cramped type in double columns with a few woodcuts at the end. Its strength was literature, especially the Long serialized novels of the famous nineteenth-century English writers.[2] It published Charles Dickens's *Bleak House,* William Makepeace Thackeray's *The Virginians*, Anthony Trollope's *Small House at Allington*, and Thomas Hardy's *Return of the Native*.[3]

By the end of the nineteenth century, it had become one of the most successful of the serious, general periodicals of the time. It reflected the growth in wealth and refinement that characterized the period. It was longer, with larger type, and lavish illustration. It published history, science, geography, literature, and three departments, one each of literary criticism (The Editor's Study), news (The Monthly Record of Current Events), and humor (The Editor's Drawer).

During this period *Harper's* became a major force in shaping America's literary tastes. William Dean Howells used his position as author of the Editor's Study from 1888 to 1894 to defend the new realism in American literature against the more romantic, melodramatic English literature that had been so popular up to that time. *Harper's* had always published works by such great American authors as Nathaniel Hawthorne, Herman Melville, Stephen Crane, Mark Twain, Bret Harte, and, of course, Howells. But during this period *Harper's* became identified as a major vehicle for native authors such as Edward Bellamy, Lefcadio Hearn, Richard Harding Davis, and J. W. De Forest.[4]

Harper's slowly became less competitive during the first two decades of the twentieth century. In 1925, however, Thomas B. Wells initiated a major change of direction for the magazine. It printed more political and social criticism and less fiction. Indeed, long, serialized fiction nearly disappeared from its pages. The typeface was simplified and all illustrations were gone, except one color, fine art reproduction at the beginning of each issue. The shift was away from genteel entertainment for the leisure classes to serious debate and commentary for the educated of any economic stratum. *Harper's* had always included articles on contemporary affairs written from a nonpolitical viewpoint. But now they reflected a clearly liberal bias and became the main focus of the magazine.[5]

Harper's gradually went further in the direction set by Wells. A *Harper's* of 1930 or 1940 was still very much like one of 1925. A typical issue from this period included several short stories; two or three serious articles on recent social, economic, or political issues; a historical or geographical article; and several departments. In all of these areas *Harper's* was able to attract the best authors, for example, Bertrand Russell, James Truslow Adams, Katherine Mansfield, Walter Lippmann, and Peter F. Drucker.

By 1950, however, *Harper's* had gradually evolved into something different. Each cover was a different color and sported a selection of the contents of the magazine, as an advertisement for its own contents. The format was taller and wider, but thinner than in the past. There were more articles, but they were, on the average, shorter. Although *Harper's* published a short story or two and several poems in each issue, they were significantly outnumbered by the non-fiction articles. Illustrations had returned; several black and white drawings adorned both articles and stories in each issue. The articles covered nearly all subjects of interest to an educated liberal of the time: communism, the presidential election, television, the poor, atomic energy. More of the articles were written by journalists and free-lance writers than by literary authors, historians, philosophers, and other more enduring authors as in the past.

In the 1960s the magazine market began to change, and *Harper's* had difficulty maintaining its preeminence. On 1 August 1967 Willie Morris was appointed editor-in-chief at the age of 32.[6] Morris attempted to reestablish *Harper's* earlier reputation as one of America's foremost literary magazines, and to increase circulation by publishing controversial material. He was moderately successful for a while, but precipitated his own termination as editor by publishing Norman Mailer's "The Prisoner of Sex," a scurrilous attack on feminism.[7]

After Morris, *Harper's* lost both subscribers and money at an even faster rate, and was nearly dissolved.[8] It was saved at the last minute, however, by the John D. and Catherine T. MacArthur Foundation and Atlantic Richfield Foundation, and became its own independent organization.[9]

The current editor, Lewis Lapham, has adapted *Harper's* format to the times. It is a leaner, simpler, better organized, more vigorously diverse publication than in the past. Issues run to around eighty pages. All the contents are fitted into one of the twelve generic departments, which regularly appear in every issue; Letters, Notebook, Harper's Index, Readings, Essay, Annotation, Report, Story, Miscellany, Review, Acrostic, and Puzzle. Notebook is an editorial by Lapham. Harper's Index measures the state of the nation by listing suggestive statistics such as the percentage of Americans who believe that hard work is the way to get rich. Readings is a section of long quotations from miscellaneous sources on any topic, for example, literature, religion, and politics. Essay is a long in-depth article on a serious social, economic, or political subject. Annotation takes a sample page of some document such as the Pentagon budget or the Nielsen ratings and explains the text in a mixture of sincerity and satire. The explanations are grouped in several distinct paragraphs around the text. Report is a medium-length article describing the author's personal experience in a place of current interest such as Guatemala or Ethiopia. It is an innovative format designed to appeal to people who have less time for reading than their parents did.

Harper's has managed to survive one civil war, five foreign wars, two bankruptcies, three publishers, radio, and television, and has one of the liveliest formats of any periodical in the information age. It is an unusual achievement for a magazine to last so long and still be viable today. At the age of 138, *Harper's* is an American institution.

Notes

1. Frederick L. Allen, "One Hundred Years of *Harper's*," *Harper's Magazine*, October 1950, p. 23.

2. Frank Luther Mott, *A History of American Magazines*, vol. 2: *1850–1865* (Cambridge: Harvard University Press, 1938), pp. 384–87.

3. Bernard De Voto, "Ninetieth Anniversary," *Harper's Magazine*, June 1940, p. 110.

4. Ibid., p. 111.

5. Mott, p. 404, and Allen, pp. 32–34.

6. "Youth for *Harper's*," *Time*, 19 May 1967, p. 56, and John Fischer, "Announcing Some Changes," *Harper's Magazine*, July 1967, p. 24.

7. "Coup at *Harper's*," *Newsweek*, 15 March 1971, p. 64; "Hang up at *Harper's*," *Time*, 15 March 1971, p. 41; D. M. Mount, "Mailer Lights Another Fire," *Publishers Weekly*, 15 February 1971, p. 55; "Morris Quits at *Harper's*," *Publishers Weekly*, 15 March 1971, p. 51.

8. Arlie Schardt and Nancy Stadtman, "*Harper's*: 1850–1980," *Newsweek*, 30 June 1980, p. 71.

9. MadaLynne Reuter, "Two Foundations Buy *Harper's*," *Publishers Weekly*, 25 July 1980, p. 81; Lewis H. Lapham, "Intimations of Mortality," *Harper's Magazine*, September 1980, pp. 8–9; "*Harper's* Reborn," *Time*, 21 July 1980, p. 62; "Angels Rescind Obit," *Newsweek*, 21 July 1980, p. 84.

Information Sources

BIBLIOGRAPHY
Allen, Frederick L. "One Hundred Years of *Harper's*." *Harper's Magazine*, October 1950, p. 23.

"Angels Rescind Obit." *Newsweek*, 21 July 1980, p. 84.

"Coup at *Harper's*." *Newsweek*, 15 March 1971, p. 64.

De Voto, Bernard. "Ninetieth Anniversary." *Harper's Magazine*, June 1940, pp. 109–12.

Fischer, John. "Announcing Some Changes." *Harper's Magazine*, July 1967, p. 24.

"Hang up at *Harper's*." *Time*, 15 March 1971, p. 41.

"*Harper's* Reborn." *Time*, 21 July 1980, p. 62.

Lapham, Lewis H. "Intimations of Mortality." *Harper's Magazine*, September 1980, pp. 8–9.

"Morris Quits at *Harper's*." *Publishers Weekly*, 15 March 1971, p. 51.

Mott, Frank Luther. *A History of American Magazines*. Vol. 2: *1850–1865*. Cambridge: Harvard University Press, 1938.

Mount, D. M. "Mailer Lights Another Fire." *Publishers Weekly*, 15 February 1971, p. 55.

Reuter, Madalynne. "Two Foundations Buy *Harper's*." *Publishers Weekly*, 25 July 1980, p. 81.

Schardt, Arlie, and Nancy Stadtman. "*Harper's*: 1850–1980." *Newsweek*, 30 June 1980, p. 71.

"Youth for *Harper's*." *Time*, 19 May 1967, p. 56.

INDEX SOURCES
> *Poole's* (1850–1906); *Readers' Guide* (1889–present); *Magazine Index* (1977–present).

LOCATION SOURCES
> Widely held and available in Microform.

Publication History

MAGAZINE TITLE AND TITLE CHANGES
> *Harper's New Monthly Magazine*, 1850–1900; *Harper's Monthly Magazine*, 1900–1939; *Harper's Magazine*, 1939–present.

VOLUME AND ISSUE DATA
> June 1850–current. Monthly. Semiannual volumes. Vol. 62, December 1880–May 1881 is vol. 1 of the British edition.

PUBLISHERS AND PLACE OF PUBLICATION
> Harper & Brothers, New York.

EDITORS
> Henry J. Raymond, 1850–1856; Alfred H. Guernsey, 1856–1869; Henry Mills Alden, 1869–1919; Thomas B. Wells, 1919–1931; Lee Foster Hartman, 1931–1941; Frederick L. Allen, 1941–1953; John Fischer, 1954–1967; Willie Morris, 1967–1971; Robert Shnayerson, 1971–1975; Lewis H. Lapham, 1975–1982; Michael Kinsley, 1982–1983; Lewis H. Lapham, 1983–present.

CIRCULATION
> 150,000.

James Hart

HEALTH

One of the more widely read popular health periodicals, *Health* magazine was founded by publishing patriarch Maxwell M. Geffen, of Family Health Magazine, in 1969. Originally titled *Family Health*, the preview issue of this magazine featured cover photographs of a young mother and daughter enjoying a peaceful moment together in the country and a laboratory scientist, linked by the promising statement: "To Feel Well, Look Better, Live Longer . . . " *Family Health* was planned as nourishment for a *public* "as hungry for current news on health care as physicians are."[1]

Based on the magazine's circulation statistics then, now, and at every point in between, the publisher's projection was indeed correct. Editor William H. White stated in issue number 1 that in advance of publication, the mailing of a subscription letter resulted in 750,000 promised subscribers. Coupled with a quarter of a million over-the-counter sales, the result was an extremely healthy million-plus circulation at the magazine's very outset.[2] *Family Health* began in 1969 with a yearly subscription rate of three dollars.

The articles in the initial issues of *Family Health* were meant to capture the interest of a general readership. Written by medical journalists and backed by an editorial advisory board consisting of physicians and scientists, the magazine featured regular departments like Trends, Month in Medicine, Ask the Doctor, and Beauty Care. The news of research, drugs, therapy, health, and beauty was covered in a casual, easy to understand writing style. Throughout the early seventies, the magazine featured such popular topics as legalizing abortion, low cholesterol foods, national health goals, heart disease, family exercise programs, cancer, contraception, and health insurance coverage.

In the January 1970 issue, the editor's statement focused on medical research developments ahead in the seventies, projecting that the decade might well be called the "Age of Medical Revolution." A cure for cancer, a vaccine to protect against hepatitis, test drugs to combat virus-caused diseases and Parkinson's disease, regulations to prevent environmental pollution, and in general, an awareness that prevention of illness might be the best cure—these were some of the dominant health issues of the era.

In 1971, the price of a subscription to *Family Health* increased one dollar, to four dollars per year. In the January issue that year, the magazine featured a special twelve-page guide to health insurance, intended to help readers assess their health insurance coverage. More significantly, *Family Health* teamed up with a leading insurance provider to create a broad income protection policy that was then made available to all subscribers.

In Bill Katz's and Berry Gargal's 1972 *Magazines for Libraries, Family Health* is described as "a general health magazine which has the largest circulation of any in this genre" (1,029,000 at that time). Katz states that "the articles and features sometimes are a bit too breezy, but the information apparently is accurate enough, and when there is doubt, the author says so." Katz notes that though the magazine does contain quite a significant amount of advertising, "the publisher will not accept tobacco or alcohol advertisements." The conclusion that Katz reaches in his 1972 review of the magazine is that it is "one of the best general, easy to understand family health magazines—and at a low price."[3]

The seventies brought changes in editorship for *Family Health*, from William H. White to Caroline Stevens to Jim Hoffman to Dalma Heyn. But a much more

visible change for the reader occurred in April 1976, when *Today's Health*
(formerly *Hygeia*), an American Medical Association (AMA) publication since
1923, merged with *Family Health* to form the uncontested leader in family health
magazines at that time, with combined readership of over six million each month
(as stated on the cover of the first combined issue). Katz reports that actual
circulation was 1,100,000 in 1978.[4] According to *Family Health* publisher Hy
Steirman, in "an open letter to *Today's Health* subscribers," the American
Medical Association decided, after fifty-four years, that it was no longer appropriate for it to be in the business of consumer publishing and so looked for
another publisher to take over. Steirman noted that by coincidence, *Family Health*
medical editor, Dr. Morris Fishbein, had founded the AMA's *Hygeia* in 1923.
Steirman's letter in this pivotal issue stated the magazine's revised goals: to keep
the public "informed on the latest in health, nutrition, and preventive medicine,"
and to help families live longer, happier, healthier lives.[5]

The late seventies saw more attention to food, nutrition, and health action
plans, though advertisements for questionable over-the-counter pep pills still
abounded. Dr. Morris Fishbein, in the May 1976 column "As We See It,"
emphasized *Family Health's* commitment to prevention of illness and to nutrition,
evidenced by long-standing columns like the one written by nutritionist Dr. Jean
Mayer. As medical editor, Fishbein traced the history of health education in the
United States, pointing to the important contribution of AMA's *Hygeia* (renamed
Today's Health in 1950) as a respected vehicle for the transmission of health
education information. The yearly subscription price then was $5.97. In Sep-
tember of 1976, Dr. Fishbein passed away, leaving his legacy of health education
writing, particularly his column "Ask The Doctor," to carry into the future.

Family Health came out with a new cover in February 1978. The design
implied a definite change in the magazine's focus, with *Family* in small letters
followed by a very bold *Health*. Hank Herman joined up as the new editor of
Family Health in May of 1980, coming from within the ranks as former managing
editor. His contributions over the next eight years provided stability during a
time of rapid change in health care issues and attitudes.

Max Geffen, founder of the magazine, died in 1980. Over the years, Geffen
carefully bought and sold some one hundred magazines (usually at a profit), yet
continued to hold the reins of *Family Health*, nurturing it throughout his career,
even after retirement.[6] Geffen's success as a publishing entrepreneur has been
attributed to his "gift for spotting and developing bright young talent and making
quick, intuitive decisions that frequently paid off in millions of dollars in profits."[7]

In 1981, to reflect values of independence, individuality, and perhaps the
single life, the magazine's name was changed from *Family Health* to simply
Health. Gene-spliced vaccines, training for fitness, salad bars, coping with stress,
and stir-frying were typical features. A regular column written by a gynecologist
and the introduction of information about a new disease called AIDS were

noteworthy inclusions in the early eighties. By this time, the cost of a yearly subscription to *Health* had risen to $15.

Katz's 1984 *Magazines for Libraries* reported that the circulation of *Health* had dropped to 800,000, most likely because of increased competition from other general health magazines. However, throughout the eighties, *Health* maintained its status as "a top choice in readable, appealing health magazines for families and a resource for teachers of health, physical fitness, and home economics."[8] A new cover design in 1986 and continued interest on the part of the magazine's staff to provide relevant health information to its audience resulted in lively, upbeat issues in the eighties.

Health retained its general nature, while many of the newer additions to the health magazine market reached out for consumers with more specialized health interests. Even with as many as twenty health-related magazines on the American market, there was still no oversupply. Health care was reported to be one of the most profitable advertising categories in 1987. No need to wonder why, with baby boomers reaching their late thirties and early forties. The desire to continue looking young and healthy, and to stay productive and on top of the job market, has become an obsession with the American people; products that enhance these qualities are selling like hotcakes used to sell. With newer magazines capturing some of this new market, *Health* readers were reported to be "older, less affluent, or less educated than (for example) the *Hippocrates* target group."[9]

A rating of thirteen health publications in 1987 gave *Health* a relatively poor report card, the lowest total score of all included in the rating. The reviewers felt that the magazine's editorial board should consist of more respected individuals in the field and that advertisements for nutrition supplements should not be included. In general, they thought *Health* to be a "poor source of health news. . . . It's essentially information for staying young and beautiful."[10]

Despite the criticism, *Health* continued to forge ahead. In 1988 the magazine got a new editor, a new cover and logo, and as throughout the years, a renewed commitment to staying at the helm of its readers' health information concerns. Coverage in 1988 included fitness fashion, skin resurfacing, genetic testing, and quality day-care, to name a few topics. The cost of a yearly subscription increased again to $22. However, in a world that values good health as a priceless commodity, the cost means nothing. The market is not yet saturated with health magazines, and as long as *Health* maintains its circulation of one million plus, it appears to be in no danger of being crowded out.

Notes

1. William H. White, in editorial of preview issue.
2. William H. White, in editorial of vol. 1, no. 1, October 1969.
3. Bill Katz and Berry Gargal, *Magazines for Libraries* 2nd ed. (New York: R. R. Bowker, 1972), p. 400.

4. Bill Katz and Berry G. Richards, *Magazines for Libraries* 3rd ed (New York: R. R. Bowker, 1978), pp. 458–459.

5. Steirman's letter appeared in the April 1976 issue.

6. "Publishing Patriarch," *Forbes*, 20 February 1978, p. 98.

7. "Maxwell M. Geffen Is Dead at 84," *New York Times Biographical Service*, October 1980, p. 1405.

8. Bill Katz and Linda Sternberg Katz, *Magazines for Libraries* 4th ed. (New York: R. R. Bowker, 1984), p. 644.

9. "Healthy Battle for Readers," *American Demographics*, February 1987, pp. 22–23.

10. "Rating the Health Advisers," *U.S. News and World Report*, 7 September 1987, pp. 54–55.

Information Sources

BIBLIOGRAPHY

"Healthy Battle for Readers." *American Demographics*, February 1987, pp. 22–23.

Katz, Bill, and Berry Gargal. *Magazines for Libraries*. 2nd ed. New York: R. R. Bowker, 1972.

Katz, Bill, and Berry G. Richards. *Magazines for Libraries*. 3rd ed. New York: R. R. Bowker, 1978.

Katz, Bill, and Linda Sternberg Katz. *Magazines for Libraries*. 4th ed. New York: R. R. Bowker, 1982.

"Maxwell M. Geffen Is Dead at 84." *New York Times Biographical Service*, October 1980, p. 1405.

"Publishing Patriarch." *Forbes*, 20 February 1978, p. 98.

"Rating the Health Advisers." *U.S. News and World Report*, 7 September 1987, pp. 54–55.

INDEX SOURCES

Readers' Guide (1977–present); *Access* (1975–present); *Cumulative Index to Nursing and Allied Health Literature* (1969–present); *General Science Index* (1978–present).

LOCATION SOURCES

Available in microform.

Publication History

MAGAZINE TITLE AND TITLE CHANGES

Health, formerly *Family Health*, incorporating *Today's Health*, formerly *Hygeia*.

VOLUME AND ISSUE DATA

Vols. 1–20, 1969–present. Monthly.

PUBLISHER AND PLACE OF PUBLICATION

Family Media, Inc., 3 Park Avenue, New York, New York.

Mary Beth Allen

HIGH FIDELITY

High Fidelity was the first magazine in America to address the interest of readers who did not exist prior to the 1940s—the audiophiles, the lovers of both music itself and the lavish and accurate reproduction of music in the home. Though recorded music of all genres already had a long and commercially successful history before *High Fidelity* was conceived, the notion of "high fidelity" did not achieve popularity until the late 1940s—roughly contiguous with the introduction of the long-playing record. Though there were special-interest magazines devoted solely to sound reproduction or music, it was *High Fidelity* that first brought together these two formerly disparate worlds in a skillful and appealing balance.

High Fidelity was the brainchild of publisher Milton B. Sleeper and editor Charles Fowler.[1] Radiocom (later Audiocom), Sleeper's publishing company, had already produced a series of magazines directed at the radio hobbyist, under constantly varying titles (*Communication Engineering, FM, FM Radio Electronics, FM and Television*, etc.). *High Fidelity's* first issue, which appeared in April of 1951, employed the same mixture of attention to both audio equipment and recorded music that the magazine still offers today. However, most of the early issues contained an evident "do-it-yourself" slant (unsurprising in view of the "hobbyist" predilections of Sleeper and Fowler). The audio components pictured in advertisements have a curiously "unfinished" look: amplifiers bristling with exposed vacuum tubes, turntables without bases, and speakers devoid of enclosures. Articles discussing home installation and construction of audio equipment cabinetry are common.

Over the next few years, serious music gradually received more emphasis. The magazine's original subtitle, *Devoted to the Interests of Audio-philes*, was changed to *The Magazine for Music Listeners* after one year, and cover illustrations devoted to music (i.e., portraits of composers) became more frequent; the space devoted to record reviews continually expanded. The magazine's immediate success warranted swift increases in publication frequency; originally a quarterly, *High Fidelity* began a bimonthly schedule with volume 2, number 2 (September-October 1952), finally becoming a monthly with volume 4, number 1 (March 1954).

The solidification of *High Fidelity* as a balanced music/audio equipment magazine came with the departure of Sleeper in 1954. Fowler took over as publisher (after a few issues with no publisher credit); associate editor John M. Conly, who frequently contributed record reviews and had previously written a highly successful music column for *Atlantic Monthly*,* became editor.[2] Conly's clear stance as a music lover set *High Fidelity* on an editorial path that continued until the late 1980s: an emphasis on the music, with equipment seen simply as a tool for its reproduction and enjoyment. This greater emphasis on music is what has distinguished *High Fidelity* from its competitors.

In 1957 *High Fidelity* was acquired by the music trade publishing giant, Billboard Publications; it was *Billboard*'s strength that led to *High Fidelity*'s acquisition, in 1964, of *Musical America*, the leading classical music magazine of the time. *Musical America*, which concentrated on music as manifested in live performance (rather than on recordings), was incorporated into *High Fidelity* as a special section printed on different paper and with separate pagination. Although the two publications did not actually "merge"—despite their physical coexistence, they remained editorially and graphically distinct—the inclusion of *Musical America* further defined *High Fidelity*'s identity as a music publication (however, it should be noted that *Musical America* was included in only the subscription edition of *High Fidelity*; the newsstand version continued as before). *Musical America* grew within its confinement, and in 1987 it separated from *High Fidelity*, though it is still published by ABC Consumer Magazines (formerly ABC Leisure Magazines, which bought *High Fidelity* from Billboard Publications in 1974 and continues to publish it today).[3]

Demographically, *High Fidelity* is aimed at moderately affluent readers who have perhaps one to five thousand dollars to spend on an audio system. This is revealed by the magazine's equipment reviews, which generally shun low-priced equipment, while leaving the ultraexpensive "high-end" products for magazines such as *Audio*.

High Fidelity's feature articles, for most of its history, have been evenly distributed between music and technical topics; they are written for the intelligent, educated layman and are often quite engaging and entertaining. The audio-oriented articles are typically deft, lively explications of such technically forbidding subjects as noise reduction and digital sampling; the result, for the reader, is that the complex world of high fidelity sound reproduction is demystified without condescension. Music articles are usually oriented toward the world of recording (for example, a review of a prominent performer's recording career), though excellent pieces on purely musical subjects appear as well. Additionally there are occasional forays into esoteric topics, such as theft of stereo systems (September 1976, written by an alleged former burglar) and improvement of the perceived performance of a stereo system by having one's ears cleaned by a physician (August 1974). Special issues devoted to a single aspect of high fidelity, such as speakers or tape recording, are frequent, and numerous how-to features provide helpful information on topics such as record cleaning and speaker placement.

High Fidelity has always eagerly covered innovation and controversy in the audio world; issues for the 1950s are filled with discussions of stereophonic versus monophonic sound, followed by the displacement of vacuum tubes by transistors in the early 1960s, the debacle of quadraphonic sound in the 1970s, the maturing of the tape cassette format in the early 1980s, and the explosion of compact disc technology in the past few years. *High Fidelity*'s treatment of new audio technology is always evenhanded, with a somewhat restrained, cautious enthusiasm; lately, the magazine has fully embraced digital sound reproduction but has been nevertheless loath to declare that the analog (LP) disc is dead.

Record reviews have been a staple of *High Fidelity* since its inception; the magazine's reviews have long been regarded as authoritative by librarians charged with developing collections of sound recordings.[4] Reviews are generally short—two, three, sometimes four paragraphs—and are always signed; they are quite erudite in tone, displaying considerable musicological knowledge on the part of the critics, yet easily accessible to the educated reader. Recordings meriting special attention are treated in longer (sometimes article-length) reviews, which generally number two or three per issue. Recent issues have also included The CD Spread, a section of one-paragraph "mini-reviews" of newly released compact discs.

Coverage of popular music in *High Fidelity* grew from reviews of a handful of Broadway show recordings in the early issues to an entire section, The Lighter Side, containing reviews of pop, rock, jazz, stage, and film music recordings. By 1977, the interest of *High Fidelity*'s readership in popular music had grown to the point that a major expansion of the popular music section was needed. The Lighter Side was transformed into Backbeat with the February 1977 issue; it was conceived as "almost like a magazine within a magazine . . . [with] its own musical, music business, and audio features, columns, and reviews."[5] With this step, *High Fidelity* essentially became a three-pronged publication, with significant interest in classical music, popular music, and audio technology.

Equipment reviews have remained prominent throughout *High Fidelity*'s history, and like the record reviews, they are considered authoritative.[6] *High Fidelity*'s equipment reports are distinguished from those of similar publications (*Stereo Review, Audio*) by being more subjectively oriented; the magazine's ultimate judgment of an audio component depends on how satisfying (to the reviewer) the listening experience actually is. This is perhaps traceable to *High Fidelity*'s long tradition of being more of a "music" magazine. Laboratory tests (currently conducted by Diversified Science Laboratories) are employed, and the reviews contain graphs and numerical information that can be intimidating to the novice, but the "hard" data is generally balanced by impressionistic remarks. Robert Long, once *High Fidelity*'s audio-video editor and now a consulting technical editor, describes the magazine's philosophy: "We approach equipment as a means to an end—reproducing music."[7]

Graphically *High Fidelity* is quite attractive; page layout is clear and uncluttered and photography is usually excellent (though, perhaps predictably, photographs of audio components are often of higher quality than those of people). The magazine has undergone a normal evolution in graphic design to keep its appearance up-to-date; most of the changes have been innocuous, the one exception being a 1985 flirtation with "new wave" design (with narrower columns, constantly shifting type styles, and increased white space) that was gradually abandoned over the next few years.

Advertisements in *High Fidelity* are almost exclusively for audio equipment; oddly enough in a magazine so concerned with recorded music, record ads are rare. Cigarette, liquor, and automobile ads, ubiquitous in many other upscale magazines, are blissfully absent. A typical issue contains about forty-four pages of advertisements, as opposed to about fifty-six pages of editorial material; currently a full-page black-and-white ad costs $12,930.

With the 1987 departure of *Musical America*, the *High Fidelity* of today immediately appears less music-oriented than it once did. Feature-length record reviews are less frequent, and articles on musical subjects not specifically related to recorded music are rare. Backbeat still continues, though in a diminished form. The development of video as a true high-fidelity medium has resulted in correspondingly greater coverage in *High Fidelity*; high-fidelity videocassette recorders and videodisc players are now reviewed alongside audio components. In short, the *High Fidelity* of the late 1980s is primarily a home audio/video technology magazine, with secondary attention given to music.[8] However, fans of the old *High Fidelity* cannot claim that they have been abandoned; the now separate *Musical America* contains record reviews, as well as an "Art and Technology" column. *High Fidelity* ceased publication with its July 1989 issue, after being purchased from ABC Consumer Magazines by Diamandis Communications Inc. (the publisher of *Stereo Review*).

Notes

1. Robert Long. "The Story of an Idea," *High Fidelity,* April 1971, pp. 46–48.

2. Ibid., p. 51.

3. ABC acquired the *Schwann Record and Tape Guides*, the leading trade discography, in 1976.

4. *High Fidelity* published *Records in Review*, an annual compilation in book form of its reviews, from 1955 to 1981.

5. Leonard Marcus, "Hello, Backbeat—Farewell, Lighter Side," *High Fidelity*, February 1977, p. 4.

6. *High Fidelity* also manifests its interest in equipment evaluation through numerous spin-off publications, both annual and one-time; the most prominent has been *Stereo*, an annual that began in 1980.

7. Robert Long, as quoted in Edward J. Foster. "High Fidelity Gurus," *Village Voice*, 9 October 1978, p. 79.

8. *High Fidelity*'s chief rival, *Stereo Review*, has as yet shown little interest in video.

Information Sources

BIBLIOGRAPHY

Clark, Robert S. "Editorial: On the Front Lines." *High Fidelity,* January 1981, p. 4.

Foster, Edward J. "High Fidelity Gurus." *Village Voice*, 9 October 1978, pp. 79–80.

Long, Robert. "The Story of an Idea." *High Fidelity*, April 1971, pp. 46–56.

Marcus, Leonard. "Hello, Backbeat—Farewell, Lighter Side." *High Fidelity*, February 1977, p. 4.

———. "*High Fidelity* weds *Schwann*." *High Fidelity*, March 1977, p. 4.

———. "Starting Out in the Fifties." *High Fidelity*, April 1976, pp. 41–42.

INDEX SOURCES

Readers' Guide to Periodical Literature (1961–present); Abridged Readers' Guide to Periodical Literature; Consumers Index; Music Index (1951–present); Magazine Index; Popular Magazine Review.

LOCATION SOURCES

Library of Congress, most medium-to-large public, and academic libraries. Available in microform.

Publication History

MAGAZINE TITLE AND TITLE CHANGES

High Fidelity (December 1958–March 1959: *High Fidelity and Audiocraft*).

VOLUME AND ISSUE DATA

Vols. 1–38, Summer 1951–present. Quarterly, Summer 1951–Summer 1952; bimonthly, September-October 1952–January-February 1954; monthly, March 1954–present.

PUBLISHER AND PLACE OF PUBLICATION

Audiocom: Milton B. Sleeper, 1951–1954; Charles Fowler, 1954–1957. Billboard Publications: Charles Fowler, 1957–1960; Warren B. Syer, 1962–1974. ABC Leisure Magazines (later ABC Consumer Magazines): Warren B. Syer, 1974–1980; Leonard Levine, 1980–1981; Steven I. Rosenbaum, 1981–1985; William Tynan, 1986–1989. Great Barrington, Massachusetts, 1951–1981; New York, 1981–1989.

EDITORS

Charles Fowler, 1951–1954; John M. Conly, 1954–1959; Roland Gelatt, 1959–1968; Leonard Marcus, 1968–1980; William Tynan, 1981–1985; Michael Riggs, 1986–present.

CIRCULATION

408,662.

H. Stephen Wright

HIGH TIMES

High Times: The Magazine of High Society (aka briefly as *High Times: The Magazine of Feeling Good*) was begun in 1974 by Tom Forcade, a veteran of the various underground media flourishing during the 1960s. In addition to founding *High Times*, Forcade established the Alternative Press Syndicate and a national distribution network for other underground magazines. *High Times* took its subtitle from the lyrics of "Kick Out the Jam," a rock song by the sixties group MC5.[1]

The magazine quickly left the underground category in terms of circulation and became mass-market within two years when it began selling 500,000 copies a month in 1976. From the beginning *High Times* was clearly and unabashedly drug-oriented. Its feature departments, articles, and advertisers clearly reflect this: an ongoing series on the best lawyers for defending people arrested on narcotics-related charges; the regular Trans High Market Quotations, which reports the going price of various drugs on the world market; and the advertisers who are almost exclusively manufacturers of drug paraphernalia—bongs, water pipes, cigarette papers, and plant growing lights. In fact, the only large, national advertisers to appear were record companies and a few other magazines that were appealing to the same market: *Rolling Stone,* * *Playboy,* * *Playgirl,* * and *Crawdaddy.* *

From the beginning a sense of being a part of an underground movement was consciously sought. Prospective subscribers were assured in the summer 1974 issue, for example, that the magazine's mailing list was protected (coded) and that the copy when delivered would appear in brown wrappers. And although drugs and drug use were clearly the focus of *High Times*, its readership was informed that while on the one hand it is best to know your dealer, some of the "best highs are not from drugs, but from far out books, records, movies, and various mental disciplines, from yoga to bio feedback."[2]

Even though its circulation and glossy, slick appearance would seem to place *High Times* out of the counterculture, its overriding drug focus and the fact that the major national distributors refused to carry it on their newsstands lent it an aura of illegality and rebellion. In addition to its subscription list, *High Times* is also sold on college campuses and in head shops nationally, which accounts for the large circulation figures. During the Carter years in particular *High Times* was politically active in calling for the legalization of marijuana. It strongly (and financially) supported NORML (the National Organization for the Reform of Marijuana Laws) for years.

The theme is further explained: "With or without marijuana people will still be getting high, whether it's from mushrooms, peyote, beer, sensory deprivation tanks, roller coaster rides or transcendental meditation. You see, *High Times* covers a lot of news about dope, but *High Times* is not a magazine about dope. It's a magazine about consciousness and awareness."[3]

Again in 1976, claiming to "always have been more than a 'dope' magazine," its editor talked of plans for "broadening editorial scope" with a broader range of contemporary and historical subjects: "more general news, more diverse features, much more music coverage than ever before. We have no desire to be limited to being the magazine of substances that people put in their mouths . . . Meanwhile, we will continue to have the best, the most accurate . . . the most wide ranging, creative, wildest, courageous coverage of dope *anywhere*."[4]

And to a large extent, this earlier goal has been realized, along with the more obvious earlier one. For example, a conscious effort was made to include literary material: excerpts from Tom Robbins's *Even Cowgirls Get the Blues* appeared in the September 1976 issue, and Charles Bukowski contributed a regular column for some time, in addition to other material. Several serialized stories appeared over the years, and a book review section (Books for your Head) was included as well. Records were regularly and extensively reviewed; a travel feature, usually closely tied to a dope theme (e.g., "A Gourmet Cocoa Taster's Tour of Peru") became a regular attraction, as did a cuisine section that offered recipes for omelets and chilis, connoisseur coffees, as well as a cannabis cookbook.

One of the areas in which the best coverage occurred was the interview section in which "Culture Heros" were featured. Even a partial list of interviewees is an impressive and incredibly eclectic one. In an era before *People Magazine*,* where else would one find such an assemblage: musicians Bob Marley, Jimmy Buffet, Deborah Harry, Dolly Parton, Ted Nugent, Tina Turner, Willie Nelson; rock groups, the Sex Pistols, DEVO; writers, Ken Kesey, Norman Mailer, Allen Ginsberg, Fran Lebowitz, Susan Sontag; an athlete, Bill Walton; comedians, Richard Pryor, the Smothers Brothers, and general celebrities—Yoko Ono and Brooke Shields.

From time to time special theme issues featuring a group of articles on a single topic appeared: a punk rock issue (February 1977), a Sex issue (October 1978), a Jamaican/Rastafarian issue (April 1983); a mushroom issue (October 1987) to name a few.

As always, though, in a magazine with the title *High Times*, the main theme is drug culture. Perhaps the most distinctive part of this magazine that is filled with distinctive parts is the color centerfold—à la *Playboy*—featuring the drug of the month. Usually, but not necessarily, the drug is featured in its natural state, in plant form. In any case, the narrative associated with this section is often the occasion of some curious mixing of metaphor. On the one hand, we have one of the above-mentioned plants referred to as "a sexy-looking marijuana plant" and on the other, a processed end-product is described as "a nice big, sexy brick of hashish." However, in 1984 ads began appearing for a marijuana flower–based perfume and cologne called "Sinsimilla," so there may be something to this vegetative eroticism. In fact, even the sedate *New Republic** observed of the pictures, "There are close-ups of cannabis buds bursting with resins and looking fairly erotic."[5]

Typical feature articles that appeared serially in *High Times* included "Dope in the Cinema," "Dope in the Comics," "Drugs in the Bible," and "Athletes on Drugs." Interestingly, for a time there was a column on drug etiquette that informed the readership of the niceties of drug socialization. Here we find articles with the provocative titles "Cocaine Courtesy," "Pill Protocol," and "Pot Politeness."

As a sort of counterpoint to the consumption-oriented features and departments, *High Times* offered a monthly feature that was written by a physician,

Dr. David Smith, who was involved with the Haight-Ashbury Free Medical Clinic. Called the "Hightime Desk Reference" (in deference to the PDR [Physician's Desk Reference] no doubt), this feature furnished technical information on a specific drug, any nicknames, use and effects, hazards, first aid, economics, and addiction liability—an abuse folio. The drugs covered ranged from the expected quaaludes, or methaqualone, and cocaine to those that would not be normally expected to be covered: caffeine pills, alcohol, and over-the-counter cold remedies.

Actually, there was some antidrug propagandizing in the pages of *High Times*, most notable immediately after Gabrielle Schang became editor in the early eighties. She described an editorial stance previously in effect that prohibited printing "anything bad about dope, not even bring-down bummer shit like angel dust, or those new boot ludes." She further explained that her editorial plans included "sweep[ing] out reckless dope journalism and open[ing] up the magazine to more kinds of highs like hang gliding . . . and honest simple love."[6]

In the eighties, it has been noted, *High Times* has become "obsessed with botany. Pages that once carried ads for roach clips, flavored rolling papers, and hookahs, now carry ads for powerful indoor 'grow lamps,' kits to detect the sex of cannabis plants. . . . The new cultural heroes are cultivators—[Ed] Rosenthal himself, author of the *Marijuana Growers Handbook*, and Jorge Cervantes, author of *Indoor Marijuana Culture*."[7] While on the one hand, *High Times* supports and advocates marijuana use and cultivation, it "does not glorify cocaine: 'The coke lifestyle, it's pretty disgusting,' says Steven Hager, executive editor."[8] Since marijuana no longer is symbolic of a rebellious or avant-grade life style, *High Times* by association has become, if not respectable, then at least more sedate, with above-mentioned columnist Ed Rosenthal being described as "the Ann Landers of the marijuana world," and its major area of interest "a major domestic cottage industry."[9]

Notes

1. [Thirteen Year History], *High Times,* June 1987, p. 41.
2. Editorial, *High Times*, Summer 1974, p. 5.
3. Editorial, *High Times*, October-November 1975, p. 6.
4. Ibid., p. 15.
5. James K. Glassman, "Going to Seed," *New Republic*, 25 August 1986, p. 13.
6. Gabrielle Schang, editorial, *High Times*, August 1980, p. 3.
7. Glassman, p. 12.
8. Ibid., p. 12.
9. Ibid., p. 12.

Information Sources

BIBLIOGRAPHY

Carter, Betsy. "High Society Rag," *Newsweek,* 8 September 1975, p. 49.
Glassman, James K., "Going to Seed," *New Republic*, 25 August 1986, pp. 11–13.

"New High," *Time*, 8 September 1975, p. 49.

"Resolution Used by County to Curb *High Times* Sales," *Folio*, November 1982, p. 16.

Schang, Gabrielle. "Opinions (an editorial)," *High Times*, August 1980, p. 3.

[Thirteen Year History], *High Times*, June 1987, pp. 41–44.

INDEX SOURCES

Not indexed.

LOCATION SOURCES

Widely held and available in microform as a part of the Bell and Howell Underground Press Collection.

Publication History

MAGAZINE TITLE AND TITLE CHANGES

High Times: The Magazine of Feeling Good, 1980–1981; otherwise, *High Times: The Magazine of High Society.*

VOLUME AND ISSUE DATA

Vol. 1, no. 1–vol. 1, no. 4, Summer 1974–Spring 1975, quarterly; vol. 1, no. 5–vol. 1, no. 7, August/September 1975–December/January 1976, bimonthly; vol. 1, no. 8–present, March 1976–present, monthly.

PUBLISHER AND PLACE OF PUBLICATION

Thomas King, 1974; Andrew Kowl, 1975–1980; Gabrielle Schang, 1980–1982; Robert Aronson, 1982–present.

EDITORS

Founding Editor, Tom Forcade; Ed Dwyer, 1974–1976; Susan Wyler, 1976; Pamela Loyd Shakespeare, 1976–1977; Glenn O'Brien, 1977–1978; Shirley Levitt, 1978–1979; Craig Pyle, 1979; Gabrielle Schang, 1980–1982; Andy Kowl, 1982; Larry Sloman, 1982–1985; John Howell, 1985–1987; Steven Hagar, 1987–present.

CIRCULATION

500,000 (1976); 250,000 (1988).

Alan Nourie

HOME JOURNAL. See TOWN AND COUNTRY

HOME MECHANIX

The magazine *Home Mechanix* has undergone many changes since it was first published. There have been changes in its format, title, publisher, editor, content, and audience.

This periodical was first published in 1928 by Fawcett Publications of Minneapolis, Minnesota. The title at this time was *Modern Mechanics and Inventions*. The publisher, W. H. Fawcett, was unsure of the potential audience for the magazine, and early volumes were intended to capture the attention of all potential readers. There were sections devoted to aviation, projects for young children, radio, amateur moviemaking, magic, automobiles, household helpers, and popular science topics. The magazine was touted as being "edited by experts," and there was a woman in charge of the household portion of the editorial board.

A very large portion of early volumes was devoted to science fiction in serial form. The most noteworthy author contributing to the magazine was Edgar Rice Burroughs. He wrote a number of short novels, and these were heavily advertised on the cover to increase sales. This technique of serial fiction was probably meant to increase the dependency of the reader on the next issue of the magazine. When an issue contained the ending of one story, the beginning of another story was included in the same issue. Another ploy used to increase sales involved staging contests that promised easy wealth to a nation stricken with economic depression. Sales techniques were aimed at newsstands. The magazine dropped fiction very early in its publication history, replacing it with accounts by famous people of their personal adventures or expertise. Examples of these famous contributors were Henry Ford, Eddie Rickenbacker, Babe Ruth, and Jack Dempsey.

There were many other titles available from the publisher. Fawcett Publications specialized in sensational magazines aimed at newsstand sales during the 1930s. Some examples of these magazines were *True Confessions, Screen Secrets, Battle Stories, Startling Detective Adventures*, and *Hollywood Mystic Magazine*.

The cover illustrations of *Modern Mechanics and Inventions* were always very sensational and resembled movie posters and comic books of that era. The portions of the magazine aimed at children and women were dropped in the first few years of publication. The target audience became adult males of low to moderate income. There were many full-page advertisements devoted to correspondence schools and get-rich-quick schemes. These were obviously very good for sales during the American depression of the 1930s. Classified advertisements were introduced in the early 1930s and have persisted throughout the history of this publication.

The articles in the magazine often speculated about sensational scientific innovations that might be in store for the future, and these were meant to spur the readers' interest in science fiction. Many articles had a "Ripley's Believe It or Not" air about them. New developments in aviation and military science were also very common topics. The quality of pictures and diagrams increased greatly after a few years of publication. Until the mid–1930s there had been many plans for flying machines that the reader was encouraged to build at home. This became a major thrust of the magazine until regulations were passed that required airplanes to be licensed. Plans for readers to build their own airplanes were soon dropped.

In 1932 the magazine's title was changed to *Modern Mechanix*; the publisher, Modern Mechanix Publishing Company, had the same mailing address as Fawcett Publications.

In the late 1930s aviation was almost completely dropped, and articles became much less sensational and more factual. The magazine became very pictorial with less text and more advertisements of higher quality. The general appearance of the magazine became much like short features that were popular in motion picture theaters of that era. In 1938 *Modern Mechanix* changed its title to *Mechanix Illustrated*, and Fawcett Publications began publishing the magazine under its new title. The drawings on the cover were replaced by color photographs at this time also. During the late 1930s, *Mechanix Illustrated* teamed with Warner Brothers to produce a number of educational short films that played in local theaters.

A new sales technique was used in 1939 when a "double your money back guarantee" was promised to readers who were not satisfied with the publication. The magazine introduced a new format in 1939 with a large section devoted entirely to plans of a very practical nature. Most of the plans involved woodworking and were very well drawn.

With the onset of World War II, the magazine began running war articles about new weaponry and military technology. New and rewarding jobs in technology were still included, with emphasis placed on wartime factory positions. The plans included in each edition maintained their practical nature, and the content of the magazine reflected the patriotic attitude of Americans whose daily lives were centered around supporting the war effort. How to better cope with rationing, make more economic use of materials in short supply due to the war, and make various small contributions to the national effort were often included as plans.

After World War II, the magazine was changed to increase its appeal to men by including many pictures of women and by focusing more on jobs in technical fields. Advertisements at this time were often for schools and technical courses that the returning soldiers might use to obtain one of these technical positions. More pages were also added to the magazine after the war.

In the 1950s, more emphasis was placed on the booming interest Americans had in the automobile. The magazine was generally composed of how-to articles, sensational and futuristic discussions of scientific discovery, and automobile articles. The automobile articles became a major thrust of the magazine. Articles dealt with new design features being introduced by the manufacturers at that time, critical evaluations of various models of automobiles, and troubleshooting tips for the home mechanic. Many members of the Fawcett family moved into upper-management positions in this decade.

In the 1960s automobiles and projects for the home became the main topics covered by the magazine, though there was still some attention paid to scientific discoveries. There was also some coverage of sporting topics for a short period. The articles and advertisements contained in the magazine became targeted at people who could afford to spend money on cars, homes, and extra possessions. The audience seems to have changed from lower-class men looking for a way to better their lives to affluent home owners with money to spend.

There must have been a great deal of competition between similar magazines at this time; *Popular Mechanics** and *Popular Science** contained similar material.[1] Content of the magazine was being shifted to appeal to an audience that had more disposable income than the previous audience. During the 1970s, less emphasis was placed on scientific discoveries and possible future uses of these discoveries. More emphasis was placed on automobiles, home, and recreation for people who had leisure time. *Electronics Illustrated*, another Fawcett Publication, was incorporated into *Mechanix Illustrated*. In 1978, *Mechanix Illustrated* was first published by CBS Publications, though marketing of the magazine was still carried out by Fawcett Marketing Services.

A major change in *Mechanix Illustrated* was implemented in 1980. The energy crisis of the late 1970s and early 1980s became a major influence on the content of the magazine. Many of the projects presented were intended to help the readers save energy in their homes and automobiles. A new logo and format were introduced, and more high-quality photographs were included with the articles. In 1983, this emphasis on energy conservation was removed because the price of oil had dropped and the tax incentives once offered for builders of solar homes and projects had been removed. A classified index to the previous year was also included as a new feature, although this index was not continued in following years.

The direction of the magazine changed again in 1984.[2] The major goal of the magazine became to give practical examples of home and automotive improvements that could be easily applied immediately. All emphasis on scientific discoveries and future technologies was removed. This change eliminated much of the competition caused by an overlap between audiences of *Popular Science* and *Mechanix Illustrated*. The magazine was narrowing its target audience to that of home and automobile owners.

Once the target audience had been narrowed and the magazine had been changed in content to address this audience, the producers of *Mechanix Illustrated* changed the name of the magazine to *Home Mechanix*. This name change was meant to attract a new audience of home owners and more clearly define the new content of the magazine.[3] In 1985, *Home Mechanix* was published by CBS Magazines.

After publishing the magazine a few years under its new name, the publishers conducted a scientific survey to determine who was being reached by their reformatted magazine.[4] The study, which interviewed 385 first-year subscribers, found that most subscribers were men, their average age was thirty-nine, the majority of them owned homes and were married, and over 60 percent were college educated.[5]

In January 1988 *Home Mechanix* was published by Diamandis Communications. Peter G. Diamandis had been president of the previous publishing company, CBS Magazines. Since February 1988 the magazine has been published by Times Mirror Magazines. It is worth noting that Times Mirror Magazines also publishes the previous major competitor, *Popular Science*.

Donald G. Cooley was the first chief editor, emerging from the panel of "expert editors." In 1934, William J. Kostka became editor, and the magazine was no longer touted as being "edited by experts." Tom Mahoney became editor for a short period in 1937, but he was replaced in the same year by Robert Hertzberg. In 1942, editorial duties were assumed by Roland Cueva and Bill Williams. Robert Hertzberg again began editing the magazine in 1945 and remained until 1948, when he was replaced by William L. Parker. Parker remained as editor until 1963, and the format of the magazine remained stable throughout this period. Robert G. Beason became editor in 1963 and remained in this position until 1980. A major change in format and intent was implemented in 1980, when editorial duties were assumed by David E. Petzal. Another major change was implemented in 1984, when Joseph R. Provey became the magazine's editor. He remained editor until 1989, when Michael Morris assumed the job.

Notes

1. A supplement was included in the January 1971 issue of *Mechanix Illustrated* that made comparisons between *Popular Mechanics, Popular Science*, and *Mechanix Illustrated*. The comparisons regarded circulation, number of pages, and percent share of the mechanical literature field. No discussion of methodology was offered to substantiate these comparisons.

2. Joseph R. Provey, "Editor's Notes: Greetings from MI's New Editor," *Mechanix Illustrated*, January 1984, p. 4.

3. Joseph R. Provey, "Letter to Readers," *Home Mechanix*, January 1985, p. 1.

4. Joseph R. Provey, "Editor's Notes," *Home Mechanix*, May 1987, p. 1.

5. Joseph R. Provey, "Editor's Notes," *Home Mechanix*, June 1987, p. 4.

Information Sources

INDEX SOURCES
> *Magazine Index* (1977–present); *Readers' Guide to Periodical Literature* (1968–present); *Consumers Index to Product Evaluations and Information Sources; Energy Information Abstracts; Energy Research Abstracts; Environment Abstracts; Popular Magazine Review.*

LOCATION SOURCES
> Available in microform.

Publication History

MAGAZINE TITLE AND TITLE CHANGES
> *Modern Mechanics and Inventions,* 1928–1932; *Modern Mechanix,* 1932–1938; *Mechanix Illustrated,* 1938–1985; *Home Mechanix,* 1985–present.

VOLUME AND ISSUE DATA
> Vols. 1–86, 1928–present. Monthly.

PUBLISHER AND PLACE OF PUBLICATION
    Fawcett Publications, 1928–1932; Modern Mechanix Publishing Company, 1932–1938; Fawcett Publishing, Inc., 1938–1978; CBS Publications, 1978–1988; Diamandis Communications, Inc., 1988; Times Mirror Magazines, 1988–present. New York, New York.
EDITORS
    Donald G. Cooley, 1929–1934; William J. Kostka, 1934–1937; Tom Mahoney, 1937; Robert Hertzberg, 1937–1942; Roland Cueva and Bill Williams, 1942–1945; Robert Hertzberg, 1945–1948; William L. Parker, 1948–1963; Robert G. Beason, 1963–1980; David E. Petzal, 1980–1984; Joseph R. Provey, 1984–1989; Michael Morris, 1989–present.
CIRCULATION
    1.5 million

Robert S. Allen

HORIZON

Horizon was launched in September 1958—published by American Horizon, a subsidiary of the American Heritage Publishing Company. Like its sister publication, *American Heritage,* Horizon* was published in hard copy for nineteen years, situations unique in modern American periodical publishing. *Horizon* was intended to be a periodical that would not be discarded after being read but would instead be proudly placed on the family bookshelf to be consulted in the future as a reference book or as a standard work. Its frame of reference was far broader than historically oriented *American Heritage*:

> Culture, the concern of this new magazine, is both achievement and dream, a work of the hands and a movement of the spirit. . . . Culture is art and ideas, past and present, taken in sum as a guide to life. . . . Culture, finally, is a birthright which we all inherit, the heritage man carries with him on his earthly voyage.[1]

The *Horizon* title and logo are noteworthy too; with "Horizon" being chosen because "it is here where earth and sky meet, that one may observe those jagged interruptions in the landscape that are the works of man." The ship of the logo is the caravel from Pieter Brueghel's painting *The Fall of Icarus*.

More specifically, *Horizon* was established to be a tool for self-improvement or self-education, a "guide to the house of culture, with its thousands of rooms." Finally, the editors elaborate on the "house of culture": "those aspects of life peculiar to high civilization—to art and ideas; to the study of man and nature; to letters; to manners and customs; and, in the long view, to political and scientific subjects as they affect civilized man." However, even though the conspectus may sound much like a humanities curriculum, it is not without some limitations: "the great concern of *Horizon* will be with our own civilization, Modern Western Variety." But this is not to say that its purview was limited to Western art. In

Horizon's second volume the first of many articles on non-Western art was published: James Michener's "Eastern Art."[2]

From its opening issue in September 1958, *Horizon* was a sumptuously produced magazine with its hardcover format, its interesting and attractive method of blending various textures of paper in the same issue, its plethora of color plates and the obvious care that it took to match authors with articles. For example, early issues contained articles by biologist Julian Huxley on population explosion; by science fiction writer Arthur C. Clarke on space and the spirit of man; by artist Ben Shahn on the French artist André François; by organist E. Power Biggs on the history and musicology of the organ; by poet Donald Hall on contemporary poetry; and by literary critic Lord David Cecil on Max Beerbohm. In addition, the first three volumes contained interviews with the following artistic and literary celebrities: Igor Stravinsky, Ernest Hemingway, Archibald MacLeish, Henry Moore, George Balanchine, and Eugène Ionesco. In this area in particular *Horizon* was ahead of its time; for at that time interviews with artists were rarely if ever published outside of little magazines. In fact, the best known of the little magazines in this respect, the *Paris Review*, began its interviews in 1953. *Horizon*, of course, reached a considerably wider audience.

Horizon began in 1958 as a bimonthly, appearing six times a year, and continued this periodicity until November 1963, when it became a quarterly. Originally its internal composition was fairly informal, with each issue being built around a substantial lead article, usually dealing with some artistic theme and accompanied by a large number of color plates. There were no formal departmental divisions in *Horizon*'s early years, but in time various configurations emerged. A specific selection included History, Art, Archaeology, Letters, Ideas, the Contemporary World, Entertainment, and Performing Arts. Later, a more condensed version emerged including Art and Architecture, History and Archaeology, the Literary Life, and Politics.

In November 1963, on the occasion of its fifth anniversary—noting its circulation of 150,000—*Horizon* shifted its frequency of publication to quarterly in an effort to lower prices without cutting the size of the publication, generally reducing its quality, or (horror of horrors) accepting advertising! The eventual decision (quarterly publication) was "to publish a little more magazine a little less often."[3]

The editors at this time (November 1963) also announced a number of projected series focused on a variety of topics: the first, by art critic John Canaday, "Great Artists and Their Worlds," was slated to continue "regularly until the subscriber has collected, in effect, a good art library."[4] So the idea of the magazine as a permanent collection—one to be referred to timelessly—was still viable. Canaday's subsequent artistic series would be worthy of special mention if only by virtue of its subjects: Albrecht Dürer, Pablo Picasso, Thomas Eakins, Giotto and Duccio di Buoninsegna, Antoine Watteau, Claude Monet, J.M.W. Turner, Gerard David, Francisco Goya, Paul Gaugin, Alexander Milne Calder, Paul Cézanne, John Constable, Polidoro de Caravaggio, Peter Paul Rubens, and

Flemish art—in addition to a number of related articles all under the title "Anatomy of a Masterpiece," in which a single work of art was analyzed in depth. Each of the Canaday pieces was accompanied by numerous full- and half-page color reproductions of the appropriate artworks being discussed. In all likelihood, no one subject has ever been treated in such depth by a single author in an American periodical. Other series were announced on architects, noted men of letters, and philosophers and men of science (all titled "Makers of Modern Thought").

The idea of using long-term series or multiple-part articles was not entirely new, for a unique series entitled "Great Confrontations" appeared in *Horizon* when it was still a bimonthly. It featured material on such figures as Pope Leo the Great versus Attila the Hun and Mary Queen of Scots versus John Knox. And in 1963 the English writer Robert Graves furnished a three-part article on the state of English letters, dealing not only with literary figures as elements of literary history, but also with their works: this in terms of poetics and stylistics, and not merely as a survey. During the sixties and early seventies *Horizon*'s editors seemingly made special efforts to match the authors of articles with appropriate subjects, considering their background. For example, we see J. B. Priestley writing on H. G. Wells; R. V. Cassill on Nathaniel Hawthorne; Peter Quennell and Anthony Burgess on various literary figures, past and present; Henry Steele Commager on American history; Malcolm Cowley on contemporary American literature; and Malcolm Muggeridge on the Webbs—Beatrice and Sidney. Often, the commentary was supplemented with numerous pages of supporting art and illustration. Other series also begun at this time included "Landmarks of Film History," which provided explications of such films as Jean Renoir's *La Grande Illusion*, Michelangelo Antonioni's *L'Avventura*, Serge Eisenstein's *Potemkin*, and Kurosawa Akira's *Rashomon*—all written by Stanley Kauffman.

The "Men of Ideas" series contained some provocative material as well, with articles on such contemporary figures as Daniel Patrick Moynihan, Michel Foucault, René Dubos, Leon Trotsky, and Herbert Marcuse—as well as Copernicus.

Another feature of the *Horizon* scene was the theme issue. For example, in spring 1968 we were given four articles on hippies and in the next issue, summer 1968, three on the environment. More elaborately developed issues also appeared: the winter 1971 *Horizon* featured six articles on children—"Children: Past and Present"—as well as a "Men of Ideas" number on educator Jean Piaget and a portfolio of paintings of children by artists ranging from Thomas Gainsborough to Picasso and Jamie Wyeth.

By January 1977 circulation, which had peaked at 150,000 in 1963, fell to 106,000 (and would ultimately fall to 78,000 by 1988). However, at this time a short-lived innovation, "Perspectives," appeared for a few issues preceding the departure from hardcover quarterly to softcover monthly. "Perspectives" consisted of contributions by three regular columnists—Bernard Levin of the *London Times*, who wrote "Against the Grain"; former *Horizon* editor Charles

Mee, who contributed book reviews in "In My Time"; and John Pfeiffer, who wrote "The Human Species" section. An example of typical contents might contain a discussion of hijackings in "Against the Grain," various reviews of new books in "In My Time," and an essay on pseudoscience (i.e., astrology) in the "Human Species."

For *Horizon*, 1977 was a watershed year on two counts: it ceased publication in its distinctive hardcover format, and it altered the publication schedule from the quarterly and bimonthly periods, which had served it well for the previous fourteen years, to monthly—in effect losing much of its uniqueness along the way. Its seasonal, almost cyclic, publication schedule and the implied permanent value of its physical state were a sad loss. However, the change was apparently not for change's sake alone, but "to allow for more flexibility and the greater use of color"; and as for the soft covers, we were told that *Horizon* "will be using new printing and binding equipment . . . a different process from the slower one required for hard cover binding, and the magazine produced in this way cannot then be bound in hard cover."[5] Also at this time, commercial advertising first appeared in the pages of *Horizon*, although some constraint and sense of decorum were applied in the matter, inasmuch as perfume, book clubs, and rather sedate liquor ads led the way. A flyer inserted into the September issue written by publisher Rhett Austell explained the rationale for including ads:

We can only continue to produce an expensive magazine if our editorial, production, and postage costs are shared by advertisers as well as subscribers. So, when we decided to publish every month instead of every other month, we let advertisers of quality products and services know that we were opening our pages to advertisements. The new *Horizon* is a natural for advertising.[6]

The magazine's focus shifted, too, from a generalized conception of "culture" to a modish particular concern with "urban life . . . including the suburbs and exurbs that depend on cities for much of their vitality."[7] One explanation of the forthcoming interests is that essentially *Horizon* at this point aspired to be an urban magazine, albeit a general one—perhaps in an attempt to appeal to numerous urban markets; at any rate, its new purview was to be "selective coverage of all the arts and thoughtful reporting on developments in and around cities."[8]

In contrast to the richly traditional culture treated in *Horizon*'s past issues, an issue from 1977 might contain material on the shopping center; squash, paddle, or racquet ball in the city; downtown Atlanta; "Saturday Night Live"; Hollywood's vision of the city as evidenced in the movie *Taxi Driver*; street art; as well as a few articles on contemporary literary figures (John C. Gardner) and artists (William de Kooning). And later in 1977 the correspondents were shifted from New York to bases in Atlanta, Boston, Chicago, Los Angeles, and Washington in this country, and London and Paris overseas. The exodus from New York reached its culmination in December 1978 when the editorial offices were moved to Tuscaloosa, Alabama, to be edited and published by the new owner,

Gray D. Boone—a move that led to a decided shift to increased coverage of the performing and visual arts, though primarily the latter. The move was explained by Boone as being "symbolic and a very real reminder that America's arts are not only in one place. America's arts are everywhere, and we intend more than ever to reflect that fact."[9] The emphasis on the visual and performing arts was evident in the new serial features "Museums You've Never Heard Of" and "USArts: Strategies for the 80's," which respectively featured lesser-known museums and art collections, even corporate collections on occasion and reports on the art scene in a particular city or state. In addition to the art coverage, dance and theater also receive regular, if not serial, coverage. So, essentially *Horizon* has thus far changed from a publication that was intended to educate and re-educate its audience in the traditional humanistic disciplines, to a slick commentator on the urban scene, to one that amounts to a museum-reporting organ enhanced by an occasional article of substance.[10] Its circulation has dropped by more than two-thirds over the years, so its readership is not a large one. What the next change will be for *Horizon*, only time can tell. One can only hope for a return to the emphases of earlier years.

Notes

1. The editors, *Horizon,* September 1958, p. 3. This is the first issue of the magazine.
2. Ibid., pp. 3–4.
3. The editors, *Horizon,* November 1963, p. 2.
4. *Standard Periodical Directory*, 11th ed., 1988, p. 338.
5. Rhett Austell, "A Message from the Publisher," *Horizon*, July 1977, insert slip.
6. Rhett Austell, "A Message from the Publisher," *Horizon*, September 1977, insert slip.
7. The editors, "A New Direction," *Horizon*, May 1977, p. 2.
8. The editors, "The Monthly Horizon," *Horizon*, September 1977, p. 2.
9. Gray D. Boone, "New Ownership, New Opportunity," *Horizon*, December 1978, p. 6. Interestingly, upon *Horizon*'s moving to Alabama, the name of the University of Alabama's head football coach—not a man generally noted for his cultural exploits—was added to the *Horizon* board of editorial advisers.
10. In all fairness, this is not a universally held view, as this recent, anonymous comment from Katz and Katz's *Magazines for Libraries* bears witness: "*Horizon* is a splendid magazine, delighting the eye and mind with excellent photography and writing."

Information Sources

BIBLIOGRAPHY
Austell, Rhett. "A Message from the Publisher." *Horizon,* July 1977, insert.
Boone, Gray D. "New Ownership, New Opportunity." *Horizon*, December 1978, p. 6.
Katz, Bill, and Linda Sternberg Katz. *Magazines for Libraries*. 4th ed. New York: R. R. Bowker, 1982.
Standard Periodical Directory. 11th ed., 1988.

INDEX SOURCES

Readers' Guide to Periodical Literature (1961–present); *America: History and Life; Historical Abstracts; Arts and Humanities Citation Index; Horizon*'s cumulative indexes. *Magazine Index* (1977–present).

LOCATION SOURCES

Widely held and available in microform.

Publication History

MAGAZINE TITLE AND TITLE CHANGES

Horizon; two subtitles: *Horizon: A Magazine of the Arts*, 1958–1970; *Horizon: The Cultural Scene*, May 1978–February, 1980; *Horizon:* The Magazine of the Arts, March, 1980–present.

VOLUME AND ISSUE DATA

Vol. 1, no. 1–vol. 5, no. 8, September 1958–November 1963, bimonthly; vol. 6, no. 1–vol. 18, no. 4, Winter 1964–Autumn 1976, quarterly; vol. 19, no. 1–vol. 20, no. 4, January 1977–December 1977, bimonthly; vol. 21, no. 1–vol. 24, no. 12, January 1978–December 1981, monthly; vol. 25, no. 1–present, January 1982–present, 10 issues a year.

PUBLISHER AND PLACE OF PUBLICATION

American Heritage Publishing Company, New York, New York, 1958–1978; Horizon Publishing, Inc., Tuscaloosa, Alabama, 1978–present.

EDITORS

Joseph J. Thorndike, Jr., 1958–1961; William Harlen Hale, 1961–1963; Marshall B. Davidson, 1964–1967; Joseph J. Thorndike, Jr., 1967–1971; Charles L. Mee, 1971–1974; Shirley Tomkievicz, 1974–1977; Otto Fuerbringer, 1977–1978; Gray D. Boone, 1978–present.

CIRCULATION

1963: 150,000; 1988: 78,000.

Alan Nourie

HYGEIA. See HEALTH

I

INTERVIEW MAGAZINE

Gossip, stars, fashion, and funk characterize *Interview,* the monthly farrago that could be found on coffee tables of national and international trendsetters in 1970, the year of its debut. Founded in 1969 by Andy Warhol as a cult magazine, *Interview* was published irregularly until 1974, when it became a monthly publication. During this same period of time, efforts were made to change the magazine's image from that of a cult magazine to an avant-garde, chic underground paper catering to a larger than cult population but never intending to be a mass-market publication.

Warhol's planning of *Interview* during the 1960s came at a time of national and international notoriety for him as a major pop art figure noted for his eccentricity. The experimental atmosphere of the 1970s was ideal for *Interview,* which provided contributors with a vehicle to express artistic freedom and opportunities for self-awareness. Therefore, *Interview* offered, as it continues to do, a forum to introduce new people, people other magazines did not write about. Frequently, well-known personalities in the visual and performing arts, politics, literature, journalism, and sports are also featured.

In an interview with Lew Grossberger in 1979, when asked why he started *Interview,* Warhol jokingly indicated that the magazine was started so that he and others could get invited to more parties.[1] However, Warhol's seriousness about the magazine was seen in his strategic hiring of Brigid Polk, of whom he was very fond and who is the daughter of Richard E. Berlin, who ran the Hearst Corporation in the 1960s, to be publisher of *Interview*. Since Brigid's father had been very effective as a publisher, Warhol reasoned that Brigid would help bring *Interview* to prominence.

As the magazine's name indicates, *Interview* was made popular by including in each issue at least one interview. When interviews are done of famous personalities, that person is interviewed when vacationing rather than while he or she is on the road preparing for a movie.

Interviews are presented in a straightforward question-and-answer format that allows authors to be kinder to their subjects than are many interviewers appearing in fan magazines. However, many interviews, especially those of famous personalities, are long and contain a lot of chitchat and trivia, which is permitted. Warhol believed that "people say more when they don't say anything. You learn more about them."[2] An attempt is also made to make the readers feel almost as though they are the tape recorders. Using this technique, therefore, the readers should feel as if they are listening to a conversation rather than to a journalist interviewing a celebrity.

A written interview profile or a taped question-and-answer session is done by the interviewer. Taping was the method preferred by Andy Warhol, who provided each interviewer with a tape recorder. Warhol also favored the pairing of "odd couples": Mick Jagger once interviewed Princess Lee Radziwill, Jagger's fashion-plate wife profiled the dress designer Yves St. Laurent, the model Lauren Hutton was taped by the late transvestite, Candy Darling.

Pairing of "odd couples" could have affected the quality of interviews. During early years, the quality of interviews was uneven primarily due to a small staff of only three to five people and a free-lance budget of $25 for each article submitted. However, by 1979, circulation had doubled and advertising had tripled. Consequently, the staff was increased to twenty-five, and $100 rather than $10 was paid for an interview. Much of the increases in circulation and advertising, plus acceptance of better interviews, can also be attributed to the hiring and training of staff to become more professional. Consequently, in 1974, Rosemary Kent was hired as a new editor. One of her ambitions was to successfully balance interviews and other materials, or as she said, "We try to balance freakiness with glamour."[3]

Freakiness has not undermined the quality of the magazine. The easy-to-read newsprint tabloid has outstanding black and white photographs and some colored ones with adequate white space in the layout. Models displayed in *Interview*, both nude and dressed, are well represented in advertisements and artistic features. Ads are classy, featuring fashion designers such as Valentino, Giorgio Armani, and Enrico Coveri. Approximately half of each issue is devoted to advertisements. The content is also well balanced, including literary works, featured interviews, current fashion trends, and musical celebrities. Current copies of *Interview* cost $2.50 for approximately 130 pages.

The person who can be considered the most instrumental in the success of *Interview Magazine* is the indomitable Andy Warhol, who was born August 6, 1928, in Pittsburgh, Pennsylvania. As a graduate of the Carnegie Institute of Technology, Warhol established himself as a commercial artist in the 1950s and 1960s and later founded the pop art movement. Throughout the 1970s, Warhol's fame as an outstanding artist continued.

Not only was Warhol a celebrated artist, he also established himself as a respected photographer, filmmaker, and author. However, he considered himself an artist first and was mainly interested in painting portraits. Almost as a sideline to these accomplishments, Andy Warhol founded *Interview Magazine*. Ironically, although he founded and published *Interview*, he admitted that he never really enjoyed being interviewed by others, nor did he relish the idea of being an interviewer. In order to compensate for this uneasiness, Warhol utilized a tape recorder when interviewing and tried to avoid asking questions of interviewees. Consequently, he felt more comfortable interviewing people who liked to talk a great deal and who would carry the conversation.

When preparing interviews for publication, Warhol strove to paint a "good" picture of those being interviewed; he did not believe in saying anything bad about anyone. Andy Warhol, a giant among pop artists and the founder and publisher of *Interview Magazine* died on February 22, 1987. *Interview Magazine*, however, continues in the tradition he began.

Notes

1. During an interview in *New York Magazine,* "Arts and Crafts with Andy Warhol," 12 November 1979, p. 54, Lew Grossberger indicated that Andy Warhol habitually lapsed into impenetrable vagueness. Therefore, Bob Colacello, then executive editor, was present during the interview to translate some of Warhol's vague statements.

2. From *New York Magazine*, "Arts and Crafts with Andy Warhol," by Lew Grossberger, 1979, p. 54. Warhol was uncomfortable interviewing and being interviewed by others.

3. "The Warhol Tapes," *Newsweek*, 22 April 1974, p. 73.

Information Sources

BIBLIOGRAPHY

Academic American Encyclopedia. vol. 20. "Warhol, Andy," by Barbara Cavaliere. Princeton: Arete Publishing Co., Grolier, 1988, pp. 29–30.

Gale Directory of Publications. Detroit: Gale Research Company, 1987. Editorial Director, Frank G. Ruffner.

Grossberger, Lew. "Arts and Crafts with Andy Warhol." *New York Magazine,* 12 November 1979.

Katz, Bill, and Linda Steinberg Katz. *Magazines for Libraries*. 5th ed. New York: R. R. Bowker, 1986.

"The Warhol Tapes." *Newsweek*, 22 April 1974, p. 73.

INDEX SOURCES

Access (1975–present); *Magazine Index* (1977–present).

LOCATION SOURCES

Available in microform.

Publication History

MAGAZINE TITLE AND TITLE CHANGES
>   *Interview*, 1969–1972; *Andy Warhol's Interview*, 1972–1974. *Interview Magazine*,
>   1975–present.

VOLUME AND ISSUE DATA
>   Vol. 1, no. 1–vol. 18, no. 10, 1970–present.

PUBLISHERS AND PLACE OF PUBLICATION
>   Interview Magazine-A.W.E. (Andy Warhol Enterprise). New York.

EDITORS
>   Glenn O'Brien and Lew Grossberger, 1971; Rosemary Kent, 1979; Robert Hayes,
>   1987; Shelley Wanger, current. Other information regarding editors was not avail-
>   able.

CIRCULATION
>   125,455.

Frances Moore-Bond

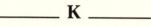

K

THE KIPLINGER MAGAZINE. See CHANGING TIMES

THE KNICKERBOCKER

The *Knickerbocker* was begun in January 1833 out of a combination of nostalgia for New York's vanishing rural past and the desire to develop a genuinely "American" literature distinct from English and European antecedents. The magazine took Dietrich Knickerbocker for its patron saint, the Dutch-American historian from Washington Irving's comic history of New York.[1] The magazine's combination of humor, topical essays, poetry, fiction, criticism, reviews, and literary gossip flourished through the 1830s, 1840s and 1850s, primarily under the editorship of Lewis Gaylord Clark, who adopted its characteristic purple cover and set its tone in his Editor's Table. As Frank Luther Mott claimed in his history of American magazines, "No American magazine has ever been regarded with more affection by its readers than was 'Old *Knick*' under [Clark's] editorship."[2]

The *Knickerbocker* published most of the important American authors of the period, from all regions of the United States. Regular contributors included the New York triumvirate of James Fenimore Cooper, William Cullen Bryant, and Washington Irving; New England writers Henry Wadsworth Longfellow, Nathaniel Hawthorne, John Greenleaf Whittier, and Oliver Wendell Holmes; and Robert Montgomery Bird from Philadelphia. Western writers James Hall, Caroline Stansbury Kirkland, Albert Pike, E.Z.C. Judson ("Ned Buntline"), and Francis Parkman were published regularly, along with Southerners William Gilmore Simms, J. M. Legare, Mary E. Lee, and Richard Henry Wilde. British contributors included William Wordsworth, Robert Southey, and Edward Bulwer-Lytton.

But the primary architects of what came to be called "Knickerbocker Literature" were mostly New Yorkers: Irving and Cooper, Irving's nephew John T. Irving ("Quod"), Charles Fenno Hoffman (Old *Knick's* first editor), James Kirke Paulding, Fitz-Greene Halleck, Joseph Rodman Drake, Robert C. Sands, John Sanderson, Lewis Gaylord Clark (editor from 1834 to 1860) and his twin brother and assistant editor, Willis Gaylord Clark, Nathaniel Parker Willis, and Rufus Wilmot Griswold.

The magazine's success and its magisterial, occasionally pompous tone drew attacks, and the Knickerbocker group, along with other New York writers, were lampooned by Edgar Allan Poe's critical review, "The Literati of New York," published in *Godey's Lady's Book* in 1846. The *Knickerbocker* failed to adjust to the new interests of the 1860s and finally ran aground in the political shoals of the Civil War, ceasing publication with the October 1865 number. The newly formed *Nation* published an obituary of Old *Knick* in December 1867, claiming that the *Knickerbocker* and its writers never succeeded in escaping their colonial backgrounds and establishing the truly American literature that had been their goal. But, in sum, the *Nation* found, the *Knickerbocker* writers "were our first crop," and, "as Americans, if we are not sorry that it exists no longer, we may very well be glad that it once existed."[3]

The *Knickerbocker* is a fascinating compendium of American intellectual and cultural life in the pre-Civil War period. Old *Knick* attempted to reflect the full range of American experience, undeterred by sectional rivalries and parochialism. Charles Fenno Hoffman was chosen as editor by the publishers, Peabody and Company, after the widely popular Washington Irving declined.[4] The first issue began with a dream vision in which the young editor spoke with Irving's fictional creation, the "Dutch Herodotus." The editor justified his new magazine to the "immortal Dietrich" by saying, "In literature . . . we find, to the neglect of our own few original models, a dotard fondness, a sickly longing for all the absurd trash of driveling sentimentality and pseudo-fashion, with which the shelves of our circulating libraries are filled from the London press" (January 1833, p. 11).

Hoffman remained as editor for only three months. Clark speculated later that he had quarreled with Peabody over the magazine's quality.[5] Hoffman was replaced by Samuel Daly Langtree, who was apparently intended to serve as acting editor until a more illustrious successor could be found. In July 1833, Timothy Flint was advertised as editor, and the publishers continued to list him through the February 1834 issue. But because of ill health, Flint did not actually begin his editorial duties until the October 1833 number, although his contributions began appearing in August.[6]

Flint's official withdrawal from the magazine was announced in the February 1834 number (pp. 159–60), but in the April number Langtree stated that during the time Flint was "announced as editor," the "precarious state" of his health had prevented him from residing in New York. Langtree said that he himself had had editorial charge of all issues "since the retirement of Mr. Hoffman in

March, 1833," with the exception of the October 1833 number, "which was edited by Mr. Flint."[7]

Clark and his partner, Clement M. Edson, bought the magazine from Peabody in April 1834. Under Clark's long editorship, the *Knickerbocker* grew by the 1850s into one of the four most influential literary periodicals, the others being *Southern Literary Messenger* (1834–1865), *Graham's** (1841–1859), and *Sartain's* (1849–1852).[8] One of Clark's major innovations was the expansion of the Editor's Table from one or two paragraphs into an editorial forum that, set in smaller type, came to occupy a third of the pages and comprise half the words by 1853.[9] The Editor's Table usually included chat with correspondents; talkative book notices; notes on the drama, music, and fine arts; clippings from contemporary newspapers; some gossip and reminiscence; selected verse (often comic); and anecdotes. The tone was generally light and humorous; representative selections were published in *Knick-Knacks from an Editor's Table* (1852).

Typically, the magazine was organized into three sections—Original Contributions (or Original Papers), Literary Notices (written primarily by Clark), and the Editor's Table. Original Contributions consisted of prose essays on a wide variety of topics (including criticism, biography, travel, history, science, art, business, women, education, and the prison system, but excluding politics until the Civil War period), humor and satire, poetry, serialized novels, short stories or tales, and translations.

Old *Knick's* taste in literature and art was conservative and conventional, a reflection of the mainstream of popular taste. *Knickerbocker* poetry is Romantic and sentimental, occasionally humorous, often sententious. The magazine tended to review better poetry than it published, but the reviews in the Literary Notices department tended toward effusive praise and long excerpts for favored authors. (See, for example, the review of Longfellow's *The Song of Hiawatha* in the December 1855 number, pages 630–32.) The magazine supported Irving, Bryant, Longfellow, and Halleck; it attacked Ralph Waldo Emerson, Bronson Alcott, and Walt Whitman.[10]

Clark's general position called for an "American" poetry, a poetry based on the American landscape and American institutions but coherent with English Romantic models. In his article "American Poets and Their Critics" in the July 1834 number, Clark defended Irving and Bryant (along with Lord Byron and Sir Walter Scott) against attacks by the poetry editor of the *American Quarterly Review*, Dr. James McHenry, essentially destroying McHenry's reputation as a critic and driving him abroad.[11] In the February 1844 number, Clark's "American Manners and American Literature" called for a "National American poetry" based on the American land, institutions, and ideals.

The most well-known *Knickerbocker* contributors of short fiction or tales were Washington Irving, Nathaniel Hawthorne, and William Dean Howells. Irving published most of his *Knickerbocker* tales during the two years he was under contract to contribute something every month, 1839–1841. Hawthorne published three of what were later republished as *Twice-Told Tales* in 1837: "The Fountain of Youth'' in January, later republished as ''Dr. Heidegger's Experiment''; ''A Bell's Biography'' in March; and ''Edward Fane's Rosebud'' in September. William Dean Howells published ''A Dream'' in the August 1861 number.

Of the other more or less minor contributors of short fiction, perhaps the best known are William Gilmore Simms, Thomas Bailey Aldrich, Fitz-James O'Brien, Timothy Flint, Harriet Prescott Spofford, James Kirke Paulding, Henry T. Tuckerman, James Hall, Henry R. Schoolcraft, Eliza Leslie, Catharine M. Sedgwick, and E.Z.C. Judson (''Ned Buntline''). Jeremiah N. Reynolds's ''Mocha Dick: or the White Whale of the Pacific,'' a source for Herman Melville's *Moby Dick*, was published in May 1839.[12] As for longer fiction, perhaps the three most popular novels serialized in the magazine were Richard B. Kimball's *The St. Leger Papers* (a combination of the Romantic novel with a tendency to philosophize and analyze), William Ware's historical romance *Zenobia*, and John T. Irving, Jr.'s mystery *The Attorney*.[13]

Travel writing became an increasingly popular genre in the late 1830s and 1840s. One early example was ''American Antiquities, with Drawings,'' a four-part series on Central America in volume 10 (1837). The foremost title published in this genre was Francis Parkman's *The Oregon Trail, or A Summer Out of Bounds*, serialized in 1847.[14]

Humor was more important in American periodicals in this period than it had ever been before, and the *Knickerbocker* was the best comic periodical of the time.[15] According to Clark, ''The present age is emphatically the Age of Fun. Everybody deals in jokes, and all wisdom is inculcated in a paraphrase'' (August 1846, p. 181). Clark introduced a great deal of humor into his commentary in the Editor's Table, and Mott called the Table one of the best comic journals ever published in America, despite its lack of illustration.[16] Clark's burlesque parody of pompous and ignorant backwoods journalism called ''The Bunkum Flagstaff and Independent Echo,'' which ran serially in 1853, was less successful.

Clark's primary models for humor were Washington Irving and Charles Lamb, and his continued praise of Oliver Goldsmith, Richard Steele, and Joseph Addison revealed the *Knickerbocker's* roots in English neoclassical wit. Among many others, Albert Pike, C. G. Leland, Frederick S. Cozzens, Donald Grant Mitchell (''Ik Marvel''), and Charles F. Briggs (''Harry Franco'') are the best remembered of Old *Knick's* humorists. But Clark's failure to wean the *Knickerbocker* from Irving and Lamb, and to publish the new American humorists of the West and Southwest (although they were reviewed, often favorably), has been seen as a telling example of the magazine's failure to adapt to changing tastes.[17] The frequent cacography, in particular, had become offensive by the 1850s.[18]

Illustration was relatively unimportant in the *Knickerbocker*. Up to 1858 there had been little attempt at illustration. In that year, in volume 52 (July-December), steel-plate engravings of notables like Oliver Wendell Holmes and Washington Irving were inserted in each number, along with woodcuts of subjects like

"Homeric Times" or "Tournament Grounds on the Rappahannoc River." More woodcuts were inserted in the following year, but the trend was discontinued.

In 1859, after the peak of the *Knickerbocker's* popularity and influence in the late 1840s and early 1850s and near the end of his long tenure as editor, Clark began running an anecdotal history of the magazine in the Editor's Table, including lengthy excerpts from past articles and sketches. The "Editorial Narrative" ran in nineteen installments from February 1859 (53:2) through January 1861 (57:1), Charles Godfrey Leland's first issue as editor. The "Excerpts" and "Intermingled Notes" ran from February through July 1861 (57:2–58:1).

According to Clark, negative reaction to a piece in his first issue (May 1834) reporting the riot that grew out of the election for mayor and common council convinced him to leave "party-squabbles to party-organs," and to occupy "*a broad neutral literary ground, on which all parties in politics, and men of all creeds in religion, might meet like brothers*" (March 1859, p. 312).

Clark printed a list of 90 contributors in the fifth installment of his history and claimed that the total list of more than 150, including "several eminent writers from abroad," was "wholly unequalled by any native periodical" (July 1859, pp. 94–95). Among the "Original Papers" that Clark singled out for mention and reprinting in excerpt because of their previous popularity were the series on "Peace Societies"; essays on science by Samuel L. Metcalf; a series of papers by James Brooks entitled "Our Own Country" and intended to "awaken in the young American a love for his own land; to fix his eyes, his thoughts, his heart, *here*" (July 1859, p. 96); "Letters from London" and "Letters from Our Village" (Pottsville, Pennsylvania) by John Sanderson of Philadelphia; E. T. Throop Martin's "Odds and Ends," sketches of street life in New York; Willis Gaylord Clark's humorous *Ollapodiana Papers*; Washington Irving's "Crayon Papers"; Nathaniel Hawthorne's "Dr. Heidegger's Experiment"; "Leaves from the Port-Folio of a Georgia Lawyer" by Robert M. Charlton; Frederick W. Shelton's satirical sketches of Long Island life and real estate speculation; James Fenimore Cooper's famous attack on John Gibson Lockhart's biography of Sir Walter Scott; "The Iron Footstep," a ghost story by Henry Carey published under the nom de plume John Waters; Frederick S. Cozzens's sketch of the Long Island South Shore, "Trout-fishing, by an Amateur"; a sample of Charles G. Leland's art criticism; the "Salmagundi" series by James K. Paulding, a descendant of the "old Knickerbockers"; Richard B. Kimball's novel, *The St. Leger Papers*; and Henry Wadsworth Longfellow's prose "Blank-Book of a Country School-Master."

Summing up his philosophy as editor in the May 1861 number, Clark said, "Not a few among the very first of writers for the Knickerbocker have been active merchants, bankers, lawyers, or other practical business-men, who jotted down, under the *true impulse*, what they had felt or what they had seen. And that's the way to *do* it" (May 1861, p. 556).

Clark's vision of the *Knickerbocker* seems largely to exclude women. But women were a large part of the magazine's target readership, and nine of the ninety contributors Clark listed in his history of the magazine are identifiable as women, a not inconsiderable percentage in a period when husbands often discouraged wives from writing for publication. Perhaps in an attempt to increase the number of women readers, articles by and about women were published with increasing frequency after Clark stepped down as editor. One example was Augusta Browne Garrett's article, "A Woman on Women," which began sarcastically, "A most delicious voluntary rung on the chimes of man's vanity is the inferiority of women" (January 1863, p. 10).

Reliable circulation figures are hard to establish for Old *Knick*. The original subscription list was 800.[19] Clark claimed that Peabody had told him and Edson when they bought the magazine in 1834 that there were 1,000 paid subscribers, when, in fact, there were only half that number (February 1837, p. 199). By 1836, Clark had raised the number to 4,000 (October 1836, p. 500). Subscriptions climbed through the 1830s and early 1840s, leveled off from about 1844 to 1851, and then increased again. The subscription price was reduced from five dollars to three in 1852, and about 6,000 new subscribers were added to the rolls that year.[20] Announcements in the magazine of increases in the number of subscribers were frequent from 1852 to 1857, and two years before he died, Samuel Hueston claimed that the readers of the *Knickerbocker* "cannot be less than a hundred and fifty thousand every month."[21]

But readers are not the same as subscribers, and the magazine was not prospering financially. Clark said in 1857, "We are pleased to say that the circle of [our] readers has never been so large, or so numerous as at this time. If all our *readers* were *paying* subscribers, we should be rich" (July 1857, p. 105). Herman Everette Spivey, trying to read between the lines of editorial announcements, estimates that the magazine had a paid circulation of "better than twenty-five thousand" at its height.[22] By comparison, most of the monthlies in the 1840s and 1850s were struggling along on 7,000 or less; *Godey's Lady's Book* set the record with a circulation of 40,000 by 1850.[23]

Given that those circulation figures were not making anyone wealthy, the *Knickerbocker* paid its contributors reasonably well, compared to other magazines of the period. Longfellow received $50 a poem. The most popular prose writers received up to $15 a page; $5 a page was more usual, and many writers (especially new or unknown ones) were not paid at all. Irving's two-year contract for 1839–1841 paid him $2,000 a year for one or two short contributions each month.[24] Clark claimed in the February 1844 number: "There is no magazine in America that has paid so large sums to distinguished native writers as the KNICKERBOCKER." He added, "Many of our more popular papers have been entirely gratuitous, unless indeed the writers consider the honorable reputation which they have established in these pages as *some* reward for intellectual exertion" (p. 198).

The decline of the *Knickerbocker* was evident by the early 1850s and marked by 1855. The financial panic of 1857 hurt the magazine, and Clark's long tenure as editor meant that Old *Knick* was slow to change in the direction of new tastes and interests. Literary Notices and Editor's Table, both of which were written primarily by Clark, became more and more perfunctory and dull after 1857.[25]

The Civil War found Old *Knick*, like many Northern periodicals with a substantial Southern circulation, trying to occupy a moderate centrist position that no longer existed. The magazine's position on slavery in the 1830s and 1840s was reformist but anti-abolitionist. An article in the October 1837 number signed "By an American" and entitled "Slavery in the United States" attacked the abolitionists and argued that "emancipation of slaves should be gradual" (p. 41). Eleven years later, an article entitled "What Should Be America's Example?" attacked the public press in the North for raising discord and sectional hostility (October 1848, pp. 347–52).

Clark's general editorial position had been to ignore political issues. But in June 1861, after the final installment of Clark's history of Old *Knick*, Leland included "A Few Words About the War" (pp. 649–52). Subsequent numbers ran essays supporting the war and advocating emancipation not as a matter of right, but as a war measure.[26] "Abolition—for the sake of the white man!" became the magazine's stated policy (November 1861, p. 287). In September 1862, Leland and his publisher, Morris Phillips, left Old *Knick* and went to Boston to found a political journal, the *Continental Monthly*.

Kinahan Cornwallis's first Editor's Table in the October 1862 number, his first issue as editor, called for "vigorous prosecution of this war for the restoration of the Federal authority in the seceded States," adding: "It is not our purpose to here discuss the causes, progress, and probable consequences of this gigantic war; we merely announce the broad rationality of our views" (p. 366). In that same issue, Cornwallis added a new column called "Notes on Current Events: Foreign and Domestic" at the end of each issue to report on the progress of the war. Clark was called back to take charge of the Editor's Table from October through December 1863, when John Holmes Agnew took over as editor.

Under Agnew's editorial leadership, Old *Knick* changed its name to the *American Monthly* and took a turn away from Cornwallis's nonpartisan stance and toward Copperhead politics, becoming a Democratic party organ (January 1864, p. 82). The April number quoted and answered a charge from the New York *Evening Post* that the magazine had become "secesh and copperhead."[27] The same issue ran an essay entitled "The Negro—His Nature and Destiny," which suggested that Great Britain and the United States plant and protect the institution of a Christian civilization in Africa, "aided by large colonies of our negroes" (April 1864, pp. 363–66). The magazine was still arguing the biblical sanction of slavery as late as January 1865.[28]

By the July 1865 number, J. P. Robens had taken over as publisher, A. J. H. Duganne had been installed as associate editor, and the magazine renamed the *Federal American Monthly* to signal another political shift. "*Federal*," according to the new editor, was chosen to signal that "The nation is intact" (61). The *Nation* commented in its 7 September number that "We have looked in vain through the "Federal American Monthly" to find any good reason for printing, publishing, or perusing it. The paper and print are very poor, and the literary matter is not worth criticism'' (p. 317).

The *Federal American Monthly* ceased publication with the October 1865 number, and Old *Knick's* thirty-two–year history came to an end. By the 1860s, ''Knickerbocker Literature'' had become a dismissive term for the colonial and pre–Civil War past. But in retrospect, any magazine that could boast of having published ''in a single number articles from Irving, Cooper, Bryant, Halleck, Longfellow, Whittier, Street, General Cass, and the 'American in Paris' [Sanderson]'' has earned a place of respect in the history of American literature.[29]

Notes

1. Washington Irving, *A History of New York from the Beginning of the World to the End of the Dutch Dynasty . . . Being the Only Authentic History of the Time that Ever Hath or Ever Will be Published. By Dietrich Knickerbocker*, 2 vols. (New York and Philadelphia: Inskeep and Bradford, 1809).

2. Frank Luther Mott, *A History of American Magazines*, vol. 1, 1741–1850 (Cambridge, Mass.: Harvard University Press, 1966–1968), p. 606.

3. [J. R. Dennett], ''Knickerbocker Literature,'' *Nation*, 5 December 1867, p. 460–61.

4. Herman Everette Spivey, ''*The Knickerbocker Magazine*, 1833–1865: A Study of Its History, Contents, and Significance'' (Ph.D. diss., University of North Carolina, 1938), pp. 9–10.

5. *Knickerbocker*, February 1859, pp. 193–200.

6. John Ervin Kirkpatrick, *Timothy Flint: Pioneer, Missionary Author, Editor, 1780–1840* (Columbus, Ohio: Arthur H. Clark, 1911), pp. 206–15, 310.

7. Editor's Table, *Knickerbocker*, April 1834, p. 320; see also Clark's ''Editorial Narrative,'' *Knickerbocker*, February 1859, pp. 193–200.

8. Irving Garwood, *American Periodicals from 1850 to 1860* (Macomb, Ill.: Western Illinois State Teachers College, 1931), p. 64.

9. Mott, pp. 609–10.

10. Spivey, p. 389.

11. *Knickerbocker*, March 1859, pp. 420–24; Mott, pp. 274–75.

12. Spivey, pp. 142–44.

13. Ibid., pp. 384–85.

14. Benjamin Franklin Fisher IV, ''The Knickerbocker,'' in *American Literary Magazines: The Eighteenth and Nineteenth Centuries*, ed. Edward E. Chielens (New York: Greenwood Press, 1986), pp. 190–91.

15. Mott, p. 424.

16. Ibid., p. 610.

17. Fisher, pp. 191–92.

18. Mott, p. 610; [Dennett], p. 460.

19. Spivey, p. 58.

20. Ibid., pp. 60–62.

21. Editor's Table, *Knickerbocker*, September 1855, p. 310; Spivey, pp. 62–63.

22. Spivey, p. 382.

23. John Tebbel, *The American Magazine: A Compact History* (New York: Hawthorne Books, 1969), pp. 51, 72–73.

24. Spivey, pp. 36–37.

25. Ibid., p. 67.

26. Mott, p. 612.

27. *American Monthly Knickerbocker*, April 1864, p. 289; see also advertisement on back cover of the July 1864 number in which "British editors" say of the magazine, "though copperhead in politics, the articles are ably written and thoroughly digested."

28. Mott, p. 613.

29. *Knickerbocker*, July 1859, p. 95; pp. 613–14.

Information Sources

BIBLIOGRAPHY

Barnes, Homer F. *Charles Fenno Hoffman*. New York: Columbia University Press, 1930.

[Clark, Lewis Gaylord]. "Editorial Narrative of the Knickerbocker Magazine" [title varies]. *Knickerbocker,* February 1859–January 1861.

[———]. "Excerpts from the Editorial and Literary Correspondence of the Knickerbocker, within the last Twenty-Five Years" [title changes to "Intermingled Notes of Knickerbocker Editorial Narrative and Correspondence" in March number]. *Knickerbocker*, February–July 1861.

———, ed. *The Knickerbocker Sketch-book: A Library of Select Literature.* New York: Burgess, Stringer, 1845.

———, ed. *Knick-Knacks from an Editor's Table.* New York: D. Appleton, 1852.

———, ed. *The Literary Remains of the Late Willis Gaylord Clark: Including the Ollapodian Papers, the Spirit of Life, and a Selection from His Various Prose and Poetical Writings.* New York: Burgess, Stringer, 1844.

"Current Literature." *Nation*, 7 September 1865, pp. 316–17. [Dennett, J. R.] "Knickerbocker Literature." *Nation*, 5 December 1867, pp. 459–61.

Dimmick, Lauretta. "Robert Weir's *Saint Nicholas*: A Knickerbocker Icon." *Art Bulletin*, September 1984, pp. 465–83.

Dunlap, Leslie W., ed. *Letters of Willis Gaylord Clark and Lewis Gaylord Clark, 1829–68.* New York: New York Public Library, 1940. Reprinted with revisions and additions from the *Bulletin of the New York Public Library*, June-December 1938.

"Filching from Old *Knick*." *Boston Aurora Borealis*, February 1849, p. 38.

Fisher, Benjamin Franklin IV. "The Knickerbocker." In *American Literary Magazines: The Eighteenth and Nineteenth Centuries*. Ed. Edward E. Chielens. New York: Greenwood Press, 1986. pp. 189–94.

Garnett, R. S. "*Moby-Dick*" and "*Mocha-Dick*." *Blackwood's Edinburgh Magazine*, December 1929, pp. 841–58.

Garwood, Irving. *American Periodicals from 1850 to 1860.* Macomb, Ill.: Western Illinois State Teachers College, 1931.

Hovey, Kenneth. "A Psalm of Life Reconsidered: The Dialogue of Western Literature and Monologue of Young America." *American Transcendental Quarterly*, March 1987, pp. 3–19.

Irving, Pierre Monroe. *The Life and Letters of Washington Irving*. 4 vols. New York: Putnam, 1862–1864. 3:147–53.

Kime, Wayne R. "The First Locomotive to Cross the Rocky Mountains: An Unidentified Sketch in the *Knickerbocker Magazine*, May 1839, by Washington Irving." *Bulletin of the New York Public Library*, vol. 76, 1972, pp. 242–50.

Kirkpatrick, John Ervin. *Timothy Flint: Pioneer, Missionary, Author, Editor, 1780–1840*. Cleveland, Ohio: Arthur H. Clark, 1911.

The Knickerbocker Gallery: A Testimonial to the Editor of the Knickerbocker Magazine From Its Contributors. Ed. John W. Francis, George P. Morris, Rufus W. Griswold, Richard B. Kimball, and Frederick W. Shelton. New York: Samuel Hueston, 1855.

"*The Knickerbocker Magazine.*" *New York Mirror*, 10 May 1834, p. 359.

Leland, Charles G. *Memoirs*. London: Heinemann, 1893. *The Letters of Willis Gaylord Clark and Lewis Gaylord Clark*. Ed. Leslie W. Dunlap. New York: New York Public Library, 1840.

[Longfellow, H. W.] "The Literary Remains of Willis Gaylord Clark." *North American Review*, July 1844, pp. 239–40.

McHaney, Thomas L. "An Early 19th Century Literary Agent: James Lawson of New York." *Papers of the Bibliographic Society of America*, second quarter, 1970, pp. 177–92.

Miller, Perry. *The Raven and the Whale: The War of Words and Wits in the Era of Poe and Melville*. New York: Harcourt, Brace, and World, 1956.

Moss, Sidney P. *Poe's Literary Battles: The Critic in the Context of His Literary Milieu*. Durham, N.C.: Duke University Press, 1963.

Mott, Frank Luther. *A History of American Magazines*. 5 vols. Cambridge, Mass.: Harvard University Press, vol. 1–5, 1957–1968.

Nethery, Wallace. *Charles Lamb in America to 1848*. Worcester, Mass.: Achilles J. St. Onge, 1963.

"The Newspaper and Periodical Press." *Southern Quarterly Review*, January 1842, p. 28.

Pennell, Elizabeth Robins. *Charles Godfrey Leland*. 2 vols. Boston: Houghton, Mifflin, 1906.

[Poe, Edgar Allan]. "The Magazines." *Broadway Journal*, July 1845, pp. 10–11.

[————]. "Our Magazine Literature." *New World*, 11, March 1843, pp. 302–3.

Pritchard, John Paul. *Literary Wise Men of Gotham: Criticism in New York, 1815–1860*. Baton Rouge: Louisiana State University Press, 1963.

Roche, Arthur John III. "A Literary Gentleman in New York: Evert A. Duyckinck's Relationship with Nathaniel Hawthorne, Herman Melville, Edgar Allan Poe, and William Gilmore Simms." Ph.D. diss., Duke University, 1973.

Sloane, David E. E., ed. *The Literary Humor of the Urban Northeast, 1830–1860*. Baton Rouge: Louisiana State University Press, 1983.

Spivey, Herman Everette. "*The Knickerbocker Magazine*, 1833–1865: A Study of Its History, Contents, and Significance." Ph.D. diss., University of North Carolina, 1938.

Tebbel, John. *The American Magazine: A Compact History*. New York: Hawthorne Books, 1969.

Thorpe, Thomas Bangs. "Lewis Gaylord Clark." *Harper's New Monthly Magazine*, March 1874, pp. 587–92.

Tomlinson, H. M. "Two Americans and a Whale." *Harper's Magazine*, April 1926, pp. 618–21.

Trout, Thomas James. "The *Knickerbocker* and German Influence." Ph.D. diss., Bowling Green State University, 1972.

Woodberry, George Edward. "Knickerbocker Era of American Letters." *Harper's Monthly Magazine*, October 1902, pp. 677–83.

INDEXES

Title index published in last number of each volume; *Poole's Index to Periodical Literature; Contents-Subject Index; Jones' Index to Legal Periodicals; A.L.A. Portrait Index.*

REPRINT EDITIONS

American Periodicals: Series 2, 1800–1850. Reels 349–61. Title: *The Knickerbocker; or, New York Monthly Magazine.* Ann Arbor, Mich.: University Microfilms, 1979. [Selected covers, some pages missing]; Serials in Microform, Order No. C4572. 15 reels. Title: *Federal American Monthly.* (New York). Ann Arbor, Mich.: University Microfilms International, 1987.

LOCATION SOURCES

According to *The Union List of Serials,* over 145 libraries hold this title, all in incomplete runs except for the Library of Congress. The New York Public Library has vols. 1–64 in paper, and vol. 65 in microfilm. All runs seen have pages missing.

Publication History

MAGAZINE TITLE AND TITLE CHANGES

(1) *The Knickerbocker, or, New York Monthly Magazine,* January 1833–September 1862 [spelled "Knickerbacker" in vol. 1] (2) *The Knickerbocker, or New-York Monthly Magazine of Literature, Art, Politics, and Society,* October-December 1862; (3) *The Knickerbocker Monthly: A National Magazine of Literature, Art, Politics, and Society,* January-June 1863; (4) *The Knickerbocker Monthly: A National Magazine of Literature, Art, Science, Politics, and Society,* July 1863–February 1864; (5) *The American Monthly Knickerbocker, Devoted to Literature, Art, Science, and Politics,* March-December 1864 [no comma after *Knickerbocker,* March-April]; (6) *The American Monthly, Devoted to Literature, Art, Science, and Politics,* January-June 1865; (7) *Federal American Monthly. Literature, Art, Science, Politics,* July-October 1865.

VOLUME AND ISSUE DATA:

Monthly. Two volumes a year. Vols. 1–66, January 1833–October 1865 (semiannual volumes). New Series begins October 1862 as vol. 1, no. 1; monthly issues numbered consecutively until no. 21, June 1864; New Series numbering begins again with no. 1, July 1864, and continues to no. 12, June 1865; New Series numbering begins again with no. 1, July 1865, and continues to no. 4, October 1865. New Series issues also carry Old Series volume and issue numbers.

PUBLISHER AND PLACE OF PUBLICATION

Peabody and Company, January 1833–April 1834; L. C. Clark and Clement M. Edson, May-June 1834; J. Disturnell, July 1834–1835; Wiley and Long, 1836; Wiley and Putnam, 1837; Clark and Edson, 1838–June 1841; John Bisco, July 1841–June 1842; John Allen, July 1842–1848; Samuel Hueston, 1849–1857; John A. Gray, 1858–1860; J. R. Gilmore, 1861; Morris Phillips, January-September

1862; Kinahan Cornwallis, October-December 1862; J. H. Elliot, January-August 1863; Kinahan Cornwallis, September 1863–February 1864; J. H. Agnew, March 1864–June 1865; J. P. Robens and the American News Company, July-October 1865: all in New York.

EDITORS

Charles Fenno Hoffman, January-March 1833; Samuel Daly Langtree, April-June 1833; Timothy Flint and S. D. Langtree, July 1833–February 1834; S. D. Langtree, March-April 1834; Lewis Gaylord Clark, May 1834–December 1860, with Willis Gaylord Clark, associate editor, 1834–1841, and James D. Noyes, associate editor, 1858–1859; Charles Godfrey Leland, January 1861–September 1862; Kinahan Cornwallis, October 1862–September 1863; K. Cornwallis and L. G. Clark, October-December 1863; John Holmes Agnew, January 1864–June 1865; J. H. Agnew and A.J.H. Duganne, July-October 1865.

CIRCULATION

800 initial subscription list; 25,000–30,000 by mid–1850s.

Daniel R. Rubey

L

LEISURE. See YANKEE

LESLIE'S MONTHLY MAGAZINE. See FRANK LESLIE'S POPULAR MONTHLY

FRANK LESLIE'S POPULAR MONTHLY

The history of *Frank Leslie's Popular Monthly* is far less controversial than that of the people who created it. Begun in 1876, the magazine was at first only one in a legion of ever-changing publications under the Frank Leslie masthead. Leslie (born Henry Carter) became famous as an illustrator who devised a clever way to drastically reduce the amount of time needed to produce engravings of current events. In an era when it could take nearly four months for a double-page engraving to be made, Leslie's process ensured unprecedented topicality within days. Prosperity in the publishing business came with *Frank Leslie's Illustrated Newspaper* in 1855, but during the 1860s his fortunes continued to prosper with the publication of the *Chimney Corner, Pleasant Hours*, and other general-interest magazines.

By 1876, Leslie was an established international success as a publisher. The *Popular Monthly*, the twelfth of his publications, offered a mix of light nonfiction and sentimental fiction not radically different from that in other, more expensive magazines. Graced by an attractive colored cover, the *Popular Monthly* of the 1870s was likely to contain a little over 100 pages per issue. Each issue was packed with features on travel, current events, one or two serials by such popular writers as Joaquin Miller and Etta Pierce, and individual short stories with titles like "Huldah's Revenge." Heavily illustrated, the magazine was an excellent value at $2.50 per year.

The *Popular Monthly* continued to flourish from its inception despite radical vicissitudes in the fortunes of its founder. To encapsulate a personal saga worthy of Etta Pierce, Leslie, within a few years, endured a scandalous divorce (1874), married former actress Miriam Folline (once known as Millie Montez), built a fabulous estate in Saratoga, went bankrupt (1877), saw his wife's past exposed in the Virginia City *Territorial Enterprise*, and died of throat cancer in 1880 at the age of fifty-nine.

Miriam Leslie inherited a debt of some $300,000 as well as the Leslie stable of publications at her husband's death. Known for her attractiveness and vivacity, Miriam Leslie personally took control of the Leslie empire and brought it back into the black within a year (helped to no small account by coverage of President Garfield's assassination). She seems to have been a remarkably able editor of the *Popular Monthly*, which she continued to edit long after selling the other Leslie publications. From a circulation of 60,000 in 1879, the *Popular Monthly* rose to 125,000 issues per number in 1887. Like her husband whose name she formally adopted in 1881, Miriam Leslie was less interested in literature than in selling magazines and did so by copying many of the traits of more expensive publications. Her formula changed little in the fifteen years of her editorship; a look at the titles in the July 1895 issue reveals "An Artist in London Town," "As Woman's Love," "Kangaroos and Kangaroo Hunting," and yet another Etta Pierce serial.

Miriam Leslie's social life continued to be newsworthy even into her old age. She added diamonds and admirers to her collections and married a fourth time (briefly) to Willie Wilde, the brother of the notorious Oscar and many years her junior. She found time for trips abroad and a lecture tour of the East and Midwest in 1890; she also authored a play based on Alexandre Dumas *fils* called "The Froth of Society."

In 1895 at age fifty-nine she attempted to retire from publishing and leased her interest in Leslie publications to a syndicate headed by Frederic Colver. Without her magic touch, however, the circulation faltered, income dropped radically, and she was requested to resume control in 1898. To boost circulation, she reduced the size of the magazine and dropped the price to ten cents an issue, at the same time redesigning the publication visually through a new printing and binding plant. Circulation reached a new high of 200,000 in 1898.

The new century brought health problems and the effects of old age to erode Miriam Leslie's editorial control of the *Popular Monthly*. Her controlling financial interest in the magazine also evaporated, and by 1903 she was out of a job, this time for good. With her retirement, the last vestiges of the Frank Leslie publishing empire began to disappear. As a millionairess and Francophile, Mrs. Leslie convinced the French government of her noble blood and renounced the use of the name Frank Leslie in favor of the Baroness de Bazus. The *Popular Monthly* lasted only a few years until it was reincarnated as the *American Magazine* in 1906. Miriam Leslie lived until 1914; the *American Magazine* lasted until the 1950s.

Information Sources

BIBLIOGRAPHY

"Frank Leslie and the Traditions and Progress of Illustrative Art." *Frank Leslie's Popular Monthly,* August 1895, pp. 253–54.
"Frank Leslie and Miriam Florence Folline Leslie." *Dictionary of American Biography.* New York: Charles Scribner's Sons, 1946.
Gambee, Bud Leslie, Jr. *Frank Leslie and His Illustrated Newspaper, 1855–1860.* Ann Arbor: University of Michigan Department of Library Science, 1964.
Mott, Frank Luther. *A History of American Magazines, vol. 3, 1865–1885.* Cambridge: Harvard University Press, 1938.
Stern, Madeleine B. *Purple Passage: The Life of Mrs. Frank Leslie.* Norman: University of Oklahoma Press, 1953.

INDEX SOURCES

> *Review of Reviews Index; Dramatic Index; Poole's* (1905–1906); *Readers' Guide* (1905–1906).

LOCATION SOURCES

> Available in microform.

Publication History

MAGAZINE TITLE AND TITLE CHANGES

> *Frank Leslie's Popular Monthly,* January 1876–February 1904; *Leslie's Monthly Magazine,* March 1904–August 1905.

VOLUME AND ISSUE DATA

> Vol. 1, no. 1, January 1876–August 1905 vol.60, no. 4. Monthly.

PUBLISHER AND PLACE OF PUBLICATION

> Frank Leslie, 1876–July 1878; Frank Leslie Publishing House, August 1878–August 1905. New York(?).

EDITORS

> Frank Leslie, 1876–1880; [Mrs. Frank Leslie] 1880–1899; Ellery Sedgwick, 1900–1905.

CIRCULATION

> 200,000 (1898).

Stephanie Childs Sigala

LIBERTY

Very few periodicals intended for a mass market dare to reflect the personal beliefs and characters of their editors. An exception was *Liberty,* an anarchist magazine edited by Benjamin Ricketson Tucker from 1881 through 1908. Though not devoted specifically to politics, literature, women's issues, or popular fiction, as were many contemporaneous periodicals, *Liberty* encompassed all of these. *Liberty* is an excellent example of a special-interest group making the most of nineteenth-century publishing practices to market its ideas to the public.

Benjamin R. Tucker was born in 1854 in South Dartmouth, Massachusetts, the son of a Quaker grocer who was turned away from the Society for marrying outside the faith. The woman he married was a Unitarian whose family was dedicated to political dissent. Tucker, if the biographical sources are to be taken at face value, was an extremely precocious child. Family tradition had it that he was able to read at the age of two, and, at four, noted an error in a biblical passage in his aunt's prayer book. Educated in Quaker schools, he refused any further religious training at the age of twelve, and at sixteen, balked at his parents' attempts to enroll him at Harvard University. His aversion to Harvard resurfaced many years later in an article in *Liberty*, in which he claimed that it was "not necessary to go to Harvard College in order to become intelligent." Harvard was "a case of atrophy, of useless survival," "a resort of the sons of wealthy people" (24 December 1881, p. 4). Instead, he attended, but did not graduate from, the Massachusetts Institute of Technology (MIT). This distaste for formal education did not, however, hinder Tucker's intellectual development, for he read voraciously the works of Herbert Spencer, Charles Darwin, John Stuart Mill, and other philosophers. There must also have been some dedication to learning foreign languages, because this skill proved a necessary ingredient in his later role as a publisher and disseminator of radical literature. Like many of his well-read contemporaries, Tucker acquired an interest in and love for literature along with his political and philosophical interests. Throughout his publishing career, Tucker read, and passed on to his readers, notes on literary authors and their works.

While at MIT, Tucker came under the influence of Josiah Warren, an influential American anarchist, and became acquainted with the writings of Pierre-Joseph Proudhon, the French libertarian socialist. The thinking of these two men helped form Tucker's views on socialism, religion, politics, economics, and women's issues. They stressed individual autonomy, abjuring all organized political and social systems. His acquaintance, at the age of eighteen, with Victoria Woodhull, a well-known advocate of free love, shaped his views on marriage and the role of women in society. Woodhull's persuasiveness on more than an intellectual level may account for Tucker's unusually progressive regard for women's individuality and intelligence in an era in which they did not yet have the right to vote.

In 1877, Tucker began his publishing career as the temporary editor of *Word*, a radical periodical advocating free love and the emancipation of women. More interested in economic reform, he relinquished this post in the same year to found the *Radical Review*. Because of economic constraints, this periodical lasted only a year, and Tucker was forced to seek employment with the *Boston Globe*, where he remained for eleven years. There, he gained valuable experience in a variety of jobs in both the editorial and production departments.

After accumulating sufficient funds, Tucker introduced the first issue of *Liberty* on Saturday, 6 August 1881. The publication's subtitle was taken from the works of Proudhon: "Liberty, not the daughter but the mother of order." The inaugural issue stated the purposes of the new periodical:

> Liberty enters the field of journalism to speak for herself because she finds no one willing to speak for her. She hears no voice that always champions her; she knows no pen that always writes in her defense; she sees no hand that is always lifted to avenge her wrongs or vindicate her rights. . . . monopoly and privilege must be destroyed, opportunity afforded, and competition encouraged. This is Liberty's work, and "Down with Authority" her war-cry. (p. 2)

The publication's editorial offices were located in Boston, and from there, Tucker expected to take on all bastions of authority, including the Catholic and Protestant churches, the Russian autocracy, and even the workers' advocate, Karl Marx. For only fifty cents a year, or two cents a copy, this fortnightly was to serve as a forum for education and the discussion of Tucker's individualist philosophy.

This first issue set the tone for all those that were to follow; irreverent, satirical, open to criticism, the magazine baited its opponents with what it dared to print. The editorial content (there was no advertising in the first issue) was a pastiche of observations, both political and literary, on the contemporary scene. The first page contained an elegiac poem and portrait of Sophie Perovskaya, the Russian anarchist who had been executed for participation in the assassination of Czar Alexander II. The lead column, Tucker's own "On Picket Duty," promised that "we shall print portraits of various heroes and heroines of revolution and radicalism" in future issues (6 August 1881, p. 1). As it turned out, the entire run of the periodical contained very few illustrations, and only one editorial cartoon, on 24 February 1894 (p. 1).

As a whole, the publication was not a single statement of Tucker's philosophy, but a rather eclectic collection of notes on the foreign and domestic press, notices of new publications, and even social events. Another column, "About Progressive People," presented somewhat gossipy reports on well-known persons such as Robert Ingersoll, Victor Hugo, Elizabeth Cady Stanton, and leaders of the anarchist movement.

Tucker made clear that this venture was a highly personal and individual one; he proclaimed that the "journal will be edited to suit its editor, not its readers" (6 August 1881, p. 1). With the cavalier attitude toward authority one often associates with the editors of modern college newspapers, Tucker offered this outrageous bit of news in the first issue, undoubtedly to provoke a response from *Liberty's* more conservative readers: "Gone from bad to worse—the young woman of Chicago, who a fortnight ago left a house of ill fame to join the church" (6 August 1881, p. 3). The daring statement had the desired effect. In the next issue, on 20 August 1881, Tucker responded to the outcry: "Nine-tenths of the occupants of Christian pulpits are prostitutes of a far worse order than the unfortunate women whom social conditions force into the service of the lusts of their male parishioners'' (p. 3).

Tucker was quick to detect, and denounce, hypocrisy. The article immediately following that quoted above reported the story of Baker Pasha, a British officer whose military exploits permitted his admittance into an officers club, despite his having allegedly forced his attentions on a young lady of his acquaintance. The editorial tone was ironic: "To this journalist we are indebted for the lesson that a man may retrieve a reputation lost in assaulting unarmed women by engaging in conflict with armed men'' (20 August 1881, p. 3).

The response to the new publication, as might be expected, was mixed. Bravely, Tucker printed responses from both ends of the political and philosophical spectrum. One reader congratulated Tucker on having "thrown down the gauntlet to the Grundys'' (3 September 1881, p. 3); some readers, however, found the new publication "not fit for outhouse use'' (4 March 1882, p. 3). Even the conventional press, including the *Boston Globe*, noted, and welcomed, *Liberty's* appearance.

Having determined that the purpose of *Liberty* was "the abolition of authority'' (20 August 1881, p. 2), Tucker suffered no qualms about personal attacks on individuals in positions of authority. As the initial issues of *Liberty* came to press, President James Garfield lay dying, the victim of an attack by Charles J. Guiteau, a disappointed office seeker. With an insensitivity most modern readers would consider astonishing, Tucker used the situation to expound upon some of his favorite themes. The outpouring of prayers and sympathy for the president aroused Tucker's contempt for religion and the automatic respect often granted to public figures by reason of their position. The president, declared Tucker, deserved pity, not undeserved praise. And of what use were the many prayers, national days of fasting, and letters of condolence to the president's wife? "God himself, being a pure fiction'' could not possibly effect a change in the president's condition (15 October 1881, p. 2). When Garfield eventually died, Tucker praised the socialists of Chicago, who adopted these resolutions in their "common-sense'' mourning:

> Resolved, That this body deeply regrets the suffering and death of the late James A. Garfield; we desire it also understood that our regret and sympathy in this case differ in no respect from that which we feel at the suffering and death of the humblest worker who is stricken in the performance of his duty. . . .
> Resolved, That as sincere grief is ever silent and undemonstrative, we cannot but protest against the present ostentatious demonstration of grief, as both insincere and unbecoming, and characteristic only of oriental and monarchical pageantry. (1 October 1881, p. 4)

Throughout the magazine's history, Tucker never hesitated to express his opinions on public figures. In 1885, he published a series of articles by Lysander Spooner, an important radical figure and contributor to *Liberty*. Spooner's essay was entitled "A Letter to Grover Cleveland on His False, Absurd, Self-contradictory, and Ridiculous Inaugural Address." The editor, armed as he was by the justice of his cause, undoubtedly felt no need to mince words.

That laws against libel were not as readily invoked a hundred years ago becomes apparent when one reads *Liberty*. In the 12 December 1885 issue, published soon after the death of railroad magnate William H. Vanderbilt, Tucker's column began with this statement: "Vanderbilt is dead. Another bad man gone right!" (p. 1). The front page of the 1 May 1886 issue ridiculed Rose Cleveland's views on modest dress for women. The editor called the president's sister a "superannuated virgin" and criticized her "prudish lunacy" in attempting to "draw the line where modesty ends and immodesty begins" (p. 1).

More important than these personal attacks, however, were Tucker's views on social and economic topics. Far from being an advocate of violence (and there parting company with certain anarchist strains), Tucker stressed the necessity for individual action, individual choice, and freedom from coercion. *Liberty* stressed these tenets and insisted that even socialism and communism impinged upon the rights of the individual. Tucker saw government and big business as major perpetrators of economic injustice, and his columns constantly "advocated the abolition of the state and with it the four major types of monopoly—those of land, money and banking, trade, and patents and copyright."[1]

When an admiring reader wrote in to suggest the establishment of a stock company to fund *Liberty*, Tucker refused, saying it would "ruin the company" (4 February 1882, p. 3). Through *Liberty's* very last issues, Tucker expressed his disapproval of such "monopolies" as the postal service, Bell Telephone, and state laws that required him to acknowledge his ownership of *Liberty*.

Mikhail Bakunin, the Russian revolutionary, was one of Tucker's heroes; in 1882 he even initiated a fund drive for the Russian nihilists in the pages of *Liberty*. The periodical faithfully reported the contributors and their contributions to the nihilists' fund-raising arm, the Red Cross Society of the People's Will. Apparently after receiving complaints about the purpose to which the monies were put, Tucker assured his readers that the funds were to support the widows and children of those who died for the cause. This support for foreign radical causes sounds strikingly relevant to us today; even more interesting is *Liberty's* opposition to British rule in Ireland. In addition to editorial comment on the issue, Tucker issued several publications on the subject. The 13 May 1882 issue of *Liberty* advertised a pamphlet by one Avery Meriwether entitled "English Tyranny and Irish Suffering." The proceeds from the ten-cent pamphlet were to benefit the Siberian exiles. On 24 October 1885, there appeared a notice of the publication of *Ireland*, by the French author Georges Sauton. This "new and thrilling romance" depicted "the story of one of the heroic struggles of the sons of Erin to lift the accursed yoke of the English" (p. 4).

Liberty often expressed in its pages the futility and error of participating in the electoral process. An article entitled "The Foolishness of Voting" in the 14

April 1883 issue expressed this notion. Although Tucker opposed women's right to vote (10 June 1882, p. 4), he defended their right to make as great fools of themselves as men (9 June 1883, p. 1).

Through the medium of *Liberty*, Benjamin Tucker was able to spread his opinions on any topic that interested him. What is remarkable is the absence of what we in the 1980s label "liberal" or "conservative" opinion; *Liberty's* editorial stance was consistent only in its thorough support of self-determination. In his advocacy of individual liberty, Tucker defended the rights of the Mormons to polygamy (22 July 1882, p. 20), and opposed legislation against pornography (27 May 1882, p. 3), but, in a seeming contradiction for a libertarian and a pacifist, appeared to support capital punishment:

> I have . . . seen it stated that capital punishment is murder in its worst form. I should like to know upon what principle of human society these assertions are based and justified. . . . Murder is an offensive act. . . . And capital punishment, however effective it may be and through whatever ignorance it may be resorted to, is a strictly defensive act,—at least in theory. . . . I insist that there is nothing sacred in the life of an invader, and there is no valid principle of human society that forbids the invaded to protect themselves in whatever way they can. (30 August 1890, p. 4)

Allied with its social and economic concerns was *Liberty's* specific interest in women's and family issues. As noted above, *Liberty* opposed women's suffrage because it violated anarchistic principles. Tucker believed that "even in so delicate a matter as that of the relations of the sexes," individualism should prevail. Anarchists "defend the right of any man or woman . . . to love each other for as long or as short a time as they can, will, or may. To them legal marriage and legal divorce are equal absurdities." Tucker felt that even women should become self-supporting, and only children had to relinquish some right to individualism "until old enough to belong to themselves" (10 March 1888, p. 3).

The interest in women's issues was perhaps an attempt to gain the readership of women; it certainly influenced *Liberty's* editorial policies. In the 17 May 1884 issue, there appeared an announcement of the publication of "interesting serial stories of a radical tendency." The new four-page section was inserted into the regular four-page publication. The first novel to appear was a translation by Benjamin Tucker, *What's To Be Done: A Romance*, by the Russian activist N. G. Tchernychewsky. Its stated purposes were to show that "woman is a human being and not an animal created for man's benefit" and "to show the superiority of free unions between men and women over the indissoluble marriage sanctioned by Church and State" (p. 2).

Though *Liberty* had not been intended as a literary magazine, the publication of literary works was certainly not foreign to the purposes and interests of its editor. From the first issues, Benjamin Tucker expressed his admiration for French author and patriot Victor Hugo. George Bernard Shaw's first American publication was in *Liberty*; Tucker pirated his essay "What's in a Name?" from the new British periodical *Anarchist*.[2] Tucker always made note of new publications, and had as strong opinions on literary matters as he did on social and economic ones. A scathing article in the 4 February 1882 issue of *Liberty* on American poets Henry Wadsworth Longfellow, James Russell Lowell, Oliver Wendell Holmes, and John Greenleaf Whittier was entitled "Our Bepuffed Litterateurs." He called them "scribbling emotionalists," "trickers-out of current thoughts and themes in pert, studied, ornamental phrase, intent mostly upon style . . . and emulating the jackdaw in the borrowed character of their plumage" (p. 4). Tucker contrasted them with the "refreshing" approach of Walt Whitman.

The same issue contains the first mention of Tucker's views on censorship. He railed against Anthony Comstock, who suppressed *House and Home*, a weekly newspaper, for advertising Dr. E. B. Foote's *Hand-Book of Health Hints and Ready Recipes* (4 February 1882, p. 1). The 26 November 1881 issue of *Liberty* announced the revised, unexpurgated edition of Walt Whitman's *Leaves of Grass*, to be published by James R. Osgood (p. 3). When the Boston post office suppressed the book in 1882, Tucker undertook its support in the interests of liberty. An advertisement in the 22 July 1882 issue of *Liberty* offered the book by mail at two dollars a copy. In his inimitable way, Tucker dared the postal authorities to prosecute him for the offense:

> To Oliver Stevens, District Attorney . . . You are hereby notified . . . that I have in my possession, and do now offer for sale, copies of the work advertised above. If you . . . believe, or affect to believe, that, in so doing, I am committing an unlawful act, you are invited to test the question whether twelve men, fairly chosen by lot, can be found in Massachusetts sufficiently bigoted, or intolerant, or hypocritical, to share with you, such belief, or affectation of belief. And, to avoid unnecessary trouble and make the evidence of sale indisputable, I offer, on receipt from any one of you of an order for a copy of the work, to deliver a copy to you in my own person, at such place in Boston as you may designate. (p. 4)

Tucker was never prosecuted for his action, and he continued to deplore the censorship of literary material. He published, on 28 November 1885, an article by Émile Zola, "*Germinal* and the Censors." Tucker realized, of course, the publicity value of being banned in Boston, or elsewhere. When the serialization of *What's To Be Done* was complete, Tucker published the work in book form. The advertisement noted that the work was banned in Russia, a Russian edition supposedly worth $600 a copy.

Like many of his contemporaries, Tucker continued to issue fiction in parts in his magazine. In addition to the aforementioned *What's To Be Done* and *Ireland, Liberty* presented the public with the decidedly minor works *The Wife of Number 4,237* by Sophie Kropotkine and *The Rag-Picker of Paris* by Felix Pyat. Many of these foreign titles were translated by Tucker himself. Some of these were not printed in *Liberty*, but were offered for sale in its pages. The most important of these was Tucker's translation of Leo Tolstoy's "Kreutzer Sonata," another work controversial in its time.

As in the first issue, poetry appeared occasionally in the pages of *Liberty*. Most of the poems were short satirical pieces, but the epic voice of anarchism did not go unheard. An advertisement for "A Good Word for the Devil: Bible Musings By an Infidel" touted this verse satire on the Bible and "Christian superstitions" as "Keen, witty, learned, powerful" (29 October 1881, p. 4). A review and excerpts from the poem were published in the next issue. "The Wind and the Whirlwind" by Wilfrid Scawen Blunt appeared on 12 July 1884, and an ad in the 26 July issue offered an "elegant and cheap" version "bound in parchment covers" for twenty-five cents (p. 8).

As *Liberty* matured, the publication and advertisement of fiction became more and more commonplace. This trend may have been due to the weakening financial stability of the periodical. This is nowhere apparent in the first issues. No ads were present in the first five numbers; with number 6 (15 October 1881), however, a series of notices for "Liberty's Library" began to appear. Though Benjamin Tucker may have been an iconoclast on social matters, when it came to economic support for his ventures, he closely resembled his fellow publishers in the pursuit of subscribers. This "library," like so many others published in the late nineteenth century, offered popular works by mail. Tucker's offerings were not popular in the usual sense, but they did appeal to populist causes and were certainly of interest to budding anarchists. The original list included sixteen titles, ranging in price from a postage stamp to $4.50. It included substantial works by Josiah Warren and Proudhon, volume 1 of Tucker's own *Radical Review*, and such tantalizing pamphlets as "So the Railway Kings Itch for an Empire" by a Red-Hot Striker, "Prostitution and the International Women's League," and "Captain Roland's Purse: How It Is Filled and How Emptied," by John Ruskin (15 October 1881, p. 4). All of these were published by Tucker himself; happily, *Liberty* provided him with adequate advertising space. As each volume of the periodical was completed, it was offered for sale as a bound volume.

The first outside advertising appeared on 20 January 1883, from the *Kansas Liberal*, a freethought journal edited by M. Harman and R. C. Walker of Valley Falls, Kansas. This had been preceded by a notice in number 31 (9 December 1882) that the editor would be vacationing and that no issue would appear until 20 January of the following year. Tucker assured his readers that the break was "not due to a lessening prosperity," but was, rather, "letting go to get a better hold" (p. 2). This was to become a favorite justification for short- or long-term suspensions of the periodical. The 20 January issue included a notice that the publication would thenceforth be monthly, rather than fortnightly. From this date onward, there were frequent fluctuations in frequency.

Tucker attempted to raise funds through a variety of methods, some typical of the fledging nineteenth-century publishing industry, some characteristic of the man dedicated to a cause. After publication of the *Kansas Liberal* ad, Tucker began to accept advertisements for various other anarchistic works by other publishers. Nearly all were socioeconomic in tenor, including other radical periodicals and pamphlet collections such as J. Bordollo's "Standard Labor Literature" (6 February 1886, p. 8). The 7 March 1891 issue offered Tucker's own fiction series, the Tendency Novels, which included the "Kreutzer Sonata" and other novels that had been serialized in *Liberty* (p. 8).

Catering to men's higher aspirations did not, apparently, resolve Tucker's fiscal woes. Number 9, on 26 November 1881, advertised a steel-plate portrait of Proudhon for seventy-five cents. To this was added a portrait of Bakunin on 18 March 1882, with the addition of a title for the series of pictures: *Liberty's* Portrait Gallery. This, too, was a common advertising ploy in the nineteenth century, and Tucker could probably justify it to himself as contributing to the anarchist cause.

A want ad for salespeople "to introduce and sell by sample a new preparation of milk" appeared in the 11 April 1885 issue (p. 8). This ad, paid for by Dr. W. K. Dyer of Boston, was the only job ad to appear in *Liberty* for many years. Not till 25 February 1893 did Tucker advertise commercial products in his publication. Page 4 of that number contained an illustrated advertisement for an "American watch" that would not "vary a minute in 30 days." The item was available from Robert H. Ingersoll and Brothers of New York City. This was followed, a month later, by an ad for Ripans tabules, good for "Biliousness, Constipation, Dyspepsia, Foul Breath, Headache, Heartburn, Loss of Appetite, Mental Depression, Painful Digestion, Pimples, Sallow Complexion, Tired Feeling," etc. (25 March 1893, p. 4). The decision to include this sort of advertising must have been difficult for Tucker, who expected his readers to have the same dedication to the spread of anarchism he had.

Tucker's naïveté in this regard, and, doubtless, a precarious financial situation, led to an entire range of demands of *Liberty's* readers. Some were simple requests to renew subscriptions; in the last number of volume 1, the editor asked his readers to get three more subscribers, and renew their own subscriptions promptly. The next issue, 14 October 1882, sounds very familiar to viewers of public television: *Liberty* offered premiums to new subscribers. For fifty cents (the usual price of the magazine), a reader could get a year's worth of *Liberty* and volume 1 of John Ruskin's *Letters to Workmen and Laborers*; for $1.00, the extra incentives were Charles Dickens's *Christmas Stories* and Thomas Carlyle's *Sartor Resartus*; for $1.50, Alfred Lord Tennyson's *Idylls of the King*, Thomas Babington Macaulay's *Essays*, and Edwin Arnold's *Light of Asia* were tacked on. The $2.00 subscriber got all of the above plus Benjamin Disraeli's *Lothair* and Louis Kossuth's *Memories of My Exile*. And, if one could spare $3.50, one could delve into Charles Knight's eight-volume *Popular History of England* as well (14 October 1882, p. 1).

The same issue announced the availability of three bound copies of volume 1, to go to the highest bidders. Ten years later, on 16 July 1892, *Liberty* printed a notice of an auction for a complete set of the first three volumes of the publication. The high bids netted $40.25 (from ''An Individualist''), $21.00, and $16.00 (3 September 1892, p. 1). *Liberty* offered various other incentives to its subscribers. These included raffles for free books and the opportunity to buy *Liberty* books and periodicals wholesale (cash in advance, of course).

After several suspensions, or ''vacations,'' Tucker apologized for delays in publication, but began a series of admonitions to his readers: ''Such delays would never occur at all, if the paper were more liberally supported. It grows in circulation, but very slowly, and, while it is thus getting its growth, each of its supporters should do double duty'' (30 October 1886, p. 1). Readers of the 4 March 1893 issue were made to feel directly responsible for the paper's problems: ''If *Liberty* under these circumstances does not soon reach a goodly circulation, it will be the fault, not of its publisher, but of its friends'' (p. 2).

There were also attempts to increase circulation through mailing lists. A reader could get three free months of *Liberty* or its German-language edition, *Libertas*, by sending in the names and addresses of twenty-five Germans of ''liberal tendencies'' (10 March 1888, p. 4). The publication of *Libertas* had been announced in the 25 February 1888 issue. This was a few scant months after the execution of the Haymarket anarchists, who had been duly commemorated in *Liberty*. The new periodical was to be edited by George and Emma Schumm of Minnesota. It would use the same format as *Liberty*, cost one dollar a year, and alternate weeks of publication with *Liberty*. It is difficult to say whether this was a sign of *Liberty's* strength, or a hint of impending economic trouble. The circulation of *Liberty* apparently reached only about six hundred,[3] but its influence was far-reaching. Just as it reprinted (often in translation) the works of foreign anarchists, foreign publications reprinted articles that had originally appeared in *Liberty*.

Liberty must have been relatively successful, if one is to judge by the geographical range of its distribution points. The 10 September 1892 issue began publishing a list of the cities in which *Liberty* had agents; these included New York, Philadelphia, Detroit, Chicago, Denver, Canton (Ohio), London, and Melbourne. During this period, the magazine was also being published weekly. There must have been some reliance on individual agents in addition to the usual direct mail offerings. In one of the last issues, Tucker placed an ad for a canvasser for *Liberty* and his other publications. The job paid ten dollars a week plus a commission of one-third on all sales. In addition to having a neat appearance, the successful applicant was required to be a ''well-grounded believer in Anarchism'' (October 1906, p. 2).

Liberty is a good example of the way in which movements outside the mainstream of political and social thought spread their ideas. From the first, *Liberty* was to be ''a channel for the diffusion of . . . needed information'' (20 August 1881, p. 1). Tucker saw the publication as an educational venture, not only with its contents, but through its urgings to readers to spread the word about anarchism. *Liberty* had an ''Anarchist letter-writing corps'' who pledged to write to a specified ''target'' on anarchism and related topics. Readers who pledged to do such writing found the targets listed in one of *Liberty's* regular columns; they were also required to report to *Liberty* if they failed in their letter-writing duties.

That some aspiring anarchists were overzealous in their preaching was evident from an article entitled "How to Help Liberty" in the 28 December 1895 issue: "Always carry some effective pamphlet, or several, to hand to chance acquaintances. . . . Recommend the leading works of Liberty's Library to the committees of public and private libraries. A little tact is perhaps permissible here" (p. 2). True believers could purchase a set of forty-eight "Anarchist stickers," which quoted "aggressive, concise Anarchistic assertions and arguments . . . to be planted everywhere as broadcast seed for thought" (December 1906, p. 64). Tucker also aggressively published anarchist books and pamphlets under his own imprint, and twice opened bookstores with reading rooms devoted exclusively to this literature.

Two of the projects that arose out of Tucker's desire to spread the gospel of anarchism would have endeared him to many a librarian. In 1892, he announced his intent to publish an index with the last number of volume 10 "to enhance the value of the complete file to its fortunate owner" (6 August 1892, p. 1). An even more interesting attempt at bibliographic control was the "Sociological Index," which appeared on the last page of *Liberty*, beginning 14 January 1893. This catalog of articles relating to the social sciences was arranged under broad topics such as belles lettres, biography, finance, and taxation. The bibliography listed author, title, periodical title (if applicable), date, and the number of words or pages. Readers could receive, at costs ranging from fifteen to seventy-five cents, clippings of these articles. They could purchase coupons instead of sending cash, and could even obtain translations of the foreign titles on the list at thirty cents per hundred words. The venture was probably intended, in part, to raise revenue, because the announcement of the column was accompanied by this request: "If every subscriber buys one clipping a week. . . . What say you, readers? Will you do it?" (14 January 1893, p. 2). The index lasted only through 24 June 1893, a period in which *Liberty* became a monthly, and an irregular one at that.

Soon after, on 24 March 1894, *Liberty* appeared with a new face. Benjamin Tucker, who often had to perform the duties of secretary and typesetter as well as editor, proposed a typographical reform—the abolition of right justification. He claimed the reform resulted in a more aesthetic, cheaper product. In addition, because it took less time to set, its universal adoption would mean "a daily addition to the world's productive power of two hundred thousand people" (p. 1). For the rest of its life, the periodical (and Tucker's other publications) appeared with ragged right edges. The typographical unions did not agree with Tucker, even though he used his reform as an ingenious application of his pursuit of the rights of the individual: "all inequality between the spaces in any given line and in the spacing of two lines in juxtaposition is eliminated" (5 May 1894, p. 12).

After the turn of the century, publication of *Liberty* became more and more erratic. No issues were published between November 1899 and December 1900.

There was another lapse from then until December 1902. In the meantime, another publishing house with a similar name had become established in New York. This apparently resulted in some loss of income for Tucker, as he cautioned readers to direct all postal communications to the " genuine *Liberty*" (December 1902, p. 2).

With volume 15, in February 1906, *Liberty* began to appear in a new, smaller format. The number of pages was increased to sixty-four (it had heretofore been from four to twelve), and it was sent via third class mail "to avoid governmental supervision, annoyance, and censorship" (p. 1). A fire destroyed the entire stock of Tucker's uninsured book-store in January 1908. He announced to his readers his intent to move to Europe and resume publication there. The last issue, published in April 1908, could scarcely sustain the defiant tone of issue number 1. It contained a maudlin story about a prostitute with the proverbial heart of gold who takes in a homeless girl on Christmas Eve. *Liberty* never resumed publication, and Benjamin Tucker died in Europe in 1939, having spent his last years filling some twenty volumes with clippings from the periodical press.[4]

Though hardly a mass-market periodical in terms of circulation, *Liberty* exerted a wide influence in anarchist circles both in the United States and abroad. A leader among the nearly 500 radical periodicals issued in the last decades of the nineteenth century,[5] it preserves in print a tradition of individualism and independence.

Notes

1. Charles A. Madison, "Benjamin R. Tucker: Individualist and Anarchist," *New England Quarterly* 16 (1943): 457.

2. Bernard Shaw, *Bernard Shaw: The Diaries, 1885–1897*, ed. Stanley Weintraub (University Park: Pennsylvania State University Press, 1896), p. 69.

3. Madison, p. 448.

4. Madison, p. 467.

5. Wendy McElroy, "Benjamin Tucker, Individualism, and Liberty: Not the Daughter but the Mother of Order," *Literature of Liberty*, vol. 4, no. 3. 1981, p. 34.

Information Sources

BIBLIOGRAPHY

DeLeon, David. *The American As Anarchist: Reflections on Indigenous Radicalism*. Baltimore: Johns Hopkins University Press, 1978.

Gutman, Herbert. "Liberty." In *The American Radical Press, 1880–1960*. Ed. Joseph R. Conlin. Westport, Conn.: Greenwood Press, 1974.

McElroy, Wendy. "Benjamin Tucker, Individualism, and Liberty: Not the Daughter but the Mother of Order." *Literature of Liberty*, 4 (Summer) 1981, pp 7–39.

———. "The Culture of Individualist Anarchism in Late Nineteenth-Century America." *Journal of Libertarian Studies*, vol. 3, no. 5 (Summer) 1981, pp. 291–304.

Madison, Charles A. "Benjamin R. Tucker: Individualist and Anarchist." *New England Quarterly* 16 (1943): 444–67.

Martin, James J. *Men Against the State: The Expositors of Individualist Anarchism in America, 1827–1908*. DeKalb, Ill.: Adrian Allen Associates, 1953.

Mott, Frank Luther. *A History of American Magazines*, vol. 3: 1865–1885. Cambridge, Mass.: Harvard University Press, 1938.

Reichert, William O. *Partisans of Freedom: A Study in American Anarchism*. Bowling Green, Ohio: Bowling Green University Popular Press, 1976.

Schuster, Eunice Minette. "Native American Anarchism: A Study of Left-Wing American Individualism." New York: AMS Press, 1970. A reprint of *Smith College Studies in History*, vol. 17, no. 1–4, 1931–1932.

Shaw, Bernard. *Bernard Shaw: The Diaries, 1885–1897*. Ed. Stanley Weintraub. University Park: Pennsylvania State University Press, 1986.

Tucker, Benjamin Ricketson. *Individual Liberty: Selections from the Writings of Benjamin R. Tucker*. Edited by C.L.S. New York: Vanguard Press, 1926.

———. *Instead of a Book, By a Man Too Busy to Write One: A Fragmentary Exposition of Philosophical Anarchism*. 2nd ed. New York: Tucker, 1897.

INDEX SOURCES

n.a.

LOCATION SOURCES

Available in microform. Reprinted by Greenwood Press.

Publication History

MAGAZINE TITLE AND TITLE CHANGES

Liberty.

VOLUME AND ISSUE DATA

Vols. 1–17, whole numbers 1–403, 1881–1908. Fortnightly, irregular.

PUBLISHER AND PLACE OF PUBLICATION

Benjamin Ricketson Tucker. Boston, 1881–1892; New York City, 1892–1908.

EDITORS

Benjamin Ricketson Tucker, 1881–1908; associate editors, A. P. Kelly, 17 May 1884–12 May 1888; Victor Yarros, 7 June 1890–13 February 1892.

CIRCULATION

n.a.

Cecile Jagodzinski

LIFE

To see life; to see the world; to eyewitness great events; . . . to see and to take pleasure in seeing; to see and be amazed to be seen and be instructed.

Thus to see, and to be shown, is now the will and new expectancy of half mankind.

To see, and to show, is the mission now undertaken by a new kind of publication, The Show-Book of the World. . . . [1]

Henry Robinson Luce's prospectus of 1936 for his new magazine, *Life*, underscored the possibilities for journalism in the great power of photography. New developments in the camera such as the invention of the superfast lens of the Leica by Paul Wolff in Germany helped to introduce "candid" techniques in picture taking, and Luce was determined to exploit the potential of this new photojournalism for his fledgling publication. He had observed the immense popularity of the movies, and the avid readership in the United States for illustrated weeklies and tabloid newspapers, and realized there was a broad audience fascinated with pictures, ripe for a ten-cent photo magazine. In 1935, Luce organized a team of photographers and journalists to plan experimental issues of the new publication. Prominent among these editors was Kurt Korff, a German publisher who had worked closely with Berlin tabloid photographer Erich Salomon to develop daring techniques in the photography of sensational political and news events.

The first issue of *Life* was preceded by numerous dry runs to test the editorial structure, the physical format, and the technical aspects of production. The first major problem in preparing the magazine was the collection of sufficient photographs; to ensure a supply of high-quality pictures, Time, Inc., made contracts with foreign agencies such as Black Star and Magnum, and struck an agreement with its biggest domestic source, Associated Press, to guarantee immediate access on an exclusive basis. Individual photographers were also sought out, among them Alfred Eisenstadt and Margaret Bourke-White, who contributed to the first issue the stunning cover photo of the Fort Peck Dam and the moving lead picture essay on the lives of the Montana shantytown workers who were building the structure. Luce appointed himself the first managing editor of his new magazine, and became preoccupied with the search for a perfect structure for *Life*. Taking as its inspiration the theme "the faces of the U.S," from a Luce publication based on the *March of Time* newsreel episodes, *Life* opened its first issue of 23 November 1936 with the photo of the birth of a baby and the caption "Life Begins." After deliberating on such names as Dime, Parade, Look, Scene, and Show-Book of the World, Luce chose the name *Life* (acquired through the purchase of the old *Life* humor magazine) as the apt title for a publication that would hold up the mirror of American society to its millions of readers.

Life was an unqualified journalistic success from its first issue, which sold out in four hours, but its first year quickly started to suffer from the financial losses that would frequently plague its existence. The circulation limit had been set at 1 million copies, and then was to gradually increase to 1.5 million copies. Production was limited by the slow printing presses then available and by the shortage of coated paper. With ad rates set too low, and a rapidly rising circulation, losses soon soared to the rate of $50,000 a week. These initial losses were recouped within a few years, after advertising rates and circulation goals were rescheduled; in any case, Luce was more concerned with a long-range editorial position for *Life* than with its immediate financial position. He attempted to map a "Life Formula" that would incorporate "Charm" and "Relaxation" as a respite from the news pattern of journalism. Thus the search for the big story would be covered by the Big News-Picture Story of the Week, and by regular departments such as On the American Newsfront and The President's Album. The first year's issues demonstrated the great possibilities in the wide range of this format, with coverage of subjects as serious as the photo essay "Georgia's Chain Gangs" (22 March 1937) to the more controversial froth of "How to Undress in Front of Your Husband" (15 February 1937). After Luce's decision in March 1937 to decentralize Time, Inc., and appoint a publisher for each of the company's magazines, *Life* acquired a new publisher, Roy Larsen. John Shaw Billings had replaced John Martin as managing editor the previous year.

It was during its coverage of World War II that *Life* matured into the prestigious reflector of the cataclysmic events that transformed the United States and the world. The photographers that the magazine added to its staff at this time—in addition to the original team of Bourke-White, Eisenstadt, Thomas McAvoy, and Peter Stackpole—formed the core of photojournalistic talent that commanded great respect from *Life's* competitors, critics, and readers. Issue after issue during the war years stunned the American public with close-ups taken under perilous conditions by *Life's* staff, who competed among themselves to obtain the most realistic portrayals of men in combat. Bourke-White's pictures of her own rescue from a torpedoed ship in the Mediterranean in 1942, Eliot Elisofon's "firsts" in photographing battle action in North Africa in November 1942, and Robert Capa's death-defying camera work of the 1944 D-Day invasion on the Normandy beaches were among the most memorable war photos that overwhelmed *Life's* readers. The heroic work of the magazine's journalists was often thwarted by such wartime obstacles as censorship and delays in the relaying of films and stories back to the United States. During this period, the popularity of the magazine, which staunchly supported the war, grew from 2.8 million copies a week in 1940 to 5.2 million at the end of the 1940s.

In the postwar years Luce again attempted a new formula in editorial direction for *Life*, which was now being read by 36 percent of all American families. The sweeping changes in the U.S. economy and society, fueled by a rapidly escalating affluence and a cold war with the Soviet Union, spurred the publisher into proposing "a greater philosophical unity" in a fourteen-page memo to *Life's* staff. Luce was especially anxious that the magazine, through its features and stories, promote "good taste in the use of the abundance of good things that our economy provides."[2] In this regard, the new department "Modern Living" would be a most appropriate vehicle to link editorial and advertising concerns in the publication.

During the short period of Joe Thorndike's editorship from 1946 to 1949, *Life* began to explore, more dramatically, cultural phenomena and intellectual trends. Series on contemporary American life and on the history of Western culture were begun in 1947; a monumental color photo essay on Michelangelo's Sistine frescoes appeared in the Christmas issue of 1949. The magazine also widened the breadth and sophistication of its news and investigative coverage. Two probing photographic essays were featured in 1945, Gordon Parks's "Harlem Gang Leader" and Eugene Smith's "Country Doctor." From 1946 to 1948 Margaret Bourke-White chronicled for *Life* the great global drama of the twin births of the nations of India and Pakistan. In late 1949, Luce's concern with the overall tone of the magazine, and especially with questionable editorial decisions on coverage of the Truman-Dewey presidential election, forced a reorganization of *Life*'s management.

Edward K. Thompson, who replaced Thorndike as managing editor in 1949, guided *Life* through its most influential period as America's foremost national magazine. Thompson's forte in journalism was the pursuit of the big story, and under his direction, *Life* focused more intently on investigative reporting and on exposés such as the McCarthy communist witchhunts in 1950, the Kefauver Committee hearings on organized crime in 1951, the trial and conviction of the Rosenbergs from 1951 to 1953, school desegregation and the ensuing protest marches in Alabama from 1954 to 1956, and the Senate hearings on labor racketeering in 1957. New departments were introduced for fashion, edited by Sally Kirkland, and for film and entertainment, edited by Mary Leatherbee and Tom Prideaux.

Thompson sought a high standard of writing for the magazine, to match the star quality of its photojournalism. In addition to the work of Evelyn Waugh, Graham Greene, Robert Penn Warren, and Carl Sandburg, *Life* featured Ernest Hemingway's *The Old Man and the Sea* in 1952, James Michener's *The Bridges at Toko-Ri* in 1953, and the memoirs of Winston Churchill, Harry S. Truman, and the Duke of Windsor over a ten-year period. The process of editing *Life* became more than ever a production of acts, with Thompson personally overseeing the layout of as many as six issues at once, pushing himself and his staff through all-night sessions to beat publishing deadlines. With news exclusives to its credit like the unique coverage of the Hungarian uprisings in 1956 and the purchase of the Project Mercury astronauts' stories in 1959, the decade of the fifties brought a satisfying balance of editorial and financial success to the magazine; *Life* reached a top net income of $17.4 million in 1956.

The 1960s brought yet another change in both editorial direction and in leadership for *Life*. Luce presented his staff with an ambitious twenty-seven–page guide, "*Life:* A New Prospectus for the Sixties," in which he proposed that the magazine be one of national purpose, in order to "Win the Cold War" and to "Create a Better America."[3] To spearhead this new nationalistic thrust, Luce appointed a new publisher in 1960, C. D. Jackson, who had worked with Dwight Eisenhower and who had helped set up Radio-Free Europe after World War II. Jackson quickly made personnel cuts in the editorial staff, froze advertising rates, and held circulation at 6.7 million to offset *Life*'s loss in profits. Striking changes in the magazine's format were made in 1961, especially in the cover, and in the layout of advertising and stories. Editorial innovations were made, such as the introduction of a column by *Life*'s first woman staff writer, Shana Alexander, and of a new department, Better Living.

In 1961 Thompson was replaced by George Hunt in the newly designated post of editor. *Life*'s issues in this decade focused on the John F. Kennedy presidency, from the election battle with Richard Nixon in 1960, through the crises with the Cuban government and the Soviet Union in 1961 and 1962, to the shattering end with the president's assassination and the investigation of the tragedy in 1963 and 1964. Hunt, an admirer of Lincoln Steffens, organized an investigative reporting team to cover the financial misdealings of both Bobby Baker, a protégé of Lyndon B. Johnson, and Abe Fortas, a Supreme Court Justice. In 1963 the magazine assigned the investigation of organized crime to Pulitzer Prize–winning reporter William Lambert. *Life* gained well-deserved respect and admiration from its readers and competition for its courageous exposés of governmental and societal corruption; its reputation as a major American news source grew world-wide with two flourishing foreign editions, *Life International* and *Life en Español*.

By the time Luce died in 1967, *Life*'s financial problems had become all too apparent. Hedley Donovan, whom Luce had appointed editorial director of *Time** in 1964, analyzed *Life*'s situation and recommended a more restricted circulation and a more specialized thrust. Even as the magazine declined economically in the late 1960s and early 1970s, it soared editorially; a more sophisticated, analytical journalistic approach and a cleaner format were developed to cover the nation's political, social, and cultural upheavals as the United States faced such divisive issues as the race riots of 1965, the escalation of the war in Vietnam in 1968, and campus strikes beginning in 1968. Talented photographers like Larry Burrows, Gjon Mili, and Lennaert Nilsson captured on film the social disruption caused by the generation gap on political issues, the innovation of mind-expanding art, and the exciting drama of medical advances.

In 1969, Ralph Graves replaced Hunt as managing editor of *Life*; it was one of the lowest fiscal points in the magazine's history. The previous year, *Life* had made the mistake of purchasing the subscription list of the defunct *Saturday Evening Post.** The resulting expansion in subscribers had forced *Life* to peg ad rates even higher to retain a high enough circulation to stay ahead of the competition. After Graves held a "summit" of the top editors and management, drastic cuts were made in 1969 and 1970 in departments such as Fashion, Sports, and Miscellany, and in personnel; Sally Kirkland, the fashion editor, and Bernie Quint, the art director, were among the highly talented and experienced staff members who were dismissed. Nonetheless, the magazine continued to triumph journalistically in these final years; the 27 June 1969 issue was devoted to a gallery of "One Week's Dead" in Vietnam, and at the end of 1970, *Life* began to publish excerpts from its exclusive transcription of Nikita Krushchev's memoirs, which had been smuggled to the magazine from the Soviet Union. In November 1971, circulation was cut back to 5.5 million to forestall financial collapse, and the year bottomed out on the farcical scam of Clifford Irving's nearly successful sale to *Life* of a nonexistent autobiography of the recluse millionaire Howard Hughes. The Irving hoax, in the wake of yet another staff reduction and following the deaths of Bourke-White, Burrows, and Leatherbee, among others, made 1972, *Life*'s last year, a demoralizing struggle for survival. The decision to end *Life* came in the fall of 1972; even if circulation were drastically cut, huge losses would still be incurred by rising postal rates and the overwhelming competition from television and special-interest publications. Corporate management kept the strictest secrecy about the shutdown because of legal restrictions on disclosure of information, but finally, on 8 December, *Life*'s crew was told that the 29 December 1972 issue would be the magazine's last.

From 1973 to 1977, *Life* reappeared in two special issues a year, ten in all. In 1978, it was reborn as a monthly publication, with Charles Whittingham as publisher and Philip Kunhardt as managing editor. The new version of *Life* is a topical feature magazine, with the photographic essay as its corner structure. Its staff is much smaller, and the source of its pictures is a pool of high-quality free-lancers like Eisenstadt, Harry Benson, Eliot Porter, George Silk, and Lennaert Nilsson. The focus of its photojournalism is not the old chase after news, but the "picture magic" that Luce had stressed when the magazine was born. Under the editorship of Kunhardt, Richard Stolley, and Judith Daniels, and with a circulation stabilized at close to two million, *Life* commands respect once more as an influential record of modern civilization, and continues to fulfill its founder's ambitions of historical importance for his "ten-cent Picture Magazine."

Notes

1. Loudon Wainwright, *The Great American Magazine* (New York: Knopf, 1986), p. 33.

2. Ibid., p. 165.

3. Curtis Prendergast and Geoffrey Colvin, *The World of Time, Inc.: The Intimate History of a Changing Enterprise, 1960–1980* (New York: Atheneum, 1986), p. 42.

Information Sources

BIBLIOGRAPHY

Bourke-White, Margaret. *Portraits of Myself.* New York: Simon and Schuster, 1963.

Cort, David. *The Sin of Henry R. Luce.* Secaucus, N.J.: Lyle Stuart, 1974.

Elson, Robert T. *Time, Inc.: The Intimate History of a Publishing Enterprise, 1923–1941.* New York: Atheneum, 1968.

———. *Time, Inc.: The Intimate History of a Publishing Enterprise, 1941–1960.* New York: Atheneum, 1973.

Life Magazine Editors. *Life: The First Fifty Years.* Boston: Little, Brown and Co., 1986.

Prendergast, Curtis, and Geoffrey Colvin. *The World of Time, Inc.: The Intimate History of a Changing Enterprise, 1960–1980.* New York: Atheneum, 1986.

Wainwright, Loudon. *The Great American Magazine.* New York: Knopf, 1986.

INDEX SOURCES
> Years 1936–1972 are indexed in *Infobank* and *Readers' Guide to Periodical Literature*. Years 1978–present are indexed in *Magazine Index, Infobank,* and *Readers' Guide*.

LOCATION SOURCES
> Many libraries.

Publication History

MAGAZINE TITLE AND TITLE CHANGES
> *Life,* 23 November 1936–29 December 1972; *Life,* October 1978–present.

VOLUME AND ISSUE DATA
> Vol. 1–73, 23 November 1936–29 December 1972, weekly. Ten special issues, two each year, 1973–1977. Vol. 1, no. 1, October 1978–present.

PUBLISHERS
> Roy E. Larsen, 1936–1945; Andrew Heiskell, 1946–1960; Charles D. Jackson, 1960–1964; Jerome S. Hardy, 1964–1970; Garry Valk, 1970–1977; Charles A. Whittingham, 1978–1987; Elizabeth P. Valk, 1987–present.

EDITORS
> John Shaw Billings, 1936–1944; Daniel Longwell, 1944–1946; Joseph J. Thorndike, 1946–1949; Edward K. Thompson, 1949–1961; George P. Hunt, 1961–1969; Ralph Graves, 1969–1972; Philip B. Kunhardt, Jr., 1973–1982; Richard B. Stolley, 1982–1985; Judith Daniels, 1985–present.

CIRCULATION
> 7.5 million (1970); 1.6 million (1987).

Diana A. Chlebek

LIPPINCOTT'S MAGAZINE

One of the so-called flagship magazines launched by the major publishing houses in the years following the Civil War, *Lippincott's* was an attractive, modestly successful magazine. Although it never achieved the stature of *Harper's*,* the major publishing-house magazine, *Lippincott's* is noteworthy for several reasons. Among these are the function it served within the history of the J. B. Lippincott Company, the quality of its writing, both fiction and nonfiction, and the tasteful appearance of the magazine.

In the mid–nineteenth century, publishing houses faced much the same dilemma they do today: some books prove profitable, others do not. At the time, publishing houses believed that a source of profit for their companies might well be the publication of magazines. Harper and Brothers was already issuing two successful magazines, and other publishers, including the Philadelphia firm J. B. Lippincott, decided to follow their lead. According to John Tebbel, the magazines served more than one purpose: "they could be used to advertise the books of the house that owned them, and serialization of a novel usually helped its hardcover sales."[1] Furthermore, the literary magazines provided authors with the possibility at least of extra income; if a novel or story was printed first in the magazines, and later in a book, there were two distinct payments for the work. Much later, near the end of the century, editor Henry Stoddart would explain his philosophy regarding the importance of the magazines: "Real talent, if it can get its products into available shape, will be heard from sooner or later, first and chiefly (as a rule) through the periodicals."[2]

Lippincott's was conceived in 1867, and first issued in January 1868. Frank Luther Mott errs in declaring John Foster Kirk the first editor. Lloyd Smith, a Philadelphia librarian, was in fact the first, and his more famous successor was Kirk, who maintained editorial responsibility from 1870 until 1884. The publisher's intent was to serialize the works of major American authors, but in July 1869 the first installment of the British novel *The Vicar of Bullhampton*, by Anthony Trollope, appeared. Subsequently, *Lippincott's* printed works of both American and British writers. The premier issue featured the first installment of Rebecca Harding Davis's *Dallas Galbraith: An American Novel*, some poetry, columns concerning travel and science, the first of a long-standing department entitled "Our Monthly Gossip," and a section of literary reviews. According to Mott, "it was one of the best-printed of American magazines; its contents, though conservative, were usually of an admirable quality."[3]

Lippincott's Magazine was to have as its forte the publication of fiction, although the house was not particularly well known for its literary publishing efforts. Rather, Lippincott was generally recognized as the publisher of the already established reference work *Lippincott's Pronouncing Gazeteer of the World*, medical reference books, including the *Dispensatory of the United States of America*, and textbooks such as Webster's *Blue Back Speller*. But each issue of *Lippincott's Magazine* contained serialized novels, and later, novelettes, printed in full in one issue; they were generally given the prized first position in the magazine. Perhaps the most well-known of the novelettes was Oscar Wilde's *The Picture of Dorian Gray*, which occupied the first 100 pages of the July 1890 issue. An earlier novel published in its entirety was Amelie Rivers's *The Quick or the Dead?*, which provoked intense controversy following its publication in April 1888.[4] In addition to Davis, Trollope, Wilde, and Rivers, fiction writers for the magazine included Ouida, Jack London, Bret Harte, and Arthur Conan Doyle. Emma Lazarus, Paul Laurence Dunbar, and Sidney Lanier contributed poetry over the years. Long the advocate of the short story form as literature, *Lippincott's* highlighted its commitment by starting a new forum for short story writers in 1911. Entitled "Short Story Masterpieces," stories were introduced and translated, when necessary, by editor J. B. Esenwein.

In addition to fiction and poetry, there were other distinguishing characteristics in the magazine. Travel pieces were always at home on the pages of *Lippincott's*. *Lippincott's* best-known tourist, Henry James, contributed six travel pieces from 1877 to 1879, including "Abbeys and Castles" (October 1877, pp. 434–42). Additionally, *Lippincott's* interested itself in the social and political; a typical article was "The National TransAlleghany Water-way," by Thompson B. Maury

(March 1873, pp. 265–76). Science, also, was of interest, as seen in "Athletics for School Children," by Dr. Luther Halsey Gurlick (August 1911, pp. 201–10). Its literary criticism was considered by Mott to be of "unusually high grade, ranking with similar work in the *Atlantic* and the *Nation*."[5] Initially, although the magazine did not carry advertisements for rival publishing houses, its unsigned literary reviews were diverse, and not limited to publications of the company. In 1891, however, the column was renamed "New Publications" and with the new title came the practice of reviewing Lippincott titles exclusively. By the end of the decade, firmly entrenched in the tradition, the section for literary reviews had become merely announcements for the company. In November 1899, the department, now called "Books of the Month," included the disparate titles *"Miss Carmichael's Conscience,"* by the Baroness von Hutten, and *System of Diseases of the Eyes*, edited by Drs. William F. Norris and Charles A. Oliver. The book review column disappeared completely from the pages of the magazine by 1903.

Lippincott's maintained nearly the same format throughout its existence. In 1885 the woodcuts that had served as the only illustration since 1869 were discontinued. The following year, it adopted the single-column format in lieu of the double column that had been used since its inception. The magazine did, however, revert to double-column pages briefly just before it ceased publication. It was in 1887 that *Lippincott's* began its practice of publishing an entire novel, called a novelette, in each issue in addition to the regular features, short stories, and poetry. These slight changes were insufficient to improve circulation, and the practice of publishing complete novels in each issue made consistently high quality difficult to maintain.

Never a star among the literary magazines, *Lippincott's* was unable to gain the wide readership enjoyed by magazines centered in the major publishing cities of New York and Boston. This is partly attributable, as has been noted, to the unfortunate fact that Philadelphia was unable to boast a large number of prominent writers of the day.[6] *Lippincott's* was, in fact, the only high-quality general magazine published in Philadelphia in the 1880s.[7] Furthermore, the publishing-house magazines (*Scribner's*,* *Putnam's*,* *Lippincott's*, the *Atlantic**) were all hard-pressed to compete with *Harper's* for a comparatively small audience. There was also the added misfortune of having to compete with the major mass-market periodicals that were coming into being at the turn of the century. It becomes painfully clear that of the publishing-house magazines, *Lippincott's* in particular was not fated to achieve prominence and success.

Lippincott's, while an attractive and fairly consistent magazine, never achieved the prosperity for which its founders hoped. Mott points out that circulation figures were never made public, and advertising in the magazine was minimal compared with that in other publications of the day.[8] After struggling for forty-five years, Lippincott sold the magazine to McBride, Nast and Company, who moved it to New York in 1914 and changed the title to *McBride's*. The periodical was not strong enough to survive, even in New York, and after its brief eight-month life as *McBride's Magazine*, it was merged with *Scribner's*.

Lippincott's was not an absolute failure, but there are several factors that contributed to its eventual demise. It was unable to match the literary quality maintained in *Harper's* and *Putnam's*, and like the other literary magazines, it could not equal the readership of the turn-of-the-century mass-market periodicals. *Lippincott's* hallmark, the publication of an entire short novel in a single issue, also eventually proved unmanageable. Finally, its base in Philadelphia disallowed consistent contribution by many major American authors. But *Lippincott's* did publish some near-classic short novels, and was able to attract quality contributions. Although the magazine did not substantially add to the prestige or the fortune of its parent and publisher, it did provide the Lippincott Company a reputation outside of that for staid reference and medical books, and J. B. Lippincott continues to publish fiction today. A relatively minor literary periodical, *Lippincott's Magazine* was, nevertheless, representative of the publishing-house, broad-appeal magazine developed in the latter part of the nineteenth century.

Notes

1. John Tebbel, *A History of Book Publishing in the United States,* vol. 2: *The Expansion of an Industry 1865–1919* (New York: Bowker, 1975), p. 14. Much of Tebbel's information is also available in a one-volume edition, *Between Covers: The Rise and Transformation of Book Publishing in America* (New York: Oxford University Press, 1987).

2. Henry Stoddart, quoted in Tebbel, p. 141.

3. Frank Luther Mott, *A History of American Magazines*, vol. 3: 1865–1885. (Cambridge: Harvard University Press, 1938), p. 396.

4. Margaret Becket, "J. B. Lippincott Company," in *Dictionary of Literary Biography*, vol. 49 (Detroit: Gale, 1986), p. 263.

5. Mott, 3:398.

6. Ibid., 4:87.

7. Ibid.

8. Ibid., 3:398–99.

Information Sources

BIBLIOGRAPHY

The Author and His Audience. Philadelphia: J. B. Lippincott, 1969.

Mott, Frank Luther. *A History of American Magazines*. 5 vol. 3: 1865–1885. Cambridge: Harvard University Press, 1938.

Tebbel, John. *A History of Book Publishing in the United States,* vol. 2: *The Expansion of an Industry 1865–1919*. New York: Bowker, 1975.

INDEX SOURCES

    Poole's (1868–1906); *Poole's Abridged; Readers' Guide to Periodical Literature* (1900–1915); *Annual Library Index; Engineering Index; Review of Reviews Index*.

LOCATION SOURCES

    Widely available. American Periodical Series. Available in microform.

Publication History

MAGAZINE TITLE AND TITLE CHANGES

Lippincott's Magazine of Literature, Science and Education, 1868–1871; *Lippincott's Magazine of Popular Literature and Science,* 1871–1885; *Lippincott's Magazine: A Popular Journal of General Literature, Science and Politics,* 1886–1903; *Lippincott's Monthly Magazine: A Popular Journal of General Literature,* 1903–1914; *Lippincott's Magazine,* 1915; *McBride's Magazine,* 1915.

VOLUME AND ISSUE DATA

Semiannual volumes. Vol. 1–96, January 1868–August 1915. Vol. 27–36 also called New Series, Vols. 1–10. Monthly.

PUBLISHERS AND PLACES OF PUBLICATION

J. B. Lippincott and Company, Philadelphia, 1868–1914; McBride, Nast and Company, New York, 1914–1915.

EDITORS

Lloyd Smith, 1868–1870; John Foster Kirk, 1870–1884; J. Bird, 1885; William Shepherd Walsh, 1885–1889; Henry Stoddart, 1889–1896; Frederic M. Bird, 1896–1898; Harrison S. Morris, 1899–1905; J. Berg Esenwein, 1905–1914; Louise Bull, 1914; Edward Frank Allen, 1914–1915.

CIRCULATION

n.a.

Jean M. Parker

LITERARY DIGEST

When the *Literary Digest* first appeared in March of 1890, it placed itself in competition with the weekly *Current Opinion* (published in Washington) and W. T. Stead's monthly *Review of Reviews** (published in London). The early *Literary Digest* featured, not excerpts from, but condensed rewritings of articles from American, Canadian, English, French, German, and Italian magazines. These rewritings, called "reviews," were arranged by general topic: the first section of the magazine included reviews in sociological, industrial, political, scientific, literary and artistic, and miscellaneous areas. A second section, called "The Press," included snippings from various newspapers about political, social, foreign, and religious topics. The back section of the magazine included several short book reviews, a brief index of periodical literature, a list of Books of the Week, and a listing of current events. The weekly's subtitle, *A Repository of Contemporaneous Thought and Research as Presented in the Periodical Literature of the World,* portrays well the portentous mission and tone the twenty-eight–page digest had set for itself.

The publisher and first editor of the *Digest,* as the magazine came to be known, was Isaac Kauffman Funk. A Lutheran clergyman whose efforts ranged from lexicography to prohibition, Funk seems to have regarded the *Digest's* condensations as useful for theologians and professional men who needed quick exposure to contemporary thought. The early *Digest* was a colorless publication, without illustrations, that gained a circulation of only a few thousand copies during its first three years.[1] The following sample from the subject index for the first volume indicates how strongly Funk's sensibilities were relayed through the early *Digest*: "creeds," "the church and doctrine," "dreams and the moral life," "New Testament criticism," "paganism." The 14 January 1893 number marks the beginning of a change in editorial strategy initiated by Funk and skillfully completed by Edward Jewitt Wheeler after 1895. Where in the early *Digest* Funk had simply listed the magazine source above each condensation, he now handled a topic (the first was "The Panama Canal Scandal") by providing an introduction and transitional material to link the various condensed newspaper and magazine reports. Of equal importance was the gradual shift from periodical to newspaper literature, the addition of illustrations, and the change in typographical format— each of which helped shift the *Digest*'s emphasis from "contemporaneous thought and research" to more mundane news.[2] The subject index from the 1895 volume reflects this attempt to address a more general audience than the first numbers: "Electrocution, how it feels," "genius, is it a disease?" "the missing link, has it been found?" "ideas, how they develop in children." This formula for composing articles about a few main events from the past week from parts of newspaper reports, documents, and commentary by weaving them together with lively introductions and transitional material was to lead the *Literary Digest* from a circulation of 3,000 to 1,500,000 and make the *Digest* "one of the greatest publishing successes in history."[3]

By 1900, Wheeler had completely redirected the *Digest* toward the news-conscious general public. The leaps in circulation from this time occur with the abruptness of a newsreel report: 63,000 in 1900; 200,000 in 1909; 400,000 in 1916; 900,000 in 1919; and 1,500,000 in 1927.[4] (Among weeklies, only the *Saturday Evening Post** had a higher circulation.) The *Digest* did not leave its format unaltered during these growth years. A department of notes and humorous columns about celebrities, fragments of newspaper editorials called "Topics in Brief," a humor section called "More or Less Pungent" (later called "Spice of Life"), a column of typographical errors from newspapers and magazines called "Slips That Pass in the Night," and "The Lexicographer's Easy Chair" written by the managing editor of Funk and Wagnalls' *Standard Dictionary* were all added between 1895 and 1905. When Wheeler left in 1915 to edit *Current Literature*, Robert J. Cuddihy became the *Digest*'s publisher and embarked on an energetic campaign of expansion. In 1906, Cuddihy bought *Public Opinion* and merged it with *Literary Digest*. The expense of Cuddihy's advertising campaign was said to have terrified his partners,[5] but the once drab weekly was now filled with advertisements. Cartoons and photographs from the paper or magazine that had originally printed them also became characteristic of the *Digest*'s format. Carefully balanced articles that quoted supporting, opposing, and independent opinions for each topic handled earned the magazine a reputation for unshakable impartiality.

While the cartoons, illustrations, features, and format helped the *Digest* gain a large readership, its coverage of World War I "probably did more to establish it in a high place among American periodicals than anything else."[6] Cuddihy used the *Digest* to collect some $10 million for relief to Belgium and the near East during World War I.[7] Professional cartographers provided colored maps of the battlegrounds and campaigns; annual summaries provided detailed histories of the war; the press corps of American and European allies, of the Central Powers, and of the neutral countries supplied coverage from their perspective; George Kennan wrote about Russian affairs; Hilaire Belloc and Frederick Palmer explained the battle of the Marne; and Dr. John H. Finley visited Palestine and Mesopotamia for the Red Cross. The digest format had the effect of putting the press corps and photography of the entire world in the service of the *Digest*. Francis Whiting Halsey was later able to compile a ten-volume book set from *Digest* articles of the time.[8]

In 1916 the *Digest* had polled members of state legislatures on their choice for the presidential nomination. This poll served as a quiet prelude to what was to be one of the magazine's most characteristic activities. In 1924, the *Digest*'s first presidential straw poll accurately predicted Calvin Coolidge's victory; in 1928, it predicted Herbert Hoover's victory; and in 1932, it predicted Franklin D. Roosevelt's victory. In each case, the winner was accurately identified and the electoral college vote was almost exact—some papers suggested calling off the elections and using the *Digest* instead.[9] Issues like veterans' bonuses, tax reduction, and Prohibition (three times) occasioned separate polls. A reporter's curiosity may have been a factor in these large straw polls, but the benefits from the polls certainly encouraged Cuddihy to continue them. The polls provided the *Digest* with interesting material to print, the predictions were themselves widely covered news that gained the *Digest* a great deal of publicity, and the *Digest* enclosed a subscription form with each of the straw ballots. Since a poll would sample opinion from as many as twenty million Americans, the *Digest*'s circulation leaps were associated with the success of its polls.[10] The *Digest* crowed often and loudly about its success with polls—this pride preceded its prediction that Alf(red) Landon would defeat Roosevelt in 1936.

The *Digest*'s use of polls for self-aggrandizement was as characteristic of the weekly as the polls themselves. The *Digest* often studied its readers and found itself important to them in a number of areas. The combination of a sturdily moral tone, impartial editorial policy, and emphasis on the value of contemporary news and thought suggested that the *Digest* might find a place in education—it was, in fact, used in some schools and even colleges. Teachers who used the *Digest* would get discounted subscriptions for their entire class: glowing testimonials from Eva Mildred Schermerham and A. Francis Trams gave the magazine credit for bringing life to their English, history, economics, or civics courses. The *Digest* printed a half dozen articles about itself as a textbook; "it can be said," proclaimed one, "that over 25,000 students, scattered over every state in the union, are now perusing the magazine extensively each week" (12

February 1916, p. 384). Another title exclaimed: "The 'Literary Digest,' We Are Informed, Makes History Study Painless" (19 April 1919, p. 61). A separate survey designed to profile the entire readership was conducted by the magazine in 1922—it sent 207,000 letters and questionnaires to subscribers. The results led the *Digest* to claim that 73 percent of its circulation was among owners, officials, executives, and professional men, "which form one of the largest groups of intelligent and affluent persons in the United States whose opinions and buying habits are influenced by one publication" (18 November 1922, p. 44).

The covers of the *Digest* during these prosperous times were often reproductions of paintings; advertisements (especially for automobiles and auto accessories) vied with photographs and political cartoons on its pages; the activity of the magazine in polling and education was itself newsworthy. By the 1930s, however, a combination of the snappy news articles in *Time** and *Newsweek,** the depression, and the Landon prediction were halting the growth of the *Digest*'s circulation and undermining the loyalty of subscribers. Despite the efforts of Arthur S. Draper, who had become the editor in 1933 and had reduced the amount of editorial comment and increased the number of articles on current topics by well-known authors, the circulation fell from 1,000,000 in 1934 to 600,000 in 1936.[11] In 1937, Funk and Wagnalls sold the *Digest* to Albert Shaw, Jr., the publisher of *Review of Reviews,** for $200,000.[12] (Less than a decade before, $5 million had been offered for 40 percent of the *Digest* stock.[13]) The first product of this wedding of the two old digests appeared on 17 July 1937; Shaw's goal was to publish an "interpretive digest of everything in print that is important"[14] in a format that had a section about the story of the week, a section of picture layouts, and a digest of magazine articles and books.

A short time later a syndicate led by George F. Havell, who had earned the nickname "the magazine doctor" for his work with failing periodicals, took over the publication from Shaw. Havell thought the *Digest*'s failure was the result of too much editorial bias; he resolved to return to the editorial neutrality of the late 1920s, to conduct no more presidential polls, and to include more special articles and big-name features.[15] As the financial problems of the *Digest* grew more desperate, Havell resorted to renting advertisers the *Digest*'s mailing list of four million present and former subscribers (at $4–$15 per 1,000 names[16]). His last measure was a test letter to 10,000 subscribers—the letter asked for a $1 gift to be credited toward their subscription as an increase in rate. Reminding its readers of the *Digest*'s former stature, the letter noted: The *Literary Digest* is not just another magazine; it is an American institution of major importance. It cannot be allowed to die.[17] Some subscribers responded with gifts of $5 or $10. But because other publishers used agents who sold the *Digest* in combination with their own magazines, they questioned this appeal for funds to their subscribers. In response to these appeals, the Audit Bureau of Circulations ruled that the *Digest* had to return contributions gained by Havell's letter—the *Digest* then petitioned for permission to reorganize under Section 77B of the Bankruptcy Act. Publication was suspended after the 19 February 1938 issue; in May, *Time* announced that it had taken over the *Digest* and would fulfill the 250,000 remaining subscriptions.[18]

The *Digest*'s failure is often tied to its mistaken Landon prediction, but the magazine was really a victim of what had made it successful. A generation of Americans had valued the orderly condensations, the serious tone, and the breadth of editorial opinion that the *Digest* had presented. A new generation viewed editorial opinion and condensation with apathy. *Time* and *Newsweek* offered news retold with the hint of an insider's knowledge—this marriage of news and gossip won the day. In a kind of obituary for the *Digest, Time* called it a "national institution, a schoolroom text, a gold mine for its publishers."[19] The *Digest* might also be viewed as a vestige of various Victorian efforts: a desire for synthesis, a sober moral presentation, an elevation of contemporary affairs to a level of supreme importance in public life. Unlike many other distinguished periodicals, whose demises were untimely, the *Digest* expired from old age.

Notes

1. Frank Luther Mott, *A History of American Magazines,* vol. 4: *1885–1905* (Cambridge: Harvard University Press, 1957), p. 571.

2. " 'Digest' Suspended," *Time,* 7 March 1938, p. 55.

3. Ibid.

4. *Ayer Directory of Publications* (Philadelphia: Ayer, 1880–1982). Data for a given year is usually found in the next year's directory.

5. "Funk and Wagnalls Sell to the 'Review of Reviews,' " *Newsweek,* 26 June 1927, p. 24.

6. Mott, p. 574.

7. " 'Digest' Digested," *Time,* 23 May 1938, p. 46.

8. Francis Whiting Halsey, *Literary Digest History of the World War,* 10 vols. (New York: Funk and Wagnalls, 1919–1920).

9. A variety of these comments are gathered in the *Literary Digest,* 17 November 1929, p. 9.

10. Mott, p. 576.

11. " 'Digest' Suspended," p. 55.

12. Ibid.

13. Mott, p. 578.

14. "Digested 'Digest' " *Time,* 28 June 1937, p. 40.

15. " 'Digest' Without Polls," *Time,* 25 October 1937, p. 71.

16. "77B," *Time,* 28 March 1938, p. 44.

17. Ibid.

18. " 'Digest' Digested," p. 46.

19. " 'Digest' Suspended," p. 55.

Information Sources

BIBLIOGRAPHY

Bostwick, Arthur E. *A Life with Men and Books.* New York: H. W. Wilson, 1939, pp. 147–64.

Drewry, John E. *Some Magazines and Magazine Makers*. Boston: Stratford, 1924.

Halsey, Francis Whiting. *Literary Digest History of the War*. 10 vols. New York: Funk and Wagnalls, 1919–1920.

Mott, Frank Luther. *A History of American Magazines,* vol. 4: *1885–1905*. Cambridge: Harvard University Press, 1957, p. 569–79.

Robinson, Claude E. *Straw Votes: A Study of Political Prediction*. New York: Columbia University Press, 1932.

INDEX SOURCES
Readers' Guide (1912–1922); *Dramatic Index; Engineering Index*.

LOCATION SOURCES
Widely available and available in microform.

Publication History

MAGAZINE TITLE AND TITLE CHANGES
The Literary Digest: A Repository of Contemporaneous Thought and Research as Presented in the Periodical Literature of the World, 1890–1899; *The Literary Digest: A Weekly Compendium of the Contemporaneous Thought of the World,* 1900–1901; *The Literary Digest,* 1902–10 July 1937, and 13 November 1937–1938; *The Digest: Review of Reviews, Incorporating the Literary Digest,* 17 July–6 November 1937.

VOLUME AND ISSUE DATA
Vols. 1–125, March 1890–19 February 1938. Weekly. Vol. 1, March-October 1890; vols. 2–14, November 1890–April 1897, semiannual volumes; vol. 15, May-December 1897; vols. 16–55, 1898–1917, regular semiannual volumes; vols. 56–113, 1918–June 1932, quarterly volumes; vols. 114–123, July 1932–June 1937, semiannual volumes; vol. 124, nos. 1–2, 3 July and 10 July 1937; new series, vol. 1, nos. 1–24, 17 July–25 December 1937; old series, vol. 125, nos. 1–8, 1 January–19 February 1938.

PUBLISHER AND PLACE OF PUBLICATION
Funk and Wagnalls, 1890–1892; Funk and Wagnalls Company (Robert J. Cuddihy, publisher, 1915–1937), 1892–1937; Review of Reviews Corporation (Albert Shaw, Jr., publisher), 1937; The Literary Digest, Inc. (George F. Havell, publisher), 1937–1938. All in New York.

EDITORS
Isaac Kauffman Funk, 1890–1895; Edward Jewitt Wheeler, 1895–1905; William Seaver Woods, 1905–1933; Arthur S. Draper, 1933–1935; Morton Savell, 1935; Wilfred John Funk, 1936–1937; Albert Shaw, Jr., 1937; David Perkins Page, 1937–1938.

CIRCULATION
1,500,000 (1927).

Glenn Anderson

LITTELL'S LIVING AGE

When Eliakim Littell founded *Littell's Living Age* in 1844, he had already established himself as a veteran of magazine publishing in America. Despite a limited formal education, he had developed a sound literary judgment through broad reading of the works of standard authors and an early apprenticeship in bookselling. With his establishment of the eclectic weekly *Philadelphia Register and National Recorder* in 1819, he originated the plan of reprinting articles, excerpts, and digests from American newspapers and periodicals and, later, from the "cream of foreign literature."[1]

Littell began the *Living Age* as a weekly in Boston with the encouragement of famous men of letters and wide cultural tastes like John Quincy Adams and George Ticknor. Like the eclectic magazines Littell had established previously, *Littell's Living Age* had the goal of introducing the great minds of the century to America. In addition, as he pointed out in the journal's prospectus, Americans would be informed of new conditions in the world abroad, "because nations seem to be hastening through a rapid process of change to some new state of things, which the mere political prophet cannot compute or foresee."[2] In fact, *Littell's* editorial strength lay in the serious material excerpted from quality British periodicals like *Blackwood's*, the *Edinburgh Review*, the *Quarterly, Fraser's*, and, later, the *Cornhill*. A variety of informational articles was the basis of the magazine's appeal, like those that appeared in its first issue in 1844: "The Cornwall Mines," "Schism in the Papacy," "Late Revolutions in Haiti," and "The Insanity of Don Quixote." A special effort was made to include all the comment of British journals on American affairs. Poetry and stories were also featured, but the fiction that appeared in *Littell's* was mostly second-rate, since the more celebrated English novelists sold their advance sheets to other publications. Selections were also reprinted from lighter serials such as Charles Dicken's *Household Words* and *All the Year Round*, Bentley's *Temple Bar* and Anthony Trollope's *St. Paul's*, along with a liberal dose of humor from *Punch*. Newspaper sources were often used, including the "thunder of the *Times*."[3]

The magazine appeared as a weekly of some sixty-four pages of double columns, with sections of "Correspondence," numbered articles, "Poetry," "Tales," and "Scraps," or short articles and news items. With little overhead expense aside from the cost of subscriptions to periodical sources, Littell's was able to maintain a low circulation of around 5,000. After Eliakim Littell died in 1870, his son, Robert, took over as publisher, and his daughter, Susan Gardner Littell, edited the magazine. The editorial policy of the journal remained unchanged, and circulation was kept around 10,000 through 1880. In 1874 the publication absorbed another periodical, *Every Saturday: A Journal of Choice Reading*.

When Robert Littell died in 1896, the family sold *Littell's* and the title was shortened to *Living Age*. Frank Foxcroft, a poet and writer who became editor and publisher, maintained the editorial policy of the Littell founders, but broadened the scope and variety of sources to include more European periodicals. The 1910 edition of the magazine, for example, featured material by Leo Tolstoy in translation and by the literary critic Edmund Gosse. In 1897, a department of notes on books and authors was added, and in 1898, *Living Age* was consolidated with a New York rival journal, *Eclectic Magazine*. From 1899 to 1900, the

Eclectic appeared in a monthly edition along with the weekly issue of *Living Age*.

In 1919, after the Atlantic Monthly Company purchased *Living Age*, Atlantic's president, Ellery Sedgwick, edited the magazine for one year, and then was succeeded by Victor S. Clark. During Clark's editorship from 1920 to 1928, the journal extended its field to include translations from periodical sources in more European countries, South America, and the Far East. The 1920 edition of *Living Age* lists contributions from *Action française, Deutsche Allgemeine, Giornale d'Italia, Heraldo de Madrid, Internationale communiste, Japan Advertiser, Moscow Pravda*, and *Statist*, among many others. In 1926, the magazine became a semimonthly.

An independent corporation in New York, the World Topics Corporation, purchased the magazine in 1928, and that year, *Living Age* appeared in a new and enlarged format as an illustrated monthly edited by John Bakeless, a former assistant of Clark's. In 1929, the magazine was changed again to a semimonthly and a smaller format without illustrations, with Quincy Howe as editor. Throughout the 1930s, the magazine continued to broaden its scope of sources and selection of news and authors. A cosmopolitan outlook on world affairs was featured through such departments as War and Peace, The World Over, and As Others See Us. Articles by and about celebrated writers and artists were highlighted: Thomas Mann, Walter De la Mare, Pío Baroja, Hilaire Belloc, Luigi Pirandello, Pablo Picasso, and J. B. Priestley. In 1938, Joseph Hilton Smyth, a journalist and free-lance writer, bought the *Living Age*, and published and edited the magazine until its abrupt demise in 1941. In 1942, Smyth, along with Irvine Harvey Williams, who had acted as president of the Living Age Corporation, and Walter G. Matheson, a staff writer, were investigated by the Federal Bureau of Investigation. All three were charged with being propaganda agents for Japan when investigations revealed that the Japanese government had provided the money for Smyth's purchase of *Living Age* in 1938, and had underwritten publication losses each month in consideration for propaganda articles to be featured in each month's issue. It was an ignominious and ironic ending for a publication that its founder, Littell, had envisioned as a bulwark against "what is bad in taste and vicious in morals."[4]

Notes

1. Frank Luther Mott, *A History of American Magazines*. Vol. 1: 1741–1850 (New York: D. Appleton and Company, 1930), p. 748.

2. Eliakim Littell, "Prospectus," quoted in "Ninety Years On," *Living Age* 346 (1934): 200.

3. Ibid.

4. Ibid.

Information Sources

BIBLIOGRAPHY
Allibone, S. Austin. *Critical Dictionary of English Literature and British and American Authors*. 3 vols. Philadelphia: Lippincott, 1858–1871.
Mott, Frank Luther. *A History of American Magazines*. vol. 1:1741–1850. New York: D. Appleton and Company, 1930– . 747–49.
"Ninety Years On." *Living Age* 346 (1934): 198–224.
INDEX SOURCES
Edward Roth, *A Complete Index to Littell's Living Age* 2 vols. Philadelphia: E. Roth, 1891. Comprising the Contents of the First 100 Volumes. *Poole's International Index to Periodicals; Readers' Guide*.
LOCATION SOURCES
Many libraries.

Publication History

MAGAZINE TITLE AND TITLE CHANGES
Littell's Living Age, 1844–1896; *Living Age,* 1897–1941.
VOLUME AND ISSUE DATA
Vols. 1–330, May 1844–September 1926, weekly; vols. 331–334, October 1926–April 1928, semimonthly; vols. 334–336, May 1928–August 1929, monthly; vols. 337–338, September 1929–July 1930, semimonthly; vols. 338–360, August 1930–1941, monthly.
PUBLISHER AND PLACE OF PUBLICATION
T. H. Carter and Company, 1844–1846; Littell, Son and Company, 1846–1896; Living Age Company, 1896–1941; Boston.
EDITORS
Eliakim Littell, 1844–1870; Robert S. Littell, 1870–1896; Ellery Sedgwick, 1896–1919; Victor S. Clark, 1920–1928; John Bakeless, 1928–1929; Quincy Howe, 1929–1938; Joseph Hilton Smyth, with Leon Bryce Bloch and Lamar Middleton, 1938–1941.
CIRCULATION
Not available.

Diana A. Chlebek

LOOK

Look is usually mentioned in tandem with another magazine renowned for its photography: *Life*.* However, the comparison is really neither an accurate nor a fair one. Despite the fact that the two were probably the best of the photo magazines, *Life* in reality aspired to be a newsmagazine (albeit a photojournalistic one) published on a weekly basis, while *Look*, because of its biweekly publication, could not and did not regularly report news, but instead developed feature articles accompanied by text.

Look was founded in January 1937 by Gardner "Mike" Cowles, a member of an Iowa family that owned numerous communications outlets including *Family Circle*,* selected trade magazines, several newspapers, and television stations. Prior to founding *Look*, Cowles was news editor for the *Des Moines Register and Tribune* when he began to notice reader response to stories that allied pictures and text. In an attempt to verify his impressions Cowles employed George Gallup to conduct his first commissioned poll for the Cowles newspapers, and Gallup's findings supported Cowles's suspicions that the text-picture alliance was far more effective than either used separately.[1] In its early years *Look* was not a "respectable" magazine. According to Fleur Cowles, because it was "categorized as barber shop reading, it was rejected by the serious advertising community."[2] Actually, for its first eighteen issues, no advertising appeared in the pages of *Look*, but its description as a male-oriented, barbershop publication is an accurate one. Its first issue featured actresses Dolores Del Rio and Joan Crawford in multiple-page coverage, as well as a regular feature, Women in the News. The next issue featured Myrna Loy and Greta Garbo; the next, Marlene Dietrich and Jean Harlow. By August 1937, in an issue featuring a plethora of female nude pictures, *Look* claimed a circulation of 1.3 million.

Photography was to remain the most important characteristic of *Look*, as its editors emphasized:

> *Look* tells stories in pictures. *Look*'s editors hunt for their unusual picture stories in the basic and important fields of screen, medicine, foreign lands, adventure, sports, inventions, crime, personalities, sociology, self-improvement, religion, beauty, movies and the stage. . . . A child can understand *Look*, yet the most intelligent, best informed adult enjoys *Look* and can learn something from it.[3]

Still, respect was some time in coming, as Gardner Cowles noted: "it grieves me to recall that the magazine was long characterized as 'sensational'—even after half of our contents, issue after issue, covered world affairs, national politics, advances in medicine and education, religion and science and the arts."[4] But paradoxically, Cowles also confesses, "Not until 1950 did *Look* begin to reach that level of quality for which I had hoped. Year by year, we improved."[5] Thirteen years is a substantial gestation period, it should be noted. Even as late as the mid-forties *Look* was being printed on paper that was little better than newsprint, and its readers were still virtually all male. In addition to the obvious negative effects male orientation had on circulation, a still more important consideration was the fact that a female readership was necessary to attract big advertisers.

Over the years *Look* was fortunate to have an unusually talented corps of associates in key positions. Leo Rosten, a long-time *Look* principal, has furnished his impressions of some of them. For example, Mike Cowles is described as the

> dominant power and personality [of *Look*] . . . a lifelong Republican and a liberal to his fingertips. . . . Cowles's dominant passion was politics . . .

he valued the entree which the editorship of a magazine that reached fifty million or more readers gave him to the inner halls of power. . . . his financial stake in newspapers outside of Iowa (in Florida and Long Island) and in radio and television stations certainly did not diminish the eagerness of presidents and monarchs and powers-behind-a-throne (or a firing squad) to receive him. . . . The industry alleged that his command of the 'nuts-and-bolts' aspects of publishing was unmatched by the editors of competitive magazines, who were not publishers as well. . . . He was at home with the budgets and the obdurate facts of finance.[6]

The man who was responsible for *Look*'s daily overall editorial operation was Daniel D. Mich, who came to *Look* from the sports pages of the *Milwaukee Journal*, worked for Cowles for many years, leaving briefly for a stint at *McCall's*,* and returned to *Look* as editor until his death in 1965. Leo Rosten describes Mich as "rough-hewn, abrupt, often abrasive. He had a fierce temper. . . . He was not diplomatic, but he was respected. He was a good administrator and a tough editor. He despised guile, fence-straddling, or laziness. He was totally fearless, a crusader for the poor and powerless. . . . He never worried about the furor that a hard-hitting article was sure to provoke. . . . [he] had an uncanny eye for photographs."[7]

William B. Arthur joined *Look*'s staff in 1946 and was managing editor until Daniel Mich's death in 1965, at which time he became editor. Described by Rosten as "a quiet man, he was easy to approach and to know. He was sentimental and . . . 'corny.' "[8]

Look's preeminence in design and layouts, artwork, and use of color and illustrations was due to its art director, Allen Hurlburt—a figure "incapable of vulgarity. He admired talent—however new, young, or offbeat. He could visualize a feature, or lay out a story, with imagination and taste. He could also turn stubborn and derisive. . . . he won more awards than any Art Director of a mass-circulation magazine."[9]

Cowles's wife, Fleur, established an independent women's section, and thereafter funneled into *Look*'s pages features never before handled with grace: "fashions, food, home decoration, art, travel . . . she fortified Mike [Cowles] in rejecting the strident and the crude, to reach for polish and . . . class. She bubbled with ideas and was undeterred by costs."[10]

Arthur Rothstein, "a much honored craftsman of the lens, headed *Look*'s staff of fifteen photographers," said Leo Rosten, who was with *Look* in an editorial capacity for twenty-two years.[11] He further notes that "in making up a typical issue, the editors saw and screened some 8,000 photographs. In thirty-five years, *Look* published over 180,000 pictures."[12]

Look, or specifically Marvin Whatmore, president of *Look*'s operations, was responsible for the development of the *Look*-Kromatic process in 1965. This process produced paper that was smoother and therefore capable of reproducing color photographs at an unequaled level in terms of brilliance, depth of hue, and color saturation and subtlety. This new process, with its capability of ten color gradations, replaced rotogravure, which used only four or five colors. Interestingly, though, in its early years *Look* attempted to strengthen its identity and even dissociate itself from *Life* on the basis of its paper. *Life* was printed on fine, coated paper—*Look* on newsprint quality. In its early promotional literature, this point was emphasized: "Don't look for coated paper or fancy printing. Look for reader interest!"[13]

Within a year after beginning publication, *Look*'s editors developed a "classification of human interest" that ultimately was reflected in the variety of departments utilized. The list was as follows:

1. Personalities

2. Romance

3. Beauty & Fashions

4. Self-Improvement

5. Child & Animal Interest

6. Movies & Stage

7. Religion

8. Health & Popular Science

9. Adventure & Travel

10. Social Problems

11. Sports

12. Curiosities & Oddities

13. Fiction.[14]

Look's table of contents late in 1938 reflects this list to a large degree; however, two departments not on the original list—Crime and Thrills—were unfortunately to set the tone for criticism of the magazine for years to come. The *New Republic,** no doubt noting *Look*'s million-plus circulation, categorized it as "a morgue and dime museum on paper. . . . We can think of no reason why *Look* should not go to a circulation of ten millions—if the supply of corpses holds out and people don't get tired of looking at them."[15] Cowles was as sensitive in 1938 as he was in 1971 of *Look*'s being labeled "sensational": "*Look* has been criticized as being sensationally thrilling. My only reply is that life itself is thrilling, and the more thrilling nature of *Look* gives it an intense reading which makes it all the more influential with its readers."[16] Actually, the truth lies somewhere in between, for in among the Ripley's Believe It or Not features and the Photo-Crime sections, *Look* very early on had begun to print photojournalistic essays on such important social issues as child labor, slums, tuberculosis, the Ku Klux Klan, and a study of war propaganda. In fact, after a few of these appeared, the *New Republic*, which had so roundly criticized *Look* earlier, became one of its strongest supporters: "*Look . . .* is the journalistic marvel of the age. . . . It has made the best pictoral study of civil liberties in the United States we have ever seen anywhere. . . . The pictures make their case convincingly; we salute *Look* for its courage in showing the seamy side of American life as well as for the skill with which it has done the job."[17] And also this: "*Look* . . . is publishing a remarkable series of photographs exposing the methods of war propagandists. . . . It is a significant and encouraging note, we feel, when a high-powered 'slick' devotes itself to editorial pictures of this admirable type."[18]

Cowles and his editorial staff never published a manifesto of editorial policy or identified a "party line," if indeed there ever was one. On the contrary, as Cowles said, "We shall never tell you what to think, but shall offer you new options to choose from. . . . We shall never attempt to mold public opinion."[19] Another observation was, "*Look* made it a matter of policy to try to please readers of all shades of opinion . . . an article with a liberal view on a current subject was usually matched with one of a more conservative view . . . 'in' material was balanced by old fashioned value oriented material."[20]

Among the various areas of the American scene that *Look* treated, one of the most influential was motion pictures. From the beginning, *Look*'s coverage of movies ranged from individual treatment of stars to reviews of pictures to a Movie Guide begun in the mid-forties that rated pictures according to appropriateness of audience—"entire family," "adults," and "adults only." At this time *Look* began giving its own movie awards, a feature that continued into the sixties and was eventually presented on television.

In 1947 *New Republic* identified what it perceived to be the Cowles formula for publishing success: "sex and crime, swathed in a sound moral lesson, or muffled by columns of serious matter." In an attempt to ameliorate the formula, the *New Republic* also claimed that Harlan Logan, *Look*'s newly hired vice-president and general manager, was "a magazine doctor" who recommended: "more serious topics, careful aim at the American family . . . elimination of synthetic gore . . . and name writers." The *New Republic* gave its own view of the composition of *Look*: "Roughly a quarter of the text of recent issues have been concerned with death, violence, blood or sex. Another quarter of conventional movie-magazine glamour; most of the rest consists of sports, quizzes, teen age doings, and fashions."[21]

Throughout the 1950s and 1960s *Look* had come into its own and was regularly publishing some of the finest photojournalism and even work by the most renowned writers of the time. Examples of subjects treated in outstanding feature articles include civil rights, the black poor, Vietnam, women's liberation, and the gay life. *Look*'s high point in this area of features was achieved in 1967 with the serial publication in four issues of William Manchester's *Death of a President*, which treated the assassination of John F. Kennedy. Some 200 million copies were sold.[22] As for outstanding and/or prominent writers, during this same time period *Look* published work by Ernest Hemingway, Marshall McLuhan, Eugene O'Neill, Pearl Buck, C. P. Snow, Norman Mailer, Archibald MacLeish, John F. Kennedy, Harry Truman, Adlai Stevenson, and two figures outside their normal forums—William F. Buckley and Gloria Steinem. The Stevenson material is particularly noteworthy in that it was commissioned by *Look* as an ongoing series of reports as Stevenson was on a world cruise visiting areas vital at the time. Hemingway's work appeared with numerous photographs on several occasions while he was on safari in Africa.

Look's circulation history is an interesting one. Its first issue had a print order of 400,000 copies, which sold out.[23] Its second issue sold over a million copies.[24] By August 1937 it claimed a circulation of 1.3 million;[25] by November, 2 million.[26] By 1953 circulation was up to 3.7 million,[27] and in 1967 it reached its peak of 7.75 million, of which some 5 million copies were mailed.[28] All told, some 4 billion copies of *Look*'s 903 issues were sold from 1937 to 1971.[29] One final note on circulation; though Cowles claimed to have cut back on circulation due to rising postal rates and production costs, the last issue of *Look* he printed (19 October 1971) still furnished subscription forms offering a year's subscription for $3.00. The original newsstand price for an issue of *Look* was ten cents in 1937, but by 1979 it had risen to $1.50.

In 1938 *Look* was guaranteeing 1.5 million readers to its advertisers and charging $3,725 a page. For its first 18 issues no advertising was published, and when it did begin, it did not use liquor or beer sponsors, although it did publish ads for virtually every tobacco company. In 1938 *Look* published a little over 400 pages of advertising. *Look*'s 1953 advertising revenue was $23 million, up from $6 million in 1946. By 1957, advertising had grown to 1,765 pages, yielding $43.4 million; in 1961, advertising decreased to 1,595 pages, but the revenue generated grew to $63.8 million. There were a variety of reasons that accounted for *Look*'s failure. Advertisers began to shift their spending from magazines to television; a strike at General Motors forced the company to cancel $9 million worth of ads in *Look*; costs of printing, paper, and distribution soared; and a huge increase in postal rates, which, since 5.5 million copies of *Look* were mailed every two weeks, had a pronounced impact. And all of these conditions were exacerbated by the fact that the country was rapidly slipping into an economic recession.

Some of the rising costs associated with *Look*'s circulation, aside from postal rate increases, can be attributed to the outmoded methods employed. For example, even in the late 1960s primitive, noncomputerized circulation, selling, and fulfillment methods were performed by 2,000 employees in Des Moines, Iowa.

In much the same way that *Life, Saturday Evening Post,** *Saturday Review,** and *Horizon** died and were reactivated under their old titles but in reduced circumstances and with less prestige, *Look* reappeared a little over seven years after it ceased publication in October 1971. The new *Look* first appeared on 9 February 1979 and was to last until August of that same year. Physically it resembled the old version—printed on slick paper—though a bit smaller, 9″ x 12″ as opposed to the old 10″ x 13″ format.

Look's new editor was Robert Gutwillig, who had worked with *Playboy** and in book publishing. *Look* reassumed a biweekly publication schedule, and its first issue appeared with two different covers: one featuring Patty Hearst for locations west of Denver, and another featuring Nelson Rockefeller for the rest of the country. As might be expected from its subtitle, *The Picture Newsmagazine, Look* still intended to feature photojournalism in its new scheme of things.[30]

Its departments were First Look, Good Look, Newslook, Look Ahead (the feature departments), and Look People. The first issue contained a portfolio of seventeen-year-old, previously unpublished pictures of Marilyn Monroe, featured exclusive coverage of the Jamestown disaster and of space-age medicine, and in the people section covered Jimmy Carter, Princess Caroline, and John McEnroe—a bag mixed enough for anyone's taste. Over the next eight biweekly issues this was to prove a typical one, with further coverage focusing on Truman Capote, Joan Miro, baseball's spring training, and the Gacy mass murders. Perhaps the most prestigious articles were three sections from the forthcoming book by Watergate Judge John Sirica.

However, by May 1979 *Look* was in financial trouble again. It was losing $1 million a month despite a circulation of 650,000 and an avowed plan to concentrate on single-copy sales in supermarkets, shopping centers, and stationery stores. In June all art, photo, and editorial personnel were fired, and the staff was reduced from 130 to 45. A new editor was hired, Jann S. Wenner of *Rolling Stone** fame. The first magazine put together by Wenner and his people appeared in July as a monthly. It was described as a "cross between *People** and a glossy version of *Rolling Stone*."[31] It was aimed at the twenty-five to thirty-nine age group, featured high-quality photography, personality profiles, a book excerpt, a movie review, and a travel feature. The personalities included (in Places and Faces) Mariel Hemingway, Nastassia Kinski, and Arthur C. Clarke. The next and final issue featured a conversation with William Styron, coverage of Sally Field and Jerry Brown, and two musical groups: the Doobie Brothers and the Bottoms Brothers.[32]

At this point a group of French investors including Daniel Filipacchi of *Paris Match* decided against a five-year plan put forth by Wenner to steadily reduce *Look*'s losses and show a profit by the next summer. The July 1979 issue, though still offering charter subscriptions at 33 percent off, was the final issue.

Notes

1. Gardner Cowles, "Foreword," in *The Look Book,* ed. Leo Rosten (New York: Abrams, 1975), pp. 17–18.

2. Fleur Cowles, *Friends and Memories* (New York: Reynal and Co., 1978), pp. 43, 47.

3. Editorial, *Look,* 17 August 1937, p. 3.

4. Gardner Cowles, pp. 17–18.

5. Ibid., p. 18.

6. Leo Rosten, "Introduction: A View From the Inside," in *The Look Book*, ed. Leo Rosten, p. 22.

7. Ibid., p. 23.

8. Ibid., p. 23.

9. Ibid., p. 23.

10. Ibid., p. 23.

11. Ibid., p. 24.

12. Ibid., p. 21.

13. Ibid., pp. 25–26.

14. Jackson Edwards, "One Every Minute," *Scribner*'s, May 1938, p. 23.

15. Quoted in Edwards, p. 102.

16. Gardner Cowles, p. 17.

17. Quoted in Edwards, p. 102.

18. Ibid., p. 102.

19. Gardner Cowles, "Look to the Future," *Look*, 10 January 1967, p. 13.

20. Don Gussow, *Divorce—Corporate Style* (New York: Ballantine Books, 1975), p. 102.

21. Dale Kramer, "Don't Make Em Mad," *New Republic*, 1 December 1947, pp. 20–23.

22. Gardner Cowles, p. 17.

23. Blurb in *Look*, 9 May 1937, p. 3.

24. Edwards, p. 102.

25. Blurb in *Look*, 17 August 1937, p. 3.

26. Blurb in *Look*, 9 November 1937, p. 3.

27. "Shakeup at *Look*," *Time*, 11 January 1954, p. 50.

28. Blurb in *Look*, 9 January 1968, p. 2.

29. Gardner Cowles, p. 17.

30. Peter Bonadventure, "The New *Look*," *Newsweek*, 12 February 1979, p. 55.

31. "*Look* Down and Possibly Out," *Newsweek*, 16 July 1979, p. 64.

32. "Split Personality: A Franco-American Look," *Time*, 12 February 1979, p. 59.

Information Sources

BIBLIOGRAPHY

Bonadventure, Peter. "The New *Look*." *Newsweek*, 12 February 1979, p. 55.

Cowles, Fleur. *Friends and Memories*. New York: Reynal and Co., 1978.

Cowles, Gardner. "Foreward." In *The Look Book*. Ed. Leo Rosten. New York: Abrams, 1975. pp. 17–18.

———. "Look to the Future." *Look*, 10 January 1967, p. 13.

Edwards, Jackson. "One Every Minute." *Scribner's*, May 1938, pp. 17–23, 102–103.

Gussow, Don. *Divorce—Corporate Style*. New York: Ballantine Books, 1975.

"Inside *Look*." *Newsweek*, 14 September 1970, pp. 73–74.

Kramer, Dale. "Don't Make Em Mad." *New Republic*, 1 December 1947, pp. 19–23.

"*Look* Down and Possibly Out." *Time*, 16 July 1979, p. 65.

Rosten, Leo. ed. *The Look Book*. New York: Abrams, 1975.

Schardt, Arlin. "*Look*: Dead Again?" *Newsweek*, 16 July 1979, p. 64.

"Split Personality: A Franco-American *Look*," *Time*, 12 February 1979, p. 59.

INDEX SOURCES
Readers' Guide to Periodical Literature; Biological Index.
LOCATION SOURCES
Widely held; also available in microform.

Publication History

MAGAZINE TITLE AND TITLE CHANGES
Subtitled *Look: The Monthly Picture Magazine,* February-May 1937, otherwise *Look Magazine*, June 1937–August 1979.
VOLUME AND ISSUE DATA
Vol. 1, no. 1–vol. 1, no. 5, February 1937–May 1937, monthly; vol. 1, no. 5–vol. 35, no. 21, 11 May 1937–19 October 1971, biweekly.
New series, vol. 1, no. 1–vol. 1, no. 8, 19 February 1979–11 June 1979, biweekly; vol. 1, no. 9–vol. 2, no. 2 [*sic*], July-August 1979, monthly.
PUBLISHER AND PLACE OF PUBLICATION
Look Inc., Des Moines, Iowa, 1937–1949; Cowles Communications, Des Moines, Iowa, 1949–1971; Look Magazine Inc., New York, 1979.
EDITORS
Vernon Pope, managing editor, 1937–1942; Harlan Logan, editor and general manager, 1942–1946; Gardner Cowles, president and editor, 1947; Gardner Cowles, editor-in-chief, 1948–1964; Daniel D. Mich, editor, 1964–1965; Gardner Cowles, editor-in-chief, 1966; William B. Arthur, editor, 1966–1971; Robert Gutwillig, editor, February 1979–June 1979; Jann S. Wenner, editor, July 1979–August 1979.
CIRCULATION
1967: 7.75 million; 1979: 650,000.

Alan Nourie

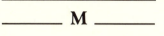

M

M magazine, subtitled *The Civilized Man*, describes itself as a publication that "devotes itself to genuine matters of style, quality, and class for men who know the difference between real turtle soup and the mock."[1] Despite pretentious blurbs like this, *M* is a good as well as a sumptuously produced magazine: "In fact, *M's* elegant look puts it in the same league with Hearst's *Town & Country.** Throughout *M* the emphasis is on the wealthy male 'to the manner born' and how he lives. Presumably, some of *M's* readers actually live that life, and the others aspire to it."[2] Categorized by *Newsweek** as "unabashedly aim [ing] at millionaires," its circulation director furnishes the following by way of elucidation: "*M* is an elitist publication (and it makes no apology for this fact). Its editorial coverage is committed to quality and excellence."[3]

In fact, "civilized," "excellence," "quality," and "the best" seem to be *M's* favorite buzzwords. One is taken, for example, on a civilized safari, taken to the best tailor, informed about the best books for Christmas or the perfect medical checkup or the civilized sports, and so on. But while *M* is competing for a readership with the other two men's fashion oriented magazines—*GQ** and *Esquire**—its typical issue is composed of 30 percent fashion despite being a transformation of *Menswear* and a Fairchild Publications product. (Fairchild also publishes *Women's Wear Daily.*) Through 1984, *M* was averaging slightly over sixty pages of advertising per issue, mainly but not exclusively devoted to menswear.

So, while targeting a 200,000-plus audience, *M* is not a mass-market magazine in the strict sense of the word (except for the circulation) and even prides itself on the opposite by virtue of its self-professed elitism, hence becoming a "demassification" organ.

While *M* is grouped with *Esquire* and *GQ* because of its concern with men's fashion, each magazine has apparently isolated particular segments of the market: "*GQ*'s readers are starting down the path to lucrative careers, *Esquire's* are well on their way, and *M's* have arrived . . . the typical *M* male is 40-years-old and has an annual salary of $67,500, as opposed to 25 years/$30,000 and 35 years/ $43,000 for *GQ* and *Esquire* respectively."[4]

In determining the composition of the magazine, the editors of *M* have gone to school on some of the other successful magazines of the day. For example, its Looking Great feature, which consists of socially oriented photographs of beautiful young women, is clearly derivative of a similarly styled feature in *Vanity Fair**; while In and Out, a listing of what writers, cars, food, drinks, sports, people, hotels, schools, and so forth are currently in vogue is similar to but not as witty as the material that *Esquire* has been providing for years. Interestingly, though, if one notices the geography of Looking Good, the implication is that no one looks very good who does not live in a few cities on the eastern seaboard of the United States or perhaps one of the major European capitals.

One of the truly unique characteristics of *M* is contained in its Entertainment section fairly regularly. Here, among the decidedly better-than-average quality features on such figures as V. S. Pritchett, Jamie Wyeth, Irving Howe, and subjects like contemporary photography and music, one finds books discussed— and not just reviews of contemporary fiction, but literary and historical master-pieces that the *M* reader is actually urged to *re-read*. What other magazine with a circulation of over a hundred thousand urges its readership to read (much less re-read) the work of Gustave Flaubert, Mark Twain, Ernest Hemingway, Alexis de Tocqueville, and Johann Wolfgang von Goethe or such individual novels as the *Sound and the Fury, Moby Dick, Jude the Obscure*, or Ford Madox Ford's tetralogy, *Parade's End?*

Another rather obsessive area of interest in *M* is things British in general; to be blunt, *M* is an Anglophile publication by any standard. For example, British-focused articles include London mens clubs, country houses in the Devons (Sussex), Dunhill cigars (the best, of course), the Duke of Edinburgh, English style, Oxford and Cambridge, London tailoring, trout fishing in Scotland, Sir Oliver Wright (the British ambassador to the United States), Southeby's auc-tioneer, Purdy guns, a round of golf at St. Andrews, London nightclubs, the Inns of Court, Winchester College (England's oldest and most exclusive public school), English country hotels, the Morgan (the British sports car), Oxford versus Cambridge rugby, British cider making, and many others.

This same fascination is carried over into the literary world as well where excellent articles on V. S. Pritchett, Martin Amis, Anthony Powell, and Dick Francis have appeared.

However, *M* is not exclusively British in its focus; in fact, it is quite inter-national in its scope when featuring important contemporary businessmen and political figures. Virtually every issue contains an in-depth article on or an interview with such figures as CBS's William Paley, Donald Kendall of Pepsico, Robert McFarlane, Walter Annenberg, Lord Carrington (secretary-general of NATO), Dick Snyder of Simon and Schuster, Peter Prescott of *Newsweek*, Akio Morita of Sony, Armand Hammer, and others of their ilk.

Because it is written and produced by its own staff, *M* is unique among the "big three" men's fashion magazines; *Esquire* and *GQ* both use outside writers heavily. *M* is also unique in its use of the theme issue: "French Style," "Italian Style," "Civilized Sports," and others. *M* is unique too in that it was successful from the first; its first issue "included a whopping 175 pages of paid advertising and a 70,000 circulation."[5] It was able to achieve this in large part because of Fairchild relations with a number of better stores: "Fairchild was able to rapidly build a following for *M* because it began with a solid list of likely subscribers," provided by stores that made their charge account lists accessible for the forthcoming magazine's use.[6]

Notes

1. "The Civilized Man is Five Years Old," *M*, August 1988, p. 54.
2. Charlene Canape, "Refashioning the Male Marketplace," *Marketing & Media Decisions*, 20 March 1985, p. 88.
3. Sara Nelson, "The Male Market Defined with a Capital M," *Advertising Age*, 5 September 1983, p. 28.
4. Canape, pp. 85–86.
5. Ibid., p. 88.
6. Ibid., p. 90.

Information Sources

BIBLIOGRAPHY
Canape, Charlene. "Refashioning the Male Marketplace." *Marketing & Media Decisions*, 20 March 1985, pp. 84–90.
Kanner, Bernice. "Peacock Alley: Life-Style Mags for Men." *New York*, 26 September 1983, pp. 24–26.
Langway, Lynn. "Courting the Clotheshound." *Newsweek*, 3 October 1983, p. 92.
Nelson, Sara. "The Male Market Defined with a Capital M." *Advertising Age*, 5 September 1983, p. 28.
Thomas, Bill. "What Does a Man Want? Four Magazines That Are Trying to Provide It." *Washington Journalism Review*, December 1984, pp. 21–23.
INDEX SOURCES
    Access.
LOCATION SOURCES
    Widely held; also available in microform.

Publication History

MAGAZINE TITLE AND TITLE CHANGES
    M: The Civilized Man, 1983–present.

VOLUME AND ISSUE DATA
    Monthly, October 1983–present.
PUBLISHER AND PLACE OF PUBLICATION
    Patrick McCarthy, 1983–1984; Ben Brontley, 1984–1988; Eugene Fahy, 1989–
    present. (All in New York, N.Y.)
EDITORS
    Kevin Doyle, 1983–1986; Michael F. Coady, 1986–1988; Thomas Moran, 1989–
    present.
CIRCULATION
    133,700.

                                                                                        Alan Nourie

MCCALL'S

In April 1976 *McCall's* celebrated 100 years of publication, which began when "James and Belle McCall published a magazine of four small pink pages—hardly more than a pamphlet—filled with information about patterns and fashion."[1] This anniversary issue was a full 300 pages, the thickest ever, to celebrate the "proud past, enduring present, and hopeful future" of the magazine. The editors noted the beginnings this way:

> Our rich heritage really goes back to the very heart of America, to northern Ohio, and Belle and James McCall. James McCall himself was an orphan who came to America in the 19th century. He had been apprenticed to a tailor in Scotland, and when he settled in Jefferson, Ohio, he opened a tailor shop of his own. He married a Jefferson woman, and together he and his wife started a pattern company. As it prospered, their horizons broadened: They began a small publication to promote their patterns. The McCalls called it *The Queen, Illustrated Magazine of Fashion.*[2]

> As the years passed, the *Queen* began to carry more than simply patterns.

> Bit by bit, there were recipes, advice about running a household, comments about current affairs. Then events took a turn for the worse; James McCall died, his business floundered. In 1892 the McCall Publishing Company went on the block at a sheriff's sale—and had to be rescued by backers who gave the failing company a new lease on life. They later gave *The Queen* a new name—*McCall's Magazine: The Queen of Fashion.* The century turned. The magazine's circulation grew to a million. By 1920 *McCall's* was not only a household word but a household necessity. Four-color fashion plates and vivid covers appeared; and writers like Rudyard Kipling and Willa Cather.[3]

Frank Luther Mott covered the history of *McCall's* (the title that appears on the cover and contents page since 1950) in depth from its inception to 1956. He noted that McCall, having previously tried in both New York and Ohio country towns to establish a business in tailoring, began his career in New York as an agent for the Royal Chart, a system for drafting dressmaking patterns. Upon returning to Ohio, he married Miss Abel, and they worked together in the dressmaking/pattern business. Mott cites a slightly different origin for the magazine from that in the anniversary issue. "It was probably in the fall of 1873 that the first number of *The Queen: Illustrating McCall's Bazar, Glove-Fitting Patterns* was issued . . . four small-folio pages on pink paper in ten monthly issues each year." As business grew, the company offered other publications with the ten monthly numbers. The summer months were the two missing issues, but the *Bazar Dressmaker* appeared twice a year with illustrations of fashions from European capitals and from New York; there were also two catalogs a year, and two "magnificent colored fashion plates."[4] Mott conjectured that Mrs. McCall edited the magazine following her husband's death in 1884, but in 1885 the editorship fell to "May Manton" (Mrs. George Bladworth), wife of one of the chief members of the McCall organization. By 1890, the McCall Publishing Company had George H. Bladworth as president, and in 1891 the title of the magazine became the *Queen of Fashion*. In 1892 Page and Ringot bought the company at a sheriff's auction and changed the name to J. H. Ringot and Company in 1893.[5]

At this point Mrs. Bladworth left as editor, to be followed by Frances M. Benson, who continued as editor even after James Henry Ottley assumed the McCall Company in 1893. [Ottley] "raised the annual subscription price to forty cents, increased the size to sixteen pages, and improved the editorial variety. Circulation responded, going to seventy-five thousand in a year."[6] In addition to fashion and patterns, the magazine began new features, including its first fiction in August 1894, and a Children's Corner, fancywork, literary notes, jokes, and editorials. In 1896 the publishers reduced the size to quarto, much like that of other women's magazines of the day. In 1897, the title became *McCall's Magazine*, and Miss E. B. Clapp assumed editorship for the next fifteen years, followed by William Griffith, the poet. "At the end of the nineties the outstanding items of content were two big fashion plates in each number, produced in brilliant chromolithography."[7] During this time circulation rose until it reached a million by 1908. In 1913 Ottley sold the corporation to White, Weld and Company, bankers. The president of the new McCall Corporation was Edward Alfred Simmons; he was succeeded a year or two later by Allen H. Richardson, by whom " . . . name writers were introduced by 1915; Editor Alice Manning bought serials and short stories from Mary Imlay Taylor, Eunice Tietjens, Nathalie Sumner Lincoln, Zona Gale, and other well-known magazinists."[8]

In February 1917 *McCall's* raised single issues to $.10 and mail subscription to between $.75 and $1.50, but advertising and circulation declined. William Bishop Warner became president of the corporation, and his changes made the difference in saving the magazine.[9] After Alice Manning came Myra G. Reed as editor (1916–1918); then Bessie Beatty, "well-known newspaper writer and foreign correspondent" (1918–1921) was followed by Harry Payne Burton, "a foreign correspondent and a feature writer for the Newspaper Enterprise Association." His mandate was to get well-known writers into *McCall's*, and he succeeded with bringing in E. Phillips Oppenheim, Robert W. Chambers, Ethel M. Dell, Emerson Hough, Samuel Merwin, Louis Joseph Vance, Arthur Somers Roche, Gilbert Parker, Dorothy Canfield, Kathleen Norris, Booth Tarkington, Mary Roberts Rinehart, Harold Bell Wright, Zane Grey, James Oliver Curwood, Joseph Hergesheimer, Juliet Wilbor Tompkins—"successful writers of the day," according to Mott.[10]

In 1924 printing transferred to Dayton, Ohio; Otis Lee Wiese became editor in January 1928 and remained in that position for more than fifty years. Initially, he brought many fine fiction pieces to the magazine and made changes in format. According to Mott, a quintet of female serialists (Margaret Ostenso, Temple Bailey, Faith Baldwin, Margaret Culkin Banning, and Alice Duer Miller) and a quintet of writers (Heywood Broun, F. Scott Fitzgerald, J. P. Marquand, Octavus Roy Cohen, and Wallace Irwin) were regular contributors, especially in the thirties.[11]

Another innovation came in 1932 when Wiese introduced the "three-way makeup": Fiction and News, Home Making, and Style and Beauty. The main advantage of this format came to the advertiser because ads were no longer exclusively in the back of the magazine. Each section had its own cover page, unique content, and unique ads. In 1950, when *McCall's* decided to discontinue the three-way format, ads still stayed in the front.[12]

In the late 1930s a small novel appeared in each issue, as well as reports on a series of youth conferences sponsored by the magazine. In 1940 a national defense section began, and after the war this space reverted to community and service kinds of projects. Also in 1940 Eleanor Roosevelt became a regular contributor, having published her memoirs serially first in *Ladies' Home Journal*, and later in *McCall's*. Prices ranged from fifteen cents in 1942 to twenty-five cents in 1946, and circulation reached four million in 1952.[13]

William Warner died in 1946 and was succeeded by Marvin Pierce. Otis Wiese was vice-president in 1949, and both publisher and editor. In the 1950s the magazine established a West Coast office and initiated a series of "personal stories." Home decoration and food ideas were increasingly prominent. "Service matter was made equal with fiction and articles."[14] And by 1956, the year of "its striking 'togetherness' program," when Mott's coverage of *McCall's* ends, circulation had reached 4,750,000.

And what was a "togetherness" program?

> The downgrading of the man of the family and the upgrading of the woman had gone so far that women became frightened and began to rebel against their power. Their magazines [were] now testing new conceptions; they [were] now trying to build up the family as a whole; no more rule by either the father or the mother, but a sharing relationship between the two. For the success of such a campaign men also must become readers of the

women's magazines. To accomplish this, the *Ladies' Home Journal* used famous writers who the editors thought would appeal to men. But it was *McCall's Magazine* which went furthest, with the slogan 'Togetherness,' a woefully sad expression, good only for wisecracks. This slogan was really born of fear on the part of the magazines—fear of losing their life's blood—circulation.[15]

The idea behind this program was that men would share more in household duties and women would become more involved in their husband's businesses. According to James Playsted Wood, in an effort to strengthen declining circulation and advertising, *McCall's* announced that it would become a magazine devoted to the woman and her family, a magazine for the household. As a result, more space was given to sex, marriage, and complete novels.[16] But apparently no more women or men than before were attracted to the new format, and sales continued to lag. Gossip suggests that because the corporation that owned *McCall's* also owned *Redbook*,* the magazine was able to survive. In 1958 suddenly a new editor, Herbert R. Mayes, who had recently resigned after twenty years as editor of *Good Housekeeping*, assumed the editorship at *McCall's*. He brought with him the concept of a seal of approval. The approval was based on use tests of products by *McCall's* editors and technicians. And the guarantee of such a magazine also began to be announced in television ads, a double bonus for manufacturers. By November of 1959 Mayes's style as an editor became apparent—in an issue termed "flash, brash, splash." Under Mayes, "togetherness" was not totally eliminated, but *McCall's* no longer tried so hard to attract men and women. *McCall's* simply became a magazine that included everybody.[17]

Since this period, *McCall's* has continued to attract a large female audience and has also continued including material that appeals to just about everybody. In the past thirty years, from the end of the fifties when togetherness was the theme to the end of the eighties when the themes are somewhat more glamorous and glitzy, the magazine has undergone some substantial changes in format and in focus. To an extent, the subtitles indicate the shifts: from *The Magazine of Togetherness* in 1959 to *First Magazine for Women* in 1960 to *The Magazine for Suburban Women* from 1974 through 1982. The current issues do not carry a subtitle, but the features for the past several years do indicate something of a focus. There is more emphasis on sensational topics and people than there was in the beginning, just as there now is in almost any magazine found on the stands. In other words, *McCall's* has simply kept up with the times, reflecting society's interests more than attempting to change them. Consistently, *McCall's* has kept pace with current trends in medicine, schooling, politics, fashion, homes, and foods. Over the course of a year these and other contemporary interests will be featured in somewhat balanced space and prominence. The approach to these and other features is from the woman's point of view, what the woman can do or should do to make a difference. An especially poignant message was that to readers from the editors upon the death of Robert Kennedy: "What Women Can Do to End Violence in America."

In the late 1950s there was teacher of the year; in the seventies woman of the year. Now there is a reader of the year. *McCall's* has tackled racism (June 1971—"A Rap on Race" by James Baldwin and Margaret Mead) and feminism, UFO's and life after death, and now AIDs and anorexia. Increasingly the cover features the more sensational feature and the headlines grab the attention of the reader, but the text of the article is invariably balanced and objective.

In 1985 *Writer* asked a number of editors of various popular magazines about the kinds of free-lance material they sought; at that time, *McCall's* was in the market for human interest narratives, personal essays, and humor pieces, all of from 1,000 to 3,000 words. A piece on The Mother's Page paid $100 for "insightful pieces"; opinion essays brought $1,000. Short stories should run 3,000 words, short short stories 2,000. For all this material, the magazine required queries for articles. Staff members wrote all service material.[18]

McCall's in the past thirty years has gone from using models on the cover to famous individuals, generally women alone or with a family member or spouse. Covers in the eighties may feature a large photo of the "lead" character in a story and several smaller photos of individuals featured in other stories. The cover is much busier than it used to be. The magazine has shown a particular interest in first ladies and first families in the last several decades, with especial attention to Jacqueline Kennedy and the entire Kennedy clan. At one time, Lynda Johnson Robb was a feature writer for the magazine, focusing more on young people than on Washington. In addition, *McCall's* has featured international leaders such as Indira Gandhi and Golda Meir; it has "starred" Princess Grace (and her family) quite frequently. More recently features have been sharper, as in "Geraldine Ferraro—Where Does She Go From Here?" Several articles concerned the Ted and Joan Kennedy marriage and subsequent divorce; and one feature in 1982 was "Jane Wyman: The First Mrs. Ronald Reagan." These and other feature articles again demonstrate more interest in the lives of public figures and more willingness to probe the sensational and highly personal incidents.

McCall's has featured more movie stars and rich and famous personalities in the magazine recently; from the late fifties right into the eighties there has been a continuing interest in Bing Crosby and his family, in Judy Garland and her family members, and in Elizabeth Taylor and her several husbands. Sophia Loren, Marilyn Monroe, Katharine Hepburn, Carol Burnett, Mary Tyler Moore, Shirley MacLaine, Marlo Thomas (spokeswoman for the McCalls' patterns at one time), and whoever is currently popular on television or at the movies are among those celebrities that *McCall's* has featured. One of the first couples to appear on the cover was Joanne Woodward and Paul Newman; one of the first men to appear alone was Alan Alda. For the past several years, particularly in the eighties, there has been widespread interest in this country in the British royal family, and Princess Diana and her children have also been featured a number of times, along with another royal daughter-in-law, Sarah Ferguson.

Regular columns have included those on diets, food, and exercise. For some years, Miss Craig demonstrated exercise tips, and Julia Child shared recipes, many of which made Miss Craig's exercise advice even more important. Beauty tips and secrets are another frequent topic of interest, as well as fashion reports. For several years the Christmas issue featured a gingerbread house on the cover and was often advertised as "our most glorious Christmas issue ever."

The magazine was originally produced to advertise McCall's patterns. That is no longer the case. Although McCall's is still a popular pattern, since the mid-eighties pattern features have not been a part of the magazine; neither, in fact, has Betsy McCall, the paper doll figure who also advertised fashion patterns. In October 1956, *Vogue*, a pattern competitor, advertised in *McCall's*: "always the smartest—now the easiest." In the early sixties McCall's introduced half sizes in patterns; in the late sixties, the magazine featured clothes designed by Givenchy for Audrey Hepburn; in the seventies there was a pattern feature on Halston clothes "anyone can make"; in the early eighties, McCall's featured Laura Ashley dresses in patterns. But the dropping of the pattern page simply indicates that women today have less time to sew; it also indicates how very changed the magazine is from the first issue in the 1870s.

Another noticeable change is in the quantity and quality of literature that has appeared in *McCall's* in the past several decades. In the late fifties and early sixties the cover often promoted the literary work in its headlines to advertise the issue contents; complete novels still could be found on occasion. Among those of interest are Sloan Wilson's *A Summer Place* (February 1958), Sheila Burnford's *The Incredible Journey* (February 1961), John Steinbeck's *The Winter of Our Discontent* (May 1961), and Herman Wouk's *Youngblood Hawke* (March 1962). In the late sixties, the magazine began to publish book excerpts, including those by Christiaan Barnard and Bernadette Devlin. Book bonuses were sometimes included. Often the works of James Herriott, Jessica Mitford, Jean Kerr, and Madeleine L'Engle appear in *McCall's*. Although literary features are still a part of the magazine, they do not occupy nearly the space that they once did. The quality of the work is still intact, however, with recent contributions by Shel Silverstein, Mario Puzo, and James Michener. That *McCall's* features fewer literary works reflects a trend in the United States to less reading altogether plus an interest in reading shorter and shorter pieces. It is unfortunate that *McCall's* and other leading magazines have not shown more leadership in attempting to reverse this trend, given the alarming literacy figures now substantiated by numerous studies.

Literary contributors from the fifties and sixties make an impressive list: Faith Baldwin, Art Buchwald, Garson Kanin, MacKinlay Kantor, John Steinbeck, William Saroyan, Harper Lee, Anne Morrow Lindbergh, Rumer Godden, John Ciardi, Pearl S. Buck, Rachel Carson, Noel Coward, Ray Bradbury, Simone de Beauvoir, Dylan Thomas, Seán O'Faoláin, James Baldwin, Morris West, Carl Sandburg, Jessamyn West, Shirley Jackson, Robert Cormier, and Judith Viorst. In the seventies, contributors included Kurt Vonnegut, Jr., Joyce Carol Oates, Arthur Miller, Mary McCarthy, Germaine Greer, Irving Stone, Sylvia Plath, Nora Ephron, Katharine Anne Porter, Gwendolyn Brooks, Earl Hamner, Jr.,

Ogden Nash, John Fowles (a chapter from *Daniel Martin*), J. R. R. Tolkien, Isaac Bashevis Singer, and Belva Plain—literary and popular writers. In the eighties there have been features on Barbara Cartland's first novel set in the United States and more recently a feature on Kate Chopin's home, "Following the Literary Trail." Perhaps with the growing interest in increased literacy, *McCall's* will return to more literature and reading material. At the present time, the reading material is more than likely to be popular, light fiction.

Between March 1963 and October 1965 circulation increased from over 6 million to over 8.4 million, but by February 1971 circulation was listed as over 7.5 million. Circulation in 1988 was 5,186,393, based on total average paid circulation during the six months prior to 31 December 1986.[19] This figure puts *McCall's* in the top 10 (number 9) among current leading U.S. magazines. Single-issue price has gone from $.35 in 1959 to the current price of $1.50 (1988). U.S. subscription price is now $13.95; add postage of $6.00 for Canada, $7.00 for Pan American countries, and $8.00 for foreign countries.

The most dramatic change in the format, however, came in February 1971 when the total size of the magazine was reduced. *Time* reported that rising paper costs and a "quantum" leap in second-class postage rates forced the shrinking of many U.S. magazines, including *McCall's*.[20] *Newsweek* noted that advertising in 1971 was at its lowest level in seven years; by cutting to 8 3/8" x 11" *McCall's* expected to save over $3 million yearly.[21] *Saturday Review* noted the change in size with regret: "In the end, consistent with contemporary patterns in American life, the quick service lunch counter may replace the full-course meal in magazine publishing. It is hardly an enchanting prospect."[22]

In the forty years from 1918 to 1959, one editor, Otis Wiese, remained at the helm; from 1959 to 1988, there have been eight editors. This fairly frequent change in leadership accounts in part for the changes in the magazine itself. Wood suggests that Herbert R. Mayes, who assumed editorship in late 1958, added more and brighter color pages and more fiction; his was the slogan, "first magazine for women."[23] In 1962, John Mack Carter followed Mayes as editor; Carter is the current editor of *Good Housekeeping*.

At the same time in the early sixties, the McCall Corporation added the *Saturday Review*** to its roster and put Norman Cousins on its board; in 1968 Cousins tried to bring a livelier, younger look to *McCall's*.[24] During those years both Robert Stein and James Fixx (famous for his books on running for fitness) were editors; Shana Alexander became the first woman to edit *McCall's* in over fifty years, but she remained for just over a year. Her fame is also perhaps more from television "Point Counterpoint" debates with news columnist James Kirk-patrick. She was followed by Patricia Carbine, who also edited for just over a year, and then left to help launch *Ms.**** During Carbine's term with *McCall's* Gloria Steinem was a frequently featured contributor. Robert Stein returned to edit in 1972 and remained as editor until 1986, when Elizabeth Sloan, current editor, took his place. Each change in leadership brought changes to the magazine; the focus today is vastly different from that of the original magazine. The focus today is an effort to retain readership in an increasingly competitive market. There are more and more magazines available today, many which appeal to a very specific female audience. *McCall's* continues to aim for a general audience, mostly female, and thus diversifies its features more than many other magazines. It leaves the "homey" focus to others such as *Good Housekeeping* and *Family Circle.** If anything, it seems to be aiming more and more for the audience perhaps attracted by magazines like *Redbook* and *Cosmopolitan.**

Notes

1. "*McCall's* Century," *McCall's*, April 1976, p. 17.
2. Ibid.
3. Ibid.
4. Frank Luther Mott, *A History of American Magazines* vol. 4: 1885–1905. (Cambridge: Harvard University Press, 1957), p. 581.
5. Ibid.
6. Ibid., p. 582.
7. Ibid.
8. Ibid., p. 583.
9. Ibid.
10. Ibid., p. 584.
11. Ibid., p. 585.
12. Ibid., p. 586.
13. Ibid., pp. 586–87.
14. Ibid., p. 587.
15. Helen Woodward, *The Lady Persuaders* (New York: Ivan Obolensky, 1960), p. 3.
16. James Playsted Wood, *Magazines in the United States* (New York: Ronald Press, 1971) p. 120.
17. Ibid., p. 143.
18. "The Changing Focus of Women's Magazines," *Writer*, November 1985, p. 25.
19. Mark S. Hoffman, ed., *The World Almanac and Book of Facts 1988* (New York: Pharos Books, 1987), p. 358.
20. "The Shrink," *Time*, 18 January 1971, p. 37.
21. "Trimming Down," *Newsweek*, 18 January 1971, pp. 54–55.
22. John Tebbel, "Time to Change Your Page Size," *Saturday Review*, 9 October 1971, p. 70.
23. Wood, pp. 122–23.
24. Ibid., p. 123.

Information Sources

BIBLIOGRAPHY
"The Changing Focus of Women's Magazines." *Writer*, November 1985, pp. 24–27.
Hoffman, Mark S., ed. *The World Almanac and Book of Facts 1988.* New York: Pharos Books, 1987, p. 358.
"*McCall's* Century." *McCall's*, April 1976.

Mott, Frank Luther. *A History of American Magazines*, vol. 4: 1885–1905. Cambridge: Harvard University Press, 1957, pp. 580–88.

"The Shrink." *Time*, 18 January 1971, p. 37.

Tebbel, John. "Time to Change Your Page Size." *Saturday Review*, 9 October 1971, p. 70.

"Trimming Down." *Newsweek*, 18 January 1971, pp. 54–55.

Wood, James Playsted. *Magazines in the United States*. New York: Ronald Press, 1971, pp. 122–23.

Woodward, Helen. *The Lady Persuaders*. New York: Ivan Obolensky, 1960.

INDEX SOURCES

Readers' Guide to Periodical Literature (1952–present); *Biography Index* (vol. 3–current); *Magazine Index* (1977–present).

LOCATION SOURCES

Library of Congress; many other libraries. Available in microform, vol. 21–present.

Publication History

MAGAZINE TITLE AND TITLE CHANGES

The Queen, 1873–1891; *The Queen of Fashion*, 1891–1897; *McCall's Magazine*, 1897–current. (Title on cover and contents page since 1950: *McCall's*.)

VOLUME AND ISSUE DATA

First issue September(?) 1873(?). Current. Monthly; annual volumes. Early volumes (1–14?) omitted January-February and July-August each year; vols. 15–21 omitted only July-August each year; vols. 22–46, September 1894–August 1919, regular annual vols. beginning with September and ending with August; vol. 47, September 1919–September 1920; vol. 48–present, October 1920–present, regular annual vols. ending with September.

PUBLISHER AND PLACE OF PUBLICATION

James McCall and Company, 1873–1890; McCall Publishing Company, 1890; Bladworth and Company, 1890–1892; Page and Ringot, 1892–1893; J. H. Ringot and Company, 1893; McCall Company (James H. Ottley, 1893–1913; White, Weld and Company, 1913–1936), 1893–1936; McCall Corporation, 1936–current. All New York, but office of publication Dayton, Ohio, 1924–current. June 1987, Working Woman of the McCall's Group.

EDITORS

James McCall and wife(?), 1873–1884; May Manton (Mrs. George H. Bladworth), 1885–1891; Frances M. Benson, 1892–1896; Miss E. B. Clapp, 1897–1911; William Griffith, 1911–1912; Alice Manning, 1912–1916; Myra G. Reed, 1916–1918; Bessie Beatty, 1918–1921; Harry P. Burton, 1921–1927; Otis L. Wiese, 1918–February 1959; Herbert R. Mayes, March 1959–February 1962; John Mack Carter, March 1962–February 1965; Robert Stein, March 1965–October 1967; James F. Fixx, November 1967–September 1969; Shana Alexander, October 1969–December 1970; Patricia Carbine, January 1971–April 1972; Robert Stein, May 1972–January 1986; A. Elizabeth Sloan, February 1986–current.

CIRCULATION
   5,353,595 (1988).

Barbara Nourie

MCCLURE'S MAGAZINE

It was in a speech by President Theodore Roosevelt in 1906 that the label of "muckraker" was coined, borrowed from John Bunyan's *Pilgrim's Progress,* to describe the journalistic investigations of some of the major newspapers and magazines of the day. By common assent, *McClure's Magazine* was the leading muckraking journal, and its founder, staff, and readers all regarded the magazine's role in the reform movement in heroic terms.

Samuel Sidney McClure was an Irish immigrant who had been raised in poverty and educated at Knox College, a New York school of evangelical Christians, where he had met John Sanborn Phillips, who was to become the cofounder of the magazine. This institution gave McClure and Phillips a background in progressive reform, instilling them with the ideals of John Brown and Abraham Lincoln. In 1893, when *McClure's* was founded, the world of publishing was undergoing drastic changes that would spur the growth of the magazine. The population of the United States had doubled, and because of the establishment and advances of public schooling, most of the population was literate and avid for specialized, current reading matter. In addition, authors were afforded protection by stricter copyright laws, and the development of services by the Post Office, such as second-class mailing privileges and free rural delivery, enabled magazine subscribers to get their issues quickly and cheaply. Another factor in the increased availability of publications was the series of technological advancements in printing, such as the development of the linotype machine and the rapid cylinder press, plus the invention of the halftone photoengraving process. Above all, a cheap and well-produced magazine became a possibility when the price of paper manufacturing fell after wood replaced cloth, and when the demand for advertising grew in the new industrial society of abundance that the United States had become at the end of the nineteenth century. Much of the initial success of *McClure's* new ten-cent magazine was based on the syndicate that he and Phillips had managed for eight years. During this period, McClure had established contact with a large number of writers in the New York literary circle, such as Thomas Bailey Aldrich, Sarah Orne Jewett, and Edward Hale, and with famous writers abroad, such as Jules Verne and Robert Louis Stevenson. Much of the literature in *McClure's* during its first two years was material already in print through syndication to American newspapers; by 1895, however, most of the syndicated features were dropped.

McClure's initially suffered a financial crisis when it began in 1893, the year of a sudden stock market crash and severe depression in the country. But within a couple of years, its popular price of fifteen cents, its well-written, informative articles, prolific advertising, and abundant use of pictures and color illustrations all combined to increase the magazine's circulation phenomenally. By May 1895, following the moves of competitors like *Cosmopolitan,** *Munsey's,* and *Godey's,* McClure cut the price of his magazine to ten cents, and the die was cast in the country for the reign of the low-priced, heavily illustrated popular monthly publication. Older, "quality" magazines like *Harper's,** *Century,* and *Scribner's,** decried the new revolution in journalism, and regarded *McClure's* and the other cheap monthlies as threats to the higher, purer literary standard that they felt they had established.[1] In fact, the comparative quality of *McClure's* was borne out in its distinguished roster of contributors: Rudyard, Kipling, William Dean Howells, Robert Louis Stevenson and Conan Doyle, among others.

Much of the popular appeal of the early issues resided in such features as the Human Documents series, devoted to portraits of famous men taken at different ages in their lives. The publication of Ida Tarbell's "Napoleon," based on pictures of the Hubbard collection, was the highlight of this series. The popularity of this feature was surpassed even further by a similar publication in 1895, "The Early Life of Lincoln," also written by Tarbell, who interviewed scores of people to create her text. These series were major factors in the magazine's leap in circulation, which by 1896 reached 250,000, putting *McClure's* ahead of all other American magazines in popularity and advertising patronage.

From the beginning, it was the quality fictional writing in the magazine that helped to establish its prestige. McClure's success and contacts with English literary agents and their writers during the years of his syndicate publication continued with the new magazine. Serials by famous authors were prominent: Stevenson's *The Ebb Tide* (1894), and Kipling's *Captains Courageous* (1896–1897), *Stalky and Co.* (1898–1899), and "Jungle Tales." Viola Roseboro, a reader for the literary department, was instrumental in the discovery of new writers such as O. Henry, whose work was sent from prison and reached national magazine publication for the first time in *McClure's* in December 1899 with "Whistling Dick's Christmas Stocking." Another Roseboro discovery was Booth Tarkington's novel *The Gentleman from Indiana.* Established short story writers like Thomas Hardy, Conan Doyle, and Joel Chandler Harris were featured, but risks were taken with unknowns such as Stephen Crane and Jack London. Literary writing in *McClure's* was strongly directed toward social concerns; notable contributors in this genre were Israel Zangwill, the Jewish writer of London ghetto life, Brand Whitlock, Henry Harland, and, above all, Josiah Flynt, an ex-convict who worked incognito as "Cigarette," and gathered material firsthand for his series, "True Stories from the Underworld," inaugurated in 1900. In the realm of nonfiction, as well, *McClure's* became known for the currency and dramatic élan of its well-researched science and travel articles. Alexander Graham Bell and Thomas Edison contributed features on scientific advancements, and there were thrilling accounts of new discoveries such as the X-ray (April 1896) and Marconi's wireless (June 1899), and of exploratory feats, such as the attempt to reach the North Pole (June 1894).

The stress on realism and immediacy in both literary and nonfiction writing in *McClure's* early years laid the groundwork for journalistic techniques of the muckraking years in the magazine's evolution. S. S. McClure had a great ability to scent the needs of the reading public. Lincoln Steffens, one of his most famous investigative reporters, characterized him as " 'the wildeditor' . . . , the receiver of the ideas of his day.' "[2] It was probably this journalistic savvy that led to the production of the landmark issue of *McClure's*, the famous muckraking issue of January 1903 that became a milestone in magazine journalism history. Since 1898, when McClure sent Ray Stannard Baker and Stephen Crane to cover the Spanish-American War, the contents of the magazine had turned perceptibly toward political reform.

In the fall of 1901, Ida Tarbell's research abilities were tapped by McClure for a series on the oil trusts, which was to become her classic, *The History of the Standard Oil Company*. Lincoln Steffens had been urged by McClure to learn how to edit the magazine by doing investigative journalism in the real world, and his observations and reporting of urban political corruption in America's heartland culminated in the series "Tweed Days in St. Louis." Finally, in late 1902, the United Mine Workers' strike in Pennsylvania hit McClure as another sign of civil lawlessness, and he assigned Ray Baker to cover the situation; Baker's observations evolved into "The Right to Work," a series of case histories of the men who refused to strike. The work of Tarbell, Steffens, and Baker all appeared in the issue of January 1903. McClure prefaced the features with an editorial statement on his magazine's fortuitous "discovery" of muckraking, concluding: "Capitalists, workingmen, politicians, citizens—all breaking the law or letting it be broken. Who is there left to uphold it? . . . — none but all of us."[3]

The muckraking years of the magazine achieved measurable journalistic and political results. By 1906 the literature of exposure as exemplified by *McClure's* was being hailed as an art by critical reviewers. Tarbell's documentation of Standard Oil's illegal dealings was instrumental in governmental investigations that led to trust-breaking legislation. The Mann Act, passed in 1910, resulted from the impact of George Kibbe Turner's exposé of the white slave trade organized by urban political machines, "The Daughters of the Poor" (1910). However, muckraking was not a great financial success for *McClure's*, and circulation did not grow rapidly over these years. In 1905, McClure made his last profit on the magazine. His vast business schemes, such as the establishment of a bank and an insurance company, called for major changes in the whole organization of the enterprise. His staff, including his partner Phillips, had not been consulted on these plans and rebelled. In 1906 Phillips, Steffens, Baker, and Tarbell, with several other staff members, left the magazine to establish their own journal, the *American*.

The new phase of *McClure's* under a reorganized staff continued to focus on muckraking. Turner was recruited to investigate and report on the corruption of city politics and the influence of machines like Tammany on all aspects of American life. Will Irwin and John Moody presented a long series, "The Masters of Capital in America," that exposed the control over American society exercised by the moguls of Wall Street. Willa Cather replaced Ida Tarbell as the major editor on *McClure's* staff. The magazine maintained its high level of literary work with Cather's stories, and contributions by established authors like London, Tarkington, Mrs. Humphrey Ward, O. Henry, and Rex Beach; a strong poetry department was managed by the poet Witter Bynner. The magazine's attractive format and vivid illustrations were sustained with work from superior artists like John La Farge, Maxfield Parrish, and Charles Dana Gibson.

By 1911, however, McClure's financial ineptness and risk taking forced a buyout of the magazine by Cameron Mackenzie and Frederick Collins. McClure remained titular editor until 1913, when Mackenzie took over. The magazine continued to feature quality literature by authors like Arnold Bennett, G. K. Chesterton, and P. G. Wodehouse, but the magazine began a financial and journalistic decline as popular interest in muckraking and public affairs waned, especially after World War I. Collins sold *McClure's* in 1919 to Herbert Kaufman, who maintained the high level of literature with work by Vicente Blasco Ibáñez, Edna Ferber, and Zane Grey. However, circulation continued to fall, and the magazine petitioned for a receiver in bankruptcy in 1921. Moody Gates of the Lupton Company took over, and brought back S. S. McClure as editor, and eventually turned the publication over to him in 1924, as it continued to lose money. The quality of the magazine had deteriorated badly, and publication was suspended after four months; it was revived again in 1925 after new financing was obtained. McClure's energetic efforts to solicit promising contributions and further financing was ineffectual, and he gave up with the January 1926 issue. The publication was revived a third time with William Randolph Hearst's money under the title *McClure's: The Magazine of Romance*, in 1926. Arthur McKeogh edited the magazine as a vulgar purveyor of cheap fiction and sensationalistic features. In 1927 under the editorship of Arthur Sullivant, the publication improved and attracted contributions from Carl Sandburg, Frazier Hunt, and Konrad Bercovici. In 1928, Hearst sold *McClure's* to James R. Quirk, who also published *Photoplay*; the old muckraking journal reappeared as the *New McClure's Magazine*. In March 1929, what had once been a serious, prestigious, and respected publication, produced by some of the greatest journalists in American magazine history, was merged into the *Smart Set*.*

Notes

1. *Independent,* 27 June 1895, p. 11.
2. Lincoln Steffens in Peter Lyons, *Success Story: The Life and Times of S. S. McClure* (New York: Scribner's, 1963), p. 268.
3. *McClure's,* January 1903, p. 335.

Information Sources

BIBLIOGRAPHY

Filler, Louis. *The Muckrakers.* University Park: Pennsylvania State University Press, 1976.

Lyons, Peter. *Success Story: The Life and Times of S. S. McClure.* New York: Scribner's, 1963.

McClure, Samuel Sidney. *My Autobiography.* New York: F. Ungar Publishing Co., 1914.

Tarbell, Ida. *All in the Day's Work.* New York: Macmillan Co., 1939.

Wilson, Harold S. *McClure's Magazine and the Muckrakers.* Princeton: Princeton University Press, 1970.

INDEX SOURCES

Each volume indexed. *Poole's Index* (1983–1906); *Readers' Guide* (1900–1916); *Index to McClure's Magazine, Vols. I–XVIII, 1893–1902* (New York: S. S. McClure, 1903).

LOCATION SOURCES

Widely available. Available in microform.

Publication History

MAGAZINE TITLE AND TITLE CHANGES

McClure's Magazine, June 1893–June 1928; *New McClure's Magazine,* July 1928–March 1929.

VOLUME AND ISSUE DATA

Vols. 1–57, June 1893–August 1924; monthly; new series: vol. 1, May-October 1925; vol. 2, November 1925–December 1926; vol. 58–62, January 1927–March 1929.

PUBLISHERS AND PLACE OF PUBLICATION

S. S. McClure Company, New York, 1893–1911 (McClure and Phillips to 1906, then McClure); McClure Publications (Frederick Collins, president), 1911–1921; McClure Publishing Company (Moody Gates, president), 1922–April 1924; McClure Press (S. S. McClure, owner), May-August 1924; S. S. McClure Company (S. S. McClure, owner), May 1925–January 1926; International Publishing (W. R. Hearst, owner), 1926–1928; Magus Publishing Company (James R. Quirk, president), 1928–1929.

EDITORS

S. S. McClure, June 1898–August 1913, March 1922–January 1926; Cameron Mackenzie, September 1913–April 1915; Frederick L. Collins, May 1915–

February 1920; Herbert Kaufman, March 1920–March 1927; Arthur McKeogh, July 1926–March 1927; James R. Quirk, July 1928–March 1929.
CIRCULATION
    250,000 (1896).

Diana A. Chlebek

MECHANIX ILLUSTRATED. See HOME MECHANIX

MODERN MATURITY

The October-November (1988) issue of *Modern Maturity* proclaims its "new leadership role as the nation's largest circulation magazine." And, indeed, if it has not already surpassed *TV Guide** and *Reader's Digest,** it may soon do so. Each member of the AARP (American Association of Retired Persons) receives six issues of *Modern Maturity,* a bimonthly magazine, each year. Spouses of AARP members are also automatically members, and the demographics supplied by the U.S. Census Bureau indicate that "senior" citizens are a rapidly increasing percentage of the total population. Originally aimed at the sixty-five and over group, *Modern Maturity* has more recently aimed successfully at the fifty-five–plus group and has been courting those over fifty since 1983. Applications pour in at the rate of as many as 8,000 a day, in many cases because of the attractive discounts on many goods and services available to members.[1]

In 1984 *Modern Maturity* national sales manager Peter Hanson estimated the fifty and over age group as representing 61 million consumers, a number that will reach 76 million by the year 2000, a 25 percent jump when the total population increase is projected at only 14 percent by the same year. He further noted that this age group buys 43 percent of all new domestic cars and 25 percent of all cosmetic and bath products.[2]

How gratified the founder of the National Retired Teachers Association (NRTA) as well as of the AARP would be! In 1947, having retired in 1944 after forty-one years of teaching, Ethel Percy Andrus founded the NRTA, and in 1950 she established the *NRTA Journal.* In 1954 she brought to fruition the first retirement residence for teachers, Grey Gables, and in 1958 she founded the AARP as well as its journal, *Modern Maturity.* Because of Dr. Andrus, the Acacias Nursing Home became a reality in 1959, and in 1967 the Andrus Apartments for convalescents were added to the existing facilities, both of which are in Ojai, California. In 1961 she had founded the Retirement Research and Welfare Association; in 1963, the Association of Retired Persons International; and in 1963, the Institute of Lifetime Learning. Dr. Andrus died in 1967.[3]

After Dr. Andrus's death, Hubert C. Pryor assumed the editorship of *Modern Maturity*; in 1982 Ian Ledgerwood became editor, and Hubert Pryor became editorial director. In 1983, Ian Ledgerwood became sole editor, and Hubert Pryor assumed duties of publishing coordinator, along with Robert E. Wood, publishing director. Three editors in thirty years represents high stability in the magazine industry.

Another interesting factor is that *Modern Maturity* has absorbed two other journals in its thirty-year history. In 1960, with volume 3, number 2, it absorbed *Journal of Lifetime Living*, and in 1981 it took in the *NRTA Journal*, a sister magazine all along. However, each year the October-November issue is sub-headed the NRTA edition.

One magazine expert decided to make a list of the thirty magazines she would choose for a public library if her budget allowed for only that number. Among the thirty that Gail Pool chose was *Modern Maturity*, for "a balanced collection for an average community." She rates it as "far better" than its nearest competition, *50 Plus*, a magazine that emphasizes "beauty" far too much for the tastes of the mature citizen.[4] Pool finds *Modern Maturity* to be "well-written and well-edited, and it succeeds in being informative without being didactic. Unfortunately, it falls short of being stimulating."[5]

The first issue in September-October 1958 stated the goals that *Modern Maturity* hoped to attain: "a forum for topics relevant to retired persons, . . . a showcase for the accomplishments of retired persons, and . . . a vehicle for a broad range of general-interest information."[6] Dr. Andrus intended to prove that life did not end at retirement and to encourage "self-renewal through activity and service."[7] Robert E. Wood, publishing director today, agrees with Dr. Andrus about the purpose for *Modern Maturity*:

> The magazine is not for old people. People were looked at as polychromatic until age 59 or 64, then bingo, they turned some age at which they were grey and all the same and on the porch whittling . . . . This new generation of older Americans has grown up with the idea that they were going to live longer and they've planned better, for the most part.[8]

As a nonprofit association magazine, *Modern Maturity* does not depend on advertising for its survival, for a large circulation is guaranteed. "The cost of this situation is a certain placidity."[9] However, in the past few years, the AARP has taken a more serious interest in selling ads. Peter Hanson, national sales manager, encourages those interested in buying ad space to "take a bite of the golden apple."[10] But there are certain considerations to be met in keeping with the goals of the original magazine. Mature models are pictured in virtually all the ads. And the kinds of products are obviously those that appeal to the mature consumer (vacations at Sun City, denture creams) and those that appeal to almost anyone (walking shoes, computers, books). *Modern Maturity* does not accept ads for cigarettes and accepts very few ads for alcoholic beverages. In addition, AARP services are promoted: health insurance, investments, pharmacy and travel services. But *Modern Maturity* is not planning to be heavily loaded with ads. "In 100 pages of our magazine, we feel there's as much reading material as *Vogue* has in 250," according to Wood.[11] He continues: "We won't publish any ad that tends to give the aura of pain, suffering, misery, old people hobbled . . . . We won't lie about anything, but we want to improve the image of aging."[12]

One long-time subscriber expresses her interest in *Modern Maturity* this way:

> I have been privileged to get *Modern Maturity* for many, many years. It covers information on a variety of subjects: health hints, gardening, recipes, insurance of all kinds, social security, and many others. I enjoy "Fun Fare" and the puzzles and look forward to each edition.[13]

Some years ago Dr. Andrus noted that *"Modern Maturity* has become for some the nearest substitute they have for a 'letter from home' and a view toward the future."[14]

The profile of the typical *Modern Maturity* reader is significant. A 1982 Simmons subscriber study revealed that 38.5 percent of the readers attended or graduated from college and that the median age is sixty-seven.[15]

With the graying of America, *Modern Maturity* has the potential to be the number 1 magazine in circulation for a number of years to come. With the shift in emphasis from those sixty-five and over to those fifty and over, and with the new attention to the advertising available, *Modern Maturity* seems to be going for that membership in a much more aggressive way than ever before. Perhaps now editorial policy can be less "middle of the road" and the magazine itself can be more "stimulating" without losing faithful readers.[16] There has been an incredible lack of attention paid to this magazine in the press to this point; "regardless of its 22 million readers (each issue is read by almost 3 people). *Modern Maturity* has what may be the lowest profile in publishing."[17] In all likelihood that is simply symptomatic of the fact that the elderly have not received their due attention in this country for some years. Those days seem to be over. The sheer increase in numbers of senior citizens will change all that. *Modern Maturity* now has the opportunity to command significant clout.

Ethel Percy Andrus once defined what AARP is and what it is not. Regarding politics, "AARP definitely does not favor or approve the program or platform of either political party or of any candidate. Also it does not limit its legislative activity to the general welfare of only its membership. It accepts no favors or support from any political party or group."[18] A 1984 survey found that 40 percent of the membership is Democratic, 40 percent of the membership is Republican, and the rest identify themselves as independent.[19] So in taking a political stand, AARP runs the risk of alienating a substantial number of its members. However, the organization, through its lobby in Washington and through *Modern Maturity*, does wield considerable clout on issues important to the elderly. Margaret Kuhn, founder of the more militant Gray Panthers, is pleased with the new activism that AARP now espouses: "AARP made a hell of a lot of money selling insurance and conveying the idea that old age is a time for having fun and taking trips.

It's good to see they now have a social conscience.''[20] A recent issue concerned cost-of-living adjustments for Social Security recipients; heavy lobbying by AARP plus Claude Pepper's threat to call for a roll call vote in the House "guaranteed" passage. No political figure wants to go on record as having voted against such a large and powerful constituency. In other matters, AARP is now urging homebuilders to consider the elderly by installing grips and nonslip surfaces.[21] The AARP is still centrist, but the possibilities are more and more obvious. With its growing circulation figures, *Modern Maturity* is sure to be a much more powerful media voice from here on into the twenty-first century.

Although Dr. Andrus passed away in 1967, and although there have been changes in the format of *Modern Maturity* and in its commercial endeavors, the magazine and its staff members still adhere to Dr. Andrus' advice. Many remember her as a "genius," as a fascinating individual who took a personal interest in her staff.[22] Her last editorial, published in the August-September 1967 issue, to some seems to have been her farewell, as if she knew that this might be her final piece. She based the essay on thoughts from Ralph Cake, "Just for the Day." She chronicled an entire year's events, leading to the September celebration of Labor Day and the value of work, no matter what, and she closed with a quote from Dr. William Osler: "Live neither in the past nor in the future, but for each day's work, absorb your entire energies and satisfy your wildest ambition." (p. 6) This seems to reflect the philosophy of the magazine itself and of the many senior citizens who value everything that the AARP does for them. Dr. Andrus lives on because of the vision that she had and because of the work that she contributed to making that vision a reality.

Notes

1. Lee Smith, "The World According to AARP," *Fortune,* 29 February 1988, p. 96.

2. *"Modern Maturity*: Sales Call," *Madison Avenue,* 26 October 1984, p. 103.

3. *The Wisdom of Ethel Percy Andrus,* compiled by Dorothy Crippen, Ruth Lana, Jean Libman Block, Thomas E. Zetkov, and Gordon Elliott (Long Beach, Calif.: National Retired Teachers Association and American Association of Retired Persons, 1968), pp. 9–12.

4. Gail Pool, "Magazines," *Wilson Library Bulletin,* February 1986, p. 55.

5. Gail Pool, "Magazines," *Wilson Library Bulletin,* November 1983, p. 220.

6. First issue quoted in Pool, p. 220.

7. Ibid., p. 221.

8. Wood quoted in Elizabeth Christian, "Retiree-Aimed Magazine Has Come of Age," *Los Angeles Times,* 17 February 1984, sec. 5, p. 1.

9. Pool, 1983, p. 221.

10. *"Modern Maturity*: Sales Call," p. 104.

11. Wood quoted in Christian, p. 1.

12. Ibid.

13. Cleo H. Livingston, of Columbia, South Carolina, is a retired schoolteacher who has subscribed to *Modern Maturity* for many years. She is quoted in a personal letter to this writer, 17 November 1988.

14. *The Wisdom of Ethel Percy Andrus*, p. 316.

15. *"Modern Maturity*: Sales Call," p. 105.

16. Pool, 1983, p. 221. Florence Gross, articles editor of *Modern Maturity*, remarked that the magazine is "decidedly middle of the road."

17. Christian, p. 1.

18. *The Wisdom of Ethel Percy Andrus*, p. 304.

19. Smith, p. 96.

20. Ibid., p. 97.

21. Ibid., p. 98.

22. Eileen Dawson, *Modern Maturity* editorial staff, in a telephone conversation on 17 August 1989.

Information Sources

BIBLIOGRAPHY

Christian, Elizabeth. "Retiree-Aimed Magazine Has Come of Age." *Los Angeles Times,* 17 February 1984, sec. 5, p. 1.

Dawson, Eileen. *Modern Maturity* editorial staff. Telephone conversation, 17 August 1989.

"Modern Maturity: Sales Call." *Madison Avenue*, 26 October 1984, pp. 102–6.

Pool, Gail. "Magazines." *Wilson Library Bulletin*, November 1983, pp. 220–21.

———. "Magazines." *Wilson Library Bulletin*, February 1986, p. 55.

Smith, Lee. "The World According to AARP," *Fortune*, 29 February 1988, pp. 96–98.

The Wisdom of Ethel Percy Andrus. Compiled by Dorothy Crippen, Ruth Lana, Jean Libman Block, Thomas E. Zetkov, and Gordon Elliott. Long Beach, Calif.: National Retired Teachers Association and American Association of Retired Persons, 1968.

INDEX SOURCES

Access (1975–present); *Magazine Index* (1977–present); *Readers' Guide* (1988–present).

LOCATION SOURCES

Available in microform.

Publication History

MAGAZINE TITLE AND TITLE CHANGES

Modern Maturity.

VOLUME AND ISSUE DATA

Bimonthly. First issue September-October, 1958.

PUBLISHER AND PLACE OF PUBLICATION

American Association of Retired Persons. Washington, D.C., 1958–1970; Long Beach, California, 1971–1986; Lakewood, California, 1986–current.

EDITORS
    Ethel Percy Andrus, 1958–1967; Hubert C. Pryor, 1967–1982; Ian Ledgerwood,
    1982–current.
CIRCULATION
    12,639,002 (1985).

Barbara Nourie

MODERN MECHANICS AND INVENTIONS. See HOME MECHANIX

MONEY

Money magazine, a monthly journal of personal finance and business, was
first published in October 1972. Its editorial philosophy was perhaps expressed
best by the last "Editor's Note" from William Rukeyser before he stepped down
as managing editor in April 1980. Rukeyser said that *Money*'s purpose was to
explain financial developments in terms of their impact on individuals and to
suggest how the public can defend itself and capitalize on opportunities.

The August 1981 issue presents a typical table of contents: a special report
on best car choices, "Picking the Best Day Care," "Collectibles: Are They on
the Verge of Collapse?," "Insurance: Toning Up Your Health Policy," "One
Family's Finances," "Tax Shelters: New Relief with R & D's," "No Way
Without a Will," and "A Buyer's Guide to California Wines."

Each February, *Money* gives a special report on taxes and a year-end performance ranking of companies listed on the New York Stock Exchange. The March
issues of election years (1976 and 1980) contained reports on candidates' personal
finances. Other noteworthy special reports have been "Job Meccas for the 80's"
(May 1978), "The Two Paycheck Life" (January 1979), "The Shabby Record
of Bank Trust Departments" (November 1980). "An Inside Look at Royal
Riches" (article on the personal finances of Prince Charles, July 1981), and
"Choosing the Best Computer for You" (November 1982).

In addition to regular articles, *Money*'s departments have included *Money*
Letter: Washington, Wall Street Letter, Shopping Center, *Money* Helps (answers
to financial inquiries), Reviewing Stand (reviews of finance books), Fund Watch,
Current Accounts (miscellaneous items regarding money and human nature),
Investment Scorecard, Money Profile (essays on individual financial experi-
ences), and others.

The 30 November 1981 issue of *Advertising Age* reported the following account
of *Money*'s success:

At a time when new magazines often come with a fanfare and go with a
whimper—sometimes only a few months later—*Money* is almost a textbook
example of how a magazine can make it if it has the backing of a large,

profitable corporation that is willing to stick with the publication through the lean years. (p. 32)

The same review noted that advertising revenues at *Money* had risen from $11.7 million in 1979 to $22 million in 1981.

Money was again reviewed in the 6 February 1984 issue of *Advertising Age* as a model imitated by other financial magazines: "*Money*'s 'how-to' approach has been imitated by many other publications—company officials point to personal finance sections in *Fortune, Forbes, Business Week,* and *Dun's Business Month*, as well as the "Money" section of *USA Today*" (p. M–5).

This how-to approach is illustrated well by Richard Eisenberg's article in the February 1986 issue entitled "Your Finances at 40." It provides specific recommendations on maintaining cash reserves, disability and health insurance, individual retirement accounts, changing careers, paying for the college education of children, and long-term investments. The essay is followed by another that illustrates the personal experiences of three "baby boomers" and their financial plans in the middle years of life.

Money's circulation has grown from an initial 225,000 copies in 1972 to 650,000 in 1976, and currently prints 1,650,000 copies.

In 1984, the editors of *Money* began to print separate issues entitled *Money Guides*. They are *Personal Finance* (1984), *Your Home* and *Planning Now for Your Successful Retirement* (1985), and *The Stock Market* and *Your IRA* (1986).

In 1986, *Money* was given the National Magazine Award for general excellence among large reviews by the American Society of Magazine Editors.

Information Sources

INDEX SOURCES
> A comprehensive index appears in each January issue; *Business Perinlishs Index* (1976–present); *Readers' Guide* (1978–present).

LOCATION SOURCES
> Widely available.

Publication History

MAGAZINE TITLE AND TITLE CHANGES
> *Money*.

VOLUME AND ISSUE DATA
> Vol. 1, October 1972–current, monthly.

PUBLISHER AND PLACE OF PUBLICATION
> Time, Inc., New York.

EDITORS
   Hedley Donovan, 1972–1979; Henry Anatole Grunwald, 1979–current.
CIRCULATION
   1.8 million (1987).

Lawrence W. Lynch

MOTHER EARTH NEWS

The most successful of the alternative-life-style magazines is *Mother Earth News*. Originally inspired by the back-to-nature movement of the late 1960s, the magazine still has plenty of vigor, claiming a paid circulation of almost 800,000.[1]

The force behind the *Mother Earth News*—Mr. Mother himself—was John Shuttleworth. In the summer of 1969 he and his wife, Jane, were doing sales-promotion work in Cleveland—and hating it. Like many others in those days, they wanted to drop out of the corporate-oriented system. Both had grown up on farms, and they wanted to buy their own and settle down.[2] But that decision, they soon became convinced, would not be one they could make on their own. They would not be able to revive the small family farm in what they saw as an increasingly corporate and centralized society. Before they could realize their dream of going back to the land, they would have to help others go back to the land.[3]

They could do that, they thought, by publishing a little newsletter in their spare time. As John sketched out the first issue, however, it became clear to him that what was needed was a magazine. They quit their public relations jobs, borrowed money, and with $1,500 in capital and a small cottage near Madison, Ohio, they put together the first issue of *Mother* in the fall and winter of 1969.[4] Their goal was nothing less than

> to change the world completely by helping all us little people throw the vested interests . . . off our backs so that we can all live richer, fuller, freer, more self-directed, self-sufficient, and self-reliant lives while encouraging us all to put the long-term interests of the planet ahead of the short-term profits of the consumer society.[5]

They not only made it past the first issue (to their surprise), but found such a demand that they spent ten years of their lives—eighteen hours a day, seven days a week, sometimes long stretches without sleep—trying to meet that demand. They filled the bimonthly magazine's pages with advice on food, health, housing, energy, and the environment. They distilled information on witching for water and milking a goat, on pruning apple trees and raising strawberries, on building a shelter or a log cabin or a teepee.

Soon *Mother*'s mailbag was bulging with ''Dear Mother'' letters—about 7,500 a month.[6] By 1978 paid circulation reached 450,000.[7] The staff increased accordingly: from the two Shuttleworths in 1969 to thirty-one people in 1972 to eighty-six people in 1978.[8]

The operation, which had been moved in 1973 to the more temperate climate of Hendersonville, North Carolina, expanded too. By 1975 it included, in addition to the magazine itself, a syndicated radio show, a syndicated newspaper column, a mail-order store, a distributing company, and a mail-order hardware store. Considerable profits were funneled back into the operation—into equipment for *Mother* and into projects such as solar energy experiments and a methane-gas–powered car.[9]

Not all of *Mother*'s readers were pleased with this expansion. Some complained that John Shuttleworth was getting involved in too many things, that he was spreading himself too thin, and that the magazine was suffering as a consequence (running stories on, for example, ham radios, which homesteaders were unlikely to own). Shuttleworth had little patience with such critics: "Either you're going to take over the world or you're not. . . . What I'm after is a power base for us. . . . And you've got to get big to do it." After all, "how many times can you tell people how to milk a goat?"[10]

Having converted the homesteaders, Shuttleworth set his sights on the suburb dwellers—there was no reason why Joe Suburb could not become more self-reliant and more conscious of the planet's fragile ecosystem.[11] But the task of broadening the magazine's appeal would be left to others. The Shuttleworths, having devoted ten years to the cause, sold the magazine to three employees in 1979.[12]

Within three years the new owners, publisher Bob Lieb, editor Bruce Woods, and president David Adams, doubled the magazine's revenues (to $20 million) and paid circulation (to 900,000 copies a year).[13] They attributed their success to having changed the magazine to appeal to changing readers, many of whom (they argued) were not ready to lead independent rural lives. Many of these readers were (they said) baby boomers who, having attained success in the corporate world, felt unsatisfied and escaped to exurban areas—at least for weekends or summers. To serve these readers, the new owners included articles not only on harvesting huckleberries and raising chickens, but also on doing aerobics and building a garden sprayer. "So what we're trying to do," said editor Woods, "is answer the needs of those people who have taken the plunge as well as those who are working in careers and looking forward to being able to do it some day."[14]

The owners also brought in a sophisticated sales team that succeeded in broadening the magazine's advertising base.[15] Soon one could see ads not only for wood-burning stoves and specialty hoes, but also for Weed Eaters and Puppy Formula. (No cigarette ads, of course, but there were ads for Jack Daniel's Whiskey and for automobiles, which may or may not be considered harmful to the body or environment.) Still, as in the Shuttleworth years, the magazine contained relatively little advertising, most of its revenues coming from its hefty $3 cover price and $18-a-year (full price) subscriptions.[16]

Despite their achievements, the owners were still under economic pressure from the buyout and themselves sought a buyer. In the fall of 1985 they sold the magazine to Owen J. Lipstein, the founder and owner of the highly successful *American Health* magazine.[17] Lipstein, noting the appeal of country music and country living, wasted no time in giving *Mother* the subtitle *The Original Country Magazine*, then poured $900,000 into design (more color, better-quality paper) and $550,000 into promotion.[18]

Nevertheless, *Mother* has not lost its purpose; it still runs articles on gardening, food, crafts, and the outdoors. Lipstein bristles at the suggestion that *Mother*'s content has been diluted. "We didn't buy this magazine to rid it of its conscience. This magazine has a mission, the distillation of information; it takes a stand." Again: "We are not changing the magazine in any major way . . . although negative political stuff [such as the suggestion that if you live in a city you are bad] will be eliminated. . . . The latter wasn't a distillation of information, it was theology."[19]

Today's circulation is down to about 750,000 from a high of over a million in 1982.[20] This drop might be attributed to a lessening of public concern about energy and to the affluence of *Mother*'s audience: the more wealth people acquire, the less likely they are to want to "do for themselves."[21] Since 1986, however, paid circulation has risen steadily (it was 745,000 in 1987; 790,000 in 1988), which suggests that Lipstein's enhancements may be having an effect.[22]

One may argue that *Mother* has "sold out to the establishment." But one may also argue that it has merely adapted to changing circumstances. A failure to adapt may explain why the *Whole Earth Catalog, Mother*'s early competitor, became extinct in 1971. In contrast, *Mother*—with a paid circulation of about 750,000 and a potential for growth—is far from extinct. Whether the current fad is communes or careers or country living, *Mother* succeeds in attracting readers who wish to lead healthy and independent lives, and who wish to do the earth a good turn by doing something good for themselves.

Notes

1. Statement of Ownership, *Mother Earth News,* January-February, 1987.

2. Mary Huntzinger, "*Mother* Spreads the Word," *McCall's*, February 1972, p. 56.

3. John N. Cole, "Mr. Mother," *Horticulture*, February 1978, p. 27.

4. Ibid., pp. 20, 27–28.

5. John Shuttleworth, "Report to *Mother's* Readers," *Mother Earth News*, November 1979, p. 44.

6. Huntzinger, p. 56.

7. Cole, p. 20.

8. Huntzinger, p. 56; Cole, p. 22.

9. Gregory Jaynes, "*Mother Earth*, Mon Amour," *New Times*, 7 February 1975, p. 49.

10. Ibid., p. 51.

11. Cole, p. 25.

12. Hermine Meinhard, "Healthy Life Makes *Mother Earth News* Robust," *Advertising Age*, 18 October 1984, p. 46. The price was reported to be about $10 million. A spokeswoman for *Mother Earth News* said that she did not know John Shuttleworth's current activities (telephone conversation with the author, 12 March 1987).

13. Sandra Salmans, "Beyond *Mother Earth News*," *New York Times*, 9 August 1983. Section D1 (late edition), 29 (National edition).

14. Meinhard, p. 46.

15. Ibid.

16. Salmans.

17. Philip H. Dougherty, "Magazine Publisher's Acquisition," *New York Times*, 21 November 1985. Section D27 (late edition), 53 (National edition).

18. Stuart J. Elliot, "*Mother Earth* Getting a Face-lift," *Advertising Age*, 5 May 1986, p. 36.

19. Ibid.

20. Statement of Ownership, *Mother Earth News*, January-February, 1983; January-February, 1987.

21. These possible explanations were cited by a *Mother Earth News* spokesman on 12 March 1987, telephone conversation with the author.

22. Statement of Ownership, *Mother Earth News*, January-February, 1988; January-February, 1989.

Information Sources

BIBLIOGRAPHY
Cole, John N. "Mr. Mother." *Horticulture,* February 1978.
Dougherty, Philip H. "Magazine Publisher's Acquisition." *New York Times*, 21 November 1985, Section D27 (Late edition), 53 (National edition).
Elliot, Stuart J. "*Mother Earth* Getting a Face-lift." *Advertising Age*, 5 May 1986, p. 36.
Huntzinger, Mary. "*Mother* Spreads the Word." *McCall's*, February 1972, p. 56.
Jaynes, Gregory. "*Mother Earth*, Mon Amour." *New Times*, 7 February 1975.
LeRoux, Margaret. "Salt of the (Mother) Earth." *Advertising Age*, 19 October 1981, sec. 2, p. S–42.
Meinhard, Hermine. "Healthy Life Makes *Mother Earth News* Robust." *Advertising Age*, 18 October 1984, p. 46.
Salmans, Sandra. "Beyond *Mother Earth News*." *New York Times*, 9 August 1983, Section D1 (Late edition), 29 (National edition).
Shuttleworth, John. "Report to *Mother's* Readers." *Mother Earth News*, November 1979, pp. 42–45.
INDEX SOURCES
   Access: The Supplementary Index to Periodicals; Magazine Index (1977–present); *Readers' Guide to Periodical Literature* (1978–present; *Alternative Press Index* (1970–1977).
LOCATION SOURCES
   Library of Congress, many other libraries. Available in microform.

Publication History

MAGAZINE TITLE AND TITLE CHANGES
> *Mother Earth News.* (1970–1986); *Mother Earth News: The Original Country Magazine.* (1986–current).

VOLUME AND ISSUE DATA
> No. 1, January 1970–present, bimonthly (six issues a year).

PUBLISHER AND PLACE OF PUBLICATION
> John Shuttleworth, 1970–1973, Madison, Ohio; John Shuttleworth, 1973–1979, Hendersonville, North Carolina; Robert M. Lieb, 1980–1985, Hendersonville, North Carolina; Owen J. Lipstein, 1986–1988, Hendersonville, North Carolina; Don W. Vergana, 1989–current, Hendersonville, North Carolina.

EDITORS
> John Shuttleworth, 1970–1979; Bruce Woods, 1980–present.

CIRCULATION
> 796,096 paid; 11,132 nonpaid.

> *David R. Kohut*

MOTHER JONES

An advertisement in the June 1980 issue of *Mother Jones* explains why its founders named their publication for the turn-of-the-century labor organizer and hell-raiser: "We loved her spirit, energy, assertiveness, and optimism, and because the things she fought for represent the values we believe in. And because she believed . . . that 'revolutions are made of hope, not despair' " (June 1980, 143). *Mother Jones* was conceived in 1974, and the first issue appeared in February 1976. According to its publishers, it became the fastest growing magazine in the United States by 1980 (January 1980, p. 16), and following a slight decline during the early 1980s, began gaining ground again by 1986. Circulation in 1986 topped 180,000, and the magazine claims readership of 2.5 people per copy, or 500,000 total readers (January 1987, p. 8). These respectable circulation figures did not prevent *Mother Jones*, dedicated initially to "confronting American Capitalism head on" (February-March 1980, p. 5), from making significant changes in marketing and design with the February-March 1989 issue. With film actress and social activist Susan Sarandon on the cover, *Mother Jones* became *The New Mother Jones: People, Politics and Other Passions.*

Self-proclaimed as a "magazine for the rest of us," *Mother Jones* is a publication of the San Francisco–based Foundation for National Progress. Richard Parker, Adam Hochschild, and Paul Jacobs established the foundation in 1974 in order to publish a magazine and create a center for radical scholarship.[1] In broad terms, though, this nonprofit foundation aims to conduct studies and research concerning problems related to the political and economic progress of American civilization. Subscribers to the magazine are members. In order to qualify for tax-exempt status, the magazine must not be commercial, but educational. From 1981 to 1983, *Mother Jones* waged a successful, albeit costly, battle with the Internal Revenue Service over this status.

The organizational structure under which *Mother Jones* operated at its start was in many ways unique. The so-called democratic management consisted of a controlling board of directors that was elected from the staff. Initially, the magazine operated largely as a committee, with no editor-in-chief, but an editorial board that made editorial decisions as a group. Each year one member of the editorial board would be elected as the managing editor: Adam Hochschild in 1976, Jeffrey Klein in 1977, Amanda Spake in 1978, and Zina Klapper in 1979. According to a statement in the April 1979 issue, this system was devised "not because of an ideological commitment to collectivity, but because it has proved an efficient way to work" (April 1979, p. 5). Similarly, the publisher was first elected by the circulation, business, and advertising employees. Publishers of *Mother Jones* who have served under this method are Richard Parker, Mark Dowie, and Jacques Marchand. Finally, as recently as June 1979, the editors stated that regarding salaries, "No one at *Mother Jones* can be paid more than twice as much as anyone else" (June 1979, p. 5).

In 1981, the group method of governance at *Mother Jones* changed and the management structure was reorganized. As a result of the change, both the publisher and the executive editor gained increased authority, and became directly accountable to the foundation board. Robin Wolaner was the first publisher to serve in this capacity; she did so until July 1985, when Don Hazen assumed the publisher's responsibilities. David Assman became publisher in 1989. Deirdre English was the first editor in 1981, a position she held until volatile 1986. In that year the editorship changed hands three times, with Michael Moore's two-issue tenure completed amid a rather ugly dispute reported in the *Nation* and in *Mother Jones's* own pages.[2] Adam Hochschild emerged as the executive editor in the final issue for the year, and held the position until Douglas Foster was appointed in 1987.

One would expect *Mother Jones's* readership to be comprised of counterculture progressives and radicals. In 1984, however, of its 220,000 subscribers, 60 percent were between twenty-five and thirty-nine years old (the typical reader was thirty-five), and the average income was a rather astonishing $43,100 per year (up from $28,400 in 1981). Readership fell along more conventional lines regarding marital status (50 percent single, 50 percent married) and sex (50 percent female, 50 percent male) (August-September 1984, p. 6). The founders of *Mother Jones* acknowledge the difficulty of publishing a magazine aimed at the wide spectrum of the magazine's readers. Originally *Mother Jones* staffers believed that their readership would not be as radical as they, so they "soft-pedaled the magazine's politics. . . . For most of [the] first year [the] pages were filled with pieces about backpacking and cooking, circuses and airline discounts" (February-March 1980, p. 5). Readers saw through this attempt to equivocate and did not like it. Consequently, this kind of article has subsequently been relatively scarce, and consumer advocacy and political articles have taken their place. And the *New Mother Jones* also features more mainstream, albeit still leftist, articles, such as the 1989 Susan Sarandon cover story.

The magazine has always carried poetry (Denise Levertov was the poetry editor for three years, 1976–1978), excerpts from novels (including *The Color Purple*, in January 1982), short stories, and music and book reviews, but its greatest recognition comes from articles that can be fairly termed "muckraking."[3] As early as 1978 the magazine won the National Magazine Award for public service for its article on the Ford Pinto gas tank explosions, "Pinto Madness" (September-October 1977, pp. 18–32), and since then similar articles have covered the Dalkon shield, smoking (cigarette advertising is no longer accepted), unrest in Central America, and issues of health care, industry, and politics. Despite a tendency toward sensational covers, and a viewpoint that has been called predictable, *Mother Jones* is consistently attractive and stylish, and articles are generally well researched.

Mother Jones's major claim to fame may well be that despite financial setbacks and amid rising conservatism, it has managed to maintain high circulation and readership. It has done so by attracting readers of diverse interests and backgrounds, appealing, according to one writer, to a "mass audience, using hardnosed advertising and marketing techniques."[4] For example, in 1986, rather than the pleas for money that had become standard end-of-the-year fare for the magazine, *Mother Jones's* mass mailing and subscription campaign included a sweepstakes, partial proceeds of which would be donated to the cause of the winner's choice. The magazine has also attempted to increase readership by reaching libraries, a campaign that was finally successful in 1988. *Mother Jones* is now indexed by the *Reader's Guide to Periodical Literature*, a standard library reference tool, after letters from readers persuaded its publisher to include the magazine.

According to Michael Andrew Scully in an early essay on *Mother Jones*, "It has managed within its pages a tentative reunion of most of [the left's] divergent sects, which in fact have little more in common than the dissatisfaction of their numbers—some with technology, some with mixed capitalism, some with the tedium of representative government, some with their parents or themselves."[5] Although issues of long-standing concern, such as Central America, are still covered in the *New Mother Jones*, the magazine now seems to be aimed at a broader audience; day care, murder cases, and interviews with celebrities now rub shoulders with old-style "muckraking." Its editor insists that the new format is aimed at "putting you in touch with the next generation of thinkers, activists, and writers" (February-March 1989, p. 3). It is too early to tell if the hard-sell approach will appear to loyal readers as a sellout, or if the new *Mother Jones* will succeed in speaking for "the next generation of thinkers."

Notes

1. "Feisty Mother," *Newsweek,* 24 April 1978, p. 111.
2. For further information see "A Family Fight Hits the Headlines," *Mother Jones,* December 1986, p. 6.
3. "Backstage," *Mother Jones,* July-August 1986: "It *is* difficult to put out a progressive magazine in a country whose progressive movements are weak and in disarray. One result has been that *Mother Jones* has mostly concentrated on Muckraking. We've carried far too little material that embodies a vision of what a truly democratic America would look like."
4. "Feisty Mother," p. 111.
5. Michael Andrew Scully, "Would Mother Jones Buy *Mother Jones?*" *Public Interest,* Fall 1978, p. 101.

Information Sources

BIBLIOGRAPHY
"Feisty Mother." *Newsweek,* 24 April 1978, p. 111.
"Mother Call." *Time,* 21 July 1980, p. 62.
Scully, Michael Andrew. "Would Mother Jones Buy *Mother Jones?*" *Public Interest,* Fall 1978, pp. 100–108.
Taft, William H. *American Magazines for the 1980s.* New York: Hastings House, 1982.
INDEX SOURCES
　　Abstracts of Popular Culture; Alternative Press Index (1976–present); *Magazine Index* (1977–present); *Media Review Index; New Periodicals Index; Popular Periodicals Index; Women Studies Abstracts; PAIS; Access* (1977–present); *Readers' Guide* (1988–present).
LOCATION SOURCES
　　Widely available. Reprint editions, University Microfilms International, Ann Arbor, Michigan. Available in microform.

Publication History

MAGAZINE TITLE AND TITLE CHANGES
　　Mother Jones: A Magazine for the Rest of Us, 1976–1988; the *New Mother Jones: People, Politics and other Passions,* 1989–present.
VOLUME AND ISSUE DATA
　　Vols. 1–10, 1976–1985, monthly except for combined issues February-March and September-October. Vol. 10, no. 9 (1985) is a combined issue for November-December. Vol. 11–present, 1986–present, monthly except for combined issues in February-March, April-May, and July-August. Ten issues per year 1976–1985; nine issues per year 1986–present.
PUBLISHER AND PLACE OF PUBLICATION
　　Foundation for National Progress, San Francisco, California. Publishers: Mark Dowie, 1980; Jacques Marchand, 1981; Robin Wolaner, 1982–1985; Don Hazen 1985–1989; David Assman, 1989–present.

EDITORS
> Adam Hochschild (managing editor), Denise Levertov (poetry editor), Paul Jacobs, Deborah Johnson, Jeffrey Klein, Joan Medlin, Richard Parker, Louise Kollenbaum, Amanda Spake, 1976; Jeffrey Klein (managing editor), Denise Levertov (poetry editor), Adam Hochschild, Richard Parker, Amanda Spake, Louise Kollenbaum, 1977; Amanda Spake (managing editor), Denise Levertov (poetry editor), Adam Hochschild, Jeffrey Klein, Louise Kollenbaum, 1978; Zina Klapper (managing editor), Adam Hochschild, Jeffrey Klein, Louise Kollenbaum, Amanda Spake, Deirdre English, 1979; Deirdre English, Adam Hochschild, Zina Klapper, Jeffrey Klein, Amanda Spake, 1980; Deirdre English (executive editor), 1981– June 1986; Michael Moore (editor, September and October), 1986; December 1986–July 1987; Douglas Foster, August 1987–present.

CIRCULATION
> 220,000.

Jean M. Parker

MS.

Ms., a magazine that grew out of the politically volatile climate of the late 1960s and early 1970s, is the most successful feminist publication in America. From its beginnings as a forty-four–page special section in a leading East Coast magazine to its current prosperous status, *Ms.* has proven that given a dedicated staff, investors unafraid to take a risk, and the right timing, even unlikely ventures may succeed admirably.

The two women behind much of this success are Gloria Steinem and Patricia Carbine. Prior to collaborating on *Ms.,* both women worked for other magazines. Steinem contributed to *Seventeen* and was an editorial consultant for *Ladies' Home Journal*; Carbine held a position of high editorial responsibility at *Look.** Job frustrations and sexist treatment resulted in their organizing a small group of women with the express goal of creating a feminist magazine that would deal with significant issues affecting, and of concern to, women.

In their first full-length issue, the Preview Issue of spring 1972, the staff outlined the mission of the magazine, declaring it to be "written for all women, everywhere, in every occupation and profession . . . women who want to humanize politics, business, education, the arts and sciences . . . in the home, the community, and the nation."[1]

Although the women possessed determination in abundance, they lacked capital. In organizing their efforts, Gloria Steinem and several others established Majority Enterprises, a corporation founded for women. Elizabeth Forsling Harris became chairwoman of the board and treasurer, and Steinem became president and secretary. The next milestone was passed when publisher Katherine Graham bought stock in *Ms.,* providing initial money for the venture. Soon after that, Clay Felker published a forty-four–page special section of *Ms.* in the 15 December 1971 issue of *New York*.* The issue hit a newsstand sales record, and *Ms*. was on its way.

Spring 1972 saw the Preview Issue of *Ms*. come out at $1.50 an issue; 300,000 copies were printed, and the *Ms*. staff expected that amount to last two months. To their delight, it sold out in eight days. With the sale of the first 300,000 issues, *Ms*. received over 36,000 subscription orders at $9.00 per year.

When Warner Communications acquired a significant but minority interest in *Ms*. that same year, the magazine was on solid ground. The combination of the support from Warner, Clay Felker, Katherine Graham, and the early subscription orders afforded *Ms*. sufficient revenue and publicity to begin regular publication.

The next issue of *Ms*.—volume 1, number 1—appeared in July 1972, selling for $1 an issue. Contributors included editor-in-chief Gloria Steinem, Germaine Greer, Carolyn Heilbrun, Jane Trahey, Del Martin, and Phyllis Lyon. Among the topics addressed were the Equal Rights Amendment, child care, lesbians, and consciousness-raising. An interview with Simone de Beauvior was also featured.

In this July 1972 issue, the *Ms*. staff outlined its policy on advertisements. The magazine emphasizes advertisements that are a service to women and that realistically reflect their lives. Ads that insult women or promote products likely to be harmful to women are not accepted.[2] (The exception to this, however, continues to be cigarette advertisements.) Aside from cigarettes, the magazine's pages contain ads for cosmetics, liquor, personal hygiene and health care products, cars, insurance, telecommunications, and food. Even in its early stages, *Ms*. did well on advertising revenue: from a figure of $19,000 in August 1972, and revenues increased to $55,000 a year later, and were up to $99,000 by October 1973.

Circulation figures have been equally impressive, especially in the early years. By the end of 1972, subscriptions were up to 175,000. February 1973 saw the circulation guarantee raised from 250,000 to 350,000. Subscriptions passed the 200,000 mark in July of that year, with an almost equal number being sold at the newsstands. By July 1974, the circulation base rate exceeded 400,000. At the end of 1986 the circulation rate for *Ms*. was 463,861—newsstand sales accounting for 38,012 and subscriptions for 444,909.[3] The 1989 price of an issue is $2.50 and a year's subscription costs $16.00.

Being a magazine intended for women, it is not surprising that the *Ms*. audience is predominantly female. Recent polls indicate that of the 1.4 million people who read *Ms*. each month, 90 percent are women. The average reader is thirty-one years old, is better educated than women reading other women's magazines, has a median household income of $40,500, and is involved in civic activities. Fifty percent of the readers are married.[4] The image projected in the pages of *Ms*. is of middle-to upper-class women, successful, professional, and primarily Caucasian. To be fair to *Ms*., it is important to note that there are women of other races in the features and advertisements, and men as well. The slur cast upon *Ms*. at a 1973 Manhattan conference on sex stereotyping, condemning *Ms*.

as "lily white and more racist" than magazines such as *Ladies' Home Journal,
Glamour*, and *Seventeen*[5] is no longer accurate or justifiable, if indeed it ever
was.

Over the years, *Ms.* has featured a variety of departments, some appearing
only occasionally, others becoming long-standing parts of the magazine. Stories
for Free Children have been especially popular, as have the Ms. Gazette (chronicling current legislation and news items), No Comment (featuring sexist ads
submitted by readers), and Poetry and Fiction. Among the poets and novelist
included in *Ms.* are Sylvia Plath, Alice Walker, Rita Mae Brown, Marilyn
French, Doris Betts, Erica Jong, and Adrienne Rich.

Ms. has proved itself unafraid to print articles on even the most controversial
topics. A list of subjects treated by *Ms.* reads like a syllabus for a survey course
in women's studies: family issues, politics and legislation, domestic violence,
economic and employment issues, lesbianism, health concerns, women and religion, and more. Some issues of the magazine are designated as special issues
that deal mainly with a single topic such as education, men, or health concerns.

Although in its first year or two, this publication left something to be desired
by way of layout and photography, *Ms.* has been and continues to be of consistent
high quality. As the pioneering magazine of the women's movement and a forum
for serious discussions on topics relevant to all people, *Ms.* is in a class by itself.

Notes

1. Subscription advertisement, *Ms.*, Preview Issue, Spring 1972, p. 113.

2. "A Personal Report from *Ms.*," *Ms.*, July 1972, p. 7.

3. *The Standard Periodical Directory*, 10th ed. (New York: Oxbridge Communications, 1987), p. 1283.

4. Philip H. Dougherty, "Advertising: Good Tidings at *Ms.*," *New York Times*, 20
October 1972, p. 66. Section L: Business and Finance.

5. Judy Klemesrud, "Some New Views on an Old Subject at a Conference on Sex
Stereotyping," *New York Times*, 9 April 1973, p. 43. Section L: Family, Food, Fashions,
Furnishings.

Information Sources

BIBLIOGRAPHY

Dougherty, Philip H. "Advertising: Good Tidings at *Ms.*" *New York Times,* 20 October
    1972.
Klemesrud, Judy. "Some New Views on an Old Subject at a Conference on Sex Ster-
    eotyping." *New York Times*, 9 April 1973, p. 43.
"A Personal Report." *Ms.*, July 1972, pp. 4–7.
"A Personal Report." *Ms.*, January 1973, pp. 96–97, 114–15.
Steinem, Gloria. *Outrageous Acts and Everyday Rebellions*. New York: Holt, Rinehart
    and Winston, 1983.
Subscription Advertisement. *Ms.*, Preview Issue, Spring 1972, p. 113.

INDEX SOURCES

Magazine Index (1977–present); *Readers' Guide* (1974–present); *Women's Studies Abstracts; Popular Periodicals Index* (1973–1974).

LOCATION SOURCES

Library of Congress and many other libraries. Available in microform.

Publication History

MAGAZINE TITLE AND TITLE CHANGES

Ms.

VOLUME AND ISSUE DATA

Preview Issue, 1972; vols. 1–15, July 1972–present, monthly.

PUBLISHER AND PLACE OF PUBLICATION

Majority Enterprise, Inc., 1972 Preview Issue; Ms. Magazine Corporation, 1972 (vol. 1, no. 1) to 1979; Ms. Foundation for Education and Communication, Inc., 1980–present. Elizabeth Forsling Harris, 1972 Preview Issue; Patricia Carbine, 1972–present, New York, New York.

EDITORS

Gloria Steinem, 1972–present.

CIRCULATION

484,809 paid (1987), 38,012 nonpaid (1986).

Sandra Wenner

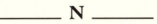

N

NATIONAL ENQUIRER

In the 1980s the *National Enquirer* is as much a national institution as motherhood, apple pie, and baseball. Compared to its youthful beginnings when it featured sports, scandals, and pin-ups, and its adolescent period when it hawked morbidity, sex, and gore; it is almost respectable in its middle age. During its sixty-three-year history it has never shirked a lawsuit. Regardless of what one might think of its sometimes tawdry tastes, morbid melodrama, and appeal to the base, it has been in the forefront of the fight for freedom of the press.

It has many imitators: the *Globe*, the *National Examiner, Weekly World News*, the *Sun, News Extra*, and the *Star*; but it is the leader of the pack in circulation with 6.1 million.

You can't miss its omnipresence at over 250,000 outlets comprised of newsstands and the supermarket, drug and convenience store chains, where it is frequently sold out. Some buy it out of curiosity, some on impulse. At the supermarket checkout counter its predominantly female readership looks furtively at the titillating headlines:

PREGNANT FERGIE DEVASTATED—DAD CAUGHT IN VICE SCANDAL

LIBERACE BOMBSHELL—BOYFRIEND TELLS ALL—WORLD EXCLU-SIVE

NEW ASTROLOGY BOMBSHELL: THE REAL SECRET ASTROLOGER WHO GUIDED PRESIDENT—THE UNTOLD STORY

STILL-MARRIED WILLIE NELSON MOVES IN WITH GIRLFRIEND 23 YEARS YOUNGER

SECRETS OF SCIENTIFIC PSYCHIC RESEARCH IN RUSSIA

BRUCE WILLIS MARRIAGE IN TROUBLE

It wasn't always like that. Until its revamping and expurgation by owner and publisher Generoso Pope, Jr. in 1968, the weekly tabloid promised a sadistic combination of "mutilation, perversion and gore":[1]

MADMAN CUT UP HIS DATE AND PUT HER BODY IN HIS FREEZER

CHEATING WIFE NAILED TO WALL

MOM USES SON'S FACE FOR AN ASHTRAY

Tabloid,[2] in its earliest meaning, referred only to a newspaper's format, that is, its small page-size, as well as its small number of pages, and in that sense all early American newspapers were tabloids.[3] In the early twentieth century on crowded subways the tabloid's compact and convenient size was almost a necessity to avoid infringing on one's neighbor's territory.[4] The word *tabloid* in addition to its meaning of physical size (9¾" x 11¾") also has the meaning of journalistic style: many pictures; short, snappy articles; and sensational headlines. Sensational headlines were important in the days before radio and television when newsboys hawked papers on the street by shouting headlines.

The *Enquirer* was founded in 1926 on a loan from William Randolph Hearst to newspaper advertising man William Griffin. The *New York Enquirer*, as it was called, featured sports and was used as a laboratory for Hearst's ideas; he took the good ones for his own papers and left the *Enquirer* with the bad ones. When circulation flagged to 17,000, Hearst sold the paper in 1952. Its buyer was sand-and-gravel millionaire Generoso Pope, Jr.[5] The twenty-eight-year-old MIT graduate was no newcomer to the newspaper business. In 1946 he turned *Il Progresso*, a faltering New York Italian-language daily founded by his father, into a money-maker.[6] "He transformed it from a horse-racing sheet into a gruesome tabloid in order to turn a profit."[7]

Circulation stalled at 1 million in 1966 as newsstand outlets slowly disappeared, and in 1968 Pope aimed at a new audience and changed his marketing strategy. Until then smut and sadism had been provided to his male readership primarily at newsstands. Now his goal was to make the *Enquirer* "respectable and then publicize the new pristine image."[8] He abruptly transformed the paper by embracing "a blend of upbeat success stories, gossip about celebrities, plus an overdose of the occult and the quasi-scientific" aimed at the supermarkets for an audience of housewives.[9] "It is at the checkout where the action is," three to four times the sales as in the magazine section of the store.[10] "It was strictly a business decision," Pope said.[11]

Circulation slowly climbed to 1.2 and then to 1.5 million in 1969, when it "displaced *Reader's Digest* at no. 5 on the newsdealers' bestseller list."[12] In 1972 circulation rose to 2.9 million, and by 1975 circulation nudged 4 million a week; 1973's gross was $17 million but in 1975 it climbed to $41 million.[13] Even with the introduction of Rupert Murdoch's New Zealand entry, the *National*

Star, the *Enquirer*'s growth did not slow. Pope anticipated a guaranteed circulation of 5 million in September 1974.[14]

Weekly circulation soared to 5.1 million as "the public's obsession with the miseries, marriages, and mismatings of celebrities" continued, and revenues were $140 million in 1983.[15] However, in November 1984, senior vice-president Neil Carey said circulation was 4.7 million and readership was 23 million.[16] Its peak issue to date: 6.7 million copies of the cover with the King, the 255 pound Elvis Presley in his coffin after his death in August 1977.[17] The bizarre interest in the death of celebrities and their ghosts was standard fare for *Enquirer* readers. In fact, a parody of the *Enquirer*'s bizarre articles published in 1967, the *Irrational Inquirer* was "all but indistinguishable from the original."[18] The *Enquirer* claims under its masthead "Largest circulation of any paper in America." But for today's reader, 85 cents brings 56 pages of articles that could be found in a dozen other magazines: celebrity recipes, health and fitness, and human interest stories.

The *Enquirer* has been involved in censorship, libel, and right-to-privacy lawsuits (the individual's right to privacy versus the public's right to know), most of which it won. In the 1980s it was almost a national pastime to sue the *Enquirer*, but in an early 1960s case, it was the New York Evening Enquirer Publishing Company that brought suit against the Chicago Transit Authority for banning the sale of some 208 publications at its station newsstands, among them the *National Enquirer*. The Transit Authority objected to the weekly tabloid that featured "photos of scantily clad women."[19]

In 1968 Marvin Varnish was awarded $20,000 by a jury in a suit against the *Enquirer*. He contended the article about his wife—"Happiest Mother Kills Her 3 Children and Herself"—in the 8 March 1964 issue was a "fictionalization and a false presentation of the tragic incident."[20]

An *Enquirer* reporter made off with five bags of Secretary of State Henry Kissinger's garbage in July 1975. Kissinger was outraged, but he did not sue.[21]

Hollywood gossip has resulted in some Hollywood libel suits by Cary Grant, Carol Burnett, Johnny Carson, and Shirley Jones and her husband Marty Ingels. The *Enquirer* has also managed to outrage Raquel Welch, Carroll O'Connor, Ed McMahon, Rory Calhoun, Rudy Vallee, Phil Silvers, and Paul Lynde. When the *Enquirer* lost a suit to Carol Burnett in a California court, the paper went to the U.S. Supreme Court, which refused to hear its appeal.[22] Burnett emerged victorious with $1.6 million, but an appellate court reduced the award to $50,000.[23]

In 1985 two *Enquirer* writers were cited for contempt when they refused to testify about interviewing Cathy Smith, accused of administering the fatal cocaine dose to actor-comedian John Belushi.[24]

Actor Eddie Murphy filed a $30-million lawsuit in 1986 against the *Enquirer* for publishing a "false and defamatory article."[25] "Miami Vice" costar Philip

Michael Thomas also filed a $14-million libel lawsuit, but a judge dismissed it in 1986, since the statute of limitations had expired.[26]

In 1988 the U.S. Supreme Court ruled 6–2 that a person's garbage bags may be searched by police without a warrant. The ruling alluded to the 1975 incident in which a *National Enquirer* reporter had taken Kissinger's garbage.[27]

Before its 1968 transformation, the *Enquirer* offered "personal ads for everyone from the sadomasochist set to foot fetishists."[28] Today its advertising extols health aids: appetite suppressants, exercise gliders, arthritis pain relievers, aspirin, shampoo, Tums, Kotex, toothpaste, and foot supports, while its four pages of classifieds have such headings as Business Opportunities; Financial, Loans, Insurance; Astrology, Religious, Recipes, Pets and Supplies, Contests & Sweepstakes, Real Estate, Books & Booklets, Buy Wholesale, Household Items, Stamps, Inventions, Of Interest to Women, Money Making Opportunities, Aviation, Safety, Investigators, Personal, Government Surplus, Coins & Medals, Work at Home, Instruction & Education, Unusual Items (a psychic amplifier), Employment Information, Health & Beauty, and Collectors' Items. New revelations of Nostradamus are promised in one ad that includes the date for the end of the world.[29] In 1983 the *Enquirer's* television ad exclaimed "Enquiring Minds Want to Know."

As D. Keith Mano so perceptively pointed out in 1977 in the *National Review*, the *Enquirer*, with its garish cover of celebrity photographs in color, is not a paper that one would find in a dentist's office, nor is it likely that one would save old *Enquirers*. Its articles are written in the second-person, *you, your*, and are never continued on another page. It is a paper for "lurid optimism, grossest good news. Like other paper products it's cheap and disposable."[30] Although Pope's goal was the bottom line, which he achieved masterfully (when sex sold, he published sex; when celebrity gossip, astrology, and the occult sold, he published these), he also fought for an admirable goal: freedom of the press.

Pope was sixty-one when he died of a heart attack on 2 October 1988.[31] In his will he stated that the paper should be sold.[32] On 13 April 1989, Boston Ventures, an investment firm, and MacFadden Holdings, which owns *True Story,** True Confessions, Modern Romances*, and *Teen Beat*, made a successful bid of $412.5 million for GP Group Inc., the parent company.[33]

Notes

1. "The *Enquirer:* Up From Smut," *Newsweek*, 21 April 1975, p. 62.

2. From the French *tabloide* meaning *tablet* or *capsule*; from that it came to mean *pressed* or *condensed*.

3. Colonial American papers were taxed by the British based on the number of pages. "The Tabloid Today," *Newsweek,* 12 May 1969, p. 69.

4. Frank Luther Mott, *American Journalism; A History: 1690–1960*. 3rd ed. (New York: Macmillan, 1962), p. 668.

5. "From Worse to Bad," *Newsweek*, 8 September 1969, p. 79.

6. "No Matter How Vile...," *Newsweek*, 18 January 1965, p. 48.

7. "Goodbye to Gore," *Time*, 21 February 1972, p. 64.

8. "From Worse to Bad," p. 79.

9. "The *Enquirer* Profits by Uplift in News," *New York Times*, 13 August 1972, p. 50.

10. "Advertising: New Magazine Tack," *New York Times*, 4 September 1974, p. 64.

11. "The *Enquirer*: Up From Smut," p. 62.

12. "From Worse to Bad," p. 79.

13. "The *Enquirer*: Up From Smut," p. 62.

14. Philip H. Dougherty, "Advertising: Selling Enquire," *New York Times*, 23 April 1974, p. 65.

15. "Now the Story Can Be Told! How Tabloids Survived the Recession," *Business Week*, 7 November 1983, p. 145.

16. "Pocket Books Series with *Enquirer* Planned," *Publishers Weekly*, 16 November 1984, p. 34.

17. "No Easy Trick; How to Spoof the *Enquirer*?" *Time*, 10 January 1983, p. 67.

18. Ibid.

19. "Publication Ban Lifted," *New York Times*, 13 July 1960, p. 47.

20. "Weekly is Fined in Privacy Case," *New York Times*, 21 March 1968, p. 43.

21. "The Man From T.R.A.S.H.," *Newsweek*, 21 July 1975, p. 16.

22. "Supreme Court Roundup: Burnett Libel Case," *New York Times*, 22 February 1984, p. 20.

23. "Sorry, Shirley," *Time*, 7 May 1984, p. 92.

24. "2 Writers in Belushi Case Cited for Contempt," *New York Times*, 8 May 1985, p. 17.

25. "Murphy Files $30 Million Suit Vs. *National Enquirer*," *Jet*, 10 February 1986, p. 62.

26. " 'Vice' Costar, Kin Sue *Natl. Enquirer*," *Variety*, 31 December 1986, p. 62.

27. Stuart Taylor, Jr., "Police May Search Person's Trash Without a Warrant, Court Rules," *New York Times*, 17 May 1988, p. 24.

28. "The *Enquirer*: Up From Smut," p. 62.

29. Michael J. Farrell, "All the Noise That Fits in Print," *National Catholic Reporter*, 19 April 1985, p. 24.

30. D. Keith Mano, "Enquiring," *National Review*, 18 February 1977, p. 309.

31. "Milestones. Died. Generoso Pope, Jr., 61," *Time*, 17 October 1988, p. 65.

32. Fabrikant, Geraldine, "Sale is Expected Soon for *National Enquirer*," *New York Times*, 14 Dec. 1988, p. D22.

33. Fabrikant, Geraldine, "Accord Reached to Acquire *National Enquirer* Publisher," *New York Times*, 14 April 1989, p. D15.

Information Sources

BIBLIOGRAPHY

"The *Enquirer* Up From Smut." *Newsweek*, 21 April 1975, p. 62.

"The *Enquirer* Profits by Uplift in News." *New York Times*, 13 August 1972, p. 50.

Fabrikant, Geraldine, "Accord Reached to Acquire *National Enquirer* Publisher," *New York Times*, 14 April 1989, p. D15.

Fabrikant, Geraldine, "Sale is Expected Soon for *National Enquirer, New York Times,*
14 Dec. 1988, p. D22.
Farrell, Michael J. "All the Noise That Fits in Print." *National Catholic Reporter,* 19
April 1985, p. 24.
"Frisco Judge Dismisses Thomas Libel Lawsuit." *Jet,* 8 June 1987, p. 32.
Reporter, 19 April 1985, p. 24.
"Frisco Judge Dismisses Thomas Libel Lawsuit." *Jet,* 8 June 1987, p. 32.
"From Worse to Bad." *Newsweek,* 8 September 1969, p. 79.
"Goodbye to Gore." *Time,* 21 February 1972, pp. 64–65.
"Hollywood Goes to War." *Time,* 21 January 1980, p. 70.
"Hollywood Stars Vs. The *Enquirer.*" *Newsweek,* 8 December 1980, p. 86.
"The Man from T.R.A.S.H." *Newsweek,* 21 July 1975, p. 16.
Mano, D. Keith. "Enquiring." *National Review,* 18 February 1977, pp. 309–10.
"Milestones. Died. Generoso Pope, Jr." *Time,* 17 October 1988, p. 65.
Mott, Frank Luther. *American Journalism; A History: 1690–1960.* 3rd ed. New York:
Macmillan, 1962.
"Murphy Files $30 Million Suit Vs. *National Enquirer.*" *Jet,* 10 February 1986, p. 62.
"No Easy Trick; How To Spoof the *Enquirer?*" *Time,* 10 January 1983, p. 67.
"No Matter How Vile . . . " *Newsweek,* 18 January 1965, p. 48.
"Now the Story Can Be Told! How Tabloids Survived the Recession." *Business Week,*
7 November 1983, pp. 145–46.
"Pocket Books Series with *Enquirer* Planned." *Publishers Weekly,* 16 November 1984,
p. 34.
"Publication Ban Lifted." *New York Times,* 13 July 1960, p. 47. Rudnitsky, Howard.
"How Gene Pope Made Millions in the Newspaper Business." *Forbes,* 16 October
1978, pp. 78–79.
"Sorry, Shirley." *Time,* 7 May 1984, p. 92.
"Supreme Court Roundup: Burnett Libel Case." *New York Times,* 22 February 1984,
p. 20.
"The Tabloid Today." *Newsweek,* 12 May 1969, p. 69.
Taylor, Stuart, Jr. "Police May Search Person's Trash Without a Warrant, Court Rules."
New York Times, 17 May 1988, p. 24.
"Trashy Journalism." *Time,* 21 July 1975, p. 40.
"2 Writers in Belushi Case Cited for Contempt." *New York Times,* 8 May 1985, p. 17.
"Vice Costar Kin Sue *Natl. Enquirer.*" *Variety,* 31 December 1986, p. 62.
"Weekly is Fined in Privacy Case." *New York Times,* 21 March 1968, p. 43.
INDEX SOURCES
    None.
LOCATION SOURCES
    Library of Congress; other libraries have partial holdings. Available on microfilm
    (1978–1981).

Publication History

MAGAZINE TITLE AND TITLE CHANGES:
The *New York Evening Enquirer,* 1926–195(?); *New York Enquirer,* 195(?)–1957;
National Enquirer, 1957–present.
VOLUME DATA
    Vols. 1–64, 1926–1989.

OWNERS
> Hearst Corporation, 1926–1952; Generoso Pope, Jr., 1952–1988; MacFadden Holdings, and Boston Ventures, 1989–present.

PUBLISHER AND PLACE OF PUBLICATION
> New York Evening Enquirer Publishing Company, Hearst Corporation. Best Medium Publishing Company, Inc. (Editorial offices have varied and include New York City, 1926–1953(?); Englewood Cliffs, N.J., 1953(?)–1971; Lantana, Florida, 1971–present.

EDITORS
> William Griffin, 1926–(?); Carl Grothmann, 1964–1967; Nat Chrzan, 1968–1969(?); current: Ian Calder, 1986–.

CIRCULATION
> 6.1 million.

Richard A. Russell

NATIONAL GEOGRAPHIC

Gilbert Grosvenor, editor of *National Geographic* from 1903 to 1954, once described the kinds of readers who contributed to its enormous success: "[Those] who long to visit faraway places, to travel adventurously, to see strange customs and races, to explore mysteries of the sea and air. Not many persons can do these things in the physical sense, but they can venture far and wide through the pages of the *National Geographic Magazine*."[1] And, indeed, for just over 100 years, millions of readers in this and other countries have traveled the world through the extraordinary photojournalism available in *National Geographic*.

The early history of the magazine is intertwined with that of the society, established by Gardiner Greene Hubbard, a Boston lawyer and financier who moved to Washington. Once established, Hubbard delegated control to Alexander Graham Bell, originally a teacher of the deaf who had tutored Hubbard's daughter Mabel whom he later married, the original Ma Bell. Bell contacted Gilbert Grosvenor, who would become his own son-in-law, to be editor. Grosvenor's son, Melville Bell Grosvenor, succeeded him, and Gilbert Melville Grosvenor, grandson of Gilbert Hovey and great-great-great-grandson of Gardiner Hubbard, is society president today. In fact, the National Geographic Society as well as the magazine has been something of a family affair.[2]

The beginnings of the magazine were irregular publications, scientific brochures. In October 1888 an announcement that explained the purpose of the magazine appeared in volume 1, number 1, to the effect that the society, "organized to increase and diffuse geographic knowledge," had decided that a magazine was one way to accomplish that goal. The magazine would include "memoirs, essays, notes, correspondence, reviews, etc.," in short, whatever material relevant to geography, submitted by any individuals, not just society members. The society itself would edit the magazine, which would appear irregularly at first; and the magazine was to be national in scope, not just local to the nation's capital. Both "leaders and followers in geographic science" were encouraged to participate.[3]

The most famous member of the early society and magazine days is, of course, Alexander Graham Bell. His interest in making the magazine comparable in popularity to those of the current market (*Harper's,* *Century, McClure's,* * and *Munsey's*) caused him to discuss the matter with Gilbert Grosvenor, who would soon thereafter be Bell's son-in-law.[4] To offer membership in the society rather than subscriptions to a magazine was also Bell's idea, one challenged in the early years but still retained (and successfully so). Both Bell and Grosvenor saw the mission of the society and its magazine as to "popularize the science of geography and take it into the homes of the people." They both insisted that such a science could be expressed in laymen's terms and interestingly so.[5]

S. S. McClure, the magazine genius of the age, was brought in as a consultant. He advised abandoning membership, moving to New York, changing the title to something less formidable, and avoiding reference to the society.[6] In addition to McClure's suggestions, Richard Watson Gilder, editor of *Century,* warned against the use of photographs, calling them "vulgar."[7] Fortunately, Grosvenor persuaded the board not to take any of this advice. But the early days were not easy ones. In fact, the Geographic Society was so poor that Grosvenor himself had to address mailing slips; after sending one 900-copy edition this way, he purchased an addressing machine.[8]

The early days of the magazine were also plagued by other problems; for example, at first the society implemented an editorship by committee process. Having once appointed Grosvenor as editor, the committee continued to test its power against his. While Grosvenor and Elsie Bell were on their honeymoon, the committee moved publication to New York. The Grosvenors rushed back to the United States, and Grosvenor returned the publication to Washington after only two issues (January and February of 1901).[9] Another controversy among the executive committee members concerned the printing of "vulgar" photoengravings, described as any that did not teach a strictly scientific lesson.[10] As the magazine found its focus in scientific articles written for the lay person, then the photography became an integral part of the total message, often even more important than the message. In 1903 the magazine published its first photo of native Filipino women, naked from the waist up. Dr. Bell advised that "prudery" should not be a part of the decision, and since this photo reflected the customs of the native women, it should be used.[11] Dr. Bell, by the way, often contributed to the magazine under the pseudonym H. A. Largelamb, unscrambled to read A. Graham Bell, so his influence was more than as adviser to Grosvenor.[12]

Over the decades the Geographic Society has sponsored innumerable explorations on land, on sea, and in the air. Rear Admiral Richard Byrd once commented that he knew of "no greater privilege" to carry the flag of the *National Geographic* other than carrying the flag of his country.[13] And of course his explorations as well as those of many others have been faithfully reported in the magazine.

One of the most exciting and controversial explorations conducted by the society was that of the discovery of the North Pole. *National Geographic* awarded its first grant in 1908 to Peary ($1,000)[14]; since that time some 3,300 such grants.[15] An executive committee offered to examine the records of reports by both Robert Edwin Peary and Frederick Albert Cook and awarded the official discovery to Peary. In the October 1909 issue both reports were published side by side. The magazine noted that before official status could be awarded, it would have to examine all records carefully. Peary submitted his, and this distinguished committee awarded the discovery to him.[16]

Grosvenor himself was one of the first to begin taking excellent photos for the magazine, beginning in 1903 with a 4-A folding Kodak he had personally paid more than a month's salary for since the magazine had no money for cameras.[17] The first color photographs were published in 1910 in a twenty-four-page series called "Scenes in Korea and China." And soon color pages were a regular part of most stories. Today *National Geographic* continues to win awards for its outstanding color photography. Also in 1910 the February cover design used for many years, through the Grosvenor editorship, was adopted: "the four portions of the globe" for the international work of the group, acorns and oak leaves to "represent the small beginning of this organization and its sturdy, consistent growth," laurel leaves for "reward for achievement" of the work of the Society and the work of all those reported in the magazine.[18]

For the most part *National Geographic* has been able to avoid controversial stands, particularly those with political overtones. This capacity to avoid controversy came from Gilbert Grosvenor's insistence that the magazine and all those who were associated with it treat all people with "an understanding heart."[19] In March 1915 Grosvenor published his seven editorial principles, earlier submitted to the board of governors: "absolute accuracy," an "abundance of beautiful, instructive, and artistic illustrations," "permanent value," avoidance of the "trivial," "nothing of a partisan or controversial character," avoidance of "everything unpleasant or unduly critical," and timeliness.[20]

Another Grosvenor decision concerned the use of advertisements. He always kept ads separate from editorial pages, and because the magazine was intended for school use and for children, he never advertised alcohol or tobacco.[21] Over the years the magazine has had countless "firsts" in photography and in discovery. The issues from the early years have many contributions from famous and distinguished individuals, all of whom shared a love for adventure and exploration: Theodore Roosevelt, William Howard Taft, Calvin Coolidge, Herbert Hoover, Peary, Roald Amundsen, Sir Ernest Henry Shackleton, Joseph Conrad, Dubose Heyward, General John Joseph Pershing, Admiral Chester William Nimitz, Charles and Anne Morrow Lindbergh, and Amelia Earhart—to name just a few.[22]

Recent contributors include Prince Philip (November 1957); William O. and Mercedes H. Douglas (January 1959); Richard M. Nixon ("Russia As I Saw It," 1959); Carl Sandburg on Lincoln (January 1960); Jacques Cousteau, General

Curtis Le May, and Dag Hammarskjöld (January 1961); Adlai Stevenson (September 1961); Alan B. Shephard's firsthand account of his flight (1961); Dr. L. S. B. Leakey, Jane Goodall, and Lyndon Baines Johnson (February 1964); Sargent Shriver on the Peace Corps (September 1964); King Hussein on Jordan (December 1964); Robert F. Kennedy (July 1965); Dwight Eisenhower on Churchill (August 1965); Carl Sagan (December 1967); Neil Armstrong, Edwin Aldrin, and Michael Collins (December 1969); Dian Fossey (January 1970); Thor Heyerdahl (January 1971); and Euell Gibbons (July 1972). In July 1976 five noted thinkers explored the future in the pages of *National Geographic*: Buckminster Fuller, Isaac Asimov, Edmund N. Bacon, Gerard Piel, and Richard F. Babcock, with *National Geographic* staffers Gilbert Grosvenor and Peter T. White. Regular contributors include each of the editors, Robert Laxalt (brother of Senator Paul Laxalt), Kenneth MacLeish, Paul Zahl, Peter Benchley, Frank Shor, Alan Villiers, Luis Marden, and many others.

The *National Geographic* supplied maps to Franklin Delano Roosevelt during World War II, and in fact, each travel article provides an accompanying map. As noted before, most members of the society treasure their magazines and maps, keeping them for years and passing them from generation to generation. In fact, according to Grosvenor, past copies of *National Geographic* are bound and saved for future reference more often than those of any other magazine in the world.[23]

But Grosvenor's commitment to avoid controversy over the years led to problems.

For years, the National Geographic ran stories about the South without even mentioning segregation, lynching, freedom marches or the Ku Klux Klan. During the rise of Hitler and Mussolini during the 1930s, it ran cheerful accounts of the renaissance of Germany and Italy without mentioning fascist and Nazi oppression.

Children growing up in the 1930s and exposed to newsreels of bread lines and dust bowls, of Japanese troops bayonetting their prisoners and Mussolini's air force bombing defenseless Ethiopian tribesmen, realized the world was not so rosy as the National Geographic painted it, and they developed a suspicion of the magazine that was to last for years.[24]

Two articles in the 100-year history of the magazine seem to have evoked the most controversy: one was about the origins of the human species based on recent discoveries of fossil bones in East Africa and the other was one on Syria suggesting that "Jews are well treated there." For the latter article, the magazine printed an apology.[25]

In 1977 Gilbert M. Grosvenor ran articles on apartheid in South Africa, separatism in Quebec, and life in Harlem—all within a six-month span. Predictably, some board members felt that such topics, although presented in a low-key, reportorial style, were inappropriate fare for *National Geographic*. But this Grosvenor, just as his grandfather had, continued coverage.[26]

Another contrast to the early days lies in prosperity. Today's *National Geographic* is quite wealthy, in part because of its status as a nonprofit educational institution. It pays taxes only on advertisement revenue. In addition to the magazine, the society now engages in numerous other ventures: $5 million annually in grants to scientific research; video production since 1965, for broadcast on public television, and three years ago for a cable television series; and, of course, educational materials for schools.[27] All activities combined bring an annual revenue of about $370 million. The membership system, suggested by Bell and implemented by Grosvenor, has led to the astounding circulation enjoyed today, surpassed by only *TV Guide* and *Readers' Digest*, both subscription/newsstand magazines. In a market in which 65 percent renewal is considered eminently successful, *National Geographic* enjoys an 85 percent renewal rate when membership subscription expires.[28] Membership is not as exclusive as one might think. Al Capone received the magazine at Alcatraz.[29]

According to those who have visited *National Geographic* headquarters, the building and the staff reflect the prosperity and the civilized demeanor so cherished by Gilbert Grosvenor. "Staff members dress well, nod and smile to one another and speak in low tones. Tousled hair and loosened ties are rare."[30] Articles often take five years from conception to publication, so the tradition of strict accuracy is also intact.

The *National Geographic* has also entered the age of computers. The mapmakers now use "a specialized computer that enables [them] to modify roads, rivers, borders and country names without wholesale revision."[31] In February 1982, however, editors used a computer to "shift" one of the Egyptian pyramids to make a better fit for the cover![32]

Regarding the written style of articles prepared for *National Geographic*, reviews are not so glowing as they are for the photography. Grosvenor insisted on first-person narrative, which still persists, all in an effort to make articles more readable for lay persons rather than for scientists. Unidentified staff members noted in an interview that they would prefer a different approach from the one now used: "Trying to extract information from those articles is a tedious process because it is not the normal expository writing, but anecdotal. . . . It appeals to the somewhat simple-minded, to families who get no other magazine. We know that nobody reads it. They just thumb through and look at the pictures. Even the staff reads it only very selectively."[33]

In 1959 Melville Grosvenor proposed color photos on the cover, a move opposed by the executive committee, but soon adopted at Grosvenor's insistence. That same year the oak-leaf border was "pruned," the yellow border narrowed and "the" and "magazine" dropped from the title.[34]

Although the magazine languished under Oliver La Gorce's editorship (1954–1957), generally because he refused to make any changes, Melville Bell Grosvenor's succession to the position of editor was called by one staff member "a cluster of Fourth of July rockets on a quiet night."[35]

In 1957, Frank Luther Mott acknowledged that some had criticized the magazine as a "picture book," but he praised it in terms so complimentary that Gilbert Grosvenor used the quote in his own history of the magazine: "There is really nothing like it in the world. . . . The *National Geographic Magazine* has long represented an achievement in editorship and management outstanding in the history of periodicals."[36]

In 1983 editor Wilbur Garrett commented on why the *National Geographic* has been so successful: "I believe it is primarily because we still fill the same need felt by that small group of thoughtful men who gave us our start almost a century ago—a need to address the insatiable human curiosity to know what makes the world tick."[37]

The good news is that *National Geographic* still deserves this praise. With an annual membership fee of $18, circulation is at 10.5 million, firmly planting *National Geographic* in the top ten magazines published in the United States. The sad news is that recent studies reveal that public knowledge of geography is at an all-time low in this country, with the eighteen to twenty-four age group least knowledgable of all those tested.[38] The work of the society and its magazine is more critical than ever. On election to the first presidency of the society, Hubbard stated: "I possess only the same general interest in the subject of geography that should be felt by every educated man."[39] With the continued work of the society and its magazine, perhaps that statement will someday come true for twentieth- and twenty-first–century citizens in this country. Long live *National Geographic*, a class act in magazine publishing for over a century. If any magazine can turn the tide, this one can.

Notes

1. Gilbert Grosvenor, *The National Geographic Society and Its Magazine* (Washington, D.C.: National Geographic Society, 1957), p. 1.

2. EF. Porter, Jr., "After a Century, the *National Geographic* Still Oozes Importance," *St. Louis Post-Dispatch*, St. Louis, Missouri, 13 March 1988, p. 14C.

3. Grosvenor, pp. 12–13.

4. Ibid., p. 22.

5. Ibid., p. 23.

6. Ibid., p. 24.

7. James Playsted Wood, *Magazines in the United States*, 3rd ed. (New York: Ronald Press, 1971), p. 396.

8. Grosvenor, p. 27.

9. Ibid., p. 34.

10. Ibid., p. 37.

11. Ibid., p. 39.

12. Ibid., p. 47.

13. Ibid., p. 7.

14. C. D. B. Bryan, *The National Geographic Society: 100 Years of Adventure and Discovery* (New York: Harry N. Abrams, 1987), p. 49.

15. Dick Thompson, "Happy 100, *National Geographic, Time*, 28 December 1987, p. 69.

16. Bryan, p. 49.

17. Grosvenor, p. 7.

18. Ibid., p. 53.

19. Ibid., p. 4.

20. Ibid., pp. 4–5.

21. Ibid., p. 56.

22. Ibid., pp. 66–67.

23. Ibid., p. 109.

24. Porter, p. 14C.

25. Ibid.

26. Ibid.

27. Ibid.

28. Ibid.

29. Ibid.

30. Ibid.

31. Thompson, p. 69.

32. Ibid., p. 70.

33. Porter, p. 14C.

34. Bryan, p. 337.

35. Ibid., p. 330.

36. Frank Luther Mott, *A History of American Magazines, 1885–1905*, vol. 4 (Cambridge: Harvard University Press, 1957), p. 632.

37. Bryan, p. 21.

38. Ibid., p. 27.

39. Kelley Griffin, "Persian Gulf Location a Mystery," for Knight-Ridder, Washington, D.C., in *The State* (Columbia, S.C.), 28 July 1988, p. 14A.

Information Sources

BIBLIOGRAPHY

Bryan, C. D. B. *The National Geographic Society: 100 Years of Adventure and Discovery*. New York: Harry N. Abrams, 1987.

Griffin, Kelley. "Persian Gulf Location a Mystery." Knight-Ridder, Washington, D.C. In *The State* (Columbia, S.C.), 28 July 1988, p. 14 A.

Grosvenor, Gilbert. *The National Geographic Society and Its Magazine*. Washington, D.C.: National Geographic Society, 1957.

Mott, Frank Luther. *A History of American Magazines, 1885–1905*. vol. 4. Cambridge: Harvard University Press, 1957, pp. 620–32.

Porter, E. F., Jr. "After a Century, the *National Geographic* Still Oozes Importance." *St. Louis Post-Dispatch,*; 13 March 1988, sec. C, pp. 1, 14.

Thompson, Dick. "Happy 100, *National Geographic*." *Time*, 28 December 1987, p. 69.

Wood, James Playsted. *Magazines in the United States*. 3rd ed. New York: Ronald Press, 1971.

INDEX SOURCES

Henry Skadsheim, comp., *Topical Index of the National Geographic Magazine, 1888–1912* (Berrien Springs, Mich., 1935); *Cumulative Indexes* (1899–1946,

1947–1951, 1952–1954, 1947–1976, published by the society); *Poole's Index*
(1889–1906); *Jones' Legal Index; Contents-Subject Index; Engineering Index*
(1907–1915); *Readers' Guide* (1888–present); *Handy Key to "National Geo-
graphics,"* Subject and Picture Locator, 1915–1981, Charles S. Underhill.

LOCATION SOURCES
Library of Congress, most libraries. Available in microform.

Publication History

MAGAZINE TITLE AND TITLE CHANGES
The National Geographic Magazine, 1888–1958; *National Geographic,* 1959–
current.

VOLUME AND ISSUE DATA
October 1888–current. Irregular, vols. 1–6, 1888–1895; vol. 1, October 1888,
April, July, and October 1889; vol. 2, April, May, June, and August 1890, April
1891; vol. 3, 28 March 1891, 29 May 1891, 28 January 1892; vol. 4, 26 March
1892, 21 March 1892, 18 March 1892, 31 March 1892, 15 May 1892, 8 February
1893; vol. 5, 7 April 1893, 20 March 1893, 29 April 1893, 10 July 1893, 31
January 1894; vol. 6, 14 February 1894, 17 March 1894, 25 April 1894, 23 May
1984, 22 June 1894, 1 November 1894, 29 December 1894, 20 April 1895.
Monthly, annual vols. 7–24, 1896–1913; monthly, semiannual vols. 25–current,
1913–current.

PUBLISHER AND PLACE OF PUBLICATION
National Geographic Society, Washington, D.C., 1888–1978. (1901–1902, published by McClure, Phillips Company, New York, for National Geographic Society, for only two months.) Corinth, Mississippi, 1978–present.

EDITORS
Henry Gannett, secretary, 1888–1890; Marcus Baker, secretary, 1891; W. J.
McGee, chairman, publication committee, 1892–1895; John Hyde, 1896–1900;
Henry Gannett, 1901–1902; Gilbert Hovey Grosvenor, 1903–1954; John Oliver
La Gorce, 1954–1957; Melville Bell Grosvenor, 1957–1967; Frederick G. Vos-
burgh, 1967–1970; Gilbert Melville Grosvenor, 1971–1980; Wilbur Garrett, 1980–
current.

CIRCULATION
10,500,000.

Barbara Nourie

NATIONAL POLICE GAZETTE

When we think of the *National Police Gazette,* if we do at all, we are likely
to think of woodcuts of actresses in tights and stories of sexual assaults and
sporting events. That is the picture of this periodical that has come down to
those of us who have never seen the original. And that impression is accurate
for most of the years (1877–1922) during which Richard K. Fox was editor and

proprietor of the magazine. But the magazine had been around for over forty years before Fox took over.

In its earliest years it had some claim to the "police" in its title, having been founded, at least in part, to aid the police and the wary citizen in the identification and apprehension or avoidance of felons and other criminals. Modeling their periodical on English police gazettes, George Wilkes and Enoch E. Camp promised to publish descriptions of criminals and accounts of crimes for the avowed purpose of revealing the identities of criminals and to supplement the work of the police.

And according to Dan Schiller, "Evidence from the *Police Gazette* itself suggests that between 1845 and 1850 the journal became the preeminent, nationally circulated newspaper for specialized crime news."[1] By November of 1850, it was claiming a circulation of over 40,000 and during this period was "a blossoming commercial concern,"[2] which had already created quite a stir on more than one occasion.

The two founders of the *National Police Gazette*, George Wilkes and Enoch E. Camp, were quite different but complementary persons. Before George Wilkes became the founding editor of the *National Police Gazette*, he had already been in trouble with the law and lawbreakers (which were not always easy to tell apart in the New York City of the 1840s) because of his work as a reporter and editor. For nearly a year he had published a small paper, the *Subterranian*, whose title suggests Wilkes's purpose of digging beneath the surface of the dung heap of the politics and crime of New York City. While he was in jail (the infamous Tombs) after his sixth arrest, he was visited by Camp, a lawyer, who proposed that with Camp's money and Wilkes's reportorial and editorial skills, they begin a journal modeled upon English police gazettes. No fewer than six such publications have been cited as models for the *National Police Gazette*, two of the most important being, perhaps, the London *Police Gazette*, an official publication founded in 1826, which contained "the Substance of all Information in Cases of Felonies, and Misdemeanors of an aggravated nature, and against Receivers of Stolen Goods, reported Thieves and offenders escaped from custody, with the time, the place and particular circumstances marking the Offence."[3] The purpose of such publicity was to help police as well as citizens in general to control crime through recognition of actual or likely offenders. The second important model was of a quite different kind; *Cleave's Weekly Police Gazette* was a famous "radical, working-class" newspaper "oriented to crime news" and to advocacy of a free press and equal laws for all classes.[4] A third dimension of the New York paper is suggested by the name of yet another English model: *Sporting and Police Gazette*.

In its first issue (13 September 1845) its Prospectus stated that the *National Police Gazette* was "devoted to the interests of the criminal police." The need was obvious: in the face of an inadequate system of crime control, "our city, and indeed the whole country, swarms with hordes of English and other thieves, burglars, pick-pockets, and swindlers." Such offenders, then, "though known to our most experienced members of the police, are entirely protected from the scrutiny of the community at large.'' Consequently, the general public is "in continual contact with miscreants who date their stationary residence from the walls of Newgate [prison], the shores of Botany Bay [penal colony,] or who have but recently left the confines of our own State Prison.'' Apparently assuming that there is no such thing as a reformed criminal, Wilkes goes on to say that it is of the "first importance that these vagabonds should be notoriously known.'' Earlier reforms had left out the press—"the mightiest conservator of social welfare"—but now the *National Police Gazette* will fill that gap, supplying to the public "all the statistics of the [police] department, both secret and otherwise.'' Everything known about felons, their names, "minute description,'' aliases, physical description, "a succinct history of their previous career, their place of residence at the time of writing, and a current account of their movements from time to time'' will be reported.[5] "The Lives of the Felons,'' a series of detailed, and often long criminal biographies, made good on the promise of the Prospectus.

Wanting to be serviceable to "The Whole country,'' the periodical promised to "open a correspondence with the principal cities and towns of the United States,''[6] and indeed the *Police Gazette* was national from its beginning, having correspondents and circulation throughout the country.

From the first, the *National Police Gazette* published advertising of a variety of kinds, though the prospectus had promised only that its advertising columns would be used for the "discovery of property lost, description of unclaimed goods taken from suspected persons, and for all the various objects connected either remotely or immediately with police affairs.''[7] The first issues did include advertisements for lost or stolen articles, as well as for a cure for rheumatism, mechanics' tools, patented trusses, bedsteads, life insurance, and a variety of other products and services.

Typically, in the weekly's earliest issues, the first two pages "flaunted the journal's prized feature—serialized criminal biographies,''—"The Lives of the Felons,'' in which "the causes, character and consequences of crime were evaluated and condemned.''[8] The last three pages were used mainly for advertising, with the middle three pages devoted to "extensive trial reports, paragraph-length news items detailing offenses committed around the nation,''[9] and an editorial. The longer stories in this middle section tended to emphasize crimes against persons (especially murder, rape, and incest) and official corruption, whereas the shorter items and "The Lives of the Felons'' series emphasized crimes against property.[10]

The weekly paper was successful from the first. Yet because it delivered on its promise to expose crime and criminals, it was often attacked, sometimes physically, by the latter and their allies in the police department. In fact, Robert Sutton, the first subject of "The Lives of the Felons,'' upon being released from jail a few months after the *Gazette* was founded, attacked the office of the paper, with a result being the death of three of his confederates. Such attacks—one of which resulted in six deaths and Wilkes's hospitalization—did not deter Wilkes from his apparently public spirited and certainly lucrative work. Yet Wilkes had other interests; in 1850 he became an assistant editor of *Spirit of the Times*, "a high class sporting paper,"[11] later becoming editor and owner. The *Police Gazette* declined, and in 1866, Wilkes sold it to former police chief George W. Matsell, with whom Wilkes had waged war in the pages of the *Gazette*. Matsell expanded or introduced features that are still identified with the *Gazette*: more pictures—especially the woodcuts that now covered virtually all of the first page; sex in stories, pictures, ads ("photographic cards for gentlemen," "manhood restored" nostrums); theater coverage, boxing and other sporting news; and as always there were the shocking crime stories. Matsell brought some life to the *Gazette*, but the sensational dailies of the period were better (or at least quicker) in reporting scandal and infamy, and the *Gazette* again declined. So in 1874, he sold out to his engravers, to whom he was deeply in debt for woodcuts.[12]

The paper probably would have died at this point had it not been for the arrival of Richard K. Fox, who was destined to turn the floundering *Gazette* into the well-known pink scandal sheet. An Irish journalist, Fox arrived in New York without money, but with ideas and energy. Going to work as an ad seller for the *Wall Street Journal*, Fox did very well. Nonetheless, he soon left the *Journal*, after discovering the ailing *Gazette*. In 1875 he went to work for it as an ad seller, but by 1877 he was its publisher and proprietor. He had gone to work for the *Gazette* with an idea, and when the operation became his through the owners' inability to pay him for his work, he revolutionized the *Gazette*. He fired the whole staff and hired first-rate writers. He expanded coverage of sex and sin—with sex scandals, sex crimes, sex pictures, sex advertising—and in 1878 began printing his sixteen pages on pale pink stock.[13] He used more and better woodcuts, including the now famous portraits of burlesque queens or stage actresses in tights, or scenes of dens of sin or crime—anything that would give his artists opportunities to create sensational pictures, whenever possible including women in revealing (for the day) poses. Crimes against women or women in battle—perhaps for the favors of a man—were favorites with his artists and reporters.

In 1879, Fox introduced the nation's first regular sports department; soon boxing coverage threatened to eclipse crime in the *Gazette*. Of course, prize fighting was illegal, and the fights were savage bare-knuckle battles, going perhaps for 100 rounds, fought as they were under London ring rules, which permitted "wrestling, gouging, kicking, and scratching."[14] The *Gazette* not only reported the fights but promoted matches and gave prizes—including championship belts to the winners. Soon the offices of the *Gazette* were the sports headquarters of the country and perhaps the world. Fox promoted or reported fights between boxers from all over the world. In all likelihood, he would have been the great John L. Sullivan's chief promoter had not Sullivan insulted Fox before they met. As a consequence of that insult, between 1882 and 1889 Fox brought every fighter he could find in any part of the world against Sullivan.

None, however, could defeat the "Strong Boy of Boston." Nonetheless, Fox made important contributions to boxing, not only with his many prizes, but also with his backing of court cases against prize fighters, which resulted in the legalization of boxing in New York.

Fox donated prizes in a vast variety of sports, and every imaginable kind of contest. Contestants included pedestrian racers, club swingers, female rifle shooters (Annie Oakley being the most famous), rowers, wrestlers, weight lifters, and so forth; nonsports competitors included champion barbers—for the fastest haircut (thirty seconds), with a prize for bravery for the cuttee—rat catchers, oyster shuckers, bartenders, hog butchers, water drinkers, teeth lifters (whatever they were), and many more.

Fox and his writers delighted in attacking the high and mighty, especially politicians and clergymen, with satirical wit. A regular feature, Religious Notes was used to report scandal or to satirize the church. In 1884, for instance, when the Iowa Conference of the Methodist Episcopal Church passed a resolution against the publication and sale of the *Police Gazette*, it was reported under Religious Notes as "a crusade against brains." For, the *Gazette* reasoned, like any other paper, it published the news of the day, and if the *Gazette* should be repressed then so should every other publication in the land other than the Bible.[15]

Theater, weird news—unusually horrible or bizarre accidents—together with fiction and not always serious editorial comment against sin and crime rounded out the *Gazette*'s coverage in the Fox years. And pictures abounded—whole two-page spreads of fine woodcuts—portraits, robberies, attacks, fighting cocks, and all manner of crimes and sensations.

Headlines from the Fox years serve to suggest the flavor of his paper: "*A New York Horror*: Lineman John Feek's Terrible Death among the Telegraph Wires Shocked to Eternity and Then Frightfully Burned in the Presence of Thousands"; "High-toned Dames Tippling"; "Whipping of a Wife-Beater"; "Because She Was Lonely. Why Mrs. Atkins Sought The Society of Men. Her Husband Objected"; "Her Young Life Ruined. Romance of Christie Jackson of Sharron Springs, N.Y. Eloped With a Rascal."

Fox's success in large part was due to his flair and imaginative originality, if not his good taste. He is said to have invented the sports page, gossip column, and the very "concept of the illustrated paper."[16] He also brought to the *Gazette* some of the best woodcut artists and reporters of his day. Legend has it that the top reporters of the top papers of New York City, hard drinkers all, would write for Fox on weekends—imprisoned in the *Gazette's* lavish offices—for good food, drinks, and $10; bylines, uncommon or pseudonym in the *Gazette*, did not reveal their identities.

When Richard K. Fox died in 1922, he was worth nearly $2 million, but the heyday of his pink paper had passed. Beginning around the turn of the century, a variety of forces made life for the *Gazette* difficult. The rise of the daily tabloids meant sin, scandal, and sensation of all kinds could be delivered daily. Later the Eighteenth Amendment closed the bars so important to the circulation of the

Gazette. And in 1922 bobbed hair became fashionable for women, bringing them into barbershops, leaving the *Gazette* with barely a place to circulate—most respectable newsstands did not carry it. Prizefighting, its old standby, did give the *Gazette* a place in the sun briefly in the 1920s, especially in 1922 when a Dempsey-Tunney match brought circulation to over 200,000. But the relatively open attitudes about sex and plenty of competition from a variety of ribald publications were costly. In 1932, the *Gazette* was sold in bankruptcy for $545. It was revived eighteen months later

> with the archaic heading and old pink paper by Mrs. Merle Williams Hersey, daughter of a Methodist clergyman and publisher of several other "hot" magazines. It was filled with confession stories and pictures of almost nudes; its leading feature was the autobiography of a burlesque "strip artist." There seemed little demand for this kind of inanity, and the *Gazette* was made a semimonthly in May 1934, and a monthly the next year, with further changes of ownership in 1935."[17]

In 1935, Harold H. Roswell became editor, made it into a slick paper monthly, and by using the same traditional *Gazette* ingredients, but by "periodically overhauling its approach,"[18] he was able to push the circulation to over 300,000 by the early 1940s.[19] He must have done something right, for he was in trouble with the postal authorities in the 1940s, and was not allowed to mail three issues. In 1968, Roswell appears to have sold the *Gazette* to J. Azaria of Montreal.[20] The latest circulation figures, for the middle seventies, are a self-reported 300,000. *Ulrich's International Periodicals Directory* for 1977–1978 lists the *National Police Gazette* at its Canadian address but does not mention the journal after that. One can only assume that the venerable tradition has died or been lost in the mists of Canada.

Notes

1. Dan Schiller, *Objectivity and the News: The Public and the Rise of Commercial Journalism* (Philadelphia: University of Pennsylvania Press, 1981), p. 102. [The author's name is normally omitted in the note when it is mentioned very closeby in the text, but the author's name here clarifies note 2.]

2. *Police Gazette* (London) 18 January 1826; quoted by Schiller, p. 97.

3. Ibid.

4. Schiller, p. 98.

5. Prospectus, quoted by Schiller, p. 101. The Prospectus was reprinted in 16 October 1845 issue; all quotations are from that issue as reprinted by Schiller.

6. Prospectus, Schiller, p. 101.

7. Ibid.

8. Schiller, pp. 102–3.

9. Ibid., p. 103.

10. Ibid.

11. Frank Luther Mott, *A History of American Magazines*, 1850–1865, vol.2 (Cambridge: Harvard University Press, 1938), p. 327.

12. Ibid., p. 328.

13. Ibid., pp. 328–29.

14. Ibid., p. 331.

15. *National Police Gazette*, 15 March 1884; reprinted in *The Police Gazette*, ed. Gene Smith and Jayne Barry Smith (New York: Simon and Schuster, 1972) pp. 58–54.

16. Gene Smith, Introduction, *The Police Gazette*, eds. Gene Smith and Jayne Barry Smith, p. 14

17. Mott, p. 337.

18. Theodore Peterson, *Magazines in the Twentieth Century* (Urbana: University of Illinois Press, 1964), p. 375.

19. Matthew Huttner, "The Police Gazette," *American Mercury*, July 1948, p. 23.

20. *Ulrich's International Periodicals Directory* for 1973 to 1974 contains two entries for *National Police Gazette*, one for Montreal and one for New York City. The meaning of this listing is unclear, but it seems unlikely that these are two different magazines.

Information Sources

BIBLIOGRAPHY

Huttner, Matthew. "The Police Gazette." *American Mercury,* July 1948, pp. 15–23.

Mott, Frank Luther. *A History of American Magazines, 1850—1865*, vol. 2. Cambridge: Harvard University Press, 1938.

Peterson, Theodore. *Magazines in the Twentieth Century*. Urbana: University of Illinois Press, 1964.

Schiller, Dan. *Objectivity and the News: The Public and the Rise of Commercial Journalism*. Philadelphia: University of Pennsylvania Press, 1981.

Smith, Gene, and Jayne Barry Smith, eds. *The Police Gazette*. New York: Simon and Schuster, 1972. Introduction by Gene Smith and Foreword by Tom Wolfe. Collection of reprints of articles and illustrations from the *National Police Gazette* of the 1870's, 1880's and 1890's; includes a complete facsimile on pink paper of the issue for 28 May 1892. Smith's introduction was also published in *American Heritage*, October 1972, p. 65–73, as "Little Visit to the Lower Depths via the Police Gazette."

Van Every, Edward. *Sins of America as "Exposed" by the Police Gazette*. New York: Frederick A. Stokes, 1931.

Sins of New York as "Exposed" by the Police Gazette. New York: Frederick A. Stokes, 1930. Reissued New York: Benjamin Blom, Inc., 1972.

INDEX SOURCES

    n.a.

LOCATION SOURCES

    American Periodical Series, Library of Congress; University of Illinois at Urbana. Available in microform, limited.

Publication History

MAGAZINE TITLE AND TITLE CHANGES

    The National Police Gazette.

VOLUME AND ISSUE DATA
>   Weekly, 1845–1934; semimonthly, 1934–1935; monthly, 1935– . Vols. 1–32
>   1845–1877, annual volumes, thereafter semiannual volumes; suspended 11
>   February 1932–5, September 1933; monthly from 5 September 1933–ca.
>   1970s.

PUBLISHERS AND PLACES OF PUBLICATION
>   Enoch E. Camp and George Wilkes, 1845–1848; George Wilkes, 1848–1866;
>   George W. Matsell and Company, 1866–1874; Herbert R. Mooney and Charles
>   A. Lederer, 1874–1877; Richard K. Fox, 1877–1922; Charles J. Fox, 1922–1932;
>   Police Gazette Corporation, owned by editors, 1933–ca. 1970s. In 1968 Harold
>   H. Roswell appears to have sold the magazine to J. Azaria of 1434 St. Catherine
>   St., W. Montreal 107, Quebec, Canada.

EDITORS
>   Same as publishers, 1845–1922; Ralph D. Robinson, 1923–1932; Merle W. Her-
>   sey, 1933–1935; Edward E. Eagle and Harold H. Roswell, 1935–1937; H. H.
>   Roswell, 1937–1968; Nat K. Perlow, 1968–?

CIRCULATION
>   11 October 1845, 8,600; after three issues, 15,000; January–February 1846,
>   20,000; September 1846, 23,000; 1889, 500,000 (thought to be an all-time high);
>   1935, 20,000 to 40,000; 1940, 83,715; 1970s, 300,000. (Most of these figures
>   are self-reported.)

Daniel Straubel

NATIONAL REVIEW

National Review includes one long feature, several short articles, several reviews of culture, a column by editor Buckley called "On the Right," and a popular crossword puzzle in each biweekly issue. In spite of this consistent format, few readers would associate the magazine with any of its individual features as strongly as with William F. Buckley, Jr., the only editor *National Review* has ever had, and with American conservatism. While *National Review's* role in the emergence of conservatism in America is the magazine's most significant achievement, one can hardly overestimate Buckley's role in this achievement. The following essay addresses the importance of *National Review* to American conservatism and neglects biographical data about Buckley (his intellectual positions form, of course, much of the history of *National Review*). Readers interested in a biographical treatment of Buckley and a review of his writing should consult Mark Royden Winchell's *William F. Buckley, Jr.* (Boston: Twayne, 1984).

Shortly after the vote was in for the 1980 presidential election, *National Review* noted: "With the election of Ronald Reagan, *National Review* assumes a new importance in American life. We become, as it were, an establishment organ; and we feel it only appropriate to alter our demeanor accordingly. This is therefore the last issue in which we shall indulge in levity. Connoisseurs of humor will have to get their yuks elsewhere. We have a nation to run" (28 November 1980, p. 1434). This characteristic lightness of tone (often the tone of the gadfly and dilettante) has never muffled the serious role played by *National Review*, the magazine that has been the dominant voice of American conservatism for thirty-three years. Since the first issue in November 1955

> no significant facet of the conservative renascence [has] escaped *NR*'s notice. Nearly every prominent conservative intellectual wrote at least one article for it; many were regular contributors. Here too, many of the crucial intramural debates on conservative thought and strategy were conducted. If any single publication mirrored and even dominated the development of the Right after the mid–50s, *National Review* was it.[1]

The major contributions *National Review* has made to American conservatism can be described in the following large categories. (1) *National Review* addressed the task of bringing together and sustaining a coalition on the Right. Since this coalition took shape in a climate wherein discussions of the "foreign" quality of conservatism in liberal America were commonplace, (2) asserting the native American content of conservative philosophy became an issue that *National Review* frequently addressed. (3) Examining the consistency of the thought of individual conservatives and denouncing self-proclaimed conservatives whose positions threatened the fragile coalition was a natural duty for the leading conservative voice—these debates and the resulting classification of the orthodox and the heterodox played a large part in defining "conservatism." Allied to this watchdog role has been (4) the resulting formulation of principles and of a vocabulary for the conservative position. From Frank Meyer's strenuously argued assertion that liberalism and communism are ideologically bound (14 June 1958, p. 566) to Joseph Sobran's eloquent appreciation of the conservative sensibility (31 December 1985, pp. 23–58), *National Review* has provided a forum wherein American conservatism has been consistently reformulated and its principles applied to the issues of the day.

To appreciate the importance of *National Review* to American conservatism, some description of the political scene of the 1950s is necessary. The American Left had, in those years, eight weekly journals to articulate liberal positions. Between 1950 and 1953, a single journal, the *Freeman*, attempted to provide this voice for the American Right. In the early 1950s, this lone conservative voice played a crucial role in focusing dissent from the Left. When the three principal editors of the *Freeman* resigned in 1953 after internal bickering and Frank Choderov, a near anarchist, became editor, conservatives keenly felt the need for a stable conservative magazine that would, like the liberal *New Republic** and *Nation* during the New Deal, reach opinion makers throughout the country. After the editorial changes in the *Freeman*, William F. Buckley, Jr., began plans to establish and edit a magazine that would reach intellectuals rather than the grass roots and would represent more than one strand of American conservative thought. George Nash provides a fine summary of the strands from which Buckley forged what was to be the conservative coalition:

> In 1945, no articulate, coordinated, self-consciously conservative intellectual force existed in the United States. There were, at most, scattered voices of protest, profoundly pessimistic about the future of their country. ... First, there were "classical liberals" or "libertarians," resisting the threat of the ever expanding State to liberty, private enterprise, and individualism. Convinced that America was rapidly drifting toward statism (socialism), these intellectuals offered an alternative that achieved some scholarly and popular influence by the mid–1950s. Concurrently and independently, a second school of thought was emerging: the "new conservatism" or "traditionalism" of such men as Richard Weaver, Peter Viereck, Russell Kirk, and Robert Nisbet. Shocked by totalitarianism, total war, and the development of secular, rootless, mass society during the 1930s and 1940s, the "new conservatives" urged a return to traditional religious and ethical absolutes and a rejection of the "relativism" which had allegedly corroded Western values and produced an intolerable vacuum that was filled by demonic ideologies. Third, there appeared militant, evangelistic anti-Communism, shaped decisively by influential ex-radicals of the 1930s, including Whittaker Chambers, James Burnham, Frank Meyer, and many more. These former men of the Left brought to the postwar Right a profound conviction that the West was engaged in a titanic struggle with an implacable adversary—Communism—which sought nothing less than conquest of the world.[2]

Buckley's success in holding together this contentious coalition was the crucial factor in establishing *National Review* as the major organ of American conservative thought. Each of the three major strands of conservative thought was represented from the magazine's first issue. Among the libertarians, Frank Choderov, Wilhelm Röpke, John Chamberlain, Max Eastman, and Frank Meyer were represented on the masthead. Traditionalists were represented by Russell Kirk, who contributed a regular column, Donald Davidson, Erik von Kuehnelt-Leddihn, and Richard Weaver. (Ortega y Gassett was to have provided an essay called "The Revolt Against the Masses.") A large number of ex-Communists and former radicals were included among the editorial staff; James Burnham, Willmoore Kendall, William Schlamm, Freda Utley, and Whittaker Chambers were among this prominent group. The themes of these groups were the themes of the magazine. The editors declared themselves libertarian in the fight against the growth of government, which they regarded as a threat to individual liberty. They were traditionalist in opposing the social engineering that tried to reshape human nature according to an ideological or scientific ideal. Several members of the editorial staff, including Buckley, openly proclaimed their Roman Catholicism and defended philosophical and moral absolutes against the plasticity of liberal thought. They were also irrevocably opposed to communism, which they characterized as "satanic"; coexistence was "neither desirable, nor possible, nor honorable" (19 November 1955, p. 6). Even more than communism, however, the intellectual enemy was liberalism.[3] Frank Meyer stated this philosophical position in an early article:

> That contemporary liberalism is in agreement with Communism on the most essential point—the necessity and desirability of socialism; that it regards all inherited value—theological, philosophical, political—as without intrinsic value or authority; that, therefore, no irreconcilable differences exist between it and Communism—only differences as to method and means; and that, in view of these characteristics of their ideology, the Liberals are unfit for the leadership of a free society, and intrinsically incapable of offering serious opposition to the Communist offensive. (14 June 1958, p. 566)

That the coalition the magazine set out to establish has endured for over thirty years is a tribute to the farsightedness of Buckley's vision. The contemporary reader of *National Review* will still find the same procapitalist, anticommunist, protraditionalist mixture—a mixture that has characterized conservatism in America.

Despite the eventual success of the coalition *National Review* sought to forge, the early editorial board was a "snakepit of sectarian controversy."[4] Several traditionalists were critical of *National Review* from the outset (among them Allen Tate, T. S. Eliot, and eventually, Russell Kirk). Kirk finally asked Buckley to take his name off the masthead. A particular complaint of the traditionalists was *National Review's* defense of Joseph McCarthy; the pragmatic nature of the anticommunist movement often brought it into conflict with the more philosophical traditionalists and libertarians. Dissent within the magazine's ranks was matched by attacks from the Left: Dwight MacDonald, in a notorious article, charged *National Review* with "vulgarity," "brutality," and "banality." The editors were "half-educated provincials" and the "intellectually underprivileged." Buckley "would make an excellent journalist if he had a little more humor, common sense, and intellectual curiosity; also if he knew how to write."[5] Despite continued internal and external sniping, Buckley has guarded *National Review* against extremists who would threaten the conservative coalition by pushing too far in their own direction. The effort required to hold such a coalition together and to recruit new talent when disgruntled veterans left was repaid by the emergence of young writers like Garry Wills, John Leonard, George F. Will, Renata Adler, Joan Didion, D. Keith Mano, and Joseph Sobran.

If establishing a conservative coalition was *National Review's* first significant achievement, working out a definition of "conservative" that would hold this coalition together became the work of the 1955–1965 period. Especially during the magazine's first four or five years, disputes about the nature of conservatism occupied the editors. Exposing inconsistencies in the positions of self-professed conservatives whose vision threatened the delicate equilibrium of American conservatism often led to lengthy disputes—the cases of the John Birch Society, Peter Viereck, and Ayn Rand, and the antagonism between Russell Kirk and Frank Meyer are examples. For several years, *National Review* attacked Robert Welch, the leader of the John Birch Society, for his wild allegations but stopped short of condemning the entire society. Finally, in a feature article in 1965 (19 October 1964, pp. 914–20; 925–29), the editors of *National Review* condemned the entire society as more damaging to the Right than communism itself. Peter Viereck, a self-styled "new conservative" who viewed liberalism as a potential ally against totalitarianism and identified Adlai Stevenson as a potential "conservative" leader, was exiled from the conservative coalition by Frank Meyer, whose article "Counterfeit at a Popular Price" (11 August 1956, p. 18) made clear that a centrist conservatism was not acceptable to the intellectual Right.[6]

The popularity of Ayn Rand raised more fundamental questions. Rand's vision, set out in a series of widely read novels, portrayed a Nietzschean world in which self-interest and free enterprise heroically defeated irrationality and collectivism. While attractive to many conservatives on the libertarian side, Rand's vision was strenuously opposed by traditionalists. In a memorable review of *Atlas Shrugged*, Whittaker Chambers denounced Rand's "dictatorial tone" and shrill dogmatism. The book, Chambers said, "consistently mistakes raw force for strength. . . . It supposes itself to be the bringer of a final revelation. Therefore, resistance to the message cannot be tolerated. . . . From almost any page of *Atlas Shrugged*, a voice can be heard, from painful necessity, commanding: 'To a gas chamber-go!' " (28 December 1957, pp. 96). Several libertarians defended Rand against Chamber's attack; many traditionalists sided with Chambers. Gary Wills's rejection of Rand's capitalistic utopia as fundamentally liberal—because of her assertion of the immediate perfectibility of mankind–became the coalition position. Rand's rejection of religion as irrational and her replacement of the cross of Christianity with the dollar sign of capitalism were not compatible with the emphasis on absolutes and transcendence that marked the *National Review's* position (27 February 1960, p. 139). This traditionalist victory was not won without the rancor of many libertarians—Max Eastman eventually demanded that his name be removed from the magazine's masthead because of his objection to its religious perspective. The battle between libertarians and traditionalists was waged, especially between Meyer and Kirk, for the better part of a decade. The result of this discussion was not a unified philosophy that satisfied each part of the coalition, but a realization that philosophical consistency was not necessary for a political program to which the various strands of conservatism could assent.[7]

The intellectual and organizational work carried out in the *National Review* in the late 1950s and early 1960s prepared the coalition that united to support Barry Goldwater's 1964 presidential candidacy. The role of *National Review* figures in Goldwater's candidacy was considerable: L. Brent Bozell (Buckley's brother-in-law) wrote *Conscience of a Conservative* for Goldwater; Russell Kirk helped prepare several of Goldwater's speeches; Milton Friedman served as his economic adviser; and Buckley, Bozell, and Meyer all endorsed his candidacy.

While Goldwater's crushing defeat sobered the short-lived euphoria at *National Review*, the style of the campaign waged against Goldwater suggested the liberal bias of the media as a new focus for conservative attention. Ronald Reagan suggested a point of departure by noting that the conservative philosophy hadn't been defeated so much as a mistaken image of it that the media had promulgated (1 December 1964, p. 1055). The willingness of the national news media to call attention to the most erratic and irresponsible accusations (Goldwater was compared to Stalin by Senator Fulbright, to Hitler by Martin Luther King and Governor Edmund Brown, and accused of psychological imbalance by many—in a survey by Ralph Ginzberg, psychiatrists who had never met Goldwater declared him unfit) awakened the *National Review* circle to the need for a more balanced voice from the media. In 1966, Buckley began his popular television series "Firing Line"; Milton Friedman became a regular columnist for *Newsweek*.* The style of Goldwater's liberal opponents in what Buckley called a "vile campaign" (6 October 1964, p. 853) also served as cement to the conservative coalition—the enemy, liberalism, had been engaged and was as fearsome as *National Review* writers had been cautioning since 1955.

The magazine's analysis of the major events of the past twenty years—the riots and unrest of the late 1960s and early 1970s, Watergate, the Carter presidency, the Reagan presidency—have not broken with the framework of conservative principle established during the first decade of *National Review*. The themes of the moral and intellectual bankruptcy of liberalism, the liberal bias of the media, and the traditional American quality of the principles of limited government, liberty under law, and Christian revelation have been consistently reformulated and reapplied. Conservatives are fond of observing that *National Review* hasn't changed, while the United States has. Certainly the magazine has found itself closer to the national mood in this decade than at any previous time; still, *National Review's* role as the tester of conservative orthodoxy and the dispatcher of the heterodox has continued, regardless of the power of the target.

Although never a physically splashy magazine, *National Review's* polysyllabic verbal pyrotechnics remain one of its most characteristic features. Ronald Reagan once said that he'd spent "many happy hours in my favorite chair, *National Review* in one hand, the dictionary in the other."[8] Buckley and the many young writers he has encouraged share the same love for the richness and complexity of the English language, and often the same wit and humor. While this style can be easily dismissed as snobbish or Ivy League, its use suggests the definition Richard Hofstadter applies to "intellectual" in *Anti-Intellectualism in American Life* (New York: Knopf, 1963). The intellectual, Hofstadter asserts, is characterized by both seriousness and playfulness toward the same subject. This recognition identifies *National Review's* intended audience and its place within American conservatism. The magazine has attempted to focus a movement of ideas—a coalition of conservative thought preparing to lend its voice to shaping the course of the nation. Whatever one's response to the magazine's politics or style, one must regard with respect *National Review's* success in focusing the conservative intellectual movement in America.

Notes

1. George H. Nash, *Conservative Intellectual Movement in America, Since 1945* (New York: Basic Books, 1976), p. 441.

2. Ibid., p. xiii.

3. Ibid., p. 149.

4. Mark Royden Winchell, *William F. Buckley, Jr.* (Boston: Twayne, 1984), p. 6.

5. Dwight MacDonald, "Scrambled Eggheads on the Right," *Commentary*, April 1956, pp. 367–73.

6. Nash, p. 156.

7. Ibid., p. 184.

8. J. Castro and E. Rudolph, "All the President's Magazine's" *Time*, 15 December 1980, p. 78.

Information Sources

BIBLIOGRAPHY

Hart, Jeffrey. *The American Dissent: A Decade of Modern Conservatism*. New York: Doubleday, 1966.

King, Larry L. "God, Man, and William F. Buckley." *Harper's*, March 1967, pp. 53–61.

MacDonald, Dwight. "Scrambled Eggheads on the Right." *Commentary*, April 1956, pp. 367–73.

Nash, George H. *Conservative Intellectual Movement in America, Since 1945*. New York: Basic Books, 1976.

Wills, Garry. *Confessions of a Conservative*. Garden City, N.Y.: Doubleday, 1979.

Winchell, Mark Royden. *William F. Buckley, Jr.* Boston: Twayne, 1984.

INDEX SOURCES

Readers' Guide (1961–present); *Magazine Index* (1977–present); *Popular Magazine Review; American Bibliography of Slavic and East European Studies; Future Survey; Catholic Periodical and Literature, Index* (1959–1962).

LOCATION SOURCES

Library of Congress, many other libraries. Available in microform.

Publication History

MAGAZINE TITLE AND TITLE CHANGES

National Review (alternate issues for 4, October 1958–4 April 1959 have title *National Review Bulletin*).

VOLUME AND ISSUE DATA

Vols. 1–39, (19 November 1955–present). Alternate issues for 4 October 1958–4 April 1959 are called vol. 1, nos. 1–14. Became biweekly in 1958.

PUBLISHER AND PLACE OF PUBLICATION

National Review, Inc., New York, New York.

EDITOR
    William F. Buckley, Jr.
CIRCULATION
    110,000.

Glenn Anderson

NEW LEADER

The *New Leader,* a journal of political opinion with a heavy emphasis on foreign affairs founded in 1924, was first edited by James Oneal. The first issue declared: "The New Leader will be a publication devoted to the Socialist Party and will aid in rebuilding the Socialist movement in the United States."[1] Between 1928 and 1935 the publication was entitled *New Leader and American Appeal.* It was originally published in a weekly newspaper format, but changed to a standard magazine format in 1950. During its formative years the publication acted as the official organ of the American Socialist party and contained contributions from well-known socialist leaders such as Eugene V. Debs and Norman Thomas, but it broke away in 1936 because of the influence of radical united-front elements within the organization.[2]

Samuel M. Levitas, an émigré Russian Jew, became general manager of *New Leader* in 1930 and was the guiding light behind the periodical for thirty years. In 1944 Levitas's name first appeared in the publication as executive editor, though William E. Bohn was listed as editor. An "old-line Socialist" whose political proposals more closely resembled "Fair Deal" pragmatism than socialism, Levitas had departed the United States in 1917 to return to his native Russia at the time of the Russian Revolution. He was soon arrested as an anti-Bolshevik, but managed to escape to Poland in 1923 and then return to the United States. The *New Leader* had already been in existence for seven years when he joined the staff.[3]

From the beginning the journal published a wide variety of democratic opinion—excluding both communism and fascism from its pages. Such notables as John Dewey, Bertrand Russell, George Orwell, Arthur Koestler, Carl Sandburg, Herbert Morrison, Leon Blum, Max Eastman, James Burnham, Walter Reuther, and James Carey wrote for the magazine. Under Levitas's editorship the *New Leader* became "America's leading liberal-labor weekly." Levitas did not pay contributors, for as he remarked to authors: "Don't expect to profit from the truth."[4]

The *New Leader*, which at its peak in the 1960s never topped a circulation of 30,000, has generally been hailed by conservatives and liberals alike for its articles. *Time** magazine referred to it as "one of the best journals of opinion in the U.S., distinguished for its international coverage and lucid reports of Soviet tyranny."[5] The *Commonweal* found it to be "a remarkable magazine,"[6] while the *National Review** found *New Leader* to be "an open forum in which a broad range of distinguished authors . . . wrote without editorial restriction.'' This was fully in keeping with Levitas's belief that the magazine should be ''dedicated without reserve to the enlightenment, not the manipulation of public opinion.''[7] Not surprisingly, the influence of *New Leader* has always been greater than its circulation would suggest.

During the 1930s and 1940s *New Leader* was notable for its anti-Stalinism and was one of the rare journals to inveigh against the liquidation of the kulaks. The journal argued that the United States was ''taken in'' at Teheran, Yalta, and Potsdam. It maintained extensive files on communist activities worldwide. It likewise fought fascism, anti-Semitism, and anti-unionism.[8]

In 1950, in order to gain new subscribers, *New Leader* went to a weekly magazine format. Soon thereafter it became a biweekly. Herb Lubalin, who had redesigned *McCall's** and the *Saturday Evening Post** for a hefty fee, contributed his services free for a further overhaul of the *New Leader* in 1961. The new journal instituted an illustrated cover with line drawings, more pictures, and better-quality paper. It was a slender periodical, but that was understandable in a venture that never made a profit but relied on the contributions of individuals and foundations to stay in print. The magazine was governed by a board of directors and had a full-time staff of only three persons. The freedom of the editor was illustrated in 1963 when Columbia professor Daniel Bell published an article critical of the anti-Negro bias of the International Ladies' Garment Workers' Union (ILGWU). The ILGWU, a financial mainstay of the *New Leader*, wrote a response but did not withdraw its financial backing.[9]

Samuel Levitas died in 1961, and was immediately succeeded by Myron Kolatch as editor. In 1963 the circulation reached 28,500. Kolatch started paying younger contributors $25 to $50 per article, but still could get articles from Spanish philosopher Salvadore de Madariaga, economist Adolf A. Berle, and theologian Reinhold Niebuhr for nothing. Into the 1970s and 1980s the *New Leader* continued to attract notable authors such as Willy Brandt, David Ben-Gurion, and Zbigniew Brzezinski. By the end of the 1970s circulation had fallen back to about 23,000, and Kolatch observed that he had learned to accept ''near-bankruptcy as a way of life.''[10]

The *New Leader*'s philosophy has been described variously as ''theoretical socialism'' or ''liberal and democratic with a small *d*.'' It has maintained a consistency over its sixty-plus years partly because it has been guided primarily by two persons since 1931. It has not been a profitable venture, but it has been a successful one, attracting notable world figures as contributors. Long indexed in the *Public Affairs Information Service Bulletin*, the *New Leader* has been included in *Readers' Guide* since 1978. By the mid–1980s it had a circulation of around 25,000. The journal, in addition to its standard political fare, contained book reviews as well as reviews of cultural events. William Katz and Linda S. Katz observed about the *New Leader*: ''The writing is not strongly biased toward the Right or Left.''[11] The *New Leader* is likely to remain a valuable source of current political opinion.

Notes

1. "The New Leader," *New Leader,* 19 January 1924 p. 10.
2. "The *New Leader* Steps Out," *Time,* 1 May 1950, pp. 60, 63.
3. "The *New Leader* Steps Out," p. 63; Theodore Peterson, *Magazines in the Twentieth Century* (Urbana: University of Illinois Press, 1964), pp. 428–29; "Samuel M. Levitas," *Who Was Who in America,* vol. 4: *1961–1968* (Chicago: Marquis-Who's Who, 1968), p. 570; "S. M. Levitas 1894–1961," *New Leader,* 9 January 1961, pp. 2–3.
4. "The *New Leader* Steps Out," p. 63.
5. "Influence Before Affluence," *Time,* 1 March 1963, p. 38;
6. "Serious But Critical," *Commonweal,* 8 September 1950, p. 525;
7. Samuel M. Levitas, RIP, *National Review,* 14 January 1961, p. 11.
8. "The *New Leader* Steps Out," p. 63; "New *New Leader,*" *Newsweek,* 15 May 1950, p. 64; Peterson, *Magazines in the Twentieth Century,* pp. 428–29.
9. "The *New Leader* Steps Out," p. 63; "Influence Before Affluence," pp. 38, 40.
10. "Influence Before Affluence," p. 38; Kolatch quoted in Anna Quindlen, "New Owners Find Magazines Costly 'Fun,' " *New York Times,* 21 March 1977, p. 29.
11. "The *New Leader* Steps Out," p. 63; William Katz and Linda S. Katz, *Magazines for Libraries,* 5th ed. (New York: R. R. Bowker, 1986), pp. 746–47.

Information Sources

BIBLIOGRAPHY
"Influence Before Affluence." *Time,* 1 March 1963, pp. 38, 40.
Katz, William, and Linda S. Katz. *Magazines for Libraries.* 5th ed. New York: R. R. Bowker, 1986, pp. 746–47.
"The New Leader." *New Leader,* 19 January 1924, p. 10
"The *New Leader* Steps Out." *Time,* 1 May 1950, pp. 60, 63.
"New *New Leader.*" *Newsweek,* 15 May 1950, p. 64.
Peterson, Theodore. *Magazines in the Twentieth Century.* Urbana: University of Illinois Press, 1964.
Quindlen, Anna. "New Owners Find Magazines Costly 'Fun.' " *New York Times,* 21 March 1977, p. 29.
"S. M. Levitas 1894–1961." *New Leader,* 9 January 1961, pp. 2–3.
"Samuel M. Levitas, RIP." *National Review,* 14 January 1961, p. 11.
"Serious But Critical," *Commonweal,* 8 September 1950, p. 525.
Tebbel, John. *The American Magazine: A Compact History.* New York: Hawthorne Books, 1969.
INDEX SOURCES
By publisher. *Readers' Guide to Periodical Literature* (1978–present); *Magazine Index* (1977–present).
LOCATION SOURCES
Stanford University, West Virginia University, many other libraries. Available in microform, limited.

Publication History

MAGAZINE TITLE CHANGES
> *New Leader and American Appeal,* 1928–1935; *New Leader,* 1924–1928, 1935–present.

VOLUME AND ISSUE DATA
> Vols. 1–70, 1924–present, weekly and biweekly.

PUBLISHER AND PLACE OF PUBLICATION
> New Leader Publishing Association, New York, New York, 1924–1936; Social Democratic Federation, New York, New York, 1936–1946; New Leader Publishing Association, New York, New York, 1946–1955; American Labor Conference on International Affairs, New York, New York, 1955–present.

EDITORS
> James Oneal, 1924–1940; William E. Bohn, 1941–1967; Samuel M. Levitas, 1944–1961; Myron Kolatch, 1961–present. Secondary sources list Levitas as editor since 1930 or 1931, yet he does not appear as an editor in the publication itself until 1944. William Bohn is listed as editor between 1941 and 1967 though Levitas and Kolatch are listed as executive editors.

CIRCULATION
> 25,000.

Ronnie W. Faulkner

THE NEW REPUBLIC

The 24 October 1988 cover of the *New Republic* shows a multicolored treehouse of leaves. Tucked among its branches is the editor Shoe, the wise old owl in the cartoon of the same name created by Jeff MacNeely. Wearing a yuppie striped tie and a brown tweed coat with patched elbows, the bespectacled Shoe, his feet propped up on a wooden rolltop desk, sits comfortably on a wooden crate. His rolltop desk is stacked to overflowing with paper, but interspersed are a few golden treasures: hardcover books. A computer monitor has been unplugged but stares down at him and the paperwork, its screen smashed in by a football. Shoe seems oblivious to the impending disaster of the precariously balanced items atop his desk. He is content to read in his red book some morsel of fine literature or intrigue.

What does the 24 October 1988 cover say about the history of the *New Republic*? Surely it says more than the headlines on the cover pronounce: "Drugs: The Koop Solution"; "Campaign '88: Judis in Mississippi, Kondracke in Ohio, Barnes in Maryland"; "The Next Economic Dunkirk"; "Fall Books"; "History in Sound Bites"; "Soviet Television"; "Vietnam"; "Harold Brodkey"; and "Painting Paris."[1] With only three weeks before federal elections, the headlines are telling for what they say and what they do *not* say. To be fair, previous issues contained extensive election coverage, but as one glances through the 24 October issue for even the slightest lingering of politics, one thing is noted:

although thin criticisms of both political parties are prevalent, the candidate with the most coverage is Republican.

Thus, the *New Republic* could appear to be taking a new twist, a new turn, in its long and famed history. From its inception in 1914, by efforts of editor Herbert Croly and funding and support from Dorothy and Willard Straight, the *New Republic: A Journal of Opinion* was described and advertised as being "the collective opinion of the editors, mainly on the political, economic, and social problems of the day."[2] Frank Luther Mott further describes the initial edition as

> a good-looking weekly of thirty-two pages quarto including self-cover. . . . The cover displayed the leading titles and authors of the issue. There were no illustrations. The journal opened with some three pages of fairly short editorial comment, and these were followed by four or five headed editorial articles . . . . Then came the signed articles known in the office as "light middles"; though by no means all of them were light, they had more variety in style and topic than the editorial section . . . . Book reviews, including Littell's "Books and Things" department, commonly occupied four or five pages. Then there were a few pages of advertising, chiefly of books. The paper sold for ten cents on the newsstands, or four dollars a year by subscription.[3]

It is difficult to trace in a few paragraphs a history rich in political fervor, social motivation, and intellectual heavyweights such as Mott and others have written extensively about. The bibliography lists in-depth works detailing the role the *New Republic* has played in the twentieth century, but a few highlights are outlined below.

At the end of its first year of publication the *New Republic* circulated among some 15,000 readers. Herbert Croly, the first editor, entertained regular contributions from Walter Lippman and Walter Weyl. John Patrick Diggins notes several beliefs of liberalism from the early writings: "freedom . . . strong government and monopolies controlled in the public interest . . . [and support of] child labor laws, an eight-hour work day, collective bargaining, a minimum wage, and workmen's compensation."[4] James Playsted Wood describes the early *New Republic* as a "liberal magazine . . . sharply critical of the social and political scene . . . the friend of labor, the foe of fascism or anything it sees as fascistic in tendency, the enemy of economic privilege, and a strong proponent and defender of civil liberties."[5]

As a critical supporter of President Woodrow Wilson's war policy, the *New Republic* grew to a circulation of between 30,000 and 43,000 during the peak of World War I.[6] But by many standards of the time, the *New Republic* was not a voice of the nation united; it instead gave the air of an elitist bunch of snobbish, leftist radicals. Editor Croly is quoted as having said that the *New Republic*'s purpose was "less to inform and entertain its readers than to start little insurrections in the realm of their convictions."[7] More often than not, these "insurrections" were for specific political causes, such as the Progressive party and Theodore Roosevelt, or President Wilson's 1916 presidential campaign. In 1920 editor Croly spoke out in favor of the Farmer-Labor Party.

In the postwar era of the 1920s, high inflation and a change to mechanical woodpulp paper stock led to increased prices and crumbling copies of the journal. When Willard Straight died, Dorothy Straight continued to support the publication financially through one deficit after another. The *New Republic* found fuel for political debate in such emotional issues as the Red Scare and the International Workers of the World (IWW). In 1924, the *New Republic* strongly supported the Progressive Party, and endorsed Robert La Follette for president.

In 1926, the *New Republic* began a new column to report on weekly Washington happenings. Frank Kent of the *Baltimore Sun* is noted as the first author of "T.R.B.," the column name and pseudonym used by him and many others to follow.[8] By 1929, in part because of the conditions of the Great Depression and in part because of the *New Republic*'s bankruptcy filing, circulation bottomed out near 10,000.[9]

In 1930 Croly died, and Bruce Bliven took over as editor-in-chief. With Bliven at the helm and George Soule close at his side, the political sphere took a more practical turn. Instead of philosophizing about utopian politics, the editors and writers acknowledged that they "were not ready to scrap the American system, much as they might criticize it."[10]

Isolationism and the belief of our "own house in order before meddling in the affairs of Europe" were prevalent views in the mid–1930s.[11] David Seideman reports that by the election of 1932 the *New Republic* displayed "disgust with both 'Republican Dee and Democratic Dum' [causing] the magazine [to ponder] . . . the radical options for the first time. Having eliminated all other possibilities, a tepid endorsement went to the Socialist [candidate], Norman Thomas."[12] While the magazine did not publicly endorse the communist candidate, William Z. Foster, prominent *New Republic* staff members did publicly endorse him outside the magazine's confines.

By the late 1930s, advertisements became more prevalent and more informative. Seideman reports,

> In any given issues, vacationers could select from a half-dozen tours to the U.S.S.R., where they might marvel at the 'outburst of enthusiasm' for the 'successful collectivization of national farms.' . . . Afterward, they could show their allegiance to the Popular Front by catching the late-night show of 'Confessions of a Nazi Spy,' starring Edward G. Robinson—the first movie promotion ever to run in the *New Republic*.[13]

Circulation gradually rose to 25,000 despite more reserved subsidies from Dorothy Straight.

With Roosevelt's New Deal and the continued emergence (or threat) of Russian politics, Mott notes that the *New Republic* had pretty well shifted "away from the 'extreme' left and about as near a conformist policy as it could ever allow itself to come.''[14] With the approach of World War II, the magazine was initially cautious in calling for intervention and a show of force.

By spring and summer of 1941, however, articles such as "The Race against Hitler" were surfacing regularly.[15] The 25 August 1941 issue "called for a declaration of war against the Axis powers.''[16] At least for a brief time, the *New Republic's* editors and political spokesmen across the country were finally, as Diggins points out, enjoying "unity in time of war.''[17] The fate of the Jewish people continued to be a popular topic during the war, although economics, racial segregation in the United States, benevolence toward Russia, and literary review continued to be covered during World War II. In a search of *Readers' Guide*, Arlene Rossen Cardozo reports that some sixty-four articles were published by national magazines during the time 1941–1944 on the Nazi problem, of which opinion magazines ran some thirty-seven articles or editorials. The *Nation* and the *New Republic* accounted for thirty of the total thirty-seven instances, with the *New Republic* responsible for eleven such articles or editorials.[18]

After World War II, Michael Whitney Straight, son of the original owners, took over as publisher. The cartoon emerged as a regular feature (not prolific, just "regular") of both political and social comment during his tenure. But the fervor, the "zing," the "sting" of political criticism at the *New Republic* took off once again in 1946 when Henry A. Wallace, who had resigned from President Truman's cabinet, was appointed editor. The possibility of a new third party was fueled by Wallace's support of Russia in the peace process. Wallace also visited Palestine and served as a distinctly prominent voice in advocating creation of a Jewish Palestine.

The magazine continued to support and promote Wallace's beliefs for some time. Circulation took off like wildfire, and a revamping of the *New Republic's* format brought up to forty-eight pages per issue packed with "sketches, cartoons (some with dabs of color), a United Nations column, labor, and farm departments, theatre and art criticisms.''[19] Circulation was reported to have been around 96,000 copies a week.[20] But when Wallace finally began his official campaign for the presidency, he was quickly phased out and dropped as editor in 1948. Two days after Wallace's last article for the *New Republic* was published, editor Straight quickly moved to endorse Supreme Court Justice William O. Douglas as the *New Republic's* choice for presidential candidate; later, Truman was endorsed.[21]

In 1950 the magazine's offices were moved from New York to Washington, D.C., primarily to be closer to the political action. The expansion and upgrading of features, printing, and style, coupled with Wallace's departure, brought financial crisis to the *New Republic* once again. Straight's targeted circulation of 300,000 fell gravely short. The *New Republic* was by no means abandoning political thought for the sake of becoming a popular, weekly news magazine, but not all the changes worked well in its favor. Staff was reduced and pages were cut; the price was raised in 1949 to 20 cents a copy ($6.50 a year).

In 1949, Wood compared the *New Republic* with the *Nation*:

> *The New Republic* [is] the more aggressive in its support of minority groups, minority opinion, and advanced thought generally. Neither magazine, until *The New Republic* in its most recent phases, has made any attempt to be popular or to entertain. Both of them have served and serve now as useful gadflies, and as antidotes to the complacency, the materialism, and the intrenched conservatism of some of the larger, more widely circulated magazines.[22]

In 1952, Bliven retired as editor. In 1953, funding from the trust set up by Willard and Dorothy Straight was cut off. Michael Straight found funding for another year from various private and independent sources and also found a new editor, Gilbert Harrison. Harrison's wife, Anne, "fell heir to well over ten million dollars of International Harvester money" in 1955.[23]

By the mid–1950s the magazine enjoyed the absence of war and a more prosperous time. Diggins quotes Alexis de Tocqueville, saying, "without a crisis of war or depression, Americans would turn away from the demands of politics to pursue their own individual interests."[24] The more comfortable and financially secure the country, spurred on by postwar growth, the more the *New Republic's* readers turned toward "more criticism of the arts, the cultural scene, the new mass culture."[25] At least for a while, political and economic commentary was held in abeyance.

It appears, however, that small seeds of "entertainment" slowly crept in between the pages of political thought, perhaps due to fiscal survival rather than "popular" journalism. Wood observes that changes were made at the *New Republic* to make it look more like a weekly news magazine. Perhaps symptomatic of the early 1950s, however, the *Nation* also underwent similar changes and difficulties. Wood states, "Neither *The New Republic* nor *The Nation* carries much advertising; consequently both operate at a financial loss. . . . They lack the physical attractiveness of the mass magazines. Because of all these limitations, they have remained periodicals for the elect and select and have failed to make their force, social, economic, or political, strongly felt."[26] Then, in 1956, Michael Straight resigned, and Gilbert Harrison became both publisher and editor. But once again, black clouds loomed, and the American News Company refused to handle the *New Republic* any longer, citing low circulation. Mott reports net paid circulation near or below 30,000 at this point.[27]

The change in content, however, was what Theodore Peterson reports as a "shift from political philosophy to political journalism. . . . [turning] from shaping events to commenting upon them."[28] Peterson further summarizes the changes developing on the political bite of the *New Republic*'s articles as contrasting with ideologies previous to World War I:

> prewar intellectuals had identified themselves with movements to fulfill the promise of American life. Intellectuals of the twenties often disassociated themselves from the shortcomings they found instead of working to

eliminate or to change them. They were detached observers, not part of the society which they professed to despise.[29]

In time of prosperity (or perhaps "lack of world war" is more correct), articles concerned with literature, music, and current affairs became more prevalent in the *New Republic*. During this time a whole array of contemporary American writers contributed regularly. These years of essays, poems, and articles are well-documented in two works, Robert B. Luce's *The Faces of Five Decades* and Reed Whittemore's *The Poet as Journalist*. Whittemore, who served as literary editor from 1969 to 1973, comments that

> mostly the magazine amazed everyone . . . by its capacity to appear on schedule when nobody could be seen doing a thing. Life was grey and quiet at the *New Republic* . . . [Harrison] was determined to be respectful of the magazine's long literary tradition, was himself an authority on early modernist literature, especially the writings of Gertrude Stein, and had no illusions about the progressive incapacity of the *New Republic*, and of weekly publications in general, to compete with TV and the big papers in being journalistically on top of everything. . . . I could therefore sit in the pleasant shabby literary office on the ground floor and look out at the poor hurrying hordes on the sidewalk as if I were simply not a part of all that.[30]

This detachment is perhaps more than the poet as journalist; it may also be, in part, a reflection of the changing times. In the years leading up to John F. Kennedy's presidency, the *New Republic* championed the idealism that seemed to have vacated American politics. Diggins notes correspondence between Adlai Stevenson and John Steinbeck, where "the quiz show scandals, G.I.s collaborating in Korea, mass conformity, cynicism, materialism, all made it appear that democratic freedom was synonymous with self-indulgence. Kennedy appealed to a country that wanted to be a little leaner—and nobler."[31]

After the elections, however, the *New Republic's* energies were turned toward civil rights issues. The *New Republic* supported Lyndon Johnson's handling of the Civil Rights Act of 1964 and the creation of VISTA (Volunteers in Service to America). Once Johnson took office, the *New Republic's* views on Vietnam were very simple: "only two options remained: get out completely, or get in much deeper."[32] By 1965 the Johnson administration fell out of favor; the articles of the *New Republic* "criticized not only the cost of war, but also the liberal ideals and leadership that had led the country into it."[33]

Whittemore notes that the Watergate era brought out a new breed of political journalist, the investigative reporter. Among them was one of the *New Republic's* finest, John Osborne. Osborne's coverage of the White House during the Nixon presidency was no small task. Martin Schram, in a eulogy of Osborne in 1981, describes the relationship between the press and the Republicans in power as "a time of perpetual thunder and storm."[34] Osborne, for his scrutinizing criticism, particularly after the breaking of the Watergate story, did consider the human aspects of Nixon the man, and at one point counted himself in the "silent majority" Nixon often referred to, particularly on issues concerning Vietnam and welfare reform.[35]

The political retrospective outlined by Diggins for the *New Republic's* seventieth anniversary issue is one of few sources to touch upon political philosophies of the last decade. Notable quotations about various presidential elections include "[Jimmy] Carter's nomination and election contributed to the *New Republic's* restiveness with Democrats"[36] and in 1980, "the *New Republic* came out for John Anderson, more out of frustration than conviction, another imperfect compromise between practicality and principle."[37] Diggins notes that despite varying political views and difficulties within both political parties, the editors at the *New Republic* found themselves as all "having studied at Harvard, as did several of the founding editors, which perhaps confirms [George] Santayana's observation that the New England mind, whether deriving from Calvinism or Judaism, bequeathed to America 'an agonized conscience.' "[38]

Diggins further comments on the neoliberal candidacy of Gary Hart versus the traditional liberal candidacy of Walter Mondale, where "the *New Republic* found itself divided between the Yuppies and their cultural elitism and the United Auto Workers and their economic needs. The debate carried on the great tradition of the *New Republic*, which has always supported security for the lower classes, opportunity for the middle class, and social responsibility for the comfortably rich."[39]

It is ironic to note that within Diggins's article lies a striking advertisement (this, in the magazine with a history of carefully selected advertisement from mostly book publishers) of half-page size placed by the Ivan F. Boesky Corporation.[40] While Boesky no doubt advertised in many journals and while the ramifications of his "business" as we know it in 1989 could not have been known in 1984, the irony is startling and gives one cause to ask, where was the *New Republic* in 1984, and where is it today in 1989? One thing is certain: the nature of the advertisements and of the product being sold have changed significantly in the 1980s.

As noted above, many of the sources used to outline this history (with the exception of Diggins) are well-documented and developed until the mid–1960s. From then on, the "change," the "swing," the "evolution," if you will, of the *New Republic* goes roughly undocumented by authors and writers, as though literary judgment were waiting for the dust of history to settle. Current literature surveyed (other than Diggins's) tends to zero in on the very things that many sources seem to end with in evaluating the 1960s: fiscal responsibility, advertising, popularity, and entertainment. I do not suggest that the *New Republic* is now competing with *Newsweek** or *People*,* but the scope of the *New Republic* today appears to reflect the blurred lines of distinction in the current national political scene.

It is no secret to state that recent history is more difficult to document, especially from a somewhat muddled perspective of the writer wading knee-deep in it. It is, nonetheless, still history in the making, and the *New Republic* is definitely still in the business of shaping, making, and documenting the social, political, economic, and literary trends in twentieth-century America.

The last several years of change at the *New Republic* can be best illustrated between the covers of the journal itself: in its articles, and in its advertising. I am particularly indebted to the work of Fred K. Paine and Nancy E. Paine for their timely bibliography on recent journal citations that outlines current historical trends in magazine publishing and advertising. The *New Republic* is, of course, not alone in its modern-day approaches to advertising and layout design changes. As early as the 1970s, several physical changes began the "overhaul" of the magazine. A change to glossy paper in 1974 adds new weight to bound volumes of the *New Republic* (something easily missed when using back issues on microfilm). In 1977–1978, significant cover changes abandon the boxed-in table-of-contents format, using the cover instead as an art vehicle to banner the theme of each issue.

Much of the more recent literature deals exclusively with the new editor in 1974, Martin Peretz. While editors can strongly shape the political tones of editorials and articles submitted, much of the fuss concerning Peretz as editor is more in the overhaul of the *New Republic* before and after his coming. James Glassman "calls this mix of thinking 'muscular liberalism.' Others call it 'conservative populism.' By whatever name, it reflects the struggle going on within both [political] parties to fashion a governing philosophy."[41] Once again, strong philosophies on both sides of the political aisle are employed together on the editorial staff. Critical issues are "the survival and well-being of democratic Israel," the following of "a party in eclipse, to a party it knows lacks force or a coherent body of ideas."[42] Michael Kinsley, the current editor, laments that the *New Republic* "is tired of trying to prove anything to anyone about labels. . . . We want to put out the best magazine we can."[43]

What is moderately conservative in 1989 was not so in 1950 or 1920; what is radically conservative was unheard of except in Nazi Germany; the label of *hawk* or *dove* is irrelevant today in a political climate that is not at war but instead embraces *Glasnost* and opening relations with Russia (reminiscent of the Russian tour advertisements from the 1940s and 1950). What is liberal? What is conservative? What is moderate? Editor Peretz simply says, "The one sure thing at this unpredictable magazine is that we will go on being unpredictable."[44]

Like the politics and economics of the nation, the staff changes, which began in the late 1960s, became increasingly complex. Fiscal problems, layout and cover changes, and position title of "publisher" or "editor" were constantly changing. Even the subtitle of the magazine was toyed with, as noted at the back of this essay.

From an advertising and fiscal point of view (even with the financial backing of Peretz and his wife), the bottom line of the 1980s is marketability and profitability. The operation must run in the black, politically or no. The acquisition of specific advertising accounts reflects significantly on the financial health *and* the political health of the magazine in which they are placed. A new marketing strategy for the *New Republic* was the addition of color "policy-maker" advertisement pages targeted specifically for readers in the Washington, D.C. area, designed to keep the magazine afloat and competitive. With such advertising ploys, however, the "labels" must change to meet the times. Jeff Dearth, the current publisher, admits "I have to worry about this dead weight of the knee-jerk liberalism label we have."[45] "He insists that the *New Republic*, named 'most insightful and thought-provoking magazine' by the readers of *Washington Journalism Review* in its annual 'Best in the Business' news awards . . . isn't as liberal as its reputation, and that conservative writers also are represented in the magazine."[46] While insisting that the *New Republic* "will not change editorially to make itself more palatable to advertisers,"[47] Peretz reportedly has already yanked out one article because of possible conflict with a major tobacco advertiser's advertisements.

Significant courting of corporate accounts, "not necessarily Republican,"[48] is also taking place, and the magazine *is* changing to reflect the lifestyle, emotions, social needs, and political philosophies of a highly targeted audience: readers who are "overeducated, overactive, and overaffluent. . . . The average reader is male (73%), at least a college graduate (87%), has an average income of $48,400 and is politically active. He is, on the average, 40 years old and spends approximately 2½ hours each week reading the *New Republic* and reads a lot of other publications as well."[49]

And so, the image of Shoe on the front cover of the 24 October 1988 issue isn't so surprising: the highly literate editor, busy, high-tech but showing some frustration with the demands of change that come with a high-tech world; tie and tennis shoes—the perfect outfit for the modern yuppie executive. The headlines are appropriate for the nonwar era of 1988, satisfying personal needs, for self-gratification: drugs, football, painting in Paris, new fall books, and television; an article for the insatiable interest in the U.S.S.R., reflecting global telecommunications (what's on Soviet television tonight?); other articles on reverse discrimination, fiscal responsibility ("Dunkirk II"), and a few mild political meanderings about Democrat Dee and Republican Dum. With most of the helpful political criticism aimed at then presidential candidate George Bush, the library magazine appears to be changing rapidly with the times.

And the advertisement and layout? The 24 October 1988 issue totals only thirty-seven ads: five airline/aerospace companies; twenty-five booksellers/vendors/publishers; and seven miscellaneous companies or corporations; there are two sketches, one poem, and a multicolor cartoon on the front cover. The more things change, the more they stay the same. . . .

Notes

1. Cover of the *New Republic*, 24 October 1988.
2. Frank Luther Mott, *A History of American Magazines*, vol. 5: Sketches of 21 Magazines, 1905–1930, (Cambridge: Harvard University Press, Belknap Press, 1938).

3. Mott, pp. 200–201.

4. John Patrick Diggins, "The New Republic and Its Times," *New Republic*, 10 December 1984, p. 26.

5. James Playsted Wood, *Magazines in the United States: Their Social and Economic Influence* (New York: Ronald Press), 1949, p. 175.

6. Mott, p. 201.

7. Ibid., p. 203.

8. Diggins, p. 36.

9. Mott, p. 213.

10. Ibid., p. 215.

11. Theodore Peterson, *Magazines in the Twentieth Century*, (Urbana: University of Illinois Press), 1964, p. 426.

12. David Seideman, "American Jitters," *New Republic*, 10 December 1984, p. 40.

13. David Seideman, "Left Turn," *New Republic*, 10 December 1984, p. 46.

14. Mott, p. 216.

15. Diggins, p. 49.

16. Ibid., p. 50.

17. Ibid.

18. Arlene Rossen Cardozo, "American Magazine Coverage of Nazi Death Camp Era," *Journalism Quarterly*, Winter 1983, pp. 716–17.

19. Mott, p. 220.

20. Peterson, p. 427.

21. Diggins, p. 54.

22. Wood, p. 176.

23. Mott, p. 222, quoted from *Time*, vol. 61, 16 March 1953, p. 95.

24. Diggins, p. 58.

25. Mott, p. 222.

26. Wood, p. 177.

27. Mott, p. 223.

28. Peterson, p. 428.

29. Ibid.

30. Reed Whittemore, *The Poet as Journalist: Life at The New Republic*, (Washington, D.C.: New Republic Book Company, 1976), p. 6.

31. Diggins, p. 60.

32. Ibid., p. 63.

33. Ibid.

34. Martin Schram, "Osborne Remembered," *New Republic*, 16 May 1981, p. 9.

35. Ibid., p. 10.

36. Diggins, p. 71.

37. Ibid., p. 72.

38. Ibid.

39. Ibid., p. 73.

40. Ibid., p. 63.

41. Robert W. Merry, "The Ferment at The New Republic," *Washington Journalism Review*, July 1985, p. 24.

42. Merry, p. 26.

43. Ibid., p. 20.

44. William A. Henry III, "Breaking the Liberal Pattern: Quirky and Provocative, The *New Republic* is Surging in Influence," *Time*, 1 October 1984, p. 78.

45. Janet Meyers, "*New Republic* Ad Pitch Leaning to Right," *Advertising Age*, 10 February 1986, p. 32.

46. Ibid.

47. Alexander Cockburn, "Chewing More Than He's Bitten Off," *Nation*, 20–27 July 1985, p. 39.

48. "Liberal Magazines Adapting to the '80s," *Folio*, May 1986, p. 53.

49. Beth Bogart, "Signs of Growth in *The New Republic*," *Advertising Age*, 17 October 1983, p. M14. Note: this reflects 1983 data.

Information Sources

BIBLIOGRAPHY

1989 Gale Directory of Publications: An Annual Guide to Newspapers, Magazines, Journals, and Related Publications, vol. 1, 1989, p. 272.

Bogart, Beth. "Signs of Growth in *The New Republic*." *Advertising Age*, 17 October 1983, pp. M11–M16.

Cardozo, Arlene Rossen. "American Magazine Coverage of the Nazi Death Camp Era." *Journalism Quarterly*, Winter 1983, pp. 717–18.

Cockburn, Alexander. "Chewing More Than He's Bitten Off." *Nation*, 20–27 July 1985, pp. 39–40.

Diggins, John Patrick. "The New Republic and Its Times." *New Republic*, 10 December 1984, pp. 23–73.

Henry, William A. III. "Breaking the Liberal Pattern: Quirky and Provocative, the *New Republic* Is Surging in Influence." *Time*, 1 October 1984, p. 78.

"Liberal Magazines Adapting to the '80s." *Folio*, May 1986, p. 53.

Luce, Robert B., ed. *The Faces of Five Decades: Selections from Fifty Years of the New Republic, 1914–1964*. New York: Simon and Schuster, 1964.

Merry, Robert W. "The Ferment at the New Republic." *Washington Journalism Review*, July 1985, pp. 22–26.

Meyers, Janet. "*New Republic* Ad Pitch Leaning to Right." *Advertising Age*, 10 February 1986, p. 32.

Mott, Frank Luther. *A History of American Magazines*, vol. 5: *Sketches of 21 Magazines, 1905–1930*. Cambridge: Harvard University Press, Belknap Press, 1938.

Paine, Fred K., and Nancy E. Paine. *Magazines: A Bibliography for Their Analysis, with Annotations and Study Guide*. Metuchen, N.J.: Scarecrow Press, 1987.

Peterson, Theodore. *Magazines in the Twentieth Century*. Urbana: University of Illinois Press, 1964.

Schram, Martin. "Osborne Remembered." *New Republic*, 16 May 1981, pp. 9–11.

Seideman, David. "American Jitters." *New Republic*, 10 December 1984, p. 40.

———. "Left Turn." *New Republic*, 10 December 1984, p. 46.

———. *The New Republic: A Voice of Modern Liberalism*. New York: Praeger Publishers, 1986.

Sherrill, Robert. "The New Regime at *The New Republic*: or, Much Ado about Martin Peretz." *Columbia Journalism Review*, March-April 1976, pp. 23–28.

Whittemore, Reed. *The Poet as Journalist: Life at The New Republic*. Washington, D.C.: New Republic Book Company, 1976.

Wood, James Playsted. *Magazines in the United States: Their Social and Economic Influence*. New York: Ronald Press, 1949.

Zwicky, Edward, ed. *Literature and Liberalism: An Anthology of Sixty Years of the New Republic*. Washington, D.C.: New Republic Book Company, 1976.

INDEX SOURCES

By publisher. *Readers' Guide to Periodical Literature* (1914–present); *Media Review Digest; Magazine Index* (1977–present).

LOCATION SOURCES

Available on microfilm from both University Microfilms International and Bell and Howell.

Publication History

MAGAZINE TITLE AND TITLE CHANGES

The New Republic: A Journal of Opinion, 1914–1969; *The New Republic: A Journal of Politics and the Arts*, 1969–1981; *The New Republic: A Weekly Journal of Opinion*, 1981–present.

VOLUME AND ISSUE DATA

Vols. 1–197, 7 November 1914–present, weekly (Saturday).

PUBLISHER AND PLACE OF PUBLICATION

Republic Publishing Company, New York (1914–1925), Herbert Croly, president. New Republic Publishing Company, New York (1925–1936): Herbert Croly, president (1925–1930); Bruce Bliven, president (1930–1936). Editorial Publications, Inc., New York (1937–1950), Washington, D.C. (1950–1951), Michael W. Straight, publisher (1946–1951). Westbury Publications, Inc., Washington, D.C., Daniel Mebane, publisher (1951–1953). New Republic, Inc., Washington, D.C. (1953–present): Gilbert A. Harrison, publisher (1953–1963, 1966): Robert B. Luce (1963–1966); Garth Hite (1966–1968); Robert J. Myers (1968–1979); Martin Peretz, publisher (1979); Robert A. Cohen, associate publisher and general manager (1979–1980), publisher (1980–1981); James K. Glassman (1981–1984); Reed Phillips, associate publisher (1984); Jeffrey L. Dearth, publisher (1985–1986), publisher and president (1986–present).

EDITORS

Herbert Croly, 1914–1930; Bruce Bliven, 1930–1946; Henry Agard Wallace, 1946–1947; Michael Whitney Straight, 1948–1956; Gilbert A. Harrison, 1956–1974; Martin Peretz, editor-in-chief, 1974–1981, with David Sanford, managing editor, 1975, and Michael Kinsley, editor, 1978; Martin Peretz, editor-in-chief and president, 1981–1986, with Morton Kondracke, executive editor, 1981, Hendrick Hertzberg, editor, 1981–1984, and Micheal Kinsley, editor, 1984–1986; Martin Peretz, editor-in-chief, 1986–present, with Michael Kinsley, editor, 1986–present.

CIRCULATION

1989: 95,973 (Gale). Annual subscription cost: $56

Susan Johns

THE NEW SUCCESS: MARDEN'S MAGAZINE. See SUCCESS

NEWSWEEK

News-Week's vol. 1 no. 1 was published February 18, 1933. Two weeks later the banks closed, business rolled to a quiet stop, with nothing but red lights ahead. Inflation, little understood, filled the air with doubt. In the middle west, the farmers' rumbling changed to riot. The United States went off the gold standard. In Europe, the Western Front, long quiet, echoed the roll of distant drums. Unemployment reached the staggering figures of 13,359,000. Yet in this, perhaps the most perilous and unsettling period in the economic history of the United States, *News-Week* built a circulation of more than 30,000 net paid.

Thus ran a full page self-advertisement on the 20 May 1933 issue of this magazine that would rank among the top three newsweeklies almost from the beginning.

That first front cover bore a collage of photos: Roosevelt elected, Hitler's Night, and Lindbergh's flight. Indeed, the first few issues of *News-Week* report news items that are strikingly similar to the news of our own days, more than fifty years later. Reports of mortgage foreclosures, the homeless under Park Avenue, Augusto César Sandino leading his rebels back to farm in Nicaragua, alimony evaders seeking moratorium while in jail, farmers striking and teachers fainting from hunger, and all the rumors of war in Europe. The new magazine claimed its stories to be "action stories, sifting, selecting, and clarifying the significant news of the week," as stated by Julian Watkins, then circulation manager, in the 25 February 1933 issue in an advertisement on the back of the front cover. Some of the early criticism of the magazine's content and style was directed at this "sifting and selecting" activity. Ben H. Bagdikian, in a series of articles on the newsmagazines published in the *Providence Journal-Bulletin*, describes *Newsweek*'s editor taking the elevator to his office and fearlessly reading the *New York Times* every morning.[1]

The first readers of *Newsweek* welcomed the magazine with fervor. "The format, the articles and pictures undoubtedly will cater to many persons who like to get the meat of all the news in a quick and interesting manner," commented one reader. (4 March 1933, p. 2) Others approved the easy-on-the-eye typography, impressive coverage of world events, and the "modern journalism" style of writing.

In 1937 the weekly *Today* absorbed *Newsweek*. Both periodicals were at the brink of bankruptcy, and the merger brought hope for continuation. *Today* was owned by Vincent Astor and edited by Raymond Moley, a former adviser to President Franklin D. Roosevelt. Malcolm Muir became editor-in-chief, bringing with him the experience in publishing and salesmanship acquired during his years as president of McGraw-Hill. The editors pledged to present the news, national and worldwide, "fairly, impartially, and with scrupulous accuracy, together with its significance and meaning," plus "opinion signed by qualified and responsible contributing editors speaking for themselves."[2] The editors adopted the slogan "the magazine of news significance," and a new era was launched.

Muir changed the title to eliminate the hyphen, and on 4 October 1937, the magazine hit the newsstands with its new cover and new features. The drama critic George Jean Nathan became contributor to Theater Week, and Sinclair Lewis wrote reviews for Book Week. Readers' responses were enthusiastic. "To me, the Periscope and Raymond Moley's editorials alone more than justify the existence of *Newsweek*," wrote a reader from California. (18 October 1937, p. 2)

During the war years and through the forties the magazine produced some outstanding articles and reports, as well as striking photography. And through the fifties—the decade that brought the demise of so many periodicals like *Collier's** and *American Magazine*—*Newsweek*, with a circulation topping the 800,000 mark, survived by making cuts in personnel, and by "trimming sail," as reported in *Time*.[3] In 1961 *Newsweek* was purchased by the Washington Post Company for some $15 million.

In 1960s brought the Summer Olympics at Rome, John F. Kennedy's election, the defection of Bernon F. Mitchell and William Martin to the Soviets, the Berlin crisis, John Glenn's orbital flight, and the U.S. involvement in Vietnam, all receiving excellent coverage. The civil rights movement, which until the end of 1962 had received only perfunctory attention in the Periscope section, rated a front cover story when James Meredith's forced enrollment at the University of Mississippi evoked rumblings of a new civil war. "The Sound and the Fury at Mississippi," an elegantly written article, echoing William Faulkner, appeared in the 15 October 1962 issue. "The Negro in America," the first in-depth study of racial problems in America by the leading newsweeklies, followed on 29 July 1963. Another issue on the Negro, 20 November 1967, recommending "what must be done," won the National Magazine Award. Also during the sixties, *Newsweek*'s coverage of the Vietnam War, the Space Age exploits, campus unrest, and President Kennedy's assassination was outstanding. Chris Welles writes in *Esquire*,

> Over the past few years, *Newsweek* has often been superior to *Time* in assessing the meaning, significance and implication of the news . . . and in recognizing many of the major trends of the 1960's, such as awakening of black aspirations, changes in the mood of the younger generation, the decline of the validity of and belief in the Cold War dialectic of anti-communism and containment. . . . *Newsweek*, uncommitted to any formal ideological position, was more receptive to deviations from traditional thinking and as a result usually covered these events with more perception and accuracy.[4]

The competition with *Time*, which had been fierce throughout the years, although haughtily unacknowledged by *Time*'s editors, peaked during the sixties, when for the first time *Newsweek* ran more domestic ad pages—3,008 to *Time*'s 2,913—and its revenue surpassed that of all major magazines. Its appeal to the younger, liberal generation, combined with ingenious packaging and advertising slogans hailing *Newsweek* as "the newsweekly that separates fact from fiction," and "the most quoted newsweekly," helped to keep the magazine "hot" in its competition with *Time*.

The 1970s brought color photography to the pages of *Newsweek*, and two new editors—Osborn Elliott and Lester Bernstein. A guest essay feature, My Turn, was added, among other improvements. Elliott, the son of a Wall Street investment counselor and himself a Harvard graduate, guided the magazine through this period of violent questioning of established authority and social upheaval without allowing his Republican-conservative outlook to interfere with the liberal tendency of his editors and correspondents.

In 1982 *Newsweek* won the National Magazine Award for General Excellence, for "its consistently high-quality reporting and editing, especially of events that require thoroughness and perspective beyond the often meager, surface coverage usually provided to the public." (Memo from the President, Spring 1983 anniversary issue) The award for Outstanding Single Topic Issue followed, for the 14 December issue in 1981 "What Vietnam Did To Us." The golden anniversary special issue in 1983—"The American Dream"—hailed more than 22 million readers worldwide.

William D. Broyles, Jr., had taken over as editor-in-chief in 1982, when the magazine suffered the most from the recession of the eighties: profits that had been in the $13 million range in 1982 dipped 13 percent. Bill Broyles's selection was unpopular with the staff, but according to Katharine Graham, spokeswoman for the Washington Post Company, Broyles did bring new life to the magazine, reorganizing the staff, creating new graphics, and enhancing *Newsweek*'s "tradition of excellence."[5] Broyles tried to focus on national and regional news involving people throughout the country, creating the new slogan—"Breaking the Mold"—but recession troubles plagued the magazine, and he resigned, under pressure, in 1984.

Controversial cover stories were plenteous early in the decade: Hitler's diaries, the Grace Kelly cover during the Palestinian massacre in September 1982 (according to *Newsweek* that same cover was a great success at the newsstands). The August 1984 AIDS cover showing two males embracing also caused quite an uproar.

Richard M. Smith was appointed editor-in-chief, and under his leadership the newsweekly has continued to compete with *Time* for popularity. The 31 December 1984 issue was dedicated to the "Year of the Yuppie," and the general trend toward the young, upwardly mobile generation continued, but generally the magazine has kept a good balance in its news reporting. Recent issues have not only covered the Bakkers' (Jim and Tammy) Holy War, and Ollie taking the Hill (Oliver North's depositions), but have also provided excellent coverage of what is new in medicine—"Revolution in Medicine" (26 January 1987)— and the aftermath of the *Challenger* tragedy—"Lost in Space: How to Get America off the Ground." (10 October 1988) "Brothers: A Portrait of Black Men in America" (23 March 1987) is also outstanding.

Notes

1. Ben H. Bagdikian, *"Newsweek:* The Magazine of News Significance," *New Republic*, 16 February 1969, p. 9. Good critical evaluation of *Time* and *Newsweek*. Reprinted from *The Providence Journal-Bulletin*.
2. Raymond Moley, "After 25 Years and Six Days," *Newsweek*, 3 November 1958, p. 112.
3. "Trimming Sail," *Time*, 1 December 1957, p. 72.
4. Chris Welles, *"Newsweek* (a Fact) Is the New Hot Book (an Opinion)," *Esquire*, November 1969, pp. 155 and 242. Welles comments on editorial practices, method of news coverage, reporting, trends, the competition with *Times*, etc.
5. Bill Sing, "Broyles Resigns as *Newsweek* Editor," *Los Angeles Times*, 5 January 1984. Source: Newsbank.

Information Sources

BIBLIOGRAPHY

Bagdikian, Ben H. *"Newsweek:* The Magazine of News Significance." *New Republic*, 16 February 1969, pp. 9–14. Reprinted from *The Providence Journal-Bulletin*, October 5–17, 1958.

Bethel, Tom. "Cold War Visitas, Guerrilla-Chic, One Grant, One Vote, *Newsweek* Gas." *American Spectator*, September 1979, pp. 5–6.

Diamond, E. "Now 'Impactweek,' " *New York*, 11 May 1987, p. 20.

Heard, Alex. "Yuppie Love." *New Republic*, 28 January 1985, pp. 10–12.

Henry, W. A. *"Newsweek*'s Outsider Bows Out." *Time*, 16 January 1984, p. 63.

"Late News from *Newsweek*: Dismissal of Editor E. Kosner." *Time*, 9 July 1979, p. 47.

Moley, Raymond. "After 25 Years and Six Days." *Newsweek*, 3 November 1958, p. 112.

Powers, John. "Mein Heart Belongs to *Newsweek*." *Washington Journalism Review*, July-August 1983, p. 70.

Sanford, David. "The Wizard of *Newsweek*." *Harper's Magazine*, August 1980, pp. 72–75.

Sing, Bill. "Broyles Resigns as *Newsweek* Editor." *Los Angeles Times*, 5 January 1984.

"Trimming Sail." *Time*, 1 December 1957, p. 72.

Welles, Chris. *"Newsweek* (a Fact) Is the New Hot Book (an Opinion)." *Esquire*, November 1969, pp. 153–155, 242–248.

INDEX SOURCES

Abstrax; Access; Book Review Index; Biology Digest; Biography Index; Computer Business; Future Surveys; Film Literature Index; Management and Marketing Abstracts; Media Review Digest; Magazine Index (1977–present); *PROMPT; Robomat; Readers' Guide to Periodical Literature* (1933–present); *Music Index* (1951–1959).

LOCATION SOURCES

Microform Bell and Howell and University Microfilms International Online from Mead Data Central, International Edition: Newsweek Inc., 25 Upper Brook St., London, W1Y 2AB.

Publication History

MAGAZINE TITLE AND TITLE CHANGES
   News-Week, 18 February 1933–27 September 1937; *Newsweek*–current.
VOLUME AND ISSUE DATA
   Vol. 1–current, 17 February 1933–current, weekly.
PUBLISHER AND PLACE OF PUBLICATION
   Newsweek, Inc., 15 July 1957; News-Week Inc., 18 February 1933–20 February
   1937; Weekly Publications 27 February 1937–8 July 1957. 444 Madison Avenue,
   New York.
EDITORS
   Samuel T. Williamson, 1933–1937; Malcolm Muir, 1937–1967; Edward Kosner,
   1967–1969; Osborn Elliott, 1970–1978; Lester Bernstein, 1979–1982; William
   Broyles, 1982–1984; Richard M. Smith, 1984–current (1987).
CIRCULATION
   3,057,000, 1989.

Heleni Pedersoli

NEW TIMES

New Times—The Feature News Magazine, a biweekly, was founded in the
fall of 1973 to fill the journalistic gap between the then thriving alternative
periodicals on the one hand and the slick newsweeklies and "often ossified
monthlies" on the other.[1] In the view of the founders, a "feature news magazine"
by definition does not attempt routinely to report all the news as a typical
newsweekly might but rather to present investigative and background stories,
and other articles focusing upon significant issues. *New Times* featured controversial stories that other news media were not reporting, such as an unflattering
profile of est (Erhard Seminars Training) founder Werner Erhard that was turned
down by *Esquire* as "too hot to handle."[2] A typical issue included many short,
factual, often "insider" or behind-the-scenes items, as well as reviews of books,
movies, music, and the arts, and news updates, such as a report on Selma ten
years after the freedom marches.

The magazine's perspective was left of center but not radical. Perhaps center-
left counterculture describes it best. Its articles were sprinkled—not filled—with
four-letter words. Though the tone of the magazine did not tend to be strident
or shrilly angry, there was anger—particularly toward big business and the
government that supports it—and toward what the editors took to be institutional
and individual incompetence and treachery in general. There was a degree of
acceptance and apparent approval of the counterculture's use of recreational
drugs, especially marijuana. An advertisement in the magazine boasted "We
published our *own* medical research on pot—'Attention—Smoking Grass May
Be Good for Your Health.' ")[3] Also there was significant emphasis upon environmental reporting and upon factual, relatively objective, writing, with many

columns and other articles expressing the individual—if somewhat predictable—views of the writer.

Although *New Times* for the most part eschewed celebrity journalism, upon its founding it signed up a roster of celebrated "New, Recent, Old Journalists,"[4] including Jimmy Breslin, Larry L. King, Studs Terkel, Nicholas von Hoffman, Murray Kempton, and Mike Royko.

But according to most observers, *New Times* proved more successful when it began to attract younger writers, whose perspectives were fresher, livelier, and perhaps more in tune with *New Times*'s potential readers. As *Time** observed in 1976, "much of *New Times*' most engaging work is by young writers. Among them: Steve Diamond, 29, whose piece on corruption in federal grain inspection was one of the first journalistic forays into that quagmire; Roger Rapoport, 29, who dissected a surgeon with $10 million in malpractice suits; Ron Rosenbaum, 29, who interviewed Fugitive Abbie Hoffman."[5]

According to its publisher, *New Times* was conceived in 1971 as a "news-oriented magazine with in-depth reporting and tough investigative journalism."[6] He cited Robert Sam Anson's article on Synanon as typical of *New Times* at its best—"a courageous reporter, lots of legwork, clean writing and a haunting, topical subject."[7] In 1978 the editors described *New Times* as reporting "news of the world, news of the nation, sports, the arts, politics, lifestyles," everything "from backstage scoops to front page leaks," and "otherwise unreported events that are really shaping our lives."[8]

The editors claimed to be fighting for "the little guy"; they sought to make waves ("The Ten Dumbest Congressmen"), and apparently they sometimes did. According to their own account, they broke the story of Secretary of Agriculture Earl Butz's racial slurs that led to his resignation, published a story that set in motion the process that freed a teenager convicted of murdering his mother, and alone interviewed jailed SLA (Symbionese Liberation Army) leaders William and Emily Harris during the Patty Hearst trial, "coming up with testimony that blew Patty's defense to bits and led to her conviction."[9]

The magazine was not without its critics. It was accused of some slipshod journalism, as in its rehash of the John Kennedy assassination, which was found to be "ragged on factual detail," and to gloss over "much of the supporting evidence for the 'lone assassin' theory."[10] To others it seemed excessively preoccupied with "drugs, conspiracies and other counter culture concerns."[11] And in its quest for circulation (which at its best topped 350,000), it wasn't above using fluff and puff and pushing its eye-catching and usually exciting graphics beyond the limits of good taste.

New Times's failure early in its sixth year was not a matter of the quality of its journalism, which in general was quite high. Rather, it was a matter of audience, advertisers, and money. The magazine business is always risky—especially for controversial magazines—and in a period of special-interest and service periodicals and a few successful revivals of the old general-interest magazines, *New Times*'s potential readers were turning elsewhere in large numbers. *New Times* sought to ride the crest of the wave of the counterculture into the "new times" the editors saw as dawning in the early 1970s or as having dawned in the 1960s. The future they envisioned included a world in which alternatives—in life styles, energy resources, technology, poisons, etc.—would make the world a freer, safer, less environmentally damaging, and in general a better place in which to live. The trouble is, the new times turned out to be characterized by self-centered materialism and status seeking and to be more like the old times (pre–1960s) than ever. The magazine, like the new times, died aborning.

Notes

1. Jonathan Z. Larsen, "Final Tribute," *New Times*, 8 January 1979, p. 92. Other gaps sometimes seen as appropriate niches for *New Times* are those among the news-weeklies and monthlies and journals of opinion. And *Time* mentioned the demographic gap "of people too old for *Rolling Stone* and too young for *Commentary*." In "Final Tribute—Time Runs out for *New Times*," *Time*, 27 November 1978, p. 100.

2. "Final Tribute—Time Runs out for *New Times*," p. 100.

3. "New Times: Think of Us as the Mighty Mouse of Magazines," *New Times*, 16 May 1975, pp. 16–17.

4. "*New Time's* Party," *Time*, 22 October 1973, p. 88.

5. "Newer Times," *Time*, 23 February 1976, p. 55.

6. George A. Hirsch, "Behind the Scenes," *New Times*, 8 January 1979, p. 4.

7. "Is News Extinct?" *New Times*, 16 October 1978, p. 9.

8. "New Times: Think of Us," pp. 16–17.

9. "Is News Extinct?," p. 9.

10. "Lean and Hungry Looks," *Newsweek*, 27 October 1975, p. 78.

11. "Newer Times," p. 55.

Information Sources

BIBLIOGRAPHY
Periodical literature, 1973–1979. (*New Times* articles cited.)
INDEX SOURCES
> *Readers' Guide to Periodical Literature* (1978–1979); *Popular Periodical Index* (1974–1977); *Access* (1975–1977); *Magazine Index* (1977–1979).

LOCATION SOURCES
> St. Louis Public Library; many other libraries. Available in microform.

Publication History

MAGAZINE TITLE AND TITLE CHANGES
> *New Times: The Feature News Magazine*, 1973–1979.

VOLUME AND ISSUE DATA
> Vol. 1, no. 1–vol. 12, no. 1, 19 October 1973–8 January 1979, biweekly.

PUBLISHER AND PLACE OF PUBLICATION
    George A. Hirsch; New Times Publishing Company, New York, New York.
EDITOR
    Jonathan Z. Larsen, 1973–1979.
CIRCULATION
    Initial, 100,000; Fall 1974, 150,000; Fall 1975, 235,000; June 1976, 300,000;
    October 1977–October 1978, 366,694; last issue, 8 January 1979, 350,000–
    355,000.

                                                                Daniel Straubel

NEW YORK

Jimmy Breslin was right about *New York* Magazine when he said in 1968, "I
think we're stuck with the thing for twenty years. You couldn't kill it with an
axe."[1] *New York* celebrated its twentieth anniversary in 1988 with four special
issues, back to back. The first, on 4 April, began with a reprise that the editors
with justifiable confidence called "The Score." Excerpts from twenty of the
magazine's cover stories, one from each year, were illustrated with snapshots
of the covers themselves, showing vividly why art directors and designers consistently give the magazine kudos.[2]

Among the cover stories featured were two that became movies: "Portrait of
an Honest Cop" (Serpico) and "Peter Maas on the Deadly Battle to Become
King of the Gypsies."[3] The excerpts supported the magazine's claim to a distinguished record of neologisms, including "radical chic," "the 'me' decade,"
"couch potato," "forever single," and "downward mobility."

It is not serendipitous that three of the excerpted cover stories were by Tom
Wolfe, ace phrase coiner and apostle of the "new journalism," which uses the
techniques of fiction to make reportage more dramatic. Wolfe was not only one
of the original writers for the magazine but also the subject of the cover story
for the 21 March 1988 issue, thereby illustrating the continuity that is a strength
of *New York* but carries the risk that future issues will have an air of déjà vu.
Skirting that danger is complicated for *New York* by its success, which has
inspired frequent imitation. In 1968, there were only a few city magazines, but
by 1982 there were 200.[4]

There were signs in 1988 that *New York* might have plateaued after two decades
of impressive growth. Whereas in its first full year of publication it had carried
972 pages of ads with revenue of $1,904,322, in 1982 there were 2,547 ad pages
with revenues of $25,500,000.[5] Particularly good years for the magazine were
1973 and 1983. In 1973 it won the National Magazine Award for reporting
excellence, with special reference to Gail Sheehy's articles on Times Square
prostitution and Herb Goro's photo essay on a lonely old man in the Bronx.
Orde Coombs's story, "Fear and Trembling in Black Streets," won the 1973
Public Service Award of the Public Relations Society of America. Alan Rich's

music articles won a Deems Taylor Award from the American Society of Composers, Authors and Publishers (ASCAP). Design director Milton Glaser and art director Walter Bernard received Awards of Distinctive Merit from the Society of Publication Designers.[6] In 1983, both circulation and advertising revenues were up, the latter by 15 percent,[7] and a 7 March 1983 article, "How Well Does Your Bank Treat You?," won that year's National Magazine Award for Service to the Individual.

New York began life in 1964 as a Sunday newspaper supplement, first to the *New York Herald Tribune* and later to its short-lived successor, the *World Journal Tribune*. When the *World Journal Tribune* folded in 1967, Clay Felker, editor of the Sunday supplement, used his severance pay to buy the copyright. Felker secured the backing of investment banker Armand Erpf and other angels for a weekly featuring writers whose names have become household words, including Jimmy Breslin, Tom Wolfe, Gloria Steinem, Adam Smith (George Goodman), and Gail Sheehy. The new publication was announced to prospective advertisers with an imaginative campaign that posted signs at all the entrances to Manhattan warning that "New York closes February 21."[8] Sixty thousand charter subscribers were enrolled after a promotion that advertised "New York on $5 a Year" and offered chances to win 1,001 prizes, including dinner with Mayor John Lindsay at Gracie Mansion.

The first issue, on 1 April 1968, carried sixty-four pages of advertising from upscale merchants like Bergdorf Goodman and Tiffany and Company and was applauded by *Time* magazine for "captur[ing] the excitement of the city in a way few other publications have."[9] It was, as it still is, glossy, *Time*-sized, and stylishly laid out. There were, and are, reviews of movies, books, theater, music, and art. A story about La Marqueta, the open-air market in Spanish Harlem, presaged *New York*'s lifelong love affair with food; some of the best writing in the magazine has been about food, thanks in part to the articulate passion of long-time contributor Gael Greene for "recurring pleasures" such as "an ethereal marinated trout, its tail proudly aloft like a vintage Cadillac fin."[10] A profile by Dick Schaap of a narcotics agent accused of selling narcotics introduced another earmark of *New York*, a tough, sophisticated attention to crime and corruption that makes it impossible ever to accuse the magazine of simplistically hyping life in the metropolis. The president of the New York Board of Trade, writing in 1981 to compliment Nicholas Pileggi on "Open City," his "honest and hard-hitting" article in the 19 January issue, says that the magazine should be "congratulated for addressing and publishing, in a factual . . . way, the problem of crime in our city."[11] A letter in the 25 April 1988 issue credits Pileggi's article "The Strange Case of Joseph Pikul" with being a catalyst for legislation dealing with the issue of temporary custody of children when one or both parents have been charged with a violent crime.[12]

In other ways, too, *New York* in 1988 resembles itself in 1968. There is still a financial column, although Adam Smith no longer writes it. Ruth Gilbert, who handled entertainment listings from the beginning, has a department called "Ruth

Recommends,'' while the entertainment listings have swelled to fifty pages since *New York* incorporated *Cue*, a forty-eight-year-old weekly entertainment and listing guide, in April 1980.

The cover story of the debut issue, Jimmy Breslin on life in New York, contrasts the insulated comfort and complacency of commuters on a New Haven train with a confrontation between a cop and two street people in Harlem, striking a note (''It was the best of times; it was the worst of times'') that the magazine has often played over the years. The cover of the 18 April 1988 issue repeats the familiar refrain: ''To live in New York in the spring of 1988 is to confront extremes of flaunted wealth and extreme poverty unknown since the Gilded Age. Never has the city seemed so full of energy and creativity—and yet so distracted and frivolous. And never in the postwar years have New Yorkers been so conscious of sharing their lives with society's depraved, desperate, and doomed.''

The chief characteristic that distinguishes the first issue of *New York* from more successful later ones is the absence of service articles. *New York* really found its identity when it began publishing stories about how to survive a variety of hassles—how to avoid being hurt in a taxi, how to pass inspection by a co-op board, when to end a relationship with a therapist, how to negotiate with landlords (not to mention how to debone shad and where to find duck eggs). Another hallmark of *New York* in its most typical and most successful mode is vivid articles on life styles—not just of the rich and famous, although there are plenty of those, but also of pimps, prostitutes, junkies, dealers, bag ladies, paramedics, cops, headhunters, rehabbers, and arsonists.

A sensitive reader of *New York* might wince at the editors' description of New Yorkers as ''frivolous'' and ''distracted,'' for it is not easy to decide whether the magazine documents those behaviors or vigorously promotes them. *New York* is glitzy; it targets affluent readers, and most of its ink is dedicated to attractive ways to spend money. There are several articles on fashion every year, as well as handsomely illustrated articles on interior design. There is an annual issue on fabulous weekends. A column appropriately called ''The Passionate Shopper'' has been replaced with a department of ''Sales and Bargains,'' but this is not proof of a new austerity: life goes on at Mortimer's and Oscar de la Renta, and *New York* is there with a photographer.

The editors of *New York* reported a little smugly on 2 December 1968 that their subscribers were travelers who liked gadgets and liquor. More than half were in business or industry, and half of those were presidents, owners, or officers. Thirteen percent of the subscribers had portfolios worth over $100,000, and 17 percent owned summer homes. Most bought over ten books a year; three-fourths regularly attended Broadway shows, art galleries, concerts, and ballets; one-third attended openings, first nights, and previews; one-fourth had post-graduate degrees.[13] Studies by Don Bowdren Research in 1979 and 1981 confirmed that the audience for local magazines is affluent, educated, and actively interested in the community.[14] *New York* was included in the 1979 study but not the 1981; *New York* no longer calls itself a city magazine.

Whereas *New York*'s first editor, Clay Felker, defined its editorial policy as "New York and good writing—that's what we are about, we want to be the weekly magazine that communicates the spirit and character of contemporary New York,"[15] *New York* now calls itself a "newsweekly" and its editorial policy states that the magazine is for "those interested in critical examination of contemporary ideas. *New York* deals regularly with such subjects as politics, business, psychology, literature, the fine arts, entertainment, home furnishing, food, wine, fashion, and a broad range of subjects."[16] Between the two statements came Rupert Murdoch, who acquired the magazine in 1977 over Felker's resistance.

From an accountant's point of view, *New York*'s editorial profile is justified; producing the editorial content is as expensive as producing that of a national newsweekly. Nevertheless, it may be doubted whether "the critical examination of contemporary ideas" is really what *New York* is about. People in the publishing industry regard it as the classic city magazine. It has twice as many subscribers as its nearest competitor, *Chicago* magazine,[17] but of course *Chicago* is not its competitor; readers are not as interested in what is going on in Chicago—or Philadelphia, Phoenix, or Fargo—as they are in what is happening in New York. *New York* is purchased by 1,821 Canadians, 993 foreigners, 17,007 residents of the Pacific states, and 400,000 buyers in between,[18] who pay $35.00 a year or $1.95 a single copy for the magazine, which comes out fifty times a year. The median age is 41.9, and 53.9 percent are women.[19] The publisher says that the magazine is read by 1.5 million people.[20] After *New York* acquired *Cue* in 1980, 78 percent of the magazine's total circulation was said to be concentrated in the New York metropolitan area.[21]

New York has had foes[22] as well as fans from the beginning, and the twentieth anniversary brought out spokesmen for both sides. The publisher of another New York magazine, who asked not to be identified, said, "You feel you have to read it . . . but it's lost its punch."[23] The problem is competition; the problem is cost; the problem is that Ed Koch is not as glamorous as John Lindsay and homelessness is not as exciting as student riots at Columbia; the problem is that New York's cultural hegemony is dwindling. *New York*'s advertising revenues were a little less than flat in 1986 and 1987, and so was circulation.[24] The four special anniversary issues were supposed to turn the tide, as was a multimagazine advertiser incentive introduced by Murdoch Magazines in January 1988 (*New York* is the flagship for twenty Murdoch titles). In the long run, however, advertising revenues may not even be half the story. Circulation now accounts for 50 percent of revenues in the magazine industry, and Paine Webber analyst J. Kendrick Noble, Jr., predicts that figure may reach 66 percent in ten years.[25]

New York tries to increase circulation by using sweepstakes, which its tests show are twice as effective as a direct mail campaign without sweepstakes.[26] Keeping subscribers after it gets them must be the mission of the editorial content. The current editor-publisher, Edward Kosner, says, "Our aim is to do stories first and to do them best, to enhance *New York*'s reputation as a haven and showcase for writers, and more than anything, to be honest and fair."[27] Kosner is the magazine's fourth editor, and his appointment in 1980 might be interpreted as a commitment by the Murdoch empire to the editorial content of *New York*. He came to the magazine after sixteen years at *Newsweek*,* culminating in four years as editor during which that publication earned an unprecedented number of journalism awards. He is married to Julie Baumgold, who was one of the original contributors to *New York*, left in 1977, and returned after Kosner became editor. Another alumnus who has come back is Pete Hamill, who wrote the cover story "Our Times" in the 4 April 1988 anniversary issue. These shifts may suggest that *New York* is trying to recover a former, more brilliant identity.

Notes

1. "Back from the Brink," *Newsweek,* 18 November 1968, p. 108.

2. "Magazines Draw Favorable Comments from Art Directors," *Advertising Age*, 14 September 1987, p. S26.

3. *New York* takes credit for starting at least six movies, including *The French Connection, Fort Apache, the Bronx, Prince of the City,* and *Saturday Night Fever* (*New York*, 18 April 1983, p. 2). Several *New York* articles have been expanded into books, among them *The Pump House Gang* and *The Electric Kool-Aid Acid Test* by Tom Wolfe, John Gruen's *The Private World of Leonard Bernstein*, and James Kunen's *The Strawberry Statement*.

4. "City and State Magazines," *Marketing and Media Decisions*, March 1982, p. 176. According to Standard Rates and Data Service, there were 23 titles in 1970 and 147 in 1984 Special Report: "City and Regional Magazines," (*Advertising Age*, 17 January 1985, p. 11).

5. Letter from the Publisher, *New York*, 18 April 1983, p. 6.

6. Between the Lines, *New York*, 8 April 1974, p. 4.

7. Patrick Reilly. " 'New York' Hits 20 with Special Issues," *Advertising Age*, 15 February 1988, p. 30.

8. Tony Brenna, "The '5 Door' Pitch to Media Buyers," *Editor and Publisher*, 20 January 1968, p. 16.

9. "New York Revival," *Time*, 5 April 1968, p. 53.

10. Gael Greene, "Rooms of Their Own," *New York*, 28 March 1988, p. 105.

11. William J. Sloboda, *New York*, 9 March 1981, p. 10.

12. Raoul Lionel Fedder, P.C., *New York*, 25 April 1988, p. 18.

13. Between the Lines, *New York*, 2 December 1968, p. 4.

14. "City and State Magazines," *Marketing and Media Decisions*, March 1982, pp. 176–84.

15. "New York Magazine Appears Again in the Spring," *Editor and Publisher*, 11 November 1967, p. 13.

16. Standard Rates and Data Service (SRDS), *Consumer Magazine and Agri-Media Rates and Data*, 27 October 1988, p. 460. The statement is described as having been received 28 February 1978.

17. Eileen Norris, "Rewriting Editorial Goals to Keep Pace with Readers," *Advertising Age*, 13 April 1987, p. S3.

18. SRDS, *Consumer Magazine and Agri-Media Rates and Data*, p. 461.

19. SRDS, *Direct Mail List Rates and Data*, 14 November 1987, p. 1418.

20. Letter from the Publisher, *New York*, 18 April 1983, p. 6.

21. Letter from the Publisher, *New York*, 14 April 1980, p. 7.

22. "This Is New York?" *Newsweek*, 8 April 1968, p. 102.

23. Reilly, p. 30.

24. Ibid.

25. "Setting Trends for Murdoch," *Marketing and Media Decisions*, April 1987, p. 24.

26. Vince Dema, "New York's Tests Reveal Some Startling Conclusions," *Direct Marketing*, February 1983, p. 59

27. Between the Lines, *New York*, 17 March 1980, p. 6.

Information Sources

BIBLIOGRAPHY

"A Day in the Life of New York," *New York*, 18 April 1983, shows *New York* at its best.

Erlanger, Steven. "Goodbye, Narcissism: A Magazine Party." *New York Times*, 19 April 1988, sec. B, p. 1.

Heckman, Lucy. "New York." *Serials Review*, January-March 1980, pp. 5–9.

Little, Stuart W. "How to Start a Magazine." *Saturday Review*, 14 June 1969, p. 52–53, 63.

INDEX SOURCES

> *Readers' Guide to Periodical Literature (1978–present); Abstrax, Film Literature Index; Magazine Index (1977–present); Media Review Digest; Popular Periodical Index (1973–1977)*.

LOCATION SOURCES

> Library of Congress, many other libraries. Available in microform from Bell and Howell and University Microfilms International.

Publication History

MAGAZINE TITLE AND TITLE CHANGES

> *New York*.

VOLUME AND ISSUE DATA

> Vols. 1–21, April 1968–present, weekly.

PUBLISHER AND PLACE OF PUBLICATION

> News America Publishing, Inc., 755 Second Ave., New York, New York 10017–5998.

EDITORS

> Clay S. Felker, 1968–1977; James Brady, January 1977–September 1977; Joe Armstrong, October 1977–March 1980; Edward Kosner, March 1980–present.

CIRCULATION

> 433,813 paid, 24,343 nonpaid.

Sandra Naiman

NEW YORK EVENING ENQUIRER. See NATIONAL ENQUIRER

THE NEW YORK TIMES MAGAZINE

Today, the *New York Times Magazine* is an acknowledged leader not only in reporting timely, thorough news features, but also in introducing the latest trends in almost every field through its advertising. An "upscale lifestyle" magazine, its advertising is aimed at the life style of the affluent of society.[1] The *Magazine's* ad pages topped *Advertising Age's* 1986 Top 100 Media Companies in the magazine sector.[2] Advertising covers products and services perceived to be desirable by the wealthy, such as travel, skin-care products, and fashion. However, when United Technologies hoped to solidify its corporate identity, it ran a series of innovative ads in the *New York Times Magazine*, the *New Yorker*, and *Time** magazine.[3] Such is the prestige of the *New York Times* and its *Magazine*.

What is now known as the *New York Times Magazine* was first printed on 6 September 1896 as the *New-York Times Sunday Magazine Supplement*. Begun less than a month after the new owner of the *New York Times*, Adolph S. Ochs, had taken control, the *Magazine* section was founded with the purpose of exploring current events. While other Sunday supplements of the time contained bland, independent stories, the *Times Sunday Magazine* focused on those events and topics that had been news in the daily papers of recent weeks.[4] The policy of following the current news has been a cardinal principle of the *Magazine* throughout its history.

In fact, Lester Markel, legendary editor and driving force behind the Sunday *Times* for over forty years, stated that the ideal Sunday paper consisted of three parts: "first, the news of the day—the news of Saturday; second, the background of the news of the week; third, something of permanent value . . . The more or less permanent touch is given . . . in the magazine and in the book review."[5] The *Magazine* was to deal with "long-range" or "spread news," as opposed to "spot news."[6] Markel explained that "the importance of the capture of Iwo [Jima] to the advance on Japan is spot news for the review [of the week]; the nature of the Japanese homeland and the large job of conquering it are spread news and something for the magazine."[7]

The early *Magazine* caused Sunday circulation to soar. Its halftone photos were of great interest to the reading public. In fact, the first scoop of the new *Magazine*, 4 July 1897, contained fifty photographs of Queen Victoria's Jubilee. The *Times Magazine* published the pictures first and published pictures of better quality than any of its competitors.[8]

Yet, its early successes did not insure the magazine's future. By 1899, the *Magazine* was discontinued due to an inadequate production plant. It was revived in June 1901, but, again, lasted only a short time (January 1904). Indeed, the

Magazine had a sporadic history from its beginning until the 1920s, changing names frequently and suffering three periods when no *Magazine* was published.

However, the exclusive pictorial coverage of Queen Victoria's Jubilee proved to be but the beginning of a long line of distinctions for the *Magazine*. When the British dirigible R–34 left for Scotland on 9 July 1919, after making the first westward, nonstop crossing of the Atlantic, it carried the first transatlantic airmail copies of the *New York Times*. The dirigible landed in Pulham, Scotland, on Sunday morning 13 July 1919, with copies of the Sunday *Times*, including the Sunday *Magazine*, bearing the same date.[9]

Such "firsts" helped to increase Sunday circulation; by 1924, Sunday circulation stood at 580,000[10] and by 1929 had reached 728,909.[11] Even at the end of 1930, when circulation and advertising had fallen off, the Sunday circulation rose by more than 12,500 copies over the previous year.[12] On 1 March 1931, in the midst of the depression, the *Times* ran 1,021,848 copies of its Sunday paper, the largest run to date in its history.[13] The magazine began color printing in 1933, and in 1936 subsumed the rotogravure picture section of the newspaper.[14]

Other distinctions came to the *Magazine* through its list of distinguished contributors. One such contributor was Anne O'Hare McCormick. In the early 1920s, McCormick wrote of Mussolini and the fascist movement. In *Magazine* articles of 5 June and 21 June 1921, she told of "violent change . . . simmering in 'the Boot.' "[15] She correctly assessed Mussolini as the rising leader of the Fascisti. In the 1950s, Robert Moses, powerful New York public official, regularly wrote feature articles for the Sunday *Times Magazine*.[16] One scoop that came quite belatedly to the *Magazine* was a 1908 interview of Kaiser William II by *Times* correspondent William Hale. The remarks of the kaiser were judged so inflammatory and racist that Adolph Ochs, after conferring with President Theodore Roosevelt and the U.S. ambassador in Berlin, decided to suppress them. The article was finally published in the *Magazine* thirty-one years later, on the eve of World War II.[17]

The *Magazine*, always drawing on current news items for its main articles, nevertheless began a stamp column in 1937, introduced crossword puzzles in 1942, and began a home furnishings section in 1943.[18] In recent years the *Times* in general, and the *Magazine* in particular, have shifted toward providing more advertising space and entertainment articles at the expense of its news space. Many of its critics feel the *Times* has abandoned its traditional news-producing role in favor of a new profit focus. Observers cite the fact that between 1935 and 1978, the number of ad columns increased by 320 percent while the number of news columns fell by 29.8 percent. Part of the shift toward a profit incentive can be explained by the fact that the family trust established in Adolph S. Ochs's will lost voting control of the New York Times Company stock in 1971, yet the ad columns to news columns ratio was moving toward increased advertising long before 1971.[19] Despite or perhaps because of the increased emphasis on advertising, the *Magazine* has been able to continue its appeal to a wide readership seeking entertainment, the latest in consumer trends, and, above all, the background for the current news.

Notes

1. Patrick Reilly, "Travel Marketing: Magazines Vie for Core Advertisers," *Advertising Age,* 25 April 1988, p. S2.
2. R. Craig Endicott, "Media Feast Fuels Growth," *Advertising Age*, 30 June 1986, p. S3.
3. Sid Karpoff, "The Big Bang Theory," *Madison Avenue*, February 1985, pp. 76–80.
4. Meyer Berger, *The Story of The New York Times, 1851–1951* (New York: Simon and Schuster, 1951), p. 116.
5. Lester Markel, *The Newspaper: Its Making and Its Meaning* (New York: Charles Scriber's Sons, 1945), p. 29.
6. Ibid., pp. 36–37.
7. Ibid., p. 37.
8. Berger, p. 558.
9. Berger, pp. 237–38.
10. Ibid., p. 270.
11. Ibid., p. 345.
12. Ibid., p. 364.
13. Ibid., p. 373.
14. Martin Walker, *Powers of the Press: Twelve of the World's Influential Newspapers* (New York: Pilgrim Press, 1982), p. 220.
15. Berger, p. 327.
16. Gay Talese, *The Kingdom and the Power* (New York: World Publishing Company, 1966), p. 101.
17. Walker, p. 218.
18. Berger, p. 560.
19. Walker, p. 232.

Information Sources

BIBLIOGRAPHY

Berger, Meyer. *The Story of the New York Times, 1851–1951*. New York: Simon and Schuster, 1951.
Davis, Elmer Holmes. *History of The New York Times, 1851–1921*. New York: New York Times, 1921.
Endicott, R. Craig. "Media Feast Fuels Growth." *Advertising Age,* 30 June 1986, pp. S2–S3.
Karpoff, Sid. "The Big Bang Theory." *Madison Avenue*, February 1985, pp. 76–80.
Markel, Lester. *The Newspaper: Its Making and Its Meaning*. New York: Charles Scribner's Sons, 1945.
The Making of a Great Newspaper: The Story of The New York Times. New York: New York Times Company, 1924.

Reilly, Patrick. "Travel Marketing: Magazines Vie for Core Advertisers." *Advertising Age*, 25 April 1988, pp. S2, S18.

Salisbury, Harrison. *Without Fear or Favor: The New York Times and Its Times*. New York: Times Books, 1980.

Talese, Gay. *The Kingdom and the Power*. New York: World Publishing Company, 1966.

INDEX SOURCES

   Readers' Guide (1940–present); *Magazine Index* (1977–present); *New York Times Index*.

LOCATION SOURCES

   Available in microform. Library of Congress and many other libraries.

Publication History

MAGAZINE TITLE AND TITLE CHANGES

   The New-York Times Sunday Magazine Supplement, 6 September 1896–29 November 1896; *The New York Times Sunday Magazine Supplement*, 6 December 1896–9 May 1897; *The New York Times Illustrated Magazine Supplement*, 16 May 1897; *The New York Times Illustrated Weekly Magazine*, 23 May 1897–20 March 1898; *The New York Times Illustrated Magazine Supplement*, 27 March 1898–3 September 1899; no magazine published, 10 September 1899–26 May 1901; *The New York Times Magazine Supplement*, 2 June 1901–24 January 1904; no magazine published, 31 January 1904–24 June 1917; *The New York Times Magazine Section*, 1 July 1917–15 February 1920; no magazine published, 22 February 1920–11 July 1920; *The New York Times Book Review and Magazine*, 18 July 1920–2 September 1923; *The New York Times Book Magazine Section*, 9 September 1923–4 April 1926; *The New York Times Magazine*, 11 April 1926–present.

VOLUME AND ISSUE DATA

   Issued weekly.

PUBLISHER AND PLACE OF PUBLICATION

   The New York Times Company, Times Building, 229 West 43rd Street, New York, New York 10036.

EDITORS

   Ralph H. Graves, 1917–1923; Lester Markel, 1923–1964; Daniel Schwarz, 1964–1972; Max Frankel, 1973–1976. In April 1976, the position of Sunday editor was abolished. Since that time, those whose duties have included editing the *New York Times Magazine* are Edward Klein, 1977–1987, and James L. Greenfield, 1987–present.

CIRCULATION

   Estimated Sunday circulation is 1,645,000.

Jane T. Bradford

NILES' WEEKLY REGISTER

Frank Luther Mott's classic study of American magazines describes *Niles' Weekly Register* as "a chief reliance of the historiographer for the first half of the nineteenth century."[1] The uniqueness and value of the *Register* derives from its duality of purpose. The *Register* not only reported significant news but also printed important documents. The prospectus for the *Register* in 1811 advertised that "its contents shall be divided into several heads—to wit, POLITICS, HISTORY, GEOGRAPHY, BIOGRAPHY—notices of ARTS and SCIENCES and MANUFACTURING, in their most liberal and extended meaning—MISCELLANY—NEWS." Hezekiah Niles, the creator and long-time editor of the *Register*, stamped the magazine with his name and molded the essentially one-man publication to fit a new need in American journalism. Unlike other magazines of the period, the *Register* was not overtly partisan to any political party and often explained opposing positions. Niles claimed in the introductory issue, "I will attach myself, as an editor, to no party but the PEOPLE's party, whose wish is '*peace, liberty and safety.*'" While the *Register* expressed Niles's views on many issues, the extent of its neutrality was comparable to that of modern newsmagazines. In fact, in many respects the *Register* may be considered a forerunner of the weekly newsmagazine of today. It was among the first publications to combine the features of newspapers and magazines.

Through most of its history the *Register* was known by its motto, "The Past— The Present—For the Future." Volume 1 had carried a quotation from Shakespeare's *Henry VIII* for its motto:

> I wish no other herald
> No other speaker of *my living actions,*
> To keep mine honor from corruption
> But such an honest chronicler.

The same concern about the future was evident in the quotation from Virgil which served as the motto from 1812 until 1817, "*Haec olim meminisse juvabit.*" Niles bound and indexed each semiannual volume as a record for the future.

For the first twenty-five years the *Register* was a moderate-sized octavo of 6⅛" x 9⅝". Each issue contained 16 pages, but the frequent 8-page supplements boosted the size of many volumes to about 500 pages. In 1836 the publication became a quarto of 8½" x 12½", and the number of columns increased from two to three. This format was continued for the final twenty-six volumes. An annual subscription cost $5 plus postage.[2] Niles used good-quality paper and type fonts, and the only complaint concerning the appearance of the *Register* seems to have been about the small type size, which occasionally strained the eyes of the readers. Italics were Niles's means for emphasizing major concerns or segments of articles, but illustrations were extremely rare. The *Register* carried no advertisements.

The *Register* faced numerous circulation problems, and its survival during an era when the average publication lasted roughly two years is remarkable. While the mails or a lack of paper held up a few issues, Hezekiah Niles was extremely punctual in mailing an issue every Saturday. The *Register* maintained a respectable circulation of 3,500 to 4,500 during most of Hezekiah Niles's term as editor. However, problems with the delinquency of payments by subscribers plagued

Niles throughout the history of the magazine. Some $40,000 in arrears was recorded in the books when he retired in 1836. Yet Niles managed to make a respectable living from his publication.

William Ogden Niles, son of Hezekiah, followed his father as editor.[3] In addition to changing the size of the publication, he moved the office of publication to Washington and revised the name to *Niles' National Register*. His term as editor lasted only about three years from 3 September 1836 to 12 October 1839. The *Register* proved too much for the younger Niles. He lacked his father's skills in condensing the news, and the move to Washington narrowed the focus to political and congressional news. When William Ogden failed to get additional printing business from Congress and could not pay the notes due his father's estate, his father's second wife decided to sell the *Register*, much to his dismay.

Jeremiah Hughes, former editor of the *Maryland Republican* and state printer of Maryland, assumed the helm of the *Register* and quickly endeavored to make up the issues missed during a two-and-a-half-month abeyance. He continued the tradition of broad coverage of national and international news, but problems with overdue accounts remained a major burden. A four-month suspension followed the issue of 26 February 1848. Hughes was sixty-five and desired to retire. His search for a buyer during this period attracted George Beatty, who purchased the *Register* and moved the publication to Philadelphia. His capital and enthusiasm kept the publication alive for two more complete volumes (74 and 75). However, the publication died after three issues of the seventy-sixth volume (5, 12, and 19 September 1849). Under Beatty the *Register* suffered its first major decline in quality as he proved totally incapable of summarizing events succinctly. He also failed to meet deadlines, and lowering the price did nothing to bring back subscribers dismayed by the uneven quality and irregular production schedule of Beatty's *Register*.

The success of the *Register* rested on the vision of Hezekiah Niles. Born in 1777, Hezekiah was raised in Wilmington, Delaware, in a Quaker family, and in 1794 he became a printer's apprentice. Three years later he established his own printing business. It failed and left him with a $25,000 debt. In 1805 he began his career as a publisher, issuing the first number of *The Apollo or Delaware Weekly Magazine* on 12 February. The final issue of the eight-page literary magazine was printed on 24 August 1805, and Niles soon moved to Baltimore, where he purchased the *Evening Post*. Under Niles the *Post* became a major exponent of the Republicans and Thomas Jefferson. This four-page paper with about three pages of advertising and very few editorials provided no hint of the new directions in which Niles would lead journalism with the *Register*. He sold the *Post* on 10 June 1811, and two weeks later the prospectus for the *Register* appeared.

Philip R. Schmidt evaluates the broad influence of Niles in national affairs; "Through the wide circulation and readership of the *Weekly Register* Niles had more influence—especially because he wrote so much of it himself—than probably ninety percent of the men who sat in Congress from 1811 to 1836."[4]

Schmidt's thesis is that the *Register* was not as purely nonpartisan as Niles himself and modern historians have claimed, but it was not stridently partisan like other contemporary publications. Niles was an ardent Jeffersonian when the *Register* first appeared, but a Whig by the 1830s. He prided himself in consistency on issues and political pragmatism. Unlike most contemporary papers, the *Register* would frequently present opposing viewpoints or documents.

The conviction of Hezekiah Niles that his *Register* would become a record for the future was well justified. He carefully indexed and stockpiled volumes for future use as reference tools, and indeed the *Register* is perhaps the most valuable source of Americana for the first half of the nineteenth century. This explains why he retained the ''book-like'' size and format throughout his twenty-five years as editor. Contemporaries held the *Register* in great esteem, and Niles went to great lengths to maintain the accuracy of his paper as well as the quality of printing. While the Congress refused requests to provide public funds to support the *Register*, public officials referred to the *Register* as the source of record for many documents. Hezekiah Niles gained the confidence of the nation. Norval Neil Luxon observes that only 2 of 149 magazines founded between 1741 and 1811 lasted as long as the *Register*.[5] The disastrous suspensions under the final two editors undermined the confidence of readers. Moreover, the growth of daily and weekly newspapers in the mid–nineteenth century spelled the end of the *Register*. Neither Hughes nor Beatty understood the special niche of the *Register* or captured the contemporary scene with the editorial flair of Hezekiah Niles, and thus the most important source documenting a critical period in the development of the new American nation came to an end.

Notes

1. Frank Luther Mott, *A History of American Magazines,* vol. 1: *1741–1850* (Cambridge: Harvard University Press, 1930), p. 268.

2. The rate was lowered to $4 for the seventy-fifth volume, but even the offer of $3 for the three issues of the seventy-sixth volume did not attract sufficient subscribers for survival. Norval Neil Luxon, *Niles' Weekly Register: News Magazine of the Nineteenth Century* (Baton Rouge: Louisiana State University Press, 1947), p. 8.

3. For information on the three editors of the *Register* who followed Hezekiah Niles, see Luxon, pp. 66–74.

4. Philip R. Schmidt, *Hezekiah Niles and American Economic Nationalism* (New York: Arno Press, 1982), p. 296.

5. Luxon, p. 305.

Information Sources

BIBLIOGRAPHY

Luxon, Norval Neil. *Niles' Weekly Register: News Magazine of the Nineteenth Century.* Baton Rouge: Louisiana State University Press, 1947.

Niles, Hezekiah. *Chronicles of the American Revolution*. Ed. Alden T. Vaughan. (Originally compiled by Hezekiah Niles as *Principles and Acts of the Revolution in America*). New York: Grosset & Dunlap, 1965.

Schmidt, Philip R. *Hezekiah Niles and American Economic Nationalism*. New York: Arno Press, 1982.

Stone, Richard Gabriel. *Hezekiah Niles as an Economist*. Johns Hopkins University Studies in Historical and Political Science, series 51, no. 5. Baltimore: Johns Hopkins University Press, 1933.

INDEX SOURCES

Index to the First Twelve Volumes, 1811–17, by publisher. Series one through four indexed in *Poole*.

LOCATION SOURCES

Available at numerous libraries, including complete microform editions.

Publication History

MAGAZINE TITLE AND TITLE CHANGES

The Weekly Register, 1811–August 1814; *Niles' Weekly Register*, September 1814–August 1837; *Niles' National Register*, September 1837–1849.

VOLUME AND ISSUE DATA

Weekly with semiannual volumes, September-February and March-August; 1st series, vols. 1–12, 1811–1817 (first issue, 7 September 1811); new [2nd] series, vols. 1–12 [13–24], 1817–1823; 3rd series, vols. 1–12 [25–36], 1823–1829; 4th series, vols. 1–14 [37–50], 1829–1836; 5th series, vols. 1–23 [51–73], 1836–1848 (suspended March-June 1848); 6th series: vol. 74, 5 July 1848–27 December 1848; vol. 75, 3 January–27 June 1849; vol. 76, incomplete, suspended July-August 1849, printed 5, 12, and 19 September 1849 (last issue, 19 September 1849). Special supplements issued for nine volumes (1, 5, 7, 8, 15, 16, 23, 38, and 43).

EDITORS/PUBLISHERS AND PLACE OF PUBLICATION

Hezekiah Niles, Baltimore, 1811–August 1836; William Ogden Niles, Washington, September 1836–October 1839; Jeremiah Hughes, Baltimore, October 1839–February 1849; George Beatty, Philadelphia, July 1848–1849.

CIRCULATION

3,500–45,000

David Haury

NORTH AMERICAN REVIEW

The *North American Review* has a rich and varied history, having gone through numerous changes and, phoenix-like, died and risen from its own ashes. It has been a bimonthly, a quarterly, a bimonthly again, a monthly, a fortnightly, and finally a quarterly. Its circulation has varied from a few hundred to a high of 76,000 in 1891 to today's 4,000. In its earlier years especially, it had an influence out of proportion with its relatively modest circulation figures.

Founded as the *North American Review and Miscellaneous Journal*[1] in Boston in 1815 as a conscious imitation of English and Scottish reviews, especially the *Quarterly Review* of London and the *Edinburgh Review*, one of its main purposes was to defend and help establish American culture in the face of European condescension and doubt of the possibility of significant cultural substance in the United States. Started by a few friends at Harvard, it was founded, according to its editor of 1817, for "the encouragement of American Literature."[2] "Literature" here should be taken in its broadest sense, for the magazine has never confined itself to belles lettres; rather its interests have consistently ranged over politics, history, economics, science, the arts, and other issues or interests of the day. Its first editor, William Tudor, who was assisted by Edward Tyrell Channing and Richard Henry Dana, wrote virtually all of the first issue. Later Channing served as editor; other prominent names among the editors include Edward Everett, James Russell Lowell, Charles Eliot Norton, Henry Adams, Henry Cabot Lodge (assistant editor), and Colonel George Harvey. More than once it has had significant political impact; it is credited, for example, in being influential in the selection of Woodrow Wilson as the Democratic presidential candidate in 1912. More than one of its early editors left political life to become editor or went into (or returned to) politics after serving as editor. The *North American Review* was once regarded as "our most prestigious magazine," but probably its most prestigious days occurred relatively early, 1870–1876, for instance, when Henry Adams served as editor. From the first it published the writing of the most prominent writers and public figures of the day. And in 1891, the *Review of Reviews** wrote that "the *North American [Review]* is regarded by more people, in all parts of the country, as at once the highest and most impartial platform upon which current public issues can be discussed, than is any other magazine or review."[3]

In its earliest years, it was almost exclusively associated with Harvard, and in its first sixty years it reflected a rather narrow academic and New England provincialism. In 1876, however, began a revolution that was to turn the quarterly "Old North" into a lively monthly. In that year a young Henry Adams was forced to resign after disagreements with the publisher. In 1877, the magazine, the circulation of which was only 1,200, was sold to Allen Thorndike Rice, a twenty-three-year-old Bostonian with money and some new ideas. First, he returned the quarterly to its original bimonthly publication schedule and made the magazine a forum of ideas. Rice said that his magazine was to be "an arena wherein any man having something valuable to say could be heard."[4] In 1878, he moved the magazine to New York City, and during the 1880s

the magazine rose to its grandest heights and best circulation figures as Rice filled its pages with the names of the world's great and with a swirling clash of opinion about the problems of the new industrial society rising in America. Henry George and David Dudley Field argued the theory of the single tax. Parkman attacked woman suffrage, and Lucy Stone, Julia Ward Howe, and Wendell Phillips, among others, defended it. J. A. Froude and Cardinal Manning debated the role of the Catholic Church, while Robert G. Ingersoll aroused a public outcry with his atheistic attack against religion in general. Walt Whitman contributed some essays. Richard Wagner talked about his life and career, and William Gladstone contributed more than a dozen articles about politics. General Pierre G. T. Beauregard reminisced about his Civil War experiences, and General Grant talked about the Nicaragua canal.[5]

Rice's emphasis upon the use of symposia to present a variety of views on controversial issues was continued after his death in 1889. Circulation was 17,000 in that year and continued to climb, reaching an all-time high of 76,000 in 1891. Topics of discussion that year included "The Indian Question," the Bacon-Shakespeare authorship debate, "The Uselessness of Flying-Machines" (Arthur Mark Cummings concluding that practical flying-machines were impossible), several questions concerning women and marriage, and "Can Lawyers Be Honest?" Frank Luther Mott summed up this period as follows:

The *Review* came more and more to cultivate a clever and somewhat sophisticated type of essay on contemporary social life, manners, and fads. Gail Hamilton had become a regular contributor in 1886. Ouida came a few years after; and Max O'Rell, Jules Clarètie, Sarah Grand, and Grant Allen wrote such pieces. The servant girl problem, the man and the girl "of the period," courtship and marriage, and the amusements and sports of the day furnished unlimited opportunities for this kind of writing. More serious was the discussion of divorce, which was analyzed in more than one symposium. Mark Twain became one of the *Review*'s most valued contributors; most of his writing done for its pages was basically serious, and even bitter—though commonly winged with barbs of wit.[6]

Today's *North American Review* keeps the symposium tradition alive. Examples of debates of recent date are 1974's collection of articles from the Conference on the rights of Nonhuman Nature and the inauguration, in 1987, of a series of articles dealing with "creativity"—"defining it, exploring it, understanding it—the articles to be written by authors, artists, scientists, architects, educators, dancers—men and women of brilliance and eccentricity and exciting bias."[7]

Throughout its history *North American Review* has been fond of calling attention to its own glory by reprinting material from its past issues. In 1915, for instance, the magazine in celebrating its centennial reprinted many pieces from its earliest issues, including William Cullen Bryant's "Thanatopsis," which first appeared in print in *North American Review*. More recently, in 1972 and 1987 respectively, the magazine gave an overview of "The Indian Question" and

"The Woman Question" by reprinting more than a hundred years of thought and discussion from the pages of the *North American Review*.

In 1935 the magazine resumed its quarterly format and returned to the longer articles on literature, history, and related topics that were characteristic of its earlier issues. But the new quarterly did not thrive, and died in 1940. Its death resulted from the discovery that Joseph Hilton Smyth, who had bought the *Review* in 1939, was an agent of and was funded by the Japanese government.

The "new" *North American Review*, established in 1964 at Cornell College, in Mount Vernon, Iowa, strives to live up to its heritage. Similar to the editor in 1817, who wrote, "this journal is not subservient to any sect religious or political,"[8] a more recent editor has written that *North American Review* doesn't wish "to make a long-term commitment to any particular muse"[9] and that the new *Review* wants to avoid being trendy. Recent editions appear to be somewhat left of center politically and have not been fond of President Ronald Reagan's administrations, especially their environmental policies.

In its reincarnation, the *North American Review* takes its name seriously, not only in terms of reminding its readers of its long and prestigious (though admittedly checkered) history, but also in its editor's resentment at its being regarded as a regional magazine in some quarters. While willing to accept the "little magazine" label (with a circulation of about 4,000 that could not be argued), the editors insist that the *North American Review* be regarded as a national magazine. They are right, of course, because even though the magazine gives attention to topics and issues of all American regions, it does not confine itself to one region or only to regional concerns.

Today's *North American Review* is lively and worthy of its distinguished heritage. It adheres to the policy of some of its early editors in encouraging new contributors, but it nonetheless publishes the work of some of the most important writers of the day. Its forms of writing are varied, as are its art and photography.

The *North American Review* publishes nonfiction, poetry, criticism—including book and film reviews, and articles on the performing arts. It gives much attention to environmental concerns, and its editors feel a strong commitment to the short story and to poetry.

Indicative of the magazine's liveliness, perhaps, is a recent editor's pointing out that in 1975, *North American Review* had published thirty short stories by twenty-nine writers and that the editors like variety and "don't want ever to be accused of having a 'stable' of writers in this magazine; not that we have any written policy, but that we are restless (some say fickle)."[10]

In 1935, Mott, in his history of the *North American Review*'s first 120 years, observed: "Its total file, amounting now to approximately one hundred and twenty thousand pages, is a remarkable repository, unmatched by that of any other magazine, of American thought."[11] The intervening years have served to enhance that file.

Notes

1. *The Words and Miscellaneous Journal* was deleted from the magazine's name in 1821.

2. *North American Review and Miscellaneous Journal*, March 1817.

3. Quoted by Frank Luther Mott, *A History of American Magazines*, vol. 2: *1850–1865* (Cambridge: Harvard University Press, 1938), p. 255.

4. Quoted by John Tebbel, *The American Magazine: A Compact History* (New York: Hawthorne Books, 1969), p. 102.

5. Tebbel, pp. 102–3.

6. Mott, p. 254.

7. About This Issue, *North American Review*, March 1987, p. 2.

8. *North American Review and Miscellaneous Journal*, March 1817.

9. About This Issue, *North American Review*, Winter 1975, p. 2.

10. Ibid.

11. "One Hundred and Twenty Years," *North American Review*, June 1935, p. 174.

Information Sources

BIBLIOGRAPHY

Anderson, Elliott, and Mary Kinzie, eds. *The Little Magazine in America: A Modern Documentary History*. Stanford, Conn.: Pushcart Press, 1978.

Mott, Frank Luther. *A History of American Magazines* vol. 2: *1850–1865*. Cambridge: Harvard University Press, 1938. Mott's sketch of *North American Review* (pp. 219–61) also appeared as "One Hundred and Twenty Years," in the *North American Review,* June 1935, pp. 144–74.

Peterson, Theodore. *Magazines in the Twentieth Century*. Urbana: University of Illinois Press, 1964.

Tebbel, John. *The American Magazine: A Compact History*. New York: Hawthorne Books, 1969.

Wood, James Playsted. *Magazines in the United States*. 3rd ed. New York: Ronald Press, 1971.

INDEX SOURCES

Old Series (1815–1940), by publisher; *Poole's Guide to Periodical Literature* (1815–1906); *Readers' Guide to Periodical Literature.* New Series (1964–), *Arts and Humanities Critical Index; Bibliography of English Language and Literature; Book Review Index; Humanities Index* (1974–present); *Index to Little Magazines* (1966–present); *Social Sciences Index* (1965–1974).

LOCATION SOURCES

Library of Congress; University of Missouri at St. Louis.

Publication History

MAGAZINE TITLE AND TITLE CHANGES

North American Review and Miscellaneous Journal, May 1815–April 1821; thereafter, *North American Review*.

VOLUME AND ISSUE DATA

Old Series: vols. 1–7, May 1815–September 1818, semiannual volumes, three numbers each; vol. 8, December 1818, March 1819; vol. 9, June and September 1819; vols. 10–183, 1820–1906, regular semiannual volumes; vol. 184, 4 January–19 April 1907; vol. 185, 3 May–16 August 1907; vol. 186, September-December 1907; vols. 187–221, January 1908–June 1925, regular semiannual volumes; vol. 222, September 1925–February 1926; vol. 223, March 1926–February 1927; vol. 224, March–December 1927; vols. 225–248, 1928–Winter 1940. New Series: vol. 1 (Old Series 249), March 1964–present. Bimonthly, May 1815–September 1818; quarterly, December 1818–October 1876; bimonthly, January 1877–December 1878; monthly, January 1879–August 1906; fortnightly, 7 September 1906–16 August 1907; monthly, September 1927–March 1934; quarterly, June 1935 to Winter 1939–1940. Monthly, March 1964–present.

PUBLISHERS AND PLACES OF PUBLICATION

Old Series: Wells and Lilly, Boston (William Tudor, owner), 1817–1820, 1824; Oliver Everett, Boston (North American Review Club, 1821–1823; Jared Sparks, 1823–1824, owners), 1821–1824; Frederick T. Gray, Boston (Jared Sparks and F. T. Gray, owners), 1825–1828; Gray and Bowen, Boston (A. H. Everett, F. T. Gray, and Charles Bowen, owners), 1830–1831; Charles Bowen, Boston (A. H. Everett and Charles Bowen, owners), 1832–1836; Otis, Broaders and Company, Boston (J. G. Palfrey, chief owner, 1836–1842; Francis Bowen, chief owner, 1843–1852), 1837–1838, 1843–1847; Ferdinand Andrews, Boston (J. G. Palfrey, chief owner), 1838–1840; James Munroe and Company, Boston (J. G. Palfrey, chief owner), 1840–1841; David H. Williams, Boston (J. G. Palfrey, chief owner), 1842; Charles C. Little and James Brown, Boston (Francis Bowen, chief owner), 1848–1852; Crosby, Nichols and Company, Boston, 1853–1863; Ticknor and Fields, Boston, 1864–1867; Fields, Osgood and Company, Boston, 1868–1869; James R. Osgood and Company, Boston (A. T. Rice, owner, 1877), 1870–1877; D. Appleton and Company, New York (A. T. Rice, owner), 1878–1880; A. T. Rice, New York, 1881–1889; Lloyd Bryce, New York, 1889–1894; North American Review Publishing Company, New York, 1895–1915; North American Review Corporation, New York, 1915–1938. (George B. M. Harvey, chief owner during his editorship); W. B. Mahony, chief owner, 1926–1938; Joseph Hilton Smyth, 1939–1940. In 1878 the magazine moved from Boston to New York.

EDITORS

William Tudor, 1815–1817; Jared Sparks, 1817–1818; Edward Tyrrel Channing, 1818–1819; Edward Everett, 1820–1823; Jared Sparks, 1824–1830; Alexander Hill Everett, 1830–1835; John Gorham Palfrey, 1836–1842; Francis Bowen, 1843–1853; Andrew Preston Peabody, 1853–1863; James Russell Lowell, 1863–1872 (with Charles Eliot Norton, 1863–1868; E. W. Gurney, 1868–1870; Henry Adams, 1870–1872); Henry Adams (with Thomas Sergeant Perry as assistant editor), 1872–1873; Henry Cabot Lodge, assistant editor, 1873–1876; Allen Thorndike Rice, 1877–1889; Lloyd Bryce, 1889–1896; David A. Munro, 1896–1899; George B. M. Harvey, 1899–1926; Walter Butler Mahony, 1926–1935; John H. G. Pell, 1935–?. New Series: Cornell College, Mount Vernon, Iowa, March 1964–November/December 1968; University of Northern Iowa, Cedar Falls, Iowa; Robert

P. Dana, March 1964–November/December 1968; Robley Wilson, Jr., Spring 1969–   . Funding for the new series has included funds from Cornell College, University of Northern Iowa, Co-ordinating Council of Literary Magazines, and the Iowa Arts Council.

CIRCULATION

1877, 1,200; 1891, 76,000; 1940, 2,798; New Series: 1967, 901; 1969, 965; 1971, 1,243; 1973, 3,110; 1974, 3,300; 1975, 2,873; 1977, 2,571; 1978, 3,300; 1979, 2,669; 1980, 3,300; 1981, 3,100; 1982, 3,300; 1983, 4,084; 1985, 4,200; 1987, 4,200.

Daniel Straubel

O

OMNI

Omni—another successful Bob (*Penthouse*) Guccione creation—came to be, according to its creator, as something "summoned up from the frost-cool morning of my youth. *Omni,* born in the breathless dreams of that long-ago child. . . . It was much smaller then . . . a joy . . . the size of a matchbox . . . a flat, thumb polished, silvery case bursting with exotic wires and tubes. . . . When I held it to my forehead, I could see the future."[1]

Notwithstanding what the mystery of this silvery case might be, *Omni* has survived almost two decades now, and will continue to "see" into the future of scientific fact and fancy. Are science and art really compatible? Judging by the glossy, silvery, colorful pages of stunning photography and artistic reproductions, perhaps *Omni* proves that they can be. Indeed, *Omni*'s greatest contribution to the futuristic/scientific milieu is this effort to enhance the awareness of patterns, colors, and the artistic creativity one can find in the lowest forms of life, or in the abstract designs of computer graphics. True to the promise of its publisher, *Omni* has displayed in its pages the best of modern and contemporary art—from Marc Chagall and Fernando Botero to Salvador Dali, Pablo Picasso, and René Magritte. The October 1986 special anniversary issue bore a futuristic Botticelli Venus on the cover. *Omni*'s graphic design and layout pays homage to symbolism, as in the silvery pages of Continuum contrasted with the red against black of the Anti-Matter column, as well as in the illustrations for the science fiction stories it publishes. *Omni* has published some of the most outstanding science fiction of our times, and the magazine has received numerous prizes for its artistic and overall quality, such as the Overseas and the Westinghouse Press awards.

According to Kathy Keeton, president of Omni Corporation, and Guccione's partner, "People are interested not in the nuts and bolts of science, but in its implications for their lives. This is really what *Omni* is all about—this and about the romance and adventure of discovery,"[2] futuristic life styles, as it were, a theme that appeals to the young, inquisitive, open-minded generation of the eighties. *Omni's* readers' profile shows a median age of twenty-nine, with a median household income of $33,000.[3] Notwithstanding its tendency to stretch the boundaries of science into the supernatural and speculative, *Omni* has been able to hold on steadily to its 892,600 (1987) circulation, counting more than 300,000 subscribers from the ranks of the college-educated young professionals.

Trying to bridge both levels of inquiry—the subjective reality of art and the objectiveness of science—is the editorial premise of *Omni*: "an original, if not controversial mixture of science, fact, fiction, fantasy and the paranormal," as noted in the October 1978 issue (p. 6). Guccione would like for his magazine to satisfy our deepest spiritual needs, and he sees religion and science, knowledge and faith, in a collision course, although some of *Omni's* own speculations defy even the boundaries of faith and belief.

Readers invited to step into the future in a charter voyage through the first collector's edition encountered such notables as Isaac Asimov, Theodore Sturgeon, and Roman Vishniac, and responded with enthusiasm: *Omni* is handsome and attractive, esthetically and intellectually. The concept of deliberately packaging summaries of the best science ("Continuum" column) with the best of science fiction is also "attractive," comments Phillip Handler, president of the National Academy of Sciences. Compliments abound, ranging from Barry Goldwater's terse "you've printed something of quality," to astronaut James B. Irwin's superlatives: "It is absolutely the best magazine I have ever read."[4] It is rather difficult to find any negative comments until recently, when upholding Guccione's staunch stand against censorship, the magazine plunged into controversy with its February issue on science versus censorship. In the June 1987 issue—"The Visitation and Other Divine Encounters"—nine fantasists unleashed their imaginations "to explore the mysterious nature of God and the effects of our religious beliefs," and the magazine joined the fray between creationists and evolutionists. A barrage of indignant comments includes the one from a reader who tells of throwing that issue in the garbage where it belonged.[5]

The August 1987 issue, "Last Rights," is a well-done, informative, and fair presentation of the right to die controversy, but Anthony Liversidge's interview with Claude Shannon—"the founding father of the electronics communication age"—leaves one chilled: "I visualize a time when we will be to robots what dogs are to humans, and I'm rooting for the machines," Shannon is quoted as saying in the August 1987 issue (p. 62).

This last year has seen some editorial slips, and negative comments, as in the April 1987 "Let's hear it for acid rain," in the Continuum section. The response from the Acid Rain Campaign coordinator for Greenpeace was sharp: "The presentation was simplistic . . . in bad taste, if not altogether misleading." The George Bugliarello interview with Frank Davidson led to the president of Brooklyn's Polytechnic University's protest that he had never called Reagan "vicious"

(May 1987). Nevertheless, *Omni* has been one of Guccione's most thriving enterprises, with over $9 million in ad revenue and its steady subscribers. Omni Publications is now diversifying into book and newsletter publishing.

According to Patrice Adcroft, *Omni's* present editor, *Longevity*, a newsletter on aging, and *Whole Mind*, on psychiatric research, are Omni's latest ventures. In the last two years *Omni* has explored video production, television shows, and telecommunications. "Omni, the New Frontier" was, according to Kathy Keeton, "an innovative television series combining the best capabilities of television with the future oriented content of *Omni* itself." The show used special effects, music and graphics to convey *Omni's* vision of the future. Although short-lived, to its creators the new experiment heralded a new age and the "end of the pedantic science show."[6]

The copies of *Omni* found at your doctor's office are editions sponsored by pharmaceutical companies, a very profitable enterprise for the magazine. *Omni's* articles, stories, games, and quizzes were available on Compuserve in 1985–1986, as well as teleconferences featuring such celebrities in the science fiction realm as Isaac Asimov.

Notes

1. *Omni,* October 1978, p. 6. First volume, first issue.
2. Diane Reese, "Penthouse: When Sex Doesn't Sell," *Folio: The Magazine for Magazine Management*, January 1987, p. 125. The best current review of *Omni*.
3. Marie Spadoni, "Science Category Is under the Microscope," *Advertising Age*, 18 October 1984, p. 38.
4. Readers' Response, *Omni*, December 1978, p. 10.
5. *Omni*, June 1987, p. 54.
6. Kathy Keeton, First Word, *Omni*, October 1981, p. 6.

Information Sources

BIBLIOGRAPHY
Bova, Ben. "How to Write for *Omni*." *Writer*, July 1981, pp. 26–28. Information on readership, philosophy, and trends.
Edel, Richard. "Magazines' Graphic Design Sets Style." *Advertising Age*, 3 October 1985, pp. 18–20.
Keeton, Kathy. First Word. *Omni*, October 1980, p. 6, and *Omni*, October 1981, p. 6.
Reese, Diane. "Penthouse: When Sex Doesn't Sell." *Folio: The Magazine for Magazine Management*, January 1987, pp. 124–28.
Spadoni, Marie. "Science Category Is under the Microscope." *Advertising Age*, 18 October 1984, p. 38.
INDEX SOURCES
    Abstrax; Access (1979–1983); *Gdlns; Magazine Index* (1978–present); *Infotrac; Popular Magazine Review* (1984–current); *Readers' Guide to Periodical Literature* (1984–present); Omni International Database.

LOCATION SOURCES
     Microformat, Bell and Howell Microforms and University Microfilms International, Online from Compuserve Videotext (1986).

Publication History

MAGAZINE TITLE AND TITLE CHANGES
     Omni, 1978–present.
VOLUME AND ISSUE DATA
     Vol. 1–current, October 1978–current, monthly.
PUBLISHER AND PLACE OF PUBLICATION
     Bob Guccione. Omni Publications International, Ltd., New York, New York.
EDITORS
     Frank Kendig, 1978–1981; Dick Teresi, 1981–1982; Ben Bova, 1983–1984; Gurney Williams III, 1984–1986; Patrice Adcroft, 1986–current.
CIRCULATION
     892,600 (1987).

Heleni Pedersoli

ONCE A WEEK. See COLLIER'S

ORGANIC GARDENING

If "magazine" can mean a container for the collection of a diversity of things, then the mind of J. I. Rodale is an appropriate place for the genesis of *Organic Gardening.* In addition to founding the magazine and writing many articles, pamphlets, and books on organic gardening, Rodale wrote a number of plays (and saw them produced in his own theater), and a number of books on a wide variety of subjects, including *Strengthening Your Memory, The Sophisticated Synonym Book, Sleep and Rheumatism,* and *Twenty Ways to Stop Smoking.*

Yet Jerome Irving Rodale is best known as founder and long-time editor of the monthly magazine that has been the flagship of the Rodale Press empire since 1942. Rodale's interest in the methods of gardening and farming now known as organic stemmed from his discovery of the work of Sir Albert Howard, the British plant breeder regarded as the father of modern organic horticulture. In 1941, after reading Howard's book, *An Agricultural Testament,* and corresponding with him, Rodale "decided that we must get a farm at once and raise as much of our family's food by the organic method as possible."[1] The farm, bought in 1941, was a "miserable piece of land," but it proved so successful that Rodale "felt that I had to share this information with the rest of the country. . . . Little did I realize what I was touching off—that I would be the one to introduce this great movement to the United States."[2] But introduce it he did. Starting with a circulation of 20,000, the magazine he founded and edited until his death in 1971 grew to over 300,000 circulation in twenty-five years, and now, forty-five years later, stands at around 1.5 million circulation and perhaps nearly three times that many readers.

The heart of organic gardening is the use of compost made from natural plant and animal materials and the use of natural pest controls. Research, especially that done at Rodale Press's own Organic Gardening and Farming Research Center, has convinced the people at *Organic Gardening* that their methods are as productive as, or more productive than, intensive chemical fertilizer and insecticide methods, widely used by modern agriculture, and a whole lot safer for both people and the environment.

From the beginning, the staples in the magazine have been practical advice to gardeners, preaching of the organic gospel, and a close, seemingly personal relationship between the editor and the reader. Even though there have been some changes in the name of the magazine over the years, "organic gardening" has always been a part of that name, and the tone of the magazine and type of content have remained remarkably consistent. Nonetheless, the magazine has managed to change with the times, shifting its emphasis somewhat over the years, while remaining faithful to its original mission.

Rodale recognized from the beginning that the movement he introduced to this country was international. In fact, Sir Albert Howard, who had done his experimental organic horticultural work in India, served as associate editor in the magazine's first years through correspondence from England. Today, the magazine continues to give attention to the international scene, especially Third World countries. "The Compost Revolution," in the August 1983 issue, for instance, reports on the efforts of the editor and others to introduce organic methods into the agriculture of Tanzania. And "Gardening Italian Style," in the April 1988 issue, profiles five home gardeners of Italy.

A typical issue today contains features on particular fruits or vegetables or special varieties thereof; on techniques for successful organic gardening; equipment reviews; question and answer columns for readers with specific gardening problems; garden calendars for six zones of the contiguous states and southern Canada; short news items, letters from readers, an editorial, and, of course, carefully selected advertising. The editorial is likely to be practical advice or a philosophical statement, or a call for action, often through one of the many organizations that the mind of the editor seems to spawn. Also, there may be sections on organic living and the organic kitchen, which extend organic principles into aspects of life other than gardening. In fact, two significant movements recently espoused in the magazine build upon such extension; one is regenerative living and the other is holistic living, both of which envision a "way of life that is simpler, less energy intensive" and that "can be created in part with one's hands."[3]

Both Jerome Irving Rodale and his son, Robert, the magazine's only editors to date, have been prolific writers and editors. Currently, articles in the magazine are usually relatively short and always carefully focused upon the interests of the readers, but earlier issues sometimes contained longer, somewhat rambling narratives by their first editor.

Even though their views have not become dominant in our culture, *Organic Gardening* remain optimistic, encouraged perhaps by certain recent trends such as increased interest in "natural" and "organically grown" food and by the fact that they are beginning to receive some cooperation from the U.S. Department of Agriculture and certain other institutions and organizations.

Over the years the magazine has supported a bewildering array of organizations of its own. In the 1940s, it created the Organic Gardening Clubs of America, with clubs in virtually every state, and the Soil and Health Foundation. More recently the editor has been active in the People's Medical Society and the Regenerative Agriculture Association.

Like his father, the current editor insists on being practical in his magazine, though he does allude to the philosophical underpinnings of organic gardening and points out that the most serious of the organic gardeners he has met tend to be a philosophical lot. In describing the concept of the holistic garden, the editor goes so far as to write of "that feeling of the inner garden."[4]

In 1987 the magazine changed its physical appearance perhaps more than ever before. Its overall dimensions were slightly reduced; there was a new, cleaner look with some experimentation with different looks for the contents page and the departments.

Name changes have reflected shifts in emphasis, either toward or away from a focus on farming—that is, large-scale use of organic methods. The word *Farming* has been added and dropped from the magazine's title. Most recently, in July 1978, *and Farming* was deleted, and a new magazine, the *New Farm*, was announced. In August 1985, *Rodale's* was added to the magazine's name, and the size of the word *organic* on the cover was significantly reduced. It was easy at a glance to read the title as *Rodale's Gardening*, as if the "organic" content of the magazine were to be given reduced emphasis; such, however, was not the case, and in September 1987, the size of the word *Rodale* was greatly reduced and *Organic* was significantly restored.

The most sweeping physical change in *Organic Gardening* came in April 1988, when the magazine showed the results of a complete format and graphics overhaul. As editor Robert Rodale observed, the magazine was given "a new size, better paper and more color."[5] In its first significant change in size the magazine went from 5" x 8" to 8" x 10". Also it began to deliver its material, basically unchanged but more geared to young, upscale tastes, in a slicker, more colorful package. And *Rodale's* was deleted from the magazine's name. In the first of the newly redesigned issues, executive editor Stevie O. Daniels observed:

> Our larger size gives you up to 35 percent more coverage of all your favorite topics—food gardening, soil care, pest control, flowers, preparing and preserving your garden bounty. In addition, you'll value regular features on environmental issues, and the important link between diet and

health. You'll also see expanded coverage of garden equipment, and special build-it projects for your yard and garden.[6]

She also wrote, "If you don't improve your garden's soil, it will become barren and die. The same is true for a magazine, which has an organic life of its own."[7] The continued life of *Organic Gardening* appears to be assured.

Notes

1. J. I. Rodale. Quoted by M. C. Goldman, "Happy Birthday, Organic Gardening," *Organic Gardening,* May 1982, p. 42.
2. Ibid, pp. 43–44.
3. Robert Rodale, "The Holistic Garden," *Organic Gardening*, May 1978, p. 38.
4. Ibid.
5. Robert Rodale, "To The Future," *Organic Gardening*, April 1988, p. 23.
6. Stevie O. Daniels, "Welcome to Change," *Organic Gardening*, April 1988, p. 5.
7. Ibid.

Information Sources

BIBLIOGRAPHY
n.a.
INDEX SOURCES
> *Abstrax; Bibliography of Agriculture; Biology Digest; Index to How to Do It Information; Readers' Guide to Periodical Literature* (1978–present); *Magazine Index* (1978–present).

LOCATION SOURCES
> St. Louis Public Library; Missouri Botanical Garden Library. Available on microform (1943–present).

Publication History

MAGAZINE TITLE AND TITLE CHANGES
> *Organic Farming and Gardening,* vol. 1, no. 1, May 1942; title changed to *Organic Gardening and Farming* in December 1942; then it appears to have been titled *Organic Gardening* until December 1954, when it combined with *Organic Farmer* and was named *Organic Gardening and Farming*; this issue is vol. 1, no. 1 of the current series. In July 1978, the title became *Organic Gardening*; in August 1985, *Rodale's Organic Gardening*; and in April 1988, *Organic Gardening*.

VOLUME AND ISSUE DATA
> Monthly. (Volume designations above.)

PUBLISHER AND PLACE OF PUBLICATION
> Rodale Press, 33 E. Minor St., Emmaus, PA. 18049.

EDITORS
    J. I. Rodale, 1942–1971; Robert Rodale, 1971–present.
CIRCULATION
    1942, 20,000; 1966, 335,000; 1978, 1,200,000; 1983, 1,310,948; 1987,
    1,333,836.

Daniel Straubel

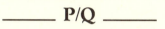

PARADE

Because Chicago sportsman Marshall Field III was losing money with his New York tabloid *PM,* he decided to salvage that paper with a thirty-two-page weekly newspaper supplement, also purchasable on the newsstands for five cents; he did so by sinking $1,950,000 into a new endeavor called *Parade.* He established a $100,000 monthly editorial budget, promising forty-three cameramen and 137 "brilliant" reporters. *Time** predicted that the probable editor of the new venture would be William McCleery, the *PM* Sunday editor, but the *PM* publisher Ralph Ingersoll was probably not to be a part of the supplement. *Time* rated the chances for this project's success "fair to good if it can reassure newspapers that it has broken with the leftist traditions of *PM.*"[1] Those predictions were somehow overly cautious because *Parade* is the only Sunday magazine of that era in print to date.

When *Parade* was launched in September 1941, the actual editor was an efficiency expert named Ross Art Lasley, who had conceived the idea. "A self-confessed ignoramus about editing," Lasley was nonetheless clever at making money, and his idea was to sell ads in *Parade* as *PM* had not done—just what Field needed given the financial bind that *PM* had caused. And the content of this Sunday supplement was interesting enough to get the attention of many newspaper publishers. *Time* quoted *Washington Post*'s publisher Eugene Mayer: "*Parade* emphasizes pretty legs, movies, theater, the more picturesque side of national defense, the more colorful reporting of *PM's* foreign correspondents— just what we have been looking for."[2]

Five years later Field offered to share ownership of *Parade* with Arthur (Red) Motley, who accepted and grabbed a new editor, Ken W. Purdy. Circulation rose from 2.1 million to 3.65 million when Purdy and Motley took over: "We've thrown the truss boys, kidney-pill artists and goiter curers out of the sheet, and have replaced them with such class A advertisers as General Foods, Arm & Hammer and Sunshine Biscuits."[3] In addition to the changes in advertising makeup, these two also emphasized human interest stories on ordinary people— apparently a winning idea given circulation increases.

One especially noteworthy human interest story appeared in a 1953 issue of *Parade*. At that time, Wallace Sprague was managing editor. He grew interested in the story of Hungarian-born Stephen Ragan, alias Michael Patrick (Stateless) O'Brien, deported twenty-two years earlier as a convicted criminal. An anonymous wanderer until September 1952, he then became a "perpetual motion" commuter on a Macao–Hong Kong ferryboat since neither city allowed him to enter. At last it seemed that Brazil would grant a visa for O'Brien, but diplomatic relations caused problems and O'Brien was assigned to cruise on a French steamer before Sprague of *Parade* finally found him a home in the Dominican Republic. Sprague paid O'Brien $350 for his first-person story. Sprague noted that "no man should be without a country." Not only was this a remarkable human interest story, but magazines such as *Parade* with copy deadlines as much as six weeks before issue rarely get to "make" much news![4]

Sunday supplements have been around since the early 1900s, but most of them were short-lived. Of the four still published in 1960 (Hearst's *American Weekly*, *This Week*, *Family Weekly*, and *Parade*), only the last two were alive in 1980. By 1985 only *Parade* remained with its original title intact when *Family Weekly* became *USA Weekend*.* The toughest times for the supplements were probably in the 1950s when advertisers were more interested in spending their money with television. At this point the survivors beefed up editorial products and began referring to themselves as Sunday magazines, castigating anyone, including agency media buyers, who called them supplements.[5] Today the competition is more from large city newspapers that produce their own Sunday magazines than from each other or from television. In addition to *Parade* and *USA Weekend*, there is the Metro group, formerly called the Sunday magazine network, which publishes fifty-two locally owned and edited Sunday magazines.[6] In 1985 *Parade* offered three major national advertisers discounts of 65 percent off for fifty-two-week schedules, a ploy the others have not yet been willing to adopt. This was in an attempt to combat the "new" competition from the sale of *Family Weekly* to the Gannett Company's *USA Today* empire. But *Parade* did not really have to worry. More newspapers defected from the new Sunday magazine than from *Parade*. *Parade* is the current circulation leader with over 31.4 million readers.

Perhaps a part of *Parade*'s success has been not only good business practice but also a kind of stability over the years. Following the editorship of Ken Purdy in the late forties, Jess Gorkin became editor and remained in that position for twenty-four years, until 1978. Soon after that time, Walter Anderson assumed the editorship and remains with *Parade* as editor to date. Gorkin said in 1966 that his aim was to "publish controversial, provocative challenging material . . . in tune with current tastes and trends."[7] As such, Personality Parade, the weekly question-answer feature for readers to ask questions of and about celebrities, has often been much more blunt with its responses than similar columns in other weeklies. Gorkin is perhaps equally remembered for his campaign in *Parade* for a direct telephone line between Washington and Moscow. When such a "hot line" became a reality in the early 1960s, President John F. Kennedy wrote to Gorkin to thank him for the idea.[8]

The unique problem facing editors of a Sunday magazine such as *Parade* is that instead of trying to please a certain type of reader, as most magazines will gear their material to a particular audience, they must try to please editors and publishers of local newspapers across the nation. Gorkin once stated that *Parade* tries to "present the facts rather than take a stand," an editorial policy determined in large measure by the nature of the format.[9] In general, over the years, *Parade* has been more of a big-city supplement, while *Family Weekly*, at least from the fifties through the seventies, was, as the name implies, more family oriented and thus suited to smaller towns in most cases. Today, such newspapers as the *St. Louis Post Dispatch* and the *Washington Post* carry *Parade* along with their own local magazines.

Today's *Parade* features a color cover photo, often of some movie star or other somewhat contemporarily famous individual, Walter Scott's Personality Parade (questions regarding the noteworthy, often with accompanying photos), perhaps a health-related feature story, On Parade (previews of "what's up this week" in movies, magazines, and children), Laugh Parade (cartoons), a food feature with recipes and color photos, Intelligence Report (facts and figures on topics of current interest), and James Brady's In Step With feature column on noted personalities—all interspersed with numerous ads, often for a total of nineteen inside pages. Most people look forward to the Sunday paper more than to daily papers; some people subscribe only to Sunday issues. Perhaps part of the reason for that extra interest is the well-done Sunday magazine, not just a supplement to the news but an important addition to leisurely Sunday reading entertainment.

Notes

1. *"PM's* Little Brother to Be Launched," *Time*, 2 June 1941, p. 51.
2. "Engineering Feat," *Time*, 18 August 1941, p. 42.
3. "Punch for *Parade*," *Time*, 7 October 1946, p. 74.
4. "One Man Parade," *Newsweek*, 2 November 1953, p. 56.
5. William F. Gloede, "Sunday Magazines Undergo Revival," *Advertising Age*, 28 July 1986, p. S8.
6. William F. Gloede, "CBS Sells Off 'Family Weekly,' " *Advertising Age*, 25 February 1985, p. 1.
7. Norman Hill, "The Last of the Red Hot Supplements," *Saturday Review*, 12 December 1970, p. 57.
8. Ibid.
9. Ibid.

Information Sources

BIBLIOGRAPHY
"Engineering Feat." *Time,* 18 August 1941, p. 42.
Gloede, William F. "CBS Sells off 'Family Weekly.' " 25 February 1985, p. 1.
————. "Sunday Magazines Undergo Revival." *Advertising Age*, 28 July 1986, p. S8.
Hill, Norman. "The Last of the Red Hot Supplements." *Saturday Review*, 12 December
      1970, pp. 56–62.
"One Man Parade." *Newsweek*, 2 November 1953, p. 56.
"*PM*'s Little Brother to Be Launched." *Time*, 2 June 1941, p. 51.
"Punch for *Parade*." *Time*, 7 October 1946, pp. 74–75.
INDEX SOURCES
      n.a.
LOCATION SOURCES
      Available in microform, 1953–present.

Publication History

MAGAZINE TITLE AND TITLE CHANGES
      Parade.
VOLUME AND ISSUE DATA
      1941–present, weekly.
PUBLISHER AND PLACE OF PUBLICATION
      Marshall Field III, 1941–1946; Arthur H. (Red) Motley, 1946–1978; Warren J.
      Reynolds, 1978–1981; Carlo Vittorini, 1981–1988. New York.
EDITORS
      Ross Lasley, 1941–1946; Ken W. Purdy, 1946–1949; Jess Gorkin, 1949–1978;
      James D. Head, 1978–1980; Walter Anderson, 1980–present.
CIRCULATION
      31.4 million (1988)

Barbara Nourie

PARENTS

The editors of *Parents* introduced the first issue with a statement entitled
"Parents, We Are Here":

This magazine has been launched because of our overwhelming conviction
that mothers and fathers would welcome such a publication. Yours is the
all-important, often bewildering, yet always loving task of caring for your
children. Ours is the privilege of helping you . . . to bring scientific findings
of the specialist concerning the child's needs of mind, body, and spirit
from birth to the twenty-first year—with simplicity and sympathy, with
humor and with understanding. We wait confidently for your response,

both as readers and contributors, to this new effort to supplement the work
that is being done to improve the race at its source—the children.[1]

Other sources, however, report a more personal reason for George Hecht's
founding a new magazine. Apparently, a prominent New York matron remarked
to Hecht that her adult children were in no way a credit to themselves or to her
because she had not known how to bring them up. After this, Hecht circulated
the leaflet "Why Another Magazine?" to determine the extent of interest in a
publication devoted to parenting; Hecht at the time was a bachelor.[2]

As founder, editor, and president of the Parents Corporation, George Joseph
Hecht has had the most profound influence of any individual associated with
Parents to date. From 1926 until 1978 at age eighty-three he maintained an
association with the magazine, and his influence is obvious throughout its history.
He is said to have commented that "there are magazines devoted exclusively to
the raising of cattle, hogs, dogs, flowers, and what not, but until now none on
the most important work of the world—the rearing of children."[3] One of his
many lifelong interests was family planning programs worldwide, especially in
underdeveloped nations. As an active member of the Population Council, for
example, he financed programs that through tax incentives benefited families
with fewer than three children in India and Bangladesh.[4] He was also devoted
to the importance of education for all children. He actively sought educators as
advisory board members and published through the cooperation of Columbia
University, the State University of Iowa, the University of Minnesota, and Yale
University–a fact proudly touted on the cover of the magazine at one time. In
1921, before launching *Parents*, Hecht published *The War in Cartoons*, and
throughout his career he championed the use of the comic strip for educational
purposes.[5]

A second, powerful influence on *Parents* came from Clara Savage Littledale,
managing editor in 1926 with the inception of the magazine. In 1951 a writer
described her as a "trim little 60 year old who doesn't like 'the idea of an
inaccessible editor.' " So accessible was she that mothers often called her at
her office for advice. One Manhattan mother called to report that her child didn't
eat his breakfast that morning. Littledale's response: "Try him on lunch." Her
career began when she was a woman's suffrage editor on Garrison Villard's *New
York Evening Post* staff. She once marched on 5th Avenue with a sign that read,
"Idiots can vote. Why Can't I?" Later she was a World War I correspondent
for *Good Housekeeping*. Just as George Hecht selected certain causes to espouse
in the pages of *Parents*, so did Littledale: better pay for teachers, school lunches,
better health examinations, and more thorough training for mothers.[6] Clara Savage Littledale died in January 1956; at that time Hecht appointed Mary E.
Buchanan as editor. She, too, had long been associated with *Parents* as managing
editor since 1930 and as first assistant to Littledale. In March 1965, when
Buchanan retired, the new editor was Dorothy Whyte Cotton, again a long-time
associate with *Parents*. In February 1971, Dorothy Cotton was succeeded by

Genevieve Millet Landau; Landau was followed briefly by Peter A. Janssen, and then in 1979 Elizabeth Crow became the editor. Throughout its more than fifty-year history, *Parents* seems to have retained a "family" feeling by appointing editors who know the magazine well.

Elizabeth Crow is the only editor of *Parents* since the time when George Hecht was publisher. She introduced herself and the "new" magazine in an article entitled "A Fresh Start: Notes on Our New Look":

> We believe that our magazine will now be more responsive to the needs of men and women who are raising children today. . . . more lively and stimulating to look at and to read. . . . In short, although we have changed, our magazine still holds a basic attitude about family life that was first expressed 52 years ago, when *Parents* was founded. It is our belief that people who believe in children believe in hope. And people who believe in parents, believe in that hope fulfilled.[7]

Crow introduced several new sections, including As They Grow columns, which discuss particular problems or concerns associated with children of a specific age. All of these changes were accompanied by a new "crew" of specialists who commented not only on children and child-rearing but on parents as adults with problems and concerns of their own. And that is probably the key difference between *Parents* under the guidance of Hecht and other editors and the new *Parents* under Crow's leadership.

A list of contributors to *Parents* since its 1926 inception reads like a who's who of the twentieth century: political figures, scholars, scientists, entertainers, all with ideas on the improvement of life for children in this country and worldwide. Beginning in January 1927, only the third issue of a young magazine originally called *Children: A Magazine for Parents*, a silhouette of small children playing appeared on the bottom of the editorial page with the quote from Philips Brooks: "The future of the race marches forward on the feet of little children." And this theme pervades the contributions included in every issue. Jane Addams of Hull House warned parents: "What children need is the protection of a community from which harmful influences and unfair temptations are removed, and this parents should work together to accomplish" (March 1927, p. 7). From these comments printed in an early issue right up to comments in the magazine today, the timeliness and significance of *Parents* remain intact. Bertrand Russell granted *Parents* several interviews, including one on bringing up children (April 1927). Vachel Lindsay introduced his daughter to the readers of *Parents* (November 1927). Mrs. Franklin D. Roosevelt contributed several times to *Parents*, but her first article was "Books I Loved as a Child" (December 1928). Dr. Maria Montessori ("Blazing New Trails in Education," April 1929), Governor Alfred E. Smith ("Educate Parents Too," May 1928), Mrs. A. A. Milne ("Now We Are Eleven," April 1932), Frances Perkins ("Our Crime Against Children," June 1933), President Franklin Roosevelt ("A Message to Parents," October 1935), Sherwood Anderson ("Give A Child Room to Grow," April 1936), Pearl

S. Buck ("What Chinese Parents Can Teach Us," November 1941), Dr. Benjamin Spock ("A Baby Doctor Advises About Thumbsucking," April 1945), Ezio Pinza ("My Career as a Father," January 1950), Bruno Bettelheim ("What Children Learn from Play," July 1964), William Saroyan ("A Small Boy's Adventure," June 1951), and Amy Vanderbilt ("Twelve Keys to Courtesy," July 1954) are among the many contributors. Other celebrities and authors who contributed include Stan Musial ("Physical Fitness for Everyone," November 1964), Frank O'Connor ("My Oedipus Complex," fiction, February 1965), John Updike ("The Alligators," fiction, September 1965), Marjorie Kinnan Rawlings ("A Mother in Mannville," fiction, April 1965), Brendan Gill ("The Knife," fiction, November 1965), Haim Ginott ("The Art of Talking with Children," October 1965), William Van Til ("Five Bold Ways to Attack the Drop-out Problem," March 1965), Hubert H. Humphrey ("Our Children Deserve the Best in Education," September 1965), Nelson A. Rockefeller ("We Honor Our Teachers," May 1966), Mrs. Lyndon B. Johnson ("Let's Work for a More Beautiful America," July 1966), Walter F. Mondale ("What Does Our Country Owe Its Children?," May 1972), Senator Edward Kennedy ("What Parents Can do to Guarantee Every Child's Right to Read," September 1973)—to mention just a few.

One interesting note is that *Parents* continued to list its staff and contributors as "Mrs." until 1975. Mrs. Franklin D. Roosevelt of 1928, however, was Mrs. Eleanor Roosevelt by 1936. As the years passed, there seemed to be an effort to use whatever name or title the contributor or staff member preferred.

One frequent contributor over several decades was Margaret Mead. In fact, in the fiftieth anniversary issue she wrote about her long association with *Parents* in "Five Decades of Writing for *Parents' Magazine*" (October 1976). One of her earliest articles was entitled "South Sea Hints on Bringing Up Children" (September 1929). After World War II she called for a panel on compulsory national service for all youth, and over the years she urged that children attain autonomy through a new kind of discipline. In 1976 she persisted in her concern for the inadequacy of the nuclear family and for children who are cut off from experiences of birth and death (October 1976).

As interesting and important as the contributors are, the ads, too, reflect the concerns and beliefs of the day. In the first issue the editors announced that the magazine accepted "only advertisements of reliable products accurately described." The second volume printed a "conscientious directory of schools and camps." Typical early ads were for Man 'o' War middies and bloomers, Lifebuoy soap, and Scot tissue. Several ads for cereals emphasized that their products helped children *gain* weight. In 1933 an ad for Mazda Sunlight Lamps proclaimed "the ultra-violet that's so important in building strong bones and teeth."

The only major controversy associated with *Parents* concerned the *Parents'* Seal of Approval on advertised products. In November 1963, 61 of the 209 ads in *Parents' Magazine* displayed the *Good Housekeeping* seal; *Parents'* seal, along with that of *Good Housekeeping*, appeared in 11.[8] In 1966 the Federal Trade Commission (FTC) ruled that

> the products certified are not always tested by experts as claimed. Some products are awarded the seal solely on the recommendation of *PM* staff members who are not qualified technicians or medical experts, or on the basis of tests and reports submitted by the applicant for the seal, or on the basis of an editorial staff decision based on the reputation of the applicant.[9]

In addition, the FTC noted that advertising contracts with *Parents* were prerequisites for the "award" of the seal. *Parents* agreed to "discontinue this misrepresentation through settlement which does not constitute an admission of violating the law."[10] In 1969 the seal no longer appeared on the cover.

In 1976, on the fiftieth anniversary of *Parents' Magazine*, the enterprise was a quite different one from the early days. There were now a book publishing company (*Parents Magazine* Press), a book club division, six separate magazines, and a film division. According to Sylvia Steinberg, the "financil security provided by the book clubs [allowed] *Parents' Magazine* Press latitude for experimentation."[11] Hecht was eighty at the time, "a courtly gentleman with a benevolent manner which thinly [veiled] an almost messianic sense of purpose," and still looking to the future; he foresaw "the challenge of communicating breakthroughs in medical research, [hoped] to discover a better way to teach morals to children, and [yearned] to establish a simplified spelling system."[12] More than a decade earlier, *Parents' Magazine* had purchased FAO Schwarz Toy Store. In 1963, Hecht stated, "*Parents' Magazine* Enterprises believes in diversification, and the acquisition of FAO Schwarz fits into our overall concept of a company devoted to the needs and interests of families with children."[13] James L. C. Ford notes that the realization that two cannot live as cheaply as one is a triumph of George Hecht: "When making up your list, remember that families with children spend more for virtually all products than any other market! 135 percent more for homes, 79 percent more for food, 72 percent more for home furnishings, 76 percent more for cars."[14]

Children: The Magazine for Parents, first issued in October 1926, sold for twenty-five cents a copy. An Ann Brockman illustration of five children appeared on the first cover, and illustrations by Brockman and others were used on the cover for several years before photographs were used. The first issue included "tips for fathers," twenty-one features of interest to mothers, menus, games, and advice. Contributors whose "stories" were published in Out of the Mouths of Babes received $1. In the beginning there was a board of editors with George Hecht as president, Clara Savage Littledale as managing editor with six other editors, three consultants, and forty-eight advisory editors from medicine, the clergy, the judiciary, academe, and science. The early issues included motion picture and book reviews plus fashions with pattern numbers. The second issue in November 1926 contained reviews of the first issue done by three "great" newspapers: the *Boston Evening Transcript*, the *New York Times*, and the *Sun*.

All reviews were positive. Another feature of the early issues was "The Thompson Twins Talk Things Over." Early numbers were approximately 50 pages long, contrasted with today's approximately 140-page length. Throughout the early period experts reacted to features from previous issues. In the first anniversary issue (October 1927) a chart showed subscription growth, and the fifth anniversary issue (October 1931) boasted more than 200,000 circulation; the tenth anniversary issue proclaimed 400,000 readers. In 1938 subscriptions sold for $2.00 a year, single issues still twenty-five cents a copy. In January 1948, subscriptions rose to $2.50 yearly, in 1950 to $3.00, finally in 1955, single issues rose to thirty-five cents a copy. In 1961, boasting a 1.85 million circulation, *Parents* sold for fifty cents a copy, $4.00 yearly; today's price is $1.95 per copy, and subscription is $20.00 annually, $27.00 for subscriptions in Canada, and $40.00 for subscriptions in all other countries. Circulation is 1,756,853.[15]

Topics covered by *Parents* have run the gamut from belief in Santa Claus to homosexuality. The subtitle "On Rearing Children from Crib to College" allowed such a range. Articles on sex education and spanking appeared in 1928, on school before age five in 1929, on influencing an unborn child in 1930, and on new careers for daughters in 1931. Beginning in 1933, a regular feature was Information Tests for Children at various ages: these tests are fascinating in that they asked so much of what today's educators call an appalling lack of "cultural literacy" in contemporary youth. Also in 1933, *Parents* crusaded vigorously for child labor laws. According to an article by then Secretary of Labor Frances Perkins in the June 1933 issue, more than one-half million children under age sixteen were gainfully employed, having left school. In Brooklyn, of a group of children illegally employed, half earned less than $4.50 per week. Many articles appeared concerning population control, and others detailed the "secret of sex determination" (June 1933). In 1937 a home development section was added, and in 1944 a miniature (4" x 5½") supplement for fathers in uniform was included. As early as 1948 an article on having a baby without anesthetics appeared. In 1951 "facts about narcotics" and books and pamphlets on alcohol were available through *Parents*. This magazine also distributed preschool and school-age programs to groups during the early 1950s. In 1961 Hecht wrote "My Wife Was Saved by a Safety Belt." As *Parents* moved through the 1960s, articles sought to address the concerns of the contemporary parent rather than to attempt to influence attitudes, and today's articles focus on topics of interest to parents as adults, not just as parents. September issues often focus on trends in education, and November issues often feature medical updates. Today's magazine is perhaps more attractive than early issues, yet it is still filled with practical and important information. As long as George Hecht was associated with the magazine, there was a definitely discernible political and social stance, an effort to persuade readers not only to a certain point of view but to action on various concerns relevant to parenting. Once Hecht left, the magazine continued its informative approach but with less zealous endorsement of potentially controversial stands. The articles throughout the history of *Parents* are informative and

interesting; perhaps this magazine should be required reading not only for all
parents but also for any other individuals who come into contact with children!

Notes

1. George J. Hecht, "Parents, We Are Here," *Children: The Magazine for Parents,*
October 1926, p. 1.

2. "George Joseph Hecht," *Current Biography 1947*, p. 287.

3. James L. C. Ford, *Magazines for Millions: The Story of Specialized Publications*
(Carbondale: Southern Illinois University Press, 1969), p. 29.

4. *Contemporary Authors*, vol. 97, p. 288.

5. *Current Biography 1947*, p. 288.

6. "*Parents'* Parent," *Time*, 24 September 1951, p. 77.

7. "A Fresh Start: Notes on Our New Look," *Parents*, 11 November 1978, p. 11.

8. Frank Luther Mott, *A History of American Magazines*, vol. 5: *Sketches of 21
Magazines 1905–1930* (Cambridge: Harvard University Press, 1968), p. 142.

9. "*Parents' Magazine* Seal Found 'Misleading' by FTC," *Publishers Weekly*, 12
December 1966, p. 31.

10. Ibid.

11. Sylvia Steinberg, "The Many Children of *Parents' Magazine*," *Publishers Weekly*,
19 July 1976, p. 83.

12. Ibid., p. 84.

13. "*Parents' Magazine* Buys FAO Schwarz Toy Store," *Publishers Weekly*, 23
September 1963, p. 38.

14. Ford, p. 30.

15. Mark S. Hoffman, ed., *The World Almanac and Book of Facts 1989* (New York:
A. Scripps Howard Co., 1988), p. 350.

Information Sources

BIBLIOGRAPHY

Contemporary Authors. vol. 97. Detroit: Gale Research, p. 234.

Ford, James L. C. *Magazines for Millions: The Story of Specialized Publications*. Carbondale; Southern Illinois University Press, 1969.

"Hecht, George Joseph." *Current Biography 1947*. New York: H. W. Wilson, pp. 286–
88, 1948.

Hoffman, Mark S., ed. *The World Almanac and Book of Facts 1989*. New York: A.
Scripps Howard Co., 1988.

Mead, Margaret. "Five Decades of Writing for *Parents' Magazine*." *Parents' Magazine*,
October 1976, p. 44.

Mott, Frank Luther. *A History of American Magazines*. Vol. 5: *Sketches of 21 Magazines
1905–1930*. Cambridge: Harvard University Press, 1968.

"*Parents' Magazine* Buys FAO Schwarz Toy Store." *Publishers Weekly*, 23 September
1963 p. 38.

"*Parents' Magazine* Seal Found 'Misleading' by FTC." *Publishers Weekly*, 12 December
1966, p. 31.

"*Parents'* Parent." *Time*, 24 September 1951, pp. 77–78.

Steinberg, Sylvia. "The Many Children of *Parents' Magazine." Publishers Weekly*, 19 July 1976, pp. 83–84.

INDEX SOURCES
  Readers' Guide to Periodical Literature (1929–present); *Education Index* (1929–1949); *Abridged Readers' Guide; Book Review Index; Biography Index.* By publisher.

LOCATION SOURCES
  Library of Congress; many other libraries. Available in microform.

Publication History

MAGAZINE TITLE AND TITLE CHANGES
  Children: The Magazine for Parents, October 1926–January 1929; *Children: The Parents' Magazine,* February 1929–July 1929; *The Parents' Magazine,* August 1929–December 1965; *Parents' Magazine and Better Homemaking,* January 1966–October 1969; *Parents' Magazine and Better Family Living,* November 1969–June 1977; *Parents' Magazine,* July 1977–December 1978; *Parents,* January 1979–current.

VOLUME AND ISSUE DATA
  October 1926–current, monthly.

PUBLISHER AND PLACE OF PUBLICATION
  George J. Hecht, October 1926–July 1978; John G. Hahn, August 1978–current. New York.

EDITORS
  Board of Editors (George J. Hecht, president; Clara Savage Littledale, managing editor), October 1926–January 1931; Clara Savage Littledale, February 1931–March 1956; Mary E. Buchanan, April 1956–February 1965; Dorothy Whyte Cotton, March 1965–December 1970; Genevieve Millet Landau, January 1971–July 1978; Peter A. Janssen, August 1978–December 1978; Elizabeth Crow, January 1979–August 1988; Ann Pleshette Murphy, September 1988–current.

CIRCULATION
  1,756,853 (1988).

Barbara Nourie

PENNSYLVANIA GRIT. See GRIT

PEOPLE WEEKLY

One of the most successful personality-oriented magazines on the market is *People Weekly,* published since 1974 by Time. Commonly referred to as *People, People Weekly* is reminiscent of the fan magazines of the 1930s and 1940s. It has the look of *Photoplay* or *Life,** yet maintains the kind of intimacy that daily newspapers enjoy with their readers. It appeared at a time when the nation was tired of heavy news items and issue-oriented journalism. Filling a void in the mass market, it is the first national weekly magazine that has been started since *Sports Illustrated* was launched in 1954. But mostly, *People* is fun. It satisfies the general public's insatiable appetite for popular trivia. As Hedley Donovan, *People*'s editor-in-chief for the first five years, put it to *Business Week*, "*People* tells things that are worth knowing, and fun to know," about people everywhere.[1]

The original concept of *People* is credited to Marian Heiskill, wife of the then chairman of the board of Time, Andrew Heiskill.[2] It is one of the first magazines to be test-marketed nationally before its official premiere. In August 1973, after a two-year development period, the Magazine Development Group at Time tested a magazine with the working title of *People of the Week* in eleven cities.[3] This test issue, with Richard Burton and Elizabeth Taylor appearing on its cover, sold at two different cover prices (ten cities at thirty-five cents and one city at fifty cents) and was accompanied by different degrees of newspaper and television publicity.[4] As described by a news release, the magazine was a "picture oriented, *Time*-size publication dedicated to report and comment on the personalities and life styles of newsworthy individuals."[5] The test issue was followed by home interviews and an October post-test evaluation of a second test issue.[6]

Encouraged by the test marketing, Time launched *People Weekly* on 25 February 1974 (with a newsstand date of 4 March). The first issue, showing Mia Farrow on the cover, had a run of 1.4 million copies and was accompanied by a half million dollar television campaign. Marketed primarily as a newsstand magazine with a cover price of thirty-five cents, it sold most of the initial run, though it did not reach its one million copies guarantee.[7]

The content and format of *People Weekly* has not changed much over the years, though story emphasis has shifted with the times. *People*'s format has always been heavily pictorial, with a conversational style to its text. Highly influenced by television, its presentation of the news has been summed up as "big pictures, few words, short takes, fast pace."[8]

If *People* reminded readers of *Life** with its pictorial style, that is not surprising, since *People*'s first managing editor was Richard Stolley, the assistant managing editor of *Life* before its 1972 demise and its managing editor after its 1982 revival. Stolley played a large part in shaping the style of *People* into its successful formula. It was his emphasis on "personality journalism" (reporting the news from the perspective of the people making the news) that appealed to *People*'s readers. As explained by Stolley, "This is a magazine devoted *entirely* to people—we don't deal with issues; we don't deal with events; we don't deal with debates. We deal *only* with human beings."[9]

The magazine is divided into neat little sections, each focusing on a different individual, whether famous or relatively unknown. Each section is introduced by a terse title describing the topic of the section; for example, "Jock" for sport figures, "Medics" for health professionals, and "Off the Screen" for movie personalities. The articles are chatty, but to the point as to what makes the subject newsworthy. Initially the balance between celebrities and unknowns was 75–25, but within a couple of years the ratio was 50–50.

Brevity has been a key to the editorial format. The magazine is meant to be read quickly, to get the gist of the story. As Richard J. Durrell, the first publisher, explains it, the reasoning behind the briefness is that "the target reader—aged 18 to 35—has been brought up on television and has a short attention span."[10] The question-and-answer interview (In His/Her Own Words section) and the cover profile are the longest articles with anywhere from 1,500 to 1,700 words each.

People has no editorial color pages. It was determined by the editorial staff from the beginning that pictures would be presented in black and white only and that color would be reserved exclusively for the cover and for advertising. This decision has remained unaltered even after fifteen years. Dick Thomas, the first director of advertising sales, stated that the reason for the black-and-white graphics "was the feeling on the part of our editors that they were dealing with the most volatile, dynamic subject in the world: people. Black and white graphics, they believed, would underscore the dynamics. For one thing, apparently the best photographers in the world agree that black and white photos of people are much more revealing, much more immediate and much more intimate than color."[11] A by-product of this decision has been the appeal to advertisers that their ads would not compete with color editorial.

The range of the types of photos that make it into *People* give the magazine its versatility. It is interesting to see how the photographers seem to have a special knack for getting their subjects to do the most unusual things. *People*'s photographic style ranges from the zany (disco queen Grace Jones snarling from behind the bars of a cage), to the sassy (fashion model Christie Brinkley rolling in the sand on a beach), to the poignant (corporate executive Mary Cunningham in a tender moment with her husband, Bill Agee, kneeling before her). *People* includes a mixture of home takes, those candid shots catching people in their own environment just being themselves, and the set up shots, the deliberate staging of the subject in a devised setting used to convey the substance of the individual or the story.

The single, most influential factor that determines the success of an issue is the cover. In a magazine where over 65 percent of the circulation comes from newsstand sales,[12] cover choice can make or break an issue. *People Weekly* from its inception has actively sought the supermarket crowd, forgoing the subscription route since increased postal rates and costly renewal notices severely hamper the profits of subscription-based magazines. The guide to selecting the subject of a cover is known as Stolley's Law. As the first managing editor puts it, "Young is better than old. Pretty is better than ugly. Rich is better than poor. TV is better than music. Music is better than movies. Movies are better than sports. And anything is better than politics."[13] This maxim changed somewhat under Patricia Ryan, *People*'s second managing editor. Under her editorship, politics was no longer considered the poor stepchild, while news-oriented covers proved to be good sellers. Still, *People* editors believe strongly that cover subjects should be recognizable to 80 percent of the American public. As Stolley pointed out, "There's an X-factor, too, of mystery and intrigue, something about that person that the reader doesn't know, but wants to know. There's a three-second decision to buy, and we need to figure who will sell."[14]

As to who sells, and who doesn't, a lot of that depends on who appeals to women, since they are the majority of buyers. Back in 1975, when 75 percent of the buyers of *People* were women,[15] Howard Cosell was the poorest selling issue, whereas covers with Cher, Princess Grace, and Elizabeth Taylor all did well.[16] In the 1980s, perennial favorites for covers include Cher, Elizabeth Taylor, Farrah Fawcett, Michael Jackson, and Jacqueline Onassis. *People*'s all-time favorite is Princess Diana, with more than twenty-five covers to her credit. Memorial issues of recent celebrity deaths often provide *People* with its best-selling issues. As of 1984, the best-selling cover in the magazine's history was the tribute to John Lennon after his assassination in 1980, and the second biggest seller was the issue featuring Princess Grace after her death in 1982.[17]

The feature sections have changed little since the first issue. Stolley added the People Picks section in the 18 April 1977 issue. It contains reviews of weekly television shows, new books, records, films, and miscellaneous events. The Take One section, with its short, anecdotal news flashes, was added under Ryan's editorship in the 21 March 1983 issue. The only feature to leave the magazine was the People Puzzle (a "find-the-celebrity's-name-within-the-letters" puzzle), which was discontinued after the 11 March 1985 issue because of the death of its creator Gerard Mosler.[18]

People underwent its first revamping in its design with the 23 January 1989 issue. Managing editor Jim Gaines wanted to give the magazine a new look without sacrificing its familiarity. The "In This Issue" section was expanded to two full pages using overlapping photos and lead-in sentences from key articles as teasers. For visual interest, the color red was used as an accent on borders and section titles to draw attention to the beginning of articles. Other changes in design were more subtle, including changes in typeface and section titles design.

From the very start, *People Weekly* was a success. In spite of not reaching its one million guarantee, *People* was able to achieve profitability by September 1975, just eighteen months after its first issue. Compare this accomplishment with the fact that *Time** needed three years before it was in the black, and *Sports Illustrated* wasn't able to claim profitability until ten years after its start-up.[19] Within two years of its existence, *People* had a rate base of 1.6 million and was one of the biggest newsstand sellers.[20] Its single copy sales were 80 percent of its total circulation, with supermarket sales comprising 60 percent of the single copy sales.[21] By the end of 1976, it neared the 2 million mark and had an estimated adult readership of over 11.5 million.[22]

Before the first issue went to press, *People* was able to obtain 300 pages of advertising commitment, with twelve to fifteen ad pages in an average sixty-two-page issue.[23] In 1975, *People* sold 1,046 pages in advertisment.[24] In 1976, ad revenues reached $16 million, almost double the previous year's revenue.

The cover price of a single issue was raised to forty cents after just seven months of publishing, and was raised again to fifty cents with the 21 July 1975 issue, where it remained for the next twenty months.

By the time *People Weekly* had reached its fifth anniversary, it had passed its sister publication *Sports Illustrated* in circulation when its rate base hit 2.3 million. In 1978, *People* ran 3,177 ad pages, ten more pages than *Time* ran in 1978, and ranked fifth among all magazines in terms of ad pages.[25] The cover price was raised to sixty cents in April 1977 and went up again one year later to seventy-five cents. In 1979, *People* started testing discount subscriptions. Its readership was estimated at 20.5 million,[26] and it ranked for the first time in the top 20 in circulation.[27]

Some of the strongest advertising categories initially were tobacco, liquor, and automobiles, which, when combined, comprised 65 percent of the ad revenues.[28] By 1979, they comprised only 45 percent of the ad revenues for *People* and dropped to 35 percent by 1983. Much of the difference was offset by increases in the food, health and beauty aids, and apparel categories, which rose from 20 percent of ad revenues in 1979 to over 33 percent in 1983.[29]

The growth of *People* in terms of ad revenue is remarkable. In its first year of operation, *People* ranked fifty-sixth in ad pages (601 pages) and fifty-seventh in ad revenue ($3.5 million). Six years later, in 1980, *People Weekly* had reached fourth in ad pages (2,430 pages) and sixth in ad revenue ($106.4 million).[30] *People* was able to climb still higher in the rankings by reaching second place in ad pages and fourth place in ad revenue in 1984.[31]

By the time *People Weekly* had reached its tenth anniversary, it had become the most profitable Time magazine in this country,[32] though *Time*,* with its international distribution was more profitable overall.[33] In July 1984, the circulation rate was 2.75 million, with an estimated 21 million adult readership.[34] By the end of the year *People* ranked second in newsstand sales, third in readership, and fifth in combined circulation and advertising revenue.[35] The rate base for the magazine was 2.85 million in October 1985.[36] This was the twelfth circulation increase in as many years. Even though ad revenues seemed to plateau by 1987, circulation continued to rise. By December 1987, the average circulation was 3.3 million, a 9 percent increase from 1986.[37] The largest issue that *People* ever published was their 15th anniversary issue (6 March 1989). It included 144 advertisements, more than twice the normal rate for a regular issue.[38]

Throughout the 1980s *People Weekly* experienced several price increases. The cover price was ninety-five cents in 1980 and had two price increases in 1982, raising it to $1.25, where it stayed for almost two and a half years. At the beginning of 1985, it once again increased its cover price, this time to $1.50. In July 1987, it attained the unusual price of $1.69, where it remained until the beginning of 1989 when it increased to $1.79. The subscription price has likewise increased during the 1980s, when the discount for an annual subscription has been anywhere from 20 to 36 percent. The current annual subscription rate listed is $61.88.

From the start, Time assumed that *People Weekly* would appeal mainly to women, since women tend to be more interested in other people's lives than men. As it correctly turned out, the majority of readers were women (58 percent) and an even higher percentage (75 percent) were the purchasers of the magazine.[39] Sixty-one percent of the readers were between the ages of eighteen and thirty-four, and had a median household income of $21,107,[40] with 48 percent having attended or graduated from college.[41] Over the years, the ratios have not changed drastically. In 1984, the median age of a *People Weekly* reader was thirty-three, with a median income of $28,000. Sixty percent of the readers were women, and 42 percent of the overall readership had attended or graduated from college.[42] In 1988, the median income was $30,769, with the median age about thirty-five years old. Women were still the primary readers, constituting 65 percent.[43]

In recent years *People Weekly* has relied less on celebrities to fill each issue. Today only 40 percent of the stories are related to the entertainment industry. The stories that are included about the stars deal more with their lives and the problems they are facing than with the trappings of being a celebrity. The uncelebrated individuals who are included are there because of their achievements or the extraordinary circumstances in which they find themselves. Either way, there is something very human in their stories that is shared by and with the reader. As Patricia Ryan stated it, "They're getting a great big chunk of America."[44]

Notes

1. "Joining the *People* Parade," *Business Week*, 16 May 1977, p. 71.

2. John Mack Carter, "The Pros Said It Couldn't Be Done, But *People*'s Making It," *Folio*, February 1976, p. 60.

3. "Time, Inc. to Test *People*," *Advertising Age*, 13 October 1973, p. 8.

4. Carter, p. 58.

5. "Time, Inc, To Test *People*," p. 8.

6. Bob Donath, "*People* Role," *Advertising Age*, 18 February 1974, p. 47.

7. Carter, p. 58.

8. Edwin Diamond, "Celebrating Celebrity," *New York*, 13 May 1985, p. 24.

9. Carter, p. 60.

10. "Joining the People Parade," p. 71.

11. Ira Ellenthal, "*People*: A Good Reason to Advertise" *Product Marketing*, 23 November 1981, p. 23.

12. Martha Nolan, "MedianLines: New and of Note," *Madison Avenue*, May 1984, p. 115.

13. Nolan, p. 115.

14. Stephen Grover, "Grocery-Day Gossip Is Ringing Up Profit at *People* Magazine," *Wall Street Journal*, 6 May 1976, p. 1.

15. Ibid.

16. Carter, p. 60.

17. Nolan, p. 115.

18. "Gerard Mosler, Puzzle Master," *People Weekly*, 11 March 1985, p. 96.

19. "Joining the *People* Parade," p. 74.

20. Carter, p. 58.

21. Bob Donath, "*People* Bullish about Its Third Year," *Advertising Age*, 1 March 1976, p. 48.

22. Richard J. Durrell, "The Men and Women behind the Cameras Are Vital to Our Continued Success," *People Weekly*, 29 November 1976, p. 3.

23. Donath, "*People* Role," p. 47.

24. Donath, "*People* Bullish," p. 48.

25. Bernice Kanner, "*People*—5 Going on 3,000,000," *Advertising Age*, 26 February, 1979, p. 76.

26. Ellenthal, p. 23.

27. *World Almanac*, 1979 ed. p. 429.

28. Donath, "*People* Bullish," p. 48.

29. Cara S. Trager, "*People* Plays into Baby Boomers' Hands," *Advertising Age*, 18 October 1984, p. 50.

30. Ellenthal, p. 23.

31. Stuart J. Elliott, "Personality Journalism Develops Sunny Disposition," *Advertising Age*, 3 October 1985, p. 27.

32. *People Weekly* is distributed in North America only.

33. Jan Benzel, "People's Choice: Managing Editor Pat Ryan," *Washington Journalism Review*, December 1984, p. 34.

34. Ibid.

35. Patricia Ryan, "Thanks a Billion," *People Weekly*, 5 March 1984, p. 1.

36. Elliott, p. 27.

37. Patrick Reilly, "*Us* Gains, *People* Profits from Lead," *Advertising Age*, 18 April 1988, p. S4.

38. Elizabeth Valk, "Publisher's Letter," *People Weekly*, 27 March 1989, p. 1.

39. Grover, p. 1.

40. Ellenthal, p. 23.

41. Nora Ephron, "Media," *Esquire*, March 1975, p. 47.

42. Trager, p. 50.

43. Reilly, p. S4.

44. Benzel, p. 36.

Information Sources

BIBLIOGRAPHY

Benzel, Jan. "People's Choice: Managing Editor Pat Ryan." *Washington Journalism Review,* December 1984, pp. 34–37.

Carter, John Mack. "The Pros Said It Couldn't Be Done, But *People's* Making It." *Folio*, February 1976, pp. 58–60.

Diamond, Edwin. "Celebrating Celebrity." *New York*, 13 May 1985, pp. 22–27.

Donath, Bob. "*People* Bullish about Its Third Year." *Advertising Age*, 1 March 1976, p. 48.

———. "*People* Role." *Advertising Age*, 18 February 1974, p. 47.

Durrell, Richard J. "The Men and Women behind the Cameras Are Vital to Our Continued Success." *People Weekly*, 29 November 1976, p. 3.

Ellenthal, Ira. "*People*: A Good Reason to Advertise." *Product Marketing*, 23 November 1981, p. 23.

Elliott, Stuart J. "Personality Journalism Develops Sunny Disposition: Popular *People* Makes Friends, Influences Rivals." *Advertising Age*, 3 October 1985, p. 27.

Emmrich, Stuart. "*People* Publisher Reflects New Time Breed." *Advertising Age*, 24 October 1983, p. 14.

Ephron, Nora. "Media." *Esquire*, March 1975.

"Gerald Mosler, Puzzle Master." *People Weekly*, 11 March 1985, p. 96.

Grover, Stephen. "Grocery-Day Gossip Is Ringing Up Profit at *People* Magazine." *Wall Street Journal*, 6 May 1976, p. 1.

"Joining the *People* Parade," *Business Week*, 16 May 1977, pp. 71–74.

Kanner, Bernice. "*People*—5 Going on 3,000,000." *Advertising Age*, 26 February 1979, p. 76.

———. "*People* Sets Ad Rate Rebate." *Advertising Age*, 3 September 1979.

Nolan, Martha. "MediaLines: New and of Note." *Madison Avenue*, May 1984, pp. 115–16.

"*People*." *American Photographer*, June 1984, pp. 39–53.

"The *People* People." *Newsweek*, 4 March 1974, pp. 88–89.

Reilly, Patrick. "*Us* Gains, *People* Profits from Lead." *Advertising Age*, 18 April 1988.

Ryan, Patricia. "Thanks a Billion." *People Weekly*, 5 March 1984, p. 1.

Span, Paula. "In the Picture: The First Decade of People Magazine." *Washington Post*, 3 March 1984, p. C1.

Taft, William H. "Mass Magazines: *Life* to *People*." In *American Magazines for the 1980s*. New York: Hastings House, 1982.

"There's New Life in the Mass Magazine." *Business Week*, 13 October 1973, pp. 84–87.

"Time, Inc. to Test *People*." *Advertising Age*, 13 October 1973, p. 8.

Trager, Cara S. "*People* Plays into Baby Boomers' Hands." *Advertising Age*, 18 October 1984, p. 50.

Valk, Elizabeth. "Publisher's Letter." *People Weekly*, 27 March 1989, p. 1.

Waters, Henry F. "The *People* Perplex." *Newsweek*, 6 June 1977, pp. 89–90.

World Almanac. 1979 ed. New York: Newspaper Enterprise Association, 1979.

INDEX SOURCES

> *Access: The Supplementary Index to Periodicals* (1975–1978); *General Periodicals Index* (1985–present); *Magazine Index* (1977–present); *Readers' Guide to Periodical Literature*, vol. 38 (March 1978/February 1979–present).

LOCATION SOURCES

> Library of Congress, many other libraries. Available in microform.

Publication History

MAGAZINE TITLE AND TITLE CHANGES
> *People Weekly,* 1974–present.

VOLUME AND ISSUE DATA
> Vol. 1–31, 4 March 1974–present, weekly.

PUBLISHER AND PLACE OF PUBLICATION
> Time, Inc., Richard J. Durrell, 4 March 1974–21 November 1983; S. Christopher Meigher III, 28 November 1983–16 December 1985; Donald M. Elliman, Jr., 23/30 December 1985–21 November 1988; Elizabeth P. Valk, 28 November 1988–present. New York, New York.

MANAGING EDITORS
> Richard B. Stolley, 4 March 1974–5 April 1982; Patricia Ryan, 12 April 1982–18 May 1987; James R. Gaines, 25 May 1987–present.

CIRCULATION
> 3,311,139 (newsstand: 1,892,969; subscription: 1,418,170 as of 31 December 1987).

Vicki L. Tate

PLAYBOY

In December 1953, Hugh M. Hefner published the first issue of his new magazine, which lacked a cover date because Hefner was unsure how long it would need to remain on the newsstands.[1] The response to the magazine was immediate and positive. From the beginning, *Playboy* proved to be a winner. Even after thirty-five years, it remains the most popular men's magazine in America.

Hugh Hefner saw that there was a terrific void within the publishing field in the area of men's magazines. His vision was to fill that void with a totally new magazine. The intent of this new magazine, which Hefner called *Playboy*, was to give the postwar urban male what he wanted, a magazine filled with sophistication and style, appealing to the mind and body of the educated man. In the mid–1950s this was the market that was not being satisfied by any of the male-oriented magazines. *Esquire** was the model for much of what Hefner tried to accomplish, but it lacked the editorial courage to continue its initial foray into the sexual realm. Other male magazines dealt in the "crude nude" market, but they lacked any sense of quality. Hefner's basic premise was that if he could create a magazine that appealed to him, it would also appeal to others. Hefner's vision of the ideal male was a suave, sophisticated man-about-town who was sexually liberated and irresistible to women. It was to this audience that *Playboy* made its pitch.

But what *Playboy* did was not new. It was a repackaging of tried-and-true material. The basic formula that Hefner used for its content was borrowed from *Esquire*: college-style humor noted for its risqué cartoons and bawdy jokes, mixed with quality fiction, fashion, and a taste for high living. The other major component came from the men's book tradition: a liberal use of the female body to tantalize and attract its readers.

Though the editorial content had played before, the one thing that made *Playboy* stand out was its attitude. No longer was sex considered to be foul and dirty. It was a natural aspect of life, to be enjoyed and relished, free from guilt.

From its inception *Playboy* made its impression on the publishing industry and found its niche in history.

Playboy began as a reflection of its time. In the middle 1950s, the restrictive social climate was becoming a chafing mantle worn by the younger generation. Having become accustomed to the Sweetheart pinups during the previous decade, men expected a certain amount of spice with the main course.

The stable economic times afforded many with a little more spending money and more leisure time in which to enjoy it. *Playboy* showed how to live in style. It catered to the new materialism that was overtaking the country; it reassured the reader that it was all right to enjoy one's pleasure. *Playboy* counseled its readers as to the appropriate wine to serve, the right style of clothes to wear, the best music to listen to, and the correct life style to enjoy. In describing what a "playboy" was, Hefner wrote in the April 1956 issue,

> He must see life not as a vale of tears, but as a happy time; he must take joy in his work, without regarding it as the end all of living; he must be an alert man, an aware man, a man of taste, a man sensitive to pleasure, a man who—without acquiring the stigma of the voluptuary or dilettante—can live life to the hilt. (p. 73)

During the first decade of *Playboy*'s existence, its focus was the promotion of this image of the good life.

In developing the concept for his new magazine, Hefner knew he needed a gimmick that would be talked about. He needed something that would give the magazine a sense of identity and instant fame. Since his financial resources were limited, Hefner did not have the means to build up a readership over a long period of time, but needed a success from the start. That successful gimmick was the "girl next door" nude. From the first issue with "Sweetheart of the Month" Marilyn Monroe, in her classic stretch pose, Hefner changed the image of the nude from the back-street, low-life bawdiness to the respectable girl you would want to meet. Gone were the nameless bodies, and in their place were the girls to dream about, complete with names, background, and identity, however contrived or fabricated.

Hefner stumbled across the concept of the "girl next door," the nice girl who wouldn't dream of posing nude—except maybe for *Playboy*. An air of respectability was instilled in all of the chosen Playmates. The reader was introduced to the current ideal girl in her natural setting—whether it was at work, at play, or engaging in some other activity. After a series of introductory pictorial vignettes, the reader finally meets her in full splendor.

In the beginning years of the magazine Playmates were always young, white, fresh, attractive, and wholesome. Over the years, the color barrier has been broken, with the occasional appearance of black or Asian women taking the top spot. In the last decade or so, glamour has been added as an important factor in the lady's appeal, but she always remains the nice, clean girl.

Standards for acceptable poses have changed since 1953. Initially the poses were meant to entice without being graphic. But during the early 1970s, due to pressure from other sexually oriented men's magazines, more explicit poses were gradually included. The first full-frontal nude pose was displayed in January 1972. Never as graphic or as raunchy as its rivals, *Playboy* retreated from the full-scale war in 1975[2] though it never returned to the relatively demure poses of the first two decades. Rather than strive for explicitness *Playboy* to this day prefers to retain the more artistic poses that have been its standard.

In addition to the monthly Playmate pictorials, *Playboy* includes supplementary pictorials as an avenue for those women not lucky enough to be chosen as a Playmate. The themes for these additions run from the promotion of movies (''Girls of James Bond''), of an occupation (''Girls on Wall Street'') or of an athletic conference (''Girls of the Big Ten''). Several celebrities have graced the pages of *Playboy* as the subject of a pictorial in order to enhance their careers or to create one. The age limitation for the supplementary pictorials is not as restrictive as it is for the Playmate. In recent years, more mature women have been shown to their fullest physical advantage.

Not known for its nonfiction features, *Playboy* has nevertheless presented numerous thought-provoking pieces in its history. In its early years most of the features were lighthearted, nonserious, unresearched opinion pieces. But as the magazine took shape and became more focused, its editorial policy likewise became more clearly defined.

Even though the emphasis has always been on the quality in content and style of the magazine, rarely in the early years did the subject matter of the nonfiction features venture into those areas that might instill guilt or invoke a sense of responsibility. As the statement of purpose in that first issue in December 1953 expressed it:

> Affairs of state will be out of our province. We don't expect to solve any world problems or prove any great moral truths. If we are able to give the American male a few extra laughs and a little diversion from the anxieties of the Atomic Age, we'll feel we've justified our existence. (p. 3)

Playboy did stray from its original intent when it found itself caught up in the changes of society. Just as the mid–1950s retreated from anything political, the mid–1960s focused on just that. *Playboy* broached several topics deemed un-fashionable by other contemporary magazines. Nat Hentoff's discussion of race relations entitled ''Through the Racial Looking Glass'' (July 1962) and inter-views with Miles Davis (September 1962) and Malcolm X (May 1963) saw print in the pre–Civil Rights Act days. Another area in which *Playboy* acted as a crusader was in its defense of the rights of the recreational drug user and the relaxation of antidrug laws. Dan Wakefield's ''The Prodigal Powers of Pot'' (August 1962) related the history and spread of marijuana use.

Though a little late in its presentation of the Vietnam War as an issue, it did provide a platform for an impressive array of dissenters whose credentials were impeccable. In the April 1967 interview with historian Arnold Toynbee, the focus was on U.S. policies in Vietnam. This was followed by Kenneth Tynan's essay, "Open Letter to an American Liberal" (February 1968), Senator William Fulbright's "For a New Order of Priorities at Home and Abroad" (July 1968), and an interview with noted peace protester Rev. William Sloane Coffin (August 1968).

As the country developed a conscience, so too did the nonfiction features, which reflected the growing awareness of responsibility to our world. *Playboy* tackled a growing list of concerns: the environment, poverty, ethics, urban conditions, space exploration, and the state of religion. The continuation of its soul-searching for the nation continued into the early 1970s before *Playboy* itself was confronted with its own set of identity crises.

In the early seventies *Playboy* showed less emphasis on moral issues of conscience. This was mostly due to the loss of articles editor James Goode and managing editor Murray Fisher,[3] both of whom were instrumental in the shaping of the previous decade's shift in editorial content. *Playboy*, caught up in the pictorial wars with its new competitors, was not able to develop an effective editorial approach to the changing economic time. Much of *Playboy*'s message had lost its relevance. For the rest of the decade, *Playboy* preferred using safe exposés of financial institutions, organized crime, politicians, and the Pentagon; it informed the readers about the world around them without preaching to them.

As the interests of the American public changed from the conscientious commitment of the 1960s and 1970s to the conspicuous consumption of the 1980s, this change was reflected in the subject matter of articles. *Playboy* returned to its original intent to entertain its readers. There was a new emphasis on relationships and male-female roles, as outlined in a seven-part series in 1982 titled "Men and Women" and Richard Rhodes's essay "Why do Men Rape?" in the April 1981 issue. Money, investments, and the role of business became recurring themes. Articles such as "The Brawning of America" by Kevin Cook (July 1982) and the "Fitness Myth" by William Barry Furlong (May 1988) reflected the continued interest in health and exercise that has typified the Me Decade.

While the quality of the magazine's nonfiction has fluctuated, fiction, on the other hand, has always been considered one of *Playboy*'s strong points. Because of the limited financial resources available to purchase new material, the early issues of *Playboy* were filled with stories available in the public domain. Using reprints of recognized authors and selected works from the classics of literature in a feature called the Ribald Classics, *Playboy* was able to offer intellectual stimulation. As financial resources improved and the magazine established a reputation for quality, it published original works from new and established writers. Since 1957, all works of fiction published by *Playboy* have been original pieces. Much of the responsibility for upgrading the fiction was due to the addition of Auguste Comte Spectorsky as editorial director in 1956.[4] His experience and background brought a touch of class and East Coast sophistication to *Playboy*. To entice the writer of quality pieces, Spectorsky offered fees of up to $2,000 for short stories,[5] drawing such literary names as Vladimir Nabokov, John Steinbeck, John Updike, James Baldwin, and Erskine Caldwell. Ray Bradbury, Arthur C. Clarke, William Saroyan, and Irwin Shaw became regular contributors. Even today top names in the literary field such as Bernard Malamud, Gabriel García Márquez, Joyce Carol Oates, Paul Theroux, and Isaac Bashevis Singer continue to add to *Playboy*'s prestige.

Many have wondered why such eminent writers would wish to lend their names to a magazine whose primary purpose was not considered to be literary. Besides the obvious financial rewards, the original incentive for many authors to publish in *Playboy* was its willingness to take stories whose themes or language other literary magazines found unsuitable or unacceptable.[6] Today the incentive is the amount of exposure a writer can gain through *Playboy*'s large circulation since its reach is still significant.

The feature that has probably had the most effect on legitimizing *Playboy* as a quality journalistic magazine is the Playboy Interview, first published in the September 1962 issue (the premier interview was with Miles Davis and conducted by the then unknown author Alex Haley).[7] The characteristic question-and-answer format and exhaustive length give a chance for readers to receive an in-depth look into the views and feelings of an extraordinary variety of people, from entertainment, politics, the arts, sports, literature, business, and public affairs. Those interviewed have ranged from the expected (sex expert Dr. Ruth Westheimer, January 1986) to the unexpected (singer and conservative causes spokesperson Anita Bryant, May 1978); from the liberal philosophy (philosopher Bertrand Russell, March 1963) to the conservative (author Ayn Rand, March 1964); from black (Rev. Martin Luther King, Jr., January 1965) to ardent white (avowed racist George Lincoln Rockwell, April 1966); and from those who dedicated their lives to helping others (humanitarian Albert Schweitzer, January 1963) to those who did not (murderer Gary Gilmore, April 1977). The timing of some interviews has added to the notoriety of the magazine. The interview with John Lennon and Yoko Ono in the January 1981 issue hit the newsstands just weeks before Lennon's untimely death. The relatively unknown ex-governor of Georgia, Jimmy Carter, caused a minor sensation when his November 1976 interview appeared during his presidential bid.

Another area in which *Playboy* has attained a good reputation is design. *Playboy* is a visual medium, not only in its pictorials, but also in its illustrations, graphics, and layout. Both Hefner and the original art editor, Art Paul, creator of the *Playboy* bunny symbol, had a keen sense of what was appealing to its readers. Though the first several issues were amateurish, they were also innovative. Throughout its history *Playboy* has maintained a sense of familiarity with consistency of typography and features, but has used its graphics and illustrations to give it a fresh, evolving look. When Art Paul retired at the end of 1982, he was replaced by associate art director Tom Staebler, who has brought a cleaner, less complicated look to both the magazine's covers and layouts. His use of simple designs and color has been effective in redefining the *Playboy* look.

Throughout its history *Playboy* has also promoted a vast array of art formats as a backdrop to its articles and features. Its promotion of the arts through its pages has been an opportunity for many artists to show their best in a highly commercial medium.

Several prominent artists have contributed to *Playboy* including Salvador Dali, Ed Pashke, Frank Gallo, and Andy Warhol. Leroy Neiman, now noted for his vibrant colorful renditions of sporting events, was an early contributor of illustrations. His Femlin character, which accompanies the Party Jokes section, made her first appearance in the August 1955 issue and is still present today. The late Patrick Nagel's Art Deco–style illustrations of elegant, erotic women became a staple of the Playboy Advisor and Forum sections. The late Alberto Vargas also found a place in the pages of *Playboy* after establishing himself at *Esquire*. His Vargas Girl came to personify the *Playboy* ideal.

There are other features besides the pictorials that have become a major drawing force of the magazine. Since its debut in 1960, one of the more successful features of the magazine has been an advice column for men known as the Playboy Advisor. This column has shown the anxieties, insecurities, and problems that plague the American male. Topics that have been approached within the column include basic points of etiquette, explanations of various persistent sexual myths, and reassurance on acceptable fashion norms.

In 1963 the Playboy Advisor was joined by the Playboy Forum, which served as a platform for the exchange of ideas raised by the Playboy Philosophy first published in the December 1962 issue. What resulted was an uninhibited discussion of sexual matters rarely seen in print. Today it is used as an educational forum for discussing issues usually related to any aspect of sex that is currently a news topic.

But the biggest continuing draw after the pictorials is the magazine's humor. Filled with cartoons, party jokes, and anecdotes, *Playboy* has tempered the serious and tantalizing with the comic or burlesque. Most of the humor uses sex as its theme, though social norms and relationships are easy targets. Some early contributors include Shel Silverstein, Jules Feiffer, Ed Sokol, and John Dempsey. Gahan Wilson's bizarre characters and off-center humor have intrigued readers for the last three decades. Other perennial favorites include Buck Brown's brash, sex-starved character known simply as Granny, and the voluptuous, bubble-headed but endearing Little Annie Fanny, who is the creation of Harvey Kurtzman and Will Elder.

Everything found within the covers of *Playboy* has catered to the image of the *Playboy* ideal. Nothing is allowed that would dispel that image. Even the advertisements must strictly adhere to the promotion of the magazine. Since the beginning, advertisements for acne cures, hair restorers, weight loss, and other similar products deemed to be in bad taste have not been accepted. The underlying assumption is that *Playboy* readers never need such products.

For the first year, *Playboy* was published without advertisements, surviving on cover price alone. It was not considered a suitable marketplace by major advertising agencies. The initial resistance of advertisers broke down in view of the success of the magazine. Also, surveys indicated that its readers were terrific consumers. In order to generate additional revenues, advertisement space was offered in the 1955 issues at the cost of $650 for black and white and $1,075 for four-color full-page advertisements.[8] In 1966, the going rate for a four-color full-page one-time ad was $27,000.[9] Today a full-page, black-and-white advertisement costs $44,740,[10] which is considerably higher than that for any other male-oriented magazine. The types of products advertised include electronics, automobiles/motorcycles, alcoholic beverages, tobacco products, fashion apparel, and personal grooming products.

As owner and editor of the magazine, Hugh Hefner is the final arbiter on all aspects of the magazine. He selects the Playmate and the corresponding photo layouts, edits the Party Jokes section, chooses the cartoons, and gives final approval on galley proofs.

From its inception *Playboy* has been a success. Of the 70,250 copies printed for the first issue, almost 54,000 copies were sold on the newsstands,[11] with a cover price of fifty cents. By the end of the first year newsstand circulation had reached 175,000.[12] Prepaid subscription rates were offered for the first time in the April 1956 issue: $6 for one year, $10 for two years, and $13 for three years. By this time *Playboy* was already selling more that 500,000 copies per month.[13] Within six years of its debut, *Playboy* passed the one million mark in circulation and had overtaken *Esquire* as the largest-selling male-oriented magazine in Amercia, a distinction it retains today.[14]

The success continued through the 1960s, with circulation reaching 3 million by the middle of the decade and 4.5 million by 1969.[15] Though there were several men's magazines on the market, many with a sexual emphasis, none of them gave *Playboy* much competition during this period.

Playboy reached its circulation peak in 1972 with its September issue selling over 7 million copies.[16] But by this time several other magazines began to chip away at *Playboy*'s seemingly invincible status. A new competitor, *Penthouse*, in four years of existence, had reached circulation of 2 million. By the end of the seventies, *Playboy*'s circulation had dropped to under 5 million,[17] where it stayed for the next five years. During this time the newsstand price doubled, from $1.00 in the early 1970s to $2.00 at the end of the decade, with a fifty-cent price increase being standard for the January anniversary issue and the December holiday issue. The basic newsstand issue price has continued to increase through the 1980s at a rate of fifty cents every couple of years. In 1988 the price per issue ranged from $4.00 to $4.50 depending on the issue. As the price of *Playboy* has increased, so, too, has the number of pages per issue. A 300-page issue is not uncommon, though most issues average around 175 pages.

Though in the last several years the circulation has continued to fall, to just over 4.1 million in 1983,[18] *Playboy* has been able to maintain its status as the most popular magazine of its kind. In 1986 it ranked sixteenth in the listing of the largest U.S. magazines in paid circulation sales (compared to *Penthouse*'s twenty-fourth ranking and *Esquire* not even making the top 100).[19]

Playboy is not just a sex magazine, nor has it ever been simply that. When *Playboy* made its first appearance on newsstands over thirty-five years ago, few could have known its effect on the publishing industry. Not many magazines have had the enormous influence it has had on redefining the standards of the men's book trade. Hugh Hefner's concept of an "entertainment" magazine that would appeal strictly to the tastes of men met the needs of an eager public.

While *Playboy* may not have had the real power to change American culture, it has shown itself to be a reflection of life styles and tastes. Many critics today no longer credit *Playboy* with the influence it once had; they believe that *Playboy* has run its course, that it is out of step with today's society. Though the related industry that sprang from the magazine has fallen on hard times, the magazine itself continues to be well regarded and well read. The transition from renegade and innovator to "elder statesman" and the standard for other men's magazines has not been an easy one. But *Playboy* continues to maintain its appeal without losing the foundation that Hefner believes to be the very basis for its existence—to entertain men.

Notes

1. Thomas Weyr, *Reaching for Paradise: The Playboy Vision of America*. New York: New York Times Books, 1978, p. 14.

2. Russell Miller, *Bunny: The Real Story of Playboy* (New York: Holt, Rinehart and Winston, 1984), pp. 170–92.

3. Weyr, pp. 170–80.

4. Miller, p. 60.

5. Ibid., p. 61.

6. Mildred Lynn Miles, *Index to Playboy* (Metuchen, N.J.: Scarecrow Press, 1970), p. x.

7. Miller, p. 121; Weyr, p. 134.

8. Miller, p. 59; Weyr, p. 32.

9. Miller, p. 135.

10. *National Directory of Magazines* (New York: Oxbridge Communications, 1988), p. 256.

11. Miller, p. 42.

12. Ibid., p. 44.

13. Weyr, p. 37.

14. Ibid., p. 43.

15. Miller, p. 170.

16. Miller, p. 189; Weyr, p. 252.

17. Miller, p. 282.

18. Ibid., p. 346.

19. Latest figures available for the second half of 1986 give the circulation for *Playboy* as 3,447,324; for *Penthouse*, 2,379,333; and for *Esquire*, 702,512. *World Almanac*, 1988, p. 358.

Information Sources

BIBLIOGRAPHY

The Art of Playboy. New York: Alfred Van Der Marck, 1985.

Brady, Frank. *Hefner.* New York: Macmillan, 1974.

Miles, Mildred Lynn. *Index to Playboy: Belles-Lettres, Articles and Humor, December 1953–December 1969.* Metuchen, N.J.: Scarecrow Press, 1970.

Miller, Russell. *Bunny: The Real Story of Playboy.* New York: Holt, Rinehart and Winston, 1984.

National Directory of Magazines. New York: Oxbridge Communications, 1988.

Playboy, vol. 1, no. 1–vol. 35, no. 9, December 1954–September 1988.

Taft, William H. "*Esquire* to the Skin Book Boom: *Playboy, Penthouse,* Others." In *American Magazines for the 1980s.* New York: Hastings House, 1982.

Weyr, Thomas. *Reaching for Paradise: The Playboy Vision of America.* New York: New York Times Books, 1978.

World Almanac and Book of Facts. New York: World Almanac, 1988.

INDEX SOURCES

Miles, Mildred Lynn, *Index to Playboy: Belles-Lettres, Articles and Humor, December 1953–December 1969.* (Metuchen, N.J.: Scarecrow Press, 1970); *Multi Media Reviews Index* (1971–1972); *Media Review Digest* (1973–present); *Film Literature Index* (1973–present); *Popular Periodical Index* (1973–present); *Access: The Supplementary Index to Periodicals* (1975–present); *Magazine Index* (1977–present); *PMR: Popular Magazine Review* (1984–present).

LOCATION SOURCES

Library of Congress, many other libraries. Available in microform.

Publication History

MAGAZINE TITLE AND TITLE CHANGES

Playboy.

VOLUME AND ISSUE DATA

Vols. 1–35, December 1953–present, monthly. March 1955 issue was not published.

PUBLISHER AND PLACE OF PUBLICATION

Playboy Enterprises, Inc., Hugh M. Hefner, 1953–present. Chicago, Illinois.

EDITOR

Hugh M. Hefner, 1953–present.

CIRCULATION

3,732,948 (newsstand: 1,317,031; subscription: 2,415,917 as of December 31, 1987, per Standard Rate and Data Service.)

Vicki L. Tate

PLAYGIRL

In April 1972, at a time when the women's movement was still new enough that it was unclear as to which of several directions it might go, *Cosmopolitan** magazine ran a centerfold of the movie star Burt Reynolds reclining on a bearskin rug in the nude. Reynolds protected his modesty with a strategically placed arm. Yet overnight, this *Cosmo* centerfold became a media and sales sensation, demonstrating the existence of a market among women for male nude photography.[1] Douglas Lambert and John Andrews, who operated the nightclub Playgirl in Garden Grove, California, near Disneyland, decided to try a magazine named after their nightclub. They had a dummy issue ready in July 1972 before Bob Guccione of *Penthouse* announced plans for a women's magazine to be called *Viva*. The first issue of *Playgirl*, of which 600,000 copies were printed, hit the newsstands 15 May 1973. According to the publishers, the magazine was in the black from that first June 1973 issue.[2] Circulation soon reached 1.1 or 1.5 million copies, depending upon which source one believes.[3]

The early issues of *Playgirl* seemed well capitalized in terms of spending for quality content. There were interviews with the novelist Thomas Tryon and the actor Hal Holbrook. There was even a piece of original fiction entitled ''Sabbatha and Solitude'' by none other than Tennessee Williams. Travel articles from such places as Amsterdam and Austria featured high quality, interesting (nonpornographic) photographs. Serious, although not overly complex or profound, articles on topics of concern to women, including breast cancer and rape, found their places among the male nudes. Only a few pages beyond the rape article in the November 1974 issue, however, was a cartoon of a woman office worker expressing her joy to her co-workers that she has just been raped in the corridor! On this and a host of subsequent occasions as well, the magazine, despite its ostensibly feminist rhetoric, seemed to misunderstand or be oblivious to important feminist issues.

Celebrity show-business men including Lyle Waggoner, George Maharis, Gary Conway, Fabian, and Fred Williamson as well as noncelebrity models showed their bodies, sometimes including their genitals, to the *Playgirl* camera, with full-frontal nudity becoming the rule for at least one model in each issue by February and March 1974.

No doubt this exposure of the male anatomy was a very important factor in causing the large corporate producers of brand name consumer goods to fear advertising in *Playgirl*.[4] The August 1973 issue carried one or two page ads for Jim Beam whiskey, Pierre Cardin men's hosiery, and the magazine *Psychology Today*,* but soon these ads appeared no more. Ads for Revlon and Maybelline cosmetics appeared and then disappeared from subsequent issues. Of all the large corporate advertisers of consumer goods, only the tobacco companies used *Playgirl* on a regular basis as a conduit to the public. Still, the magazine's advertising revenues for its second six months (December 1973–May 1974) nearly doubled the amount collected in the first six months.[5] In February 1975 there was an out-of-court settlement with the American Tobacco Company of the magazine's suit to break an early contract giving that company the back cover of every issue of the magazine. Thus the coveted back cover was freed to be used as a reward for other advertisers.[6]

To attract more advertisers who might be worried about the image of their products and companies, the editors announced in January 1976 that they would no longer accept advertising for products of an erotic nature. That summer, in order to keep up its circulation, *Playgirl* began to advertise itself in such magazines as *Redbook** and *Hairdo Ideas* and in newspapers around the country including Kansas City, Denver, and Des Moines.[7] But by the summer of 1977, the circulation, which had been dropping for two years, was down to 800,000, and advertising revenues were down 8 percent from the previous year.[8] The original owners sold *Playgirl*, now described as "financially troubled,"[9] to Stephen L. Geller and Ira Ritter, the latter a twenty-eight-year-old publishing prodigy who had been brought in as executive vice-president a year earlier.

By the fall of 1977, less money seemed to be going into the magazine's content. Much of the content and advertising seemed to be aimed at campus coeds and other young and not especially sophisticated women. In the October "Back to School" issue, there were short sketches of women in roles traditionally limited to men—captaining a Coast Guard cutter, running a leasing business, and professionally racing a speed boat. There were short fiction, a satirical article on college football, a reprint of an article from *Mother Earth News** on the kinds of typing one can do at home for money, an interview with religious cult members, and an article on women's sports scholarships. The article on choosing wines was so basic that no labels were mentioned—only a few generic names and categories. Some articles such as those on fashions and storage ideas for closets could have appeared in almost any women's magazine. Other articles including those about such electronic entertainment equipment as cassette players and phonographs seemed very much like articles in the male "skin" magazines.

The ads featured cigarettes and looks improvement—bust development, weight loss, more weight loss, fingernail strengthening, cellulite removal cream, and henna rinse. Erotic materials were back in the magazine's ads, including condoms, contraceptive foam, satin sheets, and two separate ads for Frederick's of Hollywood—the famed purveyor of naughty lingerie. To take advantage of the campus drug craze, there were ads for cigarette papers, simulated hashish and opium, and caffeine tablets. A few ads, including that for wrinkle cream, were aimed at a somewhat older audience.

In January 1978, Ritter admitted that the median age of *Playgirl*'s readers was twenty-seven, several years younger than the median age of readers of *Cosmopolitan*, *Glamour*, or *Mademoiselle*, but he claimed that his circulation was rising and that the amount of male nudity was being curtailed.[10]

Like the male skin magazines, *Playgirl* has aspired to "social significance." Thus it has presented pro and con arguments from authorities on welfare reform and other social issues. There was a series entitled "Playgirl Freedom Papers" that criticized sexism in media advertising and programming and in other places. The *Playgirl* book club featured *Our Bodies, Ourselves* on women's health and Linda Lovelace's *Ordeal*, an exposé of the pornography industry, in addition to erotica.

The magazine's closest approach to political significance came in April 1977 when *Playgirl* ran an article by Lowell Ponte, a former member of a Washington think tank who revealed some sensational facts about U.S. Army chemical and biological warfare research.[11] The editors have wanted interviews with important political figures beyond the 1979 interview given by Britain's Margaret Thatcher. They cried sexism because Jimmy Carter, George McGovern, and other politicians granted interviews to magazines featuring nude women but not to their magazine with its nude men. Usually *Playgirl*'s interviews and articles about people have dealt with Hollywood types—Burt Reynolds, Sylvester Stallone, Jacqueline Bisset, Robin Williams, Dustin Hoffman, Joan Rivers, Dudley Moore, and Liza Minnelli. Jane Fonda and the Reagans' daughter Patti Davis fit into both Hollywood and the political scene. Over the years, show business gossip and celebrity articles have seemed to wax while social significance waned and then nearly disappeared.

In format, layout, subtitle, and in so many other ways, *Playgirl* has seemed to ape Hugh Hefner's *Playboy** and Bob Guccione's *Penthouse*. *Playgirl*'s cartoons seem very much like those in *Playboy* and *Penthouse* except that they are supposedly from a woman's point of view. Some are simply reversals of tired old male-sexist jokes. The ads for T-shirts, tote bags, cigarette lighters, and other accessories carrying the *Playgirl* emblem also remind one of the male skin magazines. Along the way, as did *Penthouse, Playgirl* began to publish "erotic fantasies," often not even disguised as letters to the editor, which use Anglo-Saxon rather than Latin words to describe the genitalia if not the sex act.

By the end of 1985, the magazine's circulation had dropped below 600,000. The owners filed for bankruptcy. New owner Carl Ruderman, publisher of several less famous men's skin magazines, moved the editorial operations from Santa Monica, California, to New York. A new editor, Nancie Martin, ended full-frontal nudity with the January 1987 issue saying, "Women today are just not what they were 10 years ago."[12] Still, the big advertisers stayed away. Most of the ads continued to pitch body improvement (especially weight loss), caffeine and other energizer pills, erotic conference calls, vibrators, and pornographic videotapes of both men and women.

The latter ads introduce the question of just who buys this magazine. Critics have long charged that *Playgirl* appeals more to homosexual men than to women, a charge the editors have vigorously denied.[13] Many of the ads for pornographic videotapes are no different from ads in the men's pornographic magazines. These ads would seem to indicate much gender confusion concerning the magazine's target audience. The need to accept so much of these types of ads together with the low-quality features and articles accompanying them also means that *Playgirl* is losing the battle to be anything more than pornographic. By the magazine's fifteenth anniversary issue of June 1988 it seemed to be losing another battle. The magazine had returned to full-frontal nudity and to the display of the male models in full physical arousal. This made it seem more than ever like the publications that pornographers aim at homosexual men.

Playgirl appeared at a time when explicitly sexual material for both genders was surfacing more and more in the mainstream of American popular culture. But before the magazine had begun its second decade, a resurgence of conservatism was pushing such material to the periphery of popular culture, and the magazine came to be ever-more marginal in both a cultural and economic sense.

Notes

1. Judy Klemesrud, "She Picks the Men Who Pose in Magazine's Centerfold," *New York Times,* 2 October 1973, p. 38.
2. Philip H. Dougherty, "Advertising: Facts at Playgirl," *New York Times*, 16 July 1974, p. 53.
3. Philip H. Dougherty, "New Owners for Playgirl," *New York Times*, 28 July 1977, Section D9; and "The Girls' Magazines Claw at Each Other," *Business Week*, 17 May 1974, pp. 36–37.
4. Dougherty, "Advertising: Facts at Playgirl," p. 53.
5. Ibid.
6. Philip H. Dougherty, "Lining Up for the Back Cover," *New York Times*, 31 March 1975, p. 52.
7. Philip H. Dougherty, "Playgirl Enters New Ad Arena," *New York Times*, 21 July 1976, p. 51.
8. Dougherty, "New Owners at Playgirl," D9.
9. Philip H. Dougherty, "Changes at Playgirl," *New York Times*, 24 January 1978, p. 51.
10. Ibid.
11. "Ex-Pentagon Researcher Says the Army Waged Mock Attack on Nixon," *New York Times*, 11 March 1977, p. 10.
12. Stuart J. Elliott, " 'Playgirl' to Gird Loins for Change," *Advertising Age*, 13 October 1986, pp. 4, 107.
13. Dougherty, "Playgirl Enters New Ad Arena," p. 51.

Information Sources

BIBLIOGRAPHY

Dougherty, Philip H. "Advertising: Facts at Playgirl." *New York Times,* 16 July 1974.
———. "Changes at Playgirl." *New York Times*, 24 January 1978.
———. "Lining Up for the Back Cover." *New York Times*, 31 March 1975.
———. "New Owners for Playgirl." *New York Times*, 28 July 1977.
———. "Playgirl Enters New Ad Arena." *New York Times*, 21 July 1976.
———. "Playgirl on Way." *New York Times*, 3 May 1973.
Elliott, Stuart J. " 'Playgirl' to Gird Loins for Change." *Advertising Age*, 13 October 1986, pp. 4, 107.
"Ex-Pentagon Researcher Says the Army Waged Mock Attack on Nixon." *New York Times*, 11 March 1977.
"The Girls' Magazines Claw at Each Other." *Business Week*, 17 May 1974. pp. 36–37.
Klemesrud, Judy. "She Picks the Men Who Pose in Magazine's Centerfold." *New York Times*, 2 October 1973.

INDEX SOURCES
    Not indexed.
LOCATION SOURCES
    Widely held, but at University of Illinois at Urbana-Champaign. Available in microform, vol. 10–present.

Publication History

MAGAZINE TITLE AND TITLE CHANGES
    Playgirl: The Magazine for Women, 1973–present.
VOLUME AND ISSUE DATA
    Vol. 1, no. 1–present, August 1973–present, monthly.
PUBLISHER AND PLACE OF PUBLICATION
    Douglas Lambert, 1973–1977, Los Angeles, California; Ira Ritter, 1977–1986, Los Angeles and Santa Monica, California; Playgirl, Inc., 1987–1988, New York, New York; Louis Montesano, 1988–present, New York, New York.
EDITORS
    Marian Scott Milan, 1973–1977; Joyce Dudley Fleming, 1977; Barbara Cady, 1977–1978; Judy Lewellen, 1978–1979; Melody Sharp, 1979; Judy Lewellen, 1979–1981; Pat McGilligan, 1981–1983; Diane Grosskopf, 1983–1985; Tomasine E. Lewis, 1985–1987; Nancie S. Martin, 1987–present.
CIRCULATION
    1,042,000 (1977); 600,000 (1988).

Robert W. Frizzell

POPULAR MECHANICS

Popular Mechanics is moving toward ninety years of publication and in that time has become the standard how-to magazine for science and mechanics. Its practical approach is aimed at all age groups with generously illustrated articles on projects ranging from automobile repair to electronics. With *Popular Science** and *Home Mechanix, Popular Mechanics* is a highly successful and widely circulated magazine of considerable popular appeal.

Popular Mechanics began its life in 1902 as a weekly, subtitled *An Illustrated Weekly Review of the Mechanical Press of the World.* The entire first issue (and succeeding issues) was devoted to the how-to process on topics such as telephones, cleaning sponges, and the manufacture of car wheels. The sciences were represented as well as mechanics; an article on chewing advised the reader: "chew your food thoroughly. Mix it well with saliva. Don't rush through the meal—it comes but three times a day and you are entitled to be leisurely about it."[1] The article went on to assert that chewing gum, on the other hand, did not aid the digestive process. Science was also the subject of a brief article on quicksand. The entire contents ran for only sixteen pages in these initial issues, mixed with a few advertisements and job placement ads.

Despite its later successes and a circulation presently approaching 1.7 million, *Popular Mechanics* had a most modest beginning. The driving (and only) force behind its inception was Henry Haven Windsor, son of an Iowa minister, former editor of a small town Iowa newspaper, and editor of the *Street Railway Review* from 1892 until the inception of *Popular Mechanics*.[2] Windsor was a near visionary who saw the importance of science to the art of mechanics and the necessity for interpreting this concept to the average man. When he started *Popular Mechanics*, he did so with only five subscribers and a handful of news-stand sales. Windsor wrote the entire contents, sold the few ads, and employed a staff of only two.[3] But by September 1903, he was encouraged enough to revise the format from a weekly to a hundred-page monthly. Expansion has increased issue length, but the magazine is still a monthly. Each early issue included a news section on science and technology, a considerable section on mechanics, and a how-to section for the home do-it-yourselfer. The contents featured practical and illustrative instructions, all designed for a readership interested in the mechanics of the project—anything from simple home repairs to larger projects such as constructing electrical appliances or a seaworthy sailing craft.

One invention and scientific development that fascinated Windsor and thus was treated in several issues of his early magazine was flight. He covered the 1907 International Balloon Race from St. Louis and featured French aviator Louis Bleriot's own account of his flight across the English Channel in 1909. His interest also ran to the submarine and its future. Several issues of *Popular Mechanics* included features on how to make a glider and how to build an airplane. As science and technology advanced, Windsor's magazine added new writers but maintained its focus. The war in Europe received extensive media coverage in the United States, and *Popular Mechanics* was no exception. Numerous photographs depicted the technology that changed modern warfare, and Windsor hailed the use of airplanes in war so long predicted by poets and fiction writers. The sinking of the *Lusitania* brought a scientific explanation of the disaster, complete with illustrations and detailed drawings. In addition to the usual practical how-to articles contained on its pages, the magazine has traced the evolution of twentieth-century weaponry.

The prosperity of the decade of the 1920s was also reflected in the pages of *Popular Mechanics*. In May of 1924, Windsor died and his son, Henry H. Windsor, Jr., replaced the founder as editor and publisher. The June issue had gone to press before notice of Windsor's death could be made, but the July issue included a simple memorial to the man whose convictions now had a considerable following.

Windsor's last two editorials, printed in the July 1924 issue, chastised higher education for a lack of patriotism and strongly supported the expansion of radio. As ever, much of what Windsor believed reflected the spirit of the nation, and his son's primary aim was to continue that trend. The younger Windsor, only twenty-four when his father died, was educated in private schools and attended

Yale for less than two years.[4] He remained editor and publisher of *Popular Mechanics* until 1958, when William Randolph Hearst's organization purchased the magazine. Under Windsor Jr., *Popular Mechanics* continued to increase its circulation and size and later, in the 1940s, started publishing editions in French, Spanish, Danish, Swedish, and German.

The onset of the depression brought a new respect for the popular magazine; titles such as *Popular Science* and *Popular Mechanics* taught readers how to fix things, how to make things, and how to save and stretch what little expendable income was available to the average family. New technologies were not ignored in the issues of *Popular Mechanics*, but articles like ''Turning Junk into Money'' and on building a home for $700 or building a radio from spare and junk parts were regularly included in the 1930s. The price, twenty-five cents per issue or $2.50 for an annual subscription, remained the same during the depression, but *Popular Mechanics* did not cut down on issue length; some issues were even longer. Ads were still a most prominent feature of each issue, but a change in their form was evident. Advertisements were directed more to practical functions, such as repairing shoes or earning extra income. Somehow *Popular Mechanics* continued to grow in both appeal and circulation; and when Americans again entered global conflict in 1941, the magazine responded to the mass interest in the war, its weapons and technological changes, and the changes at home brought about by rationing and the scarcity of numerous consumer goods.

Popular Mechanics under the Windsors was more than a home repair, do-it-yourself popular magazine. It was a source of the latest scientific and technological information that appealed to a broad readership. Articles on aviation, nuclear energy, and electronic developments were commonplace. A good part of the success of the magazine was the ability to adapt to the rapidly changing world of the twentieth century. And it was this measure of success that led to the sale of *Popular Mechanics* in 1958 to the Hearst Corporation.

Windsor had been trying to sell *Popular Mechanics* for a year when the Hearst Corporation finalized the purchase in November. Paid circulation, while still well exceeding one million, had suffered a slight decline, and for the first six months of 1958, advertising revenues were down 6 percent from the same period one year earlier. In addition, the Hearst Corporation also owned ten other magazines, including *Good Housekeeping, Cosmopolitan,* Harper's Bazaar*, and *House Beautiful*.[5] Hearst named as publisher of *Popular Mechanics* Henry Chamberlaine, who had been advertising director of *Good Housekeeping*. Hearst announced that the new addition to the chain would make a broader appeal to youth, despite *Time*'s comment that ''for two generations, nearly every handy American boy read *Popular Mechanics*.''[6] Hearst realized the profitability of magazine publishing, as overall magazine circulation had grown 23 percent since 1950 while its seventeen newspapers were on a steady decline. The Hearst magazine division moved *Popular Mechanics* to New York in 1962 and sold the old Chicago building for a handsome profit. Gradual success under Hearst management is reflected in circulation statistics, from 1.3 million in 1958 to 1.4

million in 1963. By 1969, however, circulation approached 1.7 million and exceeded that figure by 1975. Today, the circulation of *Popular Mechanics* has leveled somewhat to 1,650,000, second only to *Popular Science* (1.8 million) among the science/technology how-to periodicals.[7]

Considerable credit for the increased success of *Popular Mechanics* belongs to Richard Berlin, who began with Hearst publications after World War I with a staff position on *Motor Boating*. His meteoric rise was complete by December 1930, when he was named executive vice-president and general manager of the Hearst magazine chain and ousted Ray Long as editor of *Cosmopolitan*. His power thus consolidated, Berlin successfully managed Hearst's magazine publishing operations until his retirement early in 1973.[8]

Part of the reason for Berlin's success was his inherent sense to leave well enough alone: *Popular Mechanics* maintained its do-it-yourself format. Much of the scientific innovational approach had waned with increased communication after World War II and *Popular Mechanics* under Windsor Jr. generally moved away from the emphasis on technological news of its first forty years to the home repair, individual-builder focus it has today. The magazine had evolved from being partly theoretical under the Windsors to being truly practical. Issue length had not changed drastically, from about 100 pages when it first became a monthly to about 200 pages by the 1920s. Even during the depression years and World War II *Popular Mechanics* averaged about 300 pages per issue, although continually rising costs have cut current issue length to between 120 and 170 pages; the physical size of the magazine changed, however, from 16 x 22.5 cm to 20.5 x 27.5 cm in 1975.

As with many mass-market magazines, *Popular Mechanics* has found success with the special issues centered on one theme. These issues are aimed at the consumer and include the home idea issue (begun in 1972), the car care guide (1973), the home energy issue (1977), and the outdoor living guide (1981). The single issue price, increased recently to $1.95, and odd subscription rate (13.97) keep *Popular Mechanics* in keen competition with *Popular Science* ($1.95 per issue, $13.94 annual subscription, circulation 1.8 million) and *Home Mechanix* ($1.75, $13.94, 1.2 million).

The actual physical presentation of the magazine changed very little over the early years of publication. Photography was used from the initial issue, but the majority of illustrations were sketches and drawings. But as the art of photography developed and reproduction in magazines became less expensive, *Popular Mechanics* grew with the medium. Illustrations of any sort were always generous, and remain so, due to the practical, hands-on nature of the magazine. Color photography was introduced in the late 1960s but has never replaced black-and-white photographs or illustrations. Quite often actual blueprints were substituted for sketch designs, aimed again at the reader for his (or her) personal use. As with any publication targeted at a consumer audience, advertisements were prevalent. The expansion to a 100-page monthly in September of 1903 also led to the vastly expanded use of ads. As the use of ads increased along with more articles, photography, and features, the necessity to increase staff was evident. Windsor Sr. was still very involved in the entire publication process, but by 1905 the staff had been steadily growing. More and more authors and designers participated in the production of *Popular Mechanics*, and this trend continued after the elder Windsor died. As magazine publication developed, so did *Popular Mechanics*, especially so after the Hearst takeover in 1958.

Popular Mechanics has always been a magazine aimed at practical use. Not only home projects but science news generally had a male appeal. But from its earliest years, the magazine attempted to attract female readers as well. Early photographs pictured women using dishwashers, electrical appliances, and general home mechanics. Even women's fashion drew attention from *Popular Mechanics* as early as 1910, with news of handbags, the trousers skirt, and the hobble skirt. One short piece even commented on the use of the garter to carry a small knife for self-protection. Undoubtedly, *Popular Mechanics* had a vastly predominant male audience, but the interests of women were never ignored.

With its regular hints on do-it-yourself repair, its new and innovative ideas on small and large projects, and its keeping abreast of the latest scientific and technological changes as they affect mechanics, *Popular Mechanics* remains a favorite of readers everywhere, complete with its still-published international editions.

Notes

1. "Gum Chewing vs. Food Chewing," *Popular Mechanics,* 11 January 1902, p. 5.
2. "Henry Haven Windsor," *Who Was Who in America* (Chicago: Marquis, 1943), p. 1365.
3. Edward L. Throm, *Fifty Years of Popular Mechanics, 1902–1952* (New York: Simon and Schuster, 1951), pp. ix–x.
4. "Henry Haven Windsor, Jr.," *Who Was Who in America* (Chicago: Marquis, 1968), p. 1024.
5. "Popular Mechanics Magazine Purchased by Hearst Corp.," *Wall Street Journal,* 21 November 1958, p. 8.
6. "Blood, Sweat and Marvels," *Time,* 1 December 1958, p. 43.
7. Circulation figures are taken from *Ulrich's International Periodical Directory* for the various years cited.
8. Lindsay Chaney and Michael Chieply, *The Hearsts: Family and Empire—The Later Years* (New York: Simon and Schuster, 1981), pp. 103–20.

Information Sources

BIBLIOGRAPHY
"Blood, Sweat and Marvels." *Time,* 1 December 1958, p. 43.
Bragonier, Reginald. *The Mechanics of a Magazine.* New York: Popular Mechanics, 1984.
Chaney, Lindsay, and Michael Chieply. *The Hearsts: Family and Empire—The Later Years.* New York: Simon and Schuster, 1981.

"In Memoriam." [Henry Haven Windsor] *Popular Mechanics Magazine*, July 1924,
      p. 1.
Peterson, Theodore. *Magazines in the Twentieth Century*. Urbana: University of Illinois
      Press, 1964.
"Popular Mechanics Magazine Purchased by Hearst Corp." *Wall Street Journal*, 21
      November 1958, p. 8.
Throm, Edward L. *Fifty Years of Popular Mechanics, 1902–1952*. New York: Simon
      and Schuster, 1951.
"Henry Haven Windsor." *Who Was Who in America*. Chicago: Marquis, 1943, p. 1365.
"Henry Haven Windsor, Jr." *Who Was Who in America*. Chicago: Marquis, 1968,
      p. 1024.
INDEX SOURCES
      Readers' Guide; Biography Index (1924–present); *Consumer Index; Children's
      Magazine Guide; Magazine Index* (1977–present); *Engineering Index* (1911–
      1913); *Industrial Arts Index* (1920–1923).
LOCATION SOURCES
      Library of Congress, many other libraries. Available in microform.

Publication History

MAGAZINE TITLE AND TITLE CHANGES
      *Popular Mechanics: An Illustrated Weekly Review of the Mechanical Press of the
      World*, 11 January 1902–May 1913; *Popular Mechanics Magazine*, June 1913–
      July 1959; *Popular Mechanics*, August 1959–present.
VOLUME AND ISSUE DATA
      Vols. 1–19, no. 5, 11, January 1902–May 1903, weekly and monthly, September
      1903–May 1913; vol. 19, no. 6–present, June 1913–present, monthly.
PUBLISHER AND PLACE OF PUBLICATION
      Popular Mechanics Company, Henry Haven Windsor, Sr., 1902–1924; Henry
      Haven Windsor, Jr., 1924–1958, Chicago, Illinois. Hearst Corporation, 1958–
      1962; New York, New York, 1962–present.
EDITORS
      Henry Haven Windsor, Sr., 1902–1924; Henry Haven Windsor, Jr., 1924–1958;
      Roderick M. Grant, 1959–1960; Clifford B. Hicks, 1961–1962; Don Dinwiddie,
      1962–1965; Walter Ian Fischman, editorial director, 1965–1966; Richard P. Cros-
      sley, 1966–1971; Jim Liston, 1972–1974; John A. Linkletter, editor-in-chief,
      1973–1985; Joe Oldham, editor-in-chief, 1985–present.
CIRCULATION
      1,619,778 paid; 48,063 nonpaid.

Boyd Childress and Beverley Childress

POPULAR SCIENCE: The What's New Magazine

Popular Science, changeling of the science and technology magazines, still
defies the simple label of a how-to periodical. Originally an equivalent of *Scientific American* and *Science*, it is now a competitor of *Popular Mechanics** and

Home Mechanix. Boasting of the high-quality demographics of its audience,[1] and backed by the Times Mirror empire, it has been the circulation leader in its field since 1975. A history of *Popular Science Monthly* is a technological history of the past century. Although its approach has shifted widely during the 117 years of its existence, its pages capture a microcosm of the influences of science and technology on everyday life.

Founded by Edward Livingston Youmans, a visually impaired writer and lecturer, *Popular Science Monthly* premiered in 1872 less than two weeks after its conception, with "The Study of Sociology" written by Youmans's friend Herbert Spencer.[2] Youmans wanted to disseminate scientific knowledge to an audience of educated laymen, and persuaded Appleton to publish the monthly after previously working as science editor for the weekly *Appleton's Journal*.* His earlier popular writing experience included a color chemical chart devised during the period of his greatest vision loss, the accompanying twice-revised chemistry textbook (first edition 1851), the *Handbook of Household Science* (1857), and the establishment and editorship of the INTERNATIONAL SCIENTIFIC SERIES. In *Popular Science Monthly's* first issue, Youmans wrote, "The work of creating science has been organized for centuries. . . . The work of diffusing science is clearly the next great task of civilization."[3]

Early issues of *Popular Science Monthly* consisted primarily of selections from English periodicals. "One of the most useful periodical publications now issued from the press"[4] survived the lack of original American material, charges of extreme popularization, and strident charges of atheism for its publication and de facto support of evolutionary theory. The journal became an outlet for the writings and ideas of Charles Darwin, Thomas Henry Huxley, Louis Pasteur, Ernest Rutherford, Henry Ward Beecher, William James, Thomas Edison, John Dewey, and a future editor, J. McKeen Cattell. John Shaw Billings, originator of *Index Medicus* and founder of the National Library of Medicine, summarized his work in sanitation in an article on house drainage[5] while he was still with the U.S. Surgeon General's Office. *Popular Science Monthly* covered contemporary news items relating to scientific topics such as the Tichborne claimant case, exhibitions like the Philadelphia Centennial, and early speculations about "flying machines."[6] Youmans supplemented articles with a trio of editorial departments: Literary Notices, or book reviews; the Editor's Table, for correspondence and editorials; and Miscellany. *Popular Science Monthly* was also notable in the early years for its support of the application of scientific method to sociology, psychology, and economics in addition to the natural sciences.[7]

In 1877 Edward Youmans was joined in editing *Popular Science Monthly* by his physician brother William, editor of Thomas Huxley's *Elements of Physiology and Hygiene*. To fill the demand for more articles, they started a short-lived supplement in May 1877 but ended in 1879. William succeeded to sole editorship when Edward died in 1887. A prolific writer, William was primarily responsible for the Editor's Table, writing "two or more articles [per issue] on scientific progress, scientific education, and the application of science to practical, intellectual, and moral advance.''[8] Another special feature, which William initiated and primarily composed, was a monthly biographical sketch of a leading American or European scientist or teacher of science. Fifty of these were republished as *Pioneers of Science in America* (1896). William changed Miscellany to Fragments of Science and Literary Notices to Scientific Literature. When Appleton was forced by economic reasons to sell *Popular Science Monthly* in 1900, William retired from the editorship and died a year later.

Editorial leadership was assumed by J. McKeen Cattell, academic activist, science zealot, and editor of *Science*. He also acted as publisher after 1901. Cattell was a cofounder of the American Association of University Professors in 1915 and was involved in a notorious academic freedom case in 1917. Cattell was also an advocate of the American Association for the Advancement of Science over the claims of the National Science Foundation to direct national science policy. Cattell started *American Men of Science* in 1906 and *Leaders of Education* in 1932. Under Cattell's leadership *Popular Science Monthly* maintained a balance between natural and social sciences similar to that established by the Youmans, but he combined the three miscellaneous editorial departments of the Youmans into Progress of Science, and his evangelical zeal attracted quality original articles. Progress of Science provided a forum for his views on academia and faculty control of the university as well as his views on science.

In 1915, unable to arrest *Popular Science Monthly's* decline in readership, Cattell decided to continue the erudite portion of the magazine under the title *Scientific Monthly*, published by his Science Press. The new title was considered by *Readers' Guide* and scientists of the time to be the true successor to the Youmans' journal.[9] The use of the title *Popular Science Monthly* was sold to Henry J. Fisher, Robert C. Wilson, and Oliver Capen of Modern Publishing Company, who merged it with *World's Advance*.[10] *Scientific Monthly* retained the original *Popular Science Monthly* subscription list and continued as a literate journal for laymen under the auspices of the American Association for the Advancement of Science until it was absorbed by *Science* in January 1958.

The change in publisher at this juncture cued a major shift in audience focus. Now seeking "the home craftsman and hobbyist who wanted to know something about the world of science,"[11] new editor Waldemar Kaempffert, former managing editor of *Scientific American*, added substantial illustrations, shortened the articles, and doubled the circulation in one year. "Kaempffert enjoyed telling groups of scientists on occasion that the chief function of the science writer was to 'make science so clear that the scientists could understand it.' ''[12] Kaempffert was a consistent successor to Edward Youmans in his feeling that science was "not the property of a learned class but the common possession of mankind."[13] The table of contents style of *World's Advance* was adapted with revised headings such as Aeronautics, Housekeeping Made Easy, Industrial Progress, How the War Is Being Fought (during World War I), Motor Vehicles and Their Accessories, Photography and Motion Pictures, Picture Pages, Practical Worker, Wireless Telegraphy and Telephony, and Sports and Pastimes.

Occasionally the new magazine represented such a departure from its former self that in its most sensational moments it appeared to be a *National Enquirer** of science, such as when spiritual investigators weighed ghosts and photographed phantoms (September 1921). It admitted that its seeming haphazard arrangement was designed as "mechanical vaudeville," serious subjects touching entertaining ones (June 1916, p. xii). Critics said of Kaempffert's reader that "the depths of his mind remained untouched by the importunate knocking of ideas."[14] But Kaempffert's object was for the lay reader to accept principal scientific concepts, not necessarily understand them. The pages increased to quarto size in October 1918 (vol. 93), allowing a better display of the significant photographic, illustrative material that *Popular Science Monthly* advertised as "300 pictures of inventions and discoveries" per issue. In 1919 Oliver Capen organized the Popular Science–McCall Distribution Company, later S-M News Company, in which Popular Science Monthly Publishing Company joined with McCall Company for magazine distribution.

Kaempffert departed in late 1920 to free-lance writing, the science editorship of the *New York Times*, and the first directorship of the Museum of Science and Industry in Chicago. Kenneth Payne was editor for two years but was unacknowledged on the masthead. In 1922 the fiftieth anniversary issue in May contained an article by Thomas Edison on the future marvels of radio and science. Edison was the unofficial hero of the magazine's new philosophy of the practical as well as the theoretical, and later a lengthy feature was devoted to Spencer Tracy's movie *Edison: The Man* (July 1940).

Sumner N. Blossom joined *Popular Science Monthly* as its sixth editor in 1922 during a reorganization of the publishing company. The contents were reformatted to handle a dozen feature articles with "200 important new articles in pictures" and the separately paged Home Workshop, allowing *Popular Science Monthly* to be advertised as "two magazines in one." Contests, fictional features, a serial by Houdini, popular quizzes (How Much Science Do You Know?), and They Say (brief comments on the science news of the hour) were all initiated by Blossom, as were previews of the next issue. Gus Wilson's Garage premiered in 1925. It was the longest running feature, other than PS Readers Talk Back, ending only in 1969. The "most wonderfully illustrated magazine in the world" became the "magazine of invention and discovery." Blossom's editorship covered "Lindbergh's great partner: details of the first New York to Paris plane" (August 1927); anticipation of the World War II bombings of London, Pearl Harbor, Berlin, and Hiroshima (September 1927); Albert Einstein (April 1929); the talkies (September 1928); color movies (October 1928); the first television (January 1929); and the atom smasher (January 1929). *Popular Science Monthly* continued its interest in movie technology with an article on Disney's first animated feature, *Snow White and the Seven Dwarfs* (January 1938). Circulation passed 300,000 in 1926.

Travis Hoke's brief editorship left little imprint, as did Raymond J. Brown's quiet assumption of the role in 1930 after serving as managing editor under

Blossom and Hoke. Brown steadily continued the formula of success until he moved to the editorship of *Outdoor Life*. Many changes in the formula were made in 1938 and 1939: the reduction to its former size with an increase in the number of pages and color illustrations, the absorption of *Mechanics and Handicraft*, and the return of Godfrey Hammond, former promotion manager in charge of circulation and advertising promotion, as publisher, president, and treasurer of Popular Science Publishing Company. Hammond's influence was predominant in the 1940s and 1950s, which saw the arrival of Charles McLendon, former city editor of the *New York Herald Tribune*, and his swift departure after an argument with Hammond.

Hammond felt that the keys to magazine publishing success were the importance of the subject field to advertisers, quality editorial content, and coverage of the field in comparison with competition.[15] He used his promotional experience as public relations director for the Republican National Committee during the 1944 campaign.[16]

Although *Popular Science Monthly* was building an increasing circulation throughout the 1920s and 1930s, World War II provided an opportunity for the magazine to capitalize on increased interest in science and technology. Practical advice was needed on living with wartime restrictions: how to save clothes, how to drive a car in the blackout. *Popular Science Monthly* became the "News picture magazine of science and industry," and then "a technical journal of science and industry" that concentrated on industrial contribution to the war effort. *Popular Science Monthly* appealed for paper drives and back issues for servicemen, and increased the percentage of pulp in its paper to deal with the wartime paper shortage. It took up cudgels on behalf of U.S. military technology in January 1943 in a headline article, "We don't agree, Major Desaversky, that our fighting planes failed, in response to Desaversky's II Victory through Air Power." Other unusual stories covered the technology of the "Great Escape" (October 1945) and the preservation of German rocket secrets by the United States (December 1962). Publisher Hammond's favorite story was "how the *New York Times*, the United Press, International News Service and *Time* . . . telephoned *Popular Science Monthly* the morning after the first A-bomb dropped on Hiroshima 'to ask how the blame thing worked!' "[17]

This was also the era of *Popular Science Monthly's* most flamboyant and outspoken editor, Perry Githens. He joined *Popular Science Monthly* in 1945 after a Horatio Alger–type career, starting as a copyboy for the *Boston Transcript*. Prior to 1945 Githens served as news editor for *Business Week*, promotion manager for *Liberty Magazine*, free-lance writer for *Reader's Digest*,* and an accredited war correspondent for *Time*.* Postwar editor Githens pushed how-to material out of the limelight in his concern to educate the common citizen about the social as well as the technological issues of science. His goal was to "turn out a complete yet compact notebook of science for the citizen, and an understandable manual of the mechanics of living" (February 1946, p. 6). Githens revised the title page and table of contents layout, switched from the traditional right-hand page start to the left, reduced runovers, and limited article length. He felt he was producing "a handbook for scientists who use their hands and mechanics who use their heads" (December 1946, p. 294).

Githens wanted to reach his audience personally and pioneered an informal memo-style column, To: Reader/From: Editor, chatting about the production of *Popular Science Monthly* and signed with his crayoned initials. He kept his heavy artillery for Voice of Science, his editorial column about science and the citizen. In the stinging "Don't Smear Science, Congressman!" Githens defended Dr. Edward Condon, who campaigned for civilian control of the Atomic Energy Agency, against Congressman J. Parnell Thomas, who attacked Condon in hearings before the House Committee on Un-American Activities (June 1948). Many other editorials were just as controversial, such as "An Atomic Curtain? Feasible Nonsense!" (January 1949), "The Truth about 'Experimental Animals' " (February 1949), "Why Not a Secretary of Science?" (April 1947), "Let's Quit Tin-Cup Science!" (March 1947), "Science Is a Prisoner of War" (September 1946), "Design for Dying" (October 1946), "Unhappy Birthday" (August 1946), and "Don't Arrest Science, General!," concerning censored photographs for a previously approved unclassified article (May 1946). Githens tried in both editorials and speeches to visualize for the average citizen the everyday implications of military nuclear technology, not just its destructive power. The Voice of Science section was dropped in 1950 with no explanation, and Githens left after the May 1951 issue.

Practical postwar issues were not neglected as the influence of suburbia and prefabs touched the pages of *Popular Science Monthly* (August 1946 and January 1955). Later *Popular Science Monthly* would profile the growth of horizontal hotels, i.e., motels (July 1954), the advances in color television (December 1950 and July 1954), and even preview the modern U.S. custom of taking holidays on Monday for greater business convenience instead of using the actual date (January 1955).

After the "outsider" editor experiments with McLendon and Githens, *Popular Science Monthly* returned to the in-house promotion of its editors with Volta Torrey, a writer and associate editor under Githens. In May 1952 *Popular Science* proclaimed itself "America's leading new idea magazine for 80 years." By 1955, circulation topped the World War II one million mark, and has continued to grow, more or less steadily, to its present level of two million in 1988, a far cry from the initial audience of 5,000.[18]

Torrey left in 1956 for the science desk at WGBH-TV in Boston, and was succeeded by his subordinate Howard Allaway. Allaway inaugurated You Ought to Know, a semi-editorial, and The Month in Science to provide coverage of current science news. You Ought to Know foreshadowed the Russian triumph of Sputnik's early launch (August and November 1957). During Allaway's tenure as editor, Ralph Flynn acted as *Popular Science Monthly's* publisher for two years, followed by a brief return of Hammond as publisher, before Eugene

Duffield came with experience as a director of McGraw-Hill and assistant publisher of the *Cincinnati Enquirer*.

In 1962, Robert Crossley succeeded Allaway as editor, who departed for *Consumer Reports** and NASA. John R. Whiting, formerly with *Popular Photography* and *Science Illustrated*, succeeded Duffield as publisher when Duffield assumed the presidency of Popular Science Publishing Company. Crossley improved paper quality and attracted famous names as consulting editors on special topics. Wernher von Braun's monthly feature answering readers' questions about the U.S. space program began in January 1963. He remained as space consultant until his death in 1977. The increasing interest and concern among *Popular Science* readers about the "space race" was reflected in the increasing coverage of space topics after Sputnik. Highlights included a profile of Robert Goddard (May 1959), theme sections on space and aviation (July 1962), speculation about extraterrestrial life (September 1962) including a feature by MacKinlay Kantor (January 1966), and *Popular Science's* opinion of a UFO study conducted by the University of Colorado (April 1969). Later follow-ups included a profile of the space shuttle (November 1974) and everyday uses of technology from the space program (March 1974). The information explosion, the need for science information specialists (August 1963), and engineering feats such as raising Ramses' Abu Simbel temples for protection from the Aswan Dam reservoir were also featured (March 1965).

Crossley became consulting editor and free-lancer in 1965; he left to edit *Popular Mechanics*. He was succeeded as editor-in-chief by Ernest V. Heyn, whose background was less lofty than that of previous editors, since he had worked with *Modern Screen, Photoplay, Sport, True Story,** and *Family Weekly*. Heyn was very active with the *Popular Science* Book Club, the oldest special-interest club in the nation, and one of the four largest in membership and revenue. Under Heyn, *Popular Science* wooed famous writers such as John Steinbeck and Erle Stanley Gardner, who wrote a dialogue on the pros and cons of camping (May 1967). The same issue included C. P. Gilmore's "I used a real computer at home and so will you," foreshadowing his editorship during the personal computer explosion of the 1980s. Hollywood's infatuation with gadgetry in the late 1960s was chronicled in "Crazy Gadgets of *The Man from U.N.C.L.E.*" (December 1965), cover stories on James Bond's equipment (January 1966 and June 1967), "2001: Space Odyssey" (June 1968), the car from *Chitty Chitty Bang Bang* (March 1968), and the science behind Star Trek (December 1967). Serious topics included the Northeast blackout (February 1966), the rotary engine and "Wankel fever" (April 1966), Jacques Piccard's diving laboratory (March 1968), and drugs (May 1968). Heyn later chronicled the historical technology and scientists covered by *Popular Science Monthly* in two books, *Century of Wonders* and *Fire of Genius*.

In 1967 *Popular Science Monthly* was purchased by Times Mirror as part of its diversification plan, along with *Popular Science Monthly's* companion *Outdoor Life*. The Popular Science Publishing Company acted as a subsidiary of

Times Mirror, until the separate Times Mirror Magazine division was organized in 1973. J. Michael Hadley, former publisher of *Ladies' Home Journal*, replaced Whiting as publisher, and in 1969 *Popular Science* dropped the *Monthly* and started using the consistent subtitle, "The What's New Magazine." The page size returned to "large" in February of 1970.

Heyn retired in 1971 and was succeeded by executive editor Hubert P. Luckett, who had joined *Popular Science Monthly* in 1945 as a photographer. He presided over the 100th anniversary issue in May 1972, which focused on seven technological challenges: ample energy, healthy environment, adequate housing, efficient transportation, effective information systems, increased recreation resources, and the expansion of the frontiers of knowledge. It also included special designs by Ken Isaacs, Buckminster Fuller, and Les Walker. Luckett increased the frequency of special theme issues, used occasionally in the previous decade. The early 1970s saw the beginnings of the upsurge in home entertainment equipment, the catalytic converter, the energy crisis and practical means to cope with it in daily life, the B–1 bomber, the *Apollo 13* disaster, and a "Fast-growing new hobby, real computers you assemble yourself" (November 1976). The potpourri of articles started to shift toward the current three-pronged editorial content: science and technology, consumer products from high technology, and the use of these products.[19] Publishing more science articles, Times Mirror aimed at shedding the blue-collar image for the "white coverall man when he's wearing his consumer hat."[20] Gus Wilson was dropped, and Smokey Yunick's award-winning Say Smokey became the home mechanic's advice column. Especially predominant was increasing coverage of energy, cars, outdoor recreation, and electronics in the era of the pocket calculator explosion (April 1974) and early microprocessors (March 1977). Articles about weather (September 1977), the ozone layer (June 1977), gasahol (June 1978), and fiber optics (May 1970) also became more frequent. When Hadley moved up to president in 1973, he was succeeded briefly as publisher by Edward Hagerty, Jr., then returned in 1975 before Francis Wilkinson took over as publisher in 1977.

C. P. Gilmore, electronics columnist and executive editor, replaced Luckett as editor-in-chief in 1980, when Luckett became editorial director. Gilmore's second issue highlighted electronic mail (September 1980) and the new technology section increased as the personal computer explosion, industrial robots, biomechanics, and optical discs became household words. The Voyager Saturn discoveries (March 1981) and the Russian satellite landing on Venus (November 1982) were given equal coverage. The Stealth bomber (February 1983), the asteroid that caused dinosaur extinction, and safety issues such as wind shear reflected other current interests. The late 1980s covered the technology behind the Persian Gulf mines (January 1985), the renovation of the Statue of Liberty (June 1986), superconductors (July 1987), antimatter and antigravity (July 1986), and videophones (March 1988), the latter two formerly found only in science fiction. New features include the *Popular Science* Travel Guide, starting in May

1988, and the Best of What's New, inaugurated in December 1988 to highlight 100 outstanding developments of the previous year.

In 1982, Terence E. Moyes, the former advertising director, succeeded Wilkinson as publisher and continued the campaign to increase advertising revenues. Moyes was succeeded in 1986 by Grant A. Burnett, also a former advertising director. Times Mirror's recent strategy for consolidating its magazine acquisitions has been to control men's leisure magazines. Adding *Golf Magazine* and *Ski Magazine* in 1972, and *Sporting News* in 1977, in late 1987 Times Mirror acquired *Home Mechanix*, one of *Popular Science's* closest circulation competitors, and *Field and Stream, Outdoor Life's* very successful rival.

Most of the *Popular Science* departments established in 1915 are still active today, allowing for shifts in language, technological change, and combination of similar topics. Aeronautics is now Space and Aviation; Electricity now Computers and Electronics. Science and Technology now covers Mechanical Engineering, Industrial Progress, Medicine, Surgery and Hygience, Military and Naval Science, Natural Science, and Chemistry. Cars and Driving covers Motor Vehicles and Their Accessories. Picture Pages is now the What's New Digest, a picture roundup of new products and developments. Housekeeping Made Easy, Architecture, Home Craftsman, and the Practical Worker's Department have metamorphosed into Home, Shop, and Yard and the cartoon Workless Workshop. Sports and Pastimes and Boats and Boating are now covered by Outdoor Recreation.

Anyone scanning the pages of *Popular Science Monthly* must be struck not only by the immense changes in technology, but also by the recurrence of basic themes, such as education and the environment, in spite of the major shifts in style and readership. In the Cattell scholarly era, today's antismoking concerns were anticipated in "The Smoke Nuisance" (September 1915). In June 1919, alternative energy sources for automobiles were presented in "Can you run your automobile by star power?" Coastline erosion was highlighted in November 1933. September 1920 covered labor unrest due to industrial safety problems; February 1936 queried "How dangerous is your job?" Medicine and Surgery in 1919 emphasized "decreased waistline, increased lifeline"; August 1920 covered health concerns over exhaust fumes from vehicle tubes under the Hudson. The August 1920 issue also included, in Industrial Progress, an article on William Berwick's attic laboratory at the Library of Congress for restoring manuscripts. Today's fax machines were foreshadowed by the telephoto transmission of a fugitive's photograph in January 1921. Current interest in movie stunt exploits was previously reflected in "Stunting as a Profession" (May 1921). Today we locate the *Titanic*; the 1920s speculated about the *Lusitania's* gold (August 1922). The impact of radio on electing the president in June 1924 becomes *Selling of the President*. The modern media event of rescuing a child from a well was paralleled in April 1925 by the race to take diphtheria antitoxin to Nome, Alaska. Today's concerns about technology transfer are echoed in "Is the new Russia built by America a world menace?," concerning the hiring of 2,000 American engineers (April 1931). The modern search for greater sports performance is mirrored by the reporting of "Illinois seeks new Red Grange by electric tests" (November 1931). The May 1936 issue carried an article on drugs, "Uncle Sam fights a new drug menace: marihuana." Current outcry over the lack of skilled technological professionals is foreshadowed by the vocal Githens in several editorials: "Look Behind You, Students of Science" (June 1946), "Are We Mathematically Illiterate?" (April 1946), "Let's *All* Go Back to School" (September 1948), "Why Every School Should Be a 'Trade School' " (January 1950), and "The Playing Fields of Science" (February 1950). "Straight Talk to Parents," a 1957 series that won *Popular Science Monthly* the Benjamin Franklin Award for public service, emphasized the need for excellent science and technical education *before* Sputnik made the cry a fashionable one. One of the best illustrations of the changes in style is a comparison of the two articles on Halley's comet. "Halley's Comet," in January 1910, was sparsely illustrated and academically dry in tone; "Halley-llujah," in November 1986, was dominated by color photography, reports from satellites, and a more dramatic tone.

A consistent interest device has been to take advantage of *Popular Science's* long history in comparative articles, such as "Science Catches Up with Fiction" (March 1937) and citing previous articles that led to further inventions (May 1953). As time passed, regular features such as "25, 50, 75 Years Ago in *Popular Science*" and later "30, 60, 90 Years Ago in *Popular Science*" also capitalized on history. One unique follow-up in response to reader inquiry covered the long-term results of a historic operation at Massachusetts General Hospital when a boy's completely severed arm was reattached. Ten years later, the boy was a partner in a firm specializing in auto mechanics (June 1972). PS Readers Talk Back, *Popular Science's* popular and long-running correspondence column, demonstrates the attention and expertise of the readers in the compliments, as well as the occasional error complaints. The latter are always promptly acknowledged and corrected.

The audience of *Popular Science* has been predominantly male from its inception. Female readership has increased from 2 percent of the circulation in 1972, to 20 percent in 1982, and 25 percent in 1988.[21] Even with these steady gains in its female audience, the primary target is still the male mechanical hobbyist, although *Popular Science* has been unusual for a male-oriented magazine in treating women interviewees and staffers in terms of their profession, not their sex. Attitudes of early articles were not so neutral, as evidenced in Youmans's "The Higher Education of Woman" (April 1874) and thoroughly documented in Louise Newman's *Men's Ideas/Women's Realities*. After the Edward Youmans period, articles such as "A Doctor Discusses Sex Appeal" (August 1926), "Why Men Beat Women at Sports" (November 1926), and "Why a Wife Says 'No' " (August 1956), and little appreciation of the myriad jobs of a homemaker, even with sections such as Housekeeping Made Easy, did little to attract women to *Popular Science Monthly* until these overt attitudes faded from prominence. Minority readers have been even less attracted to *Popular*

Science, seemingly due to lack of role models; the audience is only 7 percent nonwhite.[22] However unevenly distributed the readership, the editorial content has consistently been praised for accuracy and clarity of difficult topics.

Although one person's influence is difficult to measure objectively, "there is considerable evidence that as a writer on chemistry, as a lecturer on science, as an editor and as the founder of an important journal he [Youmans] was widely influential upon the growth and spread of science in America."[23] Writing in 1883, Youmans expected *Popular Science Monthly* to "hold over at least into the next century."[24] If late twentieth-century merger mania does not overtake it, one can expect that *Popular Science* will continue to publish thoroughly researched previews of future technology and its effect on everyday life well into the twenty-first century. Dare we speculate that extraterrestrials will be subscribers?

Notes

1. Over 50 percent of readers had some college education, 71 percent were married, median income was over $30,000, 79 percent were homeowners, highest index of audience penetration with over $20,000 income and in the professional and managerial ranks.

2. Eliza A. Youmans, "Sketch of Edward L. Youmans by His Sister," *Popular Science Monthly,* March 1887, p. 697.

3. "Purpose and Plan of Our Enterprise [Editor's Table]," *Popular Science Monthly,* May 1872, p. 114.

4. "Minor Topics," *New York Times,* 14 May 1872, p. 4.

5. John Shaw Billings, "House-Drainage from Various Points of View," *Popular Science Monthly,* January 1889, pp. 310–24.

6. T. W. Mather, "Flying Machines," *Popular Science Monthly,* November 1885.

7. Frank Luther Mott, "*Popular Science Monthly,* Sketch 24," *A History of American Magazines, 1865–1885* (Cambridge: Harvard University Press, 1938), pp. 495–99.

8. "Youmans, William J.," *Dictionary of American Biography,* vol. 20, pp. 616–17.

9. H. G. Good, "Edward Livingston Youmans, a National Teacher of Science (1821–1887)," *Scientific Monthly,* March 1924, p. 314.

10. Theodore Peterson, *Magazines in the Twentieth Century* (Urbana: University of Illinios Press, 1964), pp. 371–72.

11. Ibid., p. 372.

12. "Waldemar B. Kaempffert," *New York Times,* 29 November 1956, p. 34.

13. Ibid.

14. "Kaempffert, Waldemar Bernhard," *Dictionary of American Biography,* Supplement 6, 1956–1960 (New York: Scribner, 1980).

15. "Hammond, Godfrey," *Current Biography* (New York: Wilson, 1953), pp. 243–44.

16. "Godfrey Hammond, 77, Is Dead; Was Head of *Popular Science,*" *New York Times,* 20 August 1969.

17. "Hammond, Godfrey," *Current Biography,* p. 244.

18. Peterson, p. 372.

19. *1983 Annual Report*. New York: Times Mirror.

20. Israel Shenker, "Popular Science, at 100, Still Advises: Do It Yourself," *New York Times*, 25 April 1972, p. 1.

21. Ron Kolgraf and Lisa D. Loring, "What the Science/Technology Books Have to Offer," *Magazine Age*, February 1982, p. 52.

22. *Simmons 1984 Study of Media and Markets*.

23. H. G. Good, "Edward Livingston Youmans, a National Teacher of Science (1821–1887)," *Scientific Monthly*, March 1924, p. 317.

24. Ibid.

Information Sources

BIBLIOGRAPHY

"Capen, Oliver Bronson." *National Cyclopaedia of American Biography*. vol. 42, New York: J. T. White, 1958, p. 335.

"Cattell, James McKeen." *Dictionary of American Biography*. Supplement 3, 1941–1945. New York: Scribner, 1973, pp. 148–51.

"Cattell, James McKeen." *Dictionary of Scientific Biography*. vol. 3. New York: Scribner, 1971, pp. 130–31.

"Creeping War" Time, 17 May 1948, p. 71. Devers, Charlotte M., Doris B. Katz and Mary Margaret Regan. *Guide to Special Issues and Indexes of Periodicals*. 2nd ed. New York: Special Libraries Association, 1976.

"Eugene S. Duffield . . . " *New York Times,* 22 September 1974, p. 57.

Fiske, John. "Edward Livingston Youmans: The Man and his Work." *Popular Science Monthly*, May 1890, pp. 1–18.

Flint, Peter B. "Sumner N. Blossom; Former Editor Ran Publishing Concern." *New York Times Biographical Service*, March 1977.

"For Men Only" *Time,* 12 May 1947, p. 83.

Ford, James L. C. *Magazines for Millions: The Story of Specialized Publications*. Carbondale: Southern Illinois University Press, 1969.

"Godfrey Hammond, 77, Is Dead; Was Head of *Popular Science*," *New York Times*, 20 August 1969.

Good, H. G. "Edward Livingston Youmans, a National Teacher of Science (1821–1887)." *Scientific Monthly*, March 1924, pp. 306–17.

"Hammond, Godfrey." *Current Biography*. New York: Wilson, 1953, pp. 243–44.

Hart, Jack R. *The Information Empire: The Rise of the Los Angeles Times and the Times Mirror Corporation*. Washington, D.C.: University Press of America, 1981.

Heyn, Ernest V., et al. *A Century of Wonders: 100 Years of Popular Science*. Garden City, N.Y. Doubleday, 1972.

Heyn, Ernest V., et al. *Fire of Genius: Inventors of the Past Century, Based on the Files of "Popular Science Monthly" since its Founding in 1872*. Garden City, N.Y. Doubleday, 1976.

"Kaempffert, Waldemar Bernhard." *Dictionary of American Biography*. Supplement 6, 1956–1960. New York: Scribner, 1980.

Kolgraf, Ron, and Lisa D. Loring. "What the Science/Technology Books Have to Offer." *Magazine Age*, February 1982, pp. 46–55.

"Ladies Home Journal Adds Publisher Title." *New York Times*, 22 November 1967, p. 65.

Mecklin, John M. "Times Mirror's Ambitious Acquirers." *Fortune*, 1 September, 1968.

"Minor Topics," *New York Times*, 14 May 1872, p. 4.

Mott, Frank Luther. "*Popular Science Monthly*, Sketch 24." In *A History of American Magazines, 1865–1885*. Cambridge: Harvard University Press, 1938, pp. 495–99.

Newman, Louise Michele, ed. *Men's Ideas/Women's Realities: "Popular Science," 1870–1915*. New York: Pergamon Press, 1985.

Peterson, Theodore. *Magazines in the Twentieth Century*. Urbana: University of Illinois Press, 1964.

"PSM's 75th." *Newsweek*, 5 May 1947, pp. 66–67.

"Robert P. Crossley Dead at 58; Ex-Editor of *Popular Mechanics*." *New York Times Biographical Edition*. February 1972.

Shenker, Israel. "Popular Science, at 100, Still Advises: Do It Yourself." *New York Times*, 25 April 1972, p. 25.

Simmons 1984 Study of Media and Markets.

Taft, William H. *American Magazines for the 1980's*. New York: Hastings House, 1982.

Tebbel, John. *The American Magazine: A Compact History*. New York: Hawthorne Books, 1969.

"Times Mirror Co. and Popular Science." *New York Times*, 28 February 1967, p. 49.

"Times Mirror Wakes Up with a Throbbing Hangover." *Business Week*, 4 November 1985, pp. 64–68.

Treaster, Joseph B. "Howard G. Allaway, Former Journalist." *New York Times Biographical Service*. August 1980.

"Waldemar B. Kaempffert." *New York Times*, 29 November 1956, p. 34.

"Waldemar B. Kaempffert Dies." *New York Times* 28 November 1956, p. 35. Science Editor of the *Times*, 79."

Who Was Who in America.

Who's Who in America.

Wolseley, Roland E. *Understanding Magazines*. 2nd ed. Ames: Iowa State University, 1969.

"Youmans, Edward Livingston." *Dictionary of American Biography*. vol. 20. New York: Scribner, 1936, pp. 615–16.

Youmans, Eliza A. "Sketch of Edward L. Youmans by His Sister." *Popular Science Monthly*, March 1887, pp. 688–97.

"Youmans, William J." *Dictionary of American Biography*. vol. 20, New York: Scribner, 1936, pp. 616–17.

INDEX SOURCES

Poole's, (1872–1906) *Reader's Guide* (1900–present; no coverage: October 1915–December 1930), *Abridged Readers' Guide, Consumers Index, Acid Rain Abstracts, Acid Rain Annual Index, Bibliography and Index of Geology, Guidelines, Index of How To Do It Information, Magazine Index, Popular Magazine Review, Subject Index to Children's Magazines* (Children's Magazine Guide). Some volumes have semiannual or annual editorial index: subject/author. Home Workshop was indexed separately in the 1920s. Separately published indexes to vols. 1–20, 1872–1882, by title; vols. 1–40, 1872–1892, with index to supplements 1–20, by subject-title; author. Engineering Index (1884–1891, 1896–1914). (Note: *Readers' Guide* considered *Scientific Monthly* to be the continuation of *Popular Science Monthly* in 1915, and therefore did not index the "new" *Popular*

Science Monthly after October 1915. *Readers' Guide* resumed indexing of *Popular Science Monthly* with vol. 118, January. 1931.)

LOCATION SOURCES

Library of Congress, many public and academic libraries. On line availability–Dialog. Available in microform.

Publication History

MAGAZINE TITLE AND TITLE CHANGES

Popular Science Monthly, 1872–1895; 1900–1915; 1916–1969; *Appleton's Popular Science Monthly,* 1895–1900; *Popular Science Monthly and World's Advance,* October-December 1915; *Popular Science: The What's New Magazine,* 1969–present.

VOLUME AND ISSUE DATA

Vols. 1–234, May 1872–present, monthly vols. 1–66, 1872–1905, semiannual volumes beginning May and November. Vol. 67 had 8 issues, May-December 1905; vol. 68–   , 1906–   , regular semiannual volumes. There was no November issue in 1919 due to *Popular Science Monthly's* honoring of a printer's strike in New York. December 1919 and January 1920 were printed in Chicago.

After the 1915 merger with *World's Advance* the numbering of *Popular Science Monthly* was continued and *World's Advance* dropped.

SPECIAL ISSUES

Supplements 1–20, May 1877–December 1878; new issue, no. 1 (February 1879); issued separately with index.

Contemporary (1970s–): Car imports buyer's guide (February); Outdoor power equipment (March); Outdoor recreation (March); Home heating (October); Consumer electronics (November); Home improvement hardware (May, September, October).

TITLES ABSORBED

Sanitarian, July 1904; *World's Advance,* October 1915; *Mechanics and Handicraft,* February 1939. *World's Advance* was itself formerly titled *Modern Mechanics* and was a consolidation of *Popular Electricity and the World's Advance, Modern Electrics and Mechanics,* and *Electrician and Mechanic.*

PUBLISHERS AND PLACE OF PUBLICATION

D. Appleton and Company, 1872–1900.

McClure, Phillips and Company, 1900–1901.

Science Press, 1901–1915.

Modern Publishing Company, 1915–1924, H. J. Fisher, president.

Popular Science Publishing Company 1924–1967; H. J. Fisher (1924), Oliver B. Capen (1924–1930), A. L. Cole (1930–1939), Godfrey Hammond (1939–1957; 1959), Ralph H. Flynn (1957–1959), Eugene S. Duffield (1959–1962), John R. Whiting (1962–1967).

Popular Science Publishing Company as a subsidiary of Times Mirror Company, 1967–1973: J. Michael Hadley, 1968–1973.

Times Mirror Company, 1973–present: J. Michael Hadley (1973–1974), Edward F. Hagerty, Jr. (1974–1975), J. Michael Hadley (1975–1977), F. X. Wilkinson (1977–1981), Terence E. Moyes (1982–1986), Grant A. Burnett (1986–1989; John B. Crawley (1989–present). New York, New York.

NB: Prior to Godfrey Hammond, persons listed were president of the publishing company. Hammond was the first person to be listed as "publisher" in 1945.

EDITORS

Edward L. Youmans, 1872–1877; Edward L. Youmans and William J. Youmans, 1877–1887; William J. Youmans, 1887–1900; J. McKeen Cattell, 1900–1915; Waldemar Kaempffert, 1915–1920; Kenneth W. Payne, 1921–1922; Sumner N. Blossom, 1922–1929; Travis Hoke, 1929–1930; Raymond J. Brown, 1930–1940; Charles McLendon, 1941–1945; Perry Githens, 1945–1951; Volta Torrey, 1951–1956; Howard Allaway, 1956–1962; Robert P. Crossley, 1962–1964; Ernest V. Heyn, 1965–1971; Hubert P. Luckett, 1971–1980; C. P. Gilmore, 1980–present.

CIRCULATION

2,000,000 paid.

Priscilla Matthews

PREVENTION MAGAZINE

Jerome Irving Rodale envisioned a nation of people close to the natural world, healthy in body and mind through their investment in organic, unrefined foods. Rodale began publishing magazines in the 1930s to present his philosophy of life to the public. After several unsuccessful publications, all health related, he began issuing *Organic Gardening and Farming** in 1942 to advocate organic farming research. The next venture was *Prevention*, first issued in June 1950; it became most successful of all the Rodale publications and a model for other magazines and newsletters. *Executive Fitness, Body Bulletin, Women's Health, Bicycling, New Farm,* and *New Shelter* are among the Rodale publications stressing self-sufficiency and healthy living. Rodale's book division publishes thirty-five to forty-five new titles annually, and a cable television series, "Home Dynamics," began in 1981.

Rodale Press was founded in 1953, although it actually started in the 1930s when the depression forced Rodale to move his business, an electrical parts company, from New York City to Emmaus, Pennsylvania. Until interest in nutrition and natural living became widespread enough to make Rodale profitable, revenue from the electrical parts company, Lutron Electronics, kept the press alive.

The United States was not quick to grasp the relevance of Rodale's philosophy. The 1950s witnessed the rapid growth of the supermarket and the concept of a national brand, consistent in quality and packaging. Modern conveniences were the trend, not the sometimes painstaking and unreliable labor required to grow food at home. Moreover, population was shifting toward the city where space was limited for gardening. Rodale's controversial ideas alienated the supermarket shoppers and those caught up in the changing times. Many people did agree with him, however, and his audience increased until the competition was so great that supermarket managers realized that they must accommodate the need or lose customers. Rodale's patrons sought wholesome, unrefined foods and vitamin supplements for their diet.

Vitamins and commercially grown organic foods were available only through *Prevention* in the 1950s and only those who read the magazine knew about them and where to get them. Although they are now widely available, vitamins have remained the most heavily advertised products in the magazine. "You talk about gravy train for an ad manager!" said Marshall Ackerman, Rodale Press vice-president.[1] "We were making all that money running one hundred pages every month from seven advertisers. They don't make'em like that anymore!"

Circulation increased dramatically in the late 1960s, indicating a trend toward health foods and exercise. In the early 1970s, stores dedicated to selling only organically grown and unrefined foods sprang up in major cities across the United States and maintain a sizable portion of the market today. The *New York Times* reported in 1974 that the health food industry was prospering, despite soaring prices.[2] The article attributed the industry's success to the middle-class consumers' growing suspicions about major food producers and the consumers' willingness to pay higher prices for what they consider purer and more nutritious food.

Prevention's circulation increased chiefly by word of mouth. The classified advertising section of the early issues called for the "Friends of *Prevention*" to send free subscription booklets describing the magazine and its philosophy to their friends and acquaintances. In return, they received liberal commissions for subscriptions resulting from their efforts. Coded coupons in the booklets could trace each subscription to the individual Friend.[3]

It wasn't until 1980 that circulation figures were certified by the Audit Bureau of Circulations (ABC). In 1976, however, *Prevention* first advertised its circulation at "more than 1.5 million." When ABC certified 1980 circulation at 2.4 million, *Prevention* officially became the largest of Rodale's publications. Revenues jumped from $7.7 million in 1970 to $65 million in 1980, making *Prevention* the nineteenth largest monthly magazine and the second fastest growing. The company then hired Carl Byoir and Associates, a public relations firm, to promote the magazine's image and increase circulation.[4] A campaign to attract new advertisers began. By 1984, circulation was up to 3 million, and revenues were reported at $119 million, a level that *Prevention* has maintained for four years.

While advertising revenues certainly keep mass magazines alive, readership contributes just as significantly to a magazine's life span. *Prevention*'s advertising policies caused some very difficult times with advertisers, and had it not been for a loyal audience, the magazine might very well have ceased. The readership has remained distinct, providing advertisers with a clear sense of who is receiving their messages and, perhaps more important, establishing an involvement with the readers and a sense of identity. This approach to the readers and advertisers has made *Prevention* prominent among the mass-market magazines. No other magazine has been able to successfully duplicate *Prevention*.

From the content of articles and advertisements, readers can be described as active, over thirty-five, self-reliant people concerned with living life to the fullest. While it once had the reputation as material for everyone's eccentric grandparent, and the median age of subscribers in 1980 was reported at 54.7,[5] *Prevention*'s readership has grown younger. From its inception, the majority of subscribers, approximately 65 percent, have been women, most of whom are married.[6]

The relationship between the Rodale Press and advertisers has always been strained, perhaps stemming from J. I. Rodale's controversial opinions on health and food. He refused to accept ads for anything he considered harmful to health, a list including such products as tobacco, alcohol, sugary snacks, sleeping pills, laxatives, painkillers, reducing aids, anything with artificial flavoring or preservatives, processed foods, and insecticides. Rodale also rejected ads from companies that had an inferior customer service record and that promised more than they could deliver.[7]

Prospective advertisers still receive a twenty-five-page manual outlining maximum potencies and acceptable sources of ingredients for food supplements, advertising copy standards, acceptable selling methods, and packaging. Before the Food and Drug Administration required ingredients to be printed on product labels, *Prevention* had its advertisers list the ingredients in their advertising. Vitamin advertisers must use natural food rather than synthetic sources and must submit laboratory test reports. *Prevention* constantly spot-checks these products through independent laboratory analyses.[8] Maximum dosage limits must be followed since it is expected that supplemental food will be taken with the vitamins. Copy must be preventive rather than curative in nature. Rodale reserves the right to refuse any advertising without giving a reason.[9] Such strict standards annoy Madison Avenue.

For the first decade, *Prevention* accepted no display advertising, only classified ads. Some early advertisements were for "Sunflower Seed—the Miracle Food," meal flour, sweet corn, maple syrup, bed and breakfast inns with vegetarian meals, wheat, and wild berries.

Rodale's son, Robert, became publisher of *Prevention* and the president of Rodale Press in 1971 when J. I. died at the age of seventy-two. Robert has upheld his father's standards to a degree. When readership began to level off in 1980, more revenue was sought from advertising.[10] Public relations initiated an active campaign to attract more advertisers. *Prevention* was promoted in *Advertising Age*, the *Wall Street Journal*, and the *New York Times*. Public relations courted Madison Avenue with direct mail advertising and slide presentations. Chevrolet, Briggs and Stratton, Hunt-Wesson Foods, and Johnson and Johnson were some of the first major accounts to place ads in 1980.[11]

Advertising is now more varied and is aimed at a mixed readership in a wide age range. Ads are for hose, condoms, skin care products for the old and young, contour chairs, exercise aids, books, pet foods, hypoallergenic earrings, cotton clothing, health and information organizations as well as the faithful vitamins and health foods. Ads are now accepted for Lipton products, egg substitutes, laxatives, and pain relievers. Many of the large food companies have changed their production standards because of the health and fitness movement, and today it is a common marketing strategy to advertise the nutritional aspects of a food product.

In 1984, *Prevention* made another major change by adding glossy paper stock and more color. Advertising revenues had again started to decline from previous years, unusual because the magazine industry overall was achieving record results.[12] While it may have fluctuated slightly in some years, 40 per cent of the magazine's total revenues since 1980 have come from advertising and approximately 40 per cent of each issue is advertising.[13] This is another key to *Prevention*'s success: watching the trends, keeping up with or ahead of them, maintaining a philosophy, and communicating unique information in a distinctive format.

Prevention was best known for its economical, rough-hewn groundwood pages, which were meant to express an unpretentious, "just folks," common-sense personality. Although the new paper stock and color changed the look of the magazine, the format and information remained the same. Each issue is an easy to manage size, 6″ x 9″, and takes material from more than 800 medical and health journals to produce fifteen to twenty succinct articles on nutrition and health, set off by cooking advice and testimonials about spectacular cures through mind control or diet.[14]

For years a column called J. I. Rodale Said It ran quotations from early *Prevention* issues that characterized the concepts on which the magazine was based. A representative excerpt from this column is dated April 1954: "We must question every generally accepted health tenet or dogma, as rooted as it may be in the public's mind. You must observe the effect on your own bodily processes of your basic daily actions. Make your own interpretations." Rodale was a man of great vision and fairness, living the philosophy he extolled in his personal life as well as in his professional life. No vending machines or junk food outlets can be found on the Rodale premises. Instead, there are low-cost, high-quality dining rooms supplied by the company food center. The company sponsors a fitness program for all employees and in 1984 completed Energy Center, the company health club. The offices of Rodale have won many awards for the design and efficient use of space, and the decorative arts and crafts. J. I. Rodale established the "human attitude" that customers and employees should be treated like individuals, not demographic variables or dollar signs. The result of such a simple, direct, and honest approach is a happy, cooperative, and enthusiastic environment. Robert Rodale carries on these principles as successfully as his father did. The 950 staff members are given the independence to get things done quickly and move their projects ahead. Everyone is involved in decision making and has a sense of autonomy.[15]

Jerome Irving Rodale's life was not limited to the Rodale Press or the Rodale Corporation or the interests they represent. He also founded the Rodale Theater and Rodale Saturday Night Showcase Theater, both in New York City. He wrote plays ranging from children's musical comedy to serious drama, several of which were successfully produced on and off Broadway. He published books on health, but he also published several crossword puzzle dictionaries, *The Synonym Finder*, glossaries, books on strengthening the memory, *Encyclopedia of Common Diseases*, and novels.[16] He lived his vision as one who was close to the natural world, who was close to himself, and who was healthy in body and mind. His company epitomizes special-interest publishing in that its editorial message is essentially inseparable from its corporate makeup.

Notes

1. Marshall Ackerman in Stuart Elliott, "Rodale Press Getting in Shape for the 80's," *Advertising Age*, 24 December 1984, p. 4.

2. Anne Colamosca, "Health Foods Prosper, Despite Soaring Prices," *New York Times*, 17 November 1974, Sec. 3, p. 3.

3. This information comes from the inside backcover page of early issues of *Prevention Magazine*, for example the August 1950 issue. Gradually, the "Friends of Prevention" campaign was phased out.

4. Bernice Kramer. "Rodale Patiently Waiting for the World to Catch Up with It," *Advertising Age*, 21 July 1980, p. 64.

5. "Rodale Reaches Out for the Mainstream," *Business Week*, 27 October 1980, p. 85.

6. Ibid.

7. Ibid.

8. Rodale shared his philosophy and business practice techniques in editorial columns in each issue. The information here is mentioned in several such columns.

9. Elliott, p. 4.

10. Kramer, p. 64.

11. Ibid.

12. Ibid.

13. Elliott, p. 4.

14. "Rodale Reaches Out for the Mainstream," p. 85.

15. Elliott, p. 4.

16. "Jerome Irving Rodale," *Who Was Who in America,* vol. 5 (1969–73), p. 615.

Information Sources

BIBLIOGRAPHY

Colamosca, Anne. "Health Foods Prosper, Despite Soaring Prices." *New York Times*, 17 November 1974, sec. 3, p. 3.

Elliott, Stuart. "Rodale Press Getting in Shape for the 80's." *Advertising Age*, 24 December 1984, p. 4.

English, Mary McCabe. "A Word Factory Runs Its Message to the People: Rodale's Down-home Tough Belies Its Profitability." *Advertising Age*, 26 March 1984, pp. M32–M33.

Greene, Wade. "Guru of the Organic Food Cult." *New York Times Magazine*, 6 June 1971, p. 30.

Kramer, Bernice. "Rodale Patiently Waiting for the World to Catch Up with It." *Advertising Age*, 21 July 1980, p. 64.

Macmillan Directory of Leading Private Companies. 3rd ed. Wilmette, Ill.: National Register Publishing Company, 1988.

"*Prevention* Enjoys Good Health." *Madison Avenue*, December 1983, p. 84.

"Rodale Reaches Out for the Mainstream." *Business Week*, 27 October 1980, p. 85.

Writer's Market. Cincinnati: Writer's Digest Books, 1970, p. 76. Kirk Polking and Gloria Emison, editors.
INDEX SOURCES
> *Magazine Index* (1977–present); *New Periodicals Index* (1978–present); *Popular Periodical Index* (1981–present); *Readers' Guide* (1984–present).

LOCATION SOURCES
> Available in microform, 1972–present.

Publication History

MAGAZINE TITLE AND TITLE CHANGES
> *Prevention*, 1950–present.

VOLUME AND ISSUE DATA
> Vols. 1–41, June 1950–1989 (current), monthly.

PUBLISHER AND PLACE OF PUBLICATION
> Rodale Press, Inc., part of Rodale, Inc.: J. I. Rodale, 1950–1971; Robert Rodale, 1971–present. Emmaus, Pennsylvania.

EDITORS
> J. I. Rodale, 1950–1971; Robert Rodale, 1971–1988; Mark Bricklin, 1988–present.

CIRCULATION
> 2,800,000.

Patricia Palmer

PSYCHOLOGY TODAY

During the years from 1960 to 1970, mass-market magazine publishing continued to flourish in the United States in spite of the competition provided by television. Although 162 of the periodicals in existence at the time disappeared through various means (sale, merger, discontinuance), 676 new magazines appeared in the 1960s.[1] Particularly successful at this time were periodicals directed at a specialized audience and those capable of "delivering to advertisers a specific market that could not be reached specifically by any other medium."[2] One such publication, started in 1967, was directed toward a small, college-educated audience. Few predicted that *Psychology Today* would quickly become one of the nation's most successful products of the consumer magazine industry of the 1960s.

The three primary participants in the early history of *Psychology Today* were Nicolas H. Charney, John J. Veronis, and T. George Harris. Each was to make a unique contribution to the development of the magazine.

Psychology Today was begun by Nicolas Herman Charney (then aged twenty-seven) and published by C/R/M (Communications/Research/Machines), the corporation he founded in Del Mar, California, in 1967. Charney (1941–   ) received his bachelor of arts degree from the Massachusetts Institute of Technology and in 1966 a doctoral degree in biopsychology from the University of Chicago.[3] One year later he went to the small resort village of Del Mar (eighteen miles north of San Diego) with $40,000 to invest.[4] He had a strong desire to "put out a magazine, a sort of *Scientific American* of the social sciences."[5] According to Charney, "There is psychology behind all acts—eating, going to bed, and so on . . . people are curious about these things."[6] Charney's desire was to bring psychology, a discipline becoming popular, to the general public. Since 1977 he has been founder—chairman of the board of Videofashion, after owning *Saturday Review** (1971–1973), publishing *Book Digest* (1973–1975), and founding Access Communications (1976–   ).

Time-honored methods of magazine publishing were set aside by the Charney organization: a motley group of storefronts sufficed for headquarters; the dress code for the staff of five consisted of long hair and jeans; very liberal flextime was instituted. Charney raised $250,000 from friends and, within four months, sent the first issue of *Psychology Today* to the newsstands.[7]

Closely associated with Charney in his C/R/M publication venture was co-founder John James Veronis (1923–   ), who from age twenty had a succession of publishing positions: advertising director for *Popular Science,** publisher of a variety of consumer magazines including *American Home, Field and Stream, Ladies' Home Journal*, and, most recently, president of Curtis Publications' large magazine division.[8] Veronis was in charge of C/R/M's finances. He raised much additional money to keep the financially strapped corporation solvent. Veronis and Charney subsequently moved to other business ventures including ownership of *Saturday Review* in 1971.[9] In 1979 Veronis was president of *Book Digest*, a monthly condensation of best-sellers he founded after leaving *Saturday Review*.[10] Most recently he has been president of JJV Publishing Company and chairman of Veronis Suhler and Associates, investment bankers to communications, entertainment, and information industries (1981–   ).[11]

In 1968, Charney hired T. George Harris as editor of *Psychology Today*. Harris (1924–   ) received a bachelor of arts degree from Yale in 1949, and had served with *Time** magazine as correspondent and Midwest bureau chief, as well as senior editor of *Look** magazine from 1961 to 1968.[12] Among other recognitions, Harris was named Outstanding Young Man of Chicago in 1955, received a University of Kentucky Hall of Fame Award, and was a recipient of a prize for magazine journalism from the University of Missouri.[13] Although Harris had been originally hired by C/R/M to edit *Careers Today*, a periodical that folded after only four issues, he stayed with *Psychology Today* until 1976. After serving as editor of a variety of other magazines, since 1981 he has been the first editor, then editor-in-chief, and now chairman of *American Health Magazine*.[14]

From the beginning *Psychology Today* was a success. The publication was colorful and slick, with diagrams, pictures, and charts to accompany the articles. Excellent photography added to the attractive format. Professional psychologists and psychiatrists (rather than journalists) of national and international repute contributed most of the articles; however, they were strongly encouraged to make their research readable to the average nonscience reader. One editor, Jim Petersen, aged twenty three, was assigned the task of making famous scientists' writings intelligible to the educated masses.[15] All Latin words were edited out; the passive voice was changed to active; "heavier editing and a complicated ritual exchange of phone calls and letters [ensued] as the editor tried to convince the timid scholar that the brightened, clarified version [would] not damage his professional standing."[16] Each issue contained about six articles and, usually, an interview with an important scholar in the field. Both topics of current interest and those of perennial interest were included. A list of further readings accompanied most entries.

Critical comments on the new periodical were almost uniformly favorable. To sum up early sentiment Gregory A. Kimble states, "*Psychology Today* presented psychology as scientific, intelligent, idealistic, and relevant. It treated psychology with interest, respect, and enthusiasm, everything that the public and the discipline could want. Even for psychologists who were uncomfortable with the notion of popularizing psychology, the magazine was hard to resist . . . it did a spectacular job of presenting the best of psychology to the public."[17] John Tebbel, in his *The American Magazine* published in 1969, referred to the periodical as being "already highly successful."[18] Another 1969 review, although noting that the "authority of the articles is too often obscured by ponderous writing," describes the art and photography of *Psychology Today* as being "rich with color and imagination, providing a provocative—almost psychedelic—accompaniment to the text."[19] *Newsweek* writes, "By pop-translating some of the world's finest scientific minds and framing their work in eye-popping graphics, *Psychology Today* has almost overnight become one of the nation's most controversial and successful magazines . . . the *New York Times* quotes it, professors argue about it, and lots of people read it."[20] Evan Ira Farber calls it "a well-edited, attractive, reliable periodical that should be in every library and will almost certainly be used heavily."[21]

By 1971 circulation had reached 520,000 (close to that of *Harper's** and the *Atlantic Monthly** combined); ad revenue was up an astounding 143 percent in 1970, and *Psychology Today* was expected to have a $1 million profit in 1971.[22]

In 1970 Charney sold C/R/M Publications to Boise-Cascade, a large land development and wood products corporation. The selling price was $21.3 million, making *Psychology Today*'s founders rich men.[23] *Psychology Today* was sold for a second time in 1973. The purchaser was a large publisher of consumer magazines in the United States, the Ziff-Davis Publishing Company of New

York.[24] Ziff-Davis was to keep the magazine for the next decade. The American Psychological Association acquired *Psychology Today* in 1983.

In the late 1970s the quality of the magazine began to decline in several ways: (1) articles began to focus more frequently on the sensational aspects of human behavior, for example, nudity, ESP, and parapsychology; (2) the magazine had to resort to discount prices and became less profitable for Ziff-Davis; (3) paper quality was lowered; (4) editorial quality declined; (5) by 1982, *Psychology Today* had the second highest loss of advertising pages of the top 100 magazines in the United States[25] and (6) the staff was changed and reduced. One such staff change was the 1976 firing of editor Harris. Harris had been with *Psychology Today* since 1968 and had helped turn the publication into the highly profitable product ($2 million a year in net profits) that Ziff-Davis had acquired in 1973.[26] Ziff-Davis was owned by William Ziff and was run by twenty-six vice-presidents. Harris's laid-back style (reminiscent of the low-key California days), his editorial disputes, and his moving in of a Ping-Pong table into the editorial offices prompted Ziff to state, "We have created the ultimate sweatshop, one where we have eliminated the difference between work and play."[27] Harris was fired three years after Ziff-Davis bought the company that Harris had been with for eight years.

In spite of the challenges created by the ownership transition, a 1974 reader survey conducted by *Psychology Today* gave the magazine a good report card. More than 8,000 readers replied, and most were generally satisfied with the magazine. Adjectives most frequently chosen to describe the magazine were "interesting, important, responsible, useful, and good."[28] Its greatest fans were female readers; readers under age twenty-four gave *Psychology Today* slightly higher ratings than respondents in other age groups. As for educational level, the "appeal of *PT* cut across all educational levels . . . years of schooling bore no relation on any of the scales relating to the magazine's appeal."[29]

In a desperate effort to save the magazine, Ziff-Davis instituted several changes in the magazine in 1982. Nicolas Charney was brought back as editor-in-chief. The layout of the magazine was redesigned into two parts—the feature section, which contained the longer articles, and a new section called Crosstalk, which was "a magnet for information leakage—an international bulletin board on which you can find facts, ideas, opinions, and even humor."[30] The content was expanded—"especially into four areas—biology, high technology, the market-place, and people."[31] The use of computers was introduced in 1982, but a Crosstalk column notes that "most of *Psychology Today* is still written and edited with those formidable forerunners of the computer—the typewriter and the pencil."[32]

In 1983 the American Psychological Association (APA) heard rumors concerning the possible sale of *Psychology Today*. The APA, with headquarters in Washington, D.C., is a 58,000-member group founded in 1892.[33] It is a scientific and professional society of psychologists whose goals are "the advancement of psychology as a science, as a profession, and as a means of promoting human welfare.''[34] Although it has published over two dozen professional journals for many years, the association had considered publishing a magazine for the general public since 1941.[35]

The following information is taken from an account of the transactions leading up to, including, and following the acquisition of *Psychology Today* by APA from Ziff-Davis. The account was written by psychologist Gregory A. Kimble, who currently is professor emeritus of psychology at Duke University. Kimble, author of many texts in psychology, such as the frequently reprinted *Principles of General Psychology, Psychology and Learning*, and *How to Use (and Misuse) Statistics*, played an integral role in the proceedings, and has held many positions within APA.[36] His report is ''part history, part personal journal, and part white paper,'' and is based primarily on archival material of the APA.[37]

APA's main goal in publishing a popular magazine was to communicate psychology to the public, that is, to improve the public's understanding of the discipline. Since 1975 various attempts were made to launch a new magazine including a supplement to the existing *Monitor* and a trial issue of *Psychology* in 1977.[38] However, it was not until mid–1982 that APA's involvement with a popular magazine was to come to fruition. After hearing that *Psychology Today* might be for sale, APA went ahead with negotiations with great secrecy and with some dissension among members of the board. On 18 February 1983, APA bought the magazine for $3.8 million. (However, by the end of 1986 the APA had invested $12.3 million).[39] Members were notified of the purchase, and in the May 1983 issue of *Psychology Today*, President Max Siegel announced the ''Marriage'' of *Psychology Today* and the APA.[40]

A *Psychology Today* committee, chaired by Kimble, was appointed to oversee the transition and management of the magazine.[41] The transition was not smooth, as many problems arose that caused strife within APA. These problems centered around (1) the lack of money; (2) questions concerning who was actually in charge; (3) the shortage of advertising sales; (4) the weakness of the editorial content; (5) the managerial relationship between the magazine and the organization; and (6) the location of the staff—New York or Washington.[42] To partially deal with some of the financial problems, *Psychology Today* became a benefit of membership by allocating $8 of membership dues to the *Psychology Today* budget.[43]

According to Kimble, the quality of the magazine has improved since its acquisition by the APA. Editorial content is now found in four places: features, essays, Crosstalk, and book reviews. Charney was dismissed in an effort ''to get California hot-tub psychology out of the magazine and real psychology back in.''[44] Fewer opinion pieces are included, and more reader involvement is present. More stories are now by members of the research-academic community rather than by journalists.[45]

Advertising sales are currently up from the last Ziff-Davis days, although there are some problems such as the kinds of ads (that is, tobacco products and alcoholic beverages and an assortment of self-help cure-alls) that should appear in the magazine. Kimble believes that *Psychology Today* must rely on the demographic characteristics of its readers (young, affluent, well educated, and about 55 percent female)[46] to attract appropriate sponsors. Circulation is steady. Optimal circulation appears to be between 850,000 and 1,000,000 copies.[47]

Bill and Linda Sternberg Katz, in the fifth edition of their *Magazines for Libraries*, describes *Psychology Today* as "clearly written" and "the single best source of information in the field of social science available to the general public [that] attempts to achieve its goal of increasing our understanding of human behavior, albeit in a popular way."[48] Carl White writes, "It will probably provide broader coverage of the entire discipline of psychology in future years—but with the intended audience remaining the general public."[49] One indication of *Psychology Today*'s important and unique place in the field of psychology is in D. H. Borchardt and R. D. Francis's *How to Find Out in Psychology*.[50] The authors present a table showing a typology of journals "designed to draw the reader's attention to function and usage."[51] A single title under the category "Journal/magazine" appears: *Psychology Today*. An accompanying note explains that this is the only general journal/magazine of its type.[52]

The next chapter in the future of *Psychology Today* was revealed in the *Chronicle of Higher Education*. In the 16 March 1988 issue the *Chronicle* announced that the American Psychological Association had decided to sell *Psychology Today*. The sale was scheduled for 1 May 1988 to Owen J. Lipstein and T. George Harris, co-owners of *American Health* magazine. Lipstein is also the owner of *Mother Earth News*,* and Harris was the first editor of *Psychology Today*.[53] A telephone call to the office of American Psychological Association executive vice-president and chief executive officer Leonard D. Goodstein on 20 June 1988 confirmed that the sale did occur as scheduled on 1 May 1988.

During an 8 August 1989 telephone conversation with editor-in-chief T. George Harris, the author learned of a number of significant events and changes in *Psychology Today*. Mr. Harris indicated that he and Mr. Lipstein actually purchased the assets of *Psychology Today* on 12 May 1988, with Mr. Lipstein owning two-thirds of the assets, and Mr. Harris owning one-third. The new ownership company name is PT Partners L.P. Mr. Harris became editor-in-chief upon purchase, with Wray Herbert continuing as editor. In October 1988 the central office for the magazine was moved to 80 5th Avenue, New York, New York, with the Washington, D.C. office continuing until 15 December 1988. Wray Herbert now has the role of Washington, D.C. office editor. In the March 1989 issue of *Psychology Today* Ms. Julia Kagan is indicated as the new editor. One publication change under the Harris/Lipstein management has been to reduce the number of issues to ten per year by dropping the February and August issues. Another major change has been the reinstatement, where appropriate, of professional psychologists as the authors of *Psychology Today* (in contrast to the APA emphasis in which nonpsychologist journalists wrote many of the articles). Owners Harris and Lipstein have introduced a number of foreign-language versions of the publication, with the German and Italian titles currently ongoing.

Finally, Mr. Harris advised that a new subtitle has been added as of the June 1989 issue: *The Magazine of Personal Excellence*.

Notes

1. John Tebbel, *The American Magazine: A Compact History* (New York: Hawthorne Books, 1969), p. 249. From the chapter "Magazines of the Twentieth Century (1905–   )."

2. Ibid., p. 251.

3. *Who's Who in America*, 41st ed. (Chicago: Marquis Who's Who, 1980–1981), p. 598.

4. "Applied Psychology," *Newsweek*, 24 May 1971, p. 59.

5. "Synergistic Scheme of Things," *Time*, 14 February 1969, p. 65.

6. Ibid.

7. Ibid.

8. "The New Tycoons," *Newsweek*, 26 July 1971, p. 64.

9. Norman Cousins, "Report to the Readers," *Saturday Review*, 31 July 1971, p. 18.

10. "Yesterday's Wunderkinder," *Newsweek*, 25 June 1979, p. 17.

11. *Who's Who in America*, 44th ed. (Chicago: Marquis Who's Who, 1986–87), p. 2859.

12. Ibid., p. 1201.

13. Ibid.

14. Ibid.

15. "Applied Psychology," p. 59.

16. Ibid.

17. Gregory A. Kimble, "The APA-PT Connection." (Unpublished manuscript, April 1987), p. 8. (Received from *Psychology Today* and used with permission of the author.)

18. Tebbel, p. 257.

19. "Synergistic Scheme of Things," p. 65.

20. "Applied Psychology," p. 59.

21. Evan Ira Farber, et al. *Classified List of Periodicals for College Libraries*, 5th ed. revised and enlarged, Westwood, MA: F. N. Faxon Co., 1972, p. 396.

22. "Applied Psychology," p. 59.

23. Ibid.

24. "Psyched Out," *Time*, 17 May 1976, p. 78.

25. Kimble, p. 9.

26. "Psyched Out," p. 78.

27. Ibid.

28. Patrice French, "Is Psychology Today Sweet or Sour?" *Psychology Today*, September 1974, p. 112.

29. Ibid., p. 113.

30. Nicolas Charney, "Editorial," *Psychology Today*, December 1982, p. 5.

31. Ibid.

32. "Magazine Meets Computer," *Psychology Today*, March 1983, p. 88.

33. *Encyclopedia of Associations*, vol. 1, part 1 (Detroit; Gale Research Company, 1988), p. 617.

34. Ibid.
35. Kimble, p. 1.
36. *Who's Who in America*, 44th ed., p. 1524.
37. Kimble, p. i.
38. Ibid., p. 15.
39. Ibid., p. 112.
40. Max Siegel and Michael S. Pallak, "Editorial," *Psychology Today*, May 1983, p. 5.
41. Kimble, p. 48.
42. Ibid., p. 63.
43. Ibid., p. 68.
44. Ibid., p. 94.
45. Ibid., p. 42.
46. Ibid., p. 109.
47. Ibid., p. 104.
48. Bill and Linda Sternberg Katz, *Magazines for Libraries*, 5th ed. (New York: Bowker, 1986), p. 852.
49. Carl White, *Sources of Information in the Social Sciences: A Guide to the Literature*, 3rd ed. (Chicago: American Library Association, 1986), p. 453.
50. D. H. Borchardt and R. D. Francis, *How to Find Out in Psychology* (Oxford, N.Y.: Pergamon Press, 1984), p. 31.
51. Ibid.
52. Ibid.
53. "Association to Sell 'Psychology Today,' " *Chronicle of Higher Education*, 16 March 1988, p. A2.

Information Sources

BIBLIOGRAPHY

"Applied Psychology." *Newsweek*, 24 May 1971, p. 59.
"Association to Sell 'Psychology Today.' " *Chronicle of Higher Education*, 16 March 1988, p. A2.
Borchardt, D. H., and R. D. Francis. *How to Find Out in Psychology*. Oxford, N.Y.: Pergamon Press, 1984, p. 31.
Cousins, Norman. "Report to the Readers." *Saturday Review*, 31 July 1971, p. 17.
Encylopedia of Associations. vol. 1, part 1. Detroit: Gale Research, 1988, p. 617.
Farber, Evan Ira, et al. *Classified List of Periodicals for College Libraries*. 5th ed. rev. and enl. Westwood, Mass.: F. W. Faxon Co., 1972, p. 396.
French, Patrice. "Is Psychology Today Sweet or Sour?" *Psychology Today*, September 1974, p. 112–113.
Katz, Bill, and Linda Sternberg Katz. *Magazines for Libraries*. 5th ed. New York: Bowker, 1986, p. 852.
Kimble, Gregory A. "The APA-PT Connection." Unpublished manuscript, April 1987, pp. i–vii, 1–129. (Received from *Psychology Today* and used with permission of the author.)
"Magazine Meets Computer." *Psychology Today*, March 1983, p. 88.
"The New Tycoons." *Newsweek*, 26 July 1971, p. 64.

"Psyched Out." *Time*, 17 May 1976, p. 78.

Siegel, Max, and Michael S. Pallack. Editorial. *Psychology Today*, May 1983, p. 5.

"Synergistic Scheme of Things." *Time*, 14 February 1969, p. 65.

Tebbel, John. *The American Magazine: A Compact History*. New York: Hawthorne Books, 1969, p. 852.

White, Carl. *Sources of Information in the Social Sciences: A Guide to the Literature*. 3rd ed. Chicago: American Library Association. 1986, p. 453.

Who's Who in America. 41st ed. Chicago: Marquis Who's Who, 1980–81, p. 598.

Who's Who in America. 44th ed. Chicago: Marquis Who's Who, 1986–87, p. 1524, p. 2859.

"Yesterday's Wunderkinder." *Newsweek*, 25 June 1979, p. 17.

INDEX SOURCES

> *Current Contents, Excerpta Medica, Readers' Guide, Social Sciences Citation Index, Social Sciences Index, Abstrax, Book Review Index, Biology Digest, Current Christian Abstracts, Canadian Magazine Index, Current Literature in Family Planning, Exceptional Child Education Resources, Future Survey, Guide to Social Science and Religion in Periodical Literature, Higher Education Current Awareness Bulletin, Magazine Index, Popular Magazine Review, Personnel Literature, Peace Research Abstracts, Sportsearch*. Also available online. Vendor: DIALOG. (*Not* indexed in *Psychological Abstracts*.)

LOCATION SOURCES

> Widely available. Available in microform.

Publication History

MAGAZINE TITLE AND TITLE CHANGES

> *Psychology Today*, 1967–May 1989. *Psychology Today*: The Magazine of Personal Excellence, June 1989–current.

VOLUME AND ISSUE DATA

> Vol. 1, no. 1-vol. 23, no. 6, January 1967–June 1989, continuing. Monthly.

PUBLISHERS AND PLACES OF PUBLICATION

> C/R/M, Inc. (Communications/Research/Machines, Inc.), January 1967–October 1973, Del Mar, California; Ziff-Davis Publishing Company, November 1973–March 1983, New York, New York; American Psychological Association, April 1983–May 12, 1988, Washington, D.C. PT Partners L.P., May 12, 1988–present, New York, NY.

EDITORS

> Founder and editorial director, Nicholas H. Charney, December 1982–December 1983. Editors-in-chief: Nicholas H. Charney, May 1969–August 1971; T. George Harris, July 1972–June 1976; Wesley First, July 1976–December 1976. Executive editor, Howard Munson, March 1979–January 1983. Editors: Nicholas H. Charney, January 1967–April 1969; T. George Harris, May 1969–June 1972; Robert A. Poteete, July 1972–January 1973; David Maxey, February 1973–December 1976; Wesley First, January 1977–May 1977; Jack Nessel, June 1977–August 1982; Douglas Gasner, April 1983–December 1983; Patrice D. Horn, January 1984–December 1987; Wray Herbert, January 1988–February 1989 (March 1989–present: Washington Editor); Julia Kagan, March 1989–present.

CIRCULATION
896,215 mail; 85, 747 counter sales, etc.; 3,507 complimentary copies, etc.

Graham R. Walden

PUTNAM'S MONTHLY

Putnam's Monthly provided its own apologia in an Introductory at the beginning of the first number:

A man buys a Magazine to be amused—to be instructed, if you please, but the lesson must be made amusing. . . . It is because we are confident that neither Greece nor Guinea can offer the American reader a richer variety of instruction and amusement in every kind, than the country whose pulses throb with his, and whose every interest is his own, that this magazine presents itself today. The genius of the old world is affluent; we owe much to it, and we hope to owe more. But we have no less faith in the opulence of our own resources. January 1853, p. 1.

As a monthly, striving for distinction between the daily papers and the quarterly reviews, *Putnam's* placed itself in competition with *Harper's*,* which was notorious for reprinting English serials without permission. Although *Putnam's* never emerged as the victor in this competition and, after each of its three appearances, was forced to merge with another monthly, the distinction—even brilliance—of the new magazine was widely appreciated. William Makepeace Thackerary called the first series of *Putnam's* the "best magazine in the world and better than *Blackwood's*,"[1] and the *New American Cyclopaedia* later characterized the first series as the highest-quality American magazine of its time.[2]

Between its appearance in January 1853 and merger with *Emerson's United States Magazine* in 1857, the first series of *Putnam's* enjoyed both success and notoriety. Its first number sold 20,000 copies and subsequent numbers reached as many as 19,000 copies—the magazine claimed a profit of $14,000 from 1855 to 1857.[3] A steady decline in circulation (to 14,000 in 1857) combined with George Palmer Putnam's discovery in 1855 that a partner had lost company funds on wildcat speculation[4] led to the sale of *Putnam's* to Dix, Edwards, and Company, a publishing firm that failed a year later, and to the eventual merger with *Emerson's*. Revived in 1868 after the pattern of the first series, the second series of *Putnam's* never gained a circulation higher than 15,000, and since this was too few readers to avoid financial loss, George Haven Putnam sold the monthly to *Scribner's*.[5] In 1899, Putnam took over the *Critic*, which had been established eighteen years before by Jeanette and Joseph Gilder, and *Putnam's Monthly and the Critic* appeared. Again, by 1910, Putnam couldn't afford to sustain the monthly's financial losses, and it merged with the *Atlantic Monthly*.* Neither the second nor third series of *Putnam's* attained the sparkle of the first series, which combined the social commentary of George William Curtis, the political salvos of Parke Godwin, and a wealth of the best poems and stories of the time.

While claiming a distinctly American voice, the first series of *Putnam's* often seems to sound a distinctly New York voice. A series called "New York Daguerreotyped" offered a glance at the progress of New York and its architecture, with engravings illustrating the series. Subsequent glances at New York's architecture focused on mercantile New York, the benevolent institutions of New York, New York church architecture, and the educational institutions of New York. A feature begun in 1856, "The World of New York," emphasized this local flavor. One of the monthly's most popular features, satires about the current state of New York high society penned by Curtis, added to the New York tone since the escapades of the Potiphar family (around whom the satires revolved) invited speculation about the actual counterparts to its fictional characters—Mr. Gauche Boosey, Croesus, Gnu, Miss Caroline Pettitoes, and the Potiphars. Beginning in the first number with "Our Best Society" (February 1853, pp. 170–79), Curtis's satires became a strong feature and were later published separately as the *Potiphar Papers*. The buoyant tone of spirited high jinks that Curtis sustained in the Potiphar satires went a long way toward establishing a dominant tone for the new monthly. Frederick S. Cozzens assisted this lightness of tone with his "Sparrowgrass Papers," applying a combination of the comic and picturesque to sketches from rural life. The second number of *Putnam's* (February 1853) featured an article that asserted that Louis XVII, the lost dauphin of France, was living as a missionary to the Indians under the name of Eliazar Williams. An article in the April 1853 number that reviewed the reported death of the dauphin sustained the level of the controversy; the first article's title, "Have We a Bourbon Among Us?," became a catchphrase and indicates the quizzical, good-natured approach *Putnam's* took toward this "controversy." This combination—an apparent editorial stance of detachment, perhaps even amusement, juxtaposed against an author's earnest advocacy of a slightly demented issue— was later repeated when *Putnam's* printed Delia Bacon's initial attack on the authenticity of Shakespeare's authorship of the plays bearing his name (January 1856).

The Curtis-penned satires and daft controversies helped lend the early *Putnam's* a gaiety and brilliance that earned the monthly immediate distinction and recognition; another associate editor, Parke Godwin, contributed from the political side with a series of outraged attacks on President Franklin Pierce. The general political principles espoused by the magazine were those of republicanism; in fact, the first platform of the Republican party (written by Godwin) came mostly from a January 1856 article in *Putnam's*. Godwin's lively style described the "flatulent old hacks, the queasy and prurient old bawds who have so long had control of the old parties" (January 1855). The new president's (Pierce's) cabinet was "beset by as savage a crew of cormorants as ever gathered around a carcass in a desert"; their debates were "in tone, language, and spirit, as vile as the squabblers in a pot-house, or the drunken conversations of a brothel"

(September 1853). By the end of 1856, the political articles had become more radical and Godwin's invective more fierce; *DeBow's** called *Putnam's* the "leading review of the Black Republican party."[6] After the first series of *Putnam's* merged with *Emerson's*, Godwin became a political contributor to the *Atlantic Monthly** (which appeared the month after *Putnam's* disappeared).

With Curtis's social satires; Godwin's political invective; a combination of editorial notes about foreign literature, scientific news, music, and fine arts; and articles about travel, the American West, and European affairs, *Putnam's* first series might be remembered for a sophisticated editorial flair, which skirted the inhibitions of the day by satirizing them. But the monthly earned praise and authoritative status by printing the best American authors of the day and included literary criticism of penetration and intelligence. The authors whose works appear in the first series include Henry Wadsworth Longfellow, James Russell Lowell, Henry David Thoreau, Herman Melville, William Cullen Bryant, and James Fenimore Cooper. Longfellow contributed "The Warden of the Cinque Ports" to the first number; "My Lost Youth" and several lesser known poems appeared later. Lowell's "The Fountain of Youth" was also in the first number; despite the failure of "Our Own: His Wanderings and Personal Adventures," which *Putnam's* discontinued after the third installment, Lowell later contributed "A Moosehead Journal" and "Cambridge Thirty Years Ago." Bryant was represented by "Robert of Lincoln" (June 1855); Cooper's "Old Ironsides" was published posthumously (May 1853; June 1853); and Thoreau's "Excursion to Canada" in 1853 (January 1853; February 1853; March 1853) was followed by "Cape Cod" (June 1855; July 1856; August 1856). Melville was a particular favorite: a *Putnam's* review noted that the magazine "loved its step-son Melville, as if he were her own" (April 1857). *Isreal Potter* was printed in installments in 1854–1855; "Bartleby, the Scrivener" appeared in two installments in November and December of 1853; more than half a dozen of what were to be the *Piazza Tales* also appeared first in *Putnam's*. Arthur Hugh Clough was the only foreign author printed—apparently his short residence in Massachusetts won a place for his two "Letters of Parepidemus."

At the close of the first volume the following note appeared: "Every article that we have published has been paid for at a rate which their writers thought 'liberal,' all have been original, the product of American pens (June 1853, p. 204). The editors considered themselves patrons and benefactors of American writers; indeed, the writers whose work was published still rank among the major writers of American literature. The literary criticism, much of it written by Curtis, Charles A. Dana, and George Ripley during the first years, was also of high quality. An appreciation of Melville, an article about James Russell Lowell, a series about the text of Shakespeare's plays, a piece about characters in *Bleak House*—this sample gives an indication of the range of literary criticism.

The second series of *Putnam's Monthly* presented itself as a renewal of the first series: "The recollection of our former magazine . . . is still fresh in the minds of the public and . . . its reputation has served us in the renewal of the old enterprise in the present work . . . For the future, we have . . . well-stored pigeon holes of accepted articles from authors whom America has ever delighted to honor'' (January 1868, p. iii). The stated general plan of the new series, however, foreshadowed the emphasis of later volumes: the first topic listed was public policy and the last was literature. This is not to say that literature disappeared from the pages of *Putnam's* second series. James Fenimore Cooper was represented by two unpublished manuscripts (*The Eclipse* and *Battle of Plattsburg Bay*) and by ''Leaves from His Diary''; William Dean Howells contributed *No Love Lost—A Romance of Travel*; and William Cullen Bryant's poem ''Among the Trees'' appeared. One notable difference from the first series is the number of women writers whose work was printed: Elizabeth Stoddard, Julia Bears, Louisa May Alcott, Mrs. Nathaniel Hawthorne, Lucy Fountain, Phoebe Cary, and Mrs. H. B. Smith were among the many women who contributed poetry and short stories. These literary offerings, while sometimes distinguished, were not enough to disguise the greatest emphasis of the second series—articles about social issues. Charles Wyllys Elliott started a controversy over the woman's rights issue; writing under the pen name of Thom White, he earned this editor's postscript: ''A protest may surely be entered against the notion . . . of the destiny of women being marriage or—starvation'' (March 1868). One of the longest serials was a novel by Mary Clemmer Ames called *Woman's Rights*. Charlotte Bates wrote an angry article titled ''Men's Rights.'' About woman's rights and about other social questions the new *Putnam's* displays an earnest commitment which ironically marks both the most characteristic quality of the second series and the greatest divergence from the first series. Although without the wit and sparkle of the first series, the second series was well respected; *Scribner's Monthly* described it as embodying ''not only the old Knickerbocker culture and prestige, but the free spirit of modern progress and the broadest literary catholicity.''[7]

In 1898, Putnam's publishing house bought the *Critic*, an illustrated magazine edited by Jeanette Gilder and her brother, George B. Gilder. Eight years later, in October of 1906, the third series of *Putnam's Monthly*, called *Putnam's Monthly and the Critic* appeared, absorbing the *Critic* and increasing the range of covered topics. The most popular feature from the *Critic* was a regular column called ''The Lounger,'' written by Jeannette Gilder. This column consisted of a series of paragraph-length news notes about authors, performers, artists, and other prominent figures. Although several distinguished writers contributed to the monthly, including Henry James (whose *Bench of Desolation* appeared as a serial), Eden Phillpotts, and Don Marquis, the focus of the third series was on books and publishing—in this way it was more clearly linked to the interests of the Putnam's publishing firm than the first two series had been. The tone of the third series—somewhat conservative in politics and self-consciously stylish in social and cultural matters—contrasts with the earlier series, but the fate of the third series matched its predecessors. Despite earning recognition for its quality, *Putnam's* merged with the *Atlantic Monthly* in April of 1910. As the *Critic*, before being absorbed by *Putnam's*, had printed the work of Walt Whitman, H. H. Boyesen, Charles Dudley Warner, Joel Chandler Harris, Edmund Gosse, and Emma Lazarus, the third series continued the association of *Putnam's Monthly* with American literary excellence that had started with the first series in 1853.

Edward Everett Hale, reminiscing about the impact of *Putnam's* first series, wrote the following note to the editors of the third series:

> You will find it hard to make young America believe what was the thrill of joy which the green *PUTNAM*, No. 1, was received! You see,—no, you cannot see what it was,—month by month to see the dreary *Knickerbocker*, to see *Graham* and the *Southern Literary*—and to be told that these represented literary America. What young men in college read, month by month, were *Blackwood* and *Dublin University Magazine*—names unknown to young America today. And to such a constituency appeared *PUTNAM*! (1:84) October 1906, p. 84

The task *Putnam's Monthly* performed so well for American literature paralleled the task Emerson called for in "The American Scholar"—to stop casting American eyes longingly across the sea, and to recognize and develop our own national character.

Notes

1. Charles Madison, *Book Publishing in America* (New York: McGraw-Hill, 1966), p. 20.
2. "American Periodicals," *New American Cyclopaedia*, vol. 13 (New York: D. Appleton, 1861), p. 141.
3. Frank Luther Mott, *A History of American Magazines*. Vol. 2: 1850–1865 (Cambridge: Harvard University Press, 1938), p. 426.
4. Madison, p. 20.
5. George Haven Putnam, *George Palmer Putnam: A Memoir* (New York: Putnam's, 1912), p. 362.
6. *DeBow's Review*, February 1857, p. 129.
7. *Scribner's*, November 1870, p. 105.

Information Sources

BIBLIOGRAPHY
Derby, James Cephas. *Fifty Years among Authors, Books and Publishers*. New York: G. W. Carleton, 1884.
Ljungquist, Kent. "Putnam's Monthly Magazine." In *American Literary Magazines: The Eighteenth and Nineteenth Centuries*. Ed. Edward E. Chielens. New York: Greenwood Press, 1986, pp. 328–33.
Madison, Charles A. *Book Publishing in America*. New York: McGraw-Hill, 1966.

Mott, Frank Luther. *A History of American Magazines*. Vol. 2: *1850–1865*. Cambridge: Harvard University Press, 1938, pp. 419–31.

Putnam, George Haven. *George Palmer Putnam: A Memoir*. New York: Putnam's, 1912, chapters 9 and 17.

INDEX SOURCES

Poole's (1853–1870; 1906) *Readers' Guide* (1906–1910), *Jones' Index*.

LOCATION SOURCES

Library of Congress, many other Libraries. (American Periodicals, Series 3, 1850–1900. University Microfilms International, Ann Arbor. Reels 164–167.)

Publication History

MAGAZINE TITLE AND TITLE CHANGES

Putnam's Monthly Magazine of American Literature, Science, and Art, 1853–1857; *Putnam's Magazine: Original Papers on Literature, Science, Art, and National Interests*, 1868–1870; *Putnam's Monthly and the Critic: A Magazine of Literature, Art, and Life*, 1906; *Putnam's Monthly and the Reader*, 1908–1909; *Putnam's Monthly: An Illustrated Monthly of Literature, Art, and Life*, 1909–1910.

VOLUME AND ISSUE DATA

First Series, vols. 1–10, regular semiannual volumes, January 1853–September 1857. (Vol. 10 ends the series with only three numbers.) New Series, vols. 1–6, regular semiannual volumes, January 1868–November 1870. (Vol. 6 ends the series with only five numbers.) Third Series, not connected to the numbering of the earlier series. Vols. 1–7, October 1906–April 1910; each volume has six numbers except vol. 7, which has seven numbers.

PUBLISHER AND PLACE OF PUBLICATION

G. P. Putnam and Company, New York, 1853–1855; Dix and Edwards, New York, 1855–1857; Miller and Company, New York, 1857; G. P. Putnam and Sons, New York, 1868–1870; G. P. Putnam and Sons, New York, 1906–1910.

EDITORS

Charles F. Briggs (George William Curtis, Charles A. Dana, Frederick Law Olmsted, and Parke Godwin, associate editors), 1853–1857; Charles F. Briggs, 1868–1869; Edmund Clarence Stedman, 1869–1870; Parke Godwin, 1870; Jeanette Gilder and Joseph B. Gilder, 1906–1910.

CIRCULATION

20,000 (1853).

Glenn Anderson

THE QUEEN. See McCALL'S

THE QUEEN OF FASHION. See McCALL'S

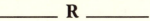

R

RAMPARTS

Ramparts began as a sedate Catholic lay quarterly in 1962, transformed itself into a mass-circulation and much-talked-about "radical slick" monthly, and died in 1975, upon facing the inevitable: mass-market magazines are paid for by advertisers, not readers.[1]

During its heyday it created many stirs and spent much money but was never able to attract and retain enough advertising to keep afloat. It lasted as long as it did only because of the infusion of large amounts of money from wealthy liberals and because it attracted the kinds of reporters and editors that make for interesting journalism.

Edward M. Keating founded *Ramparts* with his own money and his own vision. A converted Catholic, he felt the church and Catholic publishing were failing in making a difference in the world, particularly among those outside the church. His first efforts were not directed toward a mass audience. Keating's Editorial Policy statement in the first issue serves to indicate what his magazine was for a time and to suggest how different this magazine was from the transformed *Ramparts* of just a few years later:

> *Ramparts* is a journal published and edited by Catholic laymen that serves as a showcase for the creative writer and as a forum for the mature American Catholic.
>
> *Ramparts* publishes fiction, poetry, art, criticism and essays of distinction, reflecting those positive principles of the Hellenic-Christian tradition which have shaped and sustained our civilization for the past two thousand years, and which are needed still to guide us in an age grown increasingly secular, bewildered, and afraid.

Ramparts presents creative works which, besides possessing literary excellence, possess the Christian vision of man, his world, his God.

Ramparts seeks out the Christian intellectual and offers him an uninhibited opportunity to explore all the areas of the mind. *Ramparts* demands no special slanting of thought; it demands solely that its authors preserve the intellectual integrity that is their most valued possession, and that they pass this integrity on to their audience.[2]

At the magazine's beginning, Keating emphasized Catholic writers, thinkers, and artists—especially converts to Catholicism. Attention is given to John Howard Griffin, Graham Greene, Muriel Spark, and even Aubrey Beardsley. Warren Hinckle III, who was involved in the magazine from the beginning and who was later to serve as editor, wrote that the early *Ramparts'* "special heroes were the latter-day literary-type converts: Gerard Manley Hopkins, the Jesuit nature poet; the glib, dreadful G. K. Chesterton; Frederick B. (Baron) Corvo, of Hadrian VII fame; Ronald Firbank."[3] American converts published or given critical attention included several first-rate poets, among them Allen Tate, Robert Lowell, and Brother Antoninus.

From the first, there were symposia on writers or issues, in which the editors and others expressed their divergent views. The first issue contained a symposium on J. D. Salinger, for whom Keating nursed a particular distaste. Also, other serious articles (called "essays") by big names (Gabriel Marcel, "The Finality of Drama"), and poetry, often in portfolios and sometimes by important writers (Conrad Aiken), abounded. And from the first there were portfolios of art or photos, sometimes combined with poetry, as in the case of a set of woodcuts illustrating "The Ballad of Sir Patrick Spens." The portfolios were often printed on special paper, even though the art, usually religious, did not always deserve such special treatment. In other respects the earliest issue had few photos and little art of other kinds. The large-format magazine on heavy paper was mostly prose in two wide columns. The early issues used color very sparingly, with the simple cover on colored stock and at first with only a little spot color inside. Full color wasn't introduced until March 1963. All five issues of the first volume used some version of a rampart as the lone illustration on a bare front cover and a stylized Christian cross on the outside back cover.

The first volumes, then, were religious, literary, philosophical, artistic—a literary and arts magazine in some ways, perhaps in the best sense, but at the same time dull looking and perhaps taking itself a bit too seriously. Keating did not like the circulation figures, which hovered around 2,000. *Ramparts* was hardly a mass-circulation magazine at this point.

The year of the great transformation of the magazine was 1964, with the October number being the first issue of the "new" *Ramparts*. Yet Keating's editorial statement in that issue only hints at the secularization and radicalization of the magazine that was already well underway. The statement may indicate that Keating was somewhat out of touch with the direction *Ramparts* was taking.

His central concern still appears to be the failure of Catholic publishing and "the separation of men, the fragmentation of society, that results in alienation." But he sees evidence of the revival of the idea of mankind's being "one family of God," in the work and spirit of Pope John XXIII, in the efforts of fragmented Protestantism on the one hand, and some Christian and Jewish groups on the other, to find grounds for understanding and respect. On the more secular side, he sees "the desperate efforts of some whites and so many Negroes to end centuries of black bondage," and "tentative efforts to destroy poverty" in this country. Though he goes on to say that *Ramparts* offers to speak "more or less from a Catholic point of view,"[4] he has nonetheless identified two of the central issues that ignited the *Ramparts* and the protest movement of the coming decade: alienation and civil rights.

That statement reflected Keating's growing involvement in social and political issues. He published more work by distinguished writers, both Catholic and non-Catholic. He vented this dissatisfaction with the church's silent inaction on such issues as poverty, racism, and nuclear war. And yet the October 1964 statement indicates the differences between Keating's views and the more secular and radical views of Warren Hinckle and others who were to force Keating out a few years later. Though in 1964 Keating was becoming radicalized, he was to prove not radical enough.

According to Hinckle, who served as editor for five years (1965–1969), the catalyst that had pushed Keating toward radicalization was Keating's and the magazine's involvement in the controversy over Rolf Hochhuth's play *The Deputy*, early in 1964. The play, about the silence of Pope Pius XII while six million Jews died at the Nazis' hands, had caused violence throughout Europe and threatened to do the same as Broadway made preparations to present it. Hinckle came across an interview with the playwright available for publishing, and though he had to "rip apart" the spring 1964 issue, to make room for it, he did so, knowing the interview would be likely to bring national attention to *Ramparts*.[5] Keating became a leader in the effort to get Hochhuth's play on Broadway; Keating got his first taste of fame and *Ramparts* got its first significant national attention. According to Hinckle, this "experiment in activist journalism . . . became the prototype of the aggressive, extra-journalistic patterns of behavior that were a *Ramparts* hallmark in the ensuing years—a constant string of press conferences, full-page newspaper advertisements, committees, helicopter rentals, entrapments, and any and all devious and inordinate means to make our journalistic efforts effective in the face of the natural tendency of reasonable men to ignore them."[6]

In October 1964, *Ramparts* largely dropped its Catholic orientation, and became a slick monthly mass magazine with a liberal-to-radical bias. Its gurus—ad man Howard Gassage and physician Gerald Feigen—together with Keating and Hinckle, envisioned a left-of-center publication that was outside the ghetto of the underground press and that first with backers and then with national advertisers would go mass, national, and maybe even profitable. One month after that first issue of the newly incarnated *Ramparts*, circulation went from 2,500 to 10,000, and one year later its circulation was 50,000 and a few national advertisers had been signed on. In summarizing *Ramparts*' transformation, Warren Hinckle wrote, "In 1964 we were still printing the cautious counseling of Thomas Merton in praise of the methods of Gandhi; hardly two years later the editors were burning their draft cards on the cover." According to Hinckle, some were alarmed by the change: "The speed and style of such a crude metamorphosis proved more upsetting to traditional leftists than even to rightists, and thus *Ramparts* came to be viewed with alarm from both directions."[7] Further, "although *Ramparts* would continue to be described in the press as a 'Catholic layman's magazine' for the next several years, we began in that hot summer of 1964—the summer of Father DuBay's Inquisition was the summer of Harlem and the civil rights murders in Mississippi—the process of disengaging from the Catholic Church. The Church was a willing partner to the divorce. Even many radical Catholics were uneasy with *Ramparts'* kick-'em-in-the-ass style of bishop-baiting."[8]

At the time of the great transformation, a new art director, Dugald Stermer, was hired to give the magazine a whole new look. According to Hinckle, "Stermer redesigned the paper into the trend-setting, Times-Roman-typography, Push Pin studios–WPA, full-color-bleed prototype of new journalism trendiness that it was. Other magazines soon got the idea, and by the late 1960's one could line up *Evergreen Review, Harper's, Atlantic, New York* magazine, *Esquire* and *Ramparts* and be unable to tell the chicken from the egg."[9]

Ramparts had become a general magazine of satire, protest, and muckraking, rather than a primarily Catholic and literary magazine. *Ramparts* was now largely political, but it still took whatever opportunity it could find to criticize the church.

Notices from the press were mixed. In 1967, for instance, Herbert Gold, noting that *Ramparts* now "speaks for a whole style, if not a movement of 'new left' protest," observed that "the faults of erratic free-swinging—for example, its facts are often no more correct than its grammar—are redeemed by the fertility of its errors, the inventiveness of its language, its bounce and frequent hits in assaulting the way things are." And he added, "If *Ramparts* can be read with joy for its engaging youthfulness, it can perhaps also be forgiven its tottering rhetoric. The magazine is developing a steadiness."[10]

Also in 1967, Arno Karlen quoted *Ramparts*' editor as writing, "We want pieces that should be in the *New York Times* and aren't. They must be lively." But in Karlen's view *Ramparts* wanted not liveliness but "iconoclasm, controversy" and "as a result *Ramparts* has been labeled independent, New Left, Vital, silly, irresponsible, courageous. The confusion is understandable. *Ramparts* itself is confused about its identity. The staff of about twenty-five—only a third of them Catholic now—have free rein in their work, and their views range from apolitical to doctrinaire left, without any element predominating."[11] He called *Ramparts* an odd marriage "between the Left and Madison Avenue."[12]

But it was not a marriage, only a courtship that didn't lead to an engagement or a wedding.

Again according to Karlen, in the middle 1960s, "Comment gave way to block-buster reporting. Because *Ramparts* had gotten a reputation for printing what others wouldn't, people began to come to them with circulation building stories."[13] One such person was former Green Beret Don Duncan, whose cover story served as a vehicle for attacking the U.S. role in the Vietnam War. Other blockbusters included a tale of Michigan State University's serving as a front for the CIA, and a story of the "mysterious deaths" of ten people associated with the Kennedy assassination.

Circulation by August 1966 was 165,000. *Ramparts* became news across the country, and its editors and publishers used every means of publicity and promotion to build circulation and to raise funds. Advertising never did increase to the point that it could carry the magazine, but a succession of backers was found who kept the magazine afloat. Though it called itself a monthly, it missed issues. In fact, according to Warren Hinckle, "In the five years I edited *Ramparts*, there was only one year when we actually published twelve times in twelve months. I often held an edition to get an important story so that by the time the April issue was ready to come out it would be nearly May, so we would 'lose' April."[14]

In the spring of 1967, Hinckle and the *Ramparts* board ousted Keating, the magazine's founder, first editor and publisher, and long-time angel. By March of that year it was about $250,000 in debt. It announced that it would increase its prices and no longer depend on advertising.

But indebtedness was chronic at *Ramparts*. In 1969 *Time* pointed out that "*Ramparts* had been all but bankrupt from the moment it was converted in . . . [1964] from a mediocre Catholic literary quarterly into a rampaging crusader for leftist causes. It employed highly emotional writing and skilled promotion techniques to magnify its occasional and not really fresh revelations—including covert CIA funding at the National Student Association and military-financed secret research at universities. Circulation rose to a height of about 225,000."[15] A real coup was the magazine's hustling Che Guevara's diary away from competing American publishers. Yet by 1969, the magazine was $2 million in the red. Stories such as "The Menace of Barbie Dolls" or "The University on the Make or How MSU helped Arm Madame Nhu" were not designed to attract advertisers, and they didn't.

As the *New Republic* observed in 1969, *Ramparts* went through various incarnations: "cultural quarterly, a liberal Catholic bimonthly, a New Left monthly, and post-new Left biweekly."[16] The magazine had a variety of troubles, including having to scratch for material and sometimes settle for fillers, "internal quarrels, chaotic bookkeeping, and an inability—despite superb public relations talents—to attract writers with something fresh to say."[17] Nonetheless, *Ramparts* lasted past the middle of 1975. After missing the February issue, the editors optimistically wrote in their March issue: "The worst seems to be over. To us that means survival is no longer a question, though as usual it will be a struggle."[18] Yet in a May letter to subscribers, which was published in both the July and the August-September issue, the editors made an appeal for funds and stated at great length the *necessity* of the role *Ramparts* plays: "The vital principle at work here is not the liberal creed, 'If it is possible it can be arranged'; it is the radical commitment that what is necessary can be achieved."[19] Necessary or not, the voice was to be stilled. The August-September issue led off with a desperate appeal for funds, "A Matter of Life or Death," signed by all nine members of the *Ramparts* staff. It was to be death. That issue was the last.

Notes

1. Though sometimes referred to as a quarterly in these early years, the magazine was published five times a year, until the fall of 1964, when it became a "monthly," at first issuing ten numbers annually.
2. *Ramparts,* May 1962, p. 3.
3. Warren Hinckle III, *If You Have a Lemon, Make Lemonade* (New York: G. P. Putnam's Sons, 1973), p. 46.
4. "A Statement from the Publisher," *Ramparts,* October 1964, p. 3.
5. Hinckle, p. 54.
6. Ibid., p. 68.
7. Ibid., p. xii.
8. Ibid., p. 78.
9. Ibid., p. 108.
10. "Where the Action Is," *New York Times Book Review,* 19 February 1967, p. 50.
11. Arno Karlen, "O'er 'Ramparts' We Watch," *Holiday,* April 1967, p. 149.
12. Karlen, p. 15.
13. Ibid., p. 148.
14. Hinckle, p. 15.
15. "Manning the *Ramparts*—or Is It the Barricades?" *Time,* 7 February 1969, p. 42.
16. "Two for One," *New Republic,* 15 February 1969, p. 9.
17. Ibid., p. 10.
18. "A Few Words," *Ramparts,* March 1975, p. 9.
19. "An Open Letter to Our Readers," *Ramparts,* August-September 1975, p. 6.

Information Sources

BIBLIOGRAPHY
Editors of *Rampart. Eco-Catastrophe!* San Francisco: Canfield Press, 1970. A collection of articles on environmental issues originally appearing in *Ramparts.*
Hinckle, Warren III. *If You Have a Lemon, Make Lemonade.* New York: G. P. Putnam's Sons, 1973.
Gold, Herbert. "Where the Action Is." *New York Times Book Review,* 19 February 1967, p. 50.
Karlen, Arno. "O'er 'Ramparts' We Watch." *Holiday,* April 1967, pp. 147–49, 151.
"Manning the *Ramparts*—or is It the Barricades?" *Time,* 7 February 1969, p. 42.

Ridgeway, James. "The Ramparts Story: . . . Um, Very Interesting." *New York Times Magazine*, 20 April 1969, pp. 34–44.
"Two for One," *New Republic*, 15 February 1969, pp. 9–10.

INDEX SOURCES
> *Readers' Guide to Periodical Literature (1968–1975) Alternative Press Index* (1969–1975); *The Catholic Periodical Index* (1962–1966).

LOCATION SOURCES
> University of Illinois at Urbana, St. Louis Public Library, Washington University. Available in microform.

Publication History

MAGAZINE TITLE AND TITLE CHANGES
> *Ramparts.*

VOLUME AND ISSUE DATA
> Vol. 1, no.1–vol. 13, no. 10, May 1962–August-September 1975; five issues annually, 1962–October 1964; monthly (with often ten issues annually), October 1964–1975; published somewhat irregularly, 1964–1975; in 1968 the magazine was briefly published twice a month.

PUBLISHERS AND PLACES OF PUBLICATION:
> Edward M. Keating, The Layman's Press, May 1962–August 1965; Ramparts Magazine, 1965–1970; Noah's Ark, Inc., 1971–1975; Menlo Park, California, 1962–1966; San Francisco, California, 1966–1970; Berkeley, California, 1970–1975.

EDITORS
> Edward M. Keating, 1962–1965; Warren Hinckle III, ca. 1965–1969; Robert Scheer, 1969; masthead lists only groups of editors beginning in 1970.

CIRCULATION
> Summer 1964, 2,500; 1965, 10,000; August 1966, 165,000; 1967, 29,471; 1969, ca. 171,258–225,000; 1971, 122,407; 1973, 122,000; 1975, 103,469; 1977, 65,000.

Daniel Straubel

READER'S DIGEST

Reader's Digest Association has published for over sixty-five years a monthly magazine of general-interest nonfiction articles for the whole family. The association publishes the magazine in Braille, Large Print, and Talking Book editions as well as Junior editions popular in the elementary schools.

The *Digest*'s human interest and inspirational articles are generally condensed from three sources: articles written and published in other magazines, articles submitted by the readership, and commissioned articles written by the *Digest*'s own staff writers. Today probably 76 percent or more of the articles are staff written as commissioned originals.[1] The *Digest*'s editors seek to simplify complex subjects, to turn controversy into constructive action, and to offer workable solutions to problems. "The Digest believes in man's ability to change his world."[2]

The *Digest* today may be the most powerful vehicle for the printed word in the world, claiming that 100 million people read the magazine each month. The *Digest*, printed in sixteen languages and forty-one editions, has a worldwide circulation of 29 million—16 million in the United States. The median age of the readership is reported to be about forty-five.[3] The magazine is easily recognizable by its small size (5½" x 7½") and in recent years by its cover design of pastel colors. The editors, primarily founder DeWitt Wallace until his death, have been able to successfully gauge the subscribers' interests in any country where they publish. This is evidenced by the *Digest*'s astronomical circulation.

The *Digest* has been criticized severely over the years for its simplistic approach to complex ideas and problem solving. However, the *Digest* has not claimed to provide the reader with a cross section of opinion nor to delve into complex scholarly research, but as the cover of the first issue stated, there would be "thirty-one articles each month from leading magazines—each article of enduring value and interest in condensed and compact form."[4]

The Little Magazine, as its 1922 masthead proclaimed, was the product of its founder and first editor, DeWitt Wallace, and published jointly with his wife, Lila Acheson Wallace. The Wallaces maintained control until the 1970s, when much of the editorial control was released to senior editors. The influence of the owners, however, continued to be felt until their deaths; DeWitt died at the age of ninety-one in 1981, and Lila was ninety-four at her death in 1984.

Throughout its publishing history the *Digest* has come under heavy criticism for its socially and politically conservative editorial policy and/or biased viewpoints, which include attacks on big government and big labor[5] and for staff-planned and-written articles "planted" in popular magazines to be reprinted later in the *Digest*. Nevertheless, small publishers welcomed these "plantings."[6]

Another criticism leveled at their editorial policy was their refusal to provide a format for printing corrections or rebuttals, that is, letters to the editor. Also critics claimed that the condensations diluted and harmed the original manuscripts. *Digest* articles were condensed to about one-fourth the original length.[7]

Such criticisms have been levied against other digest publications at some time but most particularly against the *Reader's Digest*—perhaps simply because of its phenomenal success. The *Digest* has reported that it receives as many letters supporting its stand on controversial issues as it does opposing them. Of course, critics generally concede that all editors have the right to determine editorial policy. The *Digest* defends its "plants" because, it says, free-lance contributions or run-of-the-mill published materials would not provide sufficient material for a balance of subjects for each issue.[8]

Reader's Digest articles are not profound, but they are often controversial or crusading. These have brought criticism of sensationalism in reporting, especially the reporting of medical and scientific breakthroughs or "cures" before the

American Medical Association, the Food and Drug Administration or other reliable researchers have completed their investigations. On the medical front *Reader's Digest* has carried articles on stamping out syphilis and cigarette smoking. There have been crusading articles on promoting cheaper milk prices, safe driving practices, and conservation of our national resources.[9]

Wallace looked for articles that would appeal to a large audience of either sex and all educational levels. There has been a conscious effort to promote the self-worth of the individual, a better America, a place of respect for the United States in world affairs, and always a heavy emphasis on inspirational topics such as "miracles and achievement stories."[10]

DeWitt Wallace, a college dropout and perhaps a bit of a disappointment to his father, who was a Presbyterian minister and college president, loved to read. His curiosity was insatiable. His wife reported that he would read everything, even the fine print on menus or medicine bottles. While working as a traveling salesman, he began condensing important facts from articles of interest to himself on three-by-five slips of paper. Later, he found that he could successfully condense articles using the words of the writer but eliminating lengthy descriptions or literary embellishments.

Later when working for Webb Publishing Company, in St. Paul, Minnesota, he condensed articles of interest to farmers, which he compiled into a booklet, *Getting the Most Out of Farming,* and sold to banks as a business appreciation gift item. Wallace sold 100,000 copies, made expenses, and learned how to put out a marketable publication. While hospitalized for battle wounds incurred during World War I, he continued to polish his editorial talent. Then in 1920 he compiled condensations from *Literary Digest,* Atlantic Monthly,* National Geographic,* Scribner's,** and other popular periodicals into one volume and had several hundred copies made for distribution. He showed these copies to many magazine editors, publishers, and friends, all of whom rejected the project. Undaunted, Wallace began writing his own promotional direct-sales materials announcing his proposed publication. The folksy sales letters were aimed toward teachers, professional men and women, and especially the newly emancipated women readers. He said that the articles were chosen for their enduring value and interest and that they "would provide the reader with the means of keeping one's information account open." The country's social and educational climate was ripe for such an undertaking. Education for the masses in the United States was becoming a reality. Every State in the union had enacted a compulsory school attendance law by 1918, so a publication that endeavored to further educate and inform readers was sure to find a receptive audience.

Wallace considered the *Digest* a service to the members of the association. He also felt that the condensed articles were fulfilling the growing demand for information by the public during the 1920s when there was a growing air of national pride, enthusiasm, and self-confidence throughout the country. Believing that self-improvement was the key to success and that success could be achieved through learning, Wallace proceeded with his project.

Printed in black and white, the *Digest* had no artwork nor illustrations until November 1939, except the line drawing of a woman within a circle on the front cover. This drawing was removed later in 1942. The table of contents shifted to the outside front cover, where it remains today. Wallace did no surveys to determine readers' interests; rather he chose for condensation articles that were of interest to him. The subscriptions poured in; by 1926 they totaled 20,000, and by 1929 the *Reader's Digest* had 216,000 "members."[14]

The articles were usually positive, moral and spiritually uplifting; even the selection articles for the first issue were on topics of universal interest, that is, science and health, nature, morals and the art of living, sex, the little guy winning against great odds, and a goodly supply of humor. Today, the contents are similar, with regular features of News in Medicine, Picturesque Speech, Humor in Uniform, Campus Comedy, and Life in These United States.

Reader's Digest refused to carry any advertising in its U.S. editions until 1955. In fact, it had often carried articles attacking advertising abuses. However, with increased costs and in order to maintain its profit ratio, it surveyed its readership to determine reader preference between advertising or increased subscription costs. The result was that 80 percent favored accepting advertising.[15]

The first issue with advertising was April 1955. At that time the rate for a one-time, single-page black and white was $25,600, while the subscription rate was still $3 annually and the total circulation was 10,298,794.[16]

The *Digest* netted $351 million from advertising sources during its first decade of advertising (1955–1964). By 1987 a one-page black-and-white advertisement was $91,350, and the annual subscription had increased to $14.97. In 1985 the domestic and international editions combined produced net revenues of $565 million; the domestic advertising revenues were $110.6 million.[17] Although liquor and tobacco advertisements had been refused from the beginning, liquor advertisements finally began in 1979; cigarette and tobacco ads still are not accepted, nor is advertising permitted on the back cover. That space has been reserved for an attractive picture or art reprint suitable for coffee-table displaying.

The first foreign edition of *Reader's Digest* was published in Great Britain in 1938. Other international editions followed, first to South America during the 1940s in part to combat Nazi influence in the region. During the first international publishing all *Digest* editions consisted of translations taken from a pool of articles that had appeared in U.S. editions.[18] Today foreign editors are free to publish digests of articles of local interest. Approximately 30 percent will reflect the culture of the readers; the rest are selected from articles that originate in the *Digest*'s network of editorial offices worldwide. The international editions of *Reader's Digest* are considered somewhat more prestigious in the world market than are editions published in the United States.[19] Although the *Digest*'s subscriptions have dropped slightly from its peak in 1984, it remains the undisputed worldwide circulation leader and second only to the weekly *TV Guide** in the United States. Reader-listeners appear to have turned to magazines in recent years for practical help and to television for entertainment.[20]

Although Wallace had condensed chapters or sections of nonfiction books, it wasn't until late 1934 that a condensed book section was added as a regular feature. Some publishers feared that the appearance of a condensation would affect the total sales of the original. However, the opposite proved to be true. Wallace offered to pay a publisher five times the usual fee if sales did not increase rather than decrease. Editors who believed in the sales advantages of condensed books often made a practice of sending advance proofs to the *Digest*'s condensed book editors. The condensed book continues as an outstanding feature today.[21] The Reader's Digest Condensed Book Club followed in 1950.

DeWitt and Lila Wallace believed in the Golden Rule, helping the deserving poor and doing good works.[22] It was the founder's philosophy, the magazine's portability, its reader participation, and its pragmatic approach to problem solving that contributed to the *Digest*'s success.[23] *Reader's Digest* is still telling the world that with hard work, a positive attitude, and a spiritual faith, success is possible.

Notes

1. William H. Taft, *American Magazines for the 1980s* (New York: Hastings House, 1982), p. 156.

2. Standard Rate and Data Service, *Consumers Magazine and Agriculture*, 20 September 1987, p. 246.

3. "50 Largest Companies," *Advertising Age*, 20 June 1987, p. 59.

4. Editorial, *Reader's Digest*, February 1922, p. 1.

5. Reo M. Christenson, "Report on the *Reader's Digest*," *Columbia Journalism Review*, Winter 1965, pp. 30–36.

6. John Bainbridge, *Little Wonder: or, the Reader's Digest and How It Grew* (New York: Reynal, 1945), p. 47.

7. Ibid., p. 93.

8. Ibid., p. 269.

9. Ibid., p. 145.

10. Kenneth Stewart and John Tebbel, *Makers of Modern Journalism* (New York: Prentice-Hall, 1952), p. 442.

11. Charles W. Ferguson, "Unforgettable DeWitt Wallace," *Reader's Digest*, February 1988, pp. 178–83.

12. Ibid., pp. 180–91.

13. James Playsted Wood, *Of Lasting Interest: The Story of the Reader's Digest*, rev. ed. (Garden City, N.Y.: Doubleday, 1967), p. 26.

14. Ibid., pp. 1–50.

15. Taft, p. 56.

16. "Magazine Circulation and Rate Trends, 1940–1971," *Association of National Advertisers* (New York: Association of National Advertisers: Magazine Committee, 1972), pp. 35–45.

17. "100 Leading Media Companies," *Advertising Age*, 29 June 1987, p. 559.

18. Bainbridge, p. 118.

19. Leo Bogart, "Magazines since the Rise of Television," *Journalism Quarterly*, Spring 1956, p. 559.

20. Ibid., p. 157.

21. Wood, pp. 55–56.

22. Bainbridge, p. 22.

23. Roland E. Wollsey, *Understanding Magazines*, 2nd ed. (Ames: Iowa State University Press, 1969), p. 49.

Information Sources

BIBLIOGRAPHY

Bainbridge, John. *Little Wonder: or, the Reader's Digest and How It Grew*. New York: Reynal, 1945.

Bogart, Leo. "Magazines since the Rise of Television." *Journalism Quarterly,* Spring 1956, pp. 157–66.

Christensen, Reo M. "Report on the *Reader's Digest.*" *Columbia Journalism Review*, Winter 1965, pp. 30–36.

"The Common Touch." *Time*, 10 December 1951, p. 64.

Editorial. *Reader's Digest*, February 1922, p. 1.

Ferguson, Charles W. "Unforgettable DeWitt Wallace." *Reader's Digest*, February 1988, pp. 178–214.

"50 Largest Companies." *Advertising Age*, 20 June 1987, pp. 56–59.

Lachlan, E. C. "*Reader's Digest* Spans the Globe." *Advertising Age*, September 1984, pp. 18–20.

MacDougall, A. Kent. "*Reader's Digest* Posts Top Publishing Success since the Scriptures." *Wall Street Journal*, 17 March 1966, sec. E, p. 1.

"Magazine Circulation and Rate Trends, 1940–1971." *Association of National Advertisers*. New York: 1972, pp. 35–45.

"100 Leading Media Companies." *Advertising Age*, 29 June 1987, p. 559.

"The Reader's Digest." *Fortune*, December 1936, p. 121.

Schreiner, Samuel A., Jr. *The Condensed World of the Reader's Digest*. New York: Stein and Day, 1977, pp. 65–71.

Standard Rate and Data Service. *Consumers Magazine and Agriculture*, 20 September 1987, p. 156.

Stewart, Kenneth, and John Tebbel. *Makers of Modern Journalism*. New York: Prentice-Hall, 1952.

Taft, William H. *American Magazines for the 1980s*. New York: Hastings House, 1982.

Wollsey, Roland E. *Understanding Magazines*. 2nd ed. Ames: Iowa State University Press, 1969.

Wood, James Playsted. *Of Lasting Interest: The Story of the Reader's Digest*. rev. ed. Garden City. N.Y.: Doubleday, 1967.

INDEX SOURCES

    Readers' Guide to Periodical Literature, (1936–present); *Wall Street Journal Index; Magazine Index* (1977–present). By publisher.

LOCATION SOURCES

    Widely available. Available in microform.

Publication History

MAGAZINE TITLE AND TITLE CHANGES
> *Reader's Digest: The Little Magazine,* February 1922–July 1923; *Reader's Digest Service,* August 1923–April 1925; *Reader's Digest,* May 1925–present.

VOLUME AND ISSUE DATA
> Vol. 1–present, February 1922–present, monthly.

PUBLISHER AND PLACE OF PUBLICATION
> Reader's Digest Association, Pleasantville, New York.

EDITORS
> Lila Bell Acheson, DeWitt Wallace, and Louise M. Patterson, February 1922– March 1922; Lila Bell Acheson, DeWitt Wallace, and H. J. Cobberly, April 1922– May 1927; Lila Bell Acheson and DeWitt Wallace, 1927–1957; DeWitt Wallace and Kenneth Payne, 1957–1973; Hobart Lewis, 1973–1976; Edward T. Thompson, 1976–1984; Kenneth O. Gilmore, 1984–present.

CIRCULATION
> 16,566,650 (1987).

Katherine Shaw

REDBOOK

Redbook, originally a magazine of popular fiction, has become one of the leading women's periodicals in the United States. The first issue was published in May of 1903 by a group of Jewish businessmen in Chicago. Louis M. Stumer, Abraham R. Stumer, Benjamin J. Rosenthal, and Louis Eckstein, owners of millinery stores, restaurants, a drug store, and an office building, had at first attempted to buy out a fiction publication entitled the *10 Story Book*. Failing in this effort, they decided to start their own periodical for profit. Trumbull White, a foreign service correspondent for the *Chicago Record,* was recruited to be the first editor. White projected that it would take three years to make a profit and in that time the backers might lose $100,000. The firm of Stumer, Rosenthal, and Eckstein, with assets of $1 million, directed White to proceed with the venture.[1]

The first issue of *Redbook,* at first written *Red Book,* used zinc etchings to illustrate the stories. These looked cheap and were later replaced by tooled halftones. A photographic section was soon inserted at the beginning of each issue, which included well-known actresses of the day. The red cover and sketch of a woman clad in an evening gown, concluded one observer, "were more sensational in their suggestions than the contents of the stories warrant."[2] An editorial in the first issue noted that the magazine was designed to be "invariably wholesome, invariably decent, invariably cheerful." The editor concluded: "Red is the color of cheerfulness, of brightness, of gayety. It is the color of the most brilliant displays in nature, from sunsets to autumn foliage. Therefore THE RED BOOK."[3]

The first number of *Redbook* had a run of 40,000, of which 26,000 sold. By the end of the second year *Redbook* was already showing a profit. By 1906 it had a circulation of over 330,000. Because the issues were sold to dealers below cost, the profit came exclusively from the advertising revenues. The first issues were heavy on patent medicine ads. As the circulation grew, the prices for advertising grew, and *Redbook* became noted for ads for high-quality merchandise for the affluent.[4]

Redbook had to compete with New York periodicals for both contributors and readers. It made significant headway in the midwestern market. It started the policy of paying authors upon acceptance instead of publication. While publishing many American authors, *Redbook* soon was recognized for publishing more fiction by English authors than any periodical in America. Such authors as H. G. Wells, John Galsworthy, Jack London, Edith Wharton, Sinclair Lewis, F. Scott Fitzgerald, Pearl S. Buck, and Winston Churchill appeared in its pages. *Redbook*'s stories were aimed at the middle class, and the editors often deleted paragraphs and phrases that might offend middle-class sensibilities.[5]

Redbook was purchased by the McCall Company in 1929 and was relocated to Dayton, Ohio. For twenty years it was edited by Edwin Balmer, who edited the publication as a general-interest monthly of light fiction for both men and women. In 1937 the circulation surpassed one million, but *Redbook* lagged behind its major competitors, *American* and *Cosmopolitan*.* In the early 1940s some minor editorial changes were made. In 1948, after a loss of $400,000, a major overhaul was in order. Wade Nichols was hired as editor.[6]

Nichols, a young editor from Charlotte, North Carolina, had driven up the circulation at *Click* and *Modern Screen*. He believed that *Redbook* should appeal to "young adults," persons between the ages of eighteen and thirty-five. He emphasized stories steeped in "personal identification"—stories the reader could identify with. Nichols revamped the magazine, and by 1950 the circulation reached 2 million. In the fiftieth anniversary issue the young editor proclaimed: "Now, in the second half of this century, *Redbook* goes forward with a vast new audience. We call you Young Adults. You are the young in spirit—the believers, the hopers, the triers, the doers."[7]

Redbook was awarded the Benjamin Franklin Magazine Award in 1954 for articles dealing with security risks, academic freedom, and racial segregation. The award recognized *Redbook*'s "courageous effort to bring controversial issues before a mass audience."[8] When Nichols departed his post in 1958, Robert Stein, the new editor, continued his policies. In 1961 the periodical was indexed for the first time in *Readers' Guide*. By 1963 circulation had surpassed 3.6 million. The sixtieth anniversary issue proudly proclaimed kinship with the 1903 publication, publishing excerpts from a long and distinguished history. Five years later, under the editorship of Sey Chassler, subscriptions topped 4.5 million and *Redbook* had over 900 pages of advertising. Though *Redbook* occasionally published feminist articles, Chassler noted, "No matter what's happened women are still responsible for their families in major ways that men are not sharing."[9]

An analysis of fiction in *Redbook* in the 1970s found that *Redbook* heroines tended to be less traditional than those of other women's magazines. Also, in 1970 and 1975 the publication won the National Magazine Award for Fiction, sharing that honor with such notable publications as the *New Yorker* and the *Atlantic*.* *Redbook* authors during the period included Toni Morrison, Ann Roiphe, Mary Gordon, and Ursula K. LeGuin. Editorial policy at the time targeted women between eighteen and thirty-four who were married or planning to marry, had higher education, and who had worked or planned to do so in the future.[10]

By the 1980s circulation had declined to 3.8 million and advertising dropped from 1,600 pages to 1,000. *Redbook* saw the need to reach a new audience. "We try to appeal to the whole woman," said editor Annette Capone. "She's not just a housewife, and she's not just a career woman with kids."[11] The periodical instituted new graphics and started a campaign for a wider audience. In 1985 it launched a new appeal to the "yummy—young upwardly mobile mommy" between the ages of twenty-five and forty-four. The publisher, Alan Waxenberg, said that "the baby-boom generation is the market we're after."[12] This new effort reflected the aging of the *Redbook* reader and of the populace in general. At the same time, *Redbook* had to stake out its territory distinct from other women's magazines and to meet new competition from *People*.*[13]

Redbook's emphasis in recent years has continued to center around the married woman. The publication is still sometimes described as "wholesome." Fictional stories are accompanied by articles dealing with beauty and fashion, health and food, furnishings, and sexual matters within the context of marriage. "*Redbook*'s popularity," concluded William Katz and Linda S. Katz, "is evidence that marriage, family, children and the home continue to be the center around which many women's lives revolve."[14]

Notes

1. Herbert E. Fleming, "The Literary Interests of Chicago VI and VII," *American Journal of Sociology*, July 1906, pp. 89–91.

2. Ibid., p. 92.

3. "Redbook's First Sixty Years," *Redbook,* May 1963, p. 76.

4. Fleming, pp. 93–97.

5. Ibid., pp. 96–97; "Redbook's First Sixty Years," p. 86; Martin Bucco, "The Serialized Novels of Sinclair Lewis," *Western American Literature* 4 (1969), pp. 31–32.

6. Theodore Peterson, *Magazines in the Twentieth Century* (Urbana: University of Illinois Press, 1964), pp. 208–9.

7. Nichols quoted in "Redbook Observes Its First 50 Years," *New York Times*, 29 April 1953,; p. 27. Peterson, p. 208.

8. Peterson, pp. 208–9.

9. Chassler quoted in Esther Stineman, "Women's Magazines: Serving Up the 'New Woman' in the Same Old Ways," *Serials Review*, October-December 1979, p. 26; John Tebbel, *The American Magazine: A Compact History* (New York: Hawthorne Books, 1969), p. 250.

10. Judith Catherine Galas, "The Image of Women in Magazine Fiction: A Demographic Look at Four Women's Magazines in the 1970s" (M.S. thesis, University of Kansas, 1982), pp. 70–86, 90–96.

11. Belinda J. Oliver, "Redbook Goes for the Jugular," *Magazine Age*, February 1985, p. 69.

12. Waxenberg quoted in Stuart J. Elliott, "Yup! They're Yummies: 'Redbook' Coins Slogan for Moms," *Advertising Age*, 23 May 1985, p. 51.

13. "Redbook Zeroes in on the Women of the 80s," *Madison Avenue*, September 1983, pp. 108–12; Ira Ellenthal, "Redbook Redux," *Folio*, September 1983, p. 142.

14. William Katz and Linda S. Katz, *Magazines for Libraries*, 5th ed. (New York: R. R. Bowker, 1986), p. 992.

Information Sources

BIBLIOGRAPHY

Bucco, Martin. "The Serialized Novels of Sinclair Lewis." *Western American Literature* 4 1969, pp. 29–37.

Ellenthal, Ira. "Redbook Redux." *Folio*, September 1983, p. 142.

Elliott, Stuart J. "Yup! They're Yummies: 'Redbook' Coins Slogan for Moms." *Advertising Age*, 23 May 1985, p. 51.

Fleming, Herbert E. "The Literary Interests of Chicago VI and VII." *American Journal of Sociology*, July 1906, pp. 68–118.

Galas, Judith Catherine. "The Image of Women in Magazine Fiction: A Demographic Look at Four Women's Magazines in the 1970s." M.S. thesis, University of Kansas, 1982.

Geise, L. Ann. "The Female Role in Middle Class Women's Magazines From 1955 to 1976: A Content Analysis of Nonfiction Selections." *Sex Roles*, February 1979, pp. 51–62.

Katz, William, and Linda S. Katz. *Magazines for Libraries*. 5th ed. New York: R. R. Bowker, 1986.

Oliver, Belinda J. "Redbook Goes for the Jugular." *Magazine Age*, February 1985, pp. 69–71.

Peterson, Theodore. *Magazines in the Twentieth Century*. Urbana: University of Illinois Press, 1964.

"Redbook Observes Its First 50 Years." *New York Times*, 29 April 1953, p. 27.

"Redbook's First Sixty Years." *Redbook*, May 1963, pp. 74–86.

"Redbook Zeroes in on Women of the 80s." *Madison Avenue*, September 1983, pp. 108–12.

Stineman, Esther. "Women's Magazines: Serving Up the 'New Woman' in the Same Old Ways." *Serials Review*, October-December 1979, pp. 25–29.

Tebbel, John. *The American Magazine: A Compact History*. New York: Hawthorne Books, 1969.

INDEX SOURCES
  Readers' Guide to Periodical Literature (1961–present); *Magazine Index* (1977–present).
LOCATION SOURCES
  Library of Congress, many other libraries. Available in microform.

Publication History

MAGAZINE TITLE AND TITLE CHANGES
  Red Book, 1903–1929; *Redbook*, 1929–present.
VOLUME AND ISSUE DATA
  Vols. 1–170, 1903–present, monthly.
PUBLISHER AND PLACE OF PUBLICATION
  Redbook Company, Chicago, Illinois, 1903–1909; Consolidated Magazine Corporation, Chicago, Illinois, 1909–1929; McCall Corporation, Dayton, Ohio, 1929–1982; Hearst Corporation, New York, 1982–present. (Editorial Offices have varied and include Chicago; Dayton; Rock Island, Illinois; and Des Moines, Iowa.)
EDITORS
  Trumbull White, 1903–1906; Karl Edward Harriman, 1906–1912, 1919–1927; Ray Long, 1912–1918; Edwin Balmer, 1927–1949; Wade H. Nichols, 1949–1958; Robert Stein, 1958–1965; Sey Chassler, 1965–1978; Anne Mollegen Smith, 1978–1983; Annette Capone, 1983–present.
CIRCULATION
  3,800,000

Ronnie W. Faulkner

REVIEW OF REVIEWS

"Of the making of magazines there is no end. There are already more periodicals than anyone can find time to read. That is why I have to-day added another to the list. For the new comer is not a rival, but rather an index and a guide to all those already in existence." With these statements W. T. Stead welcomed readers to his new publication, the *Review of Reviews,* in the first issue of January 1890.[1]

By 1890 William Thomas Stead had accumulated several years of colorful journalism experience in Britain. At the age of twenty-one, Stead was appointed editor of the Darlington *Northern Echo*, a position he held for ten years. In 1880 he moved to London to edit the *Pall Mall Gazette*. As a pioneer of the "new journalism," Stead used the *Gazette* to explore controversial issues. His personal investigation of London's vice crimes landed him in jail for three months. After ten years Stead left the newspaper over a disagreement with the owners and formed the *Review of Reviews*.[2]

In launching his journal Stead envisioned "a periodical circulating throughout the English speaking world . . . read as men used to read their Bibles . . . to discover the will of God and their duty to man.'' In order to reach more of the English speaking world, Stead's plans for his journal included establishing "associates or affiliates" in all other English-language countries. Stead was able to spread his publication only to the United States in 1891 and to Australia the following year. Although the Australian *Review* was published for some time, the American version proved to be Stead's greatest satellite success, largely due to the efforts of its editor, Albert Shaw.[3]

Shaw possessed both a distinguished academic background and several years of journalism experience when he assumed the editorship of the *Review of Reviews* in the United States. Born and reared in Ohio, Shaw attended Grinnell College and began his career at the *Grinnell Herald*, the town's biweekly newspaper. Shaw left Iowa in 1882 and did graduate work at Johns Hopkins University until 1884. While at the university Shaw wrote for the *Minneapolis Tribune*, and took on full-time employment there after completing his studies. As chief editorial writer and associate editor for the *Tribune*, Shaw covered state and national politics. He also maintained his contacts in Baltimore and wrote articles for the *Dial* and the *Chautauquan*.* In 1888 Shaw toured Europe and England, where he met William Stead and contributed articles to the *Pall Mall Gazette*. After a brief return Shaw took another leave from the *Tribune* to write and teach. He was about to join the faculty of Cornell University when Stead offered him the editorship of the American edition of the *Review of Reviews*.[4]

Although Stead originally reprinted the British version of the *Review of Reviews* in New York, he soon realized the need for an American editor. By late 1890 Shaw and Stead had settled on an agreement, which was financially profitable for Shaw and which gave him a large degree of editorial control. For the first years the *Review* was very much a replica of the British publication. Tensions grew between the two men as Shaw gradually shaped the journal to his own style, relying less on Stead and more on his own writing and other contributors.[5]

Initially the *Review of Reviews* was not a journal for the common man. Shaw's subscribers tended to be conservative and included many members of the clergy as well as leaders in higher education. Shaw took pride in his *Review* being "welcomed in the families of professional men and thoughtful people quite generally." Women also made up a sizable percentage of early subscribers. In 1895–1896 the *Review* listed over 40 percent of subscribers as "ladies at their homes." With its coverage of other articles and journals, the *Review of Reviews* offered readers a faster way to keep up on current publications.[6]

Shaw intended for his magazine to be read by many segments of society. He gradually altered the format and contents of the *Review* to appeal to a broad spectrum of the population. The basic components established by Stead were kept partially intact over the years, but Shaw made his own changes in the magazine's format and makeup. In Stead's tradition each issue began with The Progress of the World. Written by Shaw and expressing his editorial opinions, the initial section was composed of several short illustrated pieces describing national and international events of the month. The Progress section was followed by a chronology entitled Record of World Events, a brief daily list of world events for the month. In 1930 the format of the chronology changed to a series of short paragraphs grouped into categories including U.S. and international events, business, labor, science, education, and sports. Another regular section, Current History in Caricature, was composed of political cartoons gleaned from other magazines and newspapers.[7]

Beyond current news events Shaw devoted a major portion of the *Review* to original articles. From the single character sketch in the early issues, Shaw gradually expanded the number and topics for his feature articles. Several articles covered major happenings including the World's Fair of 1893, the Spanish-American War, the San Francisco earthquake and fire, and World War I. The articles often were written by prominent people including many professors from Shaw's alma mater as well as government leaders such as Louis Brandeis and Elihu Root. Frank H. Simonds was the writer who covered World War I and later European political affairs for the *Review*. Although many articles concentrated on political and economic issues, other topics were featured including the arts, women's issues, social problems, and education.[8]

In comparison to other journals of the time the *Review of Reviews* did not follow the trend toward muckraking. Albert Shaw "believed in reforms, but was not a reformer." He saw his journalistic duty as collecting facts, then comparing and analyzing information, but not advocating any particular plan of action. Shaw dictated that each original article be "non-argumentative, informative and timely," effectively ruling out most of the muckrakers' contributions. The *Review* did publish articles on corruption, poverty, and the misuse of wealth, but such articles were not presented as a campaign for reform.[9]

In addition to current events and feature articles, Shaw's magazine was first and foremost a review. As such, a major portion of the magazine was devoted to summarizing and describing the contents of other magazines. Initially Shaw covered the reviewing function in two sections. Leading Articles of the Month consisted of summaries of major articles from primarily U.S. and British magazines including *Forum*,* *Atlantic Monthly*,* *Fortnightly Review*, and the *North American Review*.* In the second section, The Periodicals Reviewed, individual monthly issues of selected magazines were discussed. Since much duplication occurred in the two sections, by 1904 The Periodicals Reviewed was dropped. By 1906 Leading Articles covered thirty pages of the *Review of Reviews*, and in 1908 a separate Leading Financial Articles was added. The emphasis gradually shifted into a separate finance and business section that reviewed current business problems in addition to summarizing articles. In 1919 the separate financial section was dropped, although coverage of business issues continued. By the early 1930s the *Review* introduced a section entitled The Pulse of Business that reported on business conditions and included monthly charts and graphs of general business indices.

Leading Articles continued as a mainstay of the *Review* until 1929, when a new segment was created entitled News and Opinion Including a Survey of the

World's Periodical Literature. The new section was arranged topically and covered national and foreign affairs, finance and business, science, religion, the arts, sports, and industry. In each category articles from U.S. and foreign magazines and newspapers were summarized.

In addition to serving as a guide to other magazines, Shaw also provided his readers with information on the latest books. The New Books section varied greatly over the years, from long reviews to short annotations to simply lists of books. For the first decade the *Review* also published a brief keyword index to periodical articles from many contemporary magazines. The index ceased in 1903 after the *Readers' Guide to Periodical Literature* was established as the standard index for magazine articles.[10]

The content, structure, and length of the *Review* varied greatly over time, often in response to circulation figures and advertising revenue. The business history of the *Review* reveals its development and expansion along with its gradual decline in spite of many efforts to keep it alive.

The first issue of the *Review of Reviews* in the United States was published in April 1891 and sold for 20 cents. The following year the price was raised to 25 cents with subscriptions at $2.50, a rate that held for the next twenty-five years. Circulation statistics began in 1892 when 60,000 copies were printed per month. In the next three years the figure rose to 90,000 copies and remained at that level for the rest of the decade.[11]

The early years of the *Review* were financially difficult, but by the late 1890s advertising income increased. In 1895 the cost per page of advertising was $120, and within two years the figure had risen to $150. In July 1897 the title of the magazine became the *American Monthly Review of Reviews*, as Shaw moved another step away from the British publication.[12]

With the Spanish-American War, readership increased, and by 1901 circulation had nearly doubled to 178,200. Increases in the volume of advertising were dramatic. In 1902 there were more pages of advertising than of text, with text running about 120–130 pages. In the same year the cost of a full-page ad rose to $200. The years of 1905–1906 brought another growth spurt for the magazine. In 1906 circulation grew to 204,000 copies per month. At the same time the *Review* averaged 150 to 200 pages of ads, with the cost per page set at $225. The *Review* advertised itself as "printing more advertising than any other high grade magazine in the world." The *Review* not only increased the volume of advertising but also expanded the type of products included. In the early 1900s many ads for books and magazines were featured. According to N. W. Ayer & Sons, in the next five years advertising grew rapidly, and ad pages were divided into sections including books and educational materials, schools and colleges, financial services, and travel and recreation.[13]

Despite a slight decline in 1909, circulation remained at 200,000 until 1911, when it declined to 175,000 for about three years. The raw figures alone do not tell the entire story of how widely the magazine was read. A pre–World War I estimate indicated that each copy passed through six readers, so the actual number of readers may have been closer to one million although circulation figures were never that high.[14]

In 1916, as World War I escalated, circulation again increased, and by 1917 the *Review* reached its all-time high of over 240,000 copies per month. Advertising volume kept pace, and new ads for automobiles, office supplies, and construction companies appeared. The *Review* regularly carried cigarette ads, but accepted no liquor advertising. In January 1919 the single issue price rose to 35 cents with annual subscriptions at $4.[15]

In the decade of the 1920s the *American Review of Reviews* gradually declined. Circulation figures fluctuated sharply from 223,000 down to 205,000 and then dropped precipitously in 1923 to 150,000. To stem the marked decrease in circulation and a corresponding decline in advertising revenue, Albert Shaw, Jr., initiated a reorganization of the magazine and increased promotional efforts. The changes brought about a recovery in 1924 as circulation rose to 195,000, but neither Shaw nor his son could sustain the brief renewal. Despite increased appeals to business and travel advertisers, from 1920 to 1927 advertising income fell over $200,000 and the magazine faced its first deficit.[16]

During this time the *Review* also came up against major challenges from both the publishing and the advertising industries. By the late 1920s two divergent paths were evident in periodical publishing. A weekly magazine like the *Literary Digest* * or *Time* * was more up-to-date than a monthly review could hope to be, and many weeklies provided readers with briefer articles and more illustration. In contrast to mass-market magazines, smaller, more specialized periodicals also flourished because they were targeted for a specific group such as businessmen, hobbyists, or travelers. The *American Review of Reviews* could not measure up in either category. Shaw did not have the financial resources to expand and publish weekly. Yet the *Review* still had broader appeal and circulation than many of the specialized magazines. The increasingly sophisticated nature of advertising also contributed to the decline of the *Review*. As advertisers sought to appeal to greater numbers of people, or to the specific group most likely to purchase their product, the *Review* again found itself in the middle.[17]

Shaw tried several approaches to bolster his sagging publication. In 1929 he introduced changes in format and style. The *Review*, traditionally a small quarto, was changed to the full quarto-size page that allowed more printing and illustration options. Advertising was also easier to adapt to the larger pages, and for the first time the *Review* interspersed its ads within the text rather than grouping them at the back of the magazine. The major content change was dropping the Leading Articles section and merging its contents into the new News and Opinion section.[18]

Despite attempts to revitalize the *Review*, the onset of the depression caused severe financial problems. By 1931 advertising income had dropped by one-half, and circulation continued its downward trend. Such drastic losses necessitated cuts in the magazine down to sixty-five pages of text and ads, about one-fourth the length of the *Review* at ist its peak. The price was also reduced to 25 cents per issue, and the subscription rate was lowered to $3.[19]

Still another attempt to save the *Review* came in 1932 when Shaw acquired the publication *World's Work** and merged it with the *Review*. *World's Work* had been a major competitor of the *Review*, hence the merger eliminated a rival, but did not stop the *Review*'s continuing decline. During the final years the *Review* sought to widen its traditional scholarly audience by making a greater appeal to the business community. More advertising was aimed at businesses, as was the new Pulse of Business section.[20]

With the July 1937 issue the *Review of Reviews* ceased publication under its regular title. Shaw and his sons purchased another competing magazine, the *Literary Digest*, and merged the two under the new title of the *Digest: Review of Reviews Incorporating the Literary Digest*. The new *Digest* was issued weekly and kept the format and structure of the *Literary Digest*, adding only Shaw's editorial column from the *Review*. Due to ill health and continuing financial burdens, Shaw retired in October 1937, selling the publication to a group of editors. The magazine reverted to the name *Literary Digest*, but was issued for only a few months before it suspended publication and was eventually purchased by *Time*.[21]

As the person behind the publishing and editing of the *Review of Reviews* for forty-six years, Albert Shaw guided the magazine to a prominent position in the literary world of his era. In its heyday, the *Review* combined some of the best features of the later newsweeklies, with equally important aspects of monthly commentary and review magazines. With the demise of the *Review* the divergence between these two types of publications became a significant trend for the future of periodical publishing.

Notes

1. W. T. Stead, "Programme," *Review of Reviews,* January 1890, p. 14.

2. Albert Shaw, "William T. Stead," *American Review of Reviews*, June 1912, pp. 690–91; Piers Brendon, *The Life and Death of the Press Barons* (New York: Atheneum, 1983), pp. 75, 77–78.

3. W. T. Stead, "To All English-Speaking Folk," *Review of Reviews*, January 1890, p. 20; Frank Luther Mott, *A History of American Magazines*, 5 vols. (Cambridge: Harvard University Press, 1930–1968), 4:658–59.

4. Lloyd J. Graybar, *Albert Shaw of the "Review of Reviews": An Intellectual Biography* (Lexington: University Press of Kentucky, 1974), pp. 1–45.

5. Graybar, pp. 44–45, 47, 50–53; Mott, 4:659.

6. Graybar, pp. 49, 51, 58; *N. W. Ayer & Son's American Newspaper Annual Directory*, 1896 (Philadelphia: N. W. Ayer and Son's, 1896), p. 1435.

7. Graybar, p. 49; Mott, 4:660.

8. Graybar, pp. 61–62; Mott, 4:661–63.

9. Graybar, pp. 57, 62; Mott, 4:662; "Authors at Home," *New York Times Saturday Review of Books and Art*, 18 June 1898, p. 400.

10. Graybar, p. 61; Mott, 4:660–62.

11. Graybar, p. 203.

12. *N. W. Ayer & Son's* 1895, 1896.

13. *N. W. Ayer & Son's* 1903, p. 1557; Graybar, pp. 59, 203; Mott, 4:21, 661–662.

14. Graybar, pp. 59, 203.

15. Mott, 4:663. Mott lists the price change as occurring in 1923. Issues of the *Review* itself show the change to have taken place much earlier, in January 1919.

16. Graybar, p. 188; Mott, 4:663; Walter Dixon Anderson, "A Study of the Causes of Failure of Prominent Periodicals, 1926–1956" (M.A. thesis, University of Georgia, 1958), p. 24.

17. Graybar, pp. 187, 190; Anderson, pp. 8–10.

18. Graybar, p. 189; Anderson, p. 24.

19. Graybar, pp. 189–91.

20. Ibid., pp. 190–92; Anderson, pp. 24–25.

21. Graybar, pp. 192–93; Anderson, pp. 25–26.

Information Sources

BIBLIOGRAPHY

Anderson, Walter Dixon. "A Study of the Causes of Failure of Prominent Periodicals, 1926–1956." M.A. thesis, University of Georgia, 1958.

"Authors at Home." *New York Times Saturday Review of Books and Art,* 18 June 1898, p. 400.

Brendon, Piers. *The Life and Death of the Press Barons.* New York: Atheneum, 1983.

Graybar, Lloyd J. *Albert Shaw of the Review of Reviews: An Intellectual Biography.* Lexington: University Press of Kentucky, 1974.

Mott, Frank Luther. *A History of American Magazines.* 5 vols. Cambridge: Harvard University Press, 1930–1968.

N. W. Ayer & Son's American Newspaper Annual and Directory. Philadelphia: N. W. Ayer and Son's, 1895, 1896, 1903.

Shaw, Albert. "William T. Stead." *American Review of Reviews,* June 1912, pp. 689–95.

Stead, W. T. "Programme." *Review of Reviews,* January 1890, p. 14.

Stead, W. T. "To All English-Speaking Folk." *Review of Reviews,* January 1890, pp. 15–20.

INDEX SOURCES

Poole's Index 1889–1906, *Readers' Guide to Periodical Literature* (1890–1937); *Engineering Index* (1896–1907).

LOCATION SOURCES

Most major academic and public libraries hold at least some issues. According to *The Union List of Serials,* over 350 libraries hold this title. Available in microform.

Publication History

MAGAZINE TITLE AND TITLE CHANGES

(1) *The Review of Reviews,* January 1890–June 1897; (2) *The American Monthly Review of Reviews,* July 1897–May 1907; (3) *The American Review of Reviews,*

June 1907–1928; (4) *Review of Reviews*, 1929–August 1932; (5) *Review of Reviews and World's Work*, September 1932–July 1937.

VOLUME AND ISSUE DATA

Monthly. Vol. 1, January-June 1890; vol. 2, July-December 1890; vol. 3, January-July 1891 (March omitted, and American edition begun with April); vol. 4, August 1891–January 1892; vol. 5, February-July 1892; vol. 6, August 1892–January 1893; vol. 7, February-June 1893; vols. 8–95 (regular semiannual volumes), July 1893–June 1937; vol. 96, no. 1, July 1937.

PUBLISHER AND PLACE OF PUBLICATION

Review of Reviews, London (W. T. Stead), 1890–February 1891; Review of Reviews, New York (Albert Shaw), April 1891–1893; Review of Reviews Company, New York (Albert Shaw), 1894–January 1923; Review of Reviews Corporation, New York (Albert Shaw, Albert Shaw, Jr.), February 1923–July 1937.

EDITORS

William Thomas Stead, 1890–1891; Albert Shaw, 1891–1937.

CIRCULATION

Began at 60,000 in 1892; maximum circulation was 242,305 in 1917; in 1937, when the magazine ceased, circulation was 138,587.

Vanette Schwartz

RODALE'S ORGANIC GARDENING. See ORGANIC GARDENING

ROLLING STONE

Rolling Stone magazine, one of the foremost music-oriented publications of our day, marked its twentieth anniversary in 1987. Over the past twenty years, *Rolling Stone* has evolved from a twenty-five–cent black-and-white twenty-four–page paper to a slick full-color magazine featuring in its pages articles on culture, art, and politics as well as popular music. It is sold not only all over North America but in ninety-five foreign countries as well.

Jann S. Wenner, the force behind *Rolling Stone*, borrowed $7,500 to get the magazine underway. Wenner was greatly dissatisfied with the reporting he had been reading on rock, drugs, and the New Left, feeling that the information presented was "either myth or nonsense."[1] *Rolling Stone*, by contrast, would reflect "the changes related to rock and roll. . . . [We] hope we have something here for the artists, and the industry and every person who 'believes in the majic [*sic*] to set you free."[2]

Straight Arrow Press of San Francisco published the first issue in November 1967. From an initial press run of 40,000 and sales of only 6,000, *Rolling Stone's* circulation four years later was 250,000, 80 percent of which was newsstand sales. In 1976 the circulation figures exceeded 500,000. Today, the total circulation is over 1 million, 60 percent of which represents paid subscriptions. A one-year subscription (twenty-six issues) in 1968 cost $6.00 as compared to

$23.95 in 1987. Over the space of twenty years, the cost of a single issue has gone from twenty-five cents to $1.95.

Along with expected changes in circulation rate and price, *Rolling Stone* has undergone a number of other transitions. In 1977, the magazine's offices were moved from San Francisco to New York City for reasons of efficiency and economics. Changes in staff personnel and—most important for its readers—a shift in content also took place.

When it began, *Rolling Stone* was almost exclusively a rock-and-roll magazine that also contained a marginal number of nonmusic features. Over the years, it has broadened its scope considerably. Recent topics featured in *Rolling Stone* have included politics, AIDS, national affairs, pop psychology, nuclear energy, teen suicide, presidential races, and so on. Articles on audio and video technology are a regular part of the magazine. As one would expect, music is still the raison d'être of *Rolling Stone*.

Many well-known writers and celebrities have contributed to the magazine. Richard N. Goodwin, William Greider, Ralph J. Gleason, and Charles Perry have done articles on national affairs or social issues. Jann Wenner has written on music-oriented topics. Tom Wolfe, Truman Capote, and Jane Fonda have also been contributors. The advertisements appeal primarily to a young audience—men and women between the ages of eighteen and thirty. The ads that appear most frequently promote records, audio equipment, cars, motorcycles, cosmetics, cigarettes, and liquor Currently, the advertisements comprise 45 percent of an issue. Annual ad sales average more than $39 million.

From time to time, *Rolling Stone* has generated controversy. A particularly memorable incident took place in 1968 when the 23 November issue featured the nude photographs of John Lennon and Yoko Ono that were a part of their *Two Virgins* record album. Letters from riled readers and parents flooded the magazine's offices. Many cities and towns censored the issue. The postmaster in Englewood, New Jersey, refused to deliver copies. It even achieved the notoriety of being banned in Boston.[3]

Rolling Stone appeals mainly to two audiences, one much larger than the other. The first and larger audience consists of teens and adults who are fans of rock music. Many of these readers, an estimated 5 million, are the forty to forty-five age group who have been readers of *Rolling Stone* since it first began. The second audience consists of those who are interested in the history and/or social psychology of American popular culture from the 1960s to the present. Although the magazine's focus and informal tone may not appeal to everyone, *Rolling Stone* is excellent for what it purports to be.

Notes

1. Martin Arnold, "*Rolling Stone* Is Still Gathering Readers," *New York Times*, 22 October 1973, p. 32.

2. Alix Nelson, *"The Rolling Stone Reader"* (book review), *New York Times*, 14 April 1974, sec. 7, p. 19.

3. Jann S. Wenner, "From the Editor," *Rolling Stone*, 7 December 1968, p. 4.

Information Sources

BIBLIOGRAPHY
"Armstrong Resigns from *Rolling Stone*." *New York Times,* 28 April 1977, sec. 4, p. 9.
Dougherty, Philip H. "Advertising." *New York Times*, 26 February 1982, sec. 4, p. 13.
———. *"Rolling Stone* Adds Edition Here." *New York Times*, 6 May 1971, p. 13.
Ledbetter, Les. *"Rolling Stone* Is Tilting toward the East Coast." *New York Times*, 14 September 1976, p. 10.
Lichtenstein, Grace. "Rolling Drone, New Lampoon, Finds Little Rock in Denver." *New York Times*, 3 June 1975, p. 25.
"Notes on People." *New York Times*, 25 February 1977, sec. 2, p. 7.
INDEX SOURCES
> *Music Index* (1969–present); *Popular Periodicals Index*; *Readers' Guide* (1975, 1978–present); *Access* (1975–1978); *Magazine Index* (1977–present); *New Periodicals Index* (1977–present). By Publisher.

LOCATION SOURCES
> Library of Congress, many other libraries. Available in microform.

Publication History

MAGAZINE TITLE AND TITLE CHANGES
> *Rolling Stone.*

VOLUME AND ISSUE DATA
> Issues 1–present, November 1967–present, biweekly.

PUBLISHER AND PLACE OF PUBLICATION
> Straight Arrow Press, Jann S. Wenner, San Francisco, California, 1967–1977; New York, New York, 1977–present.

EDITOR
> Jann S. Wenner, 1967–present.

CIRCULATION
> 660,000 paid, 440,000 nonpaid.

Sandra Wenner

S

THE SATURDAY EVENING POST

The *Saturday Evening Post* is the quintessential American mass-market magazine. Its history dates from the early 1800s, earlier than most publications of any kind, and encompasses entire epochs of American history. It has risen and fallen in its appeal as a commercial publication, but it has managed to capture the feelings and aspirations of Americans more often than not.

Charles Alexander and Samuel C. Atkinson began publishing the *Saturday Evening Post* on 4 August 1821. It was begun as a weekly newspaper in Philadelphia, Pennsylvania, where it competed with weekly compilations designed for the "Sunday reader" in a time when newspapers did not publish on Sundays.

After a modest first decade, the *Post* realized some national success in the 1830s. It was sold and resold during this time until it came under the control of George Graham. He improved the appearance and the writing quality markedly during the 1840s. In 1846, Graham offered the editorship to Henry Peterson, who raised its stature during the 1850s so that its circulation approached 90,000 copies.[1]

The *Post* carried an eclectic mixture of news, politics, fiction, and human interest stories. The heart of its success during this time was the long fiction serial, usually by one Mrs. E.D.E.N. Southworth, but including Charles Dickens with *A Tale of Two Cities*. For two dollars a year, the reader got a newspaper of four pages measuring two feet by three feet.

In 1855, the *Post* became an eight-page small folio that featured fiction almost exclusively. During and after the Civil War, the *Post* declined in both circulation and quality. It was acquired by Andrew E. Smythe at a sheriff's sale in 1877 and for the next twenty years was little more than a sinecure for its owner.

Cyrus H. K. Curtis bought the *Saturday Evening Post* from Andrew Smythe in 1897 for $1,000. Curtis already owned the most successful magazine in the United States, the *Ladies' Home Journal*, and he applied the same techniques to his new acquisition. The contents were improved, the fiction was made more interesting, and a great many quality illustrations were used in the stories.

Curtis began an advertising campaign when the number of subscribers had dipped to nearly a thousand. Early in 1898, Curtis enhanced the *Post's* tenuous connection to Benjamin Franklin by claiming the *Post* had been founded by Franklin in 1728. This claim was displayed prominently on the masthead of the magazine for many years. The company went to some pains to justify this connection with Franklin in all its subsequent "history" as well as its advertising.[2]

In fact, it has been shown to be less than the truth. Frank Mott, magazine historian, concluded that "the only connection of the *Post* with the *Pennsylvania Gazette* or its illustrious early editor was the fact that it was first published from the shop in which the *Gazette* had perished six years before, and one of its founders had been a partner of the grandson of Franklin's partner, in a printing business."[3]

The price of the subscription was raised to $2.50 a year, but the single copy price was kept to a nickel. Using a prospectus on future publication plans, Curtis raised the circulation during 1898 to over 250,000. William George Jordan, an editor of the *Ladies' Home Journal* for Curtis, initially edited the *Post* while Curtis hunted for a full-time editor.

In 1898, George H. Lorimer was hired as editor of the *Post*. Lorimer became a legend in magazine publishing while leading the *Post* to its position as America's foremost weekly magazine during the next thirty years. He was solely responsible for the *Post's* editorial content. The *Post's* mixture of three major elements—business, public affairs, and romance—with liberal doses of sports, humor, illustrations, and even cartoons, was to become such a success in the marketplace that it was referred to as the "Post formula."[4]

During his time as editor, Lorimer introduced some of the most popular writers and illustrators of the next four decades to the public. The fiction of Jack London, Rudyard Kipling, and Stephen Crane graced the *Post's* pages during this period. Reminiscences of William Allen Wright, Theodore Roosevelt, and Lorimer himself were popular. In 1916, Norman Rockwell began creating the covers for the *Post* that were to number in the hundreds.

By 1913, the *Post* had over two million copies circulating each week. The Curtis Publishing Company was highly successful through the teens and twenties. Earnings in 1925 were estimated at over $16 million. The *Post's* circulation and revenues declined somewhat in the early thirties with the advent of the depression. However, by 1937, the *Post* had reached its long-held circulation goal of three million issues. It still sold for a nickel a copy.

Several major changes occurred in the thirties for the *Post* that anticipated the coming end of the pre–World War II Curtis Publishing era. Cyrus Curtis had health problems in 1932, and George Lorimer assumed the chairmanship; Curtis died in 1933. Subsequently, Lorimer retired in 1936 and died the next year. His strong hand had been felt in every aspect of the *Post's* editorial policy. In fact,

Lorimer was so in tune with the middle-class American's feelings and thoughts that the magazine was able to increase its circulation while actively opposing Franklin Delano Roosevelt's New Deal, which most Americans supported.

In 1934, Walter D. Fuller became president of the Curtis Publishing company and remained so through the forties when circulation hit 4 million copies. Wesley W. Stout succeeded Lorimer as editor in 1937. For five years, he maintained the *Post*'s standard, even increasing the use of color and illustration inside the magazine, but in 1942 he resigned amid declining revenues and circulation, perhaps resulting from the *Post*'s isolationist stance on the war and a furor over an article on Jews that was bitterly criticized.

Ben Hibbs became editor in 1942 and took the magazine through the war years with changes in nearly every aspect of its production including price, which was raised to ten cents. By 1945, then, the *Post* had the pieces in place for a new and vital magazine.

The success of the *Post* picked up again after the war. Circulation soared to over four million in 1949 and reached five million in 1955. The Curtis Publishing Company had by then fully integrated its magazine publishing from start to finish, including timber rights, paper production, printing, publishing, and circulation. The source for financing such an interdependent structure was largely from advertising revenue of the Curtis magazines.

This integrated structure had an inherent weakness. Even though it was the basis for the *Post*'s unprecedented success in the early postwar years, the *Post*'s self-sufficiency lacked true diversification. When difficult times arose in the sixties, it would prove to be the *Post*'s undoing.

With the retirement of Ben Hibbs in 1961 the *Post* entered a period of instability in both its editors and publishers—the presidents of Curtis Publishing. Although Ben Hibbs was the editor from 1942 to 1962, including a decade that was impacted by the television market and its competition for advertising dollars, the years 1962–1969 saw no less than four editors of the *Post*: Robert Fuoss, Robert Sherrad, Clay Blair, and William Emerson. The publisher's position underwent a similar period of instability, with the long tenure of Robert MacNeal being followed by the short stays of Matthew Culligan, Jess Ballew, and Stephen Kelley.

One observer has identified three major policy areas in which the new *Post* changed radically: (1) articles focused on interesting individuals as opposed to communal activities (e.g., television education, tourists, and African hospitals); (2) controversial articles (articles that show some "fight"); and (3) some curtailment of the activities of its artists and photographers by art directors.[5]

Curtis, the publisher of the *Post* and numerous other periodicals, also underwent radical changes: "When Matthew Culligan took over in 1962 he dismissed 2,200 of the company's 9,000 employees." And by 1963 the magazine that had "preached conservative Republicanism, extolled big business, and castigated Franklin Roosevelt's New Deal" became an advocate of "sophisticated muckraking'' and in the process accumulated $27,060,000 in libel suits by the year's end.[6]

Although in 1959 the *Post*'s advertising revenue was the highest ever ($97,614,442), by the early sixties it was losing millions of dollars a year. From 1961 through 1968, ''largely because of the *Post*'s problems, the parent Curtis Publishing Company had lost $62 million.''[7] Rising costs associated with production, competition by television, millions in libel suits, the loss of three million readers from subscription lists, and cut-rate subscription prices all had some effect.

Curtis Publishing was unique among publishers not only because of its size (distributor of over 100 periodicals) but also because of its diversity. It owned large tracts of timberland that fed the paper mills; it also owned and manufactured the paper that it used at its printing plant in Philadelphia. It also circulated its own material; so, it was in addition to being a publisher, also a manufacturer and a circulation company as well.

The *Post*'s success over the years was due to a number of conditions, some a direct result of the talent employed by the magazine and others that developed with the passage of time due to fortuitous circumstances of various sorts. Because of the audience it appealed to and the economic and social changes then occurring, the *Post* became an institution to millions of middle-class Americans during the early years of the twentieth century and continued to be one until roughly the mid–sixties.

After Curtis hired George H. Lorimer as editor, the *Post* began to assume institutional status. The *Post* arrived on Thursdays,

> intended for weekend reading, but nobody waited that long . . . it brought humor, sentiment, pragmatic soothsaying and a touch of romance into millions of households. In smaller towns especially, it was the prime medium of family entertainment. . . . In its pages, readers saw reflections of themselves—or, at least, what they liked to think of themselves. . . . it was the values of ordinary men—cozy domesticity, a sense of humor, a belief in decency and common sense, a faith in free enterprise—that the magazine sought to express. It distilled an almost mythic vision of small-town America that many of its readers were still living and others were already nostalgic about.[8]

Nowhere was this vision more apparent than on the *Post*'s covers—particularly in the work of artist Norman Rockwell.

Fiction always played an important role in the *Post*, and even though its targeted reader was the small-town American whose literary tastes were supposedly more bland, the work of most of the better modern American and British writers regularly appeared in its pages. For example, a partial list includes Booth Tarkington, Edith Wharton, Theodore Dreiser, John P. Marquand, Thomas Wolfe, Ring Lardner, William Faulkner, Ernest Hemingway, F. Scott Fitzgerald, Bret Harte, Jack London, and Joseph Conrad as contributors. There was also work of lesser literary value, but considerable entertainment—material by Erle Stanley Gardner, Mary Roberts Rinehart, Agatha Christie, and two series particularly identified with the *Post*, Norman Raine's adventures of Tugboat Annie, and William H. Upson's Alexander Botts and the Earthworm Tractor Company stories.

There was a formula of sorts at work in the makeup of an issue of the *Post*: usually four short stories, seven articles, one or two serial fiction pieces, and a handful of poems, usually short. Even in the sixties, when the *Post* was beginning to decline, in among its attempts at newness and variation in format, in typefaces, in editorial stances, and in editors too, the concern with providing literature for its audience was evident. Poetry was represented by the likes of Howard Nemerov, W. H. Auden, Stephen Spender, C. Day Lewis, and Robert Graves; short stories appeared from Ray Bradbury, H. E. Bates, Kurt Vonnegut, William Saroyan, Robert Penn Warren, Arthur Miller, and John O'Hara. Female literary figures were for the most part, however, quite notably absent, with Joan Didion being the exception. Serial publications by C. S. Forster and *Sand Pebbles* author Richard McKenna also appeared.

Outside of literature there was no dearth of material, if not by women, then about them—notably celebrities such as Phyllis Diller, Natalie Wood, Joanne Woodward, and Shelley Winters, as well as a healthy complement of equivalent males.

Political figures traditionally used the *Post* as a forum whenever possible, and the list of American presidents who published in the pages of the *Post* is an impressive one. Prominent public figures other than presidents occasionally found their way into the *Post* also. Arthur M. Schlesinger wrote for it on the failure of world communism; Robert Kennedy, Nelson Rockefeller, Dean Acheson, and William O. Douglas also contributed on relevant topics.

Now if the *Post* of the early part of the century advocated free enterprise, American business, and the pursuit of the American dream generally, then the "new *Post*" circa 1962 was trying to attract an audience on different grounds: noting "the decline since the mid–1940's, of the political party as a dominant factor in our political life," new editor Robert Fuoss asked, "Is our political purpose better fulfilled by those who, unencumbered by allegiance or obligation bring the full weight of reason to the sweaty but important chore of helping people make up their minds?" He wanted to make the editorial pages of the *Post* "an island of free expression."[9] The more tangible changes, described by one observer as "the European format that has been leaking into American magazines since World War I: bleed pages, lots of wasted white space, and sans-serif type,"[10] included end-to-end makeup to provide story continuity, more photographs, opinion articles, and a younger staff—and, significantly, the dropping of the bust of Ben Franklin from the masthead.

Another area in which the *Post* provided regular and extensive coverage (as well befits a periodical that had a sports editor for years) was the sports scene. Baseball and basketball provided the most coverage, and the *Post*'s fall "Pigskin

Preview'' was one of the earliest and most influential of its type; eventually it would be picked up on by *Playboy** and others. *Post* was also one of the first nonsport magazines to devote significant coverage to professional football. One sixties sports story, ''The Story of a College Football Fix,'' resulted in a $3 million libel suit against the *Post*, however.

Aside from the articles on movie stars, sports figures, politicians and the like, the *Post* regularly included in its typical issue the problem article; ''Our Flabby Youth,'' ''Real World of Divorce,'' ''Juvenile Gangs,'' and ''Thalidomide Babies'' were generally well done in comparison with similar material being published in *Life** and *Look.**

In the late 1960s, despite becoming a biweekly in 1965, actively pursuing a change of image and readership via modish content, and eliminating three million subscribers en route to achieving a '' 'class' instead of 'mass' '' audience,[11] the *Post* continued to lose millions of dollars a year. And so, in the spring of 1968 Martin S. Ackerman (aka Marty the Mortician) became president of Curtis because that company was unable to pay a $12 million debt and Ackerman offered to ''put up $5 million if he could become president of Curtis.''[12] After effecting several changes including the above-mentioned circulation reduction, Ackerman announced the last issue of the *Post* seven months later, in February 1969.

The *Post* remained dormant (not to say dead) for two years until the summer of 1971 when it was revived as a quarterly publication in Indianapolis, Indiana, by the new owner of Curtis and editor and publisher of the *Post*, an Indianapolis industrialist, Beurt SerVaas. Describing itself as the ''latest issue of the old *Post*,'' and urging readers to ''rediscover an old, old friend''[13] the new, old *Post* was filled with articles, stories, and features reprinted from earlier issues: Tugboat Annie and Alexander Boots stories, Ellery Queen, Thomas Wolfe, Hazel, and most of all, in a role resembling that of a patron saint or household deity, Norman Rockwell in every form—from reprints to interviews to special Norman Rockwell issues. The *Post* had become its former self: ''In format and much of its content, this is the homey, comfortable, non-controversial old Post of Ben Hibbs, not the later, slicker version.''[14]

Although it changed to monthly publication (actually nine issues a year) in January 1974, the *Post* kept its nostalgic emphasis in effect until September 1975, when Cory SerVaas, M.D., assumed the position of editor and publisher. At that point, although still emphasizing the magazine's rather tenuous connection with Ben Franklin, and still publishing the occasional quality piece of fiction (e.g., stories by Kurt Vonnegut and John C. Gardner), the magazine's emphasis steadily began to shift to a concern with health, health food, and religious matters—which is where it is focused at present. Organizations such as the Benjamin Franklin Literary and Medical Society and the Saturday Evening Post Society use the pages of the present-day *Post* to urge its readers to ingest a variety of health food products and support the research efforts of their organization. The advertisers seem oriented to the retirement age group, and the ads themselves are often either of the classified variety or extremely small.

Notes

1. Information on the *Post*'s early years came largely from Frank L. Mott's *History of American Magazines,* vol. 4; *1885–1905*, Cambridge: Harvard University Press, 1957, pp. 671–85.
2. Curtis Publishing Company, *A Short History of the "Saturday Evening Post"* Philadelphia: Curtis, 1953, pp. 5–22.
3. Mott, p. 683.
4. For a discussion of the Lorimer editorial style, the *Post* formula, see Mott, pp. 701–8, and John Tebbel, *George Horace Lorimer and the Saturday Evening Post*, Garden City, N.Y.: Doubleday, 1948.
5. David Cort, "Face-Lifting the Giants," *Nation*, 25 November 1961, p. 425.
6. "Death of an Institution," *Newsweek*, 20 January 1969, p. 52.
7. "The Saturday Evening Post," *Time*, 17 January 1969, p. 48.
8. Ibid.
9. Robert Fuoss, Editorial, *Saturday Evening Post*, 6 January 1962, p. 84.
10. Cort, p. 425.
11. "Death of an Institution," p. 53.
12. Otto Friedrich, Excerpt from *Decline and Fall, Harper's*, December 1969, p. 92.
13. Advertisement, *Saturday Evening Post*, September 1971, p. 92.
14. "Return of the *Post*," *Time*, 14 June 1971, p. 70.

Information Sources

BIBLIOGRAPHY

Cort, David. "Face-Lifting the Giants." *Nation,* 25 November 1961, pp. 424–26.
Curtis Publishing Company. *A Short History of the "Saturday Evening Post."* Philadelphia: Curtis Publishing Co., 1953.
———. *The Life and Times of Cyrus H. Curtis.* New York: Curtis Publishing Co., 1953.
"Death of an Institution." *Newsweek*, 20 January 1969, pp. 52–53.
Friedrich, Otto. Excerpt from *Decline and Fall. Harper's*, December 1969, pp. 92–100.
Goulder, Joseph C. *The Curtis Caper.* New York: Patmore, 1965.
Halsey, Ashley. *Illustrating for the Saturday Evening Post.* Boston: Arlington House, The Writer, 1951.
Mooney, Michael M. "The Death of the *Post*." *Atlantic*, November 1969, pp. 70–76.
Mott, Frank L. "The Saturday Evening Post." *A History of American Magazines*, vol. 4; *1885–1905*, Cambridge: Harvard University Press, 1957 pp. 671–716.
Rankin, W. Parkman, and Eugene S. Waggaman. "The Saturday Evening Post." *Business Management of General Consumer Magazines*. 2nd ed. New York: Praeger, 1984, pp. 43–75.
"Return of the *Post*." *Time*, 14 June 1971, p. 70.
"The Saturday Evening Post." *Time*, 17 January 1969, pp. 48–49.
Tebbel, John. *George Horace Lorimer and the Saturday Evening Post.* Garden City, N.Y.: Doubleday, 1948.
Wood, James. "Magazine Reflection of a Nation: *The Saturday Evening Post*." *Magazines in the United States*. 3rd ed. New York: Ronald Press, 1971, pp. 147–65.

INDEX SOURCES
    Readers' Guide to Periodical Literature, 1920–present.
LOCATION SOURCES
    Widely held; also available in microform.

Publication History

MAGAZINE TITLE AND TITLE CHANGES
    The Saturday Evening Post, 1821–1830, 1839–present; *Atkinson's Saturday Evening Post,* 1830–1832, 1833–1839; *Atkinson's Saturday Evening Post and Bulletin,* 1833; *Atkinson's Evening Post and Philadelphia Saturday News,* 1893; *The United States Saturday Post and Chronicle,* 1842–1843; *The United States Saturday Post,* 1843–1845.
VOLUME AND ISSUE DATA
    Weekly, August 1821–January 1965 with occasional missed periods and numbering variations; biweekly, January 1965–February 1969; quarterly, 1971–1974; nine issues a year, January 1974–present.
PUBLISHER AND PLACE OF PUBLICATION
    In Philadelphia: Atkinson and Alexander, 1821–1828; Samuel Coate Atkinson, 1828–1839; Du Solle and Graham, 1839–1840; G. R. Graham and Co., 1840–1843; Samuel D. Patterson and Co., 1843–1848; Deacon and Peterson, 1848–1865; H. Peterson and Co., 1865–1873; Saturday Evening Post Publishing Co., 1875; Charles I. Wickersham and Joseph P. Reed, 1875–1876; Bennet and Fitch, 1876–1877; Andrew E. Smythe, 1877–1897; Curtis Publishing Co., 1897–1962: (presidents, Cyrus H. K. Curtis, 1897–1932; George H. Lorimer, 1932–1934; Walter D. Fuller, 1934–1950; Robert E. MacNeal, 1951–1962); New York: Matthew J. Culligan, 1963–1964; Jess L. Ballew, 1964–1968; Stephen S. Kelley, 1968–1969; Curtis Publishing Co., Indianapolis, Beurt SerVaas, 1971–1975, Cory SerVaas, 1975–1982; Benjamin Franklin Literary and Medical Society, Inc., Indianapolis, Cory SerVaas, 1982–present.
EDITORS
    T. Cottrell Clarke, 1821–1826; Morton McMichael, 1826–1828; Benjamin Mathias, 1828–1839; George Rex Graham, 1839–1846; Henry Peterson, 1846–1873; R.J.C. Walker, 1874–1875; Joseph P. Reed, 1875–1876; Orlando Bennet, 1876–1877; Andrew E. Smythe, 1877–1897; William George Jordan, 1897–1899; George H. Lorimer, 1899–1936; Wesley W. Stout, 1937–1942; Ben Hibbs, 1942–1962; Robert Fuoss, 1962; Robert Sherrad, 1962; Clay Blair, 1963–1964; William A. Emerson, Jr., 1964–1969; Beurt SerVaas, 1971–1975; Cory SerVaas, 1975–present.
CIRCULATION
    6.8 million (1968); 700,000 (1988).

                        Alan Nourie and Carroll Varner

SATURDAY REVIEW

When the *Saturday Review* was founded in 1924, it was a particularly auspicious time for establishing a new literary magazine. During the 1920s, literature was gaining an increasing amount of self-conscious public attention in the country. The American cultural scene was undergoing a literary renaissance when unfamiliar forms of writing were being received with enthusiasm. In the postwar economic boom, Americans had both the leisure and the resources to appreciate a new major periodical devoted almost exclusively to books considered as literature.

The roots of the *Saturday Review* can be traced to the *Literary Review*, a weekly supplement to the *New York Evening Post*. In 1920 Henry Seidel Canby, an English professor at Yale, was asked to establish a literary review for the newspaper. With a staff of three, William Benét, Amy Loveman, and Christopher Morley, Canby built the supplement into a review of high quality and intellectual leadership, gaining an audience of 8,000 to 10,000 readers across the country. However, although the journal was considered both a critical and popular journalistic success, and the most authoritative review of serious books in America, commercial publishers criticized it as unnecessarily erudite, and a block to the success of books. When the *Post* was sold by its publisher, Thomas Lamont, to the Curtis Publishing interest in 1924, the *Literary Review* was cut from the newspaper.

Lamont, upset by the demise of the review, approached the publishers of *Time*, Henry Luce and Briton Hadden, for assistance in reestablishing the review. Lamont invested $50,000 in the new journal; Time offered its publishing facilities and its offices to house the magazine's staff; and Canby and his associates were given full editorial control. Roy Larsen, *Time*'s circulation manager, obtained the subscription list of the *Post*'s *Literary Review*; along with this established circulation, plus the subscriptions Larsen solicited from bookstores and through direct-mail, the newly founded *Saturday Review of Literature*'s circulation increased to 23,000, more than twice its independent circulation as the *Post*'s literary section.

With the same "family of minds" to assist him, Benét, Loveman, and Morley, Canby brought out the first issue of the magazine on 2 August 1924. Luce was listed as president, Canby appeared as vice-president and editor, and the others as associate and contributing editors. The review's new symbol was a phoenix rising from the ashes, an idea of Benét, who also used it in his department, Phoenix Nest. The publication's format was newspaper supplement size, three columns wide, with distinctive type; the leading editorial by Canby set forth the magazine's principles regarding literary criticism:

> In one guise a gray-bread philosopher searching for the Best, but also in the mood of youth, watching the three-ringed show under the great tent of Today—yet discriminating in both—that is the double function of criticism and this *Review*.[1]

Loveman assigned books for review, wrote reviews, and did pasteup, proofs, and final assembly of the magazine at the printer's; she also worked with new writers. Morley was the chief essayist for the *Review*, and Benét, its poetry critic. Canby was president of the American Center of the PEN Club (poets, playwrights, essayists, editors, and novelists). For a long time he had helped with the defense of foreign writers who were under political pressure and attack; he also promoted the translation and distribution of their works in the United States. Many émigré writers and critics made their first appearance or were established in America through the pages of the *Saturday Review*.

In 1925, the *Review* left *Time*'s offices and continued its existence with heavy subsidies from Thomas Lamont. By 1936, the journal's finances sharply declined when Lamont reduced his support; Canby perceived that a new course was needed for the publication, probably in the direction of current affairs. That year he resigned from his editorship of the *Review*, and Bernard De Voto, a lecturer in literature at Harvard College, succeeded him. De Voto edited the *Review* until 1938, upholding the values of the literary tradition established by Canby. He was replaced by George Stevens, who was promoted from managing editor to editor of the *Review*. After Lamont entirely withdrew his subsidy from the magazine that year, the *Review* was able to survive thanks to two new benefactors. Harrison Smith, a publisher, bought the *Review* and contributed working space; Harry Scherman, president of the Book-of-the-Month Club, helped with financing and contributed new subscribers, provided through his club's membership lists.

After 1939, the journal's title was shortened to the *Saturday Review*; at the same time, its editorial scope and thematic interests were broadened. In December, Norman Cousins was asked to join the *Review* as executive editor when Stevens left; he inherited the financial liabilities, the talented staff, and the idealistic views of the magazine's founders. Cousins viewed the editor's task as "not to raze a magnificent structure in order to get rid of the mortgage, but to retire the debt by broadening the base."[2] *Saturday Review* survived two and a half years of financial hardship until 1942, when it was purchased by E. De Golyer, a scientist, booklover, and oilman, who gave the journal editorial independence, even though his conservative views often did not coincide with its idealistic liberalism. At that time, Cousins was made editor-in-chief and began in earnest to reshape the magazine to cover arts, science, current affairs, travel, and education. To strengthen the publication's financial basis, Jack Cominsky, advertising director of the *New York Times*, was appointed advertising and business manager of the *Review*. He restructured the magazine's economic and editorial planning into long-term programs, stressing the need to diversify advertising and to make the journal less financially dependent on book publishing ads.

With the economic stability that came with De Golyer's financing and Cominsky's management, the *Review* was able to tackle new projects and broaden editorially to become a more inclusive cultural journal. Book reviews continued to be the center of the publication, reinforced, by a full-fledged review staff with specialists on the European literary scene, trade publishing, literary criticism, and children's books. The main criteria in both assigning and reviewing books were that the reviewer should not exploit himself, but interpret the subject, and that the review was to aim at the general reader, not the specialist. Over the years, features that focused on nonliterary areas of interest were added: Cleveland Amory began a "main events" column called First of the Month in 1947; Hollis Alpert and Arthur Knight began covering film in 1950; Gilbert Seldes and Lewis Shayon wrote about the broadcast media; Ivan Dimitri and Margaret Weiss reviewed photography as a fine art. Special supplements were begun in the 1940s, and a particularly innovative one on music was begun in 1947 by Irving Kolodin, the music critic, who forecast various technological changes in the recording industry. Features in a lighter vein were added and expanded; in 1942 Bennett Cerf continued Chris Morley's Trade Winds column on the publishing trade, mixing in a strong vein of humor as the distinguishing characteristic of his coverage. Horace Sutton convinced the *Review*'s editors to let him begin a travel column in 1947 called Booked for Travel; his editorial initiative made travel interest a major part of the magazine's growth. The *Review*'s end features, the Personals ads, and the Double-Crostics puzzle, begun in 1932 and in 1934, continued to be perennial favorites.

The war years helped to quicken the *Review*'s development into a journal linking the arts and ideas. The magazine acted as a countermobilization against the suppression of the free flow of ideas and rational thinking in society. For example, when Ezra Pound was granted the Bollingen Prize for poetry by the U.S. Government, the review questioned the action. The magazine handled the resulting controversy by publishing all sides of the debate, beginning with Robert Hillyer's articles, which criticized the award to Pound, who had made propaganda attacks against the United States during World War II for Mussolini's government. A later case in point was the publication in 1945 of Cousins' critical piece "Modern Man is Obsolete." The essay was prompted by the use of the atomic bomb against Japan that same year, and set the stage for the dominant editorial theme of the journal during his editorship: the nuclear issue.

During the 1950s, the *Review* became directly involved with a number of controversies that erupted from the broad debate over the impact of governmental policy concerning atomic energy. In 1956 the magazine published some of the earliest information on the effect of radioactive fallout as revealed by Barry Commoner in the evidence of milk contamination and the consequent harm to children's growth. John Lear, who joined the journal as science editor in 1956, led the charge both against the drug companies for their false advertising and inadequate testing, and against the government for enforced fluoridation of water; the latter issue, in particular, resulted in a long and bitter debate in the pages of the *Review*. An especially gratifying controversy for Cousins was the literary debate over John Ciardi's harsh review of Anne Morrow Lindbergh's poetry in the 12 June 1957 edition of the *Review*; with this issue, poetry and the values of literary criticism came into national focus.

The magazine had earlier established a reputation for itself as a vehicle for humanitarian projects. For example, in 1943 the *Review* sponsored the Hiroshima Maidens project in 1943, a four-year medical and rehabilitative treatment of Japanese girls disfigured or crippled by the bombing. A similar program of medical, surgical, and psychotherapeutic care was undertaken by the magazine from 1957 to 1959 for the Ravensbrueck Lapins, Polish women who had been used as medical guinea pigs by Nazi doctors during World War II. The money for such concerns was provided by both the readers of the *Review* and by its healthy financial resources, ably managed by an economic team of Cominsky, Nat Cohn, and Pat Patterson; De Golyer had transferred ownership of the magazine to the publishers in 1956.

Throughout the 1960s Cousins pursued his course as an itinerant editor for the *Review* in coverage of global affairs, particularly those connected with the issues of world peace. His visit to the Soviet Union in June 1959 as a speaker on world affairs in the Cultural Exchange Agreement had prompted the *Review* to sponsor the Dartmouth Conferences (1960–1964), a series of unofficial meetings between private citizens from the United States and the U.S.S.R. The 7 November 1964 issue of the *Review* featured the text of Cousin's seven-hour interview with Nikita Khrushchev on 2 April 1963, before the leader had been ousted from power. After the passage of the limited test-ban treaty by the U.S. Senate in 1963, the *Review's* editors were directly congratulated by President John Kennedy on the magazine's efforts over the years in promoting the control of nuclear testing. The lighter side of the magazine was highlighted with the introduction of Goodman Ace's humor column, "The Top of My Head," in 1964, and with a series of cartoons by Burr Schafer called "Through History with J. Wesley Smith." In 1961, a problem with the ownership structure of the magazine had been resolved when Norton Simon, the owner of *McCall's*,* offered the *Review* an affiliation with his corporation. A "pooling of interests" transaction was made, and the principal benefits to the *Review* were the use of *McCall's* printing facilities and membership in an editorial committee that met with world leaders to discuss coverage of critical issues. The *Review's* healthy financial growth in advertising revenues and circulation continued throughout the decade; by 1967, it had 510,000 readers and a staff of over one hundred.

By 1971, Cousins's ten-year contract with *McCall's* had expired, and debilitated by illness, he was ready to step down. That year, the *Review* reached a peak circulation of 650,000, and was sold to owners who divided it into four separate magazines on the arts, education, science and society. By 1972, the *Review* was in the bankruptcy courts; the venture to win the race of magazines for specialized readers and advertisers had failed. In 1973, Cousins returned to head *Saturday Review* on the basis of *World*, the magazine he had founded after leaving the *Review*. His resuscitation of the journal was defeated by the hike in postal rates that made the expense of magazine delivery and subscription solicitation by mail greater than the cost of production of the *Review*. The magazine was sold in 1977 to Carll Tucker, former drama critic of the *Village Voice*.* Tucker converted the magazine to a biweekly, but could not offset mounting financial losses of the *Review*, which never again recaptured the large following of readers that Cousins had cultivated in the 1960s through his liberal humanism and the magazine's eclectic appeal.

In 1980, in a distress sale, Robert Weingarten, owner of *Financial World*, acquired the *Review*. He changed the journal into a monthly and tried to refocus it as a newsmagazine of the arts. By June 1982 the *Review* had a circulation of 480,000, but most of the subscribers were paying a discount rate. Weingarten's attempts to cut financial losses resulted in serious undercapitalization of the magazine, which suspended publication in 1982 after a loss of $3 million. Later that year it was sold to publisher Jeffery Gluck before it slipped into bankruptcy. The new owner moved the *Review's* publication offices to Columbia, Missouri, pared subscribers to 210,000, and converted the journal to a bimonthly. Gluck's cost-cutting measures were criticized for producing a publication of inferior quality, and the magazine was once more suspended in January 1984. Two Washington-based conservatives, Frank Gannon and Paul Dietrich, bought the *Review* later that year, switched publication to a monthly schedule, and tried to change it into a review of both established and contemporary culture. The journal declined into shallow coverage of starlets and trendy stories on the arts, in an attempt to appeal to a younger generation of readers. Circulation fell to 150,000 with the May 1986 issue, and the last few issues appeared bimonthly until publication was suspended in midyear. In 1987, *Penthouse* publisher Bob Guccione bought the *Review* with plans to eventually revive the magazine, whose name remained its only real asset. *Saturday Review's* history of decline provides a striking illustration of the dilemma that has confronted so many quality literary journals in the United States: that of the successful translation of cultural values into economic worth.[3]

Notes

1. Henry Seidel Canby, quoted in Norman Cousins, *Present Tense* (New York: McGraw-Hill, 1967), p. 7.
2. Cousins, *Present Tense*, p. 20.
3. Norman Cousins, "Postmortem of the *Saturday Review*," *Center Magazine* 16 (1983): 33–40.

Information Sources

BIBLIOGRAPHY
Canby, Henry Seidel. *American Memoir*. Cambridge, Mass.: Houghton Mifflin, 1947.
Cousins, Norman. "Postmortem of the *Saturday Review*." *Center Magazine* 16 (1983): 33–40.
———. *Present Tense*. New York: McGraw-Hill, 1967.
Peterson, Theodore. *Magazines in the Twentieth Century*. Urbana: University of Illinois Press, 1964.
INDEXES
    Annual Bibliography of English Language and Literature, Magazine Index, Readers' Guide to Periodical Literature.

LOCATION SOURCES
Many libraries.

Publication History

MAGAZINE TITLE AND TITLE CHANGES
Saturday Review of Literature, 2 August 1924–21 December 1951; Saturday Review, 5 January 1952–January 1973; Saturday Review of the Arts, Saturday Review of Education, Saturday Review of the Sciences, and Saturday Review of the Society, January 1973–August 1973; Saturday Review/World, 11 September 1973–14 December 1974; Saturday Review, 11 January 1975; August-September 1986.

VOLUME AND ISSUE DATA
Vols. 1–34, 2 August 1924–29 December 1951, weekly; vols. 35–55, 5 January 1952–January 1973, weekly; vols. 1–2, no. 7, 11 September 1973–14 December 1974, weekly; vols. 5–7, 7 January 1978–April 1980, biweekly; vols. 7–9, May 1980–June 1982, monthly; vols. 10–12, March-April 1983–May-June 1986, bimonthly.

PUBLISHERS
Time, Inc., 1924–1926; Saturday Review Company, Inc., 1926–1927; Noble A. Cathcart, 1927–1939; Harrison Smith, 1940–1942; Saturday Review Associates, 1942–1952; J. R. Cominsky, 1952–1968; William D. Patterson, 1968–1971; Robert J. Moore, 1971–1972; Spencer Grin, 1972–1978; James E. Broadwater, 1979–1980; Robert Weingarten, 1980–1982; Jeffrey Gluck, 1982–1984; David Simpson, 1984–1986.

EDITORS
Henry Seidel Canby, 1924–1936; Bernard De Voto, 1936–1938; George Stevens, 1938–1939; Norman Cousins, 1939–1971; Nicholas D. Charney, 1971–1973; Norman Cousins, 1973–1978; Carll Tucker, 1979–1981; Stephen Shepard, 1981–1982; Bruce Van Wyngarden, 1983–1984; Frank Gannon and Paul Dietrich, 1984–1986.

CIRCULATION
650,000 (1971, peak).

Diana A. Chlebek

SCRIBNER'S MAGAZINE

Scribner's Magazine, one of the big four—with *Century, Harper's,** and *Atlantic Monthly**—of the quality popular journals of the late nineteenth century was first issued in January 1887. Publication was suspended after the May issue of 1939. The name was sold to the *Commentator* in 1939 and lasted under the name of *Scribner's Commentator* into the early 1940s. This magazine of the early 1940s was in no way, however, a continuation of *Scribner's Magazine*, but much more a continuation of the *Commentator*.

Intended for an educated reader, *Scribner's Magazine* was priced at twenty-five cents per copy. First editor Edward Livermore Burlingame used the twenty-five-cent price to lure new readers from the established magazines such as *The Atlantic, Harper's*, and *Century, Scribner's Magazine* sold for a quarter a copy, $3.00 a year; the others sold for thirty-five cents a copy, $4.00 a year.[1]

Another early business practice to lure more readers was that of free subscriptions to editors of weekly and small daily papers throughout the country in exchange for their printing notices for the magazines, perhaps excerpts from articles that had appeared in earlier issues.[2] This was a common practice among most of the standard monthlies. These same magazines provided posters for newssellers to display, and in the 1890s collecting the posters was popular.[3] During the same time period, many other general monthlies had joined *Scribner's Magazine* in accepting advertising. *Harper's* and *Century* charged $250 per page, *Scribner's* charged $150, and the *Atlantic* charged $100.[4] In addition, *Scribner's* had a prosperous English edition shortly after it began.[5]

Most issues contained 125–130 pages plus advertising pages at the end, until the advent of hard times in the early 1930s. The June 1889 issue contained 126 pages, plus advertising, apportioned among five articles, seven poems, one short story, a critical biography, one essay, and one novel (an installment of Stevenson's *Master of Ballantrae*, which ran serially for a year).

The quality magazines, most of which lasted at least into the 1930s, failed in large measure because of competition with the popular general audience magazines, particularly the ten-centers. Not only was price a factor, so too was content. Interestingly, as *Scribner's* became more like the popular rather than the quality magazines, it lost its audience and eventually failed entirely.[6]

Through the magazine's history it published fiction and nonfiction by established writers and also introduced works by many aspiring writers. The articles on science and travel are reminiscent of the material found in the *Smithsonian*.*

A glowing review of *Scribner's Magazine* for May 1893 appeared in the June issue of *Review of Reviews**:

The laurels of the month's race in magazine making are easier than usual to bestow, for May brings forth the long-heralded exhibition number of *Scribner's Monthly* [sic], with its important "find" of Washington's autograph narrative of the Braddock campaign, with its stories and essays by Howells, Besant, Thomas Hardy, Cable, Bret Harte and Henry James, and not least, with its goodly array of pictures that are worthy exponents of the highest stage we have reached in the art of illustrating. The magnificent volume which the Messrs. Scribners have put together with capital taste, at a time of the year when most of the journals are relapsing into summer desuetude and decreased editions, makes a landmark in the career of their magazine and is calculated to fix patriotic Americans still more comfortably in the assurance that we are first in the artistic construction of the "popular illustrated monthly." It is needless to say that this volume, on which so much care has been lavished, is timed to be an exposition number.[7]

The reviewer notes the confusion caused by the demise of the 1870–1881 *Scribner's Monthly* and the new *Scribner's Magazine*, which had attained "respectable" circulation quickly, particularly with the publication of Thackeray's letters. In 1870, Josiah Gilbert Holland and Roswell Smith, later to serve as editor and business manager, had approached Charles Scribner of the publishing firm about establishing a popular magazine. Scribner, who was to own four-tenths of the stock in the magazine company, had already offered the editorship of Scribner's periodical *Hours at Home* to Holland. Its subscription list was taken over by the new *Scribner's Monthly*.

Scribner's Monthly, edited by Dr. Josiah Gilbert Holland, was known more for its moralizing tone than was the later *Scribner's Magazine*, mostly because of the editor's own articles in the department "Topics of the Times." Edward Eggleston called him "the most popular and effective preacher of social and domestic moralities of his age," and Mott suggests that "whatever his faults, [Holland] should be named in any list of the half-dozen greatest American magazine editors."[8] Holland contributed much of the serial fiction to the *Monthly*, although in early issues he did include one piece of serial fiction by Jules Verne. Soon, however, a policy of only American serials was in place, and such noted authors as Edward Everett Hale, Henry James, Bret Harte, and George W. Cable were published. The poetry published by the *Monthly* is generally undistinguished, although Joaquin Miller and Sidney Lanier are among the well-known poets. "The Scribner achievement in the essay was more striking than that in poetry" according to Mott, although the only well-known essayist may be John Muir.[9] Associate editor Richard Watson Gilder, whose interests lay in literature and art, was influential in *Scribner's Monthly* becoming well-known for its illustrations. The most ambitious project during these years was a series of articles on "The Great South." But in 1881 three major changes took place: no longer was Scribner's associated with the publishing house, the name changed to *Century Illustrated Monthly Magazine* (a magazine that lasted under that title until 1930), and its editor Holland died. Charles Scribner's Sons (the elder Scribner having died in 1871) agreed not to start another magazine with the same title for at least five years. Six years later *Scribner's Magazine* then began.

Since the contemporary *Century* refused to publish serials of "exotic authorship," the reviewer of 1893 describes *Scribner's Magazine* as more "cosmopolitan." Another pleasant departure from practice by rival magazines at the time is *Scribner's Magazine's* once a year fiction number, " containing only imaginative work—an innovation that would seem like a revolution in *Harper's* or the *Century*."[10] Editor Burlingame is praised as the son of a diplomat who grew up in China and was educated in Germany. He is the man who each year must choose the hundred or so manuscripts "which will allow his magazine to stand unashamed by the side of the many eager rivals—not to speak of the task of deciding not to procure the nine thousand or so unsuccessful claimants!''[11] The reviewer also notes the contributions of Robert Bridges, assistant editor, O. H. Perry, art editor, and N. F. Doubleday, business manager. And he comments at length on the quality of both literary and artistic contributions in this particular May issue.

One of the major contributions both *Scribner's Monthly* and *Scribner's Magazine* seem to have made to the development of the magazine is the use of advertisements. Roswell Smith of the 1871 *Scribner's Monthly* defied a warning from Fletcher Harper to refuse advertisements; in fact, he courted them because of the need for revenue from additional sources. And *Scribner's Magazine* is now described as the "veritable cradle of magazine advertising."[12] All ads were at the back of the issue and on the back cover. They were a far cry from the slick ads in today's magazines. In *Scribner's Magazine* ads were classified by "proprietary articles," "sporting goods," and "financial." Pens, penmanship courses, pianos, typewriters, bicycles and tricycles, and patent medicines were the most popular of the ads. In addition, "the trick of running funny pictures among the advertisements, possibly invented by *Scribner's*, was to lure the reader to the back of the book where the ads lay in wait for him."[13] Interestingly, microform reprints of the magazine do not include the advertisements; one must consult the original source to see ads for items such as moustache cups and bustles. Ad space was small, "as little as two agate lines, interspersed with braver quarter-, half-, and full pages. The back cover was quartered like the coat of arms of a royal prince."[14]

Editor Burlingame not only selected outstanding fiction pieces for the magazine but also noteworthy nonfiction: the unpublished letters of Thackeray, edited by James Russell Lowell; reminiscences of General Sheridan and of Stanley, the explorer; the essays of Robert Louis Stevenson; and groups of articles on the railway, electricity and steamships. Other notable fiction and nonfiction writers who published while Burlingame was editor are innumerable, including: William Dean Howells, Henry Cabot Lodge, Henry James, George Meredith, Frank R. Stockton, George W. Cable, Bret Harte, and Theodore Roosevelt. Poets include Edwin Markham, James Russell Lowell, Amy Lowell, Edwin Arlington Robinson, Sara Teasdale, John Masefield, and James Whitcomb Riley. Illustrators include N. C. Wyeth, Charles Dana Gibson, Maxfield Parrish, H. Siddons Mowbray, LeRoy Baldridge, and James Montgomery Flagg.

Regarding the illustrations, an interesting event occurred in the 1890s regarding an article on French art that included a reproduction of a nude. " . . . a banker in upper New York State protested that at the sight of the picture a young female member of his household had 'uttered a low cry and fled from the room.' " For some years such "revealing" illustrations were called "low-cry" pictures and were not published.[15]

Among the novels published serially were *The Master of Ballantrae* by Robert Louis Stevenson, *The Amazing Marriage* by George Meredith, *Sentimental Tommy* by J. M. Barrie, *The House of Mirth* by Edith Wharton, and, in later years, *The Silver Spoon* by John Galsworthy and *A Farewell to Arms* by Ernest Hemingway.[16]

When Burlingame retired he was succeeded by Robert Bridges who had been with the magazine since its inception, primarily as assistant editor. He continued the high standards of the magazine that Burlingame established. He published from among his "remarkably large circle of friends who were noted men of achievement, and the magazine became a leader among the nontechnical publications in promoting knowledge of the new science."[17] Bridges sought a "cultivated magazine for an intelligent audience, a thought-provoking magazine for a thoughtful audience, without in any way making it a highbrow magazine for the select few."[18] He published such writers as Ernest Hemingway, Conrad Aiken, Thomas Wolfe, and Sherwood Anderson. In 1930, after forty-three years with *Scribner's*, Bridges retired.

Bridges was succeeded by Alfred S. Dashiell, assistant editor since 1923. His special interest was the short story. He established a $5,000 prize contest for the best short novel (15,000–35,000 words), to be published in a single issue. Over 1,700 manuscripts were submitted, eleven published. A second contest was held in 1932, with two first-place winners, one of whom was Thomas Wolfe. Dashiell also tried to present true-life tales of interest to Americans, again in contest form. This established the Life in the United States monthly feature.[19] "Straws in the Wind," another regular feature focused on contemporary trends in the family, the nation, the economy. Dashiell published short complete biographies of men like Thomas Edison, Joseph Lenin, and Karl Marx. William Lyon Phelps's As I Like It reviewed books, music, and drama, and in 1929 a regular book review column appeared.

In the later years better-known writers appeared—Sinclair Lewis, Erskine Caldwell, Ernest Hemingway, Marjorie Kinnan Rawlings, Langston Hughes, Kay Boyle, William Faulkner, and Thomas Wolfe. Poets included Conrad Aiken, Robinson Jeffers, William Rose Benét, Jesse Stuart, Edgar Lee Masters, Robert Frost, and Witter Bynner. Notable serials in the 1930s included Fitzgerald's *Tender Is The Night* and Hemingway's *Green Hills of Africa*.

In addition to its contribution of advertising to magazines, its stellar literary contributors, and its outstanding artwork, *Scribner's Magazine* stayed abreast of the times and often critiqued and analyzed events of the day. One outstanding piece was in the August 1905 issue, which sought to prove that "much of the sympathy for Japan in the war with Russia, so universally prevalent in America, was a result of the coloring of the news service that reaches [the United States] through English influence and manipulation" (especially Reuters News Service).[20]

Scribner's chronicled many more events that contributed significantly to the unique development of American culture. The first volume, January-June 1887, holds works on such diverse, often timely subjects as: "our defenceless [sic] coasts," the development of the steamship, our naval policy, and socialism, plus less contemporary themes such as the unpublished letters of Thackeray, the

Bayeux Tapestry, and the French Revolution. The second volume, July-December 1887, includes articles on: cyclones, the development of the American university, physical characteristics of the athlete and the typical man, and "what shall we tell the working-classes?" Throughout the 1890s *Scribner's* addressed these topics: electricity, slavery in Africa, building and loan associations, American game fishes, Theodore Roosevelt's "Rough Riders" in six installments, and the letters of Robert Louis Stevenson, also in six installments. Newly discovered records of Meriwether Lewis and William Clark, the evolution of the skyscraper, and speculation and stock exchanges were among articles in the first decade of the twentieth century. The June 1919 issue contains articles on the limits of feminine independence, the way of the Bolshevik, and personal recollections of Walt Whitman.

Volume 91, January-June 1932, includes articles on the wastefulness of American colleges, a new China, civilization in the United States, family relationships, Herbert Hoover's electibility, Japan's future, and a new political deal. The January 1937 anniversary issue looks back to each of the decades during which *Scribner's Magazine* existed to chronicle life in the United States at the time. The May 1939, "final" issue of *Scribner's Magazine*, was short, barely seventy pages, with two fictional works by Thomas Wolfe, articles on *Collier's** and Leverett Saltonstall, and regular departments: The Scribner Quiz; Life in the U.S.; Straws in the Wind; Music and Records; Wines, Spirits and Good Living; Dogs and Kennels; Books; and Education—not at all the caliber of work that *Scribner's* had once offered.

Throughout the years *Scribner's* had attempted to keep up with the trends in the magazine industry. A new typeface on special eggshell paper and a new cover appeared in 1928. In 1932 the format of the magazine was changed to a larger page size, and again a new cover was adopted. For a while illustrations were dropped entirely, but in June 1933 they returned, almost all done by Edward Shenton. In that issue, the staff noted:

> In keeping to the original policy of publishing the best that can be found to interest an intelligent American audience—in acquainting their readers with great art, great literature, the beauty of language, in keeping them informed on new modes of thought, new standards of thinking, in giving them a more thorough understanding of the problems confronting their everyday life, and in stimulating new writers of promise and publishing the work of leading authors—the editors of *Scribner's* are ever aware of their privilege. The satisfaction of the editors is shared with the satisfaction of the readers.[21]

In 1936 when Alfred Dashiell left *Scribner's* to join the staff at *Reader's Digest,** he was succeeded by Professor Harlan de Baun Logan, who had earlier analyzed *Scribner's* and offered suggestions on improving the magazine and its circulation. Logan had given this type analysis as an assignment in his New York University classes and then decided to do freelance analyses of magazines himself, including *Life,** *Liberty,** and *Vanity Fair.** His suggestions included expanding from sixty-four to ninety-six pages, using a color picture on the cover, two-column rather than three-column makeup, adding a monthly new author feature, and having fiction comprise half rather than a quarter of total entries.[22] At this point, when Logan took over, circulation had dropped to 43,000.

Logan hired Thomas Maitland Cleland, an artist who had worked on the format of *Fortune*, to help in reworking *Scribner's*. Cleland recommended that the magazine be "easy to read, . . . go against today's trend and stress art—not sex in illustrations."[23] When the "new" *Scribner's* hit the stands its price was a quarter, it was on glossy paper and *News-week* size.

In January 1937 *Scribner's* celebrated its fiftieth anniversary. At that time Frederick Lewis Allen noted three reasons to join in "the feast of congratulation and well-wishing":

> The first is that, today as yesterday, the quality magazines have an opportunity to further the cause of a really vital American literature . . . . The second reason is that they have an opportunity to throw genuine light upon the terrific problems that beset us today. . . . And the third reason is that, even in an atmosphere of crisis, they have an opportunity to deal, from time to time at least, with those enduring values which are above and beyond time and place and event, and with which *Scribner's Magazine* has dealt from the moment of its founding fifty years ago.[24]

The February 1939 issue offered a new reader a forty-word definition of *Scribner's* aim:

> Scribner's examines life in the United States, is primarily concerned with the men, media, and institutions influencing that life. Scribner's examines with fact, fiction, photographs, and art; employs all four tools in order to be realistic, incisive, important, and interesting.[25]

But in May of 1939 the publishers announced that *Scribner's* would suspend publication until the fall because of finances. Although Logan had reversed the trend of major losses, he never was able to turn a profit. One of Logan's ideas had been to distribute 50,000 free copies to top-income families every three months, but he learned one fact: "wealthy business and professional men did not read literary fiction and essays."[26] He then switched to topics of more political and current interest. In fact, he bought the magazine from Charles Scribner and Sons in 1938 and published the last year's issues himself. His net losses in March of 1939 were only $700 a month, but a slump in advertising in the 1930s led to the end of *Scribner's*. Previous losses had been as much as $25,000 per month when Logan took over, so his efforts were imminently successful, but not successful enough to keep the magazine going. In addition, circulation had risen to 100,000, not quite the 350,000 that Logan had set as a goal.[27]

In August 1939 Dave Smart, owner of *Esquire** and *Coronet,** bought *Scribner's*, for a "reputed $11,000," to boost the sales of his own magazines. At the same time, he cut the price of *Coronet*.[28] In November *Scribner's* merged with the *Commentator*; thus the May announcement that *Scribner's* would return in the fall was accurate in part.

Malcolm Cowley attempted to explain the demise of so many of the general monthly magazines in his "epitaph" for *Scribner's* in 1939. By that year magazines like *McClure's, Everybody's, Appleton's, Hampton's, Lippincott's, Munsey's*, Hearst's *International, The Metropolitan*, and *The Century* had ceased publication or were no longer read with "any excitement." Cowley explains that competition from the movies and radio partially explains the loss. But the real fault lay with commercialism in the magazine industry. "They became so commercial in spirit, so timid and deferential toward those in power, that they lost their audience, their profits and their reason for existence, all at one stroke."[29] Cowley further explained what happened specifically at *Scribner's*:

> Among the general magazines, Scribner's had stood somewhat apart. It had gone along for fifty years without being much affected by contemporary fashions; it had neither attacked business in the muckraking days nor praised it in the back-slapping that followed. Most of its reputation was due to the writers it published—Meredith, Henry James, Howells, Kipling and Stephen Crane; then Hemingway, Faulkner and Wolfe in the 1920's. It was a distinction to be printed in Scribner's and something of a distinction even to read it. For a long time the magazine had been losing money, but the publishers believed in it and the deficits were always met. . . .
>
> The point I am trying to make is that as long as Scribner's had a quality of its own, depending on the type of writing it published, there were people willing to make sacrifices in order to keep it alive. As soon as it began to imitate the new mass-circulation magazines, it had to have a mass circulation. It had to be judged by standards of strict business accounting. It had to make a profit on pain of death.[30]

Notes

1. Frank Luther Mott, *A History of American Magazines*, vol. 4: 1885–1905 (Cambridge: Harvard University Press, 1957), p. 718.

2. Ibid., p. 17.

3. Ibid., p. 19.

4. Ibid., p. 21.

5. Mott, Vol. 3: 1865–1885, p. 229. Mott uses the date 1886, an impossibility in that the magazine did not begin until 1887.

6. John Tebbel, *The American Magazine: A Compact History* (New York: Hawthorne Books, 1969), pp. 166–67.

7. "The Periodicals Reviewed," *Review of Reviews*, June 1893, p. 609.

8. Mott, vol. 3, p. 459.

9. Ibid., p. 463.

10. "The Periodicals Reviewed," p. 609.

11. Ibid.

12. Earnest Elmo Calkins. "Magazine into Marketplace," *Scribner's Magazine*, January 1937, p. 108.

13. Ibid.

14. Ibid.

15. Frederick Lewis Allen, "Fifty Years of Scribner's Magazine," *Scribner's Magazine*, January 1937, p. 21.

16. See *American Literary Magazines: The Eighteenth and Nineteenth Centuries*, ed. Edward E. Chielens (Westport, Conn.: Greenwood Press, 1986), for more detail on *Scribner's Magazine* as a literary publication.

17. Marion Ives, "Scribner's—Surveyor of the American Scene," *The Quill*, December 1935, p. 8.

18. Ibid., p. 12.

19. Ibid., p. 13.

20. George Presbury Rowell, *Forty Years An Advertising Agent* (New York: Franklin Publishing Company, 1926), pp. 338–39.

21. Ives, p. 13.

22. "Scribner's Logan Who Raked It over the Coals Is Editor Now," *News-week*, 27 June 1936, pp. 29–30.

23. "Logan and Cleland Put Out a Refurbished Monthly," *News-week*, 3 October 1936, p. 8.

24. Allen, p. 24.

25. *Scribner's Magazine*, February 1939, table of contents page.

26. "Free to be Rich," *Business Week*, 10 April 1937, p. 24.

27. "End of Scribner's," *Time*, 15 May 1939, p. 60.

28. "Scribner's to the Smoking Room," *Time*, 4 September, 1939, p. 34.

29. Malcolm Cowley, "Epitaph for Scribner's," *New Republic*, 24 May 1939, p. 77.

30. Ibid.

Information Sources

BIBLIOGRAPHY

Allen, Frederick Lewis. "Fifty Years of Scribner's Magazine." *Scribner's Magazine*. January 1937, pp. 19–24.

Calkins, Earnest Elmo. "Magazine into Marketplace." *Scribner's Magazine*. January 1937, pp. 108–117.

Cowley, Malcolm. "Epitaph for Scribner's." *New Republic*, 24 May 1939, p. 77.

"End of Scribner's." *Time*, 15 May 1939, p. 60.

"Free to be Rich." *Business Week*, 10 April 1937, p. 24.

Ives, Marion. "Scribner's-Surveyor of the American Scene." *The Quill*, December 1935, pp. 8, 12–13.

"Logan and Cleland Put Out a Refurbished Monthly." *News-week*, 3 October 1936, p. 8.

Mott, Frank Luther. *A History of American Magazines*. 5 vols. Cambridge: Harvard University Press, 1930–1968.

"Old Friends." *New York Times*, 6 May 1939, p. 16.

"The Periodicals Reviewed." *Review of Reviews*, June 1893, pp. 609, 616–17.
"Scribner's Logan Who Raked It over the Coals Is Editor Now." *News-week*, 27 June 1936, pp. 29–30.
"Scribner's Magazine Halts Publication." *New York Times*, 5 May 1939, p. 27.
"Scribner's Magazine Suspends Publication." *Publisher's Weekly*, 13 May 1939, p. 1765.
"Scribner's Paradox." *Business Week*, 13 May 1939, p. 16.
"Scribner's to the Smoking Room." *Time*, 4 September 1939, p. 34.
"Scribner's and Judge." *Newsweek*, 15 May 1939 p. 40.
Tebbel, John. *The American Magazine: A Compact History*. New York: Hawthorne Books, 1969.

INDEX SOURCES
Readers' Guide to Periodical Literature, Poole's Index, Cumulative Index, Annual *Library Index; ALA Portrait Index, Review of Reviews Annual Index, Contents-Subject Index, Engineering Index.*

LOCATION SOURCES
Library of Congress; many other libraries. Available in microform.

Publication History

MAGAZINE TITLE AND TITLE CHANGES
Scribner's Magazine. January 1887–May 1939.

VOLUME AND ISSUE DATA
January 1897–May 1939. Monthly. Volumes 1–104, regular semiannual, January 1887–December 1938; 105, January–May 1939. Merged with the Commentator in November 1939.

PUBLISHER AND PLACE OF PUBLICATION
Charles Scribner's Sons, New York, 1887–1937; Harlan Logan Associates, New York, 1937–1939.

EDITORS
Edward Livermore Burlingame, 1887–1914; Robert Bridges, 1914–1930; Alfred S. Dashiell, 1930–1936; Harlan de Baun Logan, 1936–1939.

CIRCULATION
Scribner's Magazine, peak of 200,000 in 1910–1911; 70,000 in 1924; 126,000 in 1939.

Barbara Nourie

THE SMART SET

The *Smart Set,* once a leading national monthly literary magazine devoted to the publication of poems and short stories, was the vehicle through which the careers of many prominent writers were launched. Making its debut on 10 March 1900 in New York during an era when wealth and status were wedded with intellect, *Smart Set* was designed for the rich and affluent or at least those who aspired to be like the wealthy. As reported in the *New Yorker*, the income of many of the *Smart Set* subscribers was reflected in names found on the *Social Register* and in the manner by which the affluent chose to recreate. According to the July 1905 issue of the *New Yorker*, "2,649 of the 7,816 families on its roster had left for the seashore, 3,925 had taken to the mountains or other inland resorts, and 195 were cruising on their yachts, while 847 had departed for Europe."[1]

Contributions included in the first issues of the *Smart Set* were submitted by these "fashionable ladies and gentlemen of a literary beat." *Social Register* names included Caroline Duer, Sara Van Rensselaer Cruger, Hobart Chatfield-Taylor, and Sarah Cooper Hewitt. During these early years, it became obvious that these individuals with "proper surnames" would not help sustain the magazine. The "social snobs" were more interested in reading the lackluster gazette *Town Topics* than in writing literary material.[2] Ironically, the *Smart Set, A Magazine of Cleverness*, was intended as a companion to the weekly *Town Topics, The Journal of Society*. Over the next decade, therefore, several social registrants continued to send contributions to the *Smart Set*, but more professional, mostly young and obscure writers accepted the "one cent per word for prose and twenty-five (sometimes stretched to thirty-five) cents a line for poetry."[3] Gelett Burgess, William Rose Benét, James Branch Cabell, Zona Gale, John Hall Wheeler, Jack London, Theodore Dreiser, and Sinclair Lewis were among these professionals.

The planning of the *Smart Set* was ideal. America during this era (early 1900s) had more than enough magazines, of every variety, but a journal of "cleverness" was needed. "Cleverness" reflected an attitude, whether one was wealthy himself or not, he/she needed to identify with and approve of the Gilded Age affluence that had given the United States a flourishing aristocracy of money and an expanded middle class that imitated and aspired to be aristocrats. Because of this attitude, "cleverness" could not represent avant-garde or experimental material. Avant-garde and experimental material later became a viable part of *Smart Set* especially during the H. L. Mencken and George Jean Nathan regime.

In order to accumulate "usable" literary works, *Smart Set*'s first editor, Arthur Grissom, developed a plan by which monetary prizes were awarded to potential contributors. These awards ranged from $10 for jokes to $2,000 for novelettes. Needless to say, contributions were considerable, and throughout most of the *Smart Set*'s span, there was usually an ample supply of material.

The first novelette, "The Idle Born" by Hobart Chatfield-Taylor and Reginald DeKoven established a pattern of opening the *Smart Set* with a novelette. Each issue of approximately 160 pages also included a play, several short stories and poems, and "witticisms" to fill up the bottoms of pages. Early issues rarely contained nonfictional articles until Mencken and Nathan became book reviewer and drama critic respectively.[4] They were given carte blanche by Fred Splint, managing editor, to "write what you damn well please as long as it's lively and gets attention." Thus began the Mencken-Nathan era, which lasted until the demise of the magazine. Although there were major differences in their backgrounds, education, and interests, Mencken and Nathan agreed that the individuals who ran the *Smart Set* were "a pack of asses" but they could have some "fun" with the magazine. For fifteen years not only did Mencken and Nathan write critical columns for the *Smart Set* but they also assumed several pseudonyms and contributed material to the magazine. One of their best-loved "contributors" was Owen Hatteras. Many *Smart Set* readers and contributors were unaware that Owen Hatteras was a Mencken-Nathan pseudonym. Hatteras received fan mail, invitations to lecture, to dine, and even to contribute to other journals.

Many subscribers to the magazine, those individuals who were especially content to read material reflecting their life styles, were also those who were not necessarily doers for themselves but receivers of services. Ray Womrath's cover for *Smart Set* featured an affluently dressed couple, masked Mephisto, dangled winged hearts, and impish cherub with an arrow. Each issue included ads for luxury hotels, expensive jewellers, and fashionable boutiques. By 1906, however, many of these ads gave way to ads for Milwaukee breweries and convention hotels in Atlantic City because of the plummeting circulation. About 25,000 readers left *Smart Set*, and in the next four years some 40,000 readers departed.

By 1911, the cover of *Smart Set*, now illustrated by James Montgomery Flagg, reflected the changing times. The curtseying belle now wore a more décolleté, less frilly gown; her hair was dressed in the more stylish Empire coiffure. Her tail-coated escort now looked somewhat older, definitely a more suave lothario, gallantly holding his top hat before him. However, the masked Mephisto, Cupidons, and dangling hearts appeared on the cover very much as they had on older issues. The large initial Ss of the vermillion-colored title of *Smart Set* also remained.

In attracting advertisements, *Smart Set* had been somewhat successful. During the early years, selling for twenty-five cents in an era of the ten-cent monthly, it displayed in each issue approximately two dozen pages of ads at $150 per page. Through the years, with a steady decline in circulation numbers, *Smart Set* began to attract less and less stable ads. With the sale of the magazine in 1911 to John Adams Thayer, *Smart Set* once again regained its snob appeal and exclusiveness. Thayer was superior in acquiring advertising, and by May 1912, *Smart Set* bulged with new ads. These ads became fairly firmly established; however, circulation fluctuated between 80,000 and 90,000. Eventually, *Smart Set* had to raise its cover price from twenty-five cents to thirty-five cents.

Despite some successes, *Smart Set* continued to flounder. However, the British version of *Smart Set*, with its focus on leading British socialities, continued to flourish. Many Americans did not know of the London *Smart Set*.[5]

One of the persons most responsible for the success of *Smart Set* in America was Colonel William d'Alton Mann, its originator with rights also to the London *Smart Set*. A Civil War cavalry commandant, interested in oil stocks but narrowly escaping indictment for peddling phony ones, and the proprietor of the *Mobile Register*, his first publishing venture, Mann was not beyond taking risks.

While in the South, he also tried his hand at politics—for the Southern cause—and ran as a Conservative Democrat for Congress in Mobile in 1869. He was elected by a landslide but was refused certification by Reconstruction officers. This did not deter the ambitious Mann, who decided to build his own railroad line from Mobile to New Orleans. Additionally, he patented in 1872 a "boudoir" sleeping car that became the prototype of compartmentalized sleepers. After selling his business in Europe to a Belgian partner and in America to George Pullman, who monopolized the American market, Colonel Mann sought yet another venture, publishing and editing the gossipy society weekly *Town Topics* in Manhattan. Taking the weekly over for his younger brother, Eugene, in 1891, he quickly made it a success.

As somewhat of a Fifth Avenue celebrity, he could be seen in 1900 with his long white whiskers, flaming red tie and frock coat. And, as quite a minor sideline, he became interested in developing *Smart Set* as a companion to *Town Topics*.[6] *Town Topics* was to continue with reportage, whereas *Smart Set* was intended to consist of fictional and "arty" material.

As a literary magazine from 1900 to 1924, *Smart Set* had about 2,000 contributors and published perhaps as many as 8,000 works.[7] It has had several owners: Colonel Mann (1900–1911); Adams Thayer (1911–1914); and joint ownership by Colonel Eugene R. Crowe, H. L. Mencken, and George Nathan (1914–1924). Upon *Smart Set's* sale to William Randolph Hearst in 1923, Morris Gilbert assumed the editorship. He dramatically changed the format and included "sepia-toned photographs." In 1924, the new subtitle became *True Stories from Real Life*. Acquiring *McClure's Magazine* in 1929, Hearst merged it with *Smart Set* and renamed the combined journals *The New Smart Set, The Young Woman's Magazine*. Margaret R. Sangster acquired the editorship (1929–1930), followed by Arthur Samuels in 1930. On 15 June 1930 *The New Smart Set* expired.[8]

Notes

1. Andy Logan, "That Was New York," *New Yorker*, 14 August 1965, pp. 37–91.

2. Ibid., 21 August, 1965, p. 91.

3. Carl R. Dolmetsch, *The Smart Set, A History and Anthology* (New York: Dial Press, 1966), p. 11.

4. Mencken became book reviewer in 1908; George Jean Nathan assumed the position of drama critic a year later.

5. Dolmetsch, 1966, p. 4. Colonel Mann in 1899 had incorporated his Ess Ess Publishing Company in New York and staked out publishing charters in London and Paris.

6. Logan has made extensive use of all contemporary newspaper accounts about Colonel Mann.

7. Two of the best sources of contributions to *Smart Set* other than the magazine issues are *The Smart Set Anthology* by Burton Rascoe and Groff Conklin (New York: Reynal

and Hitchcock, 1934) and *The Smart Set; A History and Anthology* by Carl R. Dolmetsch (New York: Dial Press, 1966).

8. Few libraries have complete sets of *Smart Set*. The Chicago Public Library has a partial set of original *Smart Set* issues.

Information Sources

BIBLIOGRAPHY

Dolmetsch, Carl R. *The Smart Set; A History and Anthology*. New York: Dial Press, 1966.

Goldberg, Isaac. *The Man Mencken*. New York: Simon and Schuster, 1925.

Logan, Andy. "That Was New York." *New Yorker*, August 14 and 21, 1965.

Mott, Frank Luther. *A History of American Magazines*. vol. 4: *1885–1905*. Cambridge: Harvard University Press, 1957.

Peterson, Theodore. *Magazines in the Twentieth Century*. Urbana: University of Illinois Press, 1964.

Rascoe, Burton, and Groff Conklin. *The Smart Set Anthology*. New York: Reynal and Hitchcock, 1934.

Richardson, Lyon. *A History of Early American Magazines*. New York: T. Nelson and Sons, 1931.

Tebbel, John William. *The American Magazine: A Compact History*. New York: Hawthorne Books, 1969.

Wood, James Playsted. *The Magazine in the United States*. New York: Ronald Press, 1956.

INDEX SOURCES

    n.a.

LOCATION SOURCES

    Available in microform.

Publication History

MAGAZINE TITLE AND TITLE CHANGES

    The Smart Set, A Magazine of Cleverness, March 1900–1924; *The Smart Set, True Stories From Real Life*, 1924–1929; *The New Smart Set, The Young Woman's Magazine*, 1929–June 15, 1930.

VOLUME AND ISSUE DATA

    Vols. 1–89, March 1900–April 1930.

PUBLISHER AND PLACE OF PUBLICATION

    Ess Ess Publishing Company, New York.

EDITORS

    Arthur Grissom, 1900–1901; Marvin Dana, 1901–1904; Charles Hanson Towne, 1904–1908; Col. William d'Alton Mann, 1908–1911; Norman Boyer, 1911–1913; Willard Huntington Wright, 1913–1914; Henry Louis Mencken and George Jean

Nathan, 1914–1923; Morris Gilbert, 1923–1929; Margaret R. Sangster, 1929–1930; Arthur Samuels, 1930.
CIRCULATION
165,000 (1905—peak circulation).

Frances Moore-Bond

SMITHSONIAN

In 1846 an enigmatic Englishman—James Smithson—left a bequest in his will that created, by an Act of Congress, the Smithsonian Institution, a body dedicated to "the increase and diffusion of knowledge among men," as specified by the donor. Joseph Henry, the first secretary, led the institution for over thirty years into its higher purposes of sponsoring research in the sciences, history, and the arts, publishing the results in a scholarly manner that would advance American scholarship.

In the 124th year of the institution a magazine was created, backed by a $50,000 grant, and named after its parent. The first issue came off the presses in April 1970, showing on its glossy cover the picture of two courting elephants. "It should be the task of our magazine," wrote then-secretary S. Dillon Ripley, "to add to the sum of public knowledge within the mandate of this Institution, for 'every portion throws light on all others' as Smithson asserted in the beginning."[1]

Edward K. Thompson, formerly editor of *Life*,* was lured to this job of publishing a magazine that would cater to the tastes of thousands of national associates as diverse as the pieces stored in the museum, balancing popular themes with the scholarly flavor of institutional research, things in which, in Thompson's own words, "the Smithsonian is interested, might be interested or *ought* to be interested."[2]

The magazine had a few problems in its infancy. Looking back over one decade, Edwards Park remembers the scarcity of office space and the poverty of the magazine's first quarters. He recollects the insanity of the first computer system that kept spewing hundreds of copies to the same address. "Anchorman John Chancellor," Park writes, "noted in an evening broadcast that his television studio had received a promotion letter from *Smithsonian* addressed to 'NBC News' and starting out 'Dear Mr. News . . . ' We wrote him a note offering to send the same thing to Walter Cronkite, and Chancellor wrote back again saying it was OK, he took the magazine and loved it."[3]

And so did the majority of *Smithsonian*'s first subscribers, the national associates, after perusing that first courting-elephants issue, which included articles by such authorities as microbiologist René Debos writing about the reconciliation of man and nature: "Life is an endless give-and-take with Earth and all her creatures . . . human beings are shaped, biologically and mentally, by the environment in which they develop." John W. Blassingame wrote on soul scholarship—the choices ahead for black studies. Other articles ranged from macramé to pollution to overpopulation—Stephanie Mills wearing IUDs as earrings—to the question of unleaded gasoline. And of course the cover story about the elephant-breeding project.

Psychologists and biologists used adjectives such as "fantastic, scholarly, informative, beautiful" to convey their pleasure with the new publication. There were a few negatives: "It's terrible," wrote one reader; "level of junior high student," scoffed another; "too many ads," complained a few. One reader from Auburn, Alabama, was "disappointed to encounter a *whiskey* ad"; a gentleman from South Carolina did "not care to be exposed to the garbage contained in your article on Black Studies."[4]

The quality of the artwork for the advertisements left much to be desired, and blighted the magazine in its infancy, perhaps due to the problems ad salesmen encountered, housed in a hotel of dubious repute in New York, having to share a telephone with the bookies down the street because the hotel's phone system had been destroyed by a fire.[5]

During its first decade the *Smithsonian* kept true to its pledge of leading rather than following public opinion. Fifty years from now, students of American culture may be able to browse through the first ten years and get a feeling for what occupied the minds of the national associates: the women's movement, LSD, ecology, planned parenthood, Rachel Carson's *Silent Spring*. In November 1979 the excellent coverage of the unearthing of China's first Emperor of Qin's pottery army, buried for more than 2,000 years, was an achievement. The magazine prospered, and ad revenues soared. "Its affluent readership constitutes . . . one of the most up-scale demographics in the business," reported *Newsweek*.[6] S. Dillon Ripley had stated in the first issue,

> The salvation of the world today lies neither in existentialism nor in economic development, but rather in a subtle blending of applied research—advanced technology, if you will—and humanism . . . traditional academic structures are poorly adapted to the search for new ways of examining the crises which lie in wait for us: the confrontation between the developed minority and the underdeveloped majority, the population surge which simply changes the scale of everything and depreciates old values in a quantum jump, and the relentless environmental deterioration which we are fostering.[7]

Ten years later Edwards Park looked back nostalgically on "an easier age than we live in today. But I expect that, if we can master the Eighties with the resolve of our ancestors, we can surmount the sense of anomie, sometimes of disillusion with our country and our institutions, which grips us all. May God so will it."[8] The same pessimism can be noted in James K. Page, Jr.'s column "Phenomena, Comment & Notes" as he hails the happy new decade of acid rain, nuclear threat, technological change, diminishing natural resources.[9]

The eighties started with changes in the *Smithsonian*. Edward Thompson went on an extended leave of absence, from which he never returned as editor. This cigar-smoking, Churchill-looking, mumbling man was awarded the institution's Henry Medal for "his brilliant efforts to create and sustain the quality of the magazine," as he nurtured it into a full-fledged respectable publication, and was complimented by President Jimmy Carter for doing "as much as any figure in modern journalism to help Americans learn about and enjoy the world around them."[10] Don Mosher, who had been managing editor, became editor, and Robert McAdams took over as secretary after S. Dillon Ripley's retirement. Subscriptions soared above the two million mark, and ad revenue climbed to new heights.

A sampling of this decade's earlier issues reveals a new direction, away from the idealism of the 1970s. Now we are concerned with endangered species, and ice castle sculptures, with treasure hunts and the good life expressed in the many state-of-the-art ads, directed to a generation that grew away from the earth-conscious frugality of its youth. As I read Donald Dale's essay in the January 1987 issue, "The cat could never admit her mistakes," I realized that my own generation of associates, worried about their empty nests, might have enjoyed this bland, uncontroversial diet of museum relics and the glories of the past, yet I was pleased to see improvements in the last two years in the content of articles and features and in the quality of the photography, layout, and artwork. This trend will ensure the *Smithsonian*'s survival as a herald and disseminator of culture, good taste, and scientific knowledge to its audience.

Notes

1. S. Dillon Ripley, "The View from the Castle," *Smithsonian*, April 1970, p. 2.
2. Edwards Park, "Around the Mall and Beyond," *Smithsonian*, March 1980, p. 34. An interesting history of the first ten years.
3 Ibid., p. 32.
4. Letters to the Editor, *Smithsonian*, June 1980, p. 2.
5. Park, p. 29.
6. "A Life of Its Own," *Newsweek*, 27 August 1973, pp. 76–77.
7. Ripley, p. 2.
8. S. Dillon Ripley, "The View from the Castle," *Smithsonian*, January 1980, p. 8. An interesting history of the first ten years.
9. James K. Page, Jr., "Phenomena, Comments & Notes," *Smithsonian*, March 1980, pp. 38–44.
10. Ripley, March 1980, p. 14.

Information Sources

BIBLIOGRAPHY
"Life of Its Own." *Newsweek*, 27 August 1973, pp. 76–77.
"Making Culture Pay." *Time*, 14 January 1974, p. 28.
Park, Edwards. "Around the Mall and Beyond." *Smithsonian*, March 1980, pp. 28–36.

Ripley, S. Dillon. "The View from the Castle." *Smithsonian*, April 1970, p. 2; January 1980, p. 8.

INDEX SOURCES

> *Magazine Index* (1970–present); *Readers' Guide to Periodical Literature* (1974–present); *America, History and Life* (1970–present); *Art and Archaeology Technical Abstracts; Artbibliographies Modern; Bibliography of Agriculture; Energy Information Abstracts; Environmental Abstracts; GeoRef; Historical Abstracts Part A* (Modern History Abstracts) and *Part B* (20th Century Abstracts, 1970–present); *International Aerospace Abstracts; Popular Magazine Review* 1970–present; *Reference Sources; Oceanic Abstracts; Social Sciences Citation Index; Popular Periodical Index* (1973–1974).

LOCATION SOURCES

> Microform available from University Microfilms International, Ann Arbor, Michigan; widely available.

Publication History

MAGAZINE TITLE AND TITLE CHANGES

> *Smithsonian*.

VOLUME AND ISSUE DATA

> Vol. 1–current, April 1970–current, monthly.

PUBLISHER AND PLACE OF PUBLICATION

> Smithsonian Institution National Associates, Washington, D.C.

EDITORS

> Edward K. Thompson, 1970–1981; Don Mosher, 1981–current.

CIRCULATION

> 2,302,109 (1988).

Heleni Pedersoli

SUCCESS

When *Success* began regular publication in December 1897, its cover proclaimed its purpose: the new magazine would be "an up-to-date journal of inspiration, encouragement, progress and self-help." Catalogs of qualities likely to lead to success ("purity, perseverance, patience, prudence . . . concentration, courage, character") formed an ornamental border. Every article shared a single subject: how successful people rose from poverty, deprivation, or handicap through their own determined efforts and serve as an example to others.

Orison Swett Marden, founder and editor of *Success*, was an ardent believer and proponent of the doctrine of success. His own early life was the perfect *Success* story. He was orphaned at seven and at once was bound out to a series of dour, miserly New Hampshire farmers. He had no regular education, no affection, never enough to eat. But he read Samuel Smiles's *Self-Help* and found the inspiration for his life's work. Enormous efforts earned him secondary schooling, then five academic degrees from Boston University and Harvard. Marden managed university eating clubs and Block Island hotels to finance his education and turned his $20,000 profits into a hotel fortune. A series of disasters cost him his fortune—with no sense of irony—and he began a new career writing and proselytizing about success.

Financial success was only a by-product of Marden's notion of success, which focused on character building, self-help, push, and pluck. Marden hoped to popularize his idea by founding a magazine "not only to foster success in business, but to make successful homes, successful families, successful children,"[1] but had no money. Louis Klopsch, publisher of the *Christian Herald*, shared this ideal and was persuaded to provide funding.

The contract with Klopsch gave Marden complete editorial control, and the first volume was devoted to articles, editorials, and short stories about the successful (with considerable emphasis on the triumphs of women and blacks), assertions of the magazine's own rapid success, and promotional copy: "whatever your station, your age, your circumstances, your color or nationality, SUCCESS will help you. . . . A year's subscription may make all the difference to you between success and failure. Wear threadbare clothes, economize on food, if necessary, but do not go without that which will uplift, inspire, and bring new hope and grander success into your life" (June 1898). Subscriptions were a dollar a year, ten cents a single issue, and premiums were offered for selling subscriptions. Advertising was sparse and advertising revenue low.

Circulation remained disappointing—only 50,000—and in December 1898 the format and frequency was changed to "an illustrated family weekly." Circulation rose to 75,000, but *Success* reverted to monthly publication in 1900. Klopsch was dissatisfied with the magazine's growth, and James H. McGraw (later of McGraw-Hill) replaced him as chief financial backer. McGraw introduced a new emphasis on circulation building: competitions, contests, publication of answers to readers' queries, establishment of League of Success Clubs, and the widest possible choice of premiums for selling subscriptions:[2] "We will send you any article that can be purchased in New York City," one dollar's worth of merchandise for every two subscriptions sold (October 1900). Circulation rose rapidly. By January 1901 the magazine claimed 250,000 subscribers and more than a million readers. Edward E. Higgins was appointed advertising manager and advertising space rose from fifteen pages in January 1901 to thirty-seven in December.[3]

Advertising emphasized goods and services conducive to health and success: healthful food and drink; inexpensive, neat clothing; bodybuilding and correspondence courses. Only medicines, liquor, and tobacco were excluded. In 1903 *Success* began to back its advertisements: "We will absolutely guarantee our readers against loss due to fraudulent misrepresentation in any advertisement appearing in this issue" (April). Later, the guarantee was limited to subscribers of record—another inducement to subscribe!

The incessant efforts to increase readership meant appeals to a wider audience and a blurring of editorial focus. What to Wear and How to Wear It and The

Well-dressed Man became regular features. Recipes were introduced in 1905, along with a new title, *Success Magazine*. Pretty women replaced captains of industry on the covers. Layout and artwork were attractive and expensive.[4]

And, like many other publications, *Success Magazine* turned to long muck-raking features, serialized to maintain readership. Samuel Merwin published "The Magazine Crusade" in *Success Magazine*, praising muckraking in general and in *Success*, especially Cleveland Moffet's extended "The Shameful Misuse of Wealth" (June 1906). Exposés jostled with portraits of famous beauties, advice on household economy and childrearing, humorous and inspirational verse, and fiction for children and adults.

Success constantly pledged ever-better writing, but the general literary quality was never high.[5] Marden's own writing is cloying and repetitious. But interesting people and important writers appeared among the contributors: Theodore Dreiser, who contributed steadily in the first years; Charlotte Perkins Gilman, who wrote frequently on feminist concerns; Upton Sinclair, and even P. G. Wodehouse and Buffalo Bill Cody.[6]

Occasional articles ("A College Girl's Pluck," March 1908) and Marden's own monthly editorials reiterated the central success themes, but by 1907 *Success Magazine* was essentially a general-interest publication. Higgins, the advertising manager, replaced McGraw as publisher and set about widening the audience still further. In September a Grand Educational Prize Contest was announced, offering college scholarships or elaborate trips for selling vast numbers of sub-scriptions. The plan was to at least double the circulation of 300,000: "We dare to dream that we can make *Success Magazine* . . . indispensable in the home to *all*."

The campaign failed, and *Success Magazine* began its decline. Margaret Con-nolly, a long-time employee of Marden's, loyally placed sole responsibility on the muckraking interests within the Success Company: they angered the business interests who were the advertisers and investors. But there were other contributing causes. The very Victorian themes of striving and self-help, on which *Success* had been founded, had lost much of their appeal. Even Marden's conception of success changed into the ideal of the New Thought: material gain through exercise of mental power.[7] The magazine's identity was lost in a jumble of investigative reporting, Progressive politics, household and investment advice, and fiction. *Success Magazine* was simply too small to compete as a general-interest pub-lication. New postal regulations compounded the problems by making delivery more difficult and expensive. And despite its constant reporting on dishonest investment schemes, *Success* invested heavily in one.[8] The price of single issues rose to fifteen cents in 1910, though subscriptions were held to a dollar.

In that year, a group of the muckraking writers, led by Merwin, who was then associate editor, attempted to buy Higgins out. When he refused, they formed the National Post Company, intending to publish a fiercely political biweekly. Higgins yielded in January 1911, and *Success Magazine* and its assets were used to promote the new project. The *National Post* began publication in May; in August the two magazines were merged into *Success Magazine and the National Post*. The remaining issues combined pleas for subscriptions with promises of exciting features in the coming year, but publication ceased in December 1911. Much was made, of course, of the failure of *Success*, but Marden was undeterred. In 1917 he found a new backer for a new start. The *New Success* closely resembled the original *Success*. The message was relentlessly uplifting, and Marden himself wrote much of the contents. Like its predecessor, *New Success* suffered frequent title changes and struggled to gain advertising and subscribers. Publication continued despite the founder's death in 1927 and ceased in 1928 under new ownership and a new name, *New Age Illustrated*.[9]

Notes

1. Quoted in Margaret Connolly, *The Life Story of Orison Swett Marden, A Man Who Benefited Men* (New York: Crowell, 1925), p. 209.

2. Nancy Ann McCowan Sumner, "Orison Swett Marden: The American Samuel Smiles" (Ph.D. diss., Brown University, 1982), pp. 121–22.

3. Sumner, pp. 122, 265.

4. "Success Magazine probably pays the highest price of any magazine in America for its cover designs." *Success Magazine*, December 1905.

5. Sumner, pp. 144–45.

6. Frank Luther Mott, *A History of American Magazines*, vol. 5: *Sketches of 21 Magazines, 1905–1930* (Cambridge: Harvard University Press, Belknap Press, 1968), pp. 287–90. For example, W. F. Cody, "In the West Theodore Roosevelt Won His Health and Strenuousness," January 1902, and P. G. Wodehouse, "When Doctors Disagree," March 1911.

7. Richard M. Huber, *The American Idea of Success* (New York: Crowell, 1971), pp. 145–64.

8. E. G. Lewis's The American Woman's League. Sumner, pp. 185–86.

9. Sumner, pp. 221–40, 246.

Information Sources

BIBLIOGRAPHY

Connolly, Margaret. *The Life Story of Orison Swett Marden, A Man Who Benefited Men*. New York: Crowell, 1925.

Huber, Richard M. *The American Idea of Success*. New York: McGraw-Hill, 1971.

Mott, Frank Luther. *A History of American Magazines*, vol. 5: *Sketches of 21 Magazines, 1905–1930*. Cambridge: Harvard University Press, Belknap Press, 1968.

Sumner, Nancy Ann McCowan. "Orison Swett Marden: The American Samuel Smiles." Ph.D. diss., Brown University, 1982.

INDEX SOURCES

Vols. 12–14 in *Dramatic Index*.

LOCATION SOURCES
>   *Union List of Serials in Libraries of the United States and Canada* (3d ed., 1965)
>   lists thirty-seven libraries with broken runs of one or more of the titles. Nearly
>   the entire run of *Success, Success Magazine,* and *Success Magazine and the
>   National Post* are available as reels 43–48 of *American Popular Culture, Popular
>   Periodicals in Microform* (Ann Arbor, Mich.: University Microfilms International,
>   1974–   ).

Publication History

MAGAZINE TITLE AND TITLE CHANGES
>   *Success,* 1897–1904; *Success Magazine,* 1905–June 1911; *Success Magazine and
>   the National Post,* July–December 1911; *The New Success: Marden's Magazine,*
>   1918–September 1921; *Success,* October 1921–October 1927.

VOLUME AND ISSUE DATA
>   Vols. 1–14, 1897–1911; vols. 1–2, monthly; vol. 3, weekly; vols. 4–14, monthly.
>   Vols. 1–11, 1918–1927, monthly.

PUBLISHER AND PLACE OF PUBLICATION
>   Success Company: Louis Klopsch, 1897–1900 Boston and New York. McGraw-
>   Marden Company: James H. McGraw, 1900–1907; Edward E. Higgins, 1907–
>   1911, New York. The National Post Company, Samuel Merwin, 1911. Lowery-
>   Marden Company: Frederick C. Lowery, 1918–1921, New York. Success Mag-
>   azine Corporation: Frederick C. Lowery, 1921–1927, New York. Central Mag-
>   azine Company: A.C.G. Hammersfahr, 1927–1928, Chicago.

EDITORS
>   Orison Swett Marden, 1897–1911, 1918–1924 (with Robert MacKay, 1906–1908;
>   Samuel Merwin, 1909–1910; Howard Brubaker, 1910–1911); Walter Hoff Seely,
>   1924–1925; Francis Trevelyan Miller, managing editor, 1923–1926; David Arnold
>   Balch, managing editor, 1926–1928.

CIRCULATION
>   Peaked at 500,000; low of 50,000.

>   *Linda Zieper*

SUNSET

One of the many joys of living in the West is the chance to try out the gardening,
landscaping, home improvement, cooking, camping, and travelling ideas presented in *Sunset: The Magazine of Western Living.* Though known nationally,
the magazine is produced specifically, in four different editions, for the families
of thirteen Western states. The four editions—Northwest, Central West, Southern
California and Hawaii, and Desert—are content-targeted for their particular geographical areas. An article produced for new employees in the magazine editorial
department of *Sunset* states:

>   We recognized that Western living differs from the national pattern in four
>   important ways: Western climate called for changes in gardening methods.

The possibilities in outdoor living combined with western weather and topography forced changes in architectural thinking. Western travel and recreation were as much a part of everyday living as the garden. Many Western foods and many dishes peculiar to the West were not discussed in other publications . . . by focusing on our four major fields of involvement, we can render a useful and virtually exclusive service to Westerners that neither national magazines nor local newspapers, neither television nor radio can duplicate.[1]

The history of the magazine is as colorful as the region from which it springs. *Sunset* was established in 1898 by a railroad, the Southern Pacific Company, and named after its *Sunset Express* train. It had a creed: "Publicity for the attractions and advantages of the Western Empire." Its aim was "the presentation, in a convenient form, of information concerning the great states of California, Oregon, Nevada, Texas, Louisiana, and the territories of Arizona and New Mexico . . . for the husbandman, stockman, and miner, and for the tourist and the health seeker" (May 1898, p. 1). The early issues were slim (fifteen to twenty pages) and contained articles such as "Yosemite" (May 1898) or "A Pacific Granary: Stockton California" (March 1899). Articles were profusely illustrated with black-and-white pictures and photographs. Travel information was sprinkled liberally throughout the magazine. The regularly featured Notes from Resorts column described the weather, hotel improvements, and hunting opportunities at various resorts in the West. It is great fun even now to read the notices of visitors who spent time at one resort or another. "Mr. U.S. Grant jr. [sic] and party enjoyed the ride over Smiley Heights last month" (May 1898, p. 14). Another column named Current Coin contained notes concerning expansion and development in specific cities or areas. "A cable is to be laid between San Pedro and Avalon, Catalina Island" (June 1898, p. 35). "Two hundred and fifty cars of grain and 116 cars of livestock were shipped from Gridley last year" (May 1898, p. 15).

Sunset was then a browser's magazine, with no table of contents. Short poems, clever sayings, and jokes were tucked in here and there. Though the first issue had "no advertising space to sell and comes to you unbiased,"[2] this policy soon changed. The magazine grew and began to attract regional and then national advertisers. It did not then, and never has, accepted ads for hard liquor. In 1940 it established a policy of nonacceptance for tobacco advertising as well.

May 1906 saw the publication of a very thin, eight-page issue called the "New San Francisco Emergency Edition." It was published, not on *Sunset's* presses, but at the Ferry Building in San Francisco. It contained an article written by F. H. Harriman, president of Southern Pacific, on the earthquake of 18 April. This article described the terrible damage and extolled the bravery of the citizens and military troops who worked together during this crisis. The "Greeting from the Publishers" that followed stated: "This is to announce that by reason of the recent destruction by fire of the Sunset Magazine offices on April 18th, this

Emergency Edition will be the only issue of the magazine for the month of May ... Everything was destroyed except the mailing list, a few manuscripts and contract records. The priceless stores of drawings, photographs and engravings was burned.'' In April 1908 *Sunset* published an eight-page photographic gatefold showing the rebuilt San Francisco. This was a ''publishing first.''[3]

In January of 1912 *Sunset* consolidated with the *Pacific Monthly*, a magazine promoting the Pacific Northwest region. On the title page of today's *Sunset*, ''The Pacific Monthly'' is still printed beneath the title proper.

Woodhead, Field and Company, a group of *Sunset* employees, bought the magazine in September 1914. William Woodhead, the new president, had been business manager, and Charles K. Field had been editor. *Sunset* now became more of a literary magazine, but was still a magazine of the West, featuring Western writers and espousing Western causes—even very controversial ones concerning organized labor and conservation issues. Writers such as Bret Harte, Jack London, and Sinclair Lewis contributed to *Sunset*. Stories were illustrated by artists such as Maynard Dixon and Will James. The magazine was well respected. However, without the financial backing of Southern Pacific, the literary *Sunset* never attained financial success.

In September 1928, Laurence W. Lane bought the magazine for $65,000.[4] By now *Sunset* was already in a larger format and contained colored pictures. The January 1929 issue of *Sunset* began with a two-page spread announcing in large print: ''As requested by you ... a new Sunset Magazine coming next month.'' The announcement continued: ''Advancing with modern trends, life in the West offers the utmost in living. Charming and comfortable homes are the rule. ... Gardens are not only beautiful but livable. ... The mountains, the seashore, fishing, camping, hiking are family adventures close at hand. ... The new Sunset will be vitalized by a constant stream of new ideas in the art of living.'' The February issue contained articles on camping, cooking, how to paint stucco, how to barber palm trees. It contained the Sunset Travel Service and a new column called The Kitchen Cabinet: Recipe Exchange, which is still a regular feature.

Sunset flourished under the new editorial policy. It expanded to three different editions (Northwest, Central, and Southwest) in 1932. It was financially ''in the black'' by 1938, ''the first time since Southern Pacific days''[5] and its circulation department has consistently shown profits since then. In 1940 circulation passed 250,000; in 1951 it passed 500,000; in March 1971 it reached 1 million. In 1980 the number of subscribers in the thirteen Western states reached 1.5 million, the magazine's approximate circulation today.

New columns were welcomed enthusiastically by readers and became permanent parts of the magazine. A column called Chefs of the West, featuring recipes contributed exclusively by men, was heartily endorsed and is still a regular, popular feature. A separate Book Division was established in 1949 because the books *Sunset* published, beginning with a sixty-four-page cookbook/

pamphlet in 1931, were so successful. Now *Sunset* also has a Films and Television Division.

In 1951 Sunset headquarters moved from San Francisco to Menlo Park, California. The new facility, built on the site of a land grant made by Spain to the governor of Spanish California in 1815, quickly became a showplace. The site and its facilities have been expanded several times since then. Multiple tours of the beautiful kitchens, gardens, workshops, entertainment centers, and patios are regularly scheduled every weekday except on holidays.

Sunset remains a most appealing magazine for a wide assortment of readers whose enjoyment of life is enhanced by the love of cooking or building or gardening or decorating or traveling. Any one of these interests is enough to support an addiction to *Sunset*. There are several specific editorial practices that have helped maintain the magazine's high quality. Since February of 1936 it has been totally staff written.

> The philosophy behind this move, according to SUNSET's management was based on the premise that SUNSET was an "information" publication, not a journal of opinion or fiction. Secondly, the management felt that SUNSET's continuity and authority as a reliable source of information and instruction was strengthened by foregoing individual writing credits. The editorial operation of the magazine from this point was very much a team effort. A producing editor was assigned to each story, but scouting, research and story development was the responsibility of several writers pooling their knowledge and talent.[6]

A printed statement to new employees says:

> People outside the 13 Western states pay a premium to subscribe and get no renewal notices. We don't count them in the circulation total that we charge to our advertisers—who thus receive this substantial non-Western circulation as a bonus. It's important that you understand the thinking behind this. *Sunset* has been built on a policy of *defining* the magazine's role, *limiting* its objectives, and then doing the very best job we can.[7]

Management has consistently kept its objectives in clear view. When another "first" happened at *Sunset*, the first editorial color photography in 1954, the publisher wrote: "Our future program of editorial color photography, as we see it now, will be a fairly modest one. We don't propose to use color just for lavish displays; we plan to use it where color will help make an article more understandable and more complete."[8]

Sunset is now a fat, colorful magazine filled with how-to's for the good life in the West. However, the echoes from its historical roots are still strong. Paul C. Johnson wrote, "Turning back the pages of the early *Sunsets* is a rewarding visit to a greening West, when life was simpler and filled with wonder and discovery."[9] *Sunset* still infuses its travel articles with wonder and appreciation for the beauty of the West. The conservation concern of the literary issues of the early 1900s is echoed in the published position *Sunset* took in August 1969 against the use of DDT. It is echoed again in the ninetieth anniversary issue special report, "Can the West grow wisely and well?" (May 1988).

Replete now with tables of contents and published indexes, *Sunset* is both a browser's delight and a doer's manual.[10]

Notes

1. "An Inside Look at Sunset Magazine," Pamphlet produced for New Employees in Magazine Editorial, Offices of *Sunset Magazine* (Menlo Park, Calif.: Lane Publishing Co., November 1985), p. 1.

2. *Sunset.* Vol. 1, no. 1, May 1898, p. 1.

3. *The History of Sunset* (Menlo Park, Calif.: Lane Publishing Co., 1981), p. [2].

4. Ibid., p. [3].

5. Ibid., p. [4].

6. Ibid.

7. "An Inside Look at Sunset Magazine," p. 1.

8. *The History of Sunset*, p. [6].

9. Paul C. Johnson, ed., *The Early Sunset Magazine 1899–1928* (San Francisco: California Historical Society, 1973), p. 12.

10. Joyce Covington of *Sunset*'s Public Relations Department was most helpful in supplying, during a telephone conversation on 14 October 1988, both information and printed sources for this article.

Information Sources

BIBLIOGRAPHY

"A Half-Century of Discovery: A Special Report from *Sunset*'s Publisher, *Sunset*'s Editors, Western Leaders in Business, Education, Government, the Professions, the Sciences, the Arts." *Sunset: The Magazine of Western Living*, February 1979.

The History of Sunset. Menlo Park, Calif.: Lane Publishing Co., 1981.

"An Inside Look at Sunset Magazine." Produced for New Employees in Magazine Editorial, [Offices of] *Sunset Magazine*. Menlo Park, Calif.: Lane Publishing Co., November 1985.

Johnson, Paul C., ed., *The Early Sunset Magazine 1899–1928*. A California Historical Society Anthology. San Francisco; California Historical Society, 1973.

"Welcome to *Sunset* and our 'Laboratory of Western Living.' " Pamphlet reprinted from March 1985 *Sunset Magazine*. Menlo Park, Calif.: Lane Publishing Co., 1985.

INDEX SOURCES

Abstrax; *Consumers Index; Index To How To to Do It Information; Magazine Index* (1977–present); *Popular Magazine Review*; *Readers' Guide* (1906–1930, 1953–present); *Social Science and Humanities Index* (1931–1935).

LOCATION SOURCES

Holdings at various locations. Bell and Howell Micro Photo Division; University Microfilms International, Ann Arbor, Michigan.

Publication History

MAGAZINE TITLE AND TITLE CHANGES
> *Sunset*, 1898–1912; *Sunset: The Pacific Monthly*, 1912–1943 (some variation between titles *Sunset* and *Sunset Magazine*); *Sunset: The Magazine of Western Living*, 1943–present.

VOLUME AND ISSUE DATA
> Vols. 1–181, May 1898–present, monthly.

PUBLISHER AND PLACE OF PUBLICATION
> Southern Pacific Company, 1898–1914, San Francisco, California; Woodhead, Field and Company, 1914–1928, San Francisco; L. W. Lane, Sr., Lane Publishing Company, 1929–1959, San Francisco and Menlo Park, California; L. W. Lane, Jr., Lane Publishing Company, 1959–1986, Menlo Park, California; Melvin B. Lane, Lane Publishing Company, 1986–present, Menlo Park, California.

EDITORS
> E. H. Woodman and other Southern Pacific Passenger Division Staff, 1898–1902; Charles Sedgewick Aiken, 1902–1911; Charles K. Field, 1911–1925; Charles H. Woolley, 1925–1928; Lou Richardson and Genevieve Callahan, 1928–1937; William Nichols, 1937–1939; Walter L. Doty, 1939–1954; Proctor Mellquist, 1954–1982; William Marken, 1982–present.

CIRCULATION
> Approximately 1.3–1.5 million.

Dorothy Jones

THE SURVEY

For more than half a century, *The Survey* was the nation's unrivaled journal in promoting public welfare and social reform. Directing itself toward social inquiry, it sought to accelerate change by getting "at the facts of social conditions in ways that would count."[1] The foremost outlet for the examination of critical social issues, it succeeded in influencing social thought and furthering movement toward the realization of humanistic goals in all areas of social and economic welfare.

The founding of *The Survey* was in direct response to the need for a journal that could address the concerns of professionals in the emerging field of social work. Dr. Edward Thomas Devine launched the publication in 1897 as the second official organ of the Charity Organization Society (COS) of the City of New York. The publication, then titled *Charities: A Monthly Review of Local and General Philanthropy*, was designed to provide news and information to persons engaged in philanthropic and charitable work. At the end of the first year, it became a weekly, and in March 1901, it absorbed the older organ of the New York Society, *Charities Review*. Subsequent mergers with the *Commons* (1905), the national organ of the settlement movement, and *Jewish Charity* (1906), the official paper of the United Hebrew Charities of New York, resulted in uniting conflicting ideologies and broadening the magazine's scope.

While *Charities* was primarily a newsmagazine in its early years, the Progressive era at the turn of the century served as an impetus for further expanding *Charities'* social view. Renamed *Charities and the Commons* from 1905 to 1909, it turned its attention toward the critical examination of larger social issues. Reflecting the values of a reform generation, it now sought to expose the facts of problematic social realities by undertaking "important pieces of social investigation not provided for by any existing organization."[2]

To this end, special numbers appeared on critical, sometimes controversial issues such as those on the Italian immigrants (May 1904), Negroes in the northern cities (7 October 1905), syphilis (24 June 1905), and child labor (5 October 1907). Demonstrating a respect for open and impartial discussion, *Charities*, and later the *Survey*, succeeded in bringing to the attention of thousands new findings and insights into complicated social problems.

Such early successes, however, were hardly a victory for a magazine whose concerns evolved around the corrective solution to multiple social problems. The program, now one of "social reform [and] advocacy of radical readjustment of industrial, political, educational, and religious factors,"[3] took hold when it embarked on the first comprehensive investigation of life and labor of a major metropolitan city. Financed chiefly by the newly founded Russell Sage Foundation, and directed by Paul U. Kellogg from 1907 to 1909, the project resulted in a massive compilation of data surrounding the social and economic conditions in the Pennsylvania Steel District. Published in three special numbers (January, February, and March 1909), and then more fully in six volumes by the Russell Sage Foundation, it exposed exploitive industrial and housing conditions among immigrants and other wage earners of Pittsburgh and served as an impetus for a variety of legislative reforms including the elimination of the twelve-hour workday, enactment of workmen's compensation, and the establishment of industrial safety standards.

By 1909, *Charities and the Commons* clearly needed a new name; as one subscriber put it, "In sending my subscription to *Charities and the Commons*, I want to say that I believe the name to be a heavy handicap."[4] No longer an accurate reflection of the journal's contents, the title was changed to the *Survey* in April 1909. Attention given the magazine as a result of the Pittsburgh Survey widened public awareness of its offerings, and in October 1912, it broke with the Charity Organization Society and incorporated as Survey Associates, an independent nonprofit publishing corporation. Membership, comprised of subscribers who had contributed $10 or more to the publication, included numerous associations, foundations, and businesses, as well as such notable individuals as Eleanor Roosevelt, Nelson Rockefeller, Hubert H. Humphrey, and Carl Sandburg.

In 1912, Paul Kellogg became editor-in-chief and remained so until the magazine's demise in 1952. In the spirit of the Pittsburgh Survey, Kellogg became a significant force in furthering the educative purpose of the journal and broadening its appeal. Social surveys of major metropolitan cities continued to be featured; industrial topics claimed top priority; and throughout the war much was printed on conditions in Europe and, later, reconstruction. By the end of the war, however, the weekly publication had become prohibitively expensive, and in October 1921, *Survey* split into two publications: the *Survey Midmonthly* number, which was aimed at social workers and board members, and the *Survey Graphic* number, which was directed at the intellectual layman. The *Graphic* and *Midmonthly* issues were part of the consecutive numbering of *Survey* magazine.

The *Survey Graphic* number represented Kellogg's long-time ambition for a journal that would interest a broader audience in social issues and reform. Based on the assumption that an informed constituency would move the masses toward social and political reform, Kellogg directed the new magazine toward the professionally and intellectually elite. With a regained financial base, both publications became more interesting and attractive during the 1920s than ever before. Works by notable artists appeared, and in keeping with the vision expressed by Kellogg, it continued to feature social studies and pieces by prominent individuals. Over the years, its list of contributors would include Jane Addams, Franklin Roosevelt, Samuel Fels, Roscoe Pound, Mahatma Gandhi, John Dewey, W. E. B. Du Bois, Bertrand Russell, Booker T. Washington, and Eleanor Roosevelt.

By 1929, on the eve of the Great Depression, social work was approaching full professional status. There were 4,600 social workers who belonged to forty-three chapters of the American Association of Social Workers, and twenty-five master's degree programs in social work had been established. By the latter 1920s, the *Survey Graphic* and *Midmonthly* had a combined mailing circulation of 26,000, with another 4,000 copies being sold from newsstands.[5] The *Midmonthly* had about half the circulation of the *Graphic*. Circulation, advertising, and foundation grants allowed a financial momentum to carry *The Survey* to 1932–1933 before money began to taper off.

It was at this high point of seeming prosperity that *The Survey* began a gradual descent. The depression caused two impacts. First, the financial reality meant that social workers and others could not afford the modest subscription fee. Second, the depression brought out a more radical mood among younger men and women. *The Survey*, now serving a profession dominated by caseworkers, not reformers, seemed now stodgy and unable to keep pace with rapidly changing developments. *The Survey* rarely took a partisan political position, but during the depression many articles were written by New Dealers, such as Frances Perkins and Felix Frankfurter, who defended Roosevelt's programs. The magazine's embrace of New Deal politics was criticized from the left who said that reliance on the government committed social workers to the preservation of the status quo.

In addition to the above developments, *The Survey*'s managing editor, Arthur Kellogg, Paul's brother, died unexpectedly in 1934. This threw *The Survey* operation into turmoil, and Paul squandered his declining energies in trying to meet every responsibility.

In January 1933, the *Graphic* number of *The Survey* was made a separate monthly magazine. The new *Survey Graphic* reached a circulation high of nearly 35,000. In November 1936, the *Midmonthly* was merged with *The Survey* to form the *Midmonthly Survey* (1933–1937) and later renamed the *Survey Midmonthly* (1938–1948). This new arrangement received much fanfare. *Newsweek* said together the *Graphic* and *Midmonthly* exerted "influence out of all proportion to the circulation."[6] *The Survey* granted exclusive rights to *Reader's Digest** to reprint condensed articles, bringing in additional revenue; however, the number of reprints declined over time.

Between the wars, 55 to 70 percent of the costs of running the magazines were covered by sales, one-third by the Survey Associates, and the rest by large gifts from a few donors and grants. It became increasingly difficult for the magazine to pay its expenses. By the late 1930s, long-time donors to the Survey Associates began to die off and were not replaced. The Russell Sage Foundation began to turn its attention to other matters.

By the end of the 1940s, Paul Kellogg was in ill health, and *The Survey* was in acute financial troubles. The post–World War II years brought further problems. Inflation forced subscription prices to $4 per year for each of the *Midmonthly* and *Graphic* and $6 for both. In January 1949, the two titles were merged into one, *The Survey*, with a subscription price of $5. Sales continued to decline. The economy was prosperous, and social work seemed less relevant to society's needs. New readers were difficult to recruit.

By 1950, *The Survey* ran a deficit for each issue printed. All endowment monies were exhausted. At this time Paul Kellogg had a heart attack. The remaining board of directors for Survey Associates called for an end and liquidated *The Survey*'s assets. The last issue was May 1952. Paul Kellogg had worked for the magazine for fifty years and was its editor for forty. The *New York Times* said of Kellogg, "His was the personality that made the magazine over the years a going concern."[7] The *Nation* said, "But we shall miss the *Survey*; it filled a place no other journal occupies and filled it with integrity."[8]

Notes

1. "Some Pages from the Survey Scrapbook," *Survey Graphic,* December 1937, p. 676.

2. Edward T. Devine, *When Social Work Was Young* (New York: Macmillan, 1939), p. 110.

3. Ibid., pp. 106–7.

4. "To Change the Name of *Charities and the Commons,*" *The Survey,* 27 March 1909, p. 1251.

5. Clarke A. Chambers, *Paul U. Kellogg and the Survey: Voices for Social Welfare and Social Justice* (Minneapolis: University of Minnesota Press, 1971) p. 118.

6. "Little Known Publications Celebrate 25th Anniversary As Opinion Makers," *Newsweek,* 6 December 1937, p. 35.

7. "The Survey Passes," *New York Times*, 28 May 1952, p. 28.

8. "Tribute to the 'Survey,' " *Nation*, 7 June 1952, p. 539.

Information Sources

BIBLIOGRAPHY

Chambers, Clarke A. *Paul U. Kellogg and the Survey: Voices for Social Welfare and Social Justice*. Minneapolis: University of Minnesota Press, 1971.

Devine, Edward T. *When Social Work Was Young*. New York: Macmillan, 1939.

Ehrenreich, John H. *The Altruistic Imagination: A History of Social Work and Social Policy in the United States*. Ithaca, N.Y.: Cornell University Press, 1985.

Hinding, Andrea, preparer. "An Inventory of the Papers of Paul U. Kellogg." In *Descriptive Inventories of Collections in the Social Welfare History Archives Center*. Westport, Conn.: Greenwood Press, 1970.

————. "An Inventory of the Papers of Survey Associates, Inc." In *Descriptive Inventories of Collections in the Social Welfare History Archives Center*. Westport, Conn.: Greenwood Press, 1970.

"Little Known Publications Celebrate 25th Anniversary as Opinion Makers." *Newsweek*, 6 December 1935, p. 35.

Lubove, Roy. *The Professional Altruist: The Emergence of Social Work as a Career, 1880–1930*. Cambridge: Harvard University Press, 1965.

McClymen, John F. *War and Welfare: Social Engineering in America, 1890–1925*. Westport, Conn.: Greenwood Press, 1970.

Mott, Frank Luther. *A History of American Magazines, 1885–1905*. 5 Vols. Cambridge: Harvard University Press, 1957, 4: 741–50.

"The Survey Passes." *New York Times*, 28 May 1952, p. 28.

Trattner, Walter I. *From Poor Law to Welfare State: A History of Social Welfare in America*. 2nd ed. New York: Macmillan, 1979.

"Tribute to the 'Survey.' " *Nation*, 7 June 1952, p. 539.

INDEX SOURCES

Poole's Index (1901–1906); *Readers' Guide to Periodical Literature* (1901–1952); *Index to Labor Articles; Public Affairs Information Service; Book Review Digest; Psychological Abstracts; Quarterly Cumulative Index Medicus; Biography Index*.

LOCATION SOURCES

Library of Congress, many other libraries. Available in microform (1949–1952).

Publication History

MAGAZINE TITLE AND TITLE CHANGES

Charities, 1897–October 1905; *Charities and the Commons*, November 1905–March 1909; *The Survey*, April 1909–1933, with special *Graphic* and *Midmonthly* numbers; *Midmonthly Survey*, 1933–1937; *Survey Midmonthly*, 1937–1948; *The Survey*, 1949–May 1952.

VOLUME AND ISSUE DATA

Vol. 1, 1897, monthly; vols. 2–48, no. 9, December 1898–May 1922, weekly; vols. 48, (no. 10)–68, June 1922–1932, semimonthly; vols. 69–88, 1933–May 1952, monthly.

PUBLISHER AND PLACE OF PUBLICATION
> Charity Organization Society of the City of New York, 1897–1912; Survey Associates, New York, 1912–1952.

EDITORS
> Edward Thomas Devine, 1897–1912; Paul Underwood Kellogg, 1912–1952.

CIRCULATION
> 1928: 30,000 copies: 26,000 subscription (combined total for the *Midmonthly* and *Graphic* numbers, which were sold for $3 per title or $5 for both; 16,400 individuals subscribed to both), and 4,000 newsstand copies.

Laura Schroyer and Byron Anderson

T

TEXAS MONTHLY

"It is a truth universally acknowledged, that a specialized group in possession of a good fortune must be in want of a specialized magazine." With apologies to Jane Austen, that "truth" appears to have been taken to heart by the magazine industry in the 1970s. The magazine market boomed. Regional magazines played an important part in this explosion, hoping to emulate on a smaller scale the success of the legendary *New Yorker*. One of the winners in this contest, well on its way to becoming a legend itself, is *Texas Monthly*.

Texas Monthly is either an unlikely success story or the epitome of the Hollywood musical. It was founded by a person with next to no magazine experience, planned by instinct rather than demographics, and destined to become a raging success. Michael Levy, a Wharton School graduate, sold advertising for *Philadelphia* magazine for nine months, then returned to his native Texas to attend the University of Texas Law School. While there, he developed the idea of *Texas Monthly*. Says Levy, "I came back with the idea of starting a magazine. . . . I figured out the magazine would not work in either Dallas or Houston, but it would work in the state as a whole. The state was ready for a statewide magazine."[1]

Levy admits his planning was less than scientific. "The concept of the regional magazine, at that time, wasn't a known commodity. We had no marketing studies. That would be like Alexander Graham Bell doing a marketing survey on the telephone. How could he do that if nobody had ever seen one?"[2]

Armed only with his idea, Levy set out to find an editor. After interviewing three hundred individuals, Levy chose William Broyles, a twenty-seven-year-old assistant to the superintendent of the Houston School District who had free-lanced for English and American magazines. Levy claims he again worked on intuition: "I hired him on gut instinct—because of his knowledge of the language and ability to handle people."[3]

Using capital supplied largely by Levy's father, Dallas plumbing contractor Harry Levy, the staff of approximately ten went to work. The first issue of *Texas Monthly* was published in February 1973. It featured Don Meredith on the cover, had a circulation of 10,000, and carried 2⅔ pages of advertising—mostly for local stores and radio stations.[4] The early *Texas Monthly* was a mixture of Texas issues (e.g., "The Unholy Trinity Incident," June 1973), Texas institutions (e.g., "The Best Little Old Chicken-Fried Steak in Public," May 1974), and Texas personalities (e.g., "The Lonely Blues of Duane Thomas," February 1973). Blended with these were what have become the obligatory regional magazine features: a list of places to go and things to do (Around the State) and restaurant and entertainment reviews. In July 1973 *Texas Monthly* began one of its most popular and controversial features, an annual list of the ten best and ten worst Texas legislators. Less controversial but just as entertaining are the Bum Steer Awards, which review the most dubious achievements of the past twelve months.

What made *Texas Monthly* stand out was the quality of its content. *Texas Monthly* writers have included the likes of Larry McMurtry, Larry King, and Judith Crist. The attitude adopted by the magazine also stood out: curiosity and self-analysis. Many of the stories sought to examine what Texas and Texans were, why they were that way, and what made them unique. The magazine engaged in an intelligent examination of rather than a blind celebration of its legendary state.

Also distinctive was *Texas Monthly*'s brash editorial style. The comments were bold, the headlines startling and intriguing, and the attempts to lure the reader shameless. An April 1973 article on Bruce Bowen's Houston Laboratory Theater was titled "Are You Running with Me Zeus?" The subhead read, "A young impresario is putting on a play called Dionysus in 69. It's full of blood and naked skin, so you'll like it."

The visual style, which has changed little over the years, is strong. The photography is striking, at times even dramatic. Many graphics are used, both as full-page illustrations and small insets. Major articles are regularly accompanied by a full-page illustration facing the first text page. The covers are similar to other regional magazine covers: full-size photographs (occasionally graphics) designed to catch newsstand attention and illustrate the idea of a lead story.

Texas Monthly quickly gained a national reputation. In April 1974, it received Columbia University's National Magazine Award in Specialized Journalism, the first time this award, which has been likened to an Oscar and a Pulitzer, had gone to either a first-year magazine or one not published on the East or West coasts. It has since won two more of these awards. In the mid-1970s, both *Time** and *Newsweek** featured stories on *Texas Monthly*, emphasizing the "cheeky" and "irreverent" style.[5]

Commercial success soon found Levy's magazine. By January 1974, circulation was 41,500. In two more years, it had increased to 169,600. In 1980 circulation was 250,800.[6] The most recent circulation figure is 334,523.[7] As readers increased, so did advertising. Ad pages began at 176 annually,[8] grew to 1,795 in 1980,[9] and settled to 1,271 in 1986–1987.[10]

The character and content of *Texas Monthly* changed as it grew. Slick ads for expensive stores and products (e.g., Nieman-Marcus) replaced the simpler, smaller efforts of the mid–1970s. The focal area of coverage expanded beyond the Dallas–Fort Worth/Houston/Austin triangle. Around the State now features fourteen locations, including Laredo, Lubbock, Midland-Odessa, and Beaumont–Port Arthur.

The major change in *Texas Monthly* is in its attitude. While still covering some controversial or startling stories, it does so in a more subdued manner. A larger portion of each issue now deals with personalities and life styles. The epitome of this softer focus is perhaps the fifteenth anniversary issue, "Deep in the Hearts of Texas" (February 1988), which is a collection of recollections of Texans grouped into the categories of "Lovers," "Family," "Friends," and "Community." The magazine contends it "decided to look not at institutions but at individuals. Specifically, we wanted to see how the highs and lows of the last fifteen years have affected the lives of everyday Texans. We would look deep into their hearts and determine what matters most to them, what dreams and longings shaped them. We hoped that by doing so, we would find out just what it means to be a Texan today."[11] While this is a laudable goal, the result is a disjointed series of often bland, *People*-ish profiles that leave one without an inkling of what Texans today are like, why they are special, or what has made them so.

In the winter of 1987 *Texas Monthly* made a move that can be interpreted as either an acknowledgment of its new nature or an attempt to distance itself from life-style coverage. It began publishing *Domain*, a quarterly supplement that is delivered only to subscribers in Texas. *Domain* is subtitled the *Lifestyle Magazine of Texas Monthly*. The publication features homes, gardens, good food, and interior decorating. Its articles are short, with accompanying photographs. It includes an Index, which reveals where to buy the furnishings in the issue.

Completing the change in *Texas Monthly* is its new role in relation to its home state and people. The magazine has become less of an examiner of Texas-why-and-how and more of a celebrator of Texas-by-God. While not yet blindly cheering for the Texas mythos, the magazine has lost a good portion of its critical faculty where its homeground is concerned. This loss affects not just Texans, but anyone interested in understanding the American character.

Perhaps the responsibility is time's. *Texas Monthly* has grown from an inquisitive, impulsive adolescent into a subdued, serious adult. The bad news is that *Texas Monthly* has become less distinctive and discriminating. The good news is that maturation has left *Texas Monthly* a magazine boasting good writing, a decent editorial mix, and some outstanding photography. In the end, that is more than can be said for most overnight success stories.

Notes

1. Christy Marshall, "Michael Levy," *Advertising Age*, 30 March 1981, pp. S2, S10.

2. Mike Shropshire, "The Write Stuff: 'Texas Monthly' at 10: A Past Perfect, a Future Tense?" *Dallas Morning News*, 20 February 1983, p. 4F.

3. Shropshire, p. 4F.

4. Christy Marshall, " 'Texas Monthly' Still Cheeky at 10," *Advertising Age*, 2 May 1983, p. 4.

5. "Cheeky TM," *Time*, 27 September 1976, p. 65; "The Eyes of Texas," *Newsweek*, 17 June 1974, pp. 69–70.

6. ABC Publisher's Statements and Texas Monthly Research, in Shropshire, p. 4F.

7. *Standard Rate and Data Service: Consumer Magazine and Agri-Media Rates and Data*, 27 August 1988, p. 406.

8. Shropshire, p. 1F.

9. "Ad Pages—1981," *Advertising Age*, 5 April 1982, p. M26.

10. Capell's Circulation Report, in "Shakeup and Shakeout," *Folio*, May 1988, p. 103.

11. Mimi Swartz, "Behind the Lines," *Texas Monthly*, February 1988, p. 6.

Information Sources

BIBLIOGRAPHY

"Ad Pages—1981." *Advertising Age*, 5 April 1982, p. M26.

Carpenter, Liz. "Publishing Phenomena Put Texas on Literary Map." *Austin American-Statesman*, 8 May 1977, p. E12.

"Cheeky TM." *Time*, 27 September 1976, p. 65.

Couzens, Michael. "Regional Magazines." *Folio*, May 1988.

"The Eyes of Texas." *Newsweek*, 17 June 1974, pp. 69–70.

Herold, Jean. "Texas Monthly." *Serials Review*, January—March 1977, pp. 5–11.

Mack, Toni. "Home, Sweet Home?" *Forbes*, 25 April 1983.

Marshall, Christy. "Michael Levy." *Advertising Age*, 30 March 1981.

———. " 'Texas Monthly' Still Cheeky at 10." *Advertising Age*, 2 May 1983.

Pool, Gail. "Magazines." *Wilson Library Bulletin,* March 1982, pp. 538–39, 558.

Radding, Alan. "Magazines Cross Regional Frontier." *Advertising Age*, 13 April 1987, pp. S8–S10.

"Shakeup and Shakeout." *Folio*, May 1988, pp. 101–3.

Shropshire, Mike. "The Write Stuff: 'Texas Monthly' at 10: A Past Perfect, a Future Tense?" *Dallas Morning News*, 20 February 1983.

"Texas Flair Tops 'Em All.' " *Advertising Age*, 5 April 1982, pp. M26–M27.

INDEX SOURCES

Access: The Supplementary Index to Periodicals (1975–present); *Magazine Index* (1978–present); *New Periodicals Index* (1977–1978); *Popular Magazine Review; Popular Periodical Index* (1976–present).

LOCATION SOURCES
> *Texas Monthly*—Library of Congress, many other libraries; *Domain*—University of Texas, other Texas libraries. Available in microform.

Publication History

MAGAZINE TITLE AND TITLE CHANGES
> *Texas Monthly.*

VOLUME AND ISSUE DATA
> *Texas Monthly*—vols. 1–16, February 1973–present, monthly. *Domain*—vol. 1–present, Winter 1987–present, quarterly.

PUBLISHER AND PLACE OF PUBLICATION
> Texas Monthly, Inc., Michael Levy, 1973–1988; Stephen A. Childs, 1988–present. Austin, Texas.

EDITORS
> William Broyles, 1973–1982; Gregory Curtis, 1982–present.

CIRCULATION
> 300,105 paid; 13,780 nonpaid.

Nancy Buchanan

TIME

Advertising in 1987 maintained that reading this popular periodical, self-proclaimed "the weekly newsmagazine," will provide readers with a full understanding of national, international, and other newsworthy events. Perhaps the most-often-read newsmagazine in the United States, *Time* may also be the most-often criticized. Regardless of what its critics say about this digest of weekly events, Henry R. Luce and Briton Hadden set the standard for others to follow when they issued the first *Time* on 3 March 1923.

Hadden and Luce were recent Yale graduates and had little experience as journalists when they wrote the lofty prospectus for *Time* magazine. They determined that there was a great void in the manner in which the American "busy man" was able to get information. The daily newspapers provided too much, the weekly digests too little, too selectively. According to the prospectus, "people are uninformed because no publication has adapted itself to the time which busy men are able to spend on keeping informed. . . . *Time*[will be] interested—not in how much it includes between its covers—but how much it gets off its pages into the minds of its readers." Further, Luce and Hadden hoped that their new magazine would appeal to "every man and woman in America who had the slightest interest in the world and its affairs."[1] They knew they had to compete with, among others, the popular *Literary Digest*,* which had a circulation of 1.2 million; *Time* provided competition that was so great that Time purchased the *Digest* in 1938. With the assistance of a Yale acquaintance, John Wesley Hanes, Luce and Hadden developed a plan by which *Time* would begin publication once they had raised $100,000. Although they were $14,000 short of their goal, *Time* was incorporated on 28 November 1922.[2]

On 3 March of the following year, Hadden and Luce saw the first issue of their new periodical. The premier issue was thirty-two pages long, and was divided into twenty-two departments, from National Affairs to Theatre, departments that remain largely intact. Articles were short, and generally within the goal of the prospectus of not being longer than 400 words apiece. Hadden and Luce were the magazine's editors. There were four writers, called associates, several contributing writers, including Archibald MacLeish, and Stephen Vincent Benét, the circulation and advertising managers, and a researcher. All articles were unsigned. The masthead boasted a circulation of 12,000, but as a result of errors and mishandling, only 9,000 copies of the first issue were distributed.[3] After only one year the little magazine attracted a significant amount of attention, reaching a circulation of 50,000 by October 1924, and 100,000 by December 1925. Circulation figures topped 1 million in 1942 (8 March 1948, p. 56). Publicity claimed an international readership of over 23 million in 1987, although U.S. circulation figures for 1985 were reported to be 4.6 million. *Time* maintains overseas divisions, and claims a substantial "pass-along" readership.

Hadden and Luce intended to trade the roles of business manager and editor annually, and their relationship was not without infighting and argument. It has been said that "Hadden was a journalist of facts and style; Luce's genius lay more in the spotting and measuring of trends."[4] When Hadden died in 1929 after a long illness, John S. Martin became the magazine's first managing editor, charged with the daily editorial responsibility. Luce retained the title of editor, although in a slightly different role; he thought that having a managing editor would free him from some of the more mundane aspects of running the magazine. When Luce began developing other projects, such as the hugely successful *Life*,* editors were sometimes moved from one publication to another, and Luce named himself the magazine's editor-in-chief. He retained this title and function until 1964, when Time was reorganized and Hedley Donovan assumed the role. Luce remained editorial chairman, a position rather like that of emeritus professor, until his death in 1967. Other aspects of the publishing endeavor likewise did not remain static. Until 1937, *Time* had a business manager and no publisher. It was published at Time, headquartered first in New York, then in Cleveland, and finally settling in New York in 1927. The printing of the publication has remained in Chicago since its move there in the same year. Ralph Ingersoll was named publisher in addition to his other responsibilities as general manager in 1937. The first full-time publisher of *Time* was P. I. Prentice, appointed in 1941.

Hadden has been credited with developing and forcing *Time* writers into the use of what is known as "timestyle." Although the magazine has since dropped many of these stylistic characteristics, contemporary readers will recognize many others. W. A. Swanberg describes Hadden's "editorial ingenuity" as a means of "packaging the news to make it more interesting and more salable than it was in real life."[5] Under Hadden, *Time* developed its habit of assigning a descriptive epithet to a subject (gray-thatched, gentle-spirited, pot-bellied), and of never allowing an individual to simply walk (they dashed, ambled, and shuffled) or talk (they barked, snapped, and gushed). These tactics are no longer used frequently by writers, although people still have a tendency to rush, scrawl, and blast. In addition, *Time* inverted sentences and made extensive use of alliteration. Timestyle was perceived as breezy and knowing by some, as outrageous by others.[6]

Initially *Time* made no bones about rewriting articles that had appeared in the daily newspapers—once an event appeared in the news, Hadden and Luce firmly believed, and had been advised, it was in the public domain.[7] Consequently, the magazine's writers were actually rewriters of articles that had previously appeared in the dailies, primarily in the *New York Times* and the *New York Herald Tribune*. This blatant recycling and stylizing of news stories lessened somewhat when *Time* joined the Associated Press in 1936. From this pattern of rewriting news came the development of *Time's* peculiar reporting method, called "group journalism," a phrase Luce grew to dislike. By 1948, group journalism had evolved to the extent that each article was handled by correspondents, researchers, writers, senior editors, the managing editor, and then the "checkers," whose job it was to put a dot over every word in an article in order to verify its authenticity (8 March 1948, p. 64). The story could be rewritten or simply discarded if anyone at any layer of the process challenged it.

This system has not been without its critics. In a 1981 essay, John Tirnan condemned the fact that the writers and editors of any one story may never leave the Time Life Building in New York in order to work on it.[8] Another critic wrote in 1956 that this method ensures that no writer will ever become more well known than the company he represents: "all the credit . . . goes to the corporation, never to the individual."[9] Henry A. Grunwald became the managing editor in 1968, and instituted several changes intended to counter this criticism. Although in form group journalism remained in place, contributor and writer bylines were introduced in July 1970. Stories are still submitted, however, to the give and take of cooperation between correspondent, researcher, writer, and editor.

The mechanism by which a *Time* story is submitted for publication enables the editors to make quick decisions and sudden changes should a rapidly breaking situation warrant. Writers can assemble stories efficiently based on facts and information submitted by the correspondents, some of them foreign; because the article itself is written in-house, there need not be time-consuming prepublication delays. In Curtis Prendergrast's estimation, the situation can produce, however, some problems: "every correspondent could cite instances where the process had gone wrong despite careful checking, where detail had been skewed, emphasis misplaced—where indeed *Time* had erred."[10]

The system may be a factor in a lawsuit brought against *Time* in 1984 by Israeli Minister of Defense Ariel Sharon. The case concerned a paragraph included in the 21 February 1983 cover story, "Verdict on Massacre." Sharon contended that it was absolutely false, and while the jury stated that "certain *Time* employees . . . acted negligently and carelessly in reporting and verifying the information which ultimately found its way into the published paragraph of interest in this case," a *Time* spokesman is quoted as saying, "We won, flat-out and going away."[11] The correspondent in question, David Halvey, was in Israel at the time the story was written, but the article was a composite of information written in New York.

A similar but unrelated criticism of the magazine is that it distorts or misrepresents the news by bombarding the reader with facts. This gives, according to critics, an appearance of authority that may be unjustified and misleading. In 1949 Bernard De Voto called a *Time* story "confused and misleading. Neither its alleged facts nor its judgments represent the accepted finding of scientists all over the world."[12] And as recently as 1981, Tirnan noted that readers are attracted to *Time*'s "apparent breadth (if not depth) of knowledge."[13] The criticism is not that *Time* deliberately falsifies facts, but that it uses so many that the reader has a sense that every word appearing in *Time* is absolute.

Despite the cries of critics, *Time* has had enormous staying power. An extraordinary feature of the periodical has been the consistency of the format. Today *Time* looks very much as the first issues looked. The large bold letters on the cover have changed only in size and other minor details; "the weekly newsmagazine" adorned the cover from 1923 until 1968, and it still appears on the masthead. The familiar red border on the cover first appeared in 1927 and makes a *Time* cover instantly recognizable. Articles remain short, although cover stories and infrequent special issues far exceed the 400-word goal of the prospectus. The original twenty-two departments have remained largely unchanged, although some new ones have been added, and their location in the magazine may change from time to time. In addition to the long-standing news departments, Nation, Business, Education, and Religion, among others, *Time* features its so-called back-of-the-book departments: Books, Milestones, Show Business, Music, and Cinema are among these. A popular and recurring feature has been the annual Man of the Year issue. *Time* named its first man of the year in January 1928 to spotlight Charles A. Lindbergh for his 1927 achievement. Named in the first issue of each year, the Man (Woman, People, Thing) of the Year is chosen by the editors according to this definition: "a man or woman who dominated the news that year and left an indelible mark—for good or ill—on history" (4 January 1963; pp. 10, 11). In addition to Lindbergh, men of the year have included Franklin D. Roosevelt (1932, 1934, 1941), Adolph Hitler (1938), Joseph Stalin (1939), Queen Elizabeth (1952), the Hungarian Freedom Fighter (1956), Martin Luther King, Jr. (1964), the Middle Americans (1970), and the Computer (1983).

When Hadden and Luce founded *Time*, they perceived it as a means by which ordinary Americans could get a lot of news in a little time. Eventually *Time* developed foreign divisions (Time Asia, Time Canada), so the audience has become international. Luce has been cited frequently for his elevation of what he called the American century. Part of his program was a glorification of the economic and political ideals he held, and it has been noted that *Time* is not an unbiased source. Its founders were not unprepared for this charge and even anticipated it in the prospectus. The prejudices to which they admitted included, "a general distrust of the present tendency toward increasing interference by government, a prejudice against the rising cost of government, and faith in the things that money cannot buy."[14] And in addition, *"Time* gives both sides, but clearly indicates which side it believes to have the stronger position" (8 March 1948, p. 56). Although *Time* has never endorsed a political candidate, some have charged that it exerts a great deal of power in the extent or lack of coverage it gives. On the economic side, Tirnan asserts that *"Time* is a celebration of big business, the ethos of mass consumption, and the blossoming of the 'American Century.' "[15] Likewise, Swanberg has called Luce's use of *Time* in the service of his economic views his "celebration of the tycoon."[16]

Nevertheless, *Time* is tremendously successful. It has been used in high school and college classrooms since the 1940s. It succeeded in changing the way in which many Americans got their news. Luce was indeed a man able to anticipate the interests of a diverse population, and make the most of popular trends. Luce and Hadden's dream of informing busy men has evolved into a huge publishing enterprise, and remains strong long after their deaths. In 1985 *Time* was still outselling its closest competitor, *Newsweek,** although even its editors admit that there are some things *Newsweek* does better. And while depending on *Time* for all of one's news may be rather like relying solely on the evening news, it does achieve another American goal, to paraphrase Swanberg, of preventing readers from being completely uninformed.[17] *Time* has helped satisfy the information appetite of a news-hungry world.

Notes

1. Robert T. Elson, *Time, Inc.: The Intimate History of a Publishing Enterprise 1923–1941* (New York: Atheneum, 1968), p. 7. For additional information regarding the prospectus, see "Story of an Experiment," *Time*, 8 March 1948, pp. 55–66.

2. Elson, p. 9.

3. Ibid., p. 69.

4. Henry R. Luce, *The Ideas of Henry Luce*, ed. and introd. by John K. Jessup (New York: Atheneum, 1969), p. 25.

5. W. A. Swanberg, *Luce and His Empire* (New York: Scribner's, 1972), p. 59.

6. *Time* described this style as "fresh, sassy, and sometimes impudent" in an obituary for Luce on 10 March 1967. On the other hand, Swanberg (p. 60) quotes St. John Ervine: "adjectives are used as verbs, and nouns are telescoped to such an extent that a sentence looks like a railway accident."

7. Swanberg, p. 53. Melville Stone, former Associated Press chief, "assured them that news was public property after a day or two of aging."

8. John Tirnan, "Doing *Time*," *Progressive*, August 1981, p. 48.

9. David Cort, "Once Upon a Time, Inc.: Mr. Luce's Fact Machine," *Nation*, 18 February 1956, p. 134.

10. Curtis Prendergrast and Geoffrey Colvin, *The World of Time, Inc.: The Intimate History of a Changing Enterprise*, vol. 3: *1960–1980* (New York: Atheneum, 1986), p. 106.

11. Renata Adler, *Reckless Disregard* (New York: Knopf, 1986), p. 221.

12. Bernard De Voto, "The Easy Chair," *Harper's*, May 1949, p. 57.

13. Tirnan, p. 47.

14. Elson, p. 8.

15. Tirnan, p. 47.

16. Swanberg, p. 81.

17. Ibid., p. 57.

Information Sources

BIBLIOGRAPHY

Adler, Renata. *Reckless Disregard: Westmoreland v. CBS et al.; Sharon v. Time*. New York: Knopf, 1986.

Elson, Robert T. *Time Inc.: The Intimate History of a Publishing Enterprise 1923–1941*. New York: Atheneum, 1968.

―――. *The World of Time Inc.: The Intimate History of a Publishing Enterprise*, vol. 2: *1941–1960*. New York: Atheneum, 1973.

Halberstam, David. *The Powers That Be*. New York: Knopf, 1978.

Kobler, John. *Luce: His Time, Life and Fortune*. Garden City, N.Y.: Doubleday, 1968.

Prendergrast, Curtis, and Geoffrey Colvin. *The World of Time Inc.: The Intimate History of a Changing Enterprise*, vol. 3: *1960–1980*. New York: Atheneum, 1986.

Swanberg, W. A. *Luce and His Empire*. New York: Scribner's, 1972.

INDEX SOURCES

Abstrax, Biography Index, Biology Digest, Book Review Digest, Book Review Index, Computer Business, Film Literature Index, Key to Economic Science, Magazine Index (1977–present), *Medical Review Digest, Oceanic Abstracts, Personnel Literature, Pollution Abstracts, Popular Magazine Review, PROMT, Readers' Guide to Periodical Literature* (1935–present), *Robomatix Reporter, Music Index* (1950–1958, 1976–1979).

LOCATION SOURCES

Widely available. Reprints by Bell and Howell, Microforms International, University Microfilms.

Publication History

MAGAZINE TITLE AND TITLE CHANGES

Time, the Weekly Newsmagazine.

VOLUME AND ISSUE DATA

Semiannual volumes. Vol. 1, no. 1, 3 March 1923–current, weekly.

PUBLISHERS AND PLACE OF PUBLICATION

Ralph M. Ingersoll, 1937–1939; Pierrepont Isham Prentice, 1941–1945; James Linen, 1945–1960; Bernard M. Auer, 1960–1967; James Shepley, 1967–1969; Henry Luce III, 1969–1972; Ralph Davidson, 1972–1979; John Meyers, 1978–1985; Richard B. Thomas, 1985–1986; Robert L. Miller, 1987–present.

EDITORS
    Editor-in-chief, position created in 1950: Henry R. Luce 1950–1964; Hedley
    Donovan, 1964–1979; Henry A. Grunwald, 1979–1987, Jason McManus, 1987–
    present. Editor, position began 1923, ended 1950: Briton Hadden and Henry R.
    Luce, 1923–1929 (alternating years); Henry R. Luce, 1929–1943; Henry R. Luce
    and Manfred Gottfried, 1943–1949; Thomas S. Matthews, 1949–1952. Managing
    editor, position began 1929: John S. Martin, 1929–1933; John S. Billings, 1934–
    1937; Manfred Gottfried, 1937–1943; T. S. Matthews, 1943–1949; Roy Alex-
    ander, 1949–1960; Otto Fuerbringer, 1960–1968; Henry Grunwald, 1968–1977;
    Ray Cave, 1977–1985; Jason McManus, 1986–1987; Henry Muller, 1987–present.
CIRCULATION
    4.6 million.

Jean M. Parker

TODAY'S HEALTH. See HEALTH

TOWN AND COUNTRY

Town and Country began its long history as the *Home Journal*, an illustrated
weekly founded in 1846. As the second oldest general magazine in the United
States, *Town and Country*'s longevity can be attributed to its adaptation through
the years to the specific goals and audience for which it was created.

Nathaniel Parker Willis and George P. Morris, founders of the new publication,
believed that "the workaday Republic was beginning to yield leisure for un-
economic pursuits."[1] They saw a need for a periodical "which picks, arranges,
condenses, and gives in small compass, 'the cream and substance' of the week's
wilderness of newspaper reading, while, at the same time, the greater portion
of its space is devoted to matter which is instructive, companionable and
amusing."[2] The *Home Journal* was created to promote a marriage between
intellect and fashion according to the European standard. Its purpose was to
focus on "Society" and "Literature" and to avoid, especially in that period
before the Civil War, any political issues or causes. The magazine was intended
to reach an audience characterized by Willis as "the upper ten thousand." These
were the leaders of society and those who followed the manners and tastes dictated
by them.

Willis and Morris were members of that distinctive New York society they
wished to instruct, amuse, and refine. Both men had been involved in the newspaper business separately and together before their venture into the *Home Journal*. General George Morris had been editor of the *New York Mirror*, and N. P.
Willis was famous not only as an author but also as a commentator about himself
and the elegant world in which he traveled. He developed a style of gossip that
Lucius Beebe was to make famous in more recent history. However, as the

guiding intelligence of the new periodical, Willis was able to discover, encourage, and support American literature in the 1840s.

During its early years the *Home Journal* championed Edgar Allan Poe and published such authors as Washington Irving and James Fenimore Cooper. English and European authors also appeared; some of whom, like Thomas De Quincey and Thomas Carlyle, Honoré de Balzac and Victor Hugo, were introduced for the first time to the American reader. In 1878 Henry James's short novel *Daisy Miller* was first published in the *Home Journal*. Though political causes were given no platform, the magazine did advocate the rights of women and assisted the campaign to bring grand opera to New York. By the end of the nineteenth century, the *Home Journal* had established its style and particular audience.

In 1901 the change of title from *Home Journal* to *Town and Country* signaled more than just a change in name. The goals of the founders to direct and reflect culture and taste had now been forgotten. The notion of instruction was deleted. "The intellectual wing of the 'upper ten thousand' had become too radical to read the same magazine as the rich and well-born. Or more accurately perhaps, the great new industrial fortunes were carrying the rich, with the well-born safely in train, into a paradise of super-luxury where carping intellectuals seemed too reptillian."[3] *Town and Country* became very much a peculiarly New York who's who and what's what among the wealthy. Each issue now contained a calendar of engagements, weddings, at-home days, dances, charitable entertainments, and lectures. In March of 1902, a regular feature was introduced entitled A Directory for Country Gentlemen, in which addresses of reliable stock farms, stables and breeding establishments, dog kennels, florists, nurseries, landscape architects, and breeders in poultry could be found. "The value of this comprehensive directory will be enhanced by careful discrimination in the selection of the houses and names composing it."[4]

Another special section entitled Town and Country Life included society notes on various dinners, engagement parties, and other social activities in which the names of prominent families were prominently featured. Not content keeping the reader satisfied with calendar notes, the magazine also provided a subsection called Social Movements, which gave brief notes on the travel whereabouts of society members. Photographic portraits of "leading members of society" were followed by photo essays on the "beautiful summer homes" of prestigious individuals. A special claim prefaced real estate offerings: "If you wish to buy, sell or rent high class *Country Property*, and the Summer Homes we suggest your advertising in *Town and Country*."[5] Thorstein Veblen, reflecting on this society in *The Theory of the Leisure Class*, makes this observation;

> In order to gain and to hold the esteem of men it is not sufficient merely
> to possess wealth or power. The wealth or power must be put in evidence,
> for esteem is awarded only on evidence. And not only does the evidence
> of wealth serve to impress one's importance on others and to keep their

sense of importance alive and alert, but it is of scarcely less use in building up and preserving one's self-complacency.[6]

By the middle of the 1920s, *Town and Country* became a biweekly though the contents and their style of presentation remained the same. The use of color illustrations and artwork did add a new luxury to the publication, while new features of a quasi-global nature were introduced: letters from Berlin, Paris, and London. The members of society who are mentioned regularly are no longer exclusively New Yorkers, and the photographic essays of summer homes become focused on architecture in general. Sometimes the photos portray the homes of celebrities. In 1929 the January issue spotlighted views of I Tatti, the home of Bernard Berenson.

Perhaps not surprisingly, the years of the depression hardly affected the publication. There appeared no significant changes in layout or content, nor any significant limitation of advertising as a result of the 1929 crash. Nevertheless, by 1935 the magazine was taken over by the Hearst Corporation, and Harry A. Bull, member of the prestigious New York Drama Critics Circle, was appointed editor. Under his tenure, *Town and Country* became a monthly periodical, but more importantly, the new editorial policy moved the publication back to the purpose of its founders. Once again, *Town and Country* not only reflected the taste of the time but attempted to direct it through distinguished literary contributors. Among those writers offering their talents in the thirties and forties were George Bernard Shaw, Antoine de Saint-Exupéry, Evelyn Waugh, and Somerset Maugham. In 1936 Paul Gallico and Ludwig Bemelmans became regular contributors. During this era, *Town and Country* could claim pioneering status because it introduced its readers to ballet, skiing, swing music, surrealism, and café society. The transformation the Hearst Corporation wrought in layout through more and better color photography set the magazine on the path to the glossy table-top periodical it is today.

In the decades following the 1950s when Henry B. Sell left the editorship of *Harper's Bazaar* to take over at *Town and Country*, the magazine again lost the intent of its creators but adapted to the needs of an ever-increasing audience. Advertising that before was adequate now became plentiful. The best and most expensive fashions, cars, homes, trips, clubs, and hobbies were sold in its pages. Article titles such as "The 1965 Debutantes; How They Look, Where They Go, Who They Are" and "The Establishment: Blue Chip Style, Privilege, Power and Permissiveness" reflected the life styles of the wealthy but added nothing to their understanding of themselves. The "upper ten thousand" became model consumers in a consumer society.

Town and Country in the 1980s continues to mirror the lives, interests, and purchases of the rich and powerful. Its recent issues average between 200 and 300 pages filled three-quarters full with opulent advertising. Its circulation is just under 300,000. While the magazine persists, its present and past provide invaluable social commentary not only on the affluent but also on those who would imitate them.

Notes

1. Basil Rauch, "The First Hundred Years," *Town and Country,* December 1946, p. 61.

2. Ibid., p. 59.

3. Ibid., p. 129.

4. "Editor's Comments," *Town and Country*, 15 March 1902, p. 7.

5. Ibid., p. 54.

6. Thorstein Veblen, *The Theory of the Leisure Class*, (New York: The New American Library, 1953) p. 42.

Information Sources

BIBLIOGRAPHY

Mott, Frank Luther. *A History of American Magazines. vol. 2: 1850–1865.* Cambridge: Harvard University Press, 1938.

Peterson, Theodore. *Magazines in the Twentieth Century.* Urbana: University of Illinois Press, 1956.

Wood, James. *Magazines in the United States.* 3rd ed. New York: Ronald Press, 1971.

INDEX SOURCES

    Readers' Guide to Periodical Literature, Access (1975–present), *Magazine Index* (1977–present).

LOCATION SOURCES

    University Microfilms International (1973–present). St. Louis Public Library, other libraries.

Publication History

MAGAZINE TITLE AND TITLE CHANGES

    Home Journal: An Illustrated Weekly, 1846–1901; *Town and Country,* 1901–present.

VOLUME AND ISSUE DATA

    Vols. 1–82, 1846–1928, weekly; vols. 83–91, 1928–1936, biweekly; vols. 91–142, 1936–present, monthly.

PUBLISHER AND PLACE OF PUBLICATION

    Nathaniel Parker Willis and George Pope Morris, 1846–1867, New York; Stuyvesant Company, 1867–1925, New York; Hearst Corporation, 1925–present, New York.

EDITORS

    George P. Morris and Nathaniel P. Willis, 1846–1867; Morris Phillips, 1867–1900; F. M. Munroe, 1900–1906; Thomas Hotchkiss, 1906–1908; Curtis Patterson, 1908–1910; H. J. Whigham, 1910–1935; Harry A. Bull, 1935–1949; Henry B. Sell, 1949–1967; Anthony Mazzola, 1967–1973; Frank Zachary, 1973–present.

CIRCULATION

    284,000.

Judith Bunker

TOWN WEEKLY. See GRIT

TRAVEL. See TRAVEL-HOLIDAY

TRAVEL AND CAMERA. See TRAVEL AND LEISURE

TRAVEL AND LEISURE

In an October 1975 interview with John S. Connors, president and publisher of *Travel and Leisure,* Pamela Fiori—who had been promoted to editor—stated her idea of what the magazine is all about in one word: "escape." Asked to amplify, she explained:

> I mean available escape, real escape. Escape into the lively arts, books, music, escape to a distant place, escape even into the woods behind your own house. . . . No horror stories. No toil or office intrigue. It's what *Travel and Leisure* is, as you say, all about—the landscape and mindscape of escape—and all of it's in the title.[1]

As we travel to exotic places near and far through the stunning photography, design, and layout of this magazine, we have to agree that to every person fascinated not only by the landscape of this planet of ours, but also by the diversity of its cultures, *Travel and Leisure* offers the ultimate delight, short of buying the tickets and embarking on our fantastic voyage.

The magazine's story is one of remarkable success in the marketplace. Begun in January 1971 as a free publication sent to American Express cardmembers six times a year, the magazine made the transition from 2.5 million free circulation to over a million fully paid subscriptions in less than ten years.

"Literate, briskly paced, visually pleasing but serviceable, full of surprises, and practical-minded as a c.p.a. about the escalating costs of pleasure,"[2] *Travel and Leisure* has lived up to its mission of catering to the fads and leisure pursuits of customers who read it for pleasure and entertainment, certainly, but also as a reliable source of information. "They look to us for solutions to transportation problems, for alternatives when their first-choice hotels are overbooked, and for empathy when no instant answers are available. . . . There are countless ways to measure success, but, by far, the sweetest is to have someone say 'we're here because we read about it in *Travel and Leisure*—and, by the way, we're having a wonderful time.' "[3]

The magazine's success is due, in part, to the creative energy of its level-headed editor, Pamela Fiori, one of the bright stars among young American editors. Under her leadership, the magazine became the top-quality publication it is now. When Marianne Howatson, former senior vice-president of the Magazine Publishers Association, became publisher of *Travel and Leisure*, new ventures were on the wing, such as the first overseas edition in cooperation with *Newsweek**—an English-language Asian edition that has been very successful. Plans to publish an Australian/New Zealand edition, as well as European, Canadian, and Latin American editions, are in the making.

The September 1987 issue saw more improvements: a new book look, more color photography, and new departments such as Consumer Watch, Going Shopping, and a new format in different paper stock for the Taking Off section. More tips added to its previous section Travel and Money—how to get the best rates at hotels, airlines, and cruises; Business Trip—airline clubs, passport information, custom clearance; Table for One—food for pleasure, from Palm Beach to the Côte d'Azur. Travel and Health, information on medicine's new specialties, helps travelers on such issues as risk factors involved in traveling around the world and offers suggestions on what to do for just plain old motion sickness in air or on water. And what world traveler could do without Weather Watch, the monthly report on balmy temperatures, rainfall, and humidity in various parts of the world?

There is doubtlessly no remote nook or island on this earth that *Travel and Leisure* hasn't yet explored. From Tibet to Antarctica, from Bali to Shanghai (a truly beautiful black-and-white photo essay in the August 1987 issue), the magazine caters to every whim and taste. The August 1986 issue has tips on driving in Europe, and outstanding articles on Paris's Left Bank and "Pacific Perfect Santa Barbara" in California. In the May 1987 issue you find directions on where to catch the best trout and salmon in Europe. Museum hopper? Then read all about Los Angeles's new museum of contemporary art. Teach foreign languages? *Travel and Leisure* offers a wealth of visual aids to link culture with foreign language learning, including pull-out sections from departments of tourism.

As long as airplanes fly, ships cruise, and people have money to spend in their leisure pursuits, *Travel and Leisure* promises to be around to bring the best of this world to its readers.

Notes

1. John S. Connors, "The Overture Has Been a Rousing Success," *Travel and Leisure*, October 1975. *Travel and Leisure* was one of two magazines that responded to my request for information, in this case promptly, and with a very useful package of materials from its public relations department. These are informational reports attached to each *Travel and Leisure* issue, no page numbers.

2. Ibid.
3. Ibid.

Information Sources

BIBLIOGRAPHY
Carlson, Walter. "AmEx Publishing Chief Looks to Circulation Pricing as a Priority."
  Folio: The Magazine for Magazine Management, October 1984, pp. 88–89.
Connors, John S. "The Overture Has Been a Rousing Success." *Travel and Leisure,*
  October 1975. Promotion package from *Travel and Leisure.*
"Pamela Fiori, Editor in Chief of *Travel and Leisure.*" *Folio: The Magazine for Magazine
  Management,* January 1987, pp. 49–50.
Peter, John. "American Express: Worldwide Publisher." *Folio: The Magazine for Mag-
  azine Management,* January 1987, pp. 130–33.
Spritzer, Lois, et al. "The Elements of Magazine Style." *Attenzione,* December 1985,
  pp. 41–43.
"Travel and Leisure: Top Title for Freelancers." *Folio: The Magazine for Magazine
  Management,* April 1987, p. 40.
INDEX SOURCES
  Access (1975–present), *PMR* (Popular Magazine Review), *Infotrac.*
LOCATION SOURCES
  Microformat Bell and Howell Microforms and University Microfilms International.

Publication History

MAGAZINE TITLE AND TITLE CHANGES
  Travel and Leisure, formerly *Travel and Camera.*
VOLUME AND ISSUE DATA
  Vol. 1–current, February/March 1971–current. Bimonthly, 1971–1979; monthly,
  October 1979–current.
PUBLISHER AND PLACE OF PUBLICATION
  American Express Publishing Corporation, Marianne Howatson, vice-president
  and publisher; New York.
EDITORS
  Caskie Stinnett, 1971–1975; Pamela Fiori, 1975–current.
CIRCULATION
  1,119,198 (30 June 1987).

Heleni Pedersoli

TRAVEL-HOLIDAY

Travel-Holiday was founded by George H. Daniels as *The Four-Track News*
in July 1901. It was published by the Passenger Department of the New York
Central and Hudson River Railroad as a ten-cent illustrated magazine of travel
and education. For over eighty years, *Travel-Holiday* has maintained its position

as the leading general travel magazine in the United States. It has been able to do this because of the editorial policy that aimed to serve the armchair traveler while at the same time to give those who had the means and time to travel the pertinent advice they needed. The magazine's stated aim was to provide travel, adventure, and exploration for its audience.

A half century before *Travel-Holiday's* beginning, *Gleason's Pictorial* could exclaim, "Not many years ago a man could acquire quite a reputation by crossing the Atlantic, but it does not set up a man very high to travel nowadays; everybody travels."[1] Everyone of means not only traveled, but wrote about it, too. Most periodicals of the late nineteenth century printed travel sketches, reviewed travel books, and described foreign and domestic tours. "The pictorials had an advantage of this kind, for they could make their travel articles doubly attractive."[2] *The Four-Track News*, by offering travel and education in illustrated form and at relatively reasonable prices, was able to stay in business and prosper.

Twenty years later, the publication was called *Travel* but was still carrying out the original editorial policy of its first issues. For those armchair travelers who wished to explore exotic areas of the world from the comfort of their living rooms, there were stories like "The Land of the Lapps," and the "Dark People of India's Hidden Hills." Other thrilling narratives consisted of a series of articles titled "Heart of Black Papua," by Merlin Moore Taylor. These were accounts of the author's expedition into New Guinea, which he claimed to be the first white man to explore. The tone of the series was mysterious and threatening, mentioning "deep dank jungles" and nightmares in which natives are waiting to ambush the expedition.

The periodical was now priced at thirty-five cents a copy, but the reader was getting more for his money. The issues were larger, the covers were colored painted scenes of foreign lands, and the National Travel Club advertised prominently, offering *Travel's* readers the opportunity to become active members and reap the benefits of its special advice. While the publication was long on text and short on photographs, this same text was often written by such famous authors as Hilaire Belloc on Spain and Italy, Vita Sackville-West's "The Highlands of French Savoy," and J. B. Priestley's "London's Giant Treasure Trove." It was at the time of these distinguished contributions to the publication that the first merger with another travel magazine occurred. In June 1931, *Travel* combined with *Holiday*. This periodical was identified with the American Automobile Association and had no relationship to the *Holiday* that was to merge with *Travel* in 1977.

During the 1940s, black-and-white photographs of scenic travel spots were the new cover design. Ever sensitive to the times, *Travel* responded to World War II by paring down the publication and acknowledging the limited travel opportunities. "Now that long trips are difficult to make, people throughout the United States are choosing vacation spots that are within easy reach of their homes."[3] A special feature appeared in 1942 called Background for War. This monthly entry explained the historical significance of places that first became known through the news of the war. When the end of the war finally did come, American society had changed. "Men and women of the armed forces had become accustomed to traveling, if involuntarily, during the war; presumably, they would retain the habit under pleasanter circumstances."[4] And not only would Americans have the habit of travel, but they would also have the time and money.

In the 1950s and 1960s under the editorship of Malcolm McTear Davis, the direction of the magazine was set for the active traveler. "Now, *Travel* steps forward again with this first issue of 1952. It is newly thickened, newly styled, newly geared to the demands of the modern traveler."[5] The dimensions of the magazine (8" x 10¾") became what they are today, and the publication's subtitle, *The Magazine That Roams the Globe*, was first introduced during this period. The contents of the periodical included short foreign-language phrases with their phonetic pronunciation and English translation. There were features on tours of the month, a special calendar of worldwide events for the month, a New York Broadway theater guide, and reviews of new hotels. Regular how-to articles appeared, such as "How to Stretch Your Motoring Dollar" and even "How to Obtain an Audience with the Pope."

Two successful mergers took place during the 1970s. In 1977, *Travel* merged with the monthly *Holiday*. The latter was a general travel periodical published by the Saturday Evening Post Company and had a reported circulation of 450,000. In 1979 the new *Travel-Holiday* incorporated *Travel Adviser*, a periodical that had been founded in 1976 and reported a circulation of 55,000. By the beginning of the 1980s *Travel-Holiday* could boast of a circulation in excess of 750,000.

Travel-Holiday is as responsive to its audience today as it was eighty years ago. The price remains reasonable, the text both helpful and informative, the color photography artistic and exciting. An editorial policy committed and sensitive to the best interests of its readership guarantees *Travel-Holiday* a longevity and seniority in the travel publishing business for years to come.

Notes

1. *Gleason's Pictorial* of 1853, quoted in Frank Luther Mott, *A History of American Magazines. Vol. 2: 1850–1865* (Cambridge: Harvard University Press, 1938), pp. 176–78.

2. Ibid., p. 177.

3. "Background for War," *Travel-Holiday*, July 1942, p. 27.

4. Theodore Peterson, *Magazines in the Twentieth Century* (Urbana: University of Illinois Press, 1956), p. 351.

5. Editor's Log, *Travel-Holiday*, January 1952, p. 3.

Information Sources

BIBLIOGRAPHY
Mott, Frank Luther. *A History of American Magazines. Vol. 2: 1850–1865*. Cambridge: Harvard University Press, 1938.

————. *A History of American Magazines. Vol. 4 1885–1905.* Cambridge: Harvard University Press, 1957.

Peterson, Theodore. *Magazines in the Twentieth Century.* Urbana: University of Illinois Press, 1956.

INDEX SOURCES

> *Readers' Guide to Periodical Literature* (1979–present), *Magazine Index* (1979–present).

LOCATION SOURCES

> Kent Library, Southeast Missouri State University. Available in microform (1979–present).

Publication History

MAGAZINE TITLE AND TITLE CHANGES

> *The Four-Track News,* 1901–1906; *Travel Magazine,* 1906–1910; *Travel,* 1910–1950; *Travel: The Magazine That Roams the Globe,* 1950–1977; *Travel-Holiday: The Magazine That Roams the Globe,* 1977–present.

VOLUME AND ISSUE DATA

> Vols. 1–170, July 1901–July 1988, monthly.

PUBLISHER AND PLACE OF PUBLICATION

> Passenger Department of the New York Central and Hudson River Railroad, 1901–1902, New York; Robert M. McBride and Company, 1924–1949, New Jersey; Travel Publications Inc., 1949–present, New York.

EDITORS

> George H. Daniels, 1901–?; Raymond Holden,?–1925; Edward Hale Bierstadt, 1925–1927; Coburn Gilman, 1927–1950; Malcolm McTear Davis, 1950–1972; Robert H. Rufa, 1972–1974; Barbara M. Lotz, 1974–1985; Scott Shane, 1985–present.

CIRCULATION

> 800,000.

Judith Bunker

TRUE STORY

The first and most successful of the confession magazines, *True Story* emerged from the reader mail of *Physical Culture*, publisher Bernarr Macfadden's first magazine and the vehicle for his gospel of physical fitness. As *Physical Culture* gained circulation in the late teens, it broadened its appeal by featuring advice columns and first-person narratives that addressed social and psychological as well as physical problems.[1] Macfadden's emotional editorial style encouraged readers to respond to these features on a personal level, and according to his authorized biography, many wrote letters about their own experiences to corroborate what they read in *Physical Culture*:

> Most of [the letters] had the conscious ring of public confession, such as is heard in a Salvation Army gathering, or in an old-fashioned testimony

meeting of Southern camp religionists. The folly of transgression, the terrible effects of ignorance, the girls who had not been warned by wise parents—a whole series of tragedies out of the American soil were falling, day after day, on the desk of the editor.[2]

Both Macfadden and his former wife, Mary, claimed credit for the idea of shaping these letters into a new magazine for common people that could not fail in its popular appeal because it would be written by its own readers. One of the Macfaddens hit upon the title *True Story* as the perfect expression of the new magazine's commitment to use episodes from life as its source of instructive as well as entertaining stories.

The first issue of *True Story* appeared on the newsstands in May 1919 bearing the motto "Truth is stranger than fiction" and a cover illustration of a man and a woman glaring at one another over the caption "And their love turned to hatred." If the prospective buyer were still not intrigued enough to purchase a copy, the publisher had placed a further incentive prominently under the title: "We offer $1,000.00 for your life romance."

Many were intrigued, and of a printing of 100,000, the first issue sold 60,000 copies,[3] despite a cover price of twenty cents at a time when magazines almost universally sold for ten cents a copy and most relied on subscription rather than per copy sales. For twenty cents, the reader got a book of ninety-six pages containing twelve stories with titles like "A Wife Who Awoke in Time" and "My Battle with John Barleycorn." Most of the protagonists were girls dissatisfied with their proper yet mundane lives as daughters, wives, or mothers who erred in their desire for adventure, and a few stories featured men who had committed crimes or struggled with addiction to alcohol or avarice. The consistent pattern in nearly all the stories was a fall from innocence and security as a result of the narrator's willfulness, a short period of privation and unhappiness, and repentance followed by restoration to more favorable circumstances—what became known as the sin-suffer-repent formula. To enhance the appearance of reality, *True Story's* first editor, John Brennan, illustrated the stories with posed photographs using members of his own family.

The idea of a "true" magazine proved to be phenomenally successful. Within five years, circulation of *True Story* rose to two million copies. Between 1922 and 1926, Macfadden capitalized on his success by introducing a number of new "true" magazines, including *True Romances, True Love and Romances, and True Experiences*. Young movie hopefuls like Norma Shearer, Jean Arthur, and Frederic March replaced Brennan's family in *True Story's* posed photographic illustrations. The magazine developed Hollywood ties by arranging for films based on its stories to be released in theaters simultaneously with publication, and a weekly "True Story Hour" came to radio in 1928.[4] Although Bernarr Macfadden's own favorite message to the world continued to be fitness to the extent that he insisted that all his editorial staff perform calisthenics on their desktops and in the office aisles at the beginning of each working day,[5] *True*

Story had surpassed *Physical Culture* as the financial cornerstone of Macfadden Publications.

True Story's own account of its success was that it was a magazine for and by the lower classes, people too unsophisticated and uneducated to be served by the traditional press, who were brought into new prominence by changing social and economic conditions after World War I. For people who had not read magazines before, it provided a forum in which they could share their problems.[6] Established magazines took a dimmer view of *True Story*'s role. Sex, many disapproving articles agreed, was the great attraction of confession stories; at best, they provided mindless entertainment for the mindless masses. One representative writer warned that "to pound into empty heads month after month the doctrine of comparative immunity cannot be particularly healthy" and that "it is impossible to believe that the chronic reader of 'confessions' has much traffic with good books."[7]

Both *True Story* and its detractors viewed its appeal as a new popular phenomenon, but Theodore Peterson maintained that Macfadden's success was not the result of any great stroke of originality; rather, he had "simply rediscovered what publishers had known for centuries and applied it to the magazine field. He found that a narrative of a true, highly emotional experience—a seduction, a murder—had tremendous reader appeal, especially when told in the first person. If it pointed up some lofty moral, so much the better."[8] Peterson regarded seventeenth-century broadsides that featured "true stories" of crime and passion as the first popular manifestations of the sin-suffer-repent formula, and the first novels carried the concept into the eighteenth century, for although they are understood to be fiction, novels like *Moll Flanders* are also first-person narratives that purport to be true, tell of a young woman tempted if not actually going astray, encountering passion and crime in indelicate situations, all told under the pretense of providing a moral tale to prevent others from taking the wrong path.

True Story tapped this tradition of cautionary tales that cloak intensely private, personal experiences in moral terms. The "true" in the title was understood by the magazine's own editorial to mean that its stories provided instruction, example, and advice to its readers. But beyond this moral appeal was the understanding, encouraged by enticing photographs and lurid captions, that truth was also editorial license to present all sorts of circumstances outside the social pale— wives leaving husbands, motherhood without marriage—that would be unacceptable in any other magazine format. *True Story* itself admitted that public prurience was its chief appeal; during the 1920s, it carried this statement under the masthead:

> The power of *True Story* is Truth. The names of places may be changed. There may be a slight deviation in the events depicted from the actual day by day happenings in the life of the author who writes the story: but back of each story is the fundamental truth, "this actually happened to me." And there is nothing more thrilling or engrossing than life.

Are the stories true? Evidence outside the official Macfadden accounts suggests that the confession genre really did begin with letters from the public. Even a critical 1937 article admits: "This much, at least, is undeniable: *True Story*, the first of the 'confessions,' did begin with genuine letters and, though now there is editing done and professional work bought, the flood of illiterate, exhibitionist documents continues to flow in."[9] A former editorial assistant at *True Story* wrote in 1930 that "After a while, of course, professional writers entered the field, but the first issues of the pioneer confessional magazine were made up of crude, living material, worked into some sort of shape in the office, but with care to renounce good writing rather than, say, the department store clerk who had sent in her autobiography."[10] *True Story* has solicited contributions and run contests earnestly since the first issue, including careful instructions on how to write for the magazine. This suggests that at least some stories are based on actual experiences, and a 1983 survey of forty-one writers for *True Story* showed that sixteen had in fact written of personal experiences, had never published a story before, and did not consider themselves professional writers.[11] However, the other twenty-five surveyed did consider themselves professionals, and six of those reported having more than sixty stories accepted for publication over a five-year period.[12] Clearly, over time, the most efficient way of getting at "truth" has proved to be having practiced professionals produce it according to the formula.

Editorial control at *True Story* had a rocky start, as did professional writing. Macfadden's original concept was that common people like the readers were best equipped to select stories for publication, so a reader department of part-time amateurs was organized to select from a reported 70,000 to 100,000 manuscripts per year according to two criteria: "Do you believe this story is true?" and "Does it interest you?"[13] The editorial department's responsibility had more to do with presentation than content; it was to see that the stories were "completely serious, true to life, and told in the first person in simple, homely language, and . . . [taught] a strong moral lesson."[14] The basic sin-suffer-repent formula appears to have evolved from popular taste during the 1920s, and rising circulation figures proved to the publisher that his original idea of letting the public choose its own reading material was sound. *True Story* was still an enormously popular novelty in the publishing world; it could be allowed to find its own audience.

William Jordan Rapp, editor from 1926 to 1942, showed the first signs of editorial concern about the magazine's image and responsiveness to its audience. While an occasional male-viewpoint story continued to appear, he recognized and capitalized on the fact that *True Story* appealed chiefly to women. Recipes, dress patterns, and features on raising babies, staples for women's magazines aimed at the middle classes, were introduced; and advertising, mostly for beauty products, was directed almost exclusively toward women. Rapp believed that the young women who had bought *True Story* on the newsstands in 1919 were still its audience in the late 1920s and 1930s and that they still enjoyed the sin-suffer-repent formula, but they were older, married, coping with families, and experiencing an economic depression along with the rest of the country. Marriage, motherhood, and economic security had become their chief concerns. The magazine had always targeted the lower, working, largely uneducated class as its audience, but Rapp took the trouble to reason the implications of the concerns of that class on the stories he published. He claimed to use a long-standing *True Story* feature, first called Domestic Relations Court and renamed Home Problems Forum in the 1930s, as a gauge of reader interest. In each issue a family conflict was presented, and readers were invited to write letters offering solutions for publication. Rapp drew conclusions about his readers' concerns not from the content of responses, but from volume. The situations that excited the most responses, he found, were those grounded in common experience—whether to have another child, how to cope with live-in in-laws, or why a young family should buy life insurance. Questions about how much a girl with a "past" should tell her fiancé before the wedding day were comparatively uninteresting.[15] This information suggested that for *True Story's* more mature, depression-era audience, sordid escapades were not as interesting as problems involving economic security. Tales of love and murder in the Yukon or life in an Arabian harem consequently disappeared from the magazine's pages, and the "truth" became less a promise of exotic narratives to be enjoyed vicariously than a guarantee that its stories would be grounded in real-life concerns with which its readers could easily identify. Interest in other people's problems played as large a role as ever in the magazine's appeal, but Rapp chose to emphasize the instructional aspect of this change in focus by organizing a "ministerial board" of prominent New York City clergymen to endorse the moral value of its stories, and from the 1930s, inspirational messages and anecdotes became a regular if not dominant feature.

A good part of the messianic flavor of *True Story's* leadership was lost in 1941 when accusations of misuse of company funds—allegedly in part on a failed bid for the Republican nomination for president in 1936—forced seventy-three-year-old Bernarr Macfadden's resignation. Months later it came to light that the former management had faked *True Story's* 1940 circulation figures to advertisers. Orr Jay Elder, who had dealt with fiscal management at Macfadden Publications since 1903, took over as publisher and steered the company through two years of deficits and a return to profitability in 1943.[16]

Internal financial difficulties and the wartime paper shortage put pressure on the most successful Macfadden publication to attract more revenue, principally by facing its perennially poor relations with advertisers. From the start, *True Story* had been a magazine for "persons with little education and little purchasing power, persons whom other publishers had neglected because they were not the sort that advertisers were especially interested in reaching."[17] Initially, a high cover price coupled with its fantastic newsstand circulation made up for *True Story's* lack of appeal with advertisers, but by the 1940s its novelty had worn off, its audience, though still numbering over two million, had stabilized, and the magazine had to sell its loyal following.

Toward this end, new editor Henry Lieferant capitalized on his predecessor's move toward emphasis on domestic issues and women's features to shape *True Story* into a sort of substitute women's service magazine for the lower class. The Victory Homemaker department headed by Esther Kimmel debuted in 1942, featuring "true-tested recipes" that for the first time inspired the same sort of confidence in readers that the "true stories" enjoyed. In keeping with the spirit of the war effort, home economy editorial took precedence over fashion and beauty. Articles like "Federal Income Tax for the Wage Earner" (1943) recognized the problems encountered by women working in wartime factories while managing households. The magazine even added a family feature, The National Whats-It, providing a few pages of puzzles and quizzes for children.

Market research confirmed that the traditional women's service magazines had little readership among lower-class *True Story* readers, and in fact, readers of *True Story* were unlikely to buy any of the general-interest magazines.[18] By strengthening its service departments, the magazine was able to represent itself to advertisers as providing access to a home products market that couldn't be reached through other publications. *True Story* never equaled the leading women's service magazines in its ability to draw advertising revenue; even at its peak of $5,624,000 in 1957, it lagged far behind *McCall's** and *Good Housekeeping*, both of which posted advertising revenues over $25 million.[19] Still, the home service features provided a solid if small base from which to attract advertising, and from the standpoint of readers, a bit of practical advice on running the household complemented the stories' advisory function.[20]

Subsequent editors of *True Story*, all women since 1951, have maintained the balance Lieferant initiated during the war years between stories and enough home service departments and features—making up 10 to 20 percent of each issue— to be useful to women who, the entire industry feared, would no longer buy magazines for entertainment alone. The motto "Truth is stranger than fiction" was abandoned in favor of "A Woman's guide to love and marriage" as editors dusted off and repackaged the old argument that true stories are beneficial to the reader. "Through the actual experiences of other people like themselves," a 1959 editorial message promised, "the readers of *True Story* obtain guidance and inspiration to assure their own happiness." An attempt was even made to change the label "confessions" to "family behavior magazines."

Though it failed in its attempt to rename the genre, *True Story* has succeeded in presenting itself as a women's magazine with a personal, helpful tone for a loyal core readership that has changed little since Rapp defined his audience in the late 1920s. They are still young women, married to blue-collar or low-level clerical workers, raising families, and if they work outside the home, they consider it a job rather than a career.[21] The expensive fashions, home remodeling projects, and elaborate entertaining depicted in middle-class women's service magazines are beyond their interest and economic reach. Instead, *True Story* runs features on how to keep a cake from falling or how to reorganize a closet, or a series on career alternatives for women without college degrees. Its stories pander shamelessly to the audience's time-proven appetite for romance and domestic conflict. Titles and captions often suggest verboten topics ranging from "I Was Anyone's Girlfriend" (1951) to "After Last Night, Am I a Lesbian?" (1970), or stories are based on contemporary headlines like "Surgeons Begged for My Dead Husband's Heart" (1969), "I Became a Black Woman for Six Months" (1971), and "Cocaine Killed My Husband" (1988). But beyond the "hook," stories inevitably center around the same domestic themes—rediscovery of the reliable old boyfriend, misunderstanding and making up with the teenage daughter—that have been *True Story*'s staple for decades. Its readers thrive on familiar situations that reinforce traditional values presented in the spirit of helpfulness by chatty editorials. In *True Story*, unpleasant events are borne with grace, so women with breast cancer are ennobled by their suffering but not cured, black girls who fall in love with white boys learn to accept that romance wasn't meant to be, and young wives who resent a baby's interference with their sex lives learn the joys of motherhood. Month after month, letters to the editor published in the magazine demonstrate how deeply readers appreciate and identify with *True Story*'s brand of verisimilitude.

On the basis of this unusual degree of reader trust, *True Story* has maintained its historic lead within the confession magazine field, and the acquisition of its two major rivals, *True Confessions* in 1963 and *Modern Romances* in 1978, has made it the flagship publication of a family of seven "sister" confession magazines. However, circulation figures, though still four to five times those of its sisters or its few remaining competitors from other publishers, dropped below 2 million in the 1980s for the first time since 1926 and fell to a low of 1 million in 1987. Advertising revenues, never particularly strong, dropped rapidly as soon as circulation began a downward trend, and the seven Macfadden sisters showed an operating deficit of $1.5 million in 1973 and $2.3 million in 1974. When advertising volume dropped by 21 percent in the first quarter of 1975, Macfadden-Bartell, the corporate owner, hastily sold all its Macfadden women's publications,[22] and in the midst of the fiscal confusion, the confession magazines were unable to pay their story writers for several months during 1975.[23]

Speculation on the reasons for the slumping confession market abounds. One often-cited cause is the "sexual revolution" of the 1960s that made confessions, a product of the 1920s sexual revolution, pale by comparison so that "a lot of people nowadays are doing the very things they fantasized about while reading confessions."[24] Since sex in *True Story* has never been portrayed with any degree of explicitness, this explanation seems unlikely. But potential readers probably are more sophisticated about mainstream ideas and more skeptical of the conventional wisdom found in the pages of *True Story*. Lower-class women now watch television soap operas and dramatic series that deal with domestic problems quite differently than confession stories do; instead of suffering and enduring, the protagonist on television is much more likely to put her own interests above those of her family—and she probably won't feel remorse for her actions later, either. Readers who are familiar with mainstream magazines are likely to be put off even by the appearance of *True Story*. More than 60 percent of its pages are black and white on pulp paper, with slick four-color pages reserved for advertising or the posed photographs that still head each story. For those unfamiliar with the confession genre, the titles and captions seem bizarre rather than intriguing, and every story is continued to later pages not once but many times, sometimes with less than a column of text on each page.

Economic changes discourage potential readers as well. Like general-interest women's magazines, *True Story* is geared toward the stay-at-home mother and homemaker, but lower-class women, whether by choice or necessity, have increasingly joined the work force. Traditionally, they have often bought their confession magazines on the newsstand, but *True Story*'s cover price of $1.69 compares poorly with the price of supermarket tabloids like *National Enquirer** ($.85) and *Star* ($.75), which are also aimed at lower-class women and better equipped in format to entertain readers with limited leisure time.[25]

None of these factors would discourage the avid reader of confessions who is familiar with their format. The downward trend in readership has not unduly disturbed advertisers of certain kinds of products that have enjoyed great success in confession magazines, like cigarettes or package goods marketers.[26] But it is difficult for those unfamiliar with the confession genre to view these magazines as entertainment, instruction, or a market vehicle. Having made no substantive changes in format or content since the 1940s, *True Story* is clearly in retrenchment in the 1980s, an anachronism intent on holding its traditional market and ill-equipped to communicate its appeal to either new readers or advertisers.

Notes

1. Ben Yagoda, "The True Story of Bernarr Macfadden," *American Heritage*, December 1981, p. 26.

2. Fulton Oursler, *The True Story of Bernarr Macfadden* (New York: Lewis Copeland, 1929), pp. 213–14.

3. Ibid., pp. 222–23.

4. *Prize True Story Dramas of the Air* (New York: Macfadden Book Co., 1931), pp. i–ii.

5. Emile Gauvreau, *My Last Million Readers* (New York: E. P. Dutton, 1941), p. 102–3.

6. *History and Magazines* (New York: True Story Magazine, 1941), p. [42].

7. Margaret MacMullen, "Pulps and Confession," *Harper's*, June 1937, p. 101.

8. Theodore Peterson, *Magazines in the Twentieth Century*, 2nd ed. (Urbana: University of Illinois Press, 1964), p. 296.

9. MacMullen, p. 99.

10. Irmengarde Eberle, "The New Confessional," *New Republic*, 4 June 1930, pp. 68–69.

11. Muriel G. Cantor and Elizabeth Jones, "Creating Fiction for Women," *Communication Research*, January 1983, p. 124. Since stories in *True Story* are published anonymously, *True Story* editors furnished the names of the writers surveyed.

12. Ibid., p. 128.

13. Harland Manchester, "True Stories," *Scribner's*, August 1938, p. 26.

14. Peterson, p. 299.

15. *How to Get People Excited* (New York: *True Story Magazine*, 1937), pp. 6–8.

16. "Minus Macfadden," *Newsweek*, 2 September 1946, p. 55.

17. Peterson, p. 296.

18. *The Fifth Dimension* (New York: Macfadden Publications, 1948) and many other market research reports from the publisher.

19. Peterson, p. 302.

20. Lee Rainwater, Richard P. Coleman, and Gerald Handel, *Workingman's Wife: Her Personality, World and Life Style* (New York: Oceana, 1959), p. 128.

21. Cantor and Jones, p. 120.

22. Bob Donath, "Macfadden Sale to Callahan Aids Bartell's Financial Revamp," *Advertising Age*, 21 April 1975, p. 22.

23. "Hayes B. Jacob's New York Market Letter" in *Writer's Digest* aired several complaints from writers who had not been paid for stories published in Macfadden confession magazines throughout 1975.

24. "Hayes B. Jacob's New York Market Letter," *Writer's Digest*, September 1975, p. 26.

25. Bernice Kanner, "Fan, Romance Books Face Sagging Numbers," *Advertising Age*, 9 April 1979, p. 64.

26. Ibid.

Information Sources

BIBLIOGRAPHY

Cantor, Muriel G., and Elizabeth Jones. "Creating Fiction for Women." *Communication Research,* January 1983, pp. 111–37.

Donath, Bob. "Macfadden Sale to Callahan Aids Bartell's Financial Revamp." *Advertising Age*, 21 April 1975, p. 22.

Eberle, Irmengarde. "The New Confessional." *New Republic*, 4 June 1930, pp. 68–70.

The Fifth Dimension. New York: Macfadden Publications, 1948.

History and Magazines. New York: *True Story Magazine*, 1941.

How to Get People Excited. New York: *True Story*, 1937.

Kanner, Bernice. "Fan, Romance Books Face Sagging Numbers." *Advertising Age*, 9 April 1979, pp. 22, 64.

MacMullen, Margaret. "Pulps and Confessions." *Harper's*, June 1937, pp. 94–102.

Manchester, Harland. "True Stories." *Scribner's*, August 1938, pp. 26–29, 60.

"Minus Macfadden." *Newsweek*, 2 September 1946, pp. 55–56.

Oursler, Fulton. *The True Story of Bernarr Macfadden.* New York: Lewis Copeland, 1929.

Peterson, Theodore. *Magazines in the Twentieth Century.* 2nd ed. Urbana: University of Illinois Press, 1964.

Rainwater, Lee, Richard P. Coleman, and Gerald Handel. *Workingman's Wife: Her Personality, World and Life Style.* New York: Oceana, 1959.

Yagoda, Ben. "The True Story of Bernarr Macfadden." *American Heritage*, December 1981, pp. 26–29.

INDEX SOURCES

None.

LOCATION SOURCES

Macfadden Holdings, Inc. Partial holdings: Bowling Green State University; Library of Congress; Michigan State University; University of Illinois at Urbana-Champaign; many public libraries.

Publication History

MAGAZINE TITLE AND TITLE CHANGES

True Story.

VOLUME AND ISSUE DATA

Vols. 1–138, May 1919–present, monthly.

PUBLISHER AND PLACE OF PUBLICATION

Macfadden Publications, Inc.: Bernarr Macfadden, 1919–1941; Orr J. Elder, 1941–1951; Irving S. Manheimer, 1951–1962. Macfadden-Bartell Corporation: Gerald A. Bartell, 1962–1975. Macfadden Holdings, Inc.: Peter J. Callahan, 1975–present. New York, New York.

EDITORS

John Brennan, 1919–1926(?); William Jordan Rapp, 1926–1942; Henry Lieferant, 1942–1947; Ernest V. Heyn, 1947–1950; Helen Irwin Littauer, 1950–1951; Nina Sittler Dorrance, 1951–1965; Suzanne Hilliard, 1965–1976; Helen Vincent, 1976–1987; Sue Weiner, 1987–present.

CIRCULATION

1,575,666 paid, 3,412 nonpaid.

Dena Hutto

TV GUIDE

On what calender does the week begin on Saturday and the year begin in September? The one in the offices of *TV Guide* and apparently the one in some 19 million American homes where *TV Guide* is a staple purchase weekly at the supermarket or through subscription. *TV Guide* is now the number one best-seller of all periodicals published in the United States, rivaling long-time leader *Reader's Digest*,* which surpasses *TV Guide* only when international sales in other languages are counted.

TV Guide is the brainchild of Walter H. Annenberg, who against the advice and wisdom of others in the publishing field, envisioned a periodical "dedicated to serving constructively the television viewers of America."[1] The unique feature of this periodical is that it is national and local, something no other magazine has attempted before or since on this scope.

In November 1952 Walter Annenberg noticed a full-page ad for *TV Digest* in the *Philadelphia Bulletin*, called Merrill Panitt, his administrative assistant, "to vent his annoyance at seeing the *Bulletin* get the advertisement and wanting to learn more about the advertiser.''[2] It was not unusual for Annenberg to call associates at late hours about business matters, but he did usually restrain the calls after midnight. Panitt just happened to know a little about this publication. The *Bulletin* probably received the ad rather than the *Philadelphia Inquirer* (Annenberg's newspaper) because it had a larger circulation; as for *TV Digest*, it had an approximate circulation of 180,000 weekly. Other such television magazines existed in New York and Chicago and possibly several other cities. Most of them were similar in format with local listings, and "articles were generally gushy, fan-type fare about local television personalities."[3] If one such issue impacted on higher than usual circulation, the others probably would follow the next week with a similar cover story.

Annenberg's idea, expressed in this same telephone conversation, was to print national feature material and ship this full-color section to local distributors who would insert local television listings inside the national wraparound material. Annenberg envisioned local staffs, and local and national ads. The concept was quite similar to one his father had had thirty years before for *Daily Racing Form* as a national periodical.[4]

Annenberg then decided to survey television digest-type purchases in the three cities with such publications. He actually conducted the survey personally. When he saw individuals buy this type of magazine, he introduced himself and then questioned the buyer about why he wanted such a publication. He discovered that "consumers liked the magazines' accurate listings, their convenience, and they enjoyed reading articles about the burgeoning world of television."[5] Annenberg immediately realized the possibilities of such a magazine in increasing his fortune. He further realized that television personalities would promote the magazine in return for plugs printed about their programs. Thus, the idea for a national magazine took hold and eventually became Annenberg's most lucrative success. But the idea for using print to enhance television belonged to a New Yorker named Herbert Muschel, a "scholarly-looking" fellow who often devised innovative ways for sales or services. In 1947 he designed *TeleVision Guide*, but he was unsure of how to get it on the market since most publishers found the idea "foolish." "No one, they said, would pay for such a service." However, once he met Lee Wagner, a young lawyer with ideas of his own, the first issue came out on 14 June 1948. Within a few months the two disagreed and Muschel left the magazine. For several years Wagner struggled alone with the financial problems that plagued the enterprise; he believed that the idea of such a magazine was workable, with the help of silent partners and $3 annual subscription fees. Apparently publicity agents, too, recognized the value of such a magazine and encouraged clients to grant interviews. "As a result, a picture of an entertainer on the cover of *TV Guide* as the magazine's name was later abbreviated, became so coveted that stars themselves called Wagner seeking the honor."[6]

The timing was just right when Annenberg contacted Wagner about selling the New York *TV Guide*. Wagner's legal problems with the state's attorney regarding alleged kickbacks, combined with Muschel's suit against him for never having been paid for his idea, worked in Annenberg's favor. Wagner sold to Triangle publications for about $1.5 million plus a large consulting fee. In Philadelphia Irving and Art Karowski, who operated North American Publishing Company, owned the local television digest that Annenberg wanted to purchase. At first they refused, but when they learned that Wagner had sold, they, too, sold for approximately $1 million. Chicago's *TV Forecast* was owned by four ex-GI's—Les Viahon, Norbert Dempke, John E. Groenings, and Roy V. Whiting. On learning that New York and Philadelphia had sold to the powerful Annenberg publication empire, they raised their asking price from $500,000 to $1 million in flight from Chicago to Philadelphia and got it with no arguments from Joe First, Annenberg's negotiator.[7]

Among those that Annenberg chose to lead in the organization of the new magazine was Merrill Panitt as national managing editor. Panitt later assumed the editorship from Annenberg and continues even today as a contributing editor whose pieces still appear in the feature sections. Another was Roger Clipp, whom Annenberg had asked to locate an executive to run the magazine. All the candidates he lined up were rejected, leading Annenberg to appoint Clipp (suspected by others at Triangle as Clipp's original intention all along). Clipp's value to the organization was his knowing "everyone in broadcasting." He knew just who to call whatever the situation.[8] Michael O'Neill was the new advertising director, Jim Quirk was to promote the magazine, and Alex Joseph became Panitt's assistant.

In addition to publishing the *Philadelphia Inquirer* Triangle also publishes *Seventeen*. In the early fifties the editor of *Seventeen*, Alice Thompson, refused to allow office space for *TV Guide*. Annenberg assumed that Thompson had misunderstood the need for space and personally explained the situation to her. Her response was that she had understood all along: "I don't agree with tenement journalism." Thompson's "haughty" response resulted in her immediate firing.[9] Just when Annenberg was so busy with launching the new television guide enterprise, he really didn't need the added problem of locating a new editor for *Seventeen*. But this problem resolved itself rather well, resulting in his placing his sister Enid Haupt in charge of *Seventeen*, a successful arrangement for many years to come.[10] With intense work in several major cities, Triangle published its first edition of *TV Guide* on 3 April 1953, sold 1,560,000 copies, but had very little advertising. The following week circulation slipped to 1,492,000, and for weeks to come circulation continued to decline. Advertisers were reluctant to utilize such a small magazine, small in size and in circulation. Then in September, circulation picked up, and Triangle learned that sales would always be smaller in summer because of vacations and rerun programming.[11] And this accounts for one reason that at *TV Guide* headquarters, the calendar begins with September.

Walter Annenberg's ambitions for the new magazine were enormous. He firmly believed that this was not to be a fan magazine. "His unrealistic concept of the publication was that it should become the '*Time* magazine of the television industry.' '' However, the small size and somewhat ''frivolous'' nature of the medium of television prevented that. Also, ''there were no hard-hitting articles about the TV industry, and much of the content was the fan-type pieces the publisher had contended that he hadn't wanted.'' Panitt kept raising the circulation mandate whenever reporters wanted to do articles of ''substance.''[12]

But through the years, *TV Guide* did tackle some of the tough issues regarding the new medium. A sample of such article titles includes ''*TV Guide* to Set Down Exactly What Is and Is Not Known about How Television Affects Children'' (11 October 1969), ''Television's Political Coverage . . . What Does America Think Now?'' (30 September 1972), ''Results of Nationwide Poll on TV's Morality'' (13 October 1973), and ''How America Feels about Family Viewing Time'' (5 June 1976). But one cannot help noticing that a full fifteen years passed before the magazine began running substantial and potentially critical articles about television:

> Perhaps the most controversial article published by *TV Guide* came in 1981, when the magazine printed a multi-part investigation on cocaine abuse in Hollywood that relied heavily on unnamed sources. . . . within a few months, *Time* magazine did a major piece on cocaine use, and now, . . . it's generally acknowledged that drug abuse has indeed been a problem in the TV industry.
>
> Another controversial article, titled ''Anatomy of a Smear,'' was published May 29, 1982. The cover story accused CBS News of wrongdoing in preparing a documentary on Vietnam, charges that later spurred a CBS internal investigation.
>
> Gen. William C. Westmoreland, accused in the documentary of underestimating troop strength in Vietnam, later sued CBS.[13]

In addition, after two years of surveying the nightly news network programs, *TV Guide* concluded in a 9 November 1985 story that coverage was now pro-life.

The topics covered during its now thirty-five-year history along with contributors, both regulars and free-lance, are a fascinating compendium of not only the history of the magazine but of the entire television industry. In the early days there was a negative, even hostile attitude toward television itself that spilled over to the television magazine.

> In the academic community, during the Fifties and early Sixties, television was often ridiculed as trivial and unworthy of any serious attention. In those days, a public proclamation that one did not and would not own a television set was understood to be a statement of intellectual self-purification. But when it became apparent that Presidents and Nobel winners, along with millions of fellow Americans, considered television to be a most important adjunct to their lives, much of the intellectual snobbery

tended to evaporate. By then, however, considerable damage had been done. Because most libraries, museums and academic institutions casually dismissed the upstart medium as unfit subject matter for their hallowed archives, much of television's early programming—the distinguished along with the puerile—was lost or destroyed.[14]

Similarly, these same institutions failed to collect and preserve *TV Guide*. Only two complete sets exist: one at the Library of Congress and another at *TV Guide* headquarters in Radnor, Pennsylvania. In 1977 the magazine itself microfilmed sets of the periodical for distribution to libraries.[15]

Notable contributors include John Updike, Philip Roth, James Michener, Arthur Miller, Joyce Carol Oates, and Presidents Gerald Ford, Jimmy Carter, and Ronald Reagan. In fact, Reagan's first article appeared in December 1954, "It's a Gold Rush." In April 1957, he wrote "Don't Envy the Actor," an article citing the tax problems actors encounter; naturally, there was a reply the following month about tax problems much less-monied citizens encounter. And in March 1978 another Reagan article appeared: "Do the Networks Always Short Change the 'Loyal Opposition'? "

Other writers who contributed to *TV Guide* over the years include Cleveland Amory, who wrote reviews on a regular basis from 1962 to 1976; Melvin Durslag from 1960 to the present (1988); Richard Doan from 1963 to 1976; Sally Bedell in the late seventies; Edith Efron from 1961 to 1978; Helen Feingold (food features), 1962–1977; Joseph Finnigan, 1965–1983; Neil Hickey, 1964 to the present; Dan Jenkins, 1953–1963; Eric Levin, 1973–1982; Leslie Raddatz, 1962–1978; Bob Stahl, 1953–1964; and Dwight Whitney, 1958–1984.

As noted before, perhaps more important than any article that ever appeared in *TV Guide* is the cover photograph.

> Press information specialists at television networks agree that a *TV Guide* cover is the single most important ratings builder. Performers have vied to appear on the magazine's cover since its earliest days; even Eleanor Roosevelt asked for, and was granted, that privilege.[16]

The covers of all issues during the decade of the 1970s were studied, with these conclusions: "*TV Guide* assigned a disproportionate share of coverage to regular commercial network series, ignoring the development of cable and underplaying the growth of public television. In addition, it failed to keep pace with the expansion of news and sports programming and the mini-series format."[17] These conclusions are not particularly astonishing given the consistent pattern of conservative journalism reflected in the magazine from the very beginning.

Today *TV Guide* devotes 53 percent of total listings to cable, although it wasn't until 1978 that any cable listings at all appeared, beginning with listings for HBO. A part of the impetus for increased cable attention came from Time's *TV-Cable Week*, first issued in April 1983:

Of course, *TV Guide* did not take this lying down. In 1982 it spent 40 million to expand its cable listings. . . . All of this was accomplished before the first issue of *TV-Cable Week* was in the mail. . . . With their new cable listings section in place, they were able to do a successful end run around Time's marketing strategies.

In September 1983, just five months after its debut, it was announced that *TV-Cable Week* had published its final issue.[18]

Although single-copy sales have declined, in part because of television supplements in many local newspapers and because of separate cable guides offered to cable subscribers, other best-seller periodicals have experienced similar declines, a fact attributable to the variety and increasing numbers of magazines available. The slip in single-copy sales from 1980 to 1984 for *TV Guide* is a staggering 148 million fewer copies.[19] But the magazine itself is alive and well, with greatly increased advertising money accounting for much of the success. In 1987 the magazine pulled in $331.2 million in advertising revenue, a $13 million increase over 1986.[20] Single copies now cost $.55, compared with the 1953 selling price of $.15.

One individual who objected to the way *TV Guide* advertised itself in the *New York Times* was William F. Buckley. His own description of the ad is in the inimitable Buckley style:

> . . . on the back cover of (the *New York Times*) I found a picture of myself about a half-acre in size. Way up on top the headline: "Where millions get to know/two great conversationalists." Then six leagues down, under the picture, in type so tiny only U–2 cameras can read it, the line, "Editor and novelist William F. Buckley last wrote for *TV Guide* on 'What I Didn't Tell Johnny Carson.' " Under that, in the space left over, the commercial: "An article by William F. Buckley or an ad for AT&T. Both create a dialogue with over forty million adults in *TV Guide*. Because our readers have a unique relationship with the magazine." Etc. etc. . . .
>
> The *TV Guide* caper—using a picture of an author who has written for the magazine in such a way . . . —is a maneuver against which I have formally protested, and I am willing to put it down as a fast one by nice people who, however, deserve this public rebuke.[21]

Today *TV Guide* publishes 107 editions each week, with plants in Lancaster and Scranton, Pennsylvania; Simpsonville, South Carolina; Cincinnati; Minneapolis; Dallas; Denver; and San Francisco and Merced, California.[22] And with sales approaching 19 million no one in the industry ignores *TV Guide* any more. "Each summer for more than 10 years, a limousine pulls away from NBC headquarters in New York with six programming executives aboard for the network's annual visit with *TV Guide* editors."[23] In these meetings executives from the two media discuss what kinds of programs will be on the fall schedule;

and apparently there are frequent telephone calls during the year just to keep one another apprised of changes and significant events. Everyone realizes the significance of *TV Guide* coverage of a program.

In a relatively brief period of time, then, *TV Guide* has become the leading seller among periodicals. In a highly competitive market, it maintains its position through cautious, prudent changes that reflect those changes occurring in the television industry. It really is a record of one of the most significant historical events of the twentieth century. Entire generations now relate to television people and places in a way that affects large numbers of individuals more than any other phenomenon ever has. Television characters were longer-lived in the early days, and several individuals became "family" members after years of weekly visits in American homes where there was only one television set and viewing was a family affair. For baby boomers who've come of age in the eighties, perusing the first issues of *TV Guide*, especially the all-important cover features, is a nostalgic trip: Arthur Godfrey, Sid Caesar, Dinah Shore, Giselle MacKenzie, Perry Como, Ed Sullivan, Steve Allen, the cast of "Gunsmoke," Lucy, Milton Berle, Bud Collier, Hal March, George Gobel, Loretta Young, Nanette Fabray, Patti Page, Lassie, Jackie Cooper and Cleo, Gail Storm, Jackie Gleason, Alfred Hitchcock, Jane Wyman, the Nelson family, Jack Bailey, George Burns and Gracie Allen, Walt Disney—to name just a few. Many of these names are familiar to much younger viewers because of syndicated repeats of shows from the past. But *TV Guide* has been there almost from the beginning of national broadcasting to chronicle the mass media story. And all because Walter Annenberg foresaw possibilities that no one else could envision.

In January 1989 *TV Guide* was purchased by News America Publications, Inc., a Rupert Murdoch enterprise. National offices remain in Radnor, Pennsylvania, and both the national editor David Sendler and local sections editor Roger Youman are still with the weekly magazine. But personnel as well as content changes have taken place. The magazine is no longer the wrap-around format. Articles are in the front; local listings follow. After local listings come pay-tv movie briefs, the familiar crossword puzzle, and a horoscope for the week. Some observers feel that the articles are more like those in a tabloid than in the Annenberg *TV Guide*. One critic suggests that "Murdoch has revamped the magazine with generous helpings of sensationalism and star-studded puffery, commissioning wrenching changes in format and philosophy."[24] A number of staffers and lower-level editors have resigned; many feel that *TV Guide* is too much of an advertising vehicle now. The summer of 1989 saw a sixteen-page insert of discount coupons, for example; "Murdoch just happens to own a coupon printing business as part of his empire."[25]

With increased competition from local papers, whether *TV Guide* sales continue to outpace other national magazines is questionable. Longtime *TV Guide* subscribers may not welcome the changes. On the other hand, tabloid-type publications are popular, too. Only time will tell.

Notes

1. Walter H. Annenberg, ''As We See It,'' *TV Guide,* 5 April 1958, p. 2.
2. John Cooney, *The Annenbergs* (New York: Simon and Schuster, 1982), p. 234.
3. Ibid., p. 235.
4. Ibid.
5. Ibid., p. 236.
6. Ibid., p. 237.
7. Ibid., pp. 238–39.
8. Ibid., p. 240.
9. Ibid., p. 241.
10. Ibid., p. 242.
11. Ibid., p. 243.
12. Ibid., p. 244.
13. Neill Borowski, ''A Look at the Most Heavily Read Publication on TV,'' *Electronic Media*, 9 December 1985, p. 28.
14. *TV Guide 25 Year Index*, B. P. Bradfield, ''Introduction'' (Radnor, Penn.: Triangle Publications, Inc., 1977).
15. Ibid.
16. Jean E. Dye and Mark D. Harmon, ''*TV Guide*: Images of the Status Quo, 1970–1977'' *Journalism Quarterly*, Summer-Autumn 1987, p. 627.
17. Ibid., p. 628.
18. Edward Jay Whetmore, *Mediamerica: Form Content, and Consequence of Mass Communication*, updated 3rd ed. (Belmont, Calif.: Wadsworth Publishing Co., 1987), p. 75.
19. Dan Hodges, ''The Single-Copy Slide,'' *Marketing and Media Decisions*, December 1985, p. 90.
20. Eileen Norris, ''King of the Mountain Keeps Up with Devotees,'' *Advertising Age*, 11 April 1988, p. S27.
21. William F. Buckley, ''Warning: Manipulation Ahead,'' *National Review*, 27 February 1987, p. 63.
22. Borowski, p. 28.
23. Ibid., p. 1.
24. Ray Richmond, ''Rupert Murdoch Turning *TV Guide* into a Tabloid,'' *News and Courier*, 11 August 1989, p. 14.
25. Ibid., p. 15.

Information Sources

BIBLIOGRAPHY

Annenberg, Walter H. ''As We See It.'' *TV Guide,* 2 June 1956, p. 2
———. ''As We See It.'' *TV Guide*, 5 April 1958, p. 2.
Bittner, John R. *Broadcasting and Telecommunications: An Introduction*. Englewood Cliffs, N.J.: Prentice-Hall, 1985.
Borowski, Neill. ''A Look at the Most Heavily Read Publication on TV.'' *Electronic Media*, 9 December 1985, pp. 1, 28.

Buckley, William F. "Warning: Manipulation Ahead." *National Review*, 27 February 1987, p. 63.

Compaine, Benjamin. *Who Owns the Media?* White Plains, N.Y.: Knowledge Industry Publications, 1979.

Cooney, John. *The Annenbergs*. New York: Simon and Schuster, 1982.

Dye, Jean E., and Mark D. Harmon. "*TV Guide*: Images of The Status Quo, 1970–1979." *Journalism Quarterly*, Summer-Autumn 1987, pp. 626–29.

Hodges, Dan. "The Single Copy Slide." *Marketing and Media Decisions*, December 1985, pp. 80–81.

Howard, Herbert H., and Michael S. Kievman. *Radio and TV Programming*. New York: John Wiley and Sons, 1983.

Johnson, Catherine E., ed. *TV Guide 25 Year Index*. Radnor, Penn.: Triangle Publications, Inc., 1977.

Norris, Eileen. "King of the Mountain Keeps Up with Devotees." *Advertising Age*, 11 April 1988, pp. 26–27.

Richmond, Ray. "Rupert Murdoch Turning *TV Guide* into a Tabloid." *News and Courier*, 14 August 1989, pp. 14–15.

Whetmore, Edward Jay. *Mediamerica: Form, Content, and Consequence of Mass Communication*. Updated 3rd ed. Belmont, Calif.: Wadsworth Publishing Co., 1987.

The World Almanac and Book of Facts 1988. New York: Pharos Books, 1987.

INDEX SOURCES
    TV Guide 25 Year Index (1953–1977); *TV Guide Index* (1978–1980, 1978–1982, 1983, 1984, 1985, 1986). Triangle Publications, Inc., Radnor, Pennsylvania.
LOCATION SOURCES
    Library of Congress; Triangle Publications, Inc., Radnor, Pennsylvania. Many libraries have microfilm.

Publication History

MAGAZINE TITLE AND TITLE CHANGES
    TV Guide.
VOLUME AND ISSUE DATA
    3 April 1953–current, weekly.
PUBLISHERS AND PLACE OF PUBLICATION
    Triangle Publications, Radnor, Pennsylvania, 1953–present: James T. Quirk, 1953–1969; Triangle Publications, 1969–1983; Eric G. Larson, 1983–1988; News America Publications, Inc., 1981–present.
EDITORS
    Walter H. Annenberg, 1953–January 1959; Merrill Panitt, January 1959–1974; Alexander H. Joseph, executive editor, and Merrill Panitt, editorial director, 1974–1976; Roger J. Youman, executive editor, 1976–1979; David Sendler, 1980–1981; David Sendler, national editor, and Roger J. Youman, local editor, 1982–present.
CIRCULATION
    19 million

Barbara Nourie

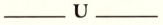

U

UNITED STATES MAGAZINE. See DEMOCRATIC REVIEW

UNITED STATES REVIEW. See DEMOCRATIC REVIEW

US

Us, a mass-circulation celebrity periodical, was founded in 1977 by the *New York Times* Company. The magazine was lightweight stuff for the *New York Times*, but Arthur Ochs Sulzberger convinced the *Times* board that *Us* would be a quick money-maker. Designed to compete with Time's very successful *People*,* it was first edited by William H. Davis. The first issue had a printing of 750,000 copies. Unfortunately, the *Times* ran the operation on a shoestring budget with little expenditure for advertising. Also, its fortnightly publication could not keep pace with the weekly gossip. For its first several years the periodical sputtered along at a loss with editors that "came and went almost as often as Billy Martin."[1] Finally, in January of 1980 *Us* made its first profit and was sold soon thereafter to Peter J. Callahan, president of Macfadden Holdings, publishers of *True Confessions* and *Photoplay*.[2]

Under the guidance of Richard Kaplan as editor and Garey T. Symington as publisher, *Us* circulation climbed to 1.1 million in 1983. Kaplan proclaimed that *Us* intended to supplant *People* as "the most popular magazine of America's Pop culture." Symington stated, "We are going to make a lot of money and we're going to treat advertisers right." Advertisers' ads always faced editorial matter, and there were no "bleed" premiums for four-color ads that ran into the fold. Despite these developments, *Us* was still regarded as a "bargain-basement version of *People* journalism."[3]

In 1985, Jann S. Wenner of *Rolling Stone** bought *Us* and became executive editor. Wenner said, "Call it what you want—gossip journalism, celebrity journalism, human-interest journalism. By any name, this has become the dominant theme of American journalism over the last five years."[4] Wenner noted his intention to continue the twice-monthly publication of *Us* despite pressures to go weekly. He introduced an all-color format and declared that *Us* intended to stick more closely to entertainment personalities than *People* does. Despite Wenner's changes, when the new *Us* hit the newsstand in June of 1985 one critic noted that "the new version even after a wholesale clean-out of the former staff, looks a lot like the old, with a prose style of lukewarm clichés and a slew of gushy celebrity profiles."[5]

By 1987 *Us*, after a vigorous campaign by Wenner, had attracted more advertisers. Nonetheless, the periodical remained a loser, with a loss of $12 million in 1986 and $7 million in 1987. Things, however, were improving, and Wenner was predicting a profit by the end of 1988.[6]

Us appeals primarily to women, 60 percent of its audience, at a median age of thirty-two and median income of $29,000.[7] A study conducted by Simmons Market Research in 1987 revealed that the typical *Us* reader was interested in fashion and was "celebrity motivated."[8] A periodical designed to entertain and amuse, *Us* still has an uphill battle ahead to compete with the mass of publications emphasizing photographs and stories about celebrities.

Notes

1. "The Times Decides We Are Not Us," *Newsweek,* 17 March 1980, p. 86; Philip H. Dougherty, "Getting Together at *Us,*" *New York Times,* 21 March 1977.

2. "The Times Decides We Are Not Us," p. 86.

3. Philip H. Dougherty, "*Us* Delays Plans to Go Weekly," *New York Times,* 10 January 1983; Edwin Diamond, "The New Gossips," *New York,* 13 May 1985, p. 22.

4. Wenner quoted in Diamond, p. 22.

5. Margot Hornblower, "It's New! It's Old! It's *Us*!" *Washington Post,* 17 June 1985; "*Us* Colors in Void in Magazine Market," *Advertising Age,* 10 June 1985, p. 10.

6. David Lieberman, "Now Star-Studded *Us* Has More Ad Pages, Too," *Business Week,* 8 June 1987, pp. 83–84.

7. Jonathan Alter, "Just Like a Rolling Stone," *Newsweek,* 17 June 1985, p. 63; David Henry, "Tough Slogging," *Forbes,* 8 September 1986, p. 76.

8. Philip H. Dougherty, "*Us* Defines Its Readers," *New York Times,* 6 October 1987.

Information Sources

BIBLIOGRAPHY
Alter, Jonathan. "Just Like a Rolling Stone." *Newsweek,* 17 June 1985, p. 63.
Diamond, Edwin. "The New Gossips." *New York,* 13 May 1985.
Dougherty, Philip H. "Getting Together at *Us.*" *New York Times,* 21 March 1977.
———. "*Us* Defines Its Readers." *New York Times,* 6 October 1987, IV, p. 26.

————. "*Us* Delays Plans to Go Weekly." *New York Times*, 10 January 1983, IV, p. 7.

Henry, David. "Tough Slogging." *Forbes*, 8 September 1986, p. 76.

Hornblower, Margot. "It's New! It's Old! It's *Us!*" *Washington Post*, 17 June 1985.

"It's *Us* vs. Them in Checkout-Counter War." *Advertising Age*, 13 May 1985, p. 14.

Lieberman, David. "Now Star-Studded *Us* Has More Ad Pages, Too." *Business Week*, 8 June 1987, pp. 83–84.

Katz, William, and Linda S. Katz. *Magazines for Libraries*. 5th ed. New York: R. R. Bowker, 1986.

"The Times Decides We Are Not Us." *Newsweek*, 17 March 1980, p. 86.

"*Us* Colors in Void in Magazine Market." *Advertising Age*, 10 June 1985, p. 10.

INDEX SOURCES
> *Readers' Guide to Periodical Literature, Access* (1986–present).

LOCATION SOURCES
> Library of Congress, Public Library of Cincinnati and Hamilton County, many other libraries. Available in microform.

Publication History

MAGAZINE TITLE AND TITLE CHANGES
> *Us,* 1977–present.

VOLUME AND ISSUE DATA
> Vols. 1–8, 1977–1985, vols. 1–3, 1985–present, biweekly. Jann Wenner, upon his takeover in 1985, started renumbering volumes from vol.1.

PUBLISHER AND PLACE OF PUBLICATION
> New York Times Company, New York, New York, 1977–1980; Macfadden Holdings, New York, New York, 1980–1985; Straight Arrow Publishers, New York, New York, 1985–present.

EDITORS
> William H. Davis, 1977; Ron Martin, 1977–1978; Sam Angeloff, 1978–1979; Jay Fitzgerald, 1979–1980; Richard Kaplan, 1980–1985; Jann S. Wenner, 1985–present.

CIRCULATION
> 1,000,000.

Ronnie W. Faulkner

USA WEEKEND

In September 1953 publisher William H. Marriott launched a new Sunday newspaper supplement, *Family Weekly,* aimed at the small-town news market and based on the recently demised supplement *Nowadays*.[1] Today that same supplement exists, entitled *USA Weekend*, purchased in 1985 by the Gannett Company, which issues *USA Today* newspapers across the country. *USA Weekend* and the other leading supplement, *Parade,** represent the only still existing such publications since the midcentury. Sunday supplements actually became a part of newspapers in the early 1900s, but by 1980 only *Parade* and *Family Weekly* remained in the market.

Interestingly, when Marriott first conceived the idea, he approached Arthur Motley, *Parade* publisher, about printing *Family Weekly*, and after initial agreement, Motley pulled out, leaving Marriott to sign a new contract with Cuneo Press. The first editor of *Family Weekly* was John B. Starr, formerly editor of the Metro Group of Sunday supplements (individual supplements for local newspapers). Marriott's advice to Starr was to aim for "a well-edited [product] with appeal for every member of the family. Higher education has raised the taste level in the small towns. These people don't give a damn what face powder Mrs. Rockefeller uses. They think for themselves now."[2]

The *Family Weekly* staff was urged to "think Midwestern" in approaching each story.[3] (Ironically, *Family Weekly* originated in New York, but *Parade* originated in Chicago.) After Starr left as editor, Ben Kartmann became editorial director. Then in 1959 Ernest Heyn became editor. His was the policy to establish writer-celebrity bylines, a practice continued by Bob Fitzgibbon in his years as editor. Heyn left to become editor of *Popular Science*,[4] and Fitzgibbon left to edit an airline magazine.[5] Following Fitzgibbon, Mort Persky edited *Family Weekly* during the early seventies. After Persky, Scott DeGarmo edited for two years, followed by Arthur Cooper, who edited for three years, and then Thomas Plate, who edited for two years until the time when Gannett purchased the magazine from CBS Magazines.

In 1985 the Gannett Company bought *Family Weekly* for approximately $40 million. There were dire predictions that *Family Weekly* would become a magazine version of the Gannett newspaper *USA Today*. And this time, the "rumor mill churned out the truth!"[6] CBS had asked originally for $60 million. It had been unable to turn around profits with its purchase in 1980. Ad pages fell 11.2 percent and ad revenues fell 10.4 percent. At the time of the Gannett purchase, twenty of its own papers were carrying rival supplement *Parade*.[7]

But within weeks a number of former *Family Weekly* executives left: editor Thomas Plate, publisher Pat Linsky, and general manager Jon Thompson. One hundred and thirty newspapers dropped the new *USA Weekend* for *Parade*, and Gannett began signing major metropolitan papers rather than continuing to court smaller markets.[8] However, *USA Weekend* boasted growing circulation in just a year: September 1986 circulation was listed as 14.2 million compared to 12.7 just a year before.

Today *USA Weekend* features a color cover, with perhaps one major photo and several inset photos, a Who's News question-answer page on the inside cover, Happy Birthday To a celebrity, a food feature, This Weekend's Passions (a hobby or other interest), This Month's Sports, This Weekend's Music spotlighting a composer or singer, This Week's Travel with tips on making travel more convenient or on places to go, What's Next with a day-by-day note of interest for the coming week, and a brief mention of what will be in the next

Sunday edition. And, of course, there are lots of ads, often of the mail-order variety. There are usually sixteen pages, including front and back cover pages.

For a time the *Chicago Tribune* issued *USA Weekend* in its Friday paper, but in January 1987 it notified Gannett of its intention to drop the magazine altogether in September of the same year. For decades these supplements have been a part of the Sunday paper, but many large metropolitan markets are now issuing their own Sunday magazines focusing on local people, places, and events. Whether the national Sunday magazines will survive yet another competitor, just as they survived the competition from television in the 1950s, is still unknown. Decreased advertising from the cigarette industry has been another blow in recent years. But Sunday magazines, originally supplements to Sunday newspapers, are still very much a part of the leisurely reading of the paper on Sunday, not yet just another workday for most Americans. As Sunday becomes more and more just another day of the week, however, the Sunday magazine may have met its most powerful competitor of all.

Notes

1. "Small Town Supplement," *Newsweek,* 22 June 1953, p. 56.
2. Ibid.
3. Norman Hill, "The Last of the Red Hot Supplements," *Saturday Review*, 12 December 1970, p. 56.
4. Ibid., p. 62.
5. Ibid., p. 57.
6. "Coke Was It among Product News Events" (Forecast and Review), *Advertising Age*, 30 December 1985, p. 3.
7. William F. Gloede, "CBS Sells Off 'Family Weekly,' " *Advertising Age*, 25 February 1985, p. 1.
8. "Coke was it," p. 3.

Information Sources

BIBLIOGRAPHY
"Coke Was It among Product News Events" (Forecast and Review). *Advertising Age,* 30 December 1985, p. 3.
Gloede, William F. "CBS Sells off 'Family Weekly.' " *Advertising Age*, 25 February 1985, p. 1.
———. "Metro Rips into 'USA Weekend,' 'Parade.' " *Advertising Age*, 19 May 1986, p. 5.
———. "Sunday Magazines Undergo Revival." *Advertising Age*, 28 July 1986, p. S8.
———. "Two Papers Plan to Drop 'Weekend.' " *Advertising Age*, 26 January 1987, p. 2.
Hill, Norman. "The Last of the Red Hot Supplements." *Saturday Review*, 12 December 1970, pp. 56–57.
"Small Town Supplement." *Newsweek*, 22 June 1953, p. 56.
"Transition." *Newsweek*, 4 March 1985, p. 64.

LOCATION SOURCES
> Often found on microfilm with the newspaper which included *Family Weekly* as a Sunday Supplement.

Publication History

MAGAZINE AND TITLE CHANGES
> *Family Weekly*, 13 September 1953–1 September 1985; *USA Weekend*, 8 September 1985–present.

VOLUME AND ISSUE DATA
> 13 September 1953–current, weekly.

PUBLISHER AND PLACE OF PUBLICATION
> William H. "Bill" Marriott, 1953–1955; Leonard S. Davidow, 1956–1965; Mort Frank, 1966–1982; Pat Linsky, 1983–1985; Gannett Company, Inc., 1985–1988 (Patricia Haegele, publisher, 1987–October 1988; Gannett, Company, Inc., November 1988–current). New York.

EDITORS
> John B. Starr, 1953–1955; Ben Kartman, editorial director, 1956–1958; Ernest Heyn, 1959–1963; Robert Fitzgibbon, 1964–July 1970; Norman M. Lobsenz, managing editor, 1971; Mort Persky, 1971–1976; Scott DeGarmo, 1976–1978; Arthur Cooper, 1979–1983; Thomas Plate, 1984; John C. Quinn, 1985–October 1988; Ron Martin, executive editor, November 1988–May 1989; John W. Walter, senior editor, June 1989–current.

CIRCULATION
> 29.5 million (1989).

Barbara Nourie

U.S. NEWS AND WORLD REPORT

In 1926 David Lawrence started a newspaper called the *United States Daily* that dealt with governmental affairs. In 1933 the publication became a weekly, the *United States News*. A magazine format was adopted in 1940. Lawrence had started another publication in 1946 called *World Report*. In 1948 the publications were merged to become *U.S. News and World Report*, and in the forty years since has consistently been the number three national newsmagazine, behind *Time** and *Newsweek** in first and second place. The comparison with the other major national newsmagazines may be a little misleading. The missions of *Time* and *Newsweek* are more closely aligned with an effort to present the many avenues of the week's events—news, culture, sports, literature, and so forth. *U.S. News and World Report*, on the other hand, has long prided itself with adhering strictly to national and international news with particular attention to the business of government.

The direction of the magazine through most of its life has been a product of the views and wishes of founder David Lawrence. Lawrence was born in Philadelphia on 25 December 1888. He was born in a room below his immigrant father's tailor shop. The family moved to Buffalo, New York, when he was a child. In the public library of Buffalo, Lawrence began reading the *Congressional Record*.[1] At fourteen Lawrence began his writing career as a sports reporter for the *Buffalo Express*. His undergraduate days were spent at Princeton University. Lawrence attended the New Jersey University from 1906 to 1910, during which he wrote for seventeen newspapers and the Associated Press—earning enough from his articles to pay tuition and board and still have $500 left. He was the only student permitted to have a telephone in his room, and perhaps as a result of the attention his articles were bringing to Princeton, Lawrence gained the friendship of Woodrow Wilson, president of the university. Two years later, when Wilson became president of the United States, the Associated Press assigned Lawrence to the White House. Lawrence had been with the Washington, D.C., staff of the Associated Press since 1910. While he rarely enjoyed private sessions with the president, aides and cabinet officers were very forthcoming.[2]

Lawrence's scoop journalism was abridged after he revealed that President Wilson's stroke had made the president "incapable of fully rational decisions."[3] In 1916 Lawrence got his own byline with the *New York Evening Post*. This ended in October 1919 (Wilson's paralytic stroke occurred in September 1919) after his White House sources were no longer forthcoming—Wilson had terminated the friendship because of Lawrence's article revealing presidential impairment. Lawrence discovered while attempting to syndicate the column himself that he needed to supply other features—"enough to keep a wire busy for eight hours."[4] He did this by supplying financial data, that is, getting exclusive rights to provide afternoon papers with quotations from the New York Stock Exchange. With the success of this service, other similar specialized services were started. Four years after the stock market crash Lawrence transferred his stock market service to the Associated Press. The North American Newspaper Alliance became the new syndicators of the Lawrence column. The remaining services were grouped under a new name—the Bureau of National Affairs.[5]

The *United States Daily* was Lawrence's next venture. It was a thirty-six-page newspaper that concerned itself solely with government—providing neither comment nor demonstrating political favoritism or ideological leaning. Edgar Kemler reports that a number of Lawrence's rich friends were the financial backers, namely, Otto Kahn, Simon Guggenheim, and Ruth Hanna McCormick of *Chicago Tribune* McCormick fame. These individuals supported the enterprise for seven years, contributing perhaps as much as $2 million. Lawrence continued with the publication for another seven years, employing his column as a vehicle for funds.[6]

In 1933 the newspaper became a weekly, and the title was changed to *United States News*. Seven years later the format was changed to a magazine with the January 1940 issue. Lawrence began another publication in 1946 called *World Report* that covered international news. In 1948 he combined *United States News* with *World Report*. The first combined issue, dated 19 March 1948, was titled

U.S. News and World Report, the ampersand was adopted with the 2 April 1948 issue.

The magazine's growth in popularity can be seen by comparing the 1939 circulation and advertising revenues with those of 1951. In 1939 *United States News* had a circulation of 87,000 with advertising revenues of $306,000. By 1951 circulation was 455,000 and advertising revenue was $4,712,000. These figures are vastly removed from those for both *Time* and *Newsweek*, but represent a very significant percentage change for *U.S. News and World Report*.[7]

As an example of how much technology has changed operating procedures and our expectations of the speed at which things can be completed, the following story shows what "quick" meant so far as getting news into print in the early 1950s. *U.S. News and World Report* publishing director John H. Sweet, responding to letters of query about how the magazine was able to get news of the Democratic Convention out in forty-two hours, speaks of the McCall Corporation printers in Dayton, Ohio, able to generate 20,000 copies an hour, with 575,000 completed in a weekend. Sweet also refers to meeting the regular train schedules for points east, but using chartered planes for the western delivery points. He goes on to say, "airplane delivery in this manner as a regular thing is, of course, still a prohibitive expense."[8]

Circulation jumped to 922,000 by 1957 and was probably over one million by 1959. Some of the features of the magazine were highlighted by Ben H. Bagdikian: lengthy tape-recorded interviews printed in question-and-answer style without comment; full texts of significant speeches; in-depth analytical articles on single topics; and use of graphics to explain news. *U.S. News and World Report* was averaging ninety pages a week of news in 1957, double that of *Time* and *Newsweek*. The figures are similarly impressive for articles on business outlook, education, science, and space.[9] Bagdikian also reports that *U.S. News and World Report* was the first to introduce the colored page and "imitation-typewriting to regular magazines."[10]

On 30 June 1962 all the stock of *U.S. News and World Report* became employee-owned. David Lawrence became chairman of the board of the profit-sharing trust and continued as editor. Lawrence had sold two previous firms to the employees: the Bureau of National Affairs and a printing company that became McArdle Printing Company. There were 435 employees at *U.S. News and World Report* when this change occurred; 285 were over thirty and had been with the company for more than one year and were members of the profit-sharing trust. Formerly the company operated as United States News Publishing Corporation, but changed in 1962 to U.S. News and World Report, Inc.[11] The circulation average for 1963 was over 1.28 million.[12] By 1968 circulation was in excess of 1.7 million.[13]

As John Tebbel suggests, a possible explanation for the success of *U.S. News and World Report* is the degree to which it differs from its rivals. The format has been distinct; forecasting and analysis have been the foci of articles. Also, the conservative audience attracted by the Lawrence editorials was also served by the rest of the publication.[14] James Playsted Wood agrees that the magazine has succeeded because it is "a foil to the contrasting beliefs and attitudes of its news magazine contemporaries."[15]

According to Evan Ira Farber, et al., writing in 1972, the periodical employed a "no-nonsense approach to the news," and gave "almost no attention to culture, entertainment or intellectual pursuits."[16] Words such as *sober* and *utilitarian* have been used by various reviewers to convey the plain, straightforward presentation of the events.

From 1933 until his death on 11 February 1973, founder David Lawrence was the editor. In the 25 June 1973 issue the periodical announced his successor: Howard Flieger. Flieger was born 11 October 1909 in Denver, Colorado. At age twenty he began his new career in Oklahoma. At twenty-five he joined the Associated Press (AP) in Missouri, moving upward to become an AP White House correspondent; he spent World War II covering President Franklin D. Roosevelt. Flieger joined *U.S. News* in 1945, and in 1946 he became managing editor of *World Report*. From 1948 to 1969 Flieger directed the international staff of *U.S. News and World Report*, and played a significant role in the writing and organizing of major stories. From 1969 to 1973 Flieger was executive editor, replacing Owen L. Scott,[17] Flieger retired from *U.S. News and World Report* in 1977, writing his last editorial the week of 7 March.[18]

Marvin L. Stone, a fifteen-year veteran with the Washington staff of the periodical, became the third editor effective with the issue of 14 March 1977. According to publisher John H. Sweet, Stone brought a total of thirty years journalism experience to the position.[19]

In 1973 *U.S. News and World Report* began a journey that was to take it to the edge of technology and realize the company significant profit. With the formation of the Atex system, in which *U.S. News and World Report* was one of the original investors, the periodical was able to generate electronically "a complete page proof with all type and graphics in position."[20] Some other users of the Atex system include *Newsweek, Forbes*, and the Government Printing Office.[21] Through the use of video display terminals (VDTs), devices that digitize black-and-white photographs, and minicomputers, the periodical is able to send copy electronically from the journalist's desk to the printer.[22] The savings in time, and the added flexibility that this system has provided, have not gone unnoticed by the competition, as witnessed by the partial list of purchasers. *U.S. News and World Report* first employed the system in its own periodical with the issue of 5 September 1977.

Atex was sold in 1981, converting the *U.S. News and World Report* original investment of $350,000 into $9 million in stock when Eastman Kodak Company purchased the corporation. By 1982 U.S. News and World Report was offering computer-based editorial services, including typesetting and page transmission—with a customer list including *Business Week, Newsweek*, Conde Nast Publications, and Hearst Publications. *U.S. News and World Report* rate base was 2.05 million, with advertising pages declining in the mid–single-digit range.[23]

The fiftieth anniversary editorial by Marvin Stone, a native Vermonter, contrasted the circulation figure of 15,040 in 1933 with the 1983 total of over two
million; mentioned that the periodical would move to new headquarters in the
fall of 1983; and repeated the fact of employee ownership of the concern. The
new headquarters building was apparently the newsmagazine's fourth move.[24]

Seven months later speculation as to who a secret potential buyer of *U.S.
News and World Report* might be was the subject of a *Newsweek* article that
mentioned Mortimer B. Zuckerman. Zuckerman was the periodical's partner in
a Washington real-estate venture—a $200 million development that includes the
new U.S. News and World Report headquarters.[25]

Newsweek seems to have led the newsmagazines in announcing Zuckerman's
$168 million bid for the "staid magazine and its entrenched staffers." The bid
apparently was three times the company's appraised value. A possible explanation as to why the sale came about may be that a large group of the owner-
employees were "near retirement and eager to collect [ownership benefits payable
at retirement], the company faced, by the same accounts, a debilitating cash
drain."[26]

The board of directors of U.S. News and World Report actually signed the
agreement with Zuckerman on 11 June 1984 for a total of $168.5 million for
all of the stock in the company. An editorial published two weeks later claimed
that the periodical was "read by nine million people every week." Included
here were all those reading someone else's copy, and such shared copies as those
in libraries, institutions, and businesses.[27]

Zuckerman was to pay about $3,000 a share in cash for the approximately
56,000 shares in the firm. Over a fifteen-year period he would pay $25 million
in deferred compensation to top executives.[28] It is worth stressing here that
Mortimer B. Zuckerman became the sole owner of the periodical. The deferred
compensation referred to above amounts to about $5 million each for editor
Marvin Stone and managing editor Lester Tanzer.[29] Zuckerman saw the purchase
of *U.S. News and World Report* as representing "a unique opportunity to be
involved in a small circle of important magazines that help set the national
agenda."[30]

An item that one critic believed that Zuckerman might wish to change was
the closing time for entries in the weekly. In 1984 the periodical went to press
on Friday, while rivals *Time* and *Newsweek* could enter stories as late as Sunday.
Also cited were the low advertising revenues for 1983, $94 million compared
with *Newsweek*'s $219 million, and $299 million for *Time*. The pretax profits
of the three major newsweeklies told an even more exaggerated story: $40 million
for *Time* (estimated), $15 million for *Newsweek*, and perhaps less than $2 million
for *U.S. News and World Report*.[31] Several more comparisons may assist in
gauging the relative size of the periodicals: an approximated editorial budget for
Time was suggested to be around $60 million a year; the figure for *U.S. News
and World Report* (again an approximation) was said to be in the neighborhood

of $15 million. In 1984 *Time* was the number 1 magazine in ad revenues earned, with *Newsweek* number 3, and *U.S. News and World Report* number 13.[32]

The *Washington Journalism Review* reported that after further discussions and modifications the sum that Zuckerman was to pay was revised downward to $153.3 million, with $2,681 for each of the 57,178 shares outstanding and an additional $22.7 million for deferred compensation to eight top managers to be paid in installments over fifteen years.[33]

The last piece of news about the periodical in 1984 was the appointment by Zuckerman of Harold Evans, foreign editor of the *Sunday Times* of London for fourteen years (1968–1982), as the "editorial director." Editor Marvin Stone still had day-to-day control. Evans said his "job [was] to assess the magazine and the role it plays." Evans attended editorial and marketing meetings.[34]

On 1 April 1985 Zuckerman installed his first handpicked editor. The fourth editor in fifty-two years, Shelby Coffey III was formerly the assistant managing editor for national news at the *Washington Post*. The former editor, Marvin Stone, retired after forty years in journalism, the last twenty-five spent at *U.S. News and World Report*. Coffey said one of his first tasks was to update the graphics.[35] Zuckerman also hired designer Walter Bernard, who had worked with Coffey on new graphics for the *Washington Post*. Harold Evans returned full-time to his former post as head of Atlantic Monthly Press (1984–1986).[36]

Coffey's salary was said to be one of the highest in print journalism, in the order of $300,000 a year. Zuckerman also hired several new columnists at this time—former Congressman Barber B. Conable and former White House communications director David Gergen.[37]

Coffey served for seventeen years with the *Washington Post*, starting in 1968. He studied American and Roman history at the University of Virginia, is the son of a prominent attorney, and the grandson of a U.S. Senator from Tennessee.[38]

Several key administrative posts were quickly filled by Zuckerman. He chose as president his friend Fred Drasner, a Washington lawyer;[39] as executive editor, Kathy Bushkin, who was Gary Hart's press secretary; and as executive vice-president, James K. Glassman, formerly publisher of the *New Republic*.[40] He also recruited Peter Bernstein, Washington editor of *Fortune* and editor of *Arthur Young's Tax Guide*, to assist in the development of the business section of *U.S. News and World Report* to compete more directly with *Business Week* and *Money*.[41] With the 29 April 1985 issue, Zuckerman named himself editor-in-chief. Zuckerman—who made his fortune in real estate development—described himself in his Who's Who entry as a publisher.[42]

Zuckerman, the son of a tobacco and candy wholesaler and grandson of an Orthodox Jewish rabbi,[43] was raised in the suburban Outremont district of Montreal.[44] His interest in U.S. public affairs was revealed at an early age through his daily purchase of the *New York Times*.[45] He received his bachelor's degree in economics and a law degree from McGill University in Montreal. He earned a master's degree from the University of Pennsylvania's Wharton School of Business and graduated in 1962 from the Harvard Law School at age twenty-four.[46] (He was lecturer and then associate professor of city and regional planning at the Harvard University Graduate School of Design from 1966 to 1974). Zuckerman then joined the Boston Development company of Cabot, Cabot, & Forbes in 1965. At age twenty-seven he became the company's chief financial officer, and by age thirty he had become a millionaire. In 1970 he left Cabot, and with a former colleague, Ed Linde, formed a private company called Boston Properties.[47] According to one source, he had accumulated a fortune estimated to be $320 million as of 1985.[48] Zuckerman became a naturalized U.S. citizen in 1977.[49] He entered the publishing world in 1980 as the president and chairman of the board of Atlantic Monthly Company in Boston.[50] (It should be noted that he is the sole owner of *The Atlantic*, formerly *The Atlantic Monthly**).

The private political views of Zuckerman may be suggested by his fund-raisers for Ted Kennedy and Gary Hart, as well as his support for Boston's local Democrats such as Mayor Kevin White.[51] He would like to spend 85 percent of his time in publishing.[52]

Covering the design changes at the three major newsweeklies, *New York* magazine suggested that a "convergence of the three is taking place," with red seeming to be the key color on the cover of all three.[53] The major change for *U.S. News and World Report* with the 1985 year-end double issue was a new section with twelve pages devoted to business and finance.[54]

Change in editors came quickly—Shelby Coffey III left the job after only nine months. He became the editor-in-chief of the *Dallas Times Herald*. It seems as though the "chemistry" between Zuckerman and Coffey ran into difficulties as a result of Zuckerman's "heavy oar" and perhaps because he felt Coffey was "hampered by his feature-page background and ill suited for the job."[55]

David Gergen became the fifth editor. A former communications director of the Reagan White House, he became *U.S. News and World Report*'s managing editor for national and international news in August 1985 and was named editor on 5 March 1986. Gergen was the staff's favorite for the editor's job. Raised in Durham, North Carolina, Gergen is a graduate of Yale and the Harvard Law School. Formerly a syndicated columnist and American Enterprise Institute fellow, Gergen has served on three White House staffs. He left the Reagan communications post in early 1984 to teach at Harvard's Kennedy School of Government.[56]

Journalist Edwin Diamond, writing for *New York* magazine, reminds the reader that politically *U.S. News and World Report* is right of center, and that demographically the readers tend to be older than those of *Time* and *Newsweek*, and that they live mostly in the "heartland."[57] Diamond also discusses job changes: Matthew Storin, a senior editor, left *U.S. News and World Report* to become editor of the *Chicago Sun-Times*; and a new executive editor, Gergen's number two, was hired by Zuckerman—Michael Ruby from *Newsweek*.[58]

The 1985 redesign divided the publication into six new sections. With all the attempt at modernization and image improvement, the publication still closes its pages on Fridays—giving rivals *Time* and *Newsweek* a clear advantage. At least one of Zuckerman's position shufflings did not work totally either. Harold Evans, former editorial director of *U.S. News and World Report*, moved on after working as Editor-in-Chief of Atlantic Monthly Press (1984–1986) to become an adviser to S. I. Newhouse at Conde Nast, working on new magazine ideas.[59] However, as a result of price-cutting on subscriptions, and by appealing to a wider audience, the circulation increased to 2,255,943.[60]

A change recently reported concerns the expansion of News You Can Use into an entire section. With the 3 August 1987 issue the section covers personal finance, taxes, careers, and travel, as well as health, nutrition, fitness, and education. President and chief executive office Fred Drasner also provided a thumbnail sketch of the *U.S. News and World Report* reader: one twice as likely as the general population to have graduated from college, twice as likely to hold a professional or managerial job, and with an income 35 percent higher than the average adult American's. A 1987 Simmons Market Research Bureau study was used by Dresner as the source for the above data. Finally, *U.S. News and World Report* teamed up with British journalist David Frost to interview the major candidates in the 1988 U.S. presidential election. Excerpts appeared in the periodical, with the interviews broadcast nationally in a weekly series of one-hour specials, and a daily series of shorter radio segments.[61]

Notes

1. Arthur Krock, "Unforgettable David Lawrence," *Reader's Digest,* January 1974, pp. 75–76. Krock won three Pulitzer Prizes in thirty-five years as Washington correspondent and columnist for the *New York Times*. He retired in 1967.

2. Edgar Kemler, "The Lawrence Riddle. The Man or the Times?" *Nation*, 19 March 1955, p. 235.

3. Ibid.

4. Ibid.

5. Ibid., p. 236.

6. Ibid.

7. "Competition—From Inside and Out—Grips Magazines," *Business Week*, 12 July 1952, p. 38.

8. John H. Sweet, "How Did You Do It?" *U.S. News and World Report*, 8 August 1952, p. 4.

9. Ben H. Bagdikian, "The Newsmagazines. I—U.S. News and World Report," *New Republic*, 2 February 1959, p. 12. Bagdikian was a reporter for the *Providence Journal-Bulletin*, where the article appeared originally.

10. Ibid., p. 16.

11. "A Statement by U.S. News and World Report, Inc.," *U.S. News and World Report*, 9 July 1962, p. 4.

12. David Lawrence, "Our 30th Anniversary," *U.S. News and World Report*, 27 May 1963, p. 108. As with each of the editorials, the following appears at the top of the

page: "(This page presents the opinion of the Editor. The news pages are written by other staff members independently of the editorial views)."

13. David Lawrence, "Our 35th Anniversary," *U.S. News and World Report*, 23 December 1968, p. 84.

14. John Tebbel, *The American Magazine: A Compact History* (New York: Hawthrone Books, 1969), p. 230. From the chapter "Magazines of the Twentieth Century (1905–   )."

15. James Playsted Wood, *Magazines in the United States*, 3rd ed. (New York: Ronald Press, 1971), p. 234.

16. Evan Ira Farber et al., *Classified List of Periodicals for College Libraries*, 5th ed., rev. and enl. (Westwood, Mass.: F. W. Faxon Co., 1972), p. 229.

17. John H. Sweet, "A Memo to Our Readers," *U.S. News and World Report*, 25 June 1973, p. 6.

18. Howard Flieger, "Sincerely Yours," *U.S. News and World Report*, 7 March 1977, p. 92.

19. John H. Sweet, "A Memo to Our Readers," *U.S. News and World Report*, 14 March 1977, p. 3.

20. "Printing by Computer: A USN and WR Gamble Pays Off," *U.S. News and World Report*, 5 September 1977, p. 58.

21. Ibid., p. 57.

22. Ibid., pp. 56–57.

23. "Diversification Is the News at U.S. News," *Business Week*, 16 August 1982, p. 32.

24. Marvin Stone, "Our Fiftieth Anniversary," *U.S. News and World Report*, 9 May 1983, p. 180.

25. "A Mystery Buyer Goes After U.S. News," *Newsweek*, 26 December 1983, p. 53.

26. David M. Alpern, Diane Weathers, and Lucy Howard, "A New Slugger for U.S. News," *Newsweek*, 18 June 1984, p. 97.

27. "For U.S. News, A New Owner to Carry It Forward" [The Editor's Page], *U.S. News and World Report*, 25 June 1984, p. 78.

28. Ibid., p. 79.

29. "Change of Command at U.S. News," *Time*, 25 June 1984, p. 75.

30. Michael Posner, "A New Face in U.S. News," *Macleans*, 25 June 1984, p. 46.

31. Edwin Diamond, "The News about 'U.S. News.' Mort Zuckerman's Big Plans," *New York*, 27 August 1984, p. 51.

32. Ibid., p. 55.

33. Bill Hogan, "Behind the Grab for U.S. News," *Washington Journalism Review*, September 1984, p. 25.

34. "English Eye. Harold Evans Scans U.S. News," *Time*, 5 November 1984, p. 72.

35. "U.S. News Gets 4th Editor in 52 Years," *U.S. News and World Report*, 1 April 1985, p. 11.

36. "Position Filled. A New Editor at U.S. News," *Time*, 1 April 1985, p. 72.

37. Jonathan Alter and Ann McDaniel, "A New Chief for U.S. News," *Newsweek*, 1 April 1985, p. 69.

38. Marvin Stone, editor, "A Final Word from Stone," *U.S. News and World Report*, 8 April 1985, p. 90.

39. Tom McNichol and Margaret Carlson, "A Developer Remodels U.S. News," *Columbia Journalism Review*, July-August 1985, p. 32.

40. Ibid., p. 33.

41. Ibid., p. 35.

42. Ibid., p. 36.

43. Joanne Lipman, "Changing Goals. Mort Zuckerman Seeks to Influence Opinion, Not Just Own Land," *Wall Street Journal*, 27 September 1985, Eastern Edition, p. 18.

44. Posner, "A New Face in U.S. News," p. 46.

45. "Change of Command at U.S. News," p. 75.

46. "For U.S. News, A New Owner to Carry It Forward," p. 79.

47. Gwen Kinkead, "Mort Zuckerman, Media's New Mogul," *Fortune*, 14 October 1985, p. 195.

48. Ibid., p. 191.

49. "Change of Command at U.S. News," p. 75.

50. *Who's Who in America*, 45th ed. (Chicago: Marquis Who's Who, 1988–89), vol. 2, p. 3418.

51. Lipman, "Changing Goals," p. 1.

52. Ibid., p. 18.

53. Edwin Diamond, "The New Newsweekly Look," *New York*, 9 December 1985, p. 20.

54. Ibid., p. 24.

55. Jonathan Alter, "The Blues at U.S. News," *Newsweek,* 27 January 1986, p. 58.

56. "David Gergen. A New Editor for U.S. News," *U.S. News and World Report*, 17 March 1986, p. 10.

57. Edwin Diamond, "The Zuckerman Report," *New York*, 22 September 1986, p. 45.

58. Ibid., p. 46.

59. Ibid.

60. Ibid., p. 47.

61. Fred Drasner, "A Message to Our Readers," *U.S. News and World Report*, 3 August 1987, p. 3.

Information Sources

BIBLIOGRAPHY

Alpern, David M., Diane Weathers, and Lucy Howard. "A New Slugger for U.S. News." *Newsweek,* 18 June 1984, p. 97.

Alter, Jonathan. "The Blues at U.S. News." *Newsweek*, 27 January 1986, p. 58.

Alter, Jonathan, and Ann McDaniel. "A New Chief for U.S. News." *Newsweek,* 1 April 1985, p. 69.

Bagdikian, Ben H. "The Newsmagazines. I—U.S. News and World Report." *New Republic*, 2 February 1959, p. 12.

"Change of Command at U.S. News." *Time*, 25 June 1984, p. 75.

"Competition—From Inside and Out—Grips Magazines." *Business Week*, 12 July 1952, p. 38.

"David Gergen. A New Editor for U.S. News." *U.S. News and World Report*, 17 March 1986, p. 10.

Diamond, Edwin. "The New Newsweekly Look." *New York*, 9 December 1985, p. 20.

————. "The News about 'U.S. News.' Mort Zuckerman's Big Plans." *New York*, 27 August 1984, p. 51.

————. "The Zuckerman Report." *New York*, 22 September 1986, p. 45

"Diversification Is the News at U.S. News." *Business Week*, 16 August 1982, p. 32.

Drasner, Fred. "A Message to Our Readers." *U.S. News and World Report*, 3 August 1987, p. 3.

"English Eye. Harold Evans Scans U.S. News." *Time*, 5 November 1984, p. 72.

Farber, Evan Ira, et al. *Classified List of Periodicals for College Libraries*. 5th ed., rev. and enl. Westwood, Mass.: F. W. Faxon Co., 1972, p. 229.

Flieger, Howard. "Sincerely Yours." *U.S. News and World Report*, 7 March 1977, p. 92.

"For U.S. News, A New Owner to Carry It Forward" [The Editor's Page]. *U.S. News and World Report*, 25 June 1984, p. 78.

Hogan, Bill. "Behind the Grab for U.S. News." *Washington Journalism Review*, September 1984, p. 25.

Kemler, Edgar. "The Lawrence Riddle. The Man or the Times?" *Nation*, 19 March 1955, p. 235.

Kinkead, Gwen. "Mort Zuckerman, Media's New Mogul." *Fortune*, 14 October 1985, p. 195.

Krock, Arthur. "Unforgettable David Lawrence." *Reader's Digest*, January 1974, pp. 75–76.

Lawrence, David. "Our 30th Anniversary." *U.S. News and World Report*, 27 May 1963, p. 108.

————. "Our 35th Anniversary." *U.S. News and World Report*, 23 December 1968, p. 84.

Lipman, Joanne. "Changing Goals. Mort Zuckerman Seeks to Influence Opinion, Not Just Own Land." *Wall Street Journal*, 27 September 1985, Eastern Edition, p. 18.

McNichol, Tom, and Margaret Carlson. "A Developer Remodels U.S. News." *Columbia Journalism Review*, July-August 1985, p. 32.

"A Mystery Buyer Goes After U.S. News." *Newsweek*, 26 December 1983, p. 53.

"Position Filled. A New Editor at U.S. News." *Time*, 1 April 1985, p. 72.

Posner, Michael. "A New Face in U.S. News." *Macleans*, 25 June 1984, p. 46.

"Printing by Computer: A USN and WR Gamble Pays Off." *U.S. News and World Report*, 5 September 1977, p. 58.

"A Statement by U.S. News and World Report, Inc." *U.S. News and World Report*, 9 July 1962, p. 4.

Stone, Marvin. "A Final Word from Stone." *U.S. News and World Report*, 8 April 1985, p. 90.

————. "Our Fiftieth Anniversary." *U.S. News and World Report*, 9 May 1983, p. 180.

Sweet, John H. "How Did You Do it?" *U.S. News and World Report*, 8 August 1952, p. 4.

————. "A Memo to Our Readers." *U.S. News and World Report*, 25 June 1973, p. 6.

————. "A Memo to Our Readers." *U.S. News and World Report*, 14 March 1977, p. 3.

Tebbel, John. *The American Magazine: A Compact History*. New York: Hawthorne Books, 1969.

"U.S. News Gets 4th Editor in 52 Years." *U.S. News and World Report*,1 April 1985, p. 11.

Who's Who in America. 45th ed. Chicago: Marquis Who's Who, 1988–89, vol. 2,
    p. 3418.
Wood, James Playsted. *Magazines in the United States.* 3rd ed. New York: Ronald Press,
    1971, p. 234.
INDEX SOURCES
    Readers' Guide (1946–present); *Magazine Index* (1977–present).
LOCATION SOURCES
    Available in microform.

Publication History

MAGAZINE TITLE AND TITLE CHANGES
    United States Daily, 1926–1933. *United States News* vol. 1, no. 1–vol. 24, no.
    2, 13 May 1933–9 January 1948. *World Report,* vol. 1, no. 1–vol. 4, no. 1, 23
    May 1946–6 January 1948. *United States News* combined with *World Report* but
    no connecting word on cover, just the two separate titles: *United States,* upper
    left, *World Report,* lower left, vol. 24, no. 3–vol. 24, no. 11, 16 January 1948–
    12 March 1948. *U.S. News and World Report,* vol. 24, no. 12–vol. 24, no. 13,
    19 March–26 March 1948. *U.S. News & World Report* (ampersand in title), vol.
    24, no. 14–present, 2 April 1948–present.
VOLUME AND ISSUE DATA
    Vol. 1, no. 1–vol. 104, no. 5, 13 May 1933–8 February 1988; continuing, weekly.
PUBLISHER AND PLACE OF PUBLICATION
    Washington, D.C. The United States News Publishing Corporation, 1933–30 June
    1962. U.S. News and World Report, Inc., 1962 to date.
EDITORS
    David Lawrence, 1933–11 February 1973; Howard Flieger, 25 June 1973–7 March
    1977; Marvin Stone, 14 March 1977–8 April 1985; Shelby Coffey III, 15 April
    1985–10 February 1986; David Gergen listed as senior managing editor (no editor
    listed), 17 February 1986–10 March 1986; David Gergen, editor, 17 March 1986–
    12 September 1988; Roger Rosenblatt, 19 September 1988–present.
CIRCULATION
    2,114,152 (1987), 2,287,061 (1988).

Graham R. Walden

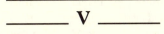

V

VANITY FAIR

While the history of *Vanity Fair* can be traced back through a series of titles to 1889, it is with the appearance of volume 1, number 1 of *Dress and Vanity Fair* in September 1913 that the magazine's unique identity began to emerge. The seeds sown in that September issue blossomed so fruitfully that four issues later, in January 1914, *Dress* was dropped from the title, which became simply *Vanity Fair*.

But from that first issue, heralded by its editors as the birth of "a new publication, with no preconceived notions and no prejudices," its guiding purpose was clear, if also ambivalent: to chronicle "the brighter side of life . . . the joy of living . . . and much, too, of its more serious aspects" (September 1913, p. 13). By celebrating "the wonder and variety of American life," its pages sought to present to readers "cheerfully, month by month, a record of current achievements in all the arts and a mirror of the progress and promise of American life" (September 1914, p. 15).

Under the editorial policies of Frank Crowninshield, who became editor in March 1914 and whose credentials included having served as publisher of the *Bookman* and art editor of the *Century*, the magazine's raison d'être occasionally took on the zealous overtones of a social missionary. *Vanity Fair* would counter the puritanical "tendency . . . of many parental warnings, admonitory sermons, and somewhat lugubrious editorials" to condemn the "increased devotion [in recent American life] to pleasure, to happiness, to dancing, to sport (in which we appear to have a laughable lead over the rest of the world), and to all forms of cheerfulness." Americans "as a nation, have come to realize the need for more cheerfulness, for hiding a solemn face, for a fair measure of pluck, and for great good humor." *Vanity Fair* would satiate that need by looking "at the highly-vitalized, electric, and diversified life of our day from the frankly cheerful angle of the optimist, or, which is much the same thing, from the mock-cheerful angle of the satirist'' (September 1914, p. 15). ''To entertain truthfully and truthfully to entertain,'' its editors boasted, '' . . . is Mission enough for any periodical'' (February 1914, p. 15).

Ironically, while propounding its purpose with such missionary enthusiasm, *Vanity Fair* left social and political abuses and evils to the ''so-called muck-rakers.'' Its only reform, the need for which was unnoticed by most, had ''nothing to do with bad government, or bad finance or bad morals.'' Rather it focused on ''the ravages of bad taste [which] are everywhere to be seen about us—in public life, in society, and in the work of many of our novelists, playwrights and artists'' (May 1914, p. 19).

While the contents of *Vanity Fair* may have implicitly attacked the bastions of ''bad taste,'' they naturally were intended to attract a select group of readers of ''discrimination and good taste.'' Denying charges of snobbery and of catering to a ''little handful of people who spend March on the Riviera, buy their dresses in Paris, send their boys to Eton, play golf at Biarritz, pass August at Newport and order their caviare [*sic*] in crates from Astrakhan on the Volga,'' the editors acknowledged that they sought to appeal to readers of ''some little sophistication . . . but not to that pseudo-sophistication bred of money alone, but rather to the sophistication which is the natural and happy result of wide travel, some little knowledge of the world and a pleasing familiarity with the five arts and the four languages'' (May 1914, p. 19). Readers of both sexes were targeted. In the pages of *Vanity Fair*, women would be given something ''never before . . . done for them by an American magazine'' : they would be given a chance to think (March 1914, p. 15). Men were advised to ''take heart,'' for in the pages of *Vanity Fair* they would find plenty of interest, including sports features and fashion news for men (January 1914, p. 13).

Modeling itself after the ''great'' English pictorial weeklies—which, its editors noted, they hoped ''to go one better'' (December 1913, p. 19)—*Vanity Fair* was to realize its mission by devoting itself to ''the more entertaining aspects of modern American life—to the theatre, to opera, art, literature, music, sport, humor, and fashion'' (May 1914, p. 19). At the center of many of these features were ''the most interesting doings of the most interesting of the People who go to make of Vanity Fair a 'very great Fair' indeed'' (January 1914, p. 13). Such diversity, which occasionally prompted its editor ''to envy those fortunate mortals whose pleasant task it is to edit such specialized and unified periodicals as, let us say, *The Iron Age*,'' would be crystallized by the editors' ''earnest attempt to avoid insincerity, puffery and vulgarity, and to tell the truth entertainingly'' (April 1914, p. 15; February 1914, p. 15).

Diversity in content alone does not account for the strength and the appeal of *Vanity Fair*. Much credit must be given to the quality of the authors who wrote for the magazine. Features by many of the foremost intellectuals, critics, essayists, poets, humorists, performers, and artists of the age appeared regularly. Notable among these were G. K. Chesterton on his vision of the future; Clarence

Darrow on the divorce problem; Julian Huxley on what science doesn't know; John Maynard Keynes on banks and the collapse of money values; Walter Lippmann with a "cheerful" view of the election; and Bertrand Russell on psychology and politics. Social and political commentaries by H. L. Mencken, Lytton Strachey, Hendrik Willem Van Loon, Frederick James Gregg, and Jay Franklin were published with some frequency. Merryle S. Rukeyser wrote regularly on the financial situation. Colette, Paul Gallico, Janet Flanner, Harold Nicholson, and Giovanni Papini were contributors, as were Drew Pearson, Clare Boothe Brokaw, and André Maurois. The panorama of essays by prominent literary figures included Sherwood Anderson's small town notes, D. H. Lawrence's answer to the question "Do Women Change?," Theodore Dreiser on the romance of power, as well as occasional reflections by F. Scott Fitzgerald, Ernest Hemingway, Thomas Mann, G. B. Shaw, Rebecca West, Gertrude Stein, and H. G. Wells. In keeping with its literary mission, *Vanity Fair* frequently published poetry by the likes of Paul Geraldy, e. e. cummings, and W. B. Yeats.

Reviews and critical essays on the arts also figured prominently in *Vanity Fair*. Reviews by critics such as Robert Sherwood, Walter Winchell, Edmund Wilson, and Hugh Walpole were complemented by the critical reflections of performers and belletristic writers of the day. Erik Satie commented on Igor Stravinsky; the photographer Robert Conlin mused on his role as the painter with the camera; Douglas Fairbanks shared his impressions of Greta Garbo; Arthur Symons reflected on the paintings of Pierre-Auguste Renoir; John Dos Passos examined a machine age theatre; Richard Le Gallienne sang the critical praises of the novelist George Moore. And so on.

In keeping with their resolution always to entertain their readers, the editors of *Vanity Fair* sought out the leading humorists of the day. On the heels of Dorothy Rothschild's thoughts on "Why I Haven't Married" came her reflections—this time as Dorothy Parker—on that "great American sport" divorce, with cartoons by Fish. Two other irreverent Algonquin Round Table members, Heywood Broun and Alexander Woolcott, joined Parker as frequent contributors. Ring Lardner, P. G. Wodehouse, Stephen Leacock, Frederick L. Allen—all were sought because they embodied the *Vanity Fair* school of "restrained and cultivated" humor rather than the exaggerated, slapstick humor to which most popular magazines had "deteriorate[d]" (May 1914, p. 19).

Vanity Fair's quest for the best extended from selecting its prose contributors to choosing its photographers. The pictures of the socially prominent at work and at play, the formal portraits of personalities of the day, and even the fashion illustrations were often works of art in themselves. Edward Steichen featured prominently among a galaxy of photographers that also included Man Ray, Florence Vandamm, and Alfred Stieglitz.

Advertising figured prominently in all the issues of *Vanity Fair*. Most ads related to fashion items though health and beauty aids also were regularly featured. An excellent cumulative index for the years 1913 through 1936 includes an index to advertisers arranged by product type. Multiple access points make this index an invaluable tool for social historians as well as for scholars in literature, the arts, and popular culture. The magazine's text is indexed by broad subjects as well as by author, by cartoonist, by photographer, and so on. Book reviews are also indexed.

In the February 1936 issue of *Vanity Fair*, its publisher Conde Nast announced that, beginning with the March issue, the magazine would be combined with its sister periodical, *Vogue*,* under whose name it would thenceforth appear. This decision, which was made because a lack of advertising support for magazines of the arts like *Vanity Fair* made them "unremunerative," spelled the end of *Vanity Fair* even though readers were assured that the editors of *Vogue* would try to "absorb certain of *Vanity Fair*'s editorial features" (February 1936, p. 11). But unlike *Vanity Fair*, which sought to balance the world of fashion with the world of literature and the arts, the editorial thrust of its successor was remorselessly on fashion.

In March 1983, Conde Nast Publications resurrected the defunct title and something denominated volume 46, number 1 of *Vanity Fair* was turned loose on the mass market. While the numbering is no doubt designed to suggest continuity between this publication and its predecessor, its similarity is titular only. No statement of purpose accompanies this premiere issue, and so the mission of its editors can be deduced only by its contents, which seem to reflect the breadth but not necessarily the depth or unified vision of its predecessor. Prominent people—politicians; dancers; actors and actresses, particularly those in movies; socialites, largely from the East Coast; novelists; members of royalty—have emerged as the focus of the magazine. For example, the cover stories of the first six issues for 1987 featured Mikhail Baryshnikov, Debra Winger, Diane Keaton, Dennis Hopper, the Calvin Kleins, and Liza Minnelli. In this new *Vanity Fair*, the focus on people appears at best to serve as a sometimes explicit, but more often implicit, reflection of current trends in the arts, society, and politics. Often, however, the focus of these portraits is diffuse, giving them the aura of "Life Styles of the Rich and Famous" gossip.

Like its putative predecessor, the new *Vanity Fair* features articles and reviews by prominent authors of the time. Calvin Trillin, Susan Sontag, Gail Sheehy, Michael Billington, Jan Morris, Nora Ephron, Stephen Jay Gould, Gore Vidal, V. S. Naipaul, Walker Percy, and Diana Trilling are among the literary stars whose work graces these pages. Occasionally excerpts from the works of contemporary novelists like Gabriel García Márquez and John Updike are included.

As in its predecessor, advertising figures prominently in this resurrected title. In fact, the advertising is so predominant that it tends to overshadow the photographs accompanying the text—photographs by contemporary artists like Lord Snowdon, Annie Liebowitz, Mick Haggerty, and Richard Avedon.

Information Sources

BIBLIOGRAPHY
Fairlie, Henry. "The Vanity of *Vanity Fair*." *New Republic*, 21 March 1983, pp. 25–30.

Kaiser, Charles. "The Making of a Magazine." *Newsweek*, 3 January 1983, pp. 65, 67.
Savory, J. "Well-Known Vanities." *American History Illustrated*, no. 9 (1978), pp. 42–46.
Unger, Craig. "Can *Vanity Fair* Live Again?" *New York*, 26 April 1982.

INDEX SOURCES
Cumulative Index, September 1913–February 1936, by publisher. *Music Index* (1983–1985); *Access* (1983–present).

LOCATION SOURCES
Illinois State University, Des Moines Public Library, Indiana University, University of Virginia, University of Wisconsin. Available in microform.

Publication History

MAGAZINE TITLE AND TITLE CHANGES
Sport, Music and Drama, 1889–1892; *Music and Drama*, 7 January–16 December 1893; *Standard and Music and Drama*, 23 December 1893–23 June 1894; *Standard*, 30 June 1894–18 December 1901; *Saturday Standard*, 21 December 1901–12 April 1902; *Vanity Fair and the Saturday Standard*, 19 April–3 May 1902; *Standard and Vanity Fair*, 2 September 1904–6 July 1912; *Dress and Vanity Fair*, September-December 1913; *Vanity Fair*, January 1914–February 1936; *Vanity Fair*, March 1983–present.

VOLUME AND ISSUE DATA
Dress and Vanity Fair, vol. 1, nos. 1–4, September–December 1913, monthly. *Vanity Fair*, vol. 1, no. 5–vol. 45, no. 6, January 1914–February 1936; vol. 46, no. 1–present, March 1983–present, monthly.

PUBLISHER AND PLACE OF PUBLICATION
Conde Nast Publications, Inc., New York, New York.

EDITORS
Unknown, September 1913–February 1914; Frank Crowninshield, March 1914–February 1936; Richard Locke, March-June 1983; Leo Lerman, July 1983–March 1984; Tina Brown, April 1984–present.

CIRCULATION
417,904.

Abigail Loomis

VILLAGE VOICE

New York's liberal weekly of politics and culture, the *Village Voice,* began in 1955 when Dan Wolf, a New School dropout and sometime *Columbia Encyclopedia* contributor on philosophy, and Ed Fancher, a psychologist, saw the need for a new publication in the Greenwich Village community. The idea was simple: give the voiceless people a voice and encourage cultural diversity. Their efforts resulted in a seminal weekly publication that influenced the direction of American journalism and by the 1960s had become "as central to the times as *Vanity Fair** to the 1920s or *Life** to the 1950s."[1] The tabloid, a hybrid of newspaper format and magazine content, promoted the "new journalism" that featured a personal narrative style and embraced a radical editorial policy that virtually gave writers free rein. It set the style for the wave of alternative weeklies and underground publications that followed, such as the *L. A. Free Press*, the *San Francisco Bay Guardian*, and the *Boston Phoenix*.

The new publication was launched by Wolf and Fancher with an initial $10,000, half of which came from the third partner, their friend Norman Mailer. Wolf was the prime mover and editor. Fancher held the position of publisher and took care of the business end of the enterprise. Mailer contributed capital, the name of the publication,[2] an occasional article, and a flagrant, controversial column for seventeen weeks during 1956.

The early *Village Voice* covered news of interest to those living in Greenwich Village while striving to be the antithesis of the *Villager*, its chief competitor and the only Village publication to succeed since the 1920s. The *Villager*'s motto read "reflecting the treasured traditions of this cherished community." The *Voice*, on the other hand, declared itself "A Weekly Newspaper Designed to be Read."[3] It became a lively forum for readers and writers appealing at first to the young, well-educated liberals, the bohemians of the 1950s, the counter-culture of the 1960s, and on to the yuppies of the 1980s.

Wolf and Fancher never claimed to know anything about publishing, and, consequently, the only policy they established was to set no policy. They ran their operation on intuition, creating an environment of freedom and independence that, despite the low pay, attracted some of New York's most talented writers. Known as a genius for "editing people, not copy,"[4] Wolf believed in the *Voice* as a writer's paper and influenced his writers' work only by sparking ideas and drawing out attitudes. He would read everything submitted, and pieces he accepted were for the most part printed without editing or alterations. In freeing up his contributors, Dan Wolf produced "more first rate writers than any other American editor over a similar period of time," according to Kevin McAuliffe, who wrote the definitive history of the *Village Voice, The Great American Newspaper*.[5] Wolf and Fancher received numerous New York Press Association awards in the late 1950s and the 1960s for achievements ranging from general excellence to excellence in advertising.

In the beginning, the *Voice* operated at a $1,000 per week loss. The first seven years it lost $50,000–$60,000, until circulation finally underwent a steady increase between 1962 and the end of the decade. It was helped considerably by the New York Typographical Union strike in 1962. The 114-day strike shut down newspapers whose contracts with the union were about to run out, and many additional newspapers went out on strike in sympathy. The void in the news market boosted the number of *Voice* readers from 17,000 to 40,000. Circulation plateaued at 25,000 after the strike, but another strike by the same union in 1965 brought circulation back up to 41,000 and it never again fell below that level. The subsequent fall of several New York papers, like the *World-Journal-Tribune*, also contributed to this period of growth.[6] Circulation grew to 138,000 by 1969, with seven out of ten issues being bought at newsstands. The

Voice was no longer just a Greenwich Village publication. It had picked up readers throughout New York City, across the country, and overseas.

Under the Wolf and Fancher ownership the price of the *Voice* increased only slightly, from five cents in 1955 to fifteen cents in 1966. Advertising began to bring in profits in the mid–1960s, after it was able to tap the local small-business market. By 1968 two-thirds of the publication was devoted to ads. A push by new owners to increase income in the 1970s jumped the price up from twenty cents to sixty cents and the ad ratio went over the 70 percent mark.

Much of the *Village Voice*'s success must be attributed to the work of the notable contributors and staff writers. Katherine Anne Porter, Ezra Pound, e.e. cummings, Allen Ginsberg, Michael Harrington, William Burroughs, Anaïs Nin, and Henry Miller were among the many distinguished names seen in the *Voice* during the fifties and sixties. Regular contributors such as Jack Newfield, Nat Hentoff, Alexander Cockburn, and Jules Fieffer can still be found in its pages. Other regulars, such as Mary Nichols, Ron Rosenbaum, Clark Whelton, Paul Cowan, Don McNeil, Lucian K. Truscott IV, Vivian Gornick, Jerry Tallmer, and Susan Brownmiller, also helped develop the tone and shape the dimensions of the *Voice*. Even the letters section contained unusually good reading, and the classified section of the *Voice* became notorious for the oddball creativity of the personal ads. Two anthologies of selected *Village Voice* pieces give a good cross section of its work: *The Village Voice Reader*, edited by Daniel Wolf and Edwin Fancher (New York: Doubleday) in 1962, and *The Village Voice Anthology: 1956–1980*, edited by Geoffrey Stokes (New York: Morrow) in 1982.

The *Voice*'s investigative reporting has often exerted an influence, especially on New York politics. Its muckracking articles and editorials helped push out the DeSapio political machine and heavily supported John Lindsay's mayoral campaign. Lead paint poisoning and the ten worst judges in New York were exposed by Newfield, and Mary Nichols championed the fight against a planned road through Washington Square. A more recent example is the annual roster of New York's ten worst landlords. The *Voice* has consistently given extensive coverage to national matters, including the sexual revolution, black activism, the civil rights demonstrations, the women's movement, the gay rights movement, Washington politics—in short, to all pressing issues of the day.

The *Voice* has always devoted considerable attention to the arts, with columns and articles on topics ranging from dance to television and the traditional fine arts to experimental visual and performance arts. Its cultural influence is perhaps best demonstrated by its early promotion of Off-Broadway and Off-Off-Broadway theater. It thoroughly covered theater activities neglected by the other media and initiated the Obie Awards, still given annually for Off-Broadway achievements. From the beginning it showed a special interest in the avant-garde, especially in its early coverage of underground film. Suitably for an innovative magazine of its generation, the *Voice* was also one of the first to adopt the new genre of rock criticism. A monthly book review insert, *VLS: The Village Voice Supplement*, was established in 1981.

In 1970, after several profitable years, Wolf and Fancher sold the weekly to Carl Burden, a young, wealthy New Yorker and aspiring politician, and Bartle Bull, his campaign manager and a Wall Street lawyer. Wolf and Fancher retained positions and some stock in the company. The daily activities stayed much the same for the staff until Burden and Bull unexpectedly merged the *Voice* with Clay Felker's *New York** in 1974. Felker, previously a reporter for *Life* and an editor for *Esquire*,* introduced some improvements in format, but the emphasis began to drift away from issues and events to personalities and life styles. The contributors were generally opposed to Felker's editorial direction, but salaries were increased, and initial defections were averted.[7]

One of Felker's attempts to expand the *Voice* was the introduction of a national edition in February 1976. The first issue made a splash with a twenty-four–page supplement devoted to Daniel Shorr's controversial piece on a secret House intelligence committee report exposing CIA incongruities, and raising the issue of executive branch leaks and journalistic ethics.[8] Despite this grand kickoff, the attempt to establish a national audience failed after only six months.

The new ownership and the changes that came with it in the 1970s brought a drop in readership and profits.[9] The publication never regained the influence it enjoyed in the 1960s. In 1977 Felker sold a majority of the *Voice* stock for $15 million to Rupert Murdoch, the Australian newspaper magnate. The staff unionized and actively opposed Murdoch's efforts to bring in a new editor. After this initial struggle, Murdoch realized it was in his interest to exempt the *Voice* from the editorial interference he generally imposed on his other publications.[10] David Schniederman was brought in as editor in 1979, and with Murdoch's forbearance, he ushered in a period of stability. The *Voice* once again became a profitable enterprise, with revenues increasing from $10.9 million in 1981 to $16.7 million in 1984 while earnings rose from $2.9 to $4.7 million.[11]

Ownership changed once again when Leonard Stern, the Hartz Mountain pet products entrepreneur, bought the publication in 1985 for $55 million. Stern sought to increase promotional activities, but did not meddle in editorial affairs. He retained David Schneiderman as editor, and although there was some debate among the staff about the future direction of the weekly, the *Voice* has continued much the same as under Murdoch.

Compounded of lengthy articles, weekly columns, editorials, reviews, and letters, the *Voice* now regularly runs over 150 pages, with more than 30 pages of classifieds and an abundance of commercial advertising. Its newsstand price is currently a dollar. The look of the *Voice* has improved considerably, with a more balanced layout, better graphics, and more recently, the use of full-color photography on the cover.

The weekly publication that influenced a generation of underground newspapers is still a provocative courier of contemporary culture. It has retained much of its traditional emphases on local and national politics, current events, and the arts, while expanding coverage of popular and social issues. Thus as it enters middle age, the *Village Voice* retains many of the attitudes and enthusiasms of its earlier days, as befits a denizen of Greenwich Village.

Notes

1. David Denby, "The Decline of the *Village Voice*," *New Republic*, 31 January 1983, p. 32.

2. Wolf and Fancher recall that Mailer chose a name from a list of possible titles, while Mailer says the title came to him while he was working on *The Deer Park*. (See Kevin McAuliffe, *The Great American Newspaper*, [New York: Charles Scribner's Sons, 1978], p. 13.)

3. Kevin McAuliffe, "Clay Felker Raises His Voice," *Columbia Journalism Review*, May-June 1975, p. 46.

4. Ellen Frankfort, *The Voice: Life at the "Village Voice"* (New York: William Morrow, 1976), p. 87.

5. Ibid. p. 141.

6. McAuliffe, *The Great American Newspaper*, pp. 127–28.

7. Ibid. p. 410.

8. David M. Alpern, Evert Clark, and Henry W. Hubbard, "A Question of Leakage," *Newsweek*, 23 February 1976, pp. 12–13.

9. McAuliffe, *The Great American Newspaper*, p. 421.

10. Michael Leapman, *Arrogant Aussie: The Rupert Murdoch Story*. (Secaucus, N.J.: Lyle Stuart, 1985), p. 112.

11. Gigi Mahon, "Hartz Content: The Good Life of Leonard Stern," *New York*, 5 May 1986, p. 47.

Information Sources

BIBLIOGRAPHY

Breen, Terry. "Comfortably Above Ground—Always Were in Fact: *Rolling Stone, Village Voice*." In *Magazine Profiles: Studies of a Dozen Contemporary Magazine Groupings*. Evanston, Ill.: Medill School of Journalism, Northwestern University, 1974, pp. 35–48.

Corry, John. "The Politics of Style." *Harper's Magazine*, November 1970, pp. 60–64.

Denby, David. "The Decline of the *Village Voice*." *New Republic*, 31 January 1983, pp. 29–34.

Frankfort, Ellen. *The Voice: Life at the "Village Voice."* New York: William Morrow, 1976.

Green, Cynthia. "The King of Hartz Mountain Polishes His Image." *Business Week*, 15 July 1985, pp. 124, 126.

Jones, Alex S. "At Village Voice, a Clashing of Visions." *New York Times*, 28 June 1985, p. B5.

Leapman, Michael. *Arrogant Aussie: The Rupert Murdoch Story*. Secaucus, N.J.: Lyle Stuart, 1985, pp. 107–14.

McAuliffe, Kevin. "Clay Felker Raises His Voice." *Columbia Journalism Review*, May-June 1975, pp. 45–54.

———. *The Great American Newspaper*. New York: Charles Scribner's Sons, 1978.

Mahon, Gigi. "Hartz Content: The Good Life of Leonard Stern." *New York*, 5 May
    1986, pp. 42–48.
Martin, Ann Ray. "The Voice of Felker." *Newsweek*, 23 June 1975, pp. 46, 51.
Rupp, Carla Marie. "Village Voice Blows Out Its 20th Candle." *Editor and Publisher*,
    1 November 1975, pp. 18–19.
Sale, J. Kirk. "The Village Voice: You've Come a Long Way, Baby, But You Got
    Stuck There." *Evergreen Review*, December 1969, pp. 25–27, 61–67.
INDEX SOURCES
    New Periodicals Index (ceased); Access, (1975–present); *Book Review Index; Film
    Literature Index; Music Index* (1976–present); *Media Review Digest; Alternative
    Press Index* (1969–1970).
LOCATION SOURCES
    Library of Congress, many other libraries. Available in microform.

Publication History

MAGAZINE TITLE AND TITLE CHANGES
    Village Voice.
VOLUME AND ISSUE DATA
    Vol. 1–present, 26 October 1955–present, weekly.
PUBLISHER AND PLACE OF PUBLICATION
    Edwin Fancher, 1955–1974; Bartle Bull, 1974–1975; Clay Felker, 1976–1977;
    William Ryan, 1977–1981; Martin Singerman and John Evans, 1982–1986; David
    Schneiderman, 1987–1988; Sally J. Cohen, 1989–present. New York, New York.
EDITORS
    Daniel Wolf, 1955–1974; Ross Wetzsteon, 1974; Thomas Morgan, 1975–1976;
    Marianne Partridge, 1976–1979; David Schneiderman, 1979–1987; Robert Freid-
    man, 1987–1988; Martin Gottlieb, 1988; Jonathan Z. Larsen, 1989–present.
CIRCULATION
    147,529.

Carole Palmer

VOGUE

Vogue had a history before Edna Chase edited it and before Conde Nast
published it, but its prestige and success were chiefly determined by this skilled
pair in the early twentieth century. Chase began in the *Vogue* circulation department in 1895, advanced to editor in 1914, and finally climbed to editor-in-
chief when *Vogue* expanded to international editions in the late 1920s. During
her thirty-seven years at the helm, Chase directed a publication that originated
as a weekly pictorial record of society under first publisher, Arthur B. Turnure.
Although *Vogue* continued to feature the haut monde, by the turn of the century
greater emphasis was being placed on fashion as a device to attract advertisers.
The ploy worked and fashion continued to be *Vogue*'s main focus after the
publication was bought by Conde Nast in 1909.

Vogue was Nast's first independent publishing effort. Having made both fame and fortune as business manager of *Collier's** between 1901 and 1907, Nast viewed *Vogue* as a testing ground for his theory of target audiences. In a famous quote Nast stated that *Vogue* editors wanted to "bait the editorial pages in such a way as to lift, out of all the millions of Americans, just the hundred thousand cultivated persons who can buy these quality goods."[1]

In the early 1920s *Vogue's* successful formula of clothes, light nonfiction, chatter, and more clothes became perfected. From a cramped small-print format, *Vogue* increasingly featured a larger photo layout and more sophisticated presentation. Although skilled artists like Georges Lepape and Christian Berard contributed an airy impressionist style in drawings, the magazine became particularly noted for its fashion photographers. In 1913, Baron de Meyer became the first of an important group that was to include Edward Steichen, Cecil Beaton, Baron Hoyningen-Huene, Andre Durst, Horst, and Irving Penn.

The layout by Mehemed Fehmy Agha and the distinctive photography established an unmistakable visual style in the 1930s and 1940s that was far more important than any attempt at content for *Vogue's* success. Although special issues occur, especially after the 1936 merger with *Vanity Fair*, articles by Thomas Wolfe or Margaret Mead were far less common than features on what to wear to the air-raid shelter (London 1939). Clothes, especially Paris clothes, were what sold *Vogue*, and during Nast's lifetime, additional pages of fashion photography and fashion advertising accounted for the more than doubling of the pages in each issue.

Chase's goal had been to "develop the taste and manners of her readers,"[2] and this conservative approach continued with little modification under successor Jessica Daves (1952–1962). In 1962, however, a revolution was at hand. By luring away Diana Vreeland from archrival *Harper's Bazaar, Vogue* had at its head one of the most powerful and eccentric forces in the fashion world. Under Vreeland, *Vogue* became identified with the exciting art and music happenings of the 1960s. A new visual momentum was created by dancing models photographed by Bert Stern, Helmut Newton, and Richard Avedon. The momentum continued with bright color, go-go graphics, and asymmetrical layouts in the text pages. This was also the era when both the society model and the professional model became household words as they were photographed by *Vogue*, shaking leonine manes and cavorting with actors in exotic locales. For those with reading on their minds, *Vogue's* departments increased as the magazine defined the chic and trendy in all aspects of its readers' lives.

Since Vreeland's day, the breathless enthusiasm of *Vogue* in the 1960s was toned down by its next editor, Grace Mirabella. Under Mirabella, a variety of spin-off books were produced with titles like *Fashion in Vogue* and *Vogue Body and Beauty Book*. In the magazine, one-page and shorter features were increased and their range expanded. Where at one time stocking styles and European travel would have predominated, subjects like health, taxes, antiques, and plants joined the featurettes on eye shadow. While no one would confuse *Vogue* with *Ms.,**

there was a somewhat greater attempt to deal with real content on a variety of topics.

A disappointing change in the Mirabella years was in the visual style of the publication. Once known for its elegance and artistic appearance, the periodical now began to look like *Glamour*, its sister publication for a college audience. The tendency to cram many small images into each page made the fashion sections far less memorable than the advertisements.

The Wintour years at *Vogue* began in December 1988, when *H. G.*'s wunderkind Anna Wintour was appointed editor. Within her first year, Wintour's presence was apparent in a more spacious and visually attractive format, as well as in the higher level of the contributors. Deborah Turbeville's murky fashion photographs of the earlier 1980s were replaced by bright and sassy footage by Patrick Demarchelier and others.

Just as the range of topics covered in the 1980s *Vogue* was expanded, so did the bulk of the magazine itself, from an average 170 pages in the early 1960s to a monster of 300–400 pages monthly. Though the proportion of advertising to text went up only 10 percent since the mid–1960s, the sheer number of advertising pages continued to increase. Edna Chase and Conde Nast would be proud parents of the present *Vogue*.

Notes

1. "The Press: Condé Nast." (obituary) *Time,* 28 September 1942, pp. 51–52.
2. Edna Woolman Chase, *Always in Vogue* (Garden City: Doubleday and Company, 1954), p. 160.

Information Sources

BIBLIOGRAPHY
Ballard, Bettina. *In My Fashion*. New York: David McKay Co., 1960.
Chase, Edna Woolman. *Always in Vogue*. Garden City: Doubleday, and Co., 1954.
———. "Fifty Years with Vogue." *Vogue,* 15 November 1943, p. 35.
Compaigne, Benjamin. *The Business of Consumer Magazines*. White Plains, N.Y.: Knowledge Publications, 1982.
Katz, Bill, and Linda Sternberg Katz. *Magazines for Libraries*. 5th ed. New York and London: R. R. Bowker Company, 1986.
Kissel, H. "Diana Vreeland—Empress of Fashion." *Horizon*, March 1980, pp. 26–27.
Mott, Frank Luther. *A History of American Magazines*. Vol. 4: *1885–1905*. Cambridge: Harvard University Press, 1957.
Peterson, Theodore. *Magazines in the Twentieth Century*. Urbana: University of Illinois Press, 1964.
Robinson, Walter G. "With the Makers of Vogue." *Vogue*, 1 January 1923, p. 74.
Ross, Josephine. *Beaton in Vogue*. London: Thames and Hudson, 1986.
Seebohm, Caroline. *The Man Who Was Vogue*. New York: Viking Press, 1982.
Vreeland, Diana. *D. V.* New York: Alfred A. Knopf, 1984.

Wood, James Playsted. *Magazines in the United States*. 3rd ed. New York: Ronald Press, 1971.

INDEX SOURCES

Readers' Guide (1953–present); *Abstrax; Biography Index; Magazine Index* (1977–present); *Popular Magazine Review*.

LOCATION SOURCES

Widely available. St. Louis Public Library. Available in microform.

Publication History

MAGAZINE TITLE AND TITLE CHANGES

Vogue, 1892–1936; *Vogue, incorporating Vanity Fair*, 1936–1983; *Vogue*, 1983–present.

VOLUME AND ISSUE DATA

December 1892 (vol. 1, no. 1–?)–January 29, 1910 (vol. 35, no. 5). weekly; February 15, 1910 (vol. 25, no. 7), semi-monthly; January, 1973 (vol. 161, no. 1)–present, monthly.

PUBLISHER AND PLACE OF PUBLICATION

Arthur Baldwin Turnure, 1892–1909; Conde Nast, 1909–1942; Iva V. S. Patcevitsch, 1942–1963 (Conde Nast Publishing purchased by Newhouse in 1957); Edwin F. Russell, 1963–1964; S. I. Newhouse, Jr., 1964–1970; Richard A. Shortway, 1970–present. New York.

EDITORS

Josephine Redding, 1892–1907; Marie Harrison, 1907–1914; Edna Woolman Chase, 1914–1952; Jessica Daves, 1952–1962; Diana Vreeland, 1963–1971; Grace Mirabella, 1971–1988; Anna Wintour, 1988–current.

CIRCULATION

1,217,453 (1985).

Stephanie Childs Sigala

W

ANDY WARHOL'S INTERVIEW. See INTERVIEW

WEEKLY REGISTER. See NILES' WEEKLY REGISTER

WHIG JOURNAL. See AMERICAN WHIG REVIEW

WILLIAMSPORT GRIT. See GRIT

WORLD REPORT. See U.S. NEWS AND WORLD REPORT

WORLD'S WORK

When Walter Hines Page began his new magazine, *World's Work,* in 1900, he was in search of new material, not the ''threshed over old straw'' that many magazines had covered for years. Page found one topic more vital and dynamic than any other, namely, ''the new impulse in American life, the new feeling of nationality, our coming to realize ourselves.'' Page saw ''greater promise in democracy'' than at any previous time in history. With this spirit of optimism, Page launched his publication in New York through the newly formed Doubleday, Page and Company publishing firm.[1]

The establishment of *World's Work*, a publication that bore his personal stamp, was the culmination of many years of work in journalism for Walter Page. Page was born in North Carolina and educated there through his beginning years at

Trinity College, which later became Duke University. Page completed his undergraduate work at Randolph-Macon College in Virginia and went on to graduate study in the classics at Johns Hopkins University. After two years of graduate work, he taught for a short time before beginning his work in journalism. Page started his newspaper work with the St. Joseph, Missouri *Gazette* and soon became its editor. Later he was hired by the *New York World*, after the paper printed a series of his articles on the South. When Joseph Pulitzer purchased the *New York World*, Page resigned along with the entire staff. He moved to North Carolina and published the Raleigh *State Chronicle* for eighteen months before giving up the unprofitable venture and returning to New York.[2]

In New York Page did free-lance writing until he found full-time employment with the *Brooklyn Union*. He later moved to the *New York Evening Post* and in 1887 was recruited by the *Forum** magazine to be its business manager. By 1891 he became the publication's editor, a position he held until 1895, when he resigned to join the *Atlantic Monthly.** The editorship of a highly respected publication such as the *Atlantic* represented a new pinnacle in Page's career. Although Page enjoyed success at the *Atlantic*, he never abandoned his desire to own, publish, and edit his own magazine.[3]

Page's opportunity came in 1899, when he joined forces with Frank Doubleday to form the Doubleday, Page and Company publishing firm. Doubleday and Page first concentrated on book publishing activities for the new company. However, given Page's background and editing experience, there was never any doubt the firm would publish magazines. "We must make a magazine," said Page, "must for the sheer love of it."[4]

By late 1900 Page had put together the first issue of *World's Work*. The magazine sold for twenty-five cents per issue with subscriptions at $3 per year. Page wanted to "make his new publication appeal to a wide audience of intelligent, everyday Americans." His purpose, as stated in the first issue, was to "convey the cheerful spirit of men who do things." Page was most impressed with those who achieved success or wealth, rather than with common laborers or average citizens. Although Page did print articles on workers from all walks of life, the magazine generally supported commercial and business interests. Even articles in *World's Work* that approached muckraking were usually published when it was "commercially feasible" to do so. Hence, in actuality, Page's magazine was aimed at the "mobile, middle class groups" who came closest to sharing Page's optimistic, achievement-oriented view of the country and the world.[5]

The early issues of *World's Work* set not only the tone and style of the publication, but also its format and content for over thirty years. From the outset *World's Work* was a current events magazine, a publication concerned with worldwide political, economic, and social happenings. Page also regularly covered education, agriculture, business, labor, immigration, travel, and the arts.[6]

Each issue began with a section entitled The March of Events, approximately twenty pages of brief news and commentary articles written almost exclusively by Page himself. In the first section Page covered topics such as the presidency, Congress, wars, conditions in other countries, labor unrest, and business trends. He also discussed more social and cultural issues including literature, the arts, national feeling, and intellectual life. By beginning *World's Work* with a news survey, Page was following the lead of many similar publications. The *Review of Reviews** began each issue with the Progress of the World. Other weekly publications such as the *Nation* and *Harper's Weekly* also began their issues with brief news surveys.[7]

Often interspersed within the March of Events was a collection of portraits or photographs. A single, full-page portrait or photo always opened the magazine. The first issue began with a portrait of Secretary of State John Hay, while later issues featured portraits of Andrew Carnegie, William McKinley, and Woodrow Wilson. Other cabinet members, diplomats, foreign heads of state, and prominent businessmen were also pictured. Beyond formal portraits, photographs of cities, buildings, monuments, and scenic areas were also included. In 1907 *World's Work* expanded its photographic coverage to include more portraits of famous people, as well as photos of notable places and events.

The portrait gallery was not the only section of *World's Work* that included illustrations. A major portion of the magazine was composed of original articles, many of which included a wide array of photographs. Illustrations in *World's Work* were exclusively photographs. The title page included some artwork, but virtually none was found in the pages of the magazine. The photos in *World's Work* were compared to those in *National Geographic** because both publications featured only photos, and remarkably similar photos showing "feats of technology and faraway places and exotic peoples."[8]

Following the March of Events, many original articles made up the remaining two-thirds of the magazine text. Most issues included ten to fifteen articles, each about six to ten pages; some only text, but many with accompanying photographs. *World's Work* offered its readers a great variety of articles on subjects from politics to the arts, from education to health, and from economics to inventions. One unique aspect of the magazine was that it printed no fiction. Although the absence of fiction may have been planned to avoid conflict with other Doubleday publications, Page viewed *World's Work* as a newsmagazine. As such, he saw his publication as "concerned with the present activities of the world and interpreting contemporary life," and for Page, including fiction was inconsistent with his philosophy and goals for the magazine.[9]

Fulfilling his concept of a newsmagazine, Page ran major articles on a range of national and international issues. *World's Work* covered U.S. and foreign politics regularly, especially election year politics in the United States. Page's background was traditionally Democratic, but in *World's Work* he supported the policies and candidacy of Republicans during the first decade of the twentieth century. The magazine ran a series on William Howard Taft in 1907 and a similar lengthy biography of Woodrow Wilson in 1911. In the 1912 election Page printed the individual platforms of Wilson, Taft, Theodore Roosevelt, and even Governor

Judson Harmon of Ohio. Following the election *World's Work* published Wilson's *The New Freedom* in a four-part series.[10]

Beyond domestic issues Page also stressed worldwide coverage and printed extensive articles on international politics. In April 1904, when the Russo-Japanese War broke out, Page shelved the issue he had planned to release and worked feverishly with his staff to put out a special war issue. Much the same scenario occurred in 1914 when Arthur Page published the best-selling issue on World War I. Beyond the major conflicts *World's Work* also published other feature articles on foreign countries including "Venezuela and the Problems It Presents" (December 1905), "Leaders of Japan" (January 1906), and "The Real Conditions at Panama" (November 1905).[11]

Business and commercial topics occupied nearly as much of *World's Work* as did political events. Page was a strong defender of U.S. business interests and an admirer of prominent business leaders. One of the early issues of April 1901 featured articles on Andrew Carnegie and J. Pierpont Morgan. In 1908 Page published Rockefeller's reminiscences, followed in 1910 by the recollections of James J. Hill.

Given Page's attitude toward business, he faced a serious dilemma when confronted with the muckraking era. *World's Work* indeed printed articles on abuses in many areas of business and industry. In May 1904 an article entitled "Our Enormous Pension Roll" began the magazine's ten-year crusade for pension reform. In 1905–1906 the magazine ran a series on abuses in the life insurance industry. Even though Page supported industrialists like Rockefeller and James J. Hill, he also published articles condemning Standard Oil's corrupt practices and exposing collusion between the railroads and powerful trusts.[12]

Page often seemed a "reluctant muckraker" because he disliked highly critical writing that offered no constructive solutions. When Page did engage in "the literature of exposure," he often balanced it with proposals to remedy the situation. After the series on life insurance abuses in 1906, *World's Work* published a virtual consumer's guide to the insurance industry, advising readers on the type of insurance to buy, warning against deceptive practices, and even evaluating various companies. By avoiding the stronger forms of muckraking, Page preserved his magazine both financially by not alienating advertisers, and journalistically by maintaining his policy of positive, progressive writing.[13]

The type of article that fit Page's philosophy best was exemplified in the "Uplift" issue of July 1904. This issue sought to "make an accurate measure of the people's progress" and featured articles on advances in business, in American cities, and in the arts.

Given his own rural upbringing, Page had long believed in the virtues of rural life and printed many articles on agriculture. In the January 1901 issue, *World's Work* published an article entitled "Going Back to the Soil," by J. P. Mowbray. The phrase was to become a continuing theme for the magazine. In November 1911 Page published the "Country Life" issue of *World's Work*, in which he offered the services of the magazine to provide information on acquiring farm land. Hundreds of letters were received. Page answered his readers' requests and stressed the attraction of farm life in articles and editorials.[14]

Page's southern roots also meant *World's Work* printed frequent articles on the region and its continuing problems. In June 1907 a special issue of *World's Work* was devoted to the South. The magazine also published articles by major black writers including Booker T. Washington, W.E.B. Du Bois, and Robert R. Moton. Doubleday, Page and Company had originally published *Up From Slavery*, and beginning in October 1910 *World's Work* serialized Washington's next work, *Chapters from My Experiences.*[15]

Education was another area of interest to Page. In 1903–1904 *World's Work* ran a series of articles on American public schools by Adele Marie Shaw. She examined many school systems from the cities of New York and Philadelphia to the country schools of Indiana and Illinois. In December 1910 the magazine sponsored a contest to attract the best articles on "The Boy (or Girl) of Tomorrow: What the School Will Do For Him (or Her)." Over 300 articles were received, and the prize winners were published in the April through July 1911 issues.[16]

World's Work lived up to its name by covering the working world from many different vantage points. In the early years the magazine explored various jobs through the "Day's Work" series. The articles began with the "Day's Work of an Arctic Hunter" in November 1900 and included the typical day of a stock-broker (July 1901), a cattle rancher (January 1902), and a schoolteacher (June 1902), as well as following a day in the regular army (January 1903). The magazine also published articles on unions, eventually taking an anti-union stance with articles such as "The Fight for Open Shop" (December 1905) and the 1913 series "The Labor War."

Beyond the range of articles in *World's Work*, the magazine also carried sections on special subjects. In covering reviews of new books and the book trade, *World's Work* used the sections entitled Appraisals of New Books and The Work of the Book World. These sections gradually diminished, and for several years no regular columns on books appeared. In the early 1920s *World's Work* resumed coverage of books with a section called The Red Letter Book Guide.

Two sections on working people were featured during the magazine's first decade. Short Stories of Men Who Work offered sketches on particular individuals or specific incidents. Among the World's Workers gave a "first hand report of the most important events and tendencies in industry and in the professions."[17]

Other special sections were carried for a few years as changes were made in the magazine. In 1905 the New Science of Business began featuring short articles on business procedures and management techniques. In 1912 to 1915 the March of the Cities chronicled the rise in prosperity, the developments in business, and the betterment of U.S. cities. In 1913 Man and His Machines presented new inventions as well as improvements in existing machines and processes.

As with many periodicals, the size, number of articles, illustrations, and overall quality of *World's Work* rose and fell with its financial and advertising fortunes.

Initially, Doubleday, Page and company did not invest great sums of money in the publication of *World's Work*. Even Page himself felt the magazine had to pay for itself shortly after it began or the firm would not continue to publish it. Fortunately for Page and his magazine, success did come quickly.[18]

World's Work began with printing 35,000 copies. Within six months there were 16,000 subscribers. The magazine contained 115 to 120 small quarto-size pages of text and illustrations, plus a section of advertising. By the end of the first year *World's Work* ran 100 pages of advertising. Perhaps 10 to 15 pages were ads for Doubleday publications. Another 20 percent of the advertising was for correspondence courses and subscriptions to books and periodicals. The remaining 60 to 70 pages of ads covered the spectrum from travel to schools, to automobiles, to consumer goods and financial services. Page ran some regular articles in the advertising section, a technique he had used as editor of the *Forum*.[19]

From its inception until 1910, Page and a staff of four people published *World's Work*. Page wrote much of the material himself, while relying on outside writers for most feature articles. The remaining staff members were two editorial assistants, a financial manager who handled the business writing, and a managing editor who served as the administrator for the publication.[20]

During the first decade, circulation increased steadily, to 64,000 in 1903 and up to 100,000 by 1907. Although exact financial figures for the magazine are difficult to determine, the publishing company was definitely prospering. The firm published other magazines including *Garden Magazine and Farming* and *Country Life in America* in addition to its book publications. In 1910 Doubleday, Page and Company, after twice outgrowing its facilities, moved to new quarters at Garden City, Long Island. In the same year the publishing firm grossed $215,000, of which *World's Work* brought in $35,000. By 1911–1912 the company's profits were up to $330,000, with *World's Work* making up $40,000, a good deal less than *Country Life*, which contributed $58,000.[21]

In 1910 circulation of *World's Work* was at 126,500, a figure that held nearly steady for the next two years. As the magazine grew, Page increased his staff of established writers. In 1905 Page's second son, Arthur, joined the magazine as a cub reporter after his graduation from Harvard. Over the years Arthur Page gradually took on more responsibility and in 1911 was named managing editor. In 1913 when his father was appointed U.S. ambassador to Great Britain, the younger Page became editor of the magazine.[22]

In 1913 Arthur Page hired Burton J. Hendrick to be his managing editor. Hendrick had many years of experience, first as a reporter and editor of the *New Haven Morning News* and the *New York Evening Post*, and later as a writer for *McClure's** magazine, where he had been for eight years prior to joining *World's Work*.[23]

Although circulation had slipped in the year immediately preceding World War I, Arthur Page and Burton Hendrick capitalized on the war to increase their readership. When the conflict broke out in Europe, the September 1914 issue was already in press. Page stopped the run and completely redesigned and rewrote the magazine into a "War Manual," 136 pages of articles on all aspects of the developing conflict. The war issue sold nearly 300,000 copies and began an increase in circulation that averaged 140,000 during the war years.[24]

In 1915 the publishing company began a Spanish edition of *World's Work*, entitled *Revista del Mundo*, a quarterly that ran for about six years. Also during World War I color illustrations were introduced. The first color portrait was of railroad magnate James J. Hill in the December 1916 issue. In 1917 color photos increased to four pages per issue. In 1918 the price of the magazine was raised to 35 cents per issue with annual subscriptions at $4. In 1919 color photos were dropped as circulation began a postwar decline until it reached a low of 104,000 in 1923. In the same year Arthur Page revised the magazine totally, once again using color photos and adding new sections. The changes revived circulation somewhat up to 116,000, but by late 1924 the color pictures were again dropped and the quality of the illustrations in general declined. More efforts were made to restructure the magazine by adding and deleting departments.[25]

In late 1926 *World's Work* suffered another blow when Arthur Page resigned to join the American Telephone and Telegraph Company as vice-president for public relations. Carl C. Dickey, who had been managing editor under Page, took over the editor's position. From this period on, *World's Work* was in a state of flux as editors came and went and changes in format were attempted. Dickey held the editor's position only until mid–1928, when Barton Currie from the *Ladies' Home Journal* was hired. Currie lasted only months, and by 1929 Russell Doubleday had taken over as editor. To his credit, Russell Doubleday, brother of the owner Frank Doubleday, tried to breathe new life into the faltering magazine. Beginning with the January 1929 issue, the magazine's format was changed to the full quarto-size pages; text and illustrations ran 140 to 200 pages, and advertising added another 60 pages or more. Due to the changes, circulation rose dramatically to 150,000, and advertising topped $500,000.[26]

The new prosperity of *World's Work* was short-lived. With the stock market crash of 1929 and the following years of economic depression, the magazine soon faced serious financial problems. By 1930 circulation was down to 127,000, and by 1932 only 77,000 copies were printed. Income from advertising dropped by over half, to $219,000. Finally, in July 1932, *World's Work* was sold to Albert Shaw, who merged it with his own *Review of Reviews*.[27]

The demise of *World's Work* was related to several factors operating at the time. As a monthly news and commentary magazine, it faced serious competition from the weekly *Time** magazine, which began in 1923. Internally the magazine was a source of conflict between Arthur Page and Frank Doubleday. In the mid–1920s, ten years before *Life** magazine appeared, Doubleday wanted his company to publish a picture magazine. Page saw the value and appeal of such a publication, but disagreed strongly when Doubleday sought to make *World's Work* into his picture publication. After Page resigned, efforts were made to turn *World's Work* into a picture showcase, but with the magazine already in decline, the efforts soon proved futile. By the late 1920s, the publishing firm as a whole made a concerted effort to rid itself of the problematic magazine publishing business and concentrate on book publishing instead. With Arthur Page, the real defender of *World's Work*, gone from the scene, there was little enthusiasm or impetus among the remaining staff to continue publication of the magazine.[28]

Notes

1. Burton J. Hendrick, *The Life and Letters of Walter H. Page*, 3 vols. (Garden City, N.Y.: Doubleday, Page and Co., 1923), 1:69.

2. Robert J. Rusnak, *Walter Hines Page and the "World's Work," 1900–1913* (Washington, D.C.: University Press of America, 1982), pp. 1–9.

3. Ibid., pp. 11–19.

4. John Milton Cooper, Jr., *Walter Hines Page: The Southerner as American, 1855–1918* (Chapel Hill: University of North Carolina Press, 1977), pp. 175–76; Walter Hines Page, "A Word on a Birthday," *World's Work*, November 1902, p. 2695.

5. Hendrick, 1:71; Walter Hines Page, "The March of Events," *World's Work*, November 1900, p. 3; Rusnak, pp. 42, 52; Cooper, p. 186.

6. Rusnak, p. 41.

7. Cooper, p. 177.

8. Ibid., pp. 181–82.

9. Ibid., pp. 179–83.

10. Frank Luther Mott, *A History of American Magazines*, 5 vols. (Cambridge: Harvard University Press, 1930–1968), 4:782; Rusnak, pp. 60–61.

11. Rusnak, p. 43; Mott, 4:783.

12. Mott, 4:777–78.

13. Cooper, pp. 184–85; Mott, 4: 777.

14. Rusnak, pp. 46, 59–60.

15. Mott, 4:789; Rusnak, pp. 44, 51.

16. Mott:, 4:776, 781; Walter Hines Page, "$500 for School Articles," *World's Work*, December 1910, p. 13719; Walter Hines Page, "The School of Tomorrow," *World's Work*, April 1911, pp. 14190–91.

17. "Among the World's Workers," *World's Work*, November 1900, p. 110.

18. Page, "A Word on a Birthday," pp. 2695–96.

19. Rusnak, pp. 28–29; Cooper, pp. 176, 185–86.

20. Cooper, p. 183.

21. Rusnak, pp. 29–30.

22. Rusnak, p. 31; Noel L. Griese, "He Walked in the Shadows: Public Relations Counsel Arthur W. Page," *Public Relations Quarterly*, Fall 1976, p. 9.

23. Cooper, p. 183; John A. Garraty and Edward T. James, eds., *Dictionary of American Biography: Supplement Four 1946–1950* (New York: Charles Scribner's Sons, 1974), s.v. "Hendrick, Burton Jesse," by Joseph Frazier Wall.

24. Mott, 4:783.

25. Mott, 4:783–84, 786.

26. Griese, p. 10; Mott, 4: 787.

27. Mott, 4:788; Theodore Peterson, *Magazines of the Twentieth Century* (Urbana: University of Illinois Press, 1956), pp. 140–41.

28. Walter Dixon Anderson, "A Study of the Causes of Failure of Prominent Periodicals, 1926–1956" (M.A. thesis, University of Georgia, 1958), pp. 36–38.

Information Sources

BIBLIOGRAPHY

"Among the World's Workers." *World's Work,* November 1900, p. 110.

Anderson, Walter Dixon. "A Study of the Causes of Failure of Prominent Periodicals, 1926–1956." M. A. thesis, University of Georgia, 1958.

Cooper, John Milton, Jr. *Walter Hines Page: The Southerner as American, 1855–1918.* Chapel Hill: University of North Carolina Press, 1977.

Garraty, John A., and Edward T. James, eds. *Dictionary of American Biography.* Supplement Four 1946–1950. New York: Charles Scribner's Sons, 1974. S. V. "Hendrick, Burton Jesse," by Joseph Frazier Wall.

Griese, Noel L. "He Walked in the Shadows: Public Relations Counsel Arthur W. Page." *Public Relations Quarterly,* Fall 1976, pp. 8–15.

Hendrick, Burton J. *The Life and Letters of Walter H. Page.* 3 vols. Garden City, N.Y.: Doubleday, Page & Co., 1923.

Mott, Frank Luther. *A History of American Magazines.* 5 vols. Cambridge: Harvard University Press, 1930–1968.

Page, Walter Hines. "$500 for School Articles." *World's Work,* December 1910, p. 13719.

———. "The March of Events." *World's Work,* November 1900, p. 3.

———. "The School of Tomorrow." *World's Work,* April 1911 pp. 14190–91.

———. "A Word on a Birthday." *World's Work,* November 1902, pp. 2695–2699.

Peterson, Theodore. *Magazines of the Twentieth Century.* Urbana: University of Illinois Press, 1956.

Rusnak, Robert J. *Walter Hines Page and the "World's Work," 1900–1913.* Washington, D.C.: University Press of America, 1982.

INDEX SOURCES

Poole's Index (1901–1906); *Readers' Guide to Periodical Literature* (1900–1932); *Engineering Index* (1901–1914).

LOCATION SOURCES

Most major academic libraries and public libraries hold some issues. According to *The Union List of Serials,* over 300 libraries hold this title. Available in microform.

Publication History

MAGAZINE TITLE AND TITLE CHANGES

The World's Work, November 1900–July 1932. Merged with *Review of Reviews* to form *Review of Reviews and World's Work,* September 1932–July 1937.

VOLUME AND ISSUE DATA

Monthly. Vols. 1–56 (semiannual volumes, May-October, November-April), May 1900–October 1928; vol. 57, November-December 1928; vols. 58–60 (annual volumes divided into Part 1, January-June, and Part 2 July-December), 1929–

1931; vol. 61, January-July 1932, complete in seven numbers. Volumes 1–22 are paged continuously, pp. 1–15010.

PUBLISHER AND PLACE OF PUBLICATION

Doubleday, Page and Company, 1900–1926; Doubleday, Doran and Company, 1927–1932. New York.

EDITORS

Walter Hines Page, 1900–1913; Arthur Wilson Page, 1913–1926; Carl C. Dickey, 1927–1928; Barton Currie, 1928–1929; Russell Doubleday, 1929–1931; Alan C. Collins, 1931–1932.

CIRCULATION

Began at 35,000 in 1900; maximum circulation was 150,000 in 1929; in 1932, when the magazine merged with *Review of Reviews,* circulation was 77,000.

Vanette Schwartz

___ Y ___

YANKEE

Yankee magazine was born in Dublin, New Hampshire, in the midst of the Great Depression as the brainchild of an out-of-work writer named Robb Sagendorph, who decided to found his own magazine as a means of getting published. Between March and September 1935, the magazine took form as a country-oriented publication celebrating the disappearing traditions and down-home philosophy of small-town New England. The magazine has remained essentially the same ever since with one important change in format, from full-size to digest, and some modernization along the way. The magazine's popularity extends far beyond the boundaries of New England, and has spawned a whole publishing empire that now includes the *Old Farmer's Almanac* (since 1941), numerous cookbooks, several hardbound anthologies, calendars, guidebooks, including *Yankee Magazine's Travel Guide to New England* (1972–   ), and three other magazines: *New England Business* (1953–   ), *Alaska* (since 1986), and *Yankee Homes* (1984–   ).

In the first issue in 1935, Robb Sagendorph wrote: "*Yankee's* destiny is the expression and perhaps, indirectly, the preservation of that great culture in which every Yank was born and by which every real Yank must live."[1] Over the years Sagendorph and the present editor, his nephew Judson Hale, Sr., have succeeded in creating an image of New England that is fondly regarded even by those who have never lived there. In fact, *Yankee* has been credited with raising the consciousness of New Englanders concerning their own heritage to the point where preservation efforts now re-create towns that are worthy of inclusion in the magazine. In 1985 Judson Hale said, "We represent the New England myth. But it's less of a myth now than it was when *Yankee* started. New England has caught on—it cleaned up the town greens, put a bandstand in the middle, painted the churches white, and kept the shopping malls outside of town."[2]

From the beginning the magazine contained articles written by professional but country-oriented authors. Traditions of the six New England states such as square dancing and bundling were rediscovered and written up in the magazine. For several years *Yankee's* emphasis was on poetry, fiction, and essays, then gradually it became more of a vehicle for folklore and nostalgia. When Judson Hale joined the staff in 1958, he reorganized the layout and design. Hale brought a preppy (Choate and Dartmouth) background and youthful enthusiasm to the magazine and has settled into life in New Hampshire with all the verve of a successful entrepreneur. Since becoming editor in 1970, when Robb Sagendorph died, he has established a standard of professionalism that continues to maintain the folksy appeal of the magazine. At the same time Sagendorph's son-in-law Rob Trowbridge became publisher, and the two have worked together as a team to keep the magazine going in the tradition of its founder, but with adaptations to modern taste.

Each issue adheres to a broad formula that includes painting, photographs, fiction, humor, people, current issues, nostalgia, history, antiques, and the home.[3] Early issues were all black and white, but as time went on, color was added. Beatrix Sagendorph, cofounder of the magazine with her husband, contributed numerous cover paintings. The color centerfold shows a typical New England scene. The tone is uplifting and positive. Feature stories are not restricted to New England settings, but generally have a regional tie-in, sometimes contrived for the occasion. Stories are often first-person accounts even when they are fictional, and have an emphasis on rural adventure, animals, and natural disasters. Nonfiction is practical, folksy, and deals only with New England. Although there have been more articles in recent years that deal with environmental and social problems, there is always an attempt to present a solution, to end on a positive note. Awards are given each year for the best fiction and poetry, and periodically for art and photography.

There are also a number of monthly departments, some of which, like the Swoppers Column (which began in 1935 when, as a joke, editor Sagendorph bartered away his pressman's false teeth), have become legendary. The other departments are a potpourri of advice, descriptions of choice real estate for sale, elusive products sought and found, and the Traveler's Journal, which provides such services as a regionwide listing of summer band concerts (July 1988). *Yankee's* recipes have been gathered into several published collections and feature regional, ethnic, and sometimes offbeat specialties.

The advertisements, one of the most popular features with readers, must be in keeping with the philosophy of the magazine or must present the product in a New England setting. Cigarette and liquor ads are not accepted, nor are products of questionable worth. Formerly the ads were for New England products, but in the mid–1970s the publisher started accepting national advertising. Ninety percent of the ads are for mail-order companies such as L. L. Bean, Deerskin, Trading Post, and hundreds of small entrepreneurs selling everything from squirrel repellent to baby cradles. Although a full-page black-and-white advertisement costs $11,660 and a color page $15,625, most of the ads are only a few lines—well within the reach of small businesses. Advertising pages have held steady in the range of 1,100 to 1,200 in recent years.[4]

Yankee's appeal is nationwide and international. The Swoppers Column engenders responses from as far away as Australia. In 1986, 65 percent of the subscribers lived outside New England,[5] 9 percent were in the West, 14 percent in the South, and 1 percent were overseas. The rest were in the Mid-Atlantic and North Central areas.[6] The subscribers, whose median age is fifty-seven, are incredibly loyal and are completely oblivious to detractors of the magazine who call it quaint and schmaltzy. Competitors who have attempted to produce regional magazines with more social relevance find that they must look somewhere other than the *Yankee* readership for subscribers. Mediamark Research reported in 1983 that *Yankee* circulates more magazines than *Fortune, Saturday Evening Post,* Forbes, Esquire,* and Business Week*. Its circulation is twice that of the *New Yorker*.[7] Subscription renewal rate exceeds 80 percent, and the publishers claim that many of those who don't renew have died. The $19.95 per year subscription rate ($1.95 per single issue) is still modest and affordable, and many subscriptions are gifts. The original subscriber list of 612 has now risen to over a million, and requires the services of over 100 computer terminals to process. The magazine continues to acknowledge each renewal, with typical Yankee shrewdness, including flyers for Yankee Publishing's numerous other publications.

In 1983 the magazine established a restoration internship program by asking each subscriber to contribute twenty-five cents to a fund to pay college students working on projects under the auspices of the National Trust for Historic Preservation. Each year approximately forty interns work for twelve weeks each on small-town and rural projects. *Yankee* readers pay 60 percent of the cost, and local community sponsors pay the rest.

The digest format continues to be *Yankee's* most distinctive feature, reinforcing its practical image as a handy magazine for the lunch box, the flight bag, or the shelves in the summer cabin. Like the *National Geographic** and *Reader's Digest,* Yankee* is difficult to throw away. It is not slick and glossy, nor would its readers have it that way. *Yankee* is like an old friend, and no doubt will continue to be for years to come.

Notes

1. Judson D. Hale, Sr., *The Best of Yankee Magazine; 50 years of New England* (Dublin, N. H., Yankee Publishing, 1985), p. 10.

2. David Shribman, "Rural New England has a Bulletin Board That Turns a Profit; Yankee Magazine Celebrates Virtues of Small Towns; Critics Find It Schmaltzy," *Wall Street Journal*, 29 October 1985, p. 20.

3. Ron Winslow, "The Pride of Yankee," *Boston Magazine*, October 1980, p. 186.

4. Hamilton Allan, "Yankee's Reach Exceeds Its Deep Roots; Magazine Shows New England to the World," *Los Angeles Times*, 17 November 1983, p. 1B, p. 14.

5. Margaret LeRoux, "Economy Writes New Chapter for Magazines," *Advertising Age*, 25 May 1986, p. S5.

6. Allan, "Yankee's Reach," p. 14.

7. Ibid.

Information Sources

BIBLIOGRAPHY

Allan, Hamilton. "Yankee's Reach Exceeds Its Deep Roots; Magazine Shows New England to the World." *Los Angeles Times,* 17 November 1983.

Carlson, Eugene. "Yankee . . . " *Wall Street Journal,* 22 February 1983.

———. "Yankee Magazine's Publishers . . . " *Wall Street Journal,* 15 April 1986.

———. "Yankee's Ingenuity: A Restoration Fee." *Wall Street Journal,* 28 February 1984.

DeVries, Hilary. "Yankee 'Swoppers' Trade Tuxedos for Spaniels and Pecans for Bamboo." *Christian Science Monitor,* 28 March 1984.

Hale, Judson D., Sr. *The Best of Yankee Magazine; 50 years of New England.* Dublin, N. H.: Yankee Publishing, 1985.

Katz, Bill, and Linda Sternberg Katz. *Magazines for Libraries.* 5th ed. New York; Bowker, 1986, p. 240 (and previous editions).

LeRoux, Margaret. "Economy Writes New Chapter for Magazines." *Advertising Age,* 25 May 1986, p. S5.

McGrath, Anne. "Yankee Fans in for a Real Treat." *Wilson Library Bulletin,* October 1985, p. 41.

Shribman, David. "Rural New England Has a Bulletin Board That Turns a Profit; Yankee Magazine Celebrates Virtues of Small Towns; Critics Find It Schmaltzy." *Wall Street Journal,* 29 October 1985.

Winslow, Ron. "The Pride of Yankee." *Boston Magazine,* October 1980, pp. 126, 182–86.

INDEX SOURCES

Access (1975–present); *Popular Magazine Review; Abstrax; Magazine Index* (1977–present); *Popular Periodical Index* (1975–present). By publisher.

LOCATION SOURCES

New York Public Library; University of Illinois Library, Urbana-Champaign. Available in microform.

Publication History

MAGAZINE TITLE AND TITLE CHANGES

Yankee: A Monthly Magazine for Yankees Everywhere (subtitle varies). Absorbed *Leisure: The Magazine of a Thousand Diversions* in 1939.

VOLUME AND ISSUE DATA

Vols. 1–8, September 1935–November 1941; vol. 9–present, August 1945–present, monthly. Suspended December 1942–July 1945. Index vols. 1–5, 1935–1939.

PUBLISHER AND PLACE OF PUBLICATION
Yankee Publishing, Inc.: Robb Sagendorph, 1935–1969; C. Robertson Trow-bridge, 1970–1989; Joseph B. Meagher, 1989–present. Dublin, New Hampshire.
EDITORS
Robb Sagendorph, 1935–1969; Judson D. Hale, Sr., 1970–present.
CIRCULATION
1,018,245.

Constance A. Fairchild

Appendix: Chronology of Mass-Market Titles

1880   The Chautauquan
1881   Liberty
1882   Argosy
       Grit
1886   Cosmopolitan
       Forum
1888   Collier's
       National Geographic
1890   Literary Digest
       Review of Reviews
1892   Vogue
1893   McClure's Magazine
1896   New York Times Magazine
1897   Success
       The Survey
1898   Sunset
1899   Everybody's Magazine
1900   The Smart Set
       World's Work
1901   Travel-Holiday
1902   Popular Mechanics
1903   Redbook
1913   Vanity Fair
1914   New Republic
1919   True Story
1920   Architectural Digest
1922   Reader's Digest
1923   Time
1924   American Mercury
       New Leader
       Saturday Review
1926   National Enquirer
       Parents
       U.S. News and World Report
1928   Mechanix Illustrated
1930   GQ: Gentleman's Quarterly
1932   Family Circle
1933   Esquire
       Newsweek
1935   Yankee

1936   Consumer Reports
       Coronet
       Life

1937   Look

1941   Parade

1942   Organic Gardening

1947   Changing Times

1949   American Heritage

1950   Prevention

1951   High Fidelity

1953   Playboy
       TV Guide
       USA Weekend

1955   Village Voice
       National Review

1956   Bon Appétit
       Horizon
       Modern Maturity

1962   Ramparts

1966   Crawdaddy

1967   Psychology Today
       Rolling Stone

1968   New York

1969   Health

1970   Early American Life
       Interview Magazine
       Mother Earth News
       Smithsonian

1971   Travel & Leisure

1972   Money
       Ms.

1973   Americana
       New Times
       Playgirl
       Texas Monthly

1974   High Times
       People Weekly

1976   Mother Jones

1977   Us

1978   Omni

1979   Geo

1983   M Magazine

Selected Bibliography

Material on individual titles will be found following the history of that title.

Allen, Frederick Lewis. "American Magazines, 1741–1941." *Bulletin of the New York Public Library*, 45, no. 5 (June 1941), pp. 439–60.

Bogart, Leo. "Magazines since the Rise of Television." *Journalism Quarterly*, Spring 1956, pp. 153–66.

Burnett, Leo. "The Mission of Magazines." *Saturday Review*, 26 December 1959, p. 52.

The Changing Face of Magazines. New York: Television Bureau of Advertising, 1959.

Cort, David. *Revolution by Cliché*. New York: Funk and Wagnalls, 1970.

Drewrey, John E. *Contemporary American Magazines*. Athens: University of Georgia Press, 1940.

————. *Some Magazines and Their Makers*. Boston: Stratford Co., 1924.

Edwards, Jackson. "One Every Minute: The Picture Magazines." *Scribner's Magazine*, May 1938, pp. 17–23.

Eight Leading Magazines: Characteristics of Their Readers and Households. Pleasantville, N.Y.: Reader's Digest, 1962.

Emery, Edwin. *The Press and America*. Englewood Cliffs, N.J.: Prentice-Hall, 1972.

Faxon, F. W., et al., eds. *Cumulated Magazine Subject Index 1907–1949*. Boston: G. K. Hall, 1964.

The Folio: 400. New Canaan, Conn.: Folio Publishing Co, annual since 1981.

Gale Directory of Publications: An annual Guide to Newspapers, Magazines, Journals, and Related Publications. Detroit: Gale Research, annual. (Formerly *Ayers Directory of Publications*.)

Garwood, Irving. *The American Periodicals from 1850 to 1860*. Macomb, Ill.: Author, 1931.

Gidal, Tim N. *Modern Photojournalism: Origin and Evolution*. New York: Collier Macmillan, 1973.

Ford, James L. C. *Magazines for Millions: The Story of Specialized Publications*. Carbondale: Southern Illinois University Press, 1969.

Hartman, E. P. "Magazines: Moulders of Opinion." *Wilson Library Bulletin*, April 1947, pp. 600–602.

Hoornstra, Jean. *American Periodicals, 1741–1900: An Index to the Microfilm Collections, American Periodical Series: The Eighteenth Century, American Periodical Series: 1800–1850, Civil War and Reconstruction: 1850–1900.* Ann Arbor, Mich.: University Microfilms International, 1979.

Iverson, William. "The Pious Pornographers." *Playboy*, October 1957, pp. 24–26.

Kerr, W. A., and H. H. Remmers. "Cultural Value of 100 Representative American Magazines." *School and Society*, 22 November 1941, pp. 476–80.

Loehwing, David A. "Back in Circulation." *Barron's*, 4 February 1963, p. 3.

Marconi, Joseph V. *Indexed Periodicals.* Ann Arbor, Mich.: Pierian Press, 1976.

Miller, Merle. "Freedom to Read: Magazines." *Survey Graphic*, December 1946, pp. 462–67.

Mott, Frank Luther. *A History of American Magazines.* 5 vols. Cambridge, Mass.: Harvard University Press, Belknap Press, 1930–1968.

————. "The Magazine Revolution and Popular Ideas in the Nineties." *Proceedings of the American Antiquarian Society*, vol. 64, part 1 (April 1954), pp. 195–214.

————. "A Twentieth Century Monster: The Mass Audience." *Saturday Review*, 8 October 1960, pp. 59–60.

Paine, Frank R., and Nancy E. Paine. *Magazines: A Bibliography for Their Analysis, with Annotations and Study Guide.* Metuchen, N. J.: Scarecrow Press, 1987.

Peterson, Theodore. *Magazines in the Twentieth Century.* Urbana: University of Illinois Press, 1964.

————. "Magazines and the Challenge of Change." *Quill*, November 1966, p. 44.

Poole, William F. *Poole's Index to Periodical Literature* (1802–1906). rev. ed. New York: Peter Smith, 1938.

Repellier, Agnes. "American Magazines." *Yale Review*, 16 (1926–1927), pp. 261–74.

Richardson, Lyon. *A History of Early American Magazines.* New York: Thomas Nelson and Sons, 1931.

Ruckner, Bryce W. *The First Freedom.* Carbondale: Southern Illinois University Press, 1968.

Schacht, John H. *A Bibliography for the Study of Magazines.* Urbana: University of Illinois College of Journalism and Communications, 1968.

————. *The Journals of Opinion and Reportage: An Assessment.* New York: Magazine Publishers Association, 1965.

Seldes, Gilbert. *The Great Audience.* New York: Viking Press, 1950.

"Special Report: Magazines," *Advertising Age*, annually in October.

Standard Periodical Directory. New York: Oxbridge Communications, Inc., annual.

Stephens, Ethel. *American Popular Magazines: A Bibliography.* Boston: Book Company, 1916.

Swan, Carroll J. *Magazines in the U.S.A.* New York: Magazine Publishers Association, 1964.

Taft, William H. *American Magazines for the 1980's.* New York: Hastings House, 1982.

Tassin, Algernon. *The Magazine in America.* New York: Dodd, Mead, 1916.

Tebbel, John. *The American Magazine: A Compact History.* New York: Hawthorne Press, 1969.

"There's Life in the Mass Magazines." *Business Week*, 13 October 1973, pp. 84–87.

Titus, Edna B. *Union List of Serials in Libraries of the United States and Canada.* 3rd ed. New York: HW. Wilson, 1965.

Ulrich's International Periodical Directory: A Classified Guide to Periodicals Foreign and Domestic. New York: R. R. Bowker, annual.

United States Library of Congress. *New Serial Titles: A Union List Of Serials.* New York and London: R. R. Bowker, 1950–

van Zuilen, A. J. *The Life Cycle of Magazines.* Uithoorn, The Netherlands: Graduate Press, 1977.

Weeks, Edward. "The Place of Magazines in America." *Quill*, September 1962, pp. 14–16.

Wolseley, Roland E. *The Changing Magazine.* New York: Hastings House, 1973.

———. *The Magazine World.* New York: Prentice-Hall, 1951.

———. *Understanding Magazines.* Ames: Iowa State University Press, 1969.

Wood, James Playsted. *Magazines in the United States.* New York: Ronald Press, 1956.

———. *Of Lasting Interest.* New York: Doubleday and Co., 1967.

Woodward, Helen. *The Lady Persuaders.* New York: Ivan Obolensky, 1960.

Index

Contributors

MARY BETH ALLEN is Assistant Undergraduate Librarian and Assistant Professor of Library Administration at the Undergraduate Library, University of Illinois at Urbana where she coordinates the bibliographic instruction program and reference service. She holds an M.A. in Teaching English as an International Language and an M.S. in Library and Information Science, both from the University of Illinois.

ROBERT S. ALLEN is currently employed by Louisiana State University as a Reference Librarian and is Library Consultant for the Louisiana Transportation Research Center. He has an M.S. in geology from Southern Illinois University and an M.S. in library and information science from the University of Illinois.

BYRON ANDERSON is assistant professor and general reference librarian at Founders Memorial Library, Northern Illinois University. He holds an M.A. and an M.L.S. from the University of Wisconsin-Milwaukee.

GLENN ANDERSON is Head, Humanities Department, at Auburn University, Ralph B. Draughon Library, Auburn, Alabama. He holds an M.A. in English from S.U.N.Y. at Albany and an M.A. in Library Science from Florida State University.

DANIEL BOICE has master's degrees in history and in library science from the University of Michigan. He is Assistant Reference Librarian at the Thomas Cooper Library at the University of South Carolina in Columbia.

JANE T. BRADFORD is an instructor and reference librarian at the duPont-Ball Library at Stetson University in DeLand, Florida. She holds a Master of Science Degree in Library and Information Science from the University of Illinois in Urbana/Champaign and a Master of Arts degree in English from Pennsylvania State University.

NANCY BUCHANAN is Assistant Instructional Services Librarian at Sterling C. Evans Library, Texas A&M University, College Station. She received an M.A. in Library Science from the University of Illinois and an M.A. in Communication from Purdue University.

JUDITH BUNKER has an M.A. in English Literature from the University of California at Los Angeles and an M.A. in anthropology from the University of California at Davis. She is an instructor in English Composition at Southeast Missouri State University.

PATRICIA A. CANNON is assistant professor in the Department of Library and Information studies at Northern Illinois University. She has an M.A. from West Texas State University, and she also holds both an M.L.S. and a Ph.D. in library and information studies from Texas Woman's University. She has published articles on education and guidance and for *The Who's Who of Nobel Prize Winners*.

BEVERLEY CHILDRESS holds a master's degree in counseling from the University of Alabama. She is the academic administrator and computer science teacher at Chambers Academy in Lafayette, Alabama.

BOYD CHILDRESS has an M.A. in history and a master of library science from the University of Alabama. He is social science reference librarian at Auburn University in Auburn, Alabama. He is the author of numerous book reviews in *Library Journal* and other review sources and of articles in the *Journal of Library History* and the *Southeastern Librarian*. At present, he is working on a history of Putnam's as a publisher of travel literature during the 1850s.

DIANA A. CHLEBEK has a Ph.D. in Comparative Literature from Cornell University. She is a bibliographer of fine arts and literature in Bierce Library at the University of Akron. She has published research on the history of journalism and on prose fiction.

KATHERINE DAHL has a master of arts in library science from the University of Minnesota and a master of science in education from the University of North Dakota. She is a reference librarian and assistant professor at the Western Illinois University Library.

CONSTANCE A. FAIRCHILD has an M.S. in library science from the University of Illinois in Urbana where she currently serves in the Reference Department. She has also been serials librarian at the University of Lagos Library,

Lagos, Nigeria, while a Peace Corps Volunteer. Since 1974 she has been a reviewer for *Library Journal* and *Reprint Bulletin-Book Reviews* in crafts and decorative arts.

RONNIE W. FAULKNER holds a Ph.D. in history from the University of South Carolina and an M.S.L.S. from the University of North Carolina at Chapel Hill. He is Librarian and Assistant Professor of History at Campbell University in Buies Creek, North Carolina. He has authored numerous articles in the fields of librarianship, history, and political science.

ROBERT W. FRIZZELL is Director, Olin C. Bailey Library at Hendrix College in Conway, Arkansas.

IRENE HANSEN is Resident Librarian in the Special Collections Department, University Library, University of Illinois at Chicago. She received her M.S. in Library and Information Science from the University of Illinois at Urbana-Champaign. She is coeditor of "Rethinking the History of Religion in Chicago: A Symposium." *The Newberry Papers in Family and Community History*, Chicago: Newberry Library, 1986.

JAMES HART is head of Public Service in the Law Library at the University of Cincinnati. He holds an M.A. in Classics and an M.S.L.S. from the University of Southern California.

DAVID HAURY is Assistant Director of the Kansas State Historical Society, Topeka, Kansas. From 1985 to 1989 he served as editor of the Newsletter of the Midwest Archives Conference and on the Kansas State Historical Records Advisory Board. His educational background includes a Ph.D. in history from Harvard University and an M.S. in library science from the University of Illinois.

DEAN HOWD is a librarian at Western Illinois University. He holds an M.A. in Theater from the University of Iowa and an M.L.S. from Rosary College.

DENA HUTTO is a cataloger and English Subject Specialist at the University of Wyoming in Laramie. She has a master of science in library and information science from the University of Illinois at Champaign-Urbana as well as advanced coursework in English.

CECILE JAGODZINSKI is head of the cataloging department for Milner Library at Illinois State University. She received the M.L.S. from the State University of New York at Buffalo and a master's degree in English from Northwestern University. She has also completed a certificate of advanced study at the University of Chicago, with a concentration in the history of the book.

SUSAN JOHNS is Systems/Circulation Librarian at the Axe Library, Pittsburg State University, Pittsburg, Kansas. She received a B.A. in English and music from Southwestern College, Winfield, Kansas, and a M.S. in library and information science from the University of Illinois, Urbana-Champaign.

DOROTHY JONES is General Reference Librarian, Coordinator of Library Services for the Physically Impaired and Coordinator of Information Services at Northern Illinois University Libraries, DeKalb, Illinois. She has an M.R.E. from Union Theological Seminary in New York and an M.L.S. from the University of California at Berkeley. She has published a number of articles on librarianship and has contributed to *American Reference Book Annual* and *Index to Reviews of Bibliographic Publications*.

DAVID R. KOHUT has an M.A. in anthropology from State University of New York at Binghamton and an M.L.S. from State University of New York at Albany. He is Social Sciences Reference Librarian at the University Library, Tennesee Technological University, Cookeville. He has published an article in *Collection Building,* prepared a resource guide for the *Book of Days 1989,* and is co-compiler of a bibliography on Latin American women authors.

ABIGAIL LOOMIS is Coordinator for Library User Education at the University of Wisconsin–Madison. She has publications on library history, library personnel issues and serial bibliographies in literature. She recently coedited a special issue of *Illinois Libraries* and has published an article on bibliographic instruction in the Fall 1987 issue of *Bookmark*.

LAWRENCE W. LYNCH has a Ph.D. in French Literature from the University of Iowa. He is Associate Professor at the University of New Mexico in Albuquerque. He is the author of numerous articles and books on eighteenth century French literature.

PRISCILLA MATTHEWS is serials Cataloging Librarian at Illinois State University. She has a master's in librarianship from the University of Washington and expects to complete her C.A.S. in Library and Information Science from the University of Illinois at Urbana-Champaign in December 1989. Previous publications include articles in *Tracings* and an article in *Illinois Libraries*.

WILLARD MOONAN is a librarian at Illinois State University. He is the author of *Martin Buber and His Critics,* Garland, 1981. He has an M.A. in Educational Psychology and an M.A. in Library Science from the University of Minnesota.

FRANCES MOORE-BOND has a Ph.D. in Education—Curriculum and Instruction from the University of Minnesota. She is librarian and learning specialist at the University of Chicago, Laboratory High School.

SANDRA NAIMAN is a subject specialist librarian at Northern Illinois University. She has a Ph.D. in English and is adjunct professor in English. She also has an M.L.S.

ALAN NOURIE has a Ph.D. in English from Southern Illinois University and an M.L.S. from the University of Illinois in Urbana. He is Associate University Librarian for Public Service and Collection Development at Illinois State University. He reviews on a regular basis for *Choice*.

BARBARA NOURIE has an M.A. in English and a Ph.D. in Curriculum, Instruction and Media from Southern Illinois University. She currently teaches in the Department of Curriculum and Instruction at Illinois State University. She reviews for *Choice* and publishes in education journals.

CAROLE PALMER has an M.L.S. from Vanderbilt University. She is Access Services Coordinator, Northern Illinois University Libraries. She is coauthor of the forthcoming *Margaret Atwood: A Reference Guide*.

PATRICIA PALMER is currently the Conservation Librarian at Washington University in St. Louis. She has a bachelor of journalism from the University of Texas at Austin and an M.S. in library and information science from the University of Illinois at Urbana-Champaign. She wrote ''Collections on the History of American Baseball,'' published by the Society for American Baseball Research as *Research Guide #9*.

JEAN M. PARKER is Reference and Bibliographic Instruction Librarian at St. Olaf College in Northfield, Minnesota. She is also assistant director of the library in a shared, half-time position. She has an M.A. in English from South Dakota State University and an M.L.S. from the University of Wisconsin. She has an article in *Collection Management* and is working on a project concerning first lines of novels for Garland Press.

HELENI PEDERSOLI has a master of arts in Comparative Literature from Auburn University and an A.M.L.S. from the University of Michigan in Ann Arbor. She is a Ph.D. candidate at the University of Maryland at College Park, where she is a bibliographer for foreign languages and literatures in Collection Management. Pedersoli has published stories, articles, and poetry, and is on the editorial board of ALA/JMR T's *Footnotes*.

LORETTA RIELLY is currently Coordinator of Library Instruction for University Libraries, Northern Illinois University. She earned an M.L.S. from NIU after teaching freshman composition at both NIU and University of Wisconsin–Platteville.

DANIEL R. RUBEY is the Humanities Librarian and Head of Periodicals at Lehman College, the City University of New York. He has a Ph.D. in English Literature and an M.L.S. from Indiana University, Bloomington, and he has published articles on medieval, Renaissance and American literature, film, literary theory, and the visual arts.

RICHARD A. RUSSELL has an M.L.S. from Clarion University. He is Assistant Professor of Library Science and Public Service Librarian at Glenville State College, Robert F. Kidd Library, Glenville, West Virginia.

LAURA SCHROYER is assistant professor and subject specialist librarian in the Research Services Division at Founders Memorial Library, Northern Illinois University. She has an M.S. from Drake University and an M.L.I.S. from the University of Wisconsin–Madison.

VANETTE SCHWARTZ holds master's degrees in library science from the University of Michigan and in American history from the University of Illinois in Urbana. She is Associate Professor and Social Sciences and Map Librarian at Milner Library, Illinois State University.

KATHERINE SHAW is associate professor division head for general information and reference librarian at Illinois State University. She holds an M.S. and an Ed. S. in Librarianship from Western Michigan University. She has served also as head librarian for the ISU Laboratory Schools.

STEPHANIE CHILDS SIGALA has an M.A. in Art History from the University of California–Los Angeles and an M.S. in Library Science from the University of Illinois. She is Head Librarian, Richardson Library, The Saint Louis Art Museum, St. Louis, Missouri. She was Serials Editor for *Art Documentation* 1985–1989 and reviews regularly for a number of publications.

DANIEL STRAUBEL has a Ph.D. degree in American literature from Kent State University. He is professor of English and mass communications at Southeast Missouri State University. His publications include articles on Melville and Hawthorne.

SHARON TABACHNICK has an M.S.L.S. from the University of Southern California.

VICKI L. TATE is a reference librarian at Illinois State University. She has a B.A. in International Relations from Knox College in Galesburg, Illinois. Her M.L.S. is from the University of Illinois.

CARROLL VARNER is an Associate University Librarian Illinois State University. He is the author of numerous articles, grants and reviews including *"Thunderbolt* on Campus: Racist Material in the Academic Library" in *Proceedings of the 5th ACRL Conference.*

NORMAN VOGT is head of the serials department at Northern Illinois University. He received his M.S.L.S. from the University of Wisconsin, Madison.

GRAHAM R. WALDEN is reference librarian at the The Ohio State University in Columbus. He has a B.A. in political science from Slippery Rock University of Pennsylvania, as well as an M.S.L.S. His M.L.S. is from the State University of New York at Albany.

SANDRA WENNER has a master of arts degree in music history and literature from the University of North Carolina at Chapel Hill and a library science degree from the University of Wisconsin–Madison. She is currently a student at the University of Wisconsin Law School.

H. STEPHEN WRIGHT has a master of music degree in instrumental conducting and a master of library science from Indiana University. He is currently music librarian at Northern Illinois University. He is active in film music research; his most recent work is *Film and TV Music 1980–1988* with James Limbacher, Scarecrow Press.

KATHY WOOD is the Agricultural Reference Librarian at R. M. Cooper Library at Clemson University in Clemson, South Carolina. Kathy has a master of science degree in Library and Information Science from the University of Illinois, Urbana-Champaign. She also holds a master of science degree in entomology from Louisiana State University.

LINDA ZIEPER is a reference/instruction librarian at Southeastern Massachusetts University, with responsibilities for the visual and performing arts. She holds an M.A. in history from the college of William and Mary, and an M.S. in library and information science from Simmons College.